THE GENERAL

Also by Jonathan Fenby

THE PENGUIN HISTORY OF MODERN CHINA: THE FALL AND RISE OF A GREAT POWER

DRAGON THRONE: THE IMPERIAL DYNASTIES OF CHINA

THE SEVENTY WONDERS OF CHINA (ED.)

ALLIANCE: THE INSIDE STORY OF HOW ROOSEVELT, STALIN AND CHURCHILL WON ONE WAR AND BEGAN ANOTHER

THE SINKING OF THE LANCASTRIA: BRITAIN'S WORST NAVAL DISASTER AND CHURCHILL'S COVER-UP

GENERALISSIMO: CHIANG KAI-SHEK AND THE CHINA HE LOST

DEALING WITH THE DRAGON: A YEAR IN THE NEW HONG KONG

ON THE BRINK: THE TROUBLE WITH FRANCE

THE GENERAL

CHARLES DE GAULLE AND THE FRANCE HE SAVED

JONATHAN FENBY

London · New York · Sydney · Toronto

A CBS COMPANY

First published in Great Britain by Simon & Schuster UK Ltd, 2010
A CBS COMPANY

1 3 5 7 9 10 8 6 4 2

Simon & Schuster UK Ltd
1st Floor
222 Gray's Inn Road
London
WC1X 8HB

www.simonandschuster.co.uk

Simon & Schuster Australia
Sydney

A CIP catalogue for this book is available
from the British Library.

ISBN: 978-1-84737-392-2

Typeset in Baskerville by M Rules
Printed in the UK by CPI Mackays, Chatham ME5 8TD

To Lola and Kate, with love

CONTENTS

PART SEVEN SHADOWS AND NIGHT

I am indebted to the staff of the [illegible] the Bibliothèque Nationale [illegible] [illegible] of Paris and [illegible] [illegible] [illegible] and the invaluable [illegible] [illegible] of French books about the [illegible] which I benefited [illegible]

ACKNOWLEDGEMENTS

My initial debt is to Christopher Sinclair-Stevenson, my agent, who pressed me for several years to write a biography of de Gaulle; after five books on China it seemed high time to turn back to France and its most important figure of the last century. Mike Jones and Simon & Schuster showed a heart-warming interest in the idea, and I am grateful to my editor, Katherine Stanton, and her colleagues, together with copy editor Richard Collins and proofreader Sue Phillpott, for their care and speed in enabling the book to appear in time for the seventieth anniversary of de Gaulle's historic 18 June appeal to resistance in 1940.

Many others assisted along the way, prominent among them André Villeneuve, who read the draft manuscript and provided research on the Second World War, Philippe Oulmont and his helpful colleagues at the Institut de Gaulle in Paris, Nathalie de Gaulle and Bernard Edinger who drew on his seemingly bottomless pool of knowledge to answer queries at the drop of an e-mail. I recalled conversations about de Gaulle with the late and invaluable André Passeron. Ginette Vincendeau was a guide to matters both cinematic and linguistic, as was Peter Graham. I am indebted, too, to Anne Boston, Coralie Poidatz and Richard Lambert for anecdotes and help. In Colombey, the Natali family provided memories as well as excellent food. Pierre Lethier pointed me to the interesting US archives on which I have drawn in chapters on the Fifth Republic. The sisters of the convent that now occupies de Gaulle's wartime home in Hampstead were welcoming.

I am indebted to the staffs of the memorials in Colombey and Paris, the Bibliothèque Nationale, the Archives Nationales and the Quai d'Orsay in Paris and, in London, at the National Archives, the British Library and the invaluable London Library with its unexpected treasure trove of French books about the period. As always, while researching and writing, I benefited from the hospitality of relatives and friends, notably Annie Besnier, Jenny and Peter Thomas and the Count of Mourjou, as well as the sympathetic encouragement of that nonpareil *belote* partner, Simon Caulkin.

I owe a great debt, naturally, to the works of those who have written at length about the General in the past, notably Jean Lacouture's monumental biography, Éric Roussel's two-volume work and Alain Peyrefitte's three-volume recounting of conversations with the President – accounts of de Gaulle tend to be no shorter than their subject. The memoirs of many who worked with the General have been an invaluable source of material as have been the works of Admiral Philippe de Gaulle, Michel Tauriac and Jean-Raymond Tournoux. I am grateful to Editions Plon for allowing me to quote from their editions of the General's notes, letters and speeches.

As always, writing took me away from family, and I am grateful to Sara and Alexander for putting up with this – to which they would reply, no doubt, that they have grown used to it. My biggest debt is to my wife who played an even greater role in this book than in previous ones. Not only did she act as first reader, researcher, translator, compiler of the Glossary of Significant People, expert on the finer points of translating the often untranslatable General, and explainer of the Gallic viewpoint, but her participation made this enterprise a real partnership for which I cannot adequately express my thanks. All I can say is that the best way to write a book is with such a companion, even if we still argue over how to render some of the subject's words into English.

INTRODUCTION

When Charles de Gaulle boarded the small plane that took him from war-torn France to London on 17 June 1940, even he could not have foreseen the way in which he was launching himself on to the world stage. He was a little-known figure, a recently promoted two-star general acting in opposition to his country's legal government in the midst of catastrophic defeat. But that flight marked the start of a trajectory which would see him save his country twice and found a republic that endures to this day, marking him out as a truly unique figure fulfilling an intense sense of manifest destiny.

He outlasted his great wartime contemporaries – Roosevelt and Stalin were both dead and Churchill in retirement when he returned to power in 1958 at the age of sixty-eight to rule France for another ten years. None had quite the same self-awareness and sense of mission, epitomised in the way he spoke of himself in the third person. 'When de Gaulle the man looks at de Gaulle the historic figure, he understands that the historic de Gaulle has to act as is expected of him,' he said. His fate was to be France's republican monarch, answering to a calling far higher than everyday politics and acting on a plane of his own. When asked if he agreed to a proposal, he replied: 'I do not agree, I decide yes or no.'

His life was more dangerous than that of most other leaders; he fought in two major wars and was the target of up to two dozen assassination attempts as President. But he declined to take precautions. In part at least, his fearlessness stemmed from his sense of the very special role he had to play. Explaining his refusal to take cover when German shells were falling around him in 1944, he told an official: 'I have a providential mission to fulfil. I think nothing will happen to me. If it does, I will have been mistaken.'[1]

A study of the ten words used most frequently in his speeches and broadcasts between 1958 and 1965 showed 'France' or 'the country' accounting for 55 per cent. The basic question, he wrote in a letter in 1963, was 'yes or no, should France be France?' His vision was pitched so high that the French were bound to disappoint him all too frequently. For de Gaulle, life was a constant struggle, and he thought his compatriots all too prone to opt for an easy existence or compromise, leading him to brand them as '*veaux*' – literally calves but best rendered into English as 'sheep'.

His identification with France was so intense that, in his mind, the 'historic' de Gaulle and the country he saw himself 'carrying on my shoulders' became one. As President, he spoke of a murmur rising around him to urge the country on, for all the world like the supernatural voices that drove Joan of Arc. When he plunged into crowds, it was more than political populism; he was exercising his human link with the nation, emerging, as the journalist Pierre Viansson-Ponté put it, with his eyes 'shining with pleasure, happy to be alive' even if the police had arrested would-be assassins on his path. For Richard Nixon, an acute admirer, he was the builder of a cathedral – France – and saw his nation as 'a sort of middle kingdom [for which] the rest of the world had meaning only if it affected France'.[2]

This identification went hand in hand with his deep belief that the nation state, not ideology or alliances, was the bedrock on which everything rested – he described himself as a 'theologian' in the matter. Sovereign independence was all; treaties were like young girls and roses; they 'last for as long as they last'. Through the first seven decades of the twentieth century, his life was intimately entwined with the country of which he wrote that he had 'a certain idea'.* In his twenties, he fought in the trenches of the First World War. In the 1930s, he waged a lonely battle to enable his country to resist Hitler's Germany. Thereafter, he raised the flag of resistance in 1940, headed the post-war government and, after a dozen years out of power, founded the Fifth Republic in 1958, staving off the very real prospect of civil war, freeing France from the quagmire of the war in Algeria and establishing a stable regime

*The phrase had been used earlier by the right-wing nationalist Maurice Barrès whom de Gaulle read and who wrote in 1920 that 'Having a certain idea of France enables us to play a certain role' (Maurice Barrès, *Mes Cahiers*, 1920, p. 880).

that has been adopted by Left and Right alike – all achieved by an extraordinary mixture of vision, stubbornness, chutzpah, political acumen and bluff.

France's characteristics and contradictions have been much rehearsed, its pride in itself, its intransigence, its historical and cultural heritage and its quasi-religious belief in the state alongside its charm, diplomatic skill and humanism. Those traits and contradictions are all to be found in the man whose personalisation of patriotism could border on the irrational.

Profoundly attached to traditional values inherited from his royalist, deeply religious parents, he referred to himself as the only revolutionary in France and deplored the way in which his compatriots called for progress but hoped that nothing would really change. Depicted by opponents as a man of the Right, he dreamed of a middle way between capitalism and Communism, and presided over a vast expansion of the public sector in his first years in government after the Liberation of 1944. A prophet of modernisation, from his advocacy of tank warfare in the 1930s to his trumpeting of the Caravelle airliner and France's motorways in the 1960s, he disliked using the telephone – the one installed at his country home was in a cubbyhole under the stairs, forcing him to bend over when he used it. He painstakingly wrote his speeches and memoirs by hand with a black fountain pen, endlessly correcting his angular script which only his daughter Élisabeth was able to read easily. As the writer and ardent Gaullist André Malraux put it, the General was a man from the day before yesterday and the day after tomorrow.[3]

He expounded grand principles and liked to appear as a leader set on a single, unwavering course, but he frequently flew trial balloons before making up his mind and on some major issues, such as Algeria, felt his way from month to month. A ruthless, calculating politician, he was a complete realist in all things, remorselessly applying cold logic; he explained his adherence to the republican democracy by his belief that it was the system to which the French were most attached and which therefore gave him the best chance of achieving unity, even if he only ran for national election once, when in his mid-seventies. A strict disciplinarian, he was one of the great rebels of his time. Demanding complete loyalty from those around him, he gave little in return. A statesman should not have friends because he would favour them and overlook their weaknesses, he told one of his ministers in the 1960s.[4]

A grand visionary, de Gaulle was also a master of improvisation, of courting danger and springing surprises, making a fetish of secrecy. He saw himself as a high-stakes poker player while mainstream French politicians contented themselves with the café card game of *belote.* He took a visceral delight in defeating opponents, telling aides during one referendum campaign: 'I'll get them. I'll stick it up their arses.' If, as Bill Clinton claimed, all great political contests are head games, Charles de Gaulle was a consummate player. He defined a statesman as 'a man capable of taking risks'. 'Nobody else would have the nerve to do what I have done,' he remarked to a minister in 1962.[5]

The General was celebrated for his intransigent refusal to bow to others – '*L'homme qui dit non*' – first in rejecting France's surrender in 1940, then in his running battles with Roosevelt and Churchill during the Second World War, in standing aloof from France's powerful political parties after the Liberation and in pursuing an independent foreign policy as he vetoed British membership of the Common Market and fought against US dominance of NATO. A man made for storms and times of great crisis, he quoted approvingly Hamlet's observation that 'Rightly to be great is not to stir without great argument'. The US Secretary of State Dean Rusk compared meetings with him to 'crawling up a mountainside on your knees, opening a little portal at the top, and waiting for the oracle to speak . . . There was never any give and take – de Gaulle gave us pronouncements from on high, but never any real discussion; he was there, he would listen – "*je vous écoute*" – and would then bid you good-bye.'[6]

He was comfortable with power, deploying it with a natural assurance – as a young man he was nicknamed 'the Constable' in reference to the senior official who ran the kingdom for the medieval monarch. He would later be compared to Louis XIV, to Bonaparte and to Stalin. During their ten hours of tête-à-tête talks only two months before the General stepped down in 1969, Nixon found him completely at home in the grandeur of the Grand Trianon Palace at Versailles from where, as de Gaulle noted, the Sun King had ruled Europe. 'He did not try to put on airs but an aura of majesty seemed to envelop him,' the US President wrote. 'His performance – and I do not use that word disparagingly – was breathtaking. At times eloquent, at other times coldly pragmatic but at all times articulate . . . he was not always right, but he was always certain.'[7]

In public, de Gaulle followed his own advice that leaders should show 'cold dignity'. His whole life, he remarked, consisted of making people do what they did not want to do. His tragedy, he noted, was that 'I respect only those who stand up to me, but I find such people intolerable.' Some detected a deep sadness in him; Churchill found a 'great capacity for feeling pain'. He harboured intense personal emotions, particularly in his love for his second daughter who suffered from Down's syndrome; without her, he said, 'perhaps I should not have done all that I have done'. While he struck many as a man who 'spoke not of doubts but of certainties', he could still be prey to internal debate about how to proceed – he was just rather good at covering this up. At regular intervals, however, he declared that his mission was done for and reached out for reassurance from trusted followers, bouncing back when they urged him to persevere, as he had known they would.

Magisterially aloof in public, the General was a shy man who could become suddenly vulnerable behind the mask he presented to the world. He was clumsy with his hands and increasingly short-sighted as he aged, forced to wear thick-lensed spectacles, which he hated. From his twenties on, he stood apart if only because of his height of 1.93 metres or six foot three inches. 'We big people, we cannot act like others,' he told the equally tall Dutch Foreign Minister Josef Luns. 'We have to give small men a lead.' As President, he remarked, 'I've always been big Charles with arms that are too long and enormous feet . . . The chairs are always too small.'[8]

He was prone to dramatic mood swings, explosions of anger and bouts of self-pity. A psychological analysis suggests that he was what is termed a constructive narcissist and a compulsive neurotic whose personality traits were channelled into achieving the ends he sought, with histrionic episodes and periodic sullen withdrawal when things were going badly. Given the stress he was under, this was hardly abnormal, and he does not seem to fit the manic depressive character loosely attributed to him by some writers.[9]

His interests were omnivorous, ranging from nuclear strategy to the breeding habits of snails; 'he wants to understand everything,' one of his closest aides, Jacques Foccart, remarked. He was proud but not vain, ready to press his case to the limits but usually knowing just when to stop. For all his grandeur, he was unfailingly courteous, always replying to authors who sent him their books with a word of praise even if the volume was *Calcium and Metabolic Bone Illnesses.* Never missing Sunday mass, he seemed bored during the services. Deeply attached to military values – he called the army the nation's 'backbone' – he applied the tactics of the battlefield to politics, but despised most generals and faced military revolts.[10]

A great teacher from his youth to those around him and then to his nation, the General deployed the French language like a weapon, though he knew the value of silence. Not a seductive speaker, he imposed himself by the force of his words and the character behind them. He rarely told an outright lie, but was masterly in obfuscation and economising with the truth. From time to time, he discarded the heritage of Corneille and Racine to take visitors aback with rough phrases and military slang.

He was personally frugal and scrupulous. 'My only enemy, and that of France, has never ceased to be money,' he told Malraux towards the end of his life. As President, he insisted on paying the telephone and electricity bills for his quarters at the Élysée Palace. His wife, Yvonne, who devoted herself to him, was equally careful about spending and about keeping the proper distance between their personal and official lives while upholding a strict code that excluded divorced people and low necklines alike – she was said never to have spoken to a journalist and melded into the crowd as she went shopping at grocery stores near the presidential palace or across the Seine on the Left Bank.[11]

Her husband was always punctual and socially punctilious. He was gallant to women; after he gave up smoking, he still carried a lighter for their cigarettes. He said that if one met an ugly woman, one should try to see her in profile so as to glimpse only half her face. He fell under the spell of Jacqueline Kennedy and Grace Kelly, and insisted that the American actress Jean Seberg be placed next to him at an official lunch after she had married the writer and diplomat Romain Gary. When

Brigitte Bardot appeared at a presidential reception in a tunic modelled on that of an eighteenth-century German grenadier, he remarked on her outfit and led her through the crowd to the buffet. But he believed that a woman was 'made to have children' and that, if the contraceptive pill was allowed, 'sex will invade everything!' Only one affair was alleged – in Poland when he was thirty and unmarried, and even that was subsequently denied by the diplomat who originally reported it. As de Gaulle himself asked the Information Minister Alain Peyrefitte, using the feminine gender for the eighth word, 'When one has had History for a friend, how could one have any others?'*[12]

He felt most at home in the bleak winters at his house in the isolated village of Colombey-les-Deux-Églises in eastern France, telling visitors that it reflected the reality of the country rather than the sunshine of Provence or the soft lands of the Loire. While he laid on lavish state ceremonies, he was not at home in the social world of Paris. He always kept up his guard in public, and usually in private, too, never appearing without a tie or jacket; the only time his son saw him in pyjamas was after he underwent a prostate operation in 1964.

Though his favourite reading was of French classical writers, notably the restless Romantic Chateaubriand, he had a taste for non-literary popular culture. He sang along with the comic troubadour Bourvil, and warbled light operetta airs in the bathroom. After watching the televised transmission of celebrations of Maurice Chevalier's eightieth birthday, he told his aide-de-camp that he shouldn't have missed the programme and launched into one of the star's standards, somewhat out of tune. Meeting his ministers after making a key broadcast during the prolonged Algerian crisis, he broke into a song by another monument of French popular music, Charles Trenet, this time getting the pitch right. He took an interest in the performances of the country's sports stars, worrying that the boxer Marcel Cerdan might lose a world title fight because he had been consorting with too many American

*The three volumes by Alain Peyrefitte of de Gaulle's conversations with him contain a treasure trove of such remarks on which this book draws. As Information Minister in the 1960s, Peyrefitte saw the President after Cabinet meetings at which he would expound at length on subjects that had just been dealt with more formally in the government sessions. Peyrefitte would usually not pass these comments on to journalists at his subsequent briefings, but noted them for future publication.

blondes, and growing angry when the national football team lost, arguing with the referee from his seat in front of the television – his wife tried to limit his viewing of matches for fear that it might send up his blood pressure dangerously.[13]

In his lifetime, de Gaulle was a highly controversial figure, both internationally and at home. His achievements often came at a cost, creating lasting enmities, suspicions and interrogations. Since his death in 1970, he has become established as the greatest French figure since Napoleon. Though he was forced to resign after losing a referendum vote in 1969, only 34 per cent of those questioned in a poll the following year expressed unhappiness with his record. While adapting the way they applied the system, his successors in the Fifth Republic have kept to the basic pattern of power set out by the General in 1958, giving him a heritage that few politicians can claim.[14]

First, his long-time Prime Minister Georges Pompidou adopted a less regal style as he moved Gaullism towards conventional conservativism before dying of cancer in 1974. Then Valéry Giscard d'Estaing sought to rule as a dashing reformist prince, only to be brought crashing to earth at the election of 1981 by economic downturn and his own superiority. For fourteen years, the Élysée was occupied by de Gaulle's major opponent, François Mitterrand, who had denounced the Fifth Republic as a permanent *coup d'état*; finally brought to power as head of a Socialist–Communist alliance, he found that he liked the office crafted by the General and manipulated it to a Florentine degree. Mitterrand's successor, Jacques Chirac, presented himself as the standard-bearer of neo-Gaullism for the end of the twentieth century but was unable to convince the French that he was the true heir rather than a new version of the pre-Gaullist political era. The current head of state, Nicolas Sarkozy, shows every sign of using Gaullist forms to the full, even if his style and approach are far from those of the founder of the regime, and loses no opportunity to appeal to the sense of national identity, importance and independence so vital for the man who installed executive government in 1958.

Every French town seems to have a street, avenue or square named after 'the Constable'. France's main airport bears his name, as does its nuclear-powered aircraft carrier. In 1970, the Place de l'Étoile in Paris, with the Arc de Triomphe at its centre, became the Place Charles de Gaulle. Large museums consecrated to the General have been opened in the military quarter of the Invalides in the capital and on the ridge above Colombey where his symbol of the Cross of Lorraine has been erected in a huge monument. When the national television station, France 2, held a poll in 2005 to pick the outstanding figure from the whole of French history, de Gaulle came out on top.

This consecration leaves many questions unanswered. Was (and is) Gaullism a coherent political creed or simply the accumulation of the actions of the man after whom it is named? Was Charles de Gaulle a visionary who influenced international affairs in a significant manner or simply an ultra-stubborn defender of France's national interests who ended up marginalising himself and his country? If he had been less intransigent and arrogant would France have played a lesser role or, on the contrary, would its influence have been increased by a more cooperative relationship with France's allies? Was he a democrat or a barely disguised autocrat who would brook no opposition and used referendums as plebiscites? Did he have a truly inclusive image of France or was his talk of a united nation a cover for statist conservatism? Was he a man so imbued with himself and his mission that he verged on irrationality, or was he the ultimate calculator using his personality and the way in which it was perceived by others as a battering ram to get what he wanted?

In short, was he a great statesman or a conjuror on a huge scale, a true founding father of present-day France, with lessons for the world, or a Wizard of Oz manipulating a giant machine of illusions? This book seeks to lay out the evidence on these and many other issues. At this stage, it may be enough to say that, in most cases, there is truth on both sides of that set of propositions. That is why Charles de Gaulle remains such a fascinating, and human, figure.

PART ONE
REACHING FOR THE HEIGHTS

1

EDGE OF THE ABYSS

I
'By myself'

On 1 June 1940, as the German army and air force swept across France, an unusually tall one-star general went to see the Prime Minister of France. The politician Paul Reynaud, an elfin-faced conservative who had been in office for ten weeks, offered him a choice: he could take command of France's tank forces or join the government as Deputy Defence Minister – Reynaud held the senior defence post. Charles de Gaulle took the second option. A historic career was launched that would parallel France's fortunes for good and ill over three decades.

As the two men talked, their country was undergoing its greatest humiliation of the twentieth century. Three weeks earlier, the German army had circumvented its main defences on the heavily fortified Maginot Line, and used the deadly combination of tanks and dive-bombers to pulverise French forces, which retreated in disarray or found themselves surrounded by the advancing enemy. The rout was all the more humiliating because France's tank force was 30 per cent larger than Germany's and included the heaviest and most powerful fighting vehicle in the world, the Char B1. In the air, the Allies again had 30 per cent superiority in numbers, and the United States had just delivered five hundred American planes, including high-quality fighters. But the Luftwaffe was as dominant as the tanks on the ground. The failure lay with the men in charge and the defensive mentality which had held sway since 1918.[1]

Millions of civilians fled from the battle areas in the intense summer heat; they were compared by the pilot and writer Antoine de Saint-Exupéry to a great anthill kicked over by a boot. Law and order broke down along roads lined with abandoned cars and lorries that had run out of petrol. The population of the city of Lille fell from 200,000 to 20,000. In the eastern city of Troyes, only thirty people were left. The crowd waiting to board trains leaving Paris stretched for a kilometre.

Officials at the Foreign Ministry carted out wheelbarrows piled with documents to burn them on the lawn. Visiting Paris for a meeting of the Allied war council, Winston Churchill found 'utter dejection' on every face. When the British Prime Minister asked where France's strategic reserve was, the commander-in-chief, Maurice Gamelin, replied against the evidence that there was none, bewailing France's 'inferiority of numbers, inferiority of equipment, inferiority of methods'.[2]

Reynaud, who barely had a parliamentary majority, sought to buttress morale by appointing the First World War hero Marshal Philippe Pétain as the number two in the government and replacing Gamelin with another figure from the last great Franco-German conflict, Maxime Weygand. Both choices were unfortunate. Pétain's defence of the fortress of Verdun in 1916 had made him into a figure revered by the French, but he thought the new war was lost and that France should sue for peace. The Marshal was eighty-four; a British general described him as looking 'senile, uninspiring and defeatist'. De Gaulle quoted the observation of the eighteenth-century writer Chateaubriand that 'old age is a wreck'. The prim, touchy Weygand wailed that he had no troops and could not hold the line. Asked why he had appointed the two old men, Reynaud replied, 'Better to have them inside than outside.'[3]

The Premier, who had opposed the appeasement of Germany before the war, insisted in speeches and radio addresses that France would continue to resist the Nazi advance; but his words rang increasingly hollow, and he was under personal pressure from his mistress who urged him to seek an armistice. His appeals for reinforcements and Royal Air Force planes received no response from Churchill as he prepared for the battle to defend Britain. On 26 May, the British began to evacuate their expeditionary force from Dunkirk. Pétain told the

American ambassador that Britain would allow the French to go on fighting to the last drop of their blood and would then sign a treaty with Hitler.[4]

To balance the two defeatist generals, Reynaud promoted a tough-minded politician, Georges Mandel, to be Interior Minister. Mandel, who carried the historic heritage of having worked with 'the Tiger', Georges Clemenceau, in the victory of 1918, stands out in photographs of the government as a solid presence in a three-piece chalk-striped suit and stiff, starched collar. He believed in fighting on, if necessary from France's territories in North Africa, but he had plenty of enemies and bore the burden of being Jewish in a country where anti-Semitism was rife.

Among the few who thought like Mandel was forty-nine-year-old Charles de Gaulle. Standing six foot three inches tall with long arms, he was physically awkward and rarely at ease. He had a little moustache, big ears and a face that bore a resemblance to that of an elephant. His handshake was surprisingly limp – 'a velvet claw', one man who met him in 1940 recalled.[5] The son of reactionary, devoutly Catholic parents, he had been a career soldier since becoming a military cadet in 1908. As a young officer, he fought in the trenches of the Western Front in the First World War, leading infantry charges with his drawn sword. Wounded three times, he was given up for dead at Verdun before being taken captive by the Germans. After acting as an adviser to the Poles in their campaign against the Soviet army in 1919–20, he became a protégé of Pétain, though they subsequently fell out, for personal reasons and because of de Gaulle's championing of armoured warfare. Great men, he had decided early on, were those ready to grab the opportunity offered by events. June 1940 was to be that moment for de Gaulle.

After commanding a tank division in two battles against the advancing Germans, he was promoted to the rank of acting brigadier general. 'Nothing counts more than this. France must be saved,' he wrote to his wife, Yvonne, from the front. In a radio broadcast, he foresaw a conflict of global dimensions from which France could emerge on the victorious side. 'We are on the edge of the abyss and you carry France on your back,' he told Reynaud on 3 June, adding that the Prime Minister had erred in appointing 'yesterday's men [who] fear me because they know I am right and have the dynamism to force their hands'. Should he become Reynaud's chief of staff? he asked. No, he replied to the offer the Prime Minister had not made, 'I intend to act with you, but by myself.'[6]

II
The last quarter of an hour

4 June 1940. As the evacuation of 200,000 British and 140,000 French from Dunkirk ended, Churchill made his speech to the House of Commons vowing to fight on the beaches and in the fields, and never to surrender. In Paris, Reynaud flirted with the idea of moving the government to a safe haven in Brittany. It was not a very sound notion since the defence of the peninsula would have required twenty divisions, which France could not muster. Still, an order was issued for work to start on setting up the communications network for an eventual transfer.

5 June. German planes bombed the outskirts of Paris. Reynaud announced de Gaulle's appointment, but also named an appeaser, Paul Baudouin, as his number two at the Foreign Ministry. Though he had greeted de Gaulle as 'a daring and energetic leader' on the battlefield, Weygand called the new Deputy Defence Minister 'a child' while the navy chief, François Darlan, said he was mad. Pétain told Churchill's envoy to France, General Sir Edward Spears: 'His vanity leads him to think the art of war has no secrets for him . . . Not only is he vain, he is ungrateful. He has few friends in the army. No wonder, for he gives the impression of looking down on everybody.' Baudouin and the head of the Prime Minister's military staff, Colonel Villelume, detected 'boundless ambition' in the general. 'But what more can he want?' Reynaud asked them. 'Your place,' they answered.[7]

6 June. Wearing his general's uniform, the new junior minister lunched with officers of his armoured Fourth Division in northern France where they had fought the Germans outside the town of Abbeville. On the battlefield, he had been a domineering, distant presence, but now he shook each officer's hand, and told them: 'I am proud of you. You know how to do your duty.'[8]

Returning to his ministry in Paris, an eighteenth-century stone *hôtel particulier* on the rue Saint-Dominique on the Left Bank of the Seine, he plotted the course of the war on a large wall map. He later recalled to a subordinate that, when he arrived, the waiting room was crammed with senior officers. They were not there to plan resistance, he added, '*all* of them had come to ask me for a promotion or a decoration'. The press greeted his appointment with enthusiasm, and, to make himself better known, he summoned photographers, leading Reynaud's chief of staff, Dominique Leca, to note that he was acting 'like a star'. De Gaulle realised France would need 'a resurrection myth' if it was to recover from defeat, and was starting to create it round himself, Leca added.[9]

8 June. In his memoirs, de Gaulle records a conversation with Weygand, whose contents the other man subsequently denied. De Gaulle's account has the commander-in-chief saying the Germans would advance to the rivers Seine and Marne, after which 'it will be over'.

'Over?' the junior general replied. 'What about the empire?'

'The empire?' Weygand answered with a despairing smile. 'That's child's talk. As for the rest of the world, when I have been beaten here, England will not wait eight days to negotiate with the Reich.' Looking de Gaulle in the eye, he added: 'Ah! If only I was sure that the Germans would leave me sufficient forces to maintain order.' Weygand wrote later that, if his smile had been despairing, it had been because de Gaulle was talking about other things instead of concentrating on the immediate situation.[10]

9 June. In his order of the day to the army Weygand declared that the 'last quarter of an hour' had come. 'Stand fast,' he advised. Reynaud instructed that a 180-kilometre line running across the frontier of Brittany should be fortified, as if there was time for that.

One of de Gaulle's responsibilities was military liaison with the British and he paid his first visit to London on 9 June to try to convince Churchill to commit more forces to the defence of France. Explaining why this was impossible, the Prime Minister launched into a virtuoso display of rhetoric delivered half in English and half in his idiosyncratic French as he strode up and down. Though de Gaulle got nowhere, the visit was important for his future. He was able to speak on behalf of his country, and made a favourable impression on his hosts as cool and collected.

On the return journey, the pilot wanted to land at Caen to avoid flying at night to Paris, where conditions might be perilous. But his passenger insisted on getting back to the capital as soon as possible. The plane put down at Le Bourget airport near Paris by the light of two flares beside the runway; the pilot was reported to have mopped sweat from his brow as the aircraft came to a halt.

At 10 p.m., the government decided to leave for the Loire Valley the following day, declaring Paris an open city. De Gaulle argued in vain that some of the administration should stay behind. The situation was like a house of cards, he thought. If everybody left, things would fall apart. His own wife and three children had moved to Brittany, where they rented two storeys in a villa in the coastal town of Carantec.[11]

10 June. 'A day of extreme anguish,' de Gaulle recalled. Italy declared war on France. Weygand handed Reynaud a note saying that the battle in metropolitan France was lost. When de Gaulle objected, the commander-in-chief asked him if he had something to propose. 'The government does not have propositions to make but orders to give' came the reply. 'I count on it to give them.'

That night, Reynaud was driven south from Paris, accompanied by de Gaulle. During the three-hour journey, the general urged the Prime Minister to replace Weygand with a commander from the front in eastern France, General Hutzinger. He was a strange choice, having been defeated by the German advance after dismissing a warning about the inadequate defences and the penetrability of the Ardennes hills through which the Panzers had burst. Still, de Gaulle argued that he had a broader view of the war than Weygand. Whether that was true or not, he would be less of an obstacle to the deputy minister.

Reynaud's car took back roads to avoid the crush of refugees on the main route. The Third Republic, established after the last defeat by the Germans in 1870, was in flight, incapable of defending the nation. Its leaders and their regime had been discredited, and they were unable to tell the truth – the official radio announced that the Prime Minister was going to join the armies but he headed in the opposite direction for the Orléans region, where Weygand had established his headquarters in the redbrick château of Briare.

Pétain joined the exodus in a Cadillac, followed by his personal doctor in a Chrysler. When the Marshal arrived at Briare at 2 a.m. no bed was available and he was driven on for two hours to the town of Gien, where he slept in a house attached to the station on a bed abandoned by a railway inspector.[12]

11 June. Meeting de Gaulle, Pétain remarked: 'You are a general now. I don't congratulate you on that. What's the meaning of rank during a defeat?' In Paris, Senator Jacques Bardoux, a stalwart of the regime whose father had been a founder of the Third Republic, went to the Interior Ministry. The gates were shut. When Bardoux asked to see Mandel, the guard replied: 'He left during the night.' 'And the President of the Republic?' 'Oh, that one left forty-eight hours ago.' 'That's sickening,' Bardoux said. 'Couldn't agree more,' the guard answered.

Churchill arrived in Orléans in a lobster-pink aeroplane for a Franco-British summit at which Pétain lamented that France was being smashed to pieces, with one-third of its 105 divisions lost. 'I am helpless,' Weygand said. 'Now is the decisive moment.'

No, Churchill replied. The decisive moment would come when Hitler hurled the Luftwaffe against Britain. 'If we can keep command of the air over our own island – that is all I ask – we will win it all back for you,' he added.

His normally sallow skin still glowing from hours spent on the field of combat, de Gaulle made a striking contrast to the other French ministers whom Spears likened to 'prisoners hauled up from some deep dungeon to hear an inevitable verdict'. Oliver Harvey, from the British embassy, described the general as 'the only calm and intelligent soldier left'. He was, Spears wrote, 'straight, direct, even rather brutal . . . a strange-looking man, enormously tall; sitting at the table, he dominated everybody else by his height . . . His heavily-hooded eyes were very shrewd. When about to speak he oscillated his head slightly, like a pendulum, while searching for words.' Spears understood why, as a young soldier, de Gaulle had gained the nickname 'the Constable'.

The junior minister's increasing prominence was signalled by a request from Churchill that he should sit at his right at dinner, to the annoyance of Weygand. The fare was soup, an omelette and a light wine followed by coffee. De Gaulle lit one cigarette from another as he preached resistance, and suggested that the French and British tank forces should be amalgamated. On his return to London, Churchill told colleagues he thought a great deal of the general.[13]

12 June. Staying in a neo-Gothic château at Azay-sur-Cher where he slept in a four-poster bed with pink curtains, de Gaulle worked on plans to move troops across the Mediterranean, and got Reynaud to agree to set up resistance centres in the Auvergne and Brittany. He made a quick trip to western France where he learned that building the necessary defences would take three months, clearly an impossible delay when the Wehrmacht's tanks were speeding across northern France. So North Africa was the only possibility for continued resistance.

'I will never sign an armistice,' he told his aide and friend, Jean Auburtin. 'It would be against French honour and interests.' When Auburtin evoked the horrors of an occupation of metropolitan France, de Gaulle replied, 'Very nasty things will happen, but would an armistice change anything? We would have against us not only Germany and Italy, but perhaps also America and Britain, and one day Russia and Japan.'

Mandel estimated that, with three undecided, the twenty-one members of the Cabinet were split equally between resistance and surrender. Pétain insisted that an armistice was essential, and Weygand spread alarm with a false report of a Communist insurrection in Paris. Though he had joined the exodus, the commander-in-chief lambasted the politicians for having left the capital, adding, according to Spears, that he intended to detain de Gaulle for having made preparations to send troops and supplies to North Africa without his approval. Those who advocated fighting on displayed only rhetorical bravery, he concluded. When Mandel objected, Weygand flounced out of the room, remarking that the ministers were mad and should be arrested – there was some evidence that he was thinking of doing this with a special troop of young soldiers.[14]

13 June. The government and the President of the Republic, Albert Lebrun, moved to a string of châteaux round Tours. To try to bolster France's will to fight, Churchill flew in for another meeting with Reynaud. Nobody met the visitors at the airport, which had been bombed the previous night. The British borrowed a car to get into the city, and, not finding the French leader in his office at the prefecture, lunched in a café. During the meal, Paul Baudouin, the leading civilian advocate of surrender, appeared to say that the situation was hopeless unless the Americans declared war on Germany.

After the British had returned to the prefecture, Reynaud turned up, his ever expressive eyebrows twitching, his face jumping with a tic. He asked for France to be released from its undertaking to Britain not to make a separate peace. Churchill replied in French that he understood the difficulties France faced, but could not agree. Twisting his remark, Baudouin spread the word that he had 'understood' in the sense of having accepted the French request.*

Reynaud did not inform the government of the meeting with Churchill. De Gaulle heard about it when he received a message from Reynaud's private secretary on his way back from his trip to Brittany. Hurrying to Tours, he managed to get to the later part of the talks. Leaving the building, Churchill saw him standing at the doorway 'solid and expressionless'. '*L'homme du destin,*' the Prime Minister said in a low voice, according to his own memoirs. The Frenchman remained impassive – he may not have heard the words or they may have been a retrospective Churchillian insertion into history.

The general then went to a Cabinet session at which he was observed to be 'pale and sober in what he said . . . a cold and passionate man'. The Deputy Prime Minister, Camille Chautemps, an expert at producing compromises, proposed a face-saving approach under which

*De Gaulle was to use the ambiguity of the verb *comprendre* to great effect in speaking to Algerian settlers two decades later. The difference was that he knew what he was doing while Churchill did not understand how his words could be twisted.

France would use a neutral channel to ask Hitler for terms and then decide whether it was ready to accept them. Pétain called an armistice 'the necessary condition for the continued existence of eternal France'. Without such an accord, he warned, the army might dissolve in panic. Countering any idea of crossing the Mediterranean, he vowed to remain in metropolitan France 'among the people of France to share their trials and misfortune'.

Reynaud went on the radio to declare: 'If it needs a miracle to save France, I believe in that miracle.' The Prime Minister's lack of resolve was proving a considerable disappointment to de Gaulle by now. According to Churchill's secretary, John Colville, during his visits to London he called the politician *ce poisson gelé* (this frozen fish) and spoke of him 'like dirt'. On the evening of 13 June, the general wrote a resignation letter. His chief of staff tipped off Georges Mandel, who asked to see him. 'We are at the start of a world war,' the Interior Minister told him. 'You will have great tasks to carry out, [with] the advantage among us of being a man who is intact. Think only of what should be done for France, and consider that, if necessary, your present job could help things.' De Gaulle agreed not to resign. Perhaps he had never really intended to do so, and was just expressing his frustration; Mandel's words were certainly calculated to appeal to his ambition and sense of destiny.

That night, Spears glimpsed Reynaud in a corridor of his château. He looked 'ghastly, with a completely unnatural expression, still and white', the British envoy recorded. The Premier's mistress, the Comtesse de Portes, described by his private secretary as 'ugly, dirty, nasty and half-demented', stalked the passages, throwing open doors to track down her man. Passing de Gaulle on her rounds, she gestured at him and said: 'What's that one doing here? Another who wants to turn himself into a politician. Let him go and lead his tanks and prove himself on the battlefield.'[15]

III
'Everything is about to collapse'

14 June. The Germans entered Paris at dawn. De Gaulle argued in favour of heading west to set up resistance in Brittany. Reynaud sent his hand luggage that way but then went to Bordeaux; his mistress had told him sharply that she was not going to sleep in a Breton farm bed.

Blocked on the road by the crowd fleeing the Germans, the Prime Minister turned pale as he heard shouts outside his car, but they were supportive – 'Hold on!' 'Long live France.' Arriving in the south-western port city, he moved into military quarters; the Comtesse de Portes ordered white tissue wall drapes. Mandel took over the prefecture, for which his mistress ordered furniture and linen to the tune of 9,760 francs. De Gaulle and Baudouin were allocated rooms at the Hôtel Splendide. That night, the general saw Pétain in the dining room, and went over to shake his hand. Neither said anything. It was the last time they met.

The general then set off on a second mission to London, to seek naval support for a troop movement to North Africa. No plane was available, so he drove through the night to take a boat from Brittany.[16]

15 June. Reynaud received a reply from Franklin D. Roosevelt to an appeal for help he had sent to Washington. It contained a broad message of support for France, but, to cater to isolationist sentiment, avoided specific commitments, and was not to be published. As the British began Operation Aerial to evacuate 100,000 support troops left in France after Dunkirk, France was ever more on its own. In the cocoon in Bordeaux, politicians intrigued in fashionable restaurants. In the Chapon Fin, the swarthy former Premier Pierre Laval, looking, as Spears put it, 'gross, flabby and high in colour' with his nicotine-stained fingers and heavy eyelids, said he would conduct negotiations with Berlin after Reynaud had borne the shame of capitulation.

Meeting in Mandel's office, a group of politicians agreed that de Gaulle, whom the Socialist Léon Blum described as 'young and ardent', should be appointed commander-in-chief to replace Weygand, and should organise a retreat to North Africa. But a majority of the Cabinet supported the proposal by Chautemps that France should get a third party to sound out Germany on its armistice terms. Reynaud turned down a British proposal that he go to London, saying he would leave only for North Africa. Pétain drafted a resignation letter to protest at the slow progress towards seeking an armistice, and discussed the composition of a new government with Admiral Darlan. That night, after upbraiding her lover once more for not having followed her advice in seeking an armistice, de Portes was said to have added, in a reference to rumours that Reynaud had Mexican blood, 'Anyway, my poor Paul, you're not even French and so you can't think as a Frenchman.' The story is that he threw two glasses of water at her.

In Brittany on his way to Britain, de Gaulle spent half an hour with his family, most of it alone with his wife, Yvonne, though he did not have time to visit his mother who was seriously ill in a nearby village. 'Things are very bad,' he said. 'Perhaps we are going to fight on in Africa, but I think it more likely that everything is about to collapse.' He added that they should be ready to leave at any time. He entrusted the family silver, linen, furs, financial securities and his papers to a local woman. Then he embraced the children and got back into his car. His son, Philippe, stood at the door watching the black Renault disappear in a cloud of dust, not knowing when he would see his father again.

From Brest, de Gaulle telephoned Bordeaux to ask for travel permits to be sent to his wife and family. He boarded a destroyer, *Milan*, insisting on being given a salute of honour as it passed France's most modern battleship, *Richelieu*, on its way out to sea. During the voyage to England, he asked the captain if he would be ready to sail under British colours. 'A French officer only fights under the French flag,' the captain replied. To which the general responded: 'Do you think it amusing, today, to be called General de Gaulle?' In the middle of the night, a crew member saw him standing rigid on deck, looking at the sea. The sailor approached de Gaulle, and their eyes met. They said nothing, but the sailor remembered him as 'preoccupied and, it seemed, very worried'.[17]

16 June. At a morning Cabinet meeting, Pétain read out his resignation letter. President Lebrun talked him out of it, but the Marshal said his continued membership of the government would depend on whether the British agreed to the proposal to sound out Berlin on armistice terms.

Arriving in Plymouth, de Gaulle and his twenty-seven-year-old aide, Geoffroy Chodron de Courcel, took the night train to London, sleeping in their seats. The general went to the Hyde Park Hotel, where he was shaving when he received a visit from the French ambassador to London, Charles Corbin, and the international official and banker Jean Monnet, who was supervising French arms purchase in London. De Gaulle and Monnet were to become fierce adversaries over Europe and French sovereignty, but, in mid-June 1940, they were united in supporting any means of keeping their country in the fight against Hitler.

This took the form of an extraordinary proposal for a Franco-British union. The idea of institutionalising cross-Channel cooperation had been explored in vague terms for several years, but now the idea canvassed by the future 'Father of Europe' and one of his colleagues, René Pleven, had reached Churchill. Though de Gaulle was later scathing about the proposition, his reaction at the time was to clutch at any straw to prevent France making peace with Hitler. He had, by his own account, already taken the initiative of ordering a ship carrying arms from the USA to France to sail instead to a British port, going well beyond the powers vested in him; subsequent evidence indicates that the boat changed course for other reasons after Britain instructed all vessels carrying supplies to France to divert to British ports.

Agreeing to go along with Monnet's proposal, the general telephoned Reynaud to say that 'something stupendous' was being prepared. Then he lunched with Churchill at the Carlton Club, assuring the Prime Minister that the French fleet would not be handed over voluntarily to the Germans. That afternoon, while de Gaulle and the ambassador waited in an adjoining room, the Cabinet approved a declaration of Franco-British union, joining the two nations indissolubly in their 'unyielding resolution in their common defence of justice and freedom, against subjection to a system which reduces mankind to a life of robots and slaves'. They would have joint defence, foreign, financial and economic policy organs, and a single War Cabinet during the conflict in charge of all their forces. Their parliaments would be associated. 'We shall conquer,' the declaration concluded.

'*Nous sommes d'accord,*' Churchill cried as he walked out of the Cabinet Room. Ministers clapped de Gaulle on the back and told him he would become commander-in-chief. '*Je l'arrangerai,*' the Prime Minister muttered. Still, the British leader again rebuffed a final appeal by the visitor to send troops and planes to France: according to Churchill's account, the Frenchman paused as he left the room, took a couple of steps back and said, in English, 'I think you are quite right.'

The union scheme was a wildly impractical initiative launched without preparation – nobody had told King George VI that his Empire was about to be merged with that of France. British policy was contradictory. A few hours before the union was proclaimed, a message had been sent to Reynaud to free France from the obligation not to seek armistice terms on its own 'but only provided that the French fleet is sailed forthwith for British harbours, pending negotiations'. This demand was peremptory in the extreme and could only fuel antagonism towards London. The bulk of the fleet was in the Mediterranean where it would be needed to protect any movement of troops to North Africa, and, though the British did not know this, Admiral Darlan had got Pétain's agreement that the warships would be kept out of German hands if the Marshal took power. As Reynaud told the ambassador, Ronald Campbell, when he handed over the message, 'It's so stupid.' He decided not to tell anybody about it.

De Gaulle telephoned Reynaud from Whitehall to read out the union declaration. Spears, who was in the room in Bordeaux, described the Premier taking down the wording with a thick pencil on sheets of paper that flew off his desk as he wrote, repeating each word, his eyebrows shooting up so far that they seemed about to merge with his neatly parted hair. When de Gaulle finished, Reynaud asked if Churchill had agreed to the declaration. The British leader took the telephone to confirm this. Speaking in English, Reynaud pledged to defend the proposal to the death. He would unveil the declaration that evening, and rout the appeasers. Spears saw Reynaud's face 'transfigured with joy . . . with a great happiness in the belief that France would now remain in the war'. He and Churchill agreed to meet the following day in the Breton port of Concarneau.

But the Comtesse de Portes read the text of the declaration as it was being typed up in the room next to Reynaud's office, and the appeasers probably had access to taps on the Prime Minister's telephone. Forewarned, they denounced a British plot to take over France's Empire and turn their country into a dominion. Pétain said union would tie

France to a corpse. Reynaud's mistress sent him a note saying she hoped he was not going to act like the fifteenth-century queen Isabel, who had signed a treaty marrying her daughter to Henry V of England and passing the royal succession to the English. The union proposal fell by the wayside without a vote. Reynaud resigned. President Lebrun called on Pétain to form a government. A straw poll of ministers showed eleven opposing an armistice and nine supporting it, with four undecided. So the Prime Minister might have won had he stood firm. But he had had enough.

Pétain had his government list ready. Weygand took the Defence Ministry. Darlan became Minister for the Marine. Laval got nothing after opposition from Weygand led to Pétain withdrawing the offer of the Foreign Ministry. Instead, the serpentine Baudouin was given the job, and immediately asked the Spanish ambassador and the papal nuncio to sound out Berlin and Rome on armistice conditions. (Questioned in a legal case in 1955, Baudouin said de Gaulle's name appeared on Pétain's first ministerial list, but was struck off at Weygand's insistence. This seems highly unlikely, and Weygand denied the story.)

'It is with a heavy heart that I tell you today that the combat must be ended,'* Pétain declared in a national broadcast, adding that he gave France 'the gift of my person to alleviate its misfortune'. He had asked the adversary 'if he is ready to seek with me, among soldiers, after the struggle and in honour, ways to put an end to the hostilities'. He tried to get Mandel to back an armistice but the former Interior Minister remained steadfastly opposed. Over lunch at the Café de Paris, the old soldier wrote on the back of the menu 'June 3 1940, first bombing of Paris, bad omen' while the politician scribbled 'June 3 1940, first bombing of Paris, first step of recovery'. There was nothing to be done with the Marshal, Mandel remarked – 'He is gaga.'

Churchill telephoned the Marshal to deliver a violent tirade against an armistice, followed by a message in which he warned the French ministers that handing over the fleet to the Germans would 'scarify their names for a thousand years of history'. For the British, the immediate

*Baudouin had the published text of the address altered to read 'we must try to stop the fighting' to lessen the weight of the defeatist message.

priority was to find a man who would continue the fight outside France. Mandel was the obvious choice, but he turned down a suggestion from Spears to fly out with the British envoy in the morning. Sitting in a large room at the prefecture lit by a single candle, he acknowledged that he might be in danger as a Jew. That was precisely why he could not leave. 'It would look as if I was afraid, as if I was running away,' he added, according to Spears. Just then, a door into the room opened and his mistress, an actress from the Comédie-Française, looked in to say that their cases were packed to move, not to London but to a hotel.

De Gaulle only learned of the failure of the union scheme and Reynaud's resignation after landing in Bordeaux in a plane put at his disposal by the British. Weygand refused to receive him, but he got to see Reynaud at 11 p.m., and said he intended to go to Britain to continue the combat. The newly resigned Premier arranged for him to receive 100,000 francs from secret government funds, though, according to one of his staff, he remarked that 'de Gaulle is doing the wrong thing; he is undisciplined'.

Accounts of what happened next vary. The Gaullist version has him pursuing a dignified course at a pace of his own choosing. On the other hand, Spears wrote of the Frenchman hailing him and Campbell in a loud whisper from behind a column as they went to their final meeting with Reynaud. Weygand intended to arrest him, de Gaulle said. By this version, he was still waiting when the two British representatives left the former Premier, and accepted an offer of a flight to London in the morning. French biographers have pooh-poohed the Spears version, saying that de Gaulle decided alone to use the British plane to return to London. The Spears imbroglio clearly does not fit with the image of a great man moving serenely towards his destiny.*

That night, the general told his staff of his decision to leave France. 'I did not want to take a whole tribe along,' he said later. This was just as well since only his aide-de-camp, de Courcel, accompanied him, though a former private secretary gave him the keys to a flat he owned in Seamore Grove† by Hyde Park.[18]

*Having been one of de Gaulle's main supporters to start with, Spears subsequently fell out with him well before he wrote his memoirs, as will be seen.

†Now Curzon Place.

17 June. When the British ambassador called on Pétain, he too found the Marshal 'completely gaga', according to the diplomat Oliver Harvey. Meanwhile, de Gaulle was driven to the airport with de Courcel. In his suitcase were a pair of trousers, four shirts and a photograph of his family. Stopping at military headquarters on the way, he raised his arms and said, 'The Germans have lost the war. They are beaten, and France must go on fighting.' Then he drove to the airfield, and boarded the two-winged Dragon Rapide aircraft.

Again the accounts differ. Spears recalled a confused exit using subterfuge in which he hauled de Gaulle into the plane at the last moment after de Courcel had stowed the luggage. The French version depicts a smooth departure, though, in a memorandum to Churchill in 1948, de Gaulle acknowledged that 'some precautions' had been undertaken. The party flew up the Atlantic coast; below them a flotilla of ships in the Loire estuary was rescuing the last British soldiers from France; the troop carrier, *Lancastria*, was bombed by a German plane and sank, with the loss of at least 3,500 lives. Then they crossed Brittany, where de Gaulle's family was and where his eighty-year-old mother was dying. The general stared imperturbably ahead, reflecting, as he told his son, on the scale of the 'adventure' he was undertaking. For somebody raised in a tradition of loyalty and service, it was appalling, he acknowledged.

When the plane landed in Jersey to refuel, Spears got a cup of coffee for the general. Taking a sip, de Gaulle thought he had been served tea. 'It was his first introduction to the tepid liquid which, in England, passes for either one or the other,' Spears wrote. 'His martyrdom had begun.'[19]

2

'I, GENERAL DE GAULLE'

I
The call

Reaching London, de Gaulle lunched with Spears at the Royal Automobile Club (RAC) in Pall Mall, and then went to Downing Street to see Churchill, who greeted him warmly in the sunny garden, and offered him the chance of broadcasting to France on the BBC once Pétain had formally sought an armistice. Despite his departure from France, the general had not entirely broken with its new government, as was evident when he cabled Bordeaux asking if he should continue to talk to the British about transferring troops to Africa and on other subjects. But he was fast moving towards accepting the consequences of what he had done. At dinner that night at Jean Monnet's home, his hostess asked him how long he expected his mission to London to last. 'Madame,' he replied, 'I am not here on a mission. I am here to save the honour of France.' At table, he called Pétain a traitor; his host asked him to lower his voice as the butler was an admirer of the Marshal. Back in the flat he had borrowed, the general walked up and down in his bedroom, smoking heavily as he considered how to proceed.

Though Churchill had been favourably impressed, he was a stranger in the country to which he had flown. Those who did know of him held varied views. At the time of his appointment to the government, *The Times* had reported that he was regarded as 'one of the most brilliant of the younger generals . . . rather aggressively "right-wing", intensely theoretical . . . clear-minded, lucid and a man of action as well as a man of dreams and abstract ideas'. The head of the Foreign Office, Sir Alexander Cadogan, remarked to colleagues that he could not tell them anything about the Frenchman 'except that he's got a head like a pineapple and hips like a woman's'. At the time of the abortive union proposal, the Prime Minister's secretary, John Colville, wondered if he would turn out to be a second Napoleon. Desmond Morton, an intelligence officer who had supplied Churchill with information before the war and then moved into Downing Street with him, called him 'a magnificent crook . . . just what we want.'[1]

De Gaulle's first full day in London, 18 June, was the anniversary of the Battle of Waterloo. In France, the official count of refugees reached six million, and the Interior Ministry announced that all urban centres with more than 20,000 inhabitants would be declared open towns. Both Washington and Moscow recognised the Pétain government. In Munich, Hitler and Mussolini met to plan the future as the Führer prepared for the assault on isolated Britain. Stalin remained in alliance with Berlin, and Soviet troops completed the occupation of Latvia and Estonia. In Chicago, Roosevelt promised American mothers that he would not send their sons to fight in a war in far-off lands.

In France, there were scattered refusals to accept the capitulation. A military commander in the Auvergne ordered his men to resist. A Communist member of the National Assembly, Charles Tillon, issued a tract declaring that 'the French people will not bear slavery'. In Chartres, the Prefect of the Eure-et-Loir department, Jean Moulin, declined to sign a proclamation handed to him by the Germans and tried to kill himself by slitting his throat to avoid giving way under torture. But most politicians and officials were less resolute.

Mandel was arrested as he finished his lunch at the Chapon Fin restaurant with his mistress, apparently on the instructions of a Pétain follower who had become Justice Minister and referred to him simply as 'the Jew'. The Marshal said he had been told that Mandel was organising a plot to prevent an armistice. After the former minister defended himself, Pétain wrote a note acknowledging the error. According to the diplomat Oliver Harvey, Mandel said he would leave on a British warship anchored in Bordeaux, with his daughter, mistress and black valet, Baba, but changed his mind and sailed with twenty-seven other parliamentarians for North Africa. The British then sent Monnet and Pleven to try to recruit the radical Socialist leader Édouard Herriot; he listened to his visitors as he dined on a rack of lamb with sorrel sauce, but decided to stay in France.[2]

In London, two men, so different in many ways but united in a stubborn belief in their own indispensability, worked through the morning of 18 June on speeches which would go down in history as expressions of the will to defy the seemingly triumphant forces of despotism. In Downing Street, Churchill put the final touches to his 'Finest Hour' address which he delivered to the House of Commons later in the day. Across central London in his small flat, de Gaulle drafted and redrafted, with a pen nib dipped into an inkwell, the broadcast address which would provide the essential foundation stone for his future.

Unknown to him, the British Cabinet, meeting in Churchill's absence, decided that the proposed broadcast would be 'undesirable' while the Foreign Office was still hoping to get the new French government to 'act in conformity with the interests of the alliance'. Duff Cooper, the Minister of Information, did not tell the general of this decision when they lunched together. However, he tipped off Spears, who went to see Churchill that afternoon to argue that de Gaulle should speak to give French resistance a focus and to try to induce the remnants of France's air force at Bordeaux to fly to Britain.

The Prime Minister told Spears he would authorise the broadcast if members of the Cabinet would change their minds. Looking 'miserable and hot', according to Colville, Spears set off to speak to them individually. His mission was successful. An addendum on top of the record of the earlier decision noted, 'Consulted one by one, Cabinet members agreed that de Gaulle should be authorised to speak.'[3]

In the flat off Park Lane, Élisabeth de Méribel, a friend of de Courcel who was employed at the French economic office in London and had been enlisted as a temporary secretary, tapped out the speech with two fingers on a portable typewriter on a small table in the entry hall. She had trouble deciphering his angular writing amid all his corrections.

In the early evening, accompanied by de Courcel, de Gaulle took a taxi to a BBC building by Oxford Circus to make the first of sixty-seven broadcasts from London during the war. He wore military uniform with leggings and polished boots. Spears and two members of the BBC staff led him to the studio where he did a sound check with a single word, 'France'. Then, his voice a little stiff, he launched into his text. He was pale, his forelock stuck to his forehead as he stared at the microphone as if speaking to a person, which, given his personalisation of his nation, he was.

His message, which went down in history as '*l'Appel du 18 juin*', was simple. 'Has the last word been said?' he asked. 'Must hope disappear? Is defeat final?' To which there was one simple answer: 'No!' France was not alone in what was a worldwide struggle, he insisted three times. It had overseas possessions, could align itself with the British Empire and 'use without limit the immense industry of the United States'. Circumspect about his own role, he simply invited French officers and soldiers who had crossed to Britain, mainly in the Dunkirk evacuation, to contact him. This was a moment to talk about the nation, not to push forward his own claims.*[4]

The general's speech was recorded and then broadcast at 10 p.m. By the time it went out, he had dined nearby at the Langham Hotel with de Courcel and gone back to his flat. His aide thought he was happier than he had been since leaving Bordeaux. To his understandable annoyance when he discovered this the following day, the BBC did not keep the recording. Very few people heard his words that night. Among them, according to a relation present in Brittany at the time, was de Gaulle's mother, a little old lady in black with heart trouble; she pulled the sleeve of a clergyman, who had alerted her to the broadcast in advance, and said 'That's my son, *Monsieur le curé*. That's my son.' Though the newspapers in Bordeaux ignored it, there were reports in the press in Lyon and Marseille. The reaction from the French government was restrained – the ambassador in London was instructed to tell the British that it was 'an unfriendly gesture' to allow a French officer to broadcast against the Pétain administration.

*See full text of speech at end of chapter.

II
God's hands

Charles de Gaulle did not suddenly erupt from nowhere in June 1940. His character and his style were already fully formed, as will be clear from the next section of this book. Otherwise, he would not have achieved what he did. June 17–18 was the moment when his long preparation for a moment of destiny was realised. But he was still displaying amazing presumption. He was a newly promoted general in a chain of command that reached up to the two eminent commanders whom he disavowed, treating one as a traitor and disregarding the other. He had no mandate from anybody to continue resistance to the Germans in defiance of a legally constituted government which was seeking an armistice. He had never been elected to any post, and had held a junior government position for just twelve days. Nobody important accompanied him to London.

The broadcast was not an immediate bid for leadership, as such. Rather, it set the stage for what was to follow. His force of character resonated from his words with their careful literary composition. He would brook no compromises and speak only the truth as he saw it. He had taken a decisive step. As he later told the faithful Gaullist Pierre Messmer, he stopped being a soldier on 18 June, in the sense that he no longer adhered to the soldier's first duty of obeying orders. He was his own man, as he would remain for the next three decades. His address thus became the foundation of Gaullism. From now on, he was the General with a capital G.

As the broadcast demonstrated, he was always a great gambler, a bluffer ready to take a supreme risk in defying Pétain and the new order in France. But, behind his arrogant intransigence, the General could be calculating in seeking to achieve his ends. Like most successful bettors, he was often considerably less headstrong than he appeared, taking care not to burn his bridges prematurely and not to expose himself unduly.

For instance, though de Gaulle denied having submitted any of his BBC speeches to the British government for approval, it is clear that he did so on at least some occasions and accepted changes. The speech he read out on 18 June dropped a reference to 'the chiefs who have been at the head of the French armies for numerous years'; the British still hoped to deal with Pétain and Weygand. The text for the following day was seen by Cadogan at the Foreign Office whose objections were relayed to Churchill; as a result, according to the mandarin, Spears 'humbly' sent him the wording of de Gaulle's broadcasts. The historian Philippe Oulmont, Research Director at the Charles de Gaulle Foundation in Paris, thinks that speech was probably not broadcast, and may have been written, or rewritten, subsequently in the form in which it was later published.

On 22 June, the Prime Minister said de Gaulle should bring the scripts of his next broadcast to Downing Street to be put to the Cabinet, which approved it without any changes. Four days later, Gladwyn Jebb of the Foreign Office was handed the text of a broadcast by de Gaulle for vetting; though he found it brilliant, he decided it violated British rules. So he hurried round to the General's hotel to suggest alterations. The Frenchman declared them '*parfaitement ri-di-cules*' but accepted them in the end in order to get on the air.[5]

Though *The Times* ran a headline, 'De Gaulle heads Free French', on 19 June, the British establishment was not convinced he was its man. The War Secretary, Anthony Eden, was supportive, as he would continue to be when he moved to the Foreign Office at the end of 1940. But two very senior diplomats, Alexander Cadogan and Robert Vansittart, had their doubts and the chief of the Imperial General Staff, Alan Brooke, was 'not much impressed', finding de Gaulle 'supercilious and self-satisfied' and 'not much use'. Colville recorded in his diary that 'it was never intended that de Gaulle should be any more than a rallying point for expatriated Frenchmen'. Duff Cooper led a delegation to Casablanca in a fresh attempt to enlist Mandel and other parliamentarians. There were also hopes that Weygand would head an administration in North Africa, which might detach itself from the Germans.[6]

On 22 June, France signed the armistice terms laid down by Hitler in the same railway carriage, in the same forest clearing at Compiègne, where Germany had surrendered in 1918. France was required to pay the costs of the occupation forces at a vastly inflated rate which absorbed 55 per cent of national revenue. The franc was devalued by 20 per cent. Germany again annexed Alsace-Lorraine. Regions it controlled included most of the nation's industry and mineral resources. In theory, the Pétain administration remained France's government; in practice, power clearly lay with the victors, and the collaborators did little more than provide an administrative and policing apparatus. In a little-noted clause in the agreement, the French consented to hand over political refugees on their territory at the demand of the Nazis; two leading German Socialists, Rudolf Breitscheid and Rudolf Hilferding, were among those taken back to Germany to their deaths.

The Pétain regime could argue that it had been left with direct authority over two-fifths of the country, and a 94,000-man army, which, however, was not permitted tanks. Apart from ships to defend the Empire, the fleet was to be put out of commission and laid up in five ports. The Marshal and Weygand pronounced the conditions 'tough but not dishonourable'. It seemed to them a lot better than continuing a hopeless war.

De Gaulle reacted with his most cutting and personal broadcast, asking what France's fate would be if the Allies won the war. 'Honour, common sense, and the superior interests of the nation command all the Free French to continue fighting wherever they are and however they can,' he added. 'I, General de Gaulle, am starting this national task here in England . . . I invite all the French who want to remain free to listen to me and to follow me.'

*

The British efforts to win support among the French establishment were doomed to failure. Having declared that Hitler would wring the neck of the British chicken, Weygand was not going to side with London against Germany. In Morocco, Mandel was packed off to a boat where Duff Cooper could not contact him. France's proconsuls in North Africa did not respond to a message from de Gaulle offering to work under them if they would oppose the Pétain regime.

So, in the end, there was no alternative to the General. He had the inestimable advantage of having made up his mind, of having won

Churchill's appreciation and of having a simple message of hope and national prestige; in the words of a later proclamation, France had lost a battle but not the war and must preserve its honour. The next four years would test whether he could make that stick, and become the embodiment of the country which he felt could not be itself without achieving grandeur. As it turned out, the blank sheet on which he operated would be an advantage, enabling him to mould the Free French movement as he wished. But, at the time, according to his recollections to his son, he wondered if he was doing something mad, 'throwing myself into the water without knowing where the bank is . . . I put myself in God's hands.'[7]

*

Original text of de Gaulle's speech, 18 June 1940:

> The leaders who, for many years, have been at the head of the French armies have formed a government. This government, alleging the defeat of our armies, has made contact with the enemy in order to stop the fighting. It is true, we were, we are, overwhelmed by the mechanical, ground and air forces of the enemy. Infinitely more than their number, it is the tanks, the aeroplanes, the tactics of the Germans which are causing us to retreat. It was the tanks, the aeroplanes, the tactics of the Germans that surprised our leaders to the point of bringing them to where they are today.
>
> But has the last word been said? Must hope disappear? Is defeat final? No!
>
> Believe me, I who am speaking to you with full knowledge of the facts, and who tell you that nothing is lost for France. The same means that overcame us can bring us victory one day. For France is not alone! She is not alone! She is not alone! She has a vast Empire behind her. She can align with the British Empire that holds the sea and continues the fight. She can, like England, use without limit the immense industry of the United States.
>
> This war is not limited to the unfortunate territory of our country. This war is not over as a result of the Battle of France. This war is a

worldwide war. All the mistakes, all the delays, all the suffering, do not alter the fact that there are, in the world, all the means necessary to crush our enemies one day. Vanquished today by mechanical force, in the future we will be able to overcome by a superior mechanical force. The fate of the world depends on it.

I, General de Gaulle, currently in London, invite the officers and the French soldiers who are located in British territory or who might end up here, with their weapons or without their weapons, I invite the engineers and the specialised workers of the armament industries who are located in British territory or who might end up here, to put themselves in contact with me.

Whatever happens, the flame of French resistance must not be extinguished and will not be extinguished.

PART TWO
THE MAKING OF A REBEL

3

'UN PETIT LILLOIS À PARIS'

The third of the five children of Henri and Jeanne de Gaulle, Charles was born on 22 November 1890, into a family that was estranged from the Republic and looked back to an older France. The de Gaulle home was in Paris, but, following tradition, his mother went to her mother's home in Lille to give birth in a context far from the hedonism of the *belle époque* in the capital.

Members of the minor aristocracy on the paternal side, the de Gaulles traced their history back to Ireland and to an ancestor who had fought the English at Agincourt. There was a division between those who thought their roots were Flemish in origin and that their name came from *van der Waulle* – 'from the rampart' – and those who traced the line back to Richard de Gaulle, a nobleman in Normandy. Prosperous inhabitants of Paris under the royalty, the family lost much of its money and assets in the Revolution of 1789.

Charles de Gaulle's grandfather, Julien, was an archivist and historian, his wife a prolific writer who turned her hand to a stream of romantic novels as well as biographies. They left Paris for Lille where Julien worked in a boarding school, but appear to have been perennially short of money. To raise cash, he sold documents which did not belong to him, and had to leave, moving back to Paris where the couple scraped a living, changing homes constantly. Fervent Catholics, they rejected the Enlightenment and the Revolution. They had a strong sense of charity and identification with those left on one side by society.

The family of de Gaulle's mother, the Maillots, settled in Lille in 1872, running factories that wove net to make curtains depicting the fables of La Fontaine. The city was a proud place, with Flemish roots dating back to 1066, its history preserved in ornate medieval buildings, its stately colonnaded fifteenth-century bourse, and its traditional carnivals. In the nineteenth century, it played a significant role in France's industrial expansion, notably in textiles and metals. With the adjoining agglomerations of Roubaix and Tourcoing, and with the coalfields of north-east France nearby, it was described as a 'French Manchester', quintupling its wealth between 1850 and 1914 as running water, electricity and gas street lighting were installed, department stores opened and a tram system linked the city with its neighbours.

The maternal grandmother, Madame Maillot-Delannoy, lived in an unostentatious house on the rue Princesse outside the city centre. The rooms were of modest size, though the mahogany dining table could be extended to seat twenty. Portraits of Irish, German and French ancestors hung in the drawing room. A veranda at the back gave on to a small courtyard. It was all very self-contained. The tradition of upright simplicity and self-sufficiency would remain with de Gaulle throughout his life, providing him with a highly conventional lifestyle within which to pursue highly unconventional ideas, his solid private existence giving him the platform from which to strut the public stage.

*

Henri and Jeanne de Gaulle had their five children in ten years – Xavier (1887), Marie-Agnès (1889), Charles (1890), Jacques (1893) and Pierre (1897). Their parents brought them up to look back to the France of the old monarchy, to the 'real' nation in contrast to the 'legal country' of the Republic. A veteran of the 1870 war with Germany, wounded in fighting outside Paris, Henri was, in the words of one biographer of his son, 'more conscious of his duties than of his privileges'. A memorial notice called him 'a representative of the old true France'. His most famous offspring described him as 'a man of thought, of culture, of tradition, imbued with the sentiment of the dignity of France'.

Henri believed that the Revolution of 1789 had been 'satanic in its essence'. A subscriber to the nationalist *Action française* newspaper, he regarded the Republic as 'vile', and condemned universal suffrage for giving equal weight to the common people and the educated elite. The de Gaulles did not sing 'La Marseillaise' or celebrate the national holiday of 14 July. Nor did Henri have any sympathy with the bourgeois capitalism which dominated France. Like most of his compatriots, he was obsessed by the idea of gaining revenge on Germany for France's defeat in 1870, which had also led to the Third Republic he so detested.

A clever, learned man, he added to the education of his children with readings of classical French and Roman texts, and instituted a regime of short speeches in Latin after grace at meals. Disapproving of motor cars, he took horse-drawn carriages rather than taxis. He also disliked fountain pens. His erudition and respect for the French language marked his son, whose extraordinary vocabulary and use of language became integral to his claim to personify the nation that spoke this tongue.[1]

Henri and Jeanne were first cousins, he twelve years older than her. They were profoundly attached to the Catholic Church. Though Henri began his career as a civil servant at the Interior Ministry, they were inevitably alienated from a regime which made religion the dividing line for politics and society, secularised schools, cemeteries and hospitals, legalised work on Sunday, introduced divorce, removed the crucifixes from law courts and outlawed Catholic orders such as the Jesuits. (Trappists were excused as their silence was thought to make them less threatening.) The de Gaulles had a social conscience and were charitable, but there could be no reconciliation between those who believed ardently in a revealed religion and a Republic which put its faith in the overwhelming power of reason and science.

Jeanne, a stronger character than her husband, was recalled by her second son as having 'an intransigent passion for the fatherland equal to her religious piety'. She and her mother imposed a puritanical regime which had no room for the theatre or dancing. If the word *amant* figured in a traditional song, they replaced it with *maman.* When given a ration card, Jeanne drew a cross against the line which said 'sex'. She was said to have despaired of the way in which her children accepted the Republic, and, in old age, called the Popular Front Prime

Minister, Léon Blum, 'a henchman of Satan'. Though he would work with Blum and become the saviour of the Republic, Charles told his sister, Marie-Agnès, shortly before his death: 'What has often reassured me . . . is the conviction that Mam would have been behind me always and in everything.'[2]

The heritage from his parents was highly significant in de Gaulle's life. There is no record of him rebelling against them. Rather, they gave him values that would remain with him even if, politically, he moved away from their strict creed. Like them, he was ready to stand aside from mainstream opinion and challenge ruling hierarchies, convinced of his rectitude. Like them, he drew strict lines between right and wrong, adopting a Manichean mindset that damned opponents and allowed for no error. Like them, he remained personally prudish, and believed that charity should be a private matter. And, like them, he was careful with money and lived modestly, suspicious of the world of business and finance. 'I have never been bourgeois,' he said. 'The bourgeoisie is wealth . . . My family and I have always been poor.'

As for religion, the piety practised by his parents was with him from the very start. A crucifix hung above the bed where Charles' mother gave birth at 4 a.m. on 22 November. Another cross stood on the mantelpiece by the cradle where the baby was laid in a lace robe. He was baptised a few hours later at the ornately decorated eighteenth-century church of Saint-André, with the Christian names Charles André Joseph Marie. His education was at Catholic schools. The first was run by the Brothers of the Christian Schools of Saint Thomas Aquinas in Paris, which he entered just before he reached the age of five, a curly-haired boy who had just started wearing trousers instead of smocks. In 1900, he moved to the Jesuit College of the Immaculate Conception in the rue de Vaugirard, which had evaded the ban on schools run by unauthorised religious congregations by turning itself into a private trust company.

Henri de Gaulle had become a master there after his ideological gulf with the Republic led him to resign from the Interior Ministry. He taught philosophy and literature, lecturing from a podium with a crucifix on the white wall behind him. The curriculum gave his second son his extensive grounding in the classics. The boy won six prizes in his last year but his elder brother, Xavier, was regarded as more clever while Charles' unruly nature led his father to remark that he was 'not what you would call a good pupil'.

Henri took his children on weekend outings from their six-room flat on the Left Bank to the Arc de Triomphe and Napoleon's tomb, to the town of Stains, where he had been wounded in the fighting in 1870, and to the public gallery at the National Assembly. Charles recalled that nothing made more of an impression on him that the symbols of France's glory – night falling on Notre-Dame Cathedral or captured enemy flags fluttering in the army bastion of Les Invalides, and the great glass dome of the Grand Palais towering across the Seine.

He was enthused by the crowd cheering France's ally, the Tsar of Russia, the Universal Exhibition of 1900 and military parades. His father ignored his wife's hostility to the theatre by giving their son a tenth-birthday present of an outing to see two of the most celebrated stars of the day, Sarah Bernhardt and Lucien Guitry, in the major new play, Edmond Rostand's *L'Aiglon*, about Napoleon's offspring – at the age of fifty-five, the great actress used all her art, and tight corsets, to play the role of a dying twenty-one-year-old man. Charles' own literary gifts were becoming apparent. He wrote a tale in verse about an encounter between a brigand and a middle-class traveller which did well in a competition in Lille. The jury told him he could be paid twenty-five francs or have the work published. He chose the latter.

When legislation against religious schools led to the closure of the College of the Immaculate Conception in 1906, Charles was sent to another Jesuit college, in Belgium, where he spent a year, learning German and visiting his sister, Marie-Agnès, who had moved to the Belgian town of Charleroi where she married an engineer in 1910. Replying to an accusation that pupils of Jesuits lacked personality, he observed: 'We will know how to show that is not the case. The future will be great because it will be moulded by our deeds.'[3]

Returning to Paris in the autumn of 1908, he was enrolled at the Collège Stanislas in Montparnasse, founded a hundred years earlier by a religious order which had been taken over by a lay administration to save it from closure but retained its religious character. By then, he had decided that he wanted to become a soldier; so he concentrated on the entry examination for the leading military school, Saint-Cyr. He wrote another short story about a love affair between a French officer and a young lady in New Caledonia, but decided to publish it under a pseudonym because of the subject matter.

To improve his German linguistic skills, he visited the Black Forest, where he saved money by staying at monasteries and with priests, went to mass at 7 a.m., and met veterans of the 1870 war, one of whom recounted the bombardment of Strasbourg with 'fanatical enthusiasm' brought on by overconsumption of schnapps. He noted how the Germans regarded the French as 'bohemians who like disorder and never agree with one another'.[4]

He kept up his links with Lille through regular visits to Madame Maillot-Delannoy, picking up the local *ch'timi* dialect, which he used to talk to dogs later in life. Though he claimed to embody the whole nation, de Gaulle was, as he once wrote, 'a man of the north'. He described himself in his youth as 'un petit Lillois à Paris', 'a little Lille boy in Paris'. For him, this was the region where France's destiny had been played out against foreign aggression. In speeches much later, he would refer to 'us people of the north'. He prized the way they had served France, and what he called their ability to confront the truth. As the writer Paul-Marie de la Gorce put it: 'When he evoked the French people, it was above all the population of the north he had in mind. When he spoke to the French, it was of the people of the north that he thought. When he chose the words with which to address them, the terms that came to him were those which struck a certain northern sensibility.'

The extended family also stayed in the north for its holidays, renting villas along the coast at Wimereux, Wimille and Malo-les-Bains, until Henri bought a large two-storey house surrounded by vines, wheat fields and truffles in the green region of the Dordogne. Getting there involved an interminable train journey across France, followed by a final stage in a horse-drawn carriage. Comfort was rudimentary. Boys and girls slept in separate dormitories. But, if Henri and Charles both wanted to get some peace and quiet on their vacations, the crush of the family was as great in the Dordogne as on the Channel. Looking at holiday photographs in later years, the General said the de Gaulles resembled the eccentric provincial family the Fenouillards, the subject of a popular illustrated book of the time. 'My father and I detested the milling around,' he recalled. 'We wanted each of us to have his own space and to be able to keep his distance.'[5]

*

The France in which de Gaulle grew up marked him profoundly. He shared the pride of his compatriots in their country's achievements. In culture, it could boast the Impressionist painters and great sculptors such as Rodin, writers of the stature of Zola, Proust, Rimbaud and Verlaine and composers like Debussy, while it led the way in the new art of the cinema. French scientists were among world leaders. The Eiffel Tower showed off France's technological skill. The Suez Canal was the work of a French entrepreneur. The Universal Exhibition in Paris in 1900 attracted fifty million people. The Bon Marché was the world's biggest department store while the Moulin Rouge, the cancan and the courtesans known as the *grandes horizontales* incarnated the racier side of the *belle époque* that visitors such as Britain's future King Edward VII found so alluring.

In 1900, the French capital hosted the Olympic Games as well as opening the first *métropolitain* underground railway line. The country was a leader in developing aviation and motor cars for tourism and sport – the first Tour de France bicycle race was staged in 1903. France's Empire covered about ten million square kilometres, encompassing some fifty million people outside the metropolitan hexagon. It stretched from the northern shores of the Mediterranean to Indochina, from the South Pacific to islands off Canada. Knowing how far their country's reach extended was a reassurance for the French that they belonged in the very first rank of nations with a 'civilising mission' by which countries in Africa and Asia would be brought the virtues of their culture and language.

De Gaulle's feelings went beyond simple pride. He vaunted nationalism as the 'most generous and disinterested' of feelings and quoted approvingly the saying of the militant polemicist Paul Déroulède, that 'the man who does not love his mother more than other mothers and his own country more than other countries loves neither his mother nor his country'. But a second national trait which was evident around 1900 also marked him through his life, and fitted naturally with his view of himself as a superior man who would be needed to save the nation. This was the concern that, for all its plus points, France was in decline and that its people and leaders were unable to live up to the greatness their state should exhibit. Men were said to be losing their masculinity, and the population as a whole to be in the grip of *neurasthénie*, a depression heading towards degeneracy. 'It is written in the destinies of this country to find its men always inferior to circumstances,' a leading politician, Jules Ferry, lamented.

The particular anxiety was the growing power of the Reich across the Rhine. The crushing defeat of France's army under Napoleon III in 1870 by the Germans, who then proclaimed their national unity in the Hall of Mirrors at Versailles, bred a preoccupation with gaining revenge, epitomised by the need to recover the lost territories of Alsace and Lorraine in the east. But there was a nagging sense of worry as Germany's population and industrial performance increased far faster than France's. Berlin challenged France's colonial position in Africa and France was obliged to join in a naval arms race that boosted military spending till it gobbled up a third of the national budget. There was also a jarring moment when expansion in Africa brought conflict with Britain on the Upper Nile in the Fashoda Incident of 1898. Deciding that it needed London's friendship against Germany, the Foreign Ministry ordered the withdrawal of its expeditionary force. For nationalists, it was a terrible humiliation; de Gaulle regarded this as the most traumatic event of his childhood.

When they looked inward, the French had plenty of reasons for concern, too. Population growth fell to near zero. Second in the European population stakes at the start of the nineteenth century, France ranked only fifth by the end of it. There were frequent warnings of moral and psychological decay, notably from alcohol and syphilis, supplemented by a jeremiad from a Dr Ludovic O'Fallowell about women bicycle riders falling prey to 'voluptuous sensations'. The country was socially backward. Living conditions outside smart metropolitan centres were often deplorable, working hours extremely long and state welfare virtually non-existent. Women were regarded as homemakers with no place in public life – and certainly not the vote, partly because of lay politicians's fears that they might back religious parties. Though France remained a major financial power and drew significant revenue from colonies, Britain clearly led in both departments. Industry stagnated between 1870 and 1895; factory output fell from 9 per cent of the world total in 1880 to 6 per cent by 1900. The middle class were greater savers, but their money went mainly into government securities and Russian loans rather than into companies.[6]

Politically, the Third Republic, given formal legal status by a one-vote majority in the National Assembly in 1875, was dominated by a broad moderate bourgeois coalition which saw lay education as the means of establishing a Republic of Reason. Any serious threat from the Left had been set aside by the crushing of the Paris Commune in 1871. The Right was disunited and badly led, though it constituted a continuing rejectionist front which dreamed of a return of the monarchy. After a crisis in 1877, the executive authority of the President of the Republic was overshadowed by that of parliament. Prime Ministers were often in a weak position since they depended on the approval of a legislature in which the division of the dominant centre into three groups made coherent majorities rare. Ministerial instability impeded major policy initiatives.

The system reflected the broad desire of the middle class for a settled existence in which awkward issues were obfuscated. This did not prevent periodic shocks. In 1888–9, a dashing general, Georges Boulanger, who had been sacked from the army for political agitation against the Republic, put himself forward as a patriot ready to revive the nation. His supporters won by-elections, drawing on anybody who had a grudge against the regime, be they royalists, rural Catholics or urban radicals – the propagandist Maurice Barrès exalted 'national socialism'. The general on the white horse lacked staying power, however. He fled to the arms of his mistress in Brussels when the government spread rumours that he was to be arrested for high treason. Though his supporters and parties of the Right did well at a national election, Boulanger remained in exile, ruined and devastated by the death of his mistress; then he shot himself on her grave.

More serious was the protracted trauma of the Dreyfus affair which split the country, sharpened the conflict between republican advocates of a lay regime and Catholic reactionaries, between anti-Semites and those who saw Jews as French people like any others. Captain Alfred Dreyfus, convicted of spying for Germany in a trumped-up case in 1894 and sent to Devil's Island in French Guiana, became a scapegoat for the enemies of the Republic, and a symbol for those who defended values they traced back to 1789. A Jew, he personified the fears of Semitic conspiracies against the nation spread by pamphleteers like Edmond Drumont whose tract, *La France Juive*, went through two hundred editions between 1886 and 1914. The virulence of attacks by the Catholic Assumptionist teaching order deepened the religious–lay divide, which was simultaneously sharpened by a toughening of the Vatican's approach towards the anti-clerical Republic.

A firm believer in the army, Dreyfus could not rouse himself to offer a strong defence which would have entailed exposing the skulduggery of the officers who accused him, while his bourgeois background and military loyalty led some left-wingers to cast him as a class enemy. His condemnation was not quashed until 1906. Even then, the divisions shown up by the affair continued when the Army Minister of a subsequent government was discovered to be using informers and Freemasons to collect damaging information about Catholic officers.

A family tradition has it that Henri de Gaulle thought Dreyfus had been wrongly convicted, but he appears to have been less concerned with the issue of the innocence or guilt of an individual and more with the way in which the army had allowed its reputation and prestige to be tarnished. For his son Charles, Dreyfus was, first and foremost, a member of the forces, regardless of race. More than half a century later, de Gaulle was told that the wife of an ambassador being posted to an Arab country was a descendant of Dreyfus. 'Yes, I know,' he cut in. 'She is the granddaughter of a French officer.' While acknowledging the miscarriage of justice in the Dreyfus affair and the 'forgeries, manoeuvres and abuses of the prosecution', he wrote that his main sorrow was about the way in which the affair acted to 'poison political life and fan political passion'. Though the crisis had been detonated by officers who fabricated the case of treason against Dreyfus and then tried to prevent the truth emerging and justice being done, de Gaulle would depict the army as the victim of 'criticisms and insults' as the military ideal was weakened and 'a so-called social ideal replaced it'.

While Émile Zola's open letter to the President of the Republic, with its ringing title of *J'accuse*, rallied the pro-Dreyfus camp, opponents of the Republic found a new voice in the *Action française* movement. Founded in 1898 under the influence of the reactionary thinker Charles Maurras, it aimed to 'strangle the wench', as the movement termed the regime. It advocated a popular monarchy to free the nation from the 'four confederates' of the 'anti-France' – Jews, Protestants, Freemasons and foreigners. The Nationalists who adopted its teachings became the largest single party on the Paris city council and had fifteen deputies elected from the capital in 1902, one proclaiming himself 'an anti-Semitic Republican' who demanded that '150,000 Jews and their lackeys, 25,000 Freemasons, stop oppressing and ruining 38 million French people'.

Others turned to socialism, syndicalism or anarchism. Religion offered a haven for some. Evangelical Catholicism flourished. The huge edifice of the Sacré-Cœur was built to float above Paris at the summit of Montmartre. The cult of Joan of Arc mushroomed as the separation of Church and state was declared in 1905. A series of scandals heightened cynicism about politicians. 'We have been continually betrayed by our teachers and our leaders,' wrote the poet Charles Péguy.[7]

Amid these fluctuating currents, the army offered the best way to serve France for an intensely patriotic young man whose background and beliefs set him at odds with the regime. De Gaulle would note the 'fascination' the army exercised on bourgeois youth. 'Officers hoped for revenge and glory,' he added. 'They were given respect.' In his memoirs, he remembered that he idealised the prospect of war that would enable him to help his country in its 'gigantic trials'. He regarded violent confrontation between nations as inevitable, and vaunted the 'virility' of citizens ready to defend their fatherland as compared to 'the love of gain and the wish for vice' provoked by prolonged peace.[8]

De Gaulle's interest in the military went back to his boyhood when he had spent his pocket money building up a collection of 1,800 toy soldiers which he used to stage great historic battles; he always commanded the French and Swiss troops. At the age of fifteen, he wrote a detailed account of a coming war with Germany, putting himself at the head of 200,000 men who won repeated victories with gallant bayonet charges amid storms of bullets. Having completed his schooling, he sat the examination to enter the military college of Saint-Cyr in 1908. He finished only 119th out of 221 successful candidates, but at least he was in France's main training school for officers.

Before going to the college, cadets spent a year with a military unit. Rather than picking a dashing colonial or cavalry outfit, de Gaulle chose the 33rd Infantry Regiment, based in Arras, just fifty-five kilometres from the family's second home in Lille. Though it had fought in Napoleon's campaigns, the 33rd was a workaday unit. Its barracks were rudimentary, discipline was slack and there was a lot of drinking. But there were practical reasons for de Gaulle's decision: his family did not have the money to enable him to pay for a horse, and he preferred northern France to North Africa or Indochina. With his confident bearing and extensive knowledge, the eighteen-year-old made a distinct impression on those around him. Explaining why he had not named the young man as a sergeant, his captain asked how he could do so to somebody who would only feel at ease as a general.

His offensive spirit chimed with the teachings of the most influential French military theorist of the day, Colonel Louis de Grandmaison, who preached the importance of willpower and offensive tactics, epitomised by the bayonet charge. But de Gaulle had a typically Spartan view of military life. Cadets could have 'neither loves, nor homes', he would recall. They were destined for tiredness, privation, uncertainties. They would be killed first and in the greatest numbers – 'and it is very good that it is thus,' he added.[9]

In October 1910, de Gaulle finished his stint in Arras and travelled in heavy rain to Versailles where Saint-Cyr was located. 'When I entered the army, it was one of the greatest things in the world,' he remembered. The daily routine was highly demanding. Reveille was at 6.30 a.m. and studies continued until 7.30 p.m. From the start, de Gaulle stood out from his comrades; his height gained him the nickname of 'the big asparagus'. At a hazing initiation ceremony, he was called out by an older cadet wielding a billiard cue. Showing the self-assurance that already marked him, he stood up calmly and impressed everybody with a rendition of the celebrated 'big nose' speech of Cyrano de Bergerac in the play of the same name – although that did not save him from being knocked down on to the backs of other youths kneeling on the floor.

Reports praised his conduct, manners, intelligence, character, attitude, zeal, military spirit and resistance to fatigue. His marching was rated highly. The only weak points were sport and shooting. He graduated thirteenth out of 210. A photograph showed him immaculate in a five-buttoned tunic and plumed helmet, with his sword. 'A highly gifted cadet,' his passing-out report noted. 'Conscientious and earnest worker. Excellent state of mind. Will make an excellent officer.' Supplementary notes by superior officers remarked on his calmness and powers of command and decision.

The newly graduated de Gaulle was keen for war to restore France's status. Everybody in the French army, from the commanding generals to the rank-and-file infantry, 'should have only one idea – advance, advance to the attack, reach the Germans and skewer them or make them run away,' he wrote. As they rushed forward, the French troops should not pause to look after their wounded, he added; 'the best service one can render to wounded comrades is to win a quick victory. Then they will be cared for, quietly and well.' Half a century later, he recalled that he had no horror of conflict with Germany. For him, it was merely an 'unknown adventure'.[10]

In September 1912, he returned from Saint-Cyr to the 33rd Regiment in Arras with the rank of second lieutenant. Capital of the Artois region, Arras had prospered as a mining and industrial town, and had a rich upper class which gave fashionable receptions and dinners in their town houses. For the second lieutenant, however, the main attraction was the commander of the 33rd Regiment, Colonel Philippe Pétain, who, he recalled in his memoirs, showed him 'what the gift and art of command were worth'. Also a man of the north, Pétain was known for rigour and independence of mind. He alienated superiors with his sarcasm and self-confidence. Though he went to mass, he said he had lost his religious faith. When asked by republican inspectors to list practising Catholic officers, he replied: 'I don't know. I'm always in the first row and I don't turn round.'

The relationship between the two men would be one of the themes of their lives for the next three and a half decades. At the start, there was mutual admiration – when the lieutenant objected to his colonel's judgement on a seventeenth-century battle, Pétain did not take umbrage but noted his subordinate's 'real value which provides fine hope for the future'. Pétain's independence of mind and blunt speaking paralleled the way in which the younger man would set out his own stall. Each was a rebel in his time, ready to risk his career as a result.

Handsome and blue-eyed, with a practically bald head, Pétain was in his mid-fifties when de Gaulle joined the regiment. He was an inveterate womaniser. 'I love two things above all else,' he said, 'sex and the infantry'; there was speculation subsequently that he and the junior officer shared a mistress. This story stemmed from a letter sent to de Gaulle in 1945 by a certain woman from Arras. Pressing his finger on the paper so hard that the nail cut into it, the General said: 'It was in her place . . . at Arras that I met Pétain.'

The colonel was moved to the command of another infantry brigade in April 1914, and was preparing to end his military career by the time war broke out, promotion to the rank of general seemingly ruled out by his unwillingness to curb his tongue. Remaining in Arras, Lieutenant de Gaulle found provincial barracks life irksome. He showed an artistic side in pencil drawings of the surrounding countryside; since photographs were still quite rare, young officers were encouraged to record the terrain round their barracks. There was no doubting the way in which he stood out. His demeanour earned him the nickname of '*le Connétable*' – 'the Constable' – the term for a high-ranking medieval functionary who led royal armies and was charged with the peace of the nation.

However, the army to which he belonged was not in the best of shape. There were mutinies. Reservists often did not turn up for training, or were exempted for agricultural work. Germany spent twice as much as France on armaments and equipment, and the size of its forces swelled; it was not until 1913 that the National Assembly introduced three-year compulsory military service to boost France's numbers from 450,000 to

750,000. The high command did not take proper account of the impact of modern weapons, such as machine guns and heavy artillery. Fortresses on France's eastern border were allowed to fall into disrepair. The head of the Staff College declared aircraft useless for the armed forces. When it was suggested that the infantry's kepis should be replaced by steel helmets, the commander-in-chief, Joseph Joffre, replied: 'We will not have time to manufacture them for I will have wrung the Boches' necks in two months.'[11]

Nor was there any evolution on the political front where ministerial infighting brought eleven changes of government between 1909 and 1914. Then, on 3 August 1914, the outbreak of war created national unity. 'There are no more parties,' wrote President Raymond Poincaré. The Left, which had been shaken by the assassination of its icon, Jean Jaurès, by a fanatic inspired by right-wing press attacks, took up the cause of fighting in a just struggle for republican values and the rights of man against Prussian imperialism. Two Socialists joined the government. Decrees for the closure of religious establishments were revoked in the name of national cohesion.

To cement that unity, it was important that France should be seen to be fighting a defensive war. 'For the sake of public opinion, let the Germans put themselves in the wrong,' concluded a Cabinet meeting as events unfolded after the assassination of the Austro-Hungarian Archduke Franz Ferdinand at Sarajevo. Berlin obliged while the mechanism of alliances in Europe propelled the Reich, the Austro-Hungarian Empire, France, Britain and Russia to war. On 2 August, the Kaiser's forces invaded Luxembourg. Poincaré declared a state of emergency. Berlin demanded free passage for its forces through Belgium, which King Albert refused. On the false pretext that French aeroplanes had bombed Nuremberg, Germany declared war on France. On 4 August, its army entered Belgium, treating the guarantee of neutrality dating back to 1839 as a scrap of paper it would not allow to stand in its way. That led Britain to declare war. Unlike 1870, France was not alone.

Poincaré proclaimed 'a sacred union in the presence of the enemy' to enable France to fight for liberty, justice and reason. The nation, the twenty-three-year-old de Gaulle wrote, would 'resume, once more, its march towards destiny' and the army could serenely await the 'days when everything will depend on it'. On 5 August, the 33rd Infantry Regiment marched out of its barracks in Arras to the local station, where it headed eastwards to confront the enemy advancing through Belgium. 'Goodbye to my rooms, my books, my keepsakes,' de Gaulle recorded in his notebook. 'How life seems more intense, how the smallest things take on a depth when all may perhaps end.' Thirty-seven years later, he told dinner companions he had become convinced that he would be killed on his first day in action. Writing to his mother at the time, however, he told her he was 'full of go and confidence' and that 'the troops are absolutely admirable'.[12]

4

WAR

I
Bayonet charge

Like France's military planners, de Gaulle had expected the Germans to attack through the Vosges mountains from Alsace and Lorraine which had been lost in the Franco-Prussian War of 1870. But the imperial high command applied (if imperfectly) the scheme drawn up by the chief of staff, Alfred Graf von Schlieffen, which ignored Belgian neutrality and tried to smash a path to north-eastern France, aiming to encircle Paris and knock the country out of the war before France's Russian ally could mobilise in the east. The job of the 33rd Infantry Regiment was to help hold this advance.

The infantrymen travelled a hundred kilometres by train, and then marched up to thirty kilometres a day. At night, the officers lodged in houses while the men slept in barns and stables. On 13 August the regiment crossed into Belgium in bright sunshine, greeted warmly by the locals and watched by an enemy spotter plane. De Gaulle, who was responsible for the regiment's catering, helped to cook dinner for fellow officers; the meal was 'very gay even if mediocre', he recorded in his diary. The soldiers then headed on through the night to the town of Dinant, where the Germans held a citadel on a cliff a hundred metres high on the left bank of the River Meuse. Reaching their destination, the troopers tried to get some rest, while de Gaulle and another junior officer purchased two eggs for each of the men under their command.[1]

At 6 a.m. on 15 August 1914, German artillery opened up. De Gaulle experienced 'two seconds of physical emotion, a tightening of my throat', but did not seek shelter. 'I was not in any way alarmed,' he recalled. He drank a cup of coffee in a roadside café, and went to sit on a street bench, walking over to a trench from time to time to exchange pleasantries with privates sheltering there. After the initial shock of their first shelling, the soldiers began to joke. Then stretcher-bearers started to pass carrying the wounded, and de Gaulle was told of the deaths of officers he knew.

Ordered to lead a bayonet charge to keep the enemy from a railway bridge, and racing forward at the head of his platoon wielding his sword under a hail of fire, he felt as if he was two people – 'one running like an automaton and the other anxiously watching him'. A bullet hit him in the knee. As he fell, a sergeant dropped on top of him, dead.

His leg numb, he crawled on, his sword dragging on the ground; later, he wondered 'how it came about that I was not riddled like a sieve'. Reaching a bridge across the Meuse, he entered a house full of wounded where a major urged everybody to start praying because they were doomed to die. The lieutenant told him to shut up, as terror-struck old women living in the house gave the soldiers coffee.

Ordered to retreat, de Gaulle limped his way back to the French line, his coat soaked in blood. He slept in an abandoned school after eating two raw eggs. It was only on the following morning that he went to the medical service; according to his son, he was left lying on a stretcher for three days without proper medical attention. Then he was driven to his sister's home in Charleroi. She came out of the house to kiss him in the car and he was taken to the station to get a train back to France. This involved a four-hour wait – still on his stretcher. Reaching Paris, he was operated on by a surgeon who told him he was fortunate not to have contracted gangrene, which would have meant amputating his leg.*

From Paris, de Gaulle was sent to a military hospital in Lyon where he underwent unspecified 'electrical' treatment before being moved to Cognac to recuperate. A story he wrote at the time told of a love affair between a lieutenant the same age as himself and his captain's wife. As

*Thirty-five years later, the Belgian who had driven him in his car wrote a letter to de Gaulle who replied by saying that he remembered the man's 'useful and kind' help (*Lettres, Complément*, p. 397).

their regiment came under fire, the captain handed the young man his pocketbook, asking him to give it to his wife if he should be killed, as he was. The lieutenant was wounded, and was taken to hospital in Lyon where the captain's widow visited him. 'She took the pocketbook and looked at it through her tears for a long while,' the story continues. 'Her husband had had it delivered to her by her lover. In her lover's eyes she read the irreparable. She moved to take the young man's hand, but he grasped both of hers and kissed them with the tenderness of a farewell.'[2]

II
War of extermination

In the month after de Gaulle was wounded, four German armies used firepower, concentration of forces and enveloping tactics to advance through north-east France. The 320,000-man First Army got to within fifty kilometres of Paris, and the government withdrew to Bordeaux, as it would do again in 1940. However, the invaders were exhausted and their lines of communication stretched to breaking point. Seeing that the First Army had left its right flank exposed, Joffre, an old-fashioned figure who declined to use the telephone, ordered a counter-offensive. In September, the French and British advanced sixty-five kilometres on a 260-kilometre line on the River Marne. Von Schlieffen's successor as chief of staff, Helmuth von Moltke, was reported to have told the Kaiser, 'Your Majesty, we have lost the war.' 'The spell was broken,' de Gaulle wrote in a history of the French army. 'For the first time in over a hundred years, France had beaten Germany in a big-scale battle. Psychologically, the game was won.'

But it was to be a very long and hugely bloody process before final victory was achieved, a process in which the young de Gaulle would be one of the millions of men who fought a conflict very different from the offensives envisaged by Colonel de Grandmaison. The siege war of the trenches became an assembly line of industrial combat which sucked in the youth of France, Britain and Germany and spat it out as dead or wounded. As the French troops did, after all, exchange their cloth kepis for metal helmets and abandoned their dashing red trousers for drab uniforms that made them stand out less, de Gaulle asked in a letter to his mother: 'What is this war except a war of extermination?'[3]

*

In October 1914, de Gaulle returned to the front. His regiment's forward trench was only forty-five metres from the Germans. Awakened by artillery shells on his first morning back, he noted how French guns fired at nearly point-blank range at houses occupied by enemy soldiers and had 'the pigs screaming as they bleed in their holes'. German snipers crouched on the roofs, 'and, as soon as a man steps out of the trench, whack!' On some days, there was compensation for the officers when the company cyclist brought them Champagne or Sauternes for lunch.

Roll calls recorded a mounting toll of dead. In a letter to his parents, Charles noted that, when he asked about any of the young officers from his class at Saint-Cyr, he was told they had been killed or wounded. Twenty years later, he recalled the effect of constant combat – 'For hours, sometimes for days, the artillery barrage pounds positions, and breaks spirits. The survivors are depressed and apathetic. Without sleep, food or water, feeling abandoned by God and man, the soldiers have one hope – that their ordeal should end quickly, no matter how.' He grew increasingly angry with the politicians in Paris as he contrasted 'the long anguish of ever-threatening death and unrelieved misery' of the soldiers with the manoeuvring and profiteering by civilians. 'Parliament is becoming more and more odious and stupid,' he wrote to his mother. 'Rather than running their departments, ministers spend all their time at debates in the National Assembly and in dealing with ludicrous requests and injunctions from any old wine merchant whom politics has turned into a deputy . . . We will be victors as soon as we have swept away this scum,* and there will be no Frenchman who will not cry with joy when that happens.' (His view of the inefficiency of the politicians in Paris was shared by Pétain who had become a general as the war revived his career; he told Poincaré that victory could only be won under a head of state

Racaille – the word that aroused great controversy when used by Nicolas Sarkozy, as Interior Minister, to refer to rioters in the Paris suburbs in 2005.

acting as a dictator.) But de Gaulle also criticised the 'grocers' in command of the troops who sacrificed men in hopeless attacks.

At the end of 1914, when France had lost 300,000 men killed and twice as many wounded or missing, the 33rd Regiment was moved to Champagne where the mud was deep and Christmas was marked by heavy shelling. De Gaulle, who had had a smart uniform made for him at the Belle Jardinière department store in Paris, was promoted to the rank of captain and decorated with the Croix de Guerre for bravery. He asked his mother to send him socks and told her that the gloves she had given him were much too small. He was impervious to danger. One day, when he was inspecting the firing line, a shell landed nearby. Two other officers threw themselves to the ground, but de Gaulle remained standing. 'Were you frightened, gentlemen?' he asked. On 10 March 1915, his left hand was hit by a shell splinter; untreated, the wound became infected and he was evacuated. In hospital in the Auvergne, he caught scarlet fever and had his pistol stolen.

Returning to his company on 14 June 1915, he supervised the strengthening of defences, told his men off for not keeping their weapons sufficiently clean, organised a communal shower, gave detailed instructions for a song and dance show to 'distract the men and raise their morale', and offered a reward of 0.05 francs for each rat killed. He punished a drunken sergeant major and complained about the failure of a cyclist from another company to salute him. He also assured his soldiers that, if he was obliged to be severe, 'your captain . . . loves you all the same'. Fifty years later, visiting the battlefront as President of the Republic, he remembered the names of men who had fought beside him. When one of those accompanying him expressed astonishment, he replied: 'If you had gone through that war, you would have known the kind of relationships established on the eve of an attack among those . . . who were going to die together a few hours later.'[4]

Heavy rain at the end of 1915 brought flooding, which, he told his mother, meant that the company 'lived like frogs'. He and his men slept in beds suspended from the ceiling of their shelters. A bombardment forced him to cancel a plan to eat venison and ortolans with the captain of a neighbouring company. For Christmas, his mother sent him boots, a waterproof coat, a waistcoat and a lamp. In February 1916, his regiment was ordered to move to the city of Verdun in Lorraine, the furthest eastern stretch of territory controlled by the French.

Three hundred and twenty kilometres east of Paris, the city and its fortress at Douaumont had resisted a German attack in 1914. Now, the two countries' armies faced one another across a bend of the Meuse. Von Moltke's successor as German chief of staff, Erich von Falkenhayn, had pinpointed it as the scene for a decisive battle in which 'the forces of France will bleed to death'.

On 21 February 1916, the Kaiser's army unleashed a bombardment of more than a million shells. Phlegmatic as ever, Joffre maintained his habit of getting plenty of sleep at the army headquarters in Chantilly, north of Paris. But his deputy, Édouard de Castelnau, witnessed the fear and chaos when he visited the battleground. He ordered that the right bank of the Meuse must be held whatever the cost, and urged the appointment of Pétain to command the defence.

Instructions were issued for the former commander of the 33rd Infantry Regiment to take on the job, but Pétain could not be found; he was in Paris seeing his mistress. An aide, Bernard Serrigny, tracked him down to the Hôtel Terminus opposite the Gare du Nord, and the two men went to see Joffre the following morning. Though the commander-in-chief told Pétain that 'things are not going badly at all', those around him were panicking that Verdun was about to fall.

Pétain set off immediately through deep snow, and found on his arrival that the enemy had taken the Douaumont fortress and were within five kilometres of the city. Despite a bout of pneumonia, the general left his bed to draw a three-line defensive plan on a map with a piece of charcoal. Telling the troops 'France has her eyes on you', he issued his war cry – 'They will not pass.'

The scale of losses soared as Pétain initiated a conveyor-belt system, known as the 'mill wheel'. Huge columns of men moved into battle in an endless procession through the mud while shell-shocked survivors were pulled back to recuperate before returning to combat. In his memoirs, Pétain recalled how their eyes 'stared into space as if transfixed by a vision of terror'. His tactic held the line, but the constant demand for more men alienated Joffre, who wanted to concentrate on a battle shaping up on the Somme. Having also got on the wrong side of Poincaré when the President visited the front, Pétain found himself moved from direct command of the battle after two months, though retaining overall authority. Still, he went down in history as 'the Victor of Verdun'.

The battle stretched for 298 days through the winter mud and summer heat. It was, wrote the poet Paul Valéry, 'a complete war in itself'. In all, 259 of France's 330 infantry regiments took part. The French suffered 378,777 dead, wounded and missing. There were 330,000 dead among the Germans, who introduced new forms of gas and sent forward units with flame-throwers bearing the insignia of a death's head. A pilot flying over the battlefield saw 'that sinister brown belt, a strip of murdered nature. It seems to belong to another world. Every sign of humanity has been swept away.' The route to and from the front became known as the *Voie Sacrée* (the Sacred Way). Only a great figure of Christ would be an appropriate monument to 'such an avalanche of conflict and sorrows', wrote the Jesuit philosopher Teilhard de Chardin, who served there as a stretcher-bearer.[5]

Four days into the battle, de Gaulle's company moved to the village of Douaumont below the fortress lost to the Germans. At 6.30 a.m. on 2 March 1916, heavy German shelling began, followed by three infantry attacks. The captain was sent out on a reconnaissance mission under heavy fire. 'The earth trembled without a pause; the noise was unbelievable,' the regimental journal recorded. 'All telephone wires had been cut and any messenger sent out was a dead man.' The shelling killed or wounded all but thirty-eight of the 180 men in de Gaulle's unit as the Germans got to within twenty metres of its position and encircled it.

'It was then that this magnificent feat was performed,' the regimental journal recorded. The captain led a charge straight at the enemy. A sergeant behind him was killed. 'There was a terrible hand-to-hand struggle in which these brave men received blows from rifle butts and bayonets from every side until they were overpowered,' according to the journal. The company perished, 'selling its life dearly and falling gloriously'. After flinging a grenade, its captain was brought down by a bayonet thrust into his right thigh – one account says he got this after jumping into a shell crater in which several Germans were sheltering. Overcome by poison gas, he passed out.

Just before entering the army in 1909, de Gaulle wrote a verse stating, 'when I have to die, I would like it to be on the battlefield'. At the age of twenty-five, it seemed that his wish had been granted. He was given up for dead. Visiting the front, his father was told that Charles had 'done his duty to the end'. 'Fell in the mêlée,' Pétain wrote in the Official Journal. 'An incomparable officer in all respects.'[6]

III
The prisoner

In fact, Captain de Gaulle had been pulled out of the shell hole by enemy soldiers and taken behind their lines, where a captured French doctor treated his wounds. Several accounts of exactly what had happened to him at Douaumont circulated in subsequent years. One version, signed by Pétain in 1919, said that, finding his company surrounded on three sides after undergoing an appalling bombardment, he 'led his men in a violent assault and fierce hand-to-hand fighting, the only solution he judged compatible with his feeling of military honour'. This, the General wrote later, went far beyond the facts; how far his reaction reflected his natural sense of propriety and personal modesty cannot be determined. In a letter to his sister in March 1916, he wrote that he had been 'wounded by a bayonet thrust, but not badly'. Much later, anti-Gaullists alleged that he had surrendered. Told of the claim, he shrugged and said nothing.

'You can guess my sadness at finishing the campaign like this!' he wrote to his parents in May 1916. Later he would say that being taken prisoner was 'a shameful misfortune which one has to avenge at any cost'. It was 'like being cuckolded'. He felt he no longer counted for anything. 'It seems to me that throughout my life, be it short or long, this regret will never leave me,' he lamented in a letter to his mother. 'May it at least guide me to think and act more and better.' In fact, his period in captivity would do much to form and confirm his character.[7]

The wounded captain was transferred by the Germans to a military hospital in Mainz, and then to a prison camp in Lower Saxony. Two months after his arrival, the guards discovered a hole in a wall which they took for an escape attempt. In reprisal, the prisoners were shut up in a communal room for all but one hour of the day, and forbidden newspapers and tobacco – Charles wrote to his father that this would enable him to give up smoking. (It did not.) He devoted himself to improving his German and studying Greek and Roman history.

As the battle of the Somme was raging on the Western Front through the second half of 1916, he was taken to Prussian Silesia and then on to a camp in a former saw mill at Szczuczyn in Lithuania for prisoners suspected of seeking to escape. De Gaulle continued the role of catering supervisor he had exercised with his regiment, ladling out soup to fellow captives. He began his day by reading German newspapers and analysing their reports. When he had finished, fellow prisoners gathered round to hear his conclusions. 'It was not a discussion,' wrote an author who obtained recollections of de Gaulle's companions. 'It was an exposition.'

His lifelong vocation as a teacher had begun. So had his voracious search for knowledge. He read as widely as possible and scrawled copious observations in his notebooks, remarking on how and why great figures of history had succeeded or failed.

Despite this intellectual activity, he yearned to escape and return to the front. Before long, he and a lieutenant began to dig an escape tunnel. When the guards found this, the French prisoners were punished as a group, which included the removal of their Russian batmen. The camp was closed down five months after de Gaulle arrived, and he was sent to the high-security Fort IX at Ingolstadt on the Danube in Bavaria, which held other French and Russian attempted escapees. The main building was closely guarded, but de Gaulle noticed that the hospital annexe for prisoners, located in the town, offered better chances of absconding. So he formulated a plan to get into the infirmary by requesting his parents send him a bottle of picric acid, supposedly to treat chilblains. He swallowed a large dose of it one night and was horrified by what he saw in the mirror the next morning. His complexion was muddy, his eyes yellow. His urine turned dark. He was afraid that he had overdone the dose. But he achieved his objective: he was sent to the hospital, where he met another French officer, Captain Dupret, who was equally intent on escaping. They decided that the best route lay through another hospital, filled with wounded from Verdun.

A French prisoner who worked as an electrician in the second hospital concealed civilian clothes there for them. For their part the two

Frenchmen suborned a German male nurse by paying him to supply them with brandy and postage stamps, and then threatening to denounce him if he did not do their bidding. He bought them a military cap, and, after what de Gaulle called 'supreme resistance', handed over his military trousers. In the afternoon of Sunday 29 October 1916, Dupret put on the cap and trousers, and a large apron, as worn by the staff. He appeared to be an attendant escorting a patient, de Gaulle. They passed the guards, and unlocked the door to the room where the civilian clothes were stowed away. Then they walked out.

Their target was the Swiss border, three hundred and twenty kilometres away. By day, they hid in the woods, moving only at night through rainy weather. They ate biscuits and chocolate from supplies they had accumulated from parcels from home. On the night of 5 November, they reached the small town of Pfaffenhofen, near Ulm, where a local festival was being celebrated. 'With our appearance and not having shaved for five days, we looked like tramps,' de Gaulle recalled. A crowd followed them, and they were arrested. Taken to Ingolstadt, de Gaulle was punished with sixty days' solitary confinement on a rudimentary diet and without reading matter in an unlit cell. He behaved himself, hoping to be moved to another detention centre from which escape would be easier. Released from solitary, he quizzed new arrivals at Ingolstadt and drew up a list of escape attempts from other camps and the reasons for their failure. On this basis, he was able to advise French soldiers being moved elsewhere of their best chances of getting away in what one successful evader dubbed his 'escape school'.*

He continued to read German newspapers, following the course of the conflict, reading between the lines for signs that the tide of war was turning and studying the conduct of military leaders. That gave him the basis for a series of lectures to fellow prisoners in which he began to formulate ideas about the failures of civilian and military command, and the fatal futility of the attrition of trench combat. As he delivered his talks in the prison camp, French soldiers at the front were showing

*The term 'escape school' was used by Marcel Diamant-Berger whose escape from the Hirschberg camp was made on the basis of recommendations by de Gaulle after he questioned prisoners who had been there. The escape of Diamant-Berger and an aviator, de Goys de Mezerac, served as inspiration for Jean Renoir's classic film *La Grande Illusion.*

what they thought of their generals' tactics by mutinying against orders to continue a failed offensive on the River Aisne in which 100,000 men were killed or wounded. They were not refusing to participate in the war, simply rebelling against losing their lives in hopeless attacks across no-man's-land.

Pétain was appointed as France's commander-in-chief in May to replace the architect of the disaster on the Aisne, Robert Nivelle. His first directive suspended large-scale attacks in depth. He then instituted a system of longer and more regular periods of leave. Though 23,000 men were found guilty of mutinous behaviour by courts martial and forty-nine were reported to have been shot, Pétain emerged with the reputation of a military leader who cared for his men, to add to the halo he had acquired at Verdun. In his prison-camp lectures, de Gaulle described his former chief as 'exceptional'. But he reserved greater praise for Joffre and the supreme Allied commander, Ferdinand Foch, a man of brilliance and self-belief that some thought verged on madness; during one battle he sent a message stating, 'My centre is giving way, my right is retreating. Situation excellent. I am attacking.'[8]

The transfer for which de Gaulle had been hoping took place in July 1917, when he was moved to the heavily guarded, moated castle of Rosenberg on a mountain cliff in Franconia. There, he received regular food parcels from his mother sent through the prisoners-of-war office in Switzerland; one neatly typed list of contents recorded the dispatch of a kilo of smoked bacon, 500 grams of sausage, tins of corned and braised beef and cassoulet, as well as condensed milk, chocolate, peas and rabbit stew. In his letters to her, he evolved a code using the first letter of each line to spell out what he wanted – civilian clothes or implements hidden in the false bottoms of tins of provisions.

On the night of 15 October 1917, a huge rainstorm broke over the castle. Calculating that this would keep the guards in their shelters, an escape group made up of de Gaulle and four other officers crossed the two moats and dropped a rope made of sheets down the forty-metre cliff beyond the outer wall. Four of them got down from there. De Gaulle was lowered after he explained that he was 'physically incapable of climbing down a smooth rope more than a few yards' – presumably on account of his height. The man who had held the rope volunteered to stay behind.

Cold and tired, the four escapees walked towards the Swiss border – as they did so, the French launched an offensive which led to the end of the battle of Verdun. After ten days, the Frenchmen stopped to rest in a pigeon loft. Farmers spotted them and alerted a soldier guarding Russian prisoners working in the nearby fields. The quartet was caught and taken back to the camp.

This fresh failure did nothing to deter de Gaulle from trying to get free once more. He made three further escape bids, the last in a laundry basket, but was recaptured each time. After one breakout, he was kept in solitary confinement for 120 days, deprived of light, heating and books, and put on survival rations. He also spent a short time in an ordinary jail after insulting a policeman who detained him.[9]

Among the other prisoners at Ingolstadt was the celebrated airman Roland Garros, who had more luck than de Gaulle in escaping back to France in early 1918 and rejoining the air force, only to be shot down and killed a month before the end of the fighting. Also in the camp was a Russian officer, Mikhail Tukhachevsky, son of tsarist nobility, who also made repeated attempts to escape and with whom, according to a fellow prisoner, de Gaulle shared a cell for a time. Tukhachevsky played mournful airs on his violin, spouted nihilist beliefs and inveighed against Jews as dogs who 'spread their fleas throughout the world'. On his fifth escape attempt, the twenty-four-year-old hothead got free and found his way back to Russia. Before he left, his French companions warned him that, as an aristocrat, he risked being shot by the Bolsheviks. 'Shot?' Tukhachevsky is said to have replied. 'I shall be a general at twenty-five.' He almost hit his target and then became head of the Red Army at the age of thirty-two. At a reunion dinner on a visit to Paris after the war, which de Gaulle attended, he is said to have remarked that he would not see them again since this time he would indeed face death when he returned home. In 1937, Stalin had him executed on the basis of forged German documents made to show that he was involved in a conspiracy with the Nazis.[10]

De Gaulle's character was by now already clear. One day in the camp, he asked a fellow prisoner, Ferdinand Plessy: 'Did you know that, fundamentally, I am a shy man?' Plessy thought that this hardly fitted with the captain's 'natural ascendancy and outstanding eloquence'.

Still, as Plessy recalled, 'he knew how to keep people at a distance. All the other young men called one another *tu*. Nobody every said *tu* to de Gaulle.' They referred to him as 'the Commander', 'Marshal of France' or the sobriquet accorded in Arras, 'the Constable'.

But then Plessy thought of de Gaulle's remark in a different context. The shower room for prisoners was an open space. So, as Plessy recalled, 'I became acquainted with the anatomy of all my companions . . . All except one: de Gaulle. What time did he choose to wash by himself? I never thought about it, but the fact is there – I never saw de Gaulle naked.' This reticence remained with him; his son recalled that his father would emerge from his bedroom fully dressed, complete with his necktie.

In his notebooks, de Gaulle honed his vision of the great man he intended to be. He wrote of the attributes a true chief had to nurture – the need to dominate himself and pay attention to small elements of everyday behaviour, as well as the importance of keeping his counsel and of developing a mystique. 'One must speak little,' he argued. 'In action one must say nothing. The chief is the one who does not speak.' It was plain whom he saw in the role of the chief. As he remarked much later to his aide-de-camp, Claude Guy: 'I always thought that I would be at the head of the state one day. Yes, that always seemed to me evident.'[11]

*

In November 1917, Georges Clemenceau, 'the Tiger', became Prime Minister of France. His call for 'total war' appealed to the Right while his republican anti-clericalism made him acceptable to the Left. The Bolshevik Revolution had taken Russia out of the conflict but the entry of the United States in April 1917 introduced a new element. As the war moved towards its end, de Gaulle fell into one of the low moods that would characterise him, often at moments when he should have been happy. In this case, he could not get over his absence from the coming victory. 'I am buried alive,' he wrote to his father. 'The other day, I read in some paper that prisoners returning to France were called "ghosts" . . . I have no illusions, I, too, shall be no more than a "ghost".'

On 1 December 1918, three weeks after the German surrender, he returned to France, having borrowed 1.90 francs from a lieutenant to upgrade his railway ticket. At his father's house in the Dordogne he met up with his three brothers who had also been in the army; miraculously, they had all survived, which their mother called 'an exceptional mark of divine favour'. They were photographed together in uniform and boots, all holding white gloves. Charles stands to attention, cigarette in hand.

He dismissed Germany's signature on the Versailles Treaty in June 1919 as 'a bad joke'. The peace agreement would be 'no more than a bad cover thrown over unrealised ambitions, hatreds that are more alive than ever, national angers that are not extinguished', he forecast. The 'odious' enemy would recover and become more arrogant. France's strength would be reduced by demobilisation and the return home of British and American troops. So his country had to hold on to the Rhineland territory occupied under the Versailles agreement, ensure that it had the world's top army, be ready to fight anew if necessary – and increase the birth rate.

His personal problem was that he had little chance to shine. He was posted to a military school for returned officers at Saint-Maixent-l'École in western France, a village he described as a dump. He fretted at the 'ocean of stupidity, laziness and administrative insolence' around him. The only silver lining was that the 'general lassitude' of his colleagues 'will, I am sure, enable me to separate myself with little ado from the sad pack,' he wrote home. His colonel told him: 'With the fine things you have done already, you can have a very good future if you wish.' All that was needed was a chance to get into action and to prove that he was no ghost.[12]

IV
Warsaw interlude

De Gaulle got his chance of action in France's next military enterprise, to help defend Poland from the advance of the Bolshevik Red Army led by his former fellow prisoner Tukhachevsky, and to impose stability on central and eastern Europe. Answering a call for volunteers from the War Ministry in Paris in February 1919, he joined a force whose numbers were planned to reach 150,000 men but never got anywhere near that. His rank was automatically raised to major in the *Chasseurs Polonai* which had fought alongside the Allies on the Western Front.

In recreating the central European nation which had been partitioned between Russia, Prussia and the Austro-Hungarian Empire at the end of the eighteenth century, the Treaty of Versailles followed the American policy of self-determination for the peoples of Europe, while also erecting buffer states on Germany's eastern flank, including Poland with its twenty-seven million people. The country was in a parlous condition. 'In parts there had been seven invasions and seven destructive retreats,' wrote the American Herbert Hoover on a relief mission there. 'Many hundreds of thousands had died of starvation. The homes of millions had been destroyed and the people in those areas were living in hovels.'

Poland's President, Josef Pilsudski, was an ardent nationalist whose adventurous career had taken him through spells as a socialist propagandist, urban fighter, leader of a spectacular cash robbery from a mail train and head of a Polish legion during the war, before being imprisoned by the Germans. Lenin saw him as a tool of Western imperialists, and calculated that, if the Red Army could march through Poland, the way would be open to spread revolution into the heartland of Europe, in particular in Germany. For France and Britain, this highly alarming prospect called for the dispatch of military advisers, while they also encouraged White Russian forces to try to undo the revolution of 1917.[13]

De Gaulle's first impression of Poland was uninspiring. He found it lacking in features of interest and consisting of big, flat, sandy plains. The weather was cold and wet. He wrote to his parents that he and his colleagues were very uncomfortable because 'everything is very dilapidated and empty of furniture after so many comings and goings of Russians, Boches, Jews'. He lost two thousand-mark notes, two pairs of shoes and most of his linen in a burglary; asking his mother for a loan, he said he was 'furious, humiliated and very embarrassed'.

But 'confidence in myself and the future has returned,' he added. He must also have been encouraged by the award of the Légion d'honneur in August 1919, for his bravery at Verdun; Pétain signed the order bestowing the decoration. The following month, he took the train to

Paris to attend the wedding of his brother, Xavier, who had become an engineer; for the occasion, he spent eight hundred francs on a new uniform with red breeches and a 'Burberry' coat. The marriage may have stirred his own feelings about his future; in a letter to his mother that November, he expressed hope that the coming year would bring him 'a family, and in the tranquillity of a deep and sanctified love the power to give to another all the happiness that a man can give'.

Though he complained repeatedly about the cost of living, de Gaulle found Warsaw very lively, filled with refugees from the Bolsheviks 'who, despite their misfortunes, amuse themselves frenetically'. The leading families 'receive us even more than we would have wanted,' he noted. His letter home with his impressions of Warsaw contained a paragraph from which a word or two was excised in the collection of his letters issued in 1980. 'In the middle of all this,' he wrote, 'countless . . . detested to death by all classes of society, all enriched by the war from which they have profited on the backs of the Russians, Boches and Poles, and pretty much ready for a social revolution from which they will draw a lot of money in exchange for some bad deeds'. The reference to the Jews is inescapable, even if the editors chose to impose political correctness.

De Gaulle's job was to train Polish officers in French military methods at a huge nineteenth-century fortress at Modlin, fifty kilometres north of Warsaw. His lectures were admired, but he longed to be sent to the front, though he described the fighting as a joke in which each side simply took turns to advance. Frustrated, he went home in April 1920; but there was no job for him in France, so he returned to Warsaw in June as chief assistant to the commander of the French military mission, General Niessel. The journey east provoked a fresh complaint about the expense of everything; he told his mother, who had loaned him five hundred francs, that train seats and baggage transport 'give rise literally to exploitation'.

In Warsaw, he took up residence in one of the city's smartest thoroughfares, Nowy-Swiat. Wearing white gloves, he became an habitué of the capital's pastry shops and cafés, sighted walking along the street holding a package of cakes suspended from a ribbon. The memoirs of a Polish ambassador to Paris, Stanislas Gajewski, allude to a 'romantic liaison' with a young noblewoman, Countess Czetwertynska, who was as small as de Gaulle was tall. They were to be seen sharing *ponski* (doughnuts) at the classic wood-panelled Café Blikle. By this account, she introduced him into society where his height was much remarked upon. 'At the same time, it was much said that he had a liaison with another young woman elsewhere in Poland,' Gajewski added. Given his age, an affair would not have been out of place. In his notes at the time, de Gaulle referred to love as 'seasoning for life'. But there is no solid evidence of any romance and Gajewski is reported to have shrugged off the story when questioned about it.[14]

De Gaulle's return from his brief sojourn in France coincided with a massive Soviet advance on Warsaw by the Red Army under Tukhachevsky, while a ruthless, hard-charging cavalry force led by Semyon Mikhailovich Budyonny wrought havoc in the south of the country. An outing to the field with Polish forces made de Gaulle pessimistic about their chances. He had a narrow escape when a Polish cavalry unit he was visiting found itself cut off on the wrong side of the River Bug, and only just got away from Russian cavalry. One rare success for the defenders came in an encounter in which their cavalry was backed by tanks. But they had too few armoured vehicles to make much difference, and most were used for static defence.

Growing Western concern led to the dispatch of Foch's former chief of staff, General Maxime Weygand, to head an Allied mission. Officially, his job was to seek a political settlement to end the war; in fact, he was to advise the Poles how to fight the Soviets. Still, it seemed that the capital must fall. Lenin created a Communist government for Poland and wrote to Stalin, the political commissar with Budyonny's army, of the prospect of striking south into Romania, Czechoslovakia, Hungary and Italy. Fifty years later, de Gaulle remembered Pilsudski as 'shattered . . . and distraught'.

Then, in what became known as 'the miracle on the Vistula', the Poles counter-attacked. Tukhachevsky's advance was held for six days in front of Warsaw by a defence reinforced with tanks while other units hit the Red Army's flank. The patriotic enthusiasm of the Poles gave them an edge against the exhausted, overextended invaders. Tukhachevsky made a serious error in trying to encircle Warsaw rather than driving the attack into the capital. Forced to retreat, the Soviets were weakened by mutinies and disintegration, suffering 200,000 casualties. Expanding into Lithuania, the Poles seemed to have the road to Moscow open before them, but Pilsudski knew better than to venture deep into Russia. An armistice was agreed on 18 October 1920.

In Paris, Weygand was hailed by compatriots as the architect of success, though he stated that 'this is a purely Polish victory'. Indeed, Pilsudski had taken little notice of him once he learned that Weygand was not bringing fresh troops. But de Gaulle wrote home that the French general had calmed the Poles down and got them to adopt a battlefield plan. Paris became Warsaw's best friend. De Gaulle stressed the importance for France of having demonstrated to the Poles 'the passionate interest we have in their cause and our resolution to help them by all means'. His own belief in nationalism could only be strengthened by their 'unusual national vigour' and the way in which 'national feeling managed to silence the voices of disorder'.

The sweeping cavalry movements, notably of Budyonny's army before it was caught in a trap by the Poles in the autumn of 1920, showed de Gaulle a form of warfare very different from what he had experienced on the Western Front. He had his first sight of tanks in action, though he wrote that the Polish command did not know how to use them properly. 'They must be used in the field in a body, not dispersed,' he added, echoing a doctrine he would elaborate in the years ahead.

As 1920 ended, it was time for de Gaulle to return home. Reports from his superiors predicted 'a very fine military future' and detected 'a collection of qualities rarely combined in the same degree: a bearing that inspires respect, a strong personality, firm character, active and cool in the presence of danger, wide culture, great intellectual value'. The only reservation concerned his 'somewhat lofty airs'. The Poles were keen for him to stay, but the major's interest in Poland dropped once the fighting ended. A place awaited him at Saint-Cyr and there was another reason to go home. A note by a French general at the end of the year recorded that 'de Gaulle wishes to return to France in order to marry'.[15]

5

'GENERATION OF CATASTROPHES'

I
Never again

The France to which de Gaulle returned from Poland was a nation drained by war, the effects of which would be felt through the following two decades. The country was, in the words of the writer Jean Giraudoux, who had been wounded several times, in the grip of 'fatigue, fatigue'. Looking back half a century later, de Gaulle depicted a nation 'exhausted by its losses and ruins, its social structure and moral balance shattered, resuming its unsteady course towards its destiny'. In turning the clock back to the pre-war regime and voting out Clemenceau for not having achieved enough for them at the peace conference, the French 'rejected greatness and returned to confusion', he added.

More than 60 per cent of men born before 1901, or 7.5 million, had fought in La Grande Guerre. France had lost 1.5 million dead – it has been estimated that, if one counts the children not born because of the war, the population deficit was double that. The death toll in relation to the population was slightly larger than that of Germany and twice that of Britain. Only one of France's 38,000 communes did not lose an inhabitant. Half the six million survivors were wounded, some mutilated, shell-shocked or confined to wheelchairs, all marked for ever. There were 670,000 war widows, their black mourning clothes a further reminder of the slaughter.

Victory had meant the recovery of Alsace-Lorraine with its two million people, but the wartime experience made the French less eager to reproduce. In the two decades after the end of the fighting, the population increased only because of immigration, notably from Italy, Poland and Spain: by the mid-1930s, France contained 2.5 million foreigners compared to 1 million before 1914. Though contraception was illegal, the law was rarely implemented, use of sheaths grew markedly, and abortions rose to 400,000 a year. The *carte famille nombreuse* was introduced to offer financial benefits to those with three or more children. But, by the mid-1930s, deaths outnumbered births and a quarter of the French were over sixty.

Four million people, or 10 per cent of the population, were estimated to be suffering from syphilis. Wine consumption was three times as great as in Italy. Public health care was poor. Though the war reduced the status of figures in authority, none of this seemed to be of much concern to the political caste which swapped jobs with great regularity – there were forty-two governments between the two world wars, with the same men on the roundabout. Though its leaders mouthed the rhetoric of progress, the dominant Radical Socialist party was socially conservative and deeply protective of the status quo, reflecting an electoral system weighed towards the middle class and rural voters. Members of parliament were valued primarily for their ability to win favours for constituents. This, and the multiplicity of parties, made it all the more difficult for policies to be changed, or even clearly defined. Though both remained committed to Marxism, a division between Socialists and Communists at a congress in Tours in 1920 fragmented the Left, and reduced pressure for measures in favour of the industrial working class.

Economic policy was usually fumbling, directed by men who cared little for the realities of the financial and commercial world. It was not that France lacked entrepreneurs – André Citroën and Louis Renault built car companies, André Michelin did the same in tyres, the Wendel Brothers ran a great metallurgy empire and François Coty prospered in perfumes. But the business world was dominated by small-scale enterprises. Agriculture employed more than 30 per cent of the population; however, landholdings were often small and French farms faced competition from the New World. A million cattle and as many sheep had been killed in the war. Mechanisation lagged; by the late 1930s, France had 35,000 tractors, a third of the number in Britain.

Industrial output in 1919 was only a little more than half its level of 1913. France lacked coal and mineral resources. Having funded the war primarily through loans and printing money rather than by taxation, the state was deeply in hock to foreigners, owing $7 billion to the USA and Britain (equivalent to $1.4 trillion today) and with a soaring trade gap. Reconstruction of devastated areas was also paid for by borrowed money. As a result, the public debt, which had totalled 31 billion francs in 1914, hit 98 billion in 1919 and 184 billion in 1924. After credits extended to France by its allies ceased in early 1919, the franc collapsed from 5.47 to the dollar to 24.70 in 1924. The theory was that the defeated enemy would pay the bill; but Germany proved adept at minimising the reparations laid out in the Versailles Treaty, and France found itself adrift in a sea of global debt.

For most people, the overriding aim was to ensure that war did not occur again, and that the Germans were deterred from attempting a fresh invasion. De Gaulle's conviction that his country had to be ready to resume fighting if necessary put him in a tiny minority. 'There is probably no other nation in Europe that [is] less warlike,' the War Minister André Maginot told the American ambassador. Though France regarded its armed forces as the most powerful on earth, the military establishment embraced a defensive strategy, seen as having the additional benefit of saving money at a time of economic uncertainty. The teaching profession, which had suffered disproportionate losses in the conflict, delivered an anti-war message to pupils while pacificism was fanned on both Left and Right by a flood of memoirs by survivors. De Gaulle noted 'an anti-war psychosis which is being carried to excess'. Pétain, who had been raised to the rank of marshal in 1918 and assumed iconic status, led the argument that a defensive approach would 'be more sparing of the blood of soldiers'.

Internationally, France felt isolated. The emergence of the Soviet Union ruled out a revival of its alliance with Moscow. There was a nagging fear that Britain would avoid involvement in a fresh war on the European mainland. The Americans retreated into isolationism and made themselves unpopular by insisting on repayment of war debts. France signed treaties with the states of central and eastern Europe to try to encircle Germany, but these nations were, for the most part, weak and unsure where their best interest lay, while the defensive strategy adopted in Paris made a nonsense of offers of military intervention to defend them. To aggravate matters, France's wartime allies wanted the recovery of Europe, which meant Germany's revival and softer treatment of the former enemy. While in Poland, de Gaulle had remarked that he belonged to 'the generation of catastrophes'. For him, the way to cope with post-war problems was to try to master the circumstances and assert leadership. But the consensus was for accommodation, at home and abroad. He was, thus, at the age of thirty, set on a collision course with the establishment and majority opinion.[1]

II
A model couple

If de Gaulle remained a supreme individualist, he gained the consolation of companionship in a courtship and marriage which faithfully reflected his milieu and provided him with a pillar for life. In a letter to his mother from Poland he had expressed his desire to raise a family, and had inquired about a cousin, Thérèse Kolb, whose charm, intelligence and delicate finesse had struck him. But it had been years since they had met, and he doubted if she would 'remember my modest person except in the most imprecise fashion'. On a trip home from Poland, he was said to have been introduced to a prospective bride in a château in northern France, but to have decided not to press his suit when he discovered that the young woman was lame. Then, on leave in Paris in October 1920, he was invited to a reception given by Madame Denquin-Ferrand, a goddaughter of his father who was also friendly with a prosperous family from Calais, the Vendroux.

Charles already knew the family's son, Jacques, with whom he had exchanged letters during the war. The Vendroux were involved in shipbuilding and ran a biscuit factory. Considerably better off than the de Gaulles, they possessed a twenty-room, eighteenth-century home in the Channel port, a country house and a château at Sept-Fontaines in the Ardennes. They also rented a flat in Paris. The paterfamilias was a Calais municipal councillor and honorary consul for six countries. Three decades later, de Gaulle's aide-de-camp, Claude Guy, recalled him reflecting how Parisian families needed an occasional injection of provincial money to keep going.

At the Denquin-Ferrand reception, Charles was introduced to Yvonne, the elder of two Vendroux daughters, a pretty, dark-haired, self-contained twenty-year-old who had spent part of the First World War in Canterbury to escape the German advance. An account by her brother, Jacques, makes it clear that the encounter was part of a scheme to bring the two young people together, but their parents told him that his sister was to think it had come about by chance.

The subject of a painting by the Dutch artist Kees van Dongen – *The Woman in Blue* – came up during the conversation at Madame Denquin-Ferrand's flat. It was on display at the autumn show at the Grand Palais, and the hostess suggested that they should make up a party to go to see it, adding that, since there was a buffet at the exhibition, they could also take tea together. The following Thursday, Charles and Yvonne joined their elders on the expedition. The others hung back on the pretext of examining other paintings to allow the soldier and the young lady to be alone. When it was time for tea, the spoon on de Gaulle's saucer slipped to the floor. He bent to retrieve it, and may have spilled a few drops of tea at Yvonne's feet.*

Charles followed up by inviting Yvonne to attend a Sunday-night ball organised by Saint-Cyr in the Hôtel des Réservoirs in Versailles, with Jacques acting as chaperone. When her brother asked what she felt about de Gaulle, she said it was up to him to declare himself first, adding, 'he's almost forty centimetres taller than me'. She had her hair done and ordered a crêpe de chine dress in periwinkle blue, which allowed a glimpse of her ankle above shiny black shoes. After some discussion, she decided not to wear jewellery. A car was hired to drive Yvonne and Jacques to Versailles.

In the hotel, Charles and Yvonne sat in armchairs 'with a proper space between them', according to her brother. Jacques bought them orange juice; de Gaulle reciprocated with a glass of champagne. The young woman spoke of her liking for the mountains and Alpine flora –

*De Gaulle stated much later that he spilled tea on her dress. Jacques Vendroux insists that this did not happen, as do the match-makers (Vendroux, *Soeur*, p. 75, Galante, p. 70, Lacouture, I, p. 62).

she had just been on a holiday during which she had hiked at three thousand metres. Charles talked about Poland and his family holidays at Wimereux on the Channel coast, a resort also patronised by the Vendroux. Though Yvonne was a good dancer, he did not invite her on to the floor. Ballroom dancing was not his style.

On the train back to Paris, Jacques asked his sister what she had thought of the evening. 'I was not at all bored,' she replied. He could see that she had been struck by de Gaulle's intelligence, presence and 'perfect education'. Three days later, she declared: 'It will be him or no one.'

The engagement was announced on 11 November, the second anniversary of the armistice. Champagne was drunk. Charles presented his fiancée with a diamond ring. They exchanged their first kiss. Writing to Yvonne's parents at the end of the year, he said he had 'the best reasons in the world to love her with all my heart' and expressed his 'immense gratitude in thinking of the treasure that you are agreeing to give me . . . Those thanks will last as long as my life . . . I hope for nothing better, nor more or less than to show myself worthy of your trust and esteem.'

The following February, he travelled to Calais to see the Vendroux family and his bride-to-be. Since there was no question of him staying under the same roof as Yvonne, he lodged in a hotel. At dinner, Monsieur Vendroux ordered a 115-year-old wine to be fetched from his cellar. After dinner, there was bridge but, by one account, de Gaulle lost his temper when the game went badly for him and thereafter nobody would partner him. Still, dates were fixed for civil and religious weddings. As was the custom, the police investigated the bride's suitability to marry a member of the armed forces: the dossier remains secret, but the findings were, evidently, positive.

At the civil wedding on 6 April 1921, the seventy-year-old mayor of Calais predicted that the groom would 'hold the precious torch he has between his hands to the end, rigorously and without weakening'. The young officer put the ring on his right hand because of the war wound to his left. For both Catholic families the real ceremony was the religious marriage the following day at the city's Gothic church of Notre-Dame. Yvonne's wedding dress was of white satin; Charles wore a sky-blue frock coat and military cap. The church was full, and police had to contain the crowd outside. There was music by Bach, Mendelssohn's Wedding March, and a sermon by an abbot. Jacques Vendroux was best man. After the ceremony, the families and their guests moved to a six-course dinner-dance accompanied by wines from Burgundy and Bordeaux and Champagne. De Gaulle joined his wife for a waltz, the only time his brother-in-law ever saw him dance. At 7 p.m., the couple took the train to Paris on their way to honeymoon on Lake Maggiore, from where they visited Milan, Venice and other historic towns of northern Italy.[2]

Returning to Paris, they moved into a three-room flat on the Boulevard de Grenelle in the 15th *arrondissement* of Paris. A soldier from a nearby barracks delivered provisions and did handy work in the morning. On Sunday nights, the couple usually dined at the Vendroux flat nearby; if Charles was in uniform, they travelled first class on the underground, as befitted an officer; otherwise they went second. The main snag with their new home was that the Métro passed outside the window; passengers would hang out of the carriages and wave. So they were happy to move to a quieter five-room flat not far away.

According to her brother, Yvonne already considered Charles a great man. By summer, she was pregnant. A keen knitter, she made vests and bootees for the child, using white wool since she did not know its gender. On 28 December 1921, a boy was born. De Gaulle was present and wrote to Jacques that it had been 'a really tough experience' for his wife. But, he added, 'our dear little Yvonne is very well and has started moving about in bed'. The boy was christened Philippe. Whether this was in homage to Pétain was not stated, but it was probably no coincidence. It was said that the Marshal would have been asked to become the godfather had he not been associated with a married woman. A photograph of him hung by the boy's bed.[3]

III
Too big for his boots

To broaden his military knowledge, de Gaulle, who reverted to the rank of captain on his return from Poland, was sent on short assignments to a tank regiment, an artillery detachment and an air force unit. Then he went to Saint-Cyr and delivered lectures on French military history since the Revolution. Tall, slim and physically awkward, his back ramrod-straight, his Adam's apple jutting out above the tight collar of his tunic, he spoke for an hour at a time without notes. He was distant, haughty and cold – his brother Xavier remarked that he must have been dropped into an ice box at birth. He retained his habit of wearing white gloves. A caricature shows him with one booted foot on a desk, riding crop in hand, while a pupil scribbles on a blackboard. His lectures showed his admiration for commanders who enhanced their nation's status, even if they were eventually defeated.

From Saint-Cyr, de Gaulle moved in May 1922 to the finishing school for French officers, the École Supérieure de la Guerre, located in the military quarter of the Champs de Mars on the left bank of the Seine, not far from his home. One of his colleagues, André Laffargue, recalled that, even if he walked like a moving statue, he took part in communal activities, 'often with originality and humour', adding his 'rather sepulchral voice' to those of his companions when they sang on outings. Another colleague noted what he termed his 'Oxford irony'. Sitting by a hedge during a field exercise one day, a fellow officer told de Gaulle that he thought he was headed for 'a very great destiny'. The captain did not immediately respond, but then replied, 'Yes . . . me, too.' In a group photograph taken at the war school, he seems apart from those around him. Jacques Vendroux remembered that at around this time his brother-in-law began to intimidate the family-in-law.

Not surprisingly, his manner rubbed his superiors up the wrong way. On an exercise in eastern France, in which he was put in charge of an army unit, a colonel enquired where its supporting forces were deployed. De Gaulle called on one of his junior officers to supply the answer.

'But it was you I asked, de Gaulle,' the colonel interjected.

'*Mon Colonel*, you entrusted me with the responsibility of an army corps command,' the captain replied. 'If, on top of that, I had to take on those of my subordinates, my mind would not be free enough to fulfil my mission.' The colonel was enraged and later noted that 'unfortunately, he spoils his undoubted qualities by his excessive self-belief and his attitude of a king in exile.'

The feeling that de Gaulle was simply too full of himself was reinforced at the beginning of 1924 when he published his first book, *La discorde chez l'ennemi* (*The Enemy's House Divided*). Its theme was the destructive effect of the errors of the German high command. The analysis was unexceptional, but his pedagogical tone in laying out lessons for 'our military chiefs of tomorrow' can only have increased the irritation at his superior ways. He added to this with a twenty-two-page pamphlet arguing that warfare was essentially an empirical exercise and so abstract lines set down in advance should be avoided – such planning was the basis on which the French high command proceeded with its defensive strategy.

There was a clear echo in all this of his father's attitude to the Republic; Henri and Charles both believed in order but insisted on being free to follow their own paths. Neither was ready to suffer those they regarded as fools, even if they were hierarchical superiors. The price for such independence was that, at the end of the course at the École Supérieure, the young officer was not given the 'very good' mark needed to join the general staff. Even worse, his 'good' ranking was, it was reported, only achieved when Pétain intervened on his behalf. De Gaulle's reaction to his grade was forthright. 'Those fools of the war school,' he was heard to say. 'I will only go back into that filthy place if I am in charge. Then you'd see how everything would change.'[4]

By then, Yvonne had given birth to a second child, Élisabeth. When he could get away from his duties, de Gaulle joined the Vendroux clan at its château at Sept-Fontaines. A colonel at a local garrison loaned him a horse on which he took long rides. The family made motor-car trips through the Ardennes. The captain played badminton, and went hunting for the first time, killing a hare with a rifle bought for him by his father-in-law and sharing in large picnics in the forests. But he also found time to go through dossiers as he sat in a deck-chair under a tree in the garden, or to work on his manuscripts. Jacques Vendroux recalls him reading Friedrich Nietzsche's *Thus Spoke Zarathustra* in a shaded corner of the terrace on a beautiful August morning; he interrupted his reading to help Philippe's wobbly attempts to walk, smiling at his son.

IV
Politics as usual

While de Gaulle worked his way through the military college, France experienced a series of government crises revolving around the treatment of Germany and involving two major politicians who, in their very different ways, epitomised the era. The Prime Minister of 1922, Aristide Briand, made the search for a lasting settlement in Europe his principal objective, earning him the sobriquet 'the apostle of peace'. An affable, womanising humanist, corpulent, with thick, wavy white hair, a large moustache and a cigarette invariably in the corner of his mouth, he was twenty-six times a minister and eleven times Prime Minister. His great rival, the wartime President, Raymond Poincaré, a trim, spade-bearded, hardworking lawyer who radiated logic and precision, advocated a tougher line with the defeated enemy and lavished affection on his pet cats and dogs in the absence of children. Briand knew nothing and understood everything, one diplomat remarked; Poincaré knew everything and understood nothing.

Briand's government fell after going along with a British proposal for France to join wholeheartedly in the reconstruction of Europe, which would mean a moratorium on the reparation payments it received from Germany that were falling behind schedule. Poincaré took over, and in January 1923 sent military engineers, backed by troops, to occupy factories and mines in the industrial bastion of the Ruhr. There was peaceful resistance from the Germans. Britain disapproved but the move was popular in France. If there is no record of de Gaulle's thoughts about the crisis, there can be little doubt that he backed Poincaré's conduct. He had always insisted on the need to force Germany to live up to obligations imposed at Versailles, and classed Briand as a man who had 'shamefully denationalised' France's domestic and foreign policy.

By September, Poincaré's hard line appeared to have worked as Berlin called off the resistance. The central bank in Berlin reformed the Weimar Republic's currency, swingeing economy measures were introduced and the Chancellor, Gustav Stresemann, told Paris and London that Germany would resume supplies of coal under the reparations programme. Opposition within the Weimar Republic included Hitler's attempted coup in Munich.[5]

Considering he had won and wanting to mend fences with Britain, Poincaré agreed to an examination of the reparations issue which led to a plan that called for withdrawal from the Ruhr and a rescheduling of German payments. But, as the mark stabilised, international speculators staged a run on the franc, which fell sharply. To restore state finances, the Prime Minister raised loans from British and American banks, cut civil service jobs and increased taxes. That gained him a breathing space, but the centre-left opposition staged a powerful campaign for a general election in May 1924, on slogans such as 'For peace', 'For the ordinary people', 'Against the power of money'. The so-called Cartel of the Left (essentially a centrist grouping) took 328 of the 582 National Assembly seats. The third major political figure of the time, the Radical Socialist Édouard Herriot, whose party was the biggest in the lower house of parliament, became Prime Minister. The government roundabout that followed set a trend which showed why people like de Gaulle despaired of French politics and its practitioners.

Herriot, a former university lecturer, was a fitting representative of what came to be known as 'the Republic of the teachers'. A pipe-smoking gastronome, as befitted the mayor of the food capital of Lyon, he was an artful operator adept at reaching the deals that underpinned the regime, a cultured but lazy figure prone to put style above substance and focus on electoral success rather than fundamental policies. In this, he reflected his party, which never had the membership numbers of the Socialists or the Communists, but exerted greater power through its core position in the network of high-level political relationships at the heart of the Third Republic.

The tricky financial situation Herriot's administration inherited was aggravated by the anti-capitalist rhetoric of its Socialist allies, who had 103 seats in the National Assembly. The franc fell further, and a run on state bonds escalated, impoverishing many middle-class voters. The public debt rose. So did inflation. The government blamed the crisis on the forces of finance – the 'wall of money' – and announced a forced loan from the rich. The moderate wing of the Cartel defected. Poincaré delivered a biting speech in the Senate, where the government was defeated.

Herriot's successor, Paul Painlevé, a mathematician as well as a politician, was another skilled political operator. He left foreign affairs to Briand, who negotiated the Treaty of Locarno which united the West European allies, Germany and the states of central and east Europe. Briand and Stresemann received a joint Nobel peace prize. The Foreign Minister's standing was such that he remained in his post at the Quai d'Orsay until his death in 1932. At the end of 1925, he became Prime Minister yet again, but the financial crisis escalated further. The 'apostle of peace' was no economist and his government was forced to step down.

After a shambling attempt by Herriot to form an administration, Poincaré was appointed Prime Minister once more. Government spending was cut and taxes increased. The franc stabilised, and then doubled in value against the dollar. Gold reserves rose. France had found its champion in adversity. This experience left two legacies. First, a strong currency became a watchword, put above other economic and financial concerns as a matter of basic patriotism. That brought higher tariffs to keep out imports and led industry to depend increasingly on domestic sales rather than exports. Second, the way that politicians swapped jobs – or, in Briand's case, proved unmovable – bred contempt and anti-republican feelings. Street demonstrations sprouted; extremist splinter groups emerged. The Republic might have found a financial saviour in Poincaré, but the regime was increasingly on the defensive.

V
Purgatory and revenge

Though he approved of the harsh treatment of Germany and wrote scornfully of the 'dreams of Locarno', de Gaulle was not impressed by Poincaré whom he described as 'half-big, half-honest, half-understanding'. Nobody, except perhaps Pétain, lived up to the expectations of the thirty-six-year-old captain, or was capable of fulfilling the destiny France deserved. Much later, de Gaulle would say that the Marshal had become intellectually dead by the mid-1920s, but this seems to have been the product of hindsight and their subsequent differences. At the time, he saw the Victor of Verdun as his model and master.

The old man's status was such that he was known as the 'Imperator', though, in a letter to his mistress in 1919, he put his successes down to an awareness of his limitations. Two decades later, Pétain would remark that he never took more care of a young officer than he did of de Gaulle. In an inscription to his photograph which hung by the bed of Philippe de Gaulle, the Marshal wrote of his wish that the boy would combine all the qualities and gifts of his father.[6]

On the basis of his relatively low passing-out mark at the École Supérieure, de Gaulle was sent to a French unit stationed at Mainz in the occupied Rhineland, where he was put in charge of supplies. That purgatory was short-lived, thanks to Pétain who called him back to Paris to join his staff on the superior war council. The older man could only see the exile of his protégé as an indirect rebuff to himself, and, once the captain was back in France, made sure his career moved ahead at a smart pace. De Gaulle became Pétain's 'pen officer', writing material for the Marshal. He had a room to himself, which soon reeked from his chain-smoking. He worked in civilian clothes, walking to his office wearing a bowler hat and carrying a walking stick which he waved as if writing in the air.

Pétain showed his trust and favour by asking the young man to write a book for him on the history of the French army, to be entitled *Le Soldat.* The draft of the first chapters was so satisfactory that he changed only a few words. 'The substance is faultless,' he added in a letter to his ghost. But nobody was to know the true authorship. 'It is agreed, is it not, that you do not tell anyone of this work, which is to remain between ourselves,' the Marshal added in a postscript. A further sign of favour came when he took the captain with him on a trip to Verdun – before they left, he told friends that he was going to travel 'with the most intelligent officer in the French army and find out what he would have done had he been on the [German] side'.

Though de Gaulle regarded himself as a member of the 'house of Pétain', the book which the Marshal had commissioned him to put together caused tension between them. After his initial approval, the old man criticised the manuscript, judging that one of the seven chapters was 'uniformly catastrophic' since it did not conform to his view of the First World War. In addition, de Gaulle appears to have resented being relegated to the anonymity of ghost. On one occasion, another member of the staff saw de Gaulle stride from the Marshal's office 'on edge and in the grip of cold anger'.

Still, the older man was intent on hitting back at those who had given his protégé such a low graduation mark at the war school. Pétain told the head of the establishment that de Gaulle was due a gesture of compensation, 'and me, too'. At 10.30 a.m. on 7 April 1927, in full dress uniform, including sword and his habitual white gloves, de Gaulle strode into the school's auditorium. Pétain stood aside to let him go first, and then took the chair. The captain put his cap on the table in front of him, laid his sword beside it and removed his gloves, and began to speak in his high, rasping tone.

Emphasising the importance of 'contingency', he pointed to the variable factors of war, starting with the adversary who might move in unexpected ways. 'What has happened before will never happen again,' de Gaulle argued. Great leaders were those who moved beyond set hierarchies and regulations to take individual action, aware of the risks but ready to accept them. They were predestined to assume charge, tough people who lacked 'surface seduction' and were not always easy to get on with as they organised themselves for struggles, challenges and great events. Developing themes he had first set down when a prisoner of war, he said it was essential for such leaders to keep their distance from others, 'to exercise self-control and to be cold'. Even if their superiority was implicitly accepted, they were rarely loved, he noted.

In a subsequent lecture, he expanded on his concept of leadership, speaking of men who exuded authority from birth and who needed to foster a certain mystique in order to maintain their prestige, 'for people have little reverence for that which they know too well'. They had to be able to deal with unplanned events. 'There are moments when free men break through determinism and open up new paths – one gets the history one deserves.' His delivery left his listeners in little doubt about whose future career he was describing, even if he might also have been seen as paying tribute to Pétain, who had remained nonconformist and individual but had still risen to the top of the army. The principal of the military school, General Hering, recalled that his colleagues were incredulous at the speaker's arrogance and insolence.

De Gaulle thought he had triumphed. In a letter to his father, he wrote that he had made a very big impression. Still, he was aware of the enmity he provoked. 'My supporters jubilated, neutral people smiled, and the sharks who navigate round the ship waiting for me to fall into the water to devour me moved a good distance away,' he added.

On the Marshal's recommendation, de Gaulle was raised to the rank of major; he remarked to a friend that, while promotion was nice, the real thing was to make one's mark. He also received a further decoration for his war service and the medal given to escaped prisoners of war. He accompanied Pétain on a visit to inaugurate a war memorial at Dinant in Belgium, where he had been wounded in 1914. The head of the French infantry referred to him as 'a future generalissimo' as he was posted back to Germany to command an elite unit in France's army of occupation.

VI
Anne

Yvonne was pregnant with their third child when the family moved in late 1927 to Trier, Germany's oldest city, close to the border with Luxembourg and birthplace of Karl Marx. They occupied a small villa by the River Moselle, with an Austrian governess for the children. A loan from the Vendroux family enabled Charles to have a black Citroën, which he once backed into a ditch and had to have pulled out by a horse. He walked to work in the morning, lunched alone, but fraternised with his young junior officers in the evening, usually discussing history. 'He stood out not so much because of his size but because of his ego, which glowed from afar,' a witness recalled. This witness also sensed his 'extraordinary loneliness'. 'Beyond his excursions into history, what could the major say?' he wondered. 'Who could he talk to? What about?'

The couple's third child, Anne, was born on New Year's Day 1928. It soon became evident that she suffered from Down's syndrome. Yvonne's mother ascribed this to the shock her daughter felt when, out walking while heavily pregnant, she witnessed a street brawl between German war veterans and men from her husband's battalion. De Gaulle and his wife did not seek to hide Anne's condition, but nor was it something to be talked about. For the most part, they kept the suffering within their close-knit family, devoting themselves to her wellbeing. 'We ourselves would give up everything in the way of ambition, fortune etc., if that could improve our little Anne's health,' Madame de Gaulle wrote to a friend when her second daughter was a year old.

Just before the outbreak of the Second World War, Charles told the Catholic writer Henri Daniel-Rops of the 'heavy cross' he and his wife carried because of Anne's condition. 'It was deeply moving,' the author recalled. The parents never thought of putting Anne in an institution, instead looking for family homes where they thought she would be as happy as possible and engaging a dedicated carer. Treatment with ultra-violet rays was tried but did no good.

De Gaulle's devotion to Anne was enormous; it was said that the only word the girl managed to say properly was 'papa'. The family's maid remembered seeing him playing on all fours with her on holiday at Wissant, singing a song which went 'You are beautiful, Mademoiselle; not you, Sir'. A photograph taken in Brittany in 1933 catches him in a deck-chair on the sand, dressed in a dark suit, white shirt and tie and wearing a homburg, with Anne sitting on his thighs. She wears a light-coloured playsuit and a floppy white hat fastened with a braid under her chin. Her father grasps her forearms, the index finger of his right hand touching her left thumb. She stares at him with bulbous eyes and a grave expression. He concentrates on his daughter completely, his mouth slightly open as if murmuring something to her.

Returning home from work, Charles would go straight to her room, taking her on his knees, kissing her face, singing to her and complementing her on her dresses. She particularly liked to play with his military cap, dropping off to sleep with it in her arms. His niece recalled that Anne sometimes gripped his cheeks so vigorously that he was left with red marks. When posted to Metz just before the outbreak of the war, he asked for the gates of the botanical gardens to be opened for him at 7 p.m. when the weather was fine so that he could walk round with Anne without anybody else turning to stare at her. A young officer under his command noted how, when their unit was out on manoeuvres, de Gaulle ordered a car each night to take him 140 kilometres to see Anne, rocking her gently in his arms till he had to leave at dawn to return to his post.

In 1945, Yvonne established an Anne de Gaulle Foundation for

Down's syndrome children in a château bought for the purpose outside Paris, and, after his daughter's death in 1948, de Gaulle kept her framed photograph with him. His character was already stoic, but her tribulations contributed an additional emotional layer to a man whose concealment of his personal sentiments did not mean that they were not deep. With her, he could lift a corner on his feelings. 'One is always more attached to a fragile child than to a normal child,' he remarked in 1962 to the Information Minister Alain Peyrefitte, whose daughter was in a coma after being hit by a car. His biographer Jean Lacouture reported that one of his doctors, whom he does not identify, said he heard his patient say: 'Without Anne, perhaps I should not have done all that I have done. She gave me so much heart and spirit.' As he led his tank division into battle in 1940, de Gaulle spoke to the chaplain of his affection for her. 'For a father, believe me, it is a very great trial. But for me, this child is also a blessing, she is my joy, she has helped me to rise above all setbacks and all honours, and always to aim higher.'[7]

6

THE CONSTANT REBEL

I
Falling out

Quite apart from the tragedy of his second daughter, de Gaulle was generally discontented in Trier, finding the daily routine boring and dismissing his colleagues as imbeciles.

He was a harsh disciplinarian and did not hesitate to invoke his connection with Pétain when superiors tried to countermand his orders. His bitterness towards the 'riffraff' of politicians grew. All in all, and with consideration for his personal tragedy, Charles de Gaulle was not a particularly agreeable fellow to know or to work with.

Nor was his relationship with the Marshal what it had been. Two dinners in Paris at his patron's invitation had been glacial, largely, it appears, because Yvonne made clear her disapproval of the old man's marriage to a divorced woman, who had been his mistress. The discovery that another officer had been asked to comment on the book de Gaulle had been ghosting set off an explosion in January 1928. He wrote a letter insisting that his role should be acknowledged in a preface.

The Marshal sent a placatory response, but then lost patience with the whole matter, throwing the manuscript into his safe. The spell was broken on both sides. That left de Gaulle without a protector when the French occupation army was disbanded as relations with Germany improved. In keeping with the vision he had of himself throughout his life as a teacher, he wanted to return to Paris to become a senior lecturer at the war school. But, despite a glowing farewell from his commanding general, his previous time at the college led staff members to threaten to resign en masse if he was appointed. Instead, Corsica and one of France's colonies in Africa were mentioned as possible destinations. 'They have had enough of me; they want to get rid of me,' de Gaulle told his family. In the end his destination in October 1929 was Beirut.[1]

The posting to the Levant made him part of an episode of French colonialism with League of Nations trappings which buttressed his country's belief that it had a special role to play in the Near East, particularly in Syria and Lebanon. France's presence there in the 1920s, with 15,000 of its own soldiers and a local force of 13,000 men, was the result of a secret accord reached in 1916 with Britain, known as the Sykes–Picot Agreement after the two diplomats who negotiated it. After the defeat and dismembering of the Ottoman Empire, Britain took what is today Jordan, south Iraq and a small area around Haifa. France got responsibility for 150,000 square kilometres in Syria, Lebanon, south-east Turkey and northern Iraq, with a population of 3.6 million in all.

France was welcomed by the Christians in Lebanon, but had a much tougher time in Syria, facing a rebellion by the Druze in 1925. Bombing of undefended villages increased resentment as did shelling of a populous district of Damascus. Things were a lot calmer by the time de Gaulle and his family arrived aboard an old steamship at the end of 1929. They moved into spacious quarters in a new house in the Druze district of Beirut, with high ceilings and large windows. There were marble columns and flower-patterned armchairs. Philippe attended a Jesuit college while Élisabeth learned to read at a school run by nuns. The family went to mass at the church of St Louis each Sunday.

Yvonne spent much of her time looking after her second daughter. 'Little Anne is doing well and making some progress,' de Gaulle wrote to his parents. Their landlady recalled 'a charming and very united couple. One never heard raised voices from their home. The major was friendly and generous.' He rose early to walk to his office, and read and wrote a lot, particularly after dinner. Needless to say, the de Gaulles did not participate in the more exotic features of the 'Paris of the Levant', which made the posting attractive for some of his fellow officers.

As far as domestic French politics were concerned, de Gaulle took some comfort at the formation of a new government at the end of 1929 under an energetic, modernising conservative, André Tardieu, a former associate of Clemenceau. In a letter to his father, he hoped that the new Prime Minister would grab his chance and reverse Briand's policies, which he characterised as 'a dead dog floating on the water'. In charge of operations and intelligence, he was soon off on trips to Aleppo, where he noted with surprise that it was cold in the evening, and to the River Tigris, where he felt 'a certain emotion' as he dipped his hands in the water. On one occasion, his vehicle broke down in the middle of the desert; a photograph shows him in uniform and boots standing by as the driver repairs the engine, a cigarette between his lips, his thumbs looped round his belt. On another trip, his car sank into sodden sand after heavy rains and he had to sleep in the open.

Letters on his travels in late November 1929 attest to his tenderness for his wife. From Aleppo, he wrote to his 'Dear little beloved wife' to tell her of his progress to the Euphrates, the Turkish border and Tripoli. He asked her to send him 'a little word'. 'I love you with all my heart,' he signed off. Everybody asked him if she was not concerned by his departure on expeditions, he went on. 'I reply with the truth, that is to say "no"; I think that perhaps she was, but that she is so brave and courageous that she pretends to be happy.' 'Never will I forget how much you have supported me,' he concluded.[2]

II
The planner

In November 1931 de Gaulle returned to Paris to join the secretariat of the *Conseil supérieur de la guerre* at the centre of French military planning. He drew up a study of economic mobilisation in which he noted the scope of the US industrial machine and the way in which the Fascist system in Italy 'allows the authorities to extract all that existing sources can provide, without reserve or consideration for other interests'. Reflecting on the growth of economic direction, mass production, government intervention in everyday life and the emergence of organised youth, he concluded that 'the military type of organisation is becoming the symbol of our new times in Europe'.

The de Gaulles moved into an apartment in an eight-storey stone-faced building with a tiled entrance hall, stucco wall decorations and a balcony on the busy, tree-lined Boulevard Raspail with a *métropolitain* railway station outside. The Collège Stanislas was round the corner. Montparnasse, home to new art and literature, was up the road, but there is no record of the couple having participated in its bohemian, smart-set life; the *Années folles* of Paris, with their innovative, turbulent, edgy, artistic life, passed them by. The only outing recorded for them was to the operetta *Rose Marie* which de Gaulle remembered with pleasure.* The flat was old-fashioned; they had radiators installed to prevent Anne catching colds in winter.[3]

In their absence in the Levant, the Tardieu government in which de Gaulle had placed his hopes had begun building the defensive line in eastern France proposed by Pétain as long ago as 1922. This now became known as the Maginot Line after the War Minister, a Verdun veteran who had been crippled in the battle and boasted that 'like my leg, I won't bend'. Stretching over 240 kilometres, it had three defensive lines, heavily reinforced artillery positions, pillboxes, tank traps and a warren of tunnels, railways and living quarters buried twenty metres beneath the surface, complete with cinemas and hospitals. It represented the acme of static defence, but its efficacy depended on the enemy attacking where it was located.

Under Weygand, who had become chief of staff, motorisation of cavalry and infantry units began, but the high command held back from creating independent armoured units, seeing the role of the vehicles as being to protect the infantry. With military service shortened, defensive strategy continued to dominate thinking, which fitted neatly with Briand's efforts to promote détente in Europe by overseeing the evacuation of the Rhineland and circulating a memorandum on European union. De Gaulle judged that the evacuation meant France had lost control and would have to retreat steadily from the gains of the Versailles Treaty.

In 1931, the world depression fully hit France. Industrial output dropped by nearly 20 per cent that year; agricultural prices collapsed; unemployment soared; more than a hundred banks closed. The

*When it was revived in Paris during his presidency, he thought of going to see it but his aides advised that the new version was too vulgar for his taste (Tauriac, *Vivre*, p. 330).

Governor of the Bank of France, Émile Moreau, played a highly nationalist game; he was described by an English note-taker at a meeting as 'stupid, obstinate, devoid of imagination and generally of understanding but a magnificent fighter for narrow and greedy ends', but his policies were popular as the franc remained stable and foreign capital was attracted to French markets. While Moreau and successive governments pursued the Poincaré legacy of keeping the franc strong, deflation gripped the nation.

Tardieu proposed a big increase in public spending on Keynesian lines, but his activism and self-confidence brought him too many enemies and his administration was defeated. In terms which echoed de Gaulle's persistent complaint, Tardieu wrote of the 'corrupt condition into which the principle and the spirit of the institutions have fallen', which he regarded as being as serious as the threat from Germany. The revolving door of governments without firm parliamentary majorities asserted itself with a vengeance, with nine changes of Prime Minister in four years. As the British diplomat Robert Vansittart put it, becoming Prime Minister was 'a thing that may happen to anyone in French politics'.[4]

*

In May 1932, de Gaulle's father died. Two months later, he published another book, *Le fil de l'épée,* based on his 1927 lectures at the war school under Pétain's patronage. The book developed his pet themes in language that sometimes teeters between high literature and grandiloquence, at least for those unaccustomed to the rhetoric in which he was steeped. He drew a picture of a 'man of character' waiting to assume the role of a national saviour, exalting the leader to whom people would turn in a crisis 'as iron towards the magnet'. 'When the crisis comes, it is he who is followed, it is he who raises the burden with his own arms, though they may break in doing so, and carries it on his shoulders, though they may crack under it,' he added. Such a leader may be criticised as vain and undisciplined, but 'asperity is the failing of powerful characters'. 'As soon as matters grow serious and the danger urgent, as soon as the safety of the nation requires immediate initiative . . . a kind of tidal wave sweeps the man of character to the forefront.'[5]

Despite this fresh portrait of the leader he aspired to be, de Gaulle was still a marginal figure. However, his independence of mind, dubbed 'legitimist disobedience' by the writer Raoul Girardet, did not hold back his career. He was promoted to the rank of lieutenant colonel at the end of 1932. He had a settled bourgeois family life based on solid values. But members of the officer corps were set apart from society in many ways. They could not vote or belong to a political party. They were expected to obey orders without question and to accept the ultimate wisdom of figures like Pétain or Weygand who believed that 'nothing needs to be created; everything exists'. Pay fell below pre-war levels in real terms – this was a particular burden for the de Gaulles, given the cost of caring for Anne. Politically, the Left was suspicious of the military as the potential source of a coup, the Socialist Vincent Auriol declaring that the army must 'disarm and disarm again, always disarm'.

In the masculine military world, wives were expected to play a respectful secondary role, to be dutiful Catholics and mothers. Yvonne fitted the bill to perfection, devoted to the smooth running of the household so that her husband could concentrate on his work. She never went out without wearing a hat and played the piano in a mechanical manner, 'with memory but not melody' as her son put it. Her brother noted how perfectly the table was set when he visited. The de Gaulles entertained rarely – hardly more than one cocktail party and two dinner parties a year. When they were alone, she provided the stews and offal Charles preferred.

This suited her husband perfectly. His attitude to women was generally conventional. Unpractical himself, he would tease them for being unable to make machines and for not knowing how to read road maps. According to his son, he saw the waltz as a symbol of the relationship, with the woman yielding voluntarily to the lead given by her partner 'who protects his dancer at the same time as clasping her'. Still, as Philippe recalls, he had a high appreciation of female intelligence and contrasted the all-round antennae of women with the single-mindedness of men. 'They inspire feelings in all senses, to the heights and depths, towards children and towards men,' he wrote. 'They assure love from the beginning of life to its conclusion and, in the end, they govern our existence.'

As a parent, de Gaulle was a strict patriarch. His son remembered that he received a slap for daring to call his father by his first name.

When Philippe asked him how much he earned, he sent the boy packing. Philippe and Élisabeth were educated at Catholic establishments. Their father checked their reports carefully, gave them learning tests during the holidays and had them recite passages from French literature. He usually accompanied his son to his school near his own office. He taught Philippe 'La Marseillaise' when the boy was five, in contrast to his own father who rejected the republican hymn. The teenage boy was given pocket money to cover his journeys on public transport and two visits to the cinema per month. The cash was dispensed by Yvonne; Philippe wrote later that his father would have found it 'in bad taste' to hand it out himself.

Shortage of money meant that de Gaulle bought a suit only every other year and his wife hunted for bargains in the sales, sometimes with her husband. To economise, he sold his car, while Yvonne would not throw out her husband's old shirts until she was sure that she could not reverse the cuffs. On Sundays they went to mass and took the children, whom Charles referred to in letters to his wife as '*les Babies*', for walks in the Bois de Boulogne – a photograph shows de Gaulle sitting on a chair on a path through the woods with Anne on his knees. Holidays were usually spent with the rest of the family either at the country homes of the Vendroux or in rented villas on the Channel coast where everybody shared the costs.

As had been his habit since youth, de Gaulle read constantly, concentrating on the French classics. His knowledge of literature shaped his own writing. His texts were composed to be read out from a lecture podium. The contrast between the soaring ambition in his tracts about leadership and the flat routine of his daily life is obvious. But the second formed a solid platform for the first, and Yvonne's support was essential in that. 'Who are you, *mon Général*?' one of his followers would ask in 1961. 'Who am I? You know that I am the husband of Madame de Gaulle,' came the reply. The feeling was reciprocal. According to a journalist who followed the de Gaulles closely, late in his life Yvonne spoke at length one evening about her home town. Her husband broke in to say she made him think of the Tudor Queen Mary who said she had Calais engraved on her heart. 'On my heart,' Yvonne was said to have answered, 'it is true that you would find the name of Calais, but you would also, and above all, find yours, Charles.'[6]

III
Threatening world, new home

As de Gaulle worked on military planning, the world was becoming an ever more dangerous place. Hitler was moving towards taking power in Germany to add a second Fascist power to Mussolini's Italy. Japan had grabbed Manchuria and was expanding into northern China. The Great Depression set off a wave of beggar-thy-neighbour protectionism. Economic decline hit France's international standing. Military spending was cut by 32 per cent between 1931 and 1935. De Gaulle lamented the 'infirmity' of the French state, and pointed to the defensive strategy as a source of weakness. He thought the only sure ally in a future war with Germany would be Poland and perhaps Romania, Belgium and Yugoslavia – he believed that Britain and the United States would initially maintain neutrality. Still he felt that, if it could withstand the initial shock of an attack from the east, his country would gain the upper hand in time, helped by the resources of its colonies.

He also suggested that it might be useful to create a 'Latin Union' of France, Spain, Portugal, Italy and Belgium to balance the influence of the Anglo-Saxon powers. He regretted that Soviet rule in Moscow prevented a revival of the alliance with Russia. 'The world is moving and devouring itself,' he wrote to a friend in June 1934. 'All the same, let us not complain. Despite everything, our generation will have the privilege of being present at events of such a scale that no other, except perhaps at the Great Flood, will have seen so many great things in so little time!'[7]

More prosaically, he and Yvonne found new roots when they bought a country home, a country house called La Boisserie in the small village of Colombey-les-Deux-Églises in the Haute-Marne department in eastern France. At 50,000 francs, La Boisserie was too expensive for them, but the owner allowed them to pay in annuities for so long as she lived. Despite this, the de Gaulles had to borrow money to meet the payments. The financial pressure increased when, at the time of the purchase, Philippe fell ill with an appendicitis complicated by peritonitis, which meant he had to undergo expensive hospital treatment. But, after three years, the former owner drowned in her bath, and the family was secure in the home in which de Gaulle would ultimately die.

The two-storey house was set in wooded grounds with a fine view over fields to thick forests. Electricity had just been installed in part of the building though some rooms were still lit by oil lamps. There was no running water – a small well in the garden provided some but most was brought by tanker from the city of Troyes. Despite the lack of amenities, Charles and Yvonne thought Anne would be happy there, benefiting from the tranquil countryside and grounds. De Gaulle was photographed helping her to walk by the trees. In one shot, he stands with his right hand stretched down to support her; in another, he looks at her with his hand on his heart. In both, in keeping with his formality, he is in a suit and tie while she wears a white dress and bootees.

The village lay near the Abbey of Clairvaux where St Bernard had built up the Cistercian order and laid out the rules of the Christian nobility, the Knights Templar. The only telephone in the village was at the post office and the only refrigerator at the butcher's. There was a café-bar, and the five hundred inhabitants owned two cars between them. Most were farmers and agricultural labourers, growing wheat and raising cattle. The war memorial bore the names of sixteen men who had died between 1914 and 1918.

Until 1946, the family used the house only for summer holidays – the winters in the Haute-Marne were harsh, with frequent fog and driving rain. They got on good terms with the locals, presenting gifts at births and marriages, and inquiring after the health of the elderly. One of the two churches that lent the village its name had been sold off and built over during the French Revolution. The de Gaulles regularly attended mass at the other, a squat edifice dating back to the eleventh century with a curved ceiling and six chandeliers. Its stained-glass windows depicted Saint Louis and Joan of Arc, who was said to have passed through on her way from eastern France to Orléans to save France and its monarchy from the English. More recently, Russian troops had penetrated as far as the valley below the village towards the end of the Napoleonic Wars but had fled when they heard that the Emperor himself was arriving to organise a counter-attack.[8]

IV
Tank man

Published in May 1934, de Gaulle's third book *Vers l'armée de métier* (*The Army of the Future*) was a watershed, focusing on practical means to ensure France's military safety through the development of armoured forces and a professional army of 100,000 men. This broke with the defensive orthodoxy of the high command; the author saw the Maginot Line as part of the overall battle plan rather than as simply an instrument of static defence. In his memoirs, de Gaulle wrote of how painful he found the rupture with accepted military thinking after twenty-five years spent under military rules. But, once again, there was a barely disguised personal note to his theories. The 'strategic battering ram' of his new model army should be led by a 'master', 'a man strong enough to impose himself, clever enough to seduce, big enough for a big undertaking'.

He argued that the indiscipline of his compatriots meant there was a need for 'a special body of men firmly welded together' whose isolation would save the nation from its 'internal poisons' and the perils of politics. These 100,000 men, acting as a spearhead for a conscript army, would be technically skilled in modern warfare. Their key weapon would be the tank, which restored the art of surprise and manoeuvre allied with 'the relentlessness of machinery', bringing a return of military quality as opposed to the quantitative warfare of 1914–18.

The lieutenant colonel was far from the first military theoretician to recognise the role of mechanised, mobile armour used in a solid formation as a striking force on its own, rather than being dispersed to assist infantry. The battle of Cambrai in 1917 on the Western Front had shown the force of tanks, leading a French general, Jean-Baptiste Estienne, to rank their battlefield appearance as equal in importance to the advent of gunpowder. A plan for an armoured force was submitted to the French high command in 1928; it was still being considered six years later. The military theorists Basil Liddell Hart and General Sir John Fuller developed similar ideas across the Channel.

De Gaulle had witnessed the sweeping cavalry movements of the war in Poland, and had already taken his distance from the static defensive strategy espoused by his superiors. He spent a brief time at a tank base in France in 1921 and gate-crashed a meeting of former tank officers chaired by General Estienne. But there is no evidence that he thought about armoured vehicles before he read an article in a 1932 edition of a veterans' journal in which a friend, Lucien Nachin, wrote a positive review of *Le fil de l'épée.* The anonymous piece foresaw the role of armour on the battlefield; de Gaulle wrote to Nachin that the 'original manner' of the article would be expanded in his own work.

His book received good reviews and the author persuaded sympathetic writers to place articles developing his ideas in the press. The editor of *L'Écho de Paris* singled de Gaulle out as 'one of the strongest personalities among that corps of officers who will be called on to become great leaders'. But half the print run of 1,500 was given away. The military establishment was hostile: one leading general published an article arguing that a motorised force would be stopped by hedges and ravines. De Gaulle's commanding officer refused him permission to publish an article on the creation of a professional army in the official military journal. The Defence Minister feared that public opinion would see a conflict between his proposal and the conscript army on which France depended. The reaction was to be expected – military spending on horse fodder was four times as much as on petrol. 'The army, by its very nature, resists change,' de Gaulle wrote. 'Since it lives by stability, by conformity, by tradition, the army instinctively fears anything that tends to modify its structure.' Nonconformist notions were not welcome; in a speech in 1934, Pétain said that 'France has greater need of work, conscience, and self-sacrifice than of ideas. Ideas too often divide while effort unites.'

Nor did leading politicians offer support. The Left was particularly hostile to the idea of an elite corps which might be tempted to stage a coup. It would have been even more dubious had it known of a letter in which de Gaulle wrote that France's 'economic, political and moral crisis is, little by little, pushing the question of public order to the forefront . . . the creation of a specialised corps is not only necessary to meet the external conditions of the time but also meets the coming necessities of internal order.'

A receptive response came from a circle of thinkers grouped around an independent-minded colonel, Émile Mayer, an early prophet of the importance of aviation in warfare. Mayer, now in his eighties, undoubtedly appealed to de Gaulle for the way in which he had set out unorthodox thinking, which held back his promotion. In a dedication on an article he sent to the old man, de Gaulle described himself as a disciple. He wrote a stream of letters to him, noting at one point that, while they differed on some matters such as Mayer's belief that Germany would use chemical weapons dropped from aircraft to wipe out the French population, he valued Mayer's benevolence towards him.

De Gaulle's friend Lucien Nachin, the self-educated son of a policeman, also belonged to the Mayer circle. Finding advancement in the army blocked by his lack of educational qualifications, he had left the forces to work in the Paris public transport system, though he remained an acute observer of military matters. His importance in the evolution of de Gaulle's military thinking was crucial, if unacknowledged. He was the author of the anonymous article on armoured warfare in the journal he sent to his friend in 1932.

De Gaulle also attracted support from a range of newspaper commentators in France, and his ideas were noted by specialists abroad. Tukhachevsky congratulated the author at the reunion dinner for prisoners at Ingolstadt, and had the book translated into Russian. It was read in Germany, among others by the future Panzer general Heinz Guderian, who wrote an article on very similar lines in a German military magazine in 1936, invoking de Gaulle. In 1945, a French officer found a copy of the book at Hitler's headquarters, annotated favourably by the Führer. A note about how de Gaulle championed armoured warfare was tucked inside.[9]

V
Republic under siege

While de Gaulle was immersed in military theory, France's political life became tense. Anti-regime leagues of the far right became increasingly active as the economic depression bit ever deeper. In the countryside, where yields were the lowest among major European producers, peasant discontent boosted support for the Communist Party in some regions, but the main beneficiary was Henri Dorgères, the son of a butcher from the north, who organised a populist movement of the Right with the slogan *Haut les fourches!* (Raise your pitchforks!). An impassioned orator, Dorgères gave the depressed farmers a voice, and claimed half a million members for his movement, which ran its own security force, the Greenshirts.

Financial scandals rocked the regime when politicians were linked with major frauds. The most sensational involved a refugee from Ukraine, Serge Alexandre Stavisky, known as *le beau Sasha* (Handsome Sasha). A one-time singer and operator of a gambling den, he had issued a tide of bonds from the municipal pawnshop he managed in the south-western town of Bayonne. The security for these was allegedly a set of emeralds owned by the former Empress of Germany. The jewels were made of glass; the bonds were worthless. Arrested, Stavisky bought himself political protection and ensured press silence by purchasing advertising space. At the end of 1933, however, he fled, and was found dying from a gunshot wound in an Alpine chalet. Police said he had committed suicide; many, however, thought he had been killed to prevent him spilling the beans on his highly placed associates. The affair took a fresh twist when an investigating magistrate was found cut in three on a railway line. The fact that Stavisky was Jewish and the incumbent Premier, Camille Chautemps, a Mason fed the prejudices of the far right. Its demonstrations brought down the government.

As protests swelled, the Prime Minister, the Radical Édouard Daladier, sacked the rightist Paris police prefect, Jean Chiappe, who was suspected of encouraging them. He also dismissed the head of the Comédie-Française which had been staging Shakespeare's *Coriolanus*, regarded as an anti-democratic play. The Interior Minister announced that demonstrators would be shot. But this did not stop the 60,000-strong *Action française* members and its rough-house youth branch, the *Jeunesses patriotes* (Patriotic Youth), or the biggest league, the *Croix de Feu* (Cross of Fire), consisting largely of ex-servicemen, which claimed 400,000 adherents.

The rightists staged thirteen demonstrations in January 1934. Then, on the night of 6 February, a crowd estimated at 40,000 converged on the Place de la Concorde and tried to march across the bridge over the Seine to storm the National Assembly. Police held them back in six hours of fighting which took some fifteen lives and injured more than a thousand. Inside the parliamentary building, deputies came to blows.

Losing the support of his Radical colleagues and facing opposition from the judiciary and the police, Daladier resigned, marking a victory for street action. The seventy-year-old Gaston Doumergue, who had been Prime Minister before the First World War, came back from his estate in the south of France to form a 'government of public safety' which included Tardieu and Pétain as Defence Minister – it was said that the only reason it had so many members in their seventies was that all the eighty-year-old politicians were dead.

Amid fears that the leagues would make a grab for power, Socialists and Communists put aside their divisions to stage a mass rally in the capital; nine died in clashes with police. But the only man who might have emerged as a French Mussolini, the *Croix de Feu* chief Colonel François de La Rocque, insisted on adhering to republican legality. Still, political polarisation deepened. De La Rocque put forward a seductive programme under the slogan *Social d'abord!* (Social matters first!), calling for reform of parliament, cooperation between industries, an alliance between capital and labour, a minimum wage, paid holidays, votes for women and resistance to Germany. The Left staged hundreds of demonstrations against what it portrayed as the rise of Fascism.

On Bastille Day, 14 July 1935, 20,000 *Croix de Feu* followers marched from the Place de la Concorde to the Arc de Triomphe while ten times as many from the Left paraded between the classic squares of the Nation and Bastille.* Even if order was restored, the Third Republic was on its deathbed, de Gaulle believed. This made the army's 'moral spirit' more necessary than ever, he felt; if anything was to be done for the nation, it would start with the forces. But he remained an outsider, his isolation underlined when Pétain did not include him on his staff as the Defence Minister – some reports said the old man thought of doing so but gave up the idea when his chief aide threatened to resign if such an appointment were made. However, at the end of 1934, de Gaulle finally met a politician who could help him to have a greater impact on France's future.[10]

*On the same day, Alfred Dreyfus was buried in the cemetery of Montparnasse.

VI
The connection

Born in 1878, 1,100 metres up in the French Alps, into a family that had earned a fortune in textiles, Paul Reynaud made his mark as a lawyer before joining the army at the start of the First World War. He was evacuated from the front in the early months of the fighting because of an attack of pleurisy and joined the office of the Prime Minister. In peacetime, he became a star of the Paris Bar, with his sharp voice, logical style and mastery of dossiers. Elected to the National Assembly, he emerged as a prominent independent centre-right politician, sitting in governments in the early 1930s. Economics was his speciality; he served as Finance Minister under Tardieu.

However, his support for a devaluation of the franc put him at odds with the mainstream devotion to a strong currency. His tough attitude towards Germany ran counter to the Briand-inspired search for European entente. His support for an alliance with Moscow repelled the Right while his economic liberalism and opposition to a shorter working week brought him the hostility of the Left. His self-satisfied air grated. For de Gaulle, however, Reynaud's self-confidence and stubbornness made him an ideal standard-bearer.

A member of the Émile Mayer circle, the lawyer Jean Auburtin, sent Reynaud a copy of the officer's latest book at the end of 1934. A week later, the politician asked to meet de Gaulle. On 5 December, the lieutenant colonel called at Reynaud's home in Paris's 17th *arrondissement*. The host was struck by the 'quiet assurance' of his visitor, enhanced by the look in his deep-set brown eyes. When de Gaulle asked him to make a speech in parliament putting forward the proposals in his book, Reynaud said he was up to his neck in his devaluation campaign, and would find somebody else to pursue the military issue.

'Useless,' de Gaulle replied. 'I've already looked. It will be you or no one.'

'All right, I'm listening,' Reynaud said.

He recalled that de Gaulle delivered his argument with 'such power and such clarity that I was won over by the man and his plan'. Conjuring up a neat image, Reynaud concluded that the professional army should be the spearhead of the French forces while the conscript army acted as a shaft. After an hour, he broke off to see another visitor, leaving de Gaulle with his Oxford-educated political aide, Gaston Palewski, a rotund, dark-complexioned man who was impressed by the soldier's calm 'superiority'. The two went to lunch, in a restaurant of de Gaulle's choosing. The meal was mediocre, but they talked till four in the afternoon, and Palewski decided to use any influence he had to spread de Gaulle's ideas.

Auburtin also arranged meetings for de Gaulle with his other political contacts, including some of the Left, such as Marcel Déat, a one-time rising star in the Socialist party who had left its ranks to form his own group, and who wrote an article in support of the *Armée de métier*. But the Reynaud connection was to prove much the most important in de Gaulle's future. Hearing of his death during a Cabinet meeting in 1966, the General leaned across to a minister and murmured, 'Was Paul Reynaud of more service to de Gaulle than the other way round? History will tell.'

Reynaud's interest in de Gaulle's ideas was heightened by the way events were moving in Europe. Germany reoccupied the Saarland, which had been detached from it at Versailles. Hitler repudiated the military clauses of that treaty as a whole, introduced compulsory military service and speeded up rearmament. France did nothing. At the start of a stream of seventy letters de Gaulle wrote to Reynaud over the following six years, he passed on information from the Defence Ministry that Germany had three armoured Panzer divisions and would have three more by 1936, all organised on the lines he had laid out in his book. 'I do not dwell on the sadness that may be felt by an officer who, having laid out a rescue plan for his country, sees this plan implemented in full by the eventual enemy and neglected by the army to which he belongs,' he added. While on manoeuvres in the Alps, he sent Reynaud comparative figures on modern tanks in the German and French armies – 2,000 to 620. The divulgation of such confidential information showed how he felt himself above the routine discipline of the army; one letter included a postscript blatantly marked 'secret'.[11]

Having won over Reynaud, de Gaulle hoped that a parliamentary debate in mid-March 1935, on extending conscription from one to two years to make up for France's lack of numbers, would provide a platform from which his ideas could gain wider political backing. In his speech, Reynaud laid out the need for a shock force like the one being built up in Germany. But the argument got nowhere. The Prime Minister, Pierre-Étienne Flandin, told a colleague Reynaud's speech was idiotic. For the Radicals, Daladier denounced the dangers for the nation of a professional shock force. The leader of the SFIO Socialists, Léon Blum, insisted that the army's role must be simply defensive while his party's newspaper, *Le Populaire*, accused Reynaud of being ready to provoke Germany with which, it added, France could not struggle, for demographic and industrial reasons. Blum wrote later that, when Reynaud argued that the armoured force envisaged by de Gaulle would be an effective element in maintaining collective security, he told his colleagues that this was correct, but in an undertone.

The Defence Minister, General Maurin, wondered how anybody could favour offensive warfare when France was spending so much on the Maginot Line. 'Would we be so mad as to advance beyond this barrier into who knows what kind of adventure?' he asked in a perfect example of why France's attempt to build alliances in central and eastern Europe carried so little weight. The military high command insisted that France had quite enough motorised troops, and accused de Gaulle of wanting to divide the army. An eminent veteran of the First World War, General Debeney, declared that the only thing that mattered was to defend the north-eastern frontier as strongly as possible. In an anonymous magazine piece, a three-star general expounded the view that it was normal for the Germans to have Panzer divisions because they were by nature offensive-minded, 'but France, peaceful and defensive, can only be anti-motorisation'. Pétain weighed in to argue that tanks and planes did not change the fundamentals of warfare, and that France's security depended on the continuous line of fortifications in the east.

Reynaud's idea of creating a special corps on de Gaulle's lines got nowhere. Nor did he succeed with a legislative proposal in 1935 for six heavy armoured divisions and one light division, to be operational by April 1940 (as it turned out, three weeks before the German invasion), which the parliamentary commission on the army rejected as 'contrary to logic and history'. The need for armoured forces as such could not be denied. So a division was formed; the issue was whether it should protect the infantry or be given the independent existence.

De Gaulle lavished praise bordering on obsequiousness on Reynaud, characterising his speeches, some of which he had written, as 'magnificent', 'decisive' and 'magisterial'. But, though de Gaulle wrote subsequently that his ideas were gaining ground because of concern at Germany's military build-up, the hostility at the Defence Ministry remained high. A senior civil servant recalled that, when he mentioned de Gaulle's name to generals, it was as if he had spoken of 'the village idiot'.

Visiting Reynaud one day, de Gaulle said his career was destroyed since his name had been removed from those being considered for promotion to the rank of full colonel. When Reynaud raised the matter with Daladier, who had succeeded Maurin at the Defence Ministry and begun to increase military spending, he was told that de Gaulle's record was not as good as that of other candidates. The politician informed his collaborator, who pulled from his pocket a list of his citations and decorations. Reynaud went back to see Daladier and handed him the list. De Gaulle became a full colonel at the end of 1937.[12]

VII
The Popular Front

In a letter to Reynaud on the last day of 1936, de Gaulle could only hope that 'your year' was opening, to enable both to influence French policy. There was, however, little evidence of this. Paris had reacted limply to Mussolini's invasion of Ethiopia, seeking an understanding with the dictator in Rome. Though France concluded a pact with the Soviet Union, there was no practical effect, and it gave Hitler a pretext to reoccupy the Rhineland in March; among the towns the Wehrmacht entered was de Gaulle's former temporary home of Trier. The government of a cultivated Verdun veteran, Albert Sarrault, did nothing.

As commander-in-chief, Maurice Gamelin, an intellectual soldier with sensitive political reactions, insisted that France could only match German strength if there was a general mobilisation which, with elections looming, the politicians could not contemplate. The army was run down by falling numbers of conscripts due to the low birth rate. There was little coordination between branches of the military. Communications technology was backward. Morale was low – a confidential internal report in 1934 spoke of 'debility' that deprived the forces of vitality. 'France wants peace, fears war, does not conceal that fear, and will be forced to take the consequences,' the US embassy reported to Washington. Paris appealed to treaties and to the British, neither of which offered any succour. Inaction seemed the wisest course. 'War is absolutely crazy,' remarked the celebrated actor Louis Jouvet. 'But there will be no war.'[13]

Elections in May 1936 resulted in a Popular Front government under the leadership of Léon Blum, bringing together Socialists and Radicals on a programme of social, educational and labour reform. With Communist backing, it saw a great outburst of rejoicing as France got its first truly left-wing government. From the start, the new administration had to cope with the militancy of its grassroots supporters. Two million workers spontaneously occupied factories and staged mass rallies.

The result was an agreement that established collective bargaining rights, set the working week at forty hours and granted a 10–12 per cent pay rise. A raft of reforms followed. The Bank of France was made more accountable; the school leaving age was raised from thirteen to fourteen; measures were introduced to help farmers. Nationalisation of the railways and of arms and aviation factories began. In the colonies, an amnesty freed 7,000 of the 10,000 political prisoners in Indochina where a Communist-led rising had been put down in 1929–30. French workers were guaranteed two weeks' annual holiday – *les congés payés* (paid holidays). Cheap railway tickets were available for vacations, leading to a rash of cartoons showing bourgeois vacationers reacting with horror at the arrival of people who had never seen the sea before. Membership of the Socialist SFIO party soared.

However, expectations soon clashed with economic realities. The franc was devalued. Capital fled. Inflation soared; civil servants and pensioners were hit hardest as their revenues lagged behind those of industrial workers. The inflexible nature of the new labour system produced bottlenecks, given the shortage of skilled staff. Output fell – at a time when German production was rising fast.

The economic situation forced the government to declare a 'pause' in its reform programme while Blum's caution about aiding the Republicans in the Spanish civil war for fear of widening Left–Right divisions in France split his supporters. Spending on public works dropped, while the increasingly threatening context in Europe led to a fresh rise in the arms budget. The target was to double the country's military capacity in four years, producing the irony of the united Left, many of whose supporters abhorred the thought of war, giving guns priority over butter.

As he considered France's military needs, Blum received de Gaulle at his official residence in the Hôtel Matignon. In his memoirs, he spoke of his visitor as being 'all of one piece' both morally and physically, expounding his ideas in a slow, measured tone. The Prime Minister compared him to Clemenceau 'because, for them, action represents a vital necessity'.

According to de Gaulle's account, Blum assured him of his interest in the soldier's ideas.

'But you fought against them,' his visitor observed.

'One changes one's point of view when one becomes head of the government,' came the reply.

Though Blum was constantly interrupted by telephone calls, the two men spoke about what France would do if Hitler marched on Vienna, Prague or Warsaw. Simple, said de Gaulle with sarcasm: the reserves would be called up and the country would watch the subjugation of Europe from behind its battlements. He summed up his impression of Blum the following day as 'power of understanding, 100; power of action, 1'.

The Right attacked the Popular Front relentlessly. Industrialists formed committees to undermine the government's reforms, and funded extremist groups. Blum was denounced as a Jew who was doing Moscow's bidding. Anti-Communism easily shaded into a benevolent view of the Fascist dictators, expressed in the saying 'Better Hitler than Blum'. A particularly savage campaign targeted the Interior Minister, Roger Salengro, who was accused of having deserted to the Germans during the First World War. Though a military inquiry disproved the claims, the accusations continued to the point where the minister committed suicide in his home in Lille.

Amid all this, Pétain decided it was time to set out his concerns about the state of the nation in a speech on the twentieth anniversary of the battle of Verdun in June 1936. He submitted the draft to Blum and was outraged when it came back with key passages deleted, including his assertion that, having won the war, France was on the brink of losing the peace. Nor did Blum agree to the Marshal's wish to have his speech broadcast on national radio.

Though toned down, the words were pointed enough. 'The physical and mental health of the French people required important reforms,' Pétain declared. Failure to protect the family had led to a worrying degree of social disequilibrium. Profound changes were needed to revive the family, school and army. The night before he delivered the speech, the Marshal told his doctor that honest men should replace the politicians of the Third Republic, and that he might be their standard-bearer. He gained an unlikely supporter in the shape of one of France's numerous former prime ministers, Pierre Laval. The stocky, white-tied, broken-toothed Auvergnat was always ready to try something that offered him an opportunity to get an edge – it was noted, too, that his name was a palindrome. Despite having participated in the system to the full, he now said he thought that the existing parliamentary regime could not continue and would henceforth be ready to draw on the prestige of the Victor of Verdun.

The Communists played a canny game, with the Kremlin pulling the wires. The PCF had vastly boosted its parliamentary representation and its trade union federation united with the Socialist labour organisation. But, having won substantial advances, the party wanted to avoid doing anything that might frighten the Radical Socialists and impede rearmament against Hitler's Germany. By not joining the government it was able to claim credit for wage increases and social reforms while remaining free to criticise Blum for not going far enough and for not committing himself to the fight against Franco.

The pause in reforms reduced popular enthusiasm for the Popular Front government, which encountered fresh economic troubles as the run on the franc resumed. After right-wing leagues had been banned, Colonel de La Rocque of the *Croix de Feu* formed a new political party, the *Parti social français* (French Social Party), leading to a big demonstration by left-wingers in March 1937. To maintain order, police opened fire, killing seven people and wounding several hundred. The main trade union federation called a one-day general strike in protest. Blum asked parliament for authority to impose financial policy by decree. The Senate refused, and the Prime Minister resigned. He returned to office the following March, at the time of Hitler's Anschluss, union with Austria, but failed to put together a majority and resigned within a month.[14]

VIII
The Marshal and Munich

Blum was succeeded by Daladier, who remained popular. In keeping with his nickname 'the Bull of the Vaucluse', after his home department in southern France, the burly Radical could thump the table in defence of French interests, but then invariably caved in, deepening de Gaulle's pessimism about the outlook for his country. Writing to his mother, the colonel warned that Poland was playing a double game with Germany and was worthless. Britain had its fleet, but no army and a backward air force. The need to bring together all Hitler's opponents made an alliance with the Soviet Union unavoidable, 'whatever horror we have for its regime,' he added. Hitler's ultimate aim was to crush France, though his 'very skilful' propaganda had persuaded many French people that he would leave them alone so long as he was allowed to conquer central Europe and Ukraine.

His relations with Pétain took a further turn for the worse when the Victor of Verdun did not use a draft of a speech about Foch which he had written for the old man to deliver when he took the other Marshal's seat in the Académie-Française. The two soldiers had been rivals, so Pétain was not pleased by the praise de Gaulle lavished on Foch's offensive spirit and imaginative grasp of the battlefield. Matters then deteriorated further when de Gaulle proposed to publish a book on the history of the French army which reprised some elements from the earlier work he had undertaken for Pétain. He asked his former mentor to contribute a preface.

After an edgy exchange of letters, the Marshal suggested a Sunday morning meeting at his home in Paris. He opened the door himself, dressed in civilian clothes. Philippe de Gaulle, who accompanied his father, remembered that Pétain's handshake lacked warmth. De Gaulle read from a copy of his manuscript, and the old man took an emollient line. But then he asked for the manuscript to be left for him to read. His guest refused. Pétain said he was giving him an order. De Gaulle replied that he could issue an order on a military matter, not on a literary one. When the Marshal insisted, the visitor saluted and left. The book was published soon afterwards without a preface from the old hero but with a few words of appreciation in the author's note.

Pétain, who was about to become France's ambassador to Spain, remained indignant. He contributed a preface to a volume that relegated tank warfare to 'the realm of dreams', writing that an attack by armoured vehicles would be stopped by mines, anti-tank weapons and natural obstacles. When the director of a political science college in Paris discussed with him the idea of holding a course on military matters, and suggested that it might be conducted by de Gaulle, he replied: 'I know de Gaulle well. He is an ambitious man, and very ill bred.'

For his part, de Gaulle disparaged Pétain for accepting the ambassadorship to Spain as evidence of 'senile ambition'. 'It's terrible and pathetic,' he added. 'He's no longer in a condition to take on responsibility.' In his notebook, he set down a series of verdicts on the man who had once signed his obituary eulogy – 'Covers the wretchedness of his solitude with pride . . . Too sure of himself ever to give up . . . inscrutable with a hint of irony which he uses to protect his thoughts and his peace . . . more greatness than virtue.' The divorce between the two soldiers was thus confirmed well before they went their different ways in 1940.[15]

*

When France and Britain made a temporary show of force that deterred Hitler from taking all Czechoslovakia in 1938, panic spread in France at the prospect of war. There were dire warnings of Paris being obliterated by air raids. The Louvre was closed, and its contents packed into storage cases. People fought for seats on trains and traffic jams blocked roads away from Paris as people fled. In the capital, in Dijon and Strasbourg, mobs attacked Jewish shops shouting, 'Down with the Jewish war!'

De Gaulle's regiment was moved forward to positions on the German frontier. But after Britain and France signed the agreement at Munich that ceded the Sudetenland to the Reich in September 1938, his troops were told to pull back. Before they left, local people covered their vehicles with flowers. As they drove to their base, de Gaulle suddenly appeared in a car. 'The flowers in the ditch!' he ordered. 'If you think the time to celebrate has come, you are mistaken. You're mad.'

But for the bulk of his compatriots the only reaction was relief, even if the agreement meant the end of the strategy of building a ring of allies on Germany's eastern flank. After the experience of the Popular Front, many on the Right regarded the Socialists and Communists as a worse threat than Hitler and believed France could co-exist with the Nazi regime while the traditional pacificism of the SFIO militated against any attempt by Blum to urge a tougher line in foreign policy. Though industrial companies with investments in central Europe favoured a tough stance towards Hitler, major business figures like Louis Renault and leading banks backed appeasement.

The Foreign Minister, Georges Bonnet, described by observers as resembling a snake both physically and in his policies, argued that France could not afford to compete with Germany and so should try to buy off Hitler. During the pre-Munich crisis, he advised: 'Let us not be heroic. We are not up to it.' He let the Germans know that France was 'indifferent' to eastern Europe, and, when his Nazi counterpart visited Paris, made sure Jewish members of the government did not attend the receptions. The lack of a moral sense – or any sense of where France was heading – was caught in Jean Renoir's classic film *La règle du jeu*, which was banned as being too demoralising when war did loom. The nation, in the words of the writer Julien Green, was in 'a nightmare of fear'.[16]

Daladier, who had lived down to a description of him by a trade union leader as a bull with the horns of a snail, had been happy to follow Britain's lead in appeasing Hitler – a quarter of a century later, de Gaulle would invoke this as evidence of the need for an independent foreign policy. The Radical Premier was said to have feared that he might be lynched on his return from Munich for having betrayed an ally; instead, he was cheered by a crowd at the airport, leading him to mutter, 'Imbeciles! If they only knew what they are cheering.' De Gaulle denounced the agreement with Hitler as 'an irreparable disaster'; with tanks, France could have broken through the German Siegfried Line, he told his family. 'We have capitulated without fighting when faced with the insolent demands of the Germans . . . the series of humiliations continues,' he wrote to Yvonne in September 1938.

'It will continue with the abandoning of our colonies, then of Alsace etc unless an upsurge of honour wakes up the nation and puts the traitors in the doghouse,' he went on. 'Thanks to today's capitulation we will gain a short breathing space, like the old Madame du Barry begging on the revolutionary scaffold "A little moment more, Mr Executioner!" . . . Bit by bit, we are becoming accustomed to retreat and humiliation, to the point at which it becomes second nature. We drink the chalice down to the dregs.' In protest, he gave up smoking 'until the cannon shot', a vow which he ended at the pact between Germany and the Soviet Union in August 1939.[17]

His fury at the Munich accord was accompanied a few days later by his sorrow at the death of Émile Mayer. Suffering from heart pains, the old man wrote in his diary 'Today, my death', asked to be left alone and died a few hours later. De Gaulle's military commitments prevented him attending the funeral, but he spoke to mutual acquaintances of his esteem for 'this eminent and excellent man'. In later years, his aide, Olivier Guichard, recalled that Mayer's name was 'the only one from that era which I heard the General utter with some degree of emotion'. The lieutenant colonel joined a group of Catholics, including the writer François Mauriac, which backed a weekly, *Temps présent*, that was critical of the right-wing dictators; this was no move to the Left but was still an independent step for a soldier who wrote to Jean Auburtin that Fascism had found a way of overcoming social antagonisms, but 'how can one accept a social balance whose price is the death of freedom?'

He could take some comfort politically, however, from the return of Reynaud to a government headed by Daladier. Though the two politicians did not get on, and their mistresses detested one another, de Gaulle's friend became Justice Minister, and had the pleasure of seeing the government put into effect the devaluation he had long advocated. In November 1938, he moved to the Finance Ministry, warning the nation in a broadcast that it was 'going blindfold towards an abyss'. He introduced an austerity programme, raised taxes and chipped away at Popular Front measures such as the forty-hour working week, insisting that, since France lived in the capitalist system, it must operate by the laws of profits, individual risk, free markets and growth through competition. A Communist-led general strike flopped. State finances improved and industrial output jumped while unemployment and inflation declined. Military spending was raised. But another abyss lay ahead.[18]

IX
'Colonel Motors'

In June 1937 de Gaulle had been appointed to command a tank regiment based in Metz, where he lived alone while Yvonne remained in Colombey. He maintained a modest lifestyle. The kitchen was the only room in the house which was properly heated in winter. He continued to wear white gloves, which he changed three times a day.

He was clear how he intended to use his armoured force if war came. During field manoeuvres, he told officers that, if they encountered a solidly defended village, they should go round it and continue their advance without waiting for the infantry. This brought him criticism from the military governor of the city, General Henri Giraud, and from the commander-in-chief, Gamelin, who said armour was needed only for flanking action or for an occasional spectacular operation. 'When rules are stupid, they should be cancelled and changed,' the colonel told his superior, saluting. Writing to the publisher of *France and Her Army* (De Gaulle's book of 1938 in which he treats his country's military history in broad sweeping terms) he suggested a publicity pen portrait of himself 'in helmet and combat gear amidst his battle engines and less surprised than anybody by current events'. Reynaud noted that his collaborator, who had gained the nickname of 'Colonel Motors', had evolved into 'a war chief, an intellectual melded with a fighting animal'.[19]

The advance of the Fascist powers continued as 1939 unfolded. In January, Franco's forces clinched victory in the Spanish civil war. In March, using the pretext of Slovak discontent with rule from Prague, Germany occupied Czechoslovak territory not taken at the time of Munich. Italy invaded Albania. Such advances finally brought a reaction from Paris and London, with guarantees of territorial integrity extended to Poland by Britain and to Romania and Greece by both powers. But France's military leaders were unperturbed. In July 1939, the former chief of staff, Maxime Weygand, proclaimed the army 'a more effective force than at any moment in its history. Its materiel is first rate, its fortifications are first class, its morale is excellent, its High Command remarkable. No one among us wants war, but I affirm that if we are compelled to win victory again, we will win it.' Though the Socialist rebel and pacifist Marcel Déat attracted a lot of attention with an article entitled 'Do we have to die for Danzig?', a poll showed that three-quarters of those questioned were ready to do just that. A defence loan collected six billion francs in six hours. Reservists were called up. Communist newspapers were banned.

On 1 September 1939, Hitler invaded Poland. The following day, de Gaulle was appointed tank commander of France's Fifth Army in Alsace. His vehicles were deployed in the pattern he had fought against, attached to infantry units rather than being concentrated into a single force as he wished. The only action he led was a small raid on a German frontier post on 12 September. From his command post at Wangenbourg, which was visited by President Lebrun, he sent Reynaud reports and recommendations. He did not think the Germans would attack for a long time. Having got France to mobilise, their interest lay in letting it stew in its own juice while they acted elsewhere, he added.

But, after a dinner in Paris organised by Reynaud, he told Blum of his fear that the high command would persist in believing that the Germans could not repeat their performance in Poland in the west. 'Everything remains to be done and if we do not act in time, we will lose this war in a miserable fashion; we will lose it by our own fault,' he warned.[20]

*

For Christmas 1939 de Gaulle went to snow-bound Colombey to spend the holiday with his wife and Anne while Philippe and Élisabeth stayed in Paris. Those few days together in the country were the last moments of relaxation and peace he would have for years to come. On Christmas Eve, according to Yvonne's biographer Geneviève Moll, Yvonne noticed that the bird bath in the garden was frozen, so Charles took out hot water to melt the ice. Wearing a heavy cape, she followed him, carrying a coat which she made him put on. Then they walked down the alleys of the garden, arm in arm, their feet crunching in the snow. Looking back, they saw the birds feeding. That night, they attended midnight mass, singing with the local farmers and praying for the safety of France.[21]

7

DEBACLE

I
Rebuffed again

Back on the offensive in January 1940, de Gaulle made another attempt to get his ideas across with a pamphlet entitled *L'avènement de la force mécanique* (*The Advent of Mechanised Forces*) in which he warned of a political, economic, social and moral crisis so deep and widespread that it was bound to lead to a complete upheaval which would affect the structure of states. Mechanical warfare was exactly proportional to the 'colossal dimension' of this revolution. 'It is high time that France draws the conclusions,' he added.

The colonel had his pamphlet run off on a roneotype machine and sent copies to eight hundred leading figures. Blum wrote, 'I now understood everything', and passed a copy to General Georges, the number two in the French army, who replied that he read it with very great interest. But the bulk of the establishment remained hostile. The following month, a decision was taken to organise French tanks into four armoured divisions, with de Gaulle in command of one based in the north-east. This did nothing to diminish his pessimism. 'This war is lost; we must now prepare to win the next one – with machines,' he told a delegation of British MPs, whom he kept standing out in the snow for two hours watching his tanks going up and down hills.

But politics seemed, at last, to be moving in his direction, though it would prove a false dawn. On 19 March 1940, a parliamentary vote forced the Daladier government to resign, and President Lebrun called on Reynaud to form a new one. After backstairs lobbying in the National

Assembly, de Gaulle's associate managed to muster a majority, of just one vote. Even in war, the Third Republic politicians could not end their squabbling.

The new Premier's fragile position in parliament meant that he had to juggle between the factions in his coalition and put up with Daladier as Defence Minister. Some of those in the administration advocated seeking an agreement with Mussolini. Colonel Villelume, the chief of the Prime Minister's military staff, thought the conflict a great mistake. The pro-German Comtesse de Portes complicated her lover's life, not hesitating to telephone him in the middle of meetings and reading secret documents in bed. In his notebooks, Reynaud said later that she was trying to help him and described her as having been led astray by her desire to be in with young people, 'and to distance herself from Jews and old politicians'. In a conversation with the historian Henri Amouroux in 1963, de Gaulle called her a 'goose . . . like all women who get into politics'.*

Georges Mandel, the Minister for Colonies who took the toughest pro-war line, urged Reynaud to get rid of incompetents, starting with Gamelin, whom the Prime Minister described as 'an old woman'. When Daladier told him on 16 May that the French must attack, the commander-in-chief replied that he had no reserves for the purpose.

'So this is the destruction of the French army,' the Defence Minister replied.

'Yes, it is the destruction of the French army,' Gamelin concurred. But Daladier would not agree to sack him.

Not surprisingly, the Defence Minister was highly hostile to de Gaulle, as were de Portes and Villelume. Daladier, who had pronounced trench warfare to be 'the first and last word in military art', had declined even to look at his pamphlet. When told that Reynaud proposed to appoint de Gaulle Secretary to the War Cabinet, the Radical Socialist leader said: 'If de Gaulle comes here, I will leave this office, I will walk down the stairs, and I will telephone Paul Reynaud to tell him to put him in my place.' Again, the Prime Minister gave way. So the job went to the suave banker Paul Baudouin, a protégé of his mistress and a leading

**Dindon* was his word.

apostle of seeking peace with Germany. 'Experience shows that I was wrong,' Reynaud acknowledged later.[1]

The failure of the Allied expedition to Norway, designed to counter Germany's invasion of Denmark and the sealing of Baltic ports in early April 1940, put Reynaud's administration at even greater risk. (De Gaulle marked the German success down as further proof that his theories of modern warfare were correct since it was 'one more victory down to mechanised force. Unfortunately, once more, this victory is German.') In early May 1940, the Prime Minister finally went on the offensive, proposing Gamelin's dismissal at a Cabinet meeting. Daladier dissented. Since the Radical party kept the government in power, Reynaud offered to resign. President Lebrun asked him to keep this secret until a new administration was formed.

Before this could be done, the Wehrmacht advanced into Belgium, the Netherlands and Luxembourg at dawn on 10 May. Two hours later, executing the long-standing plan to which Gamelin remained faithful, French troops crossed into Belgium, expecting the decisive battle to take place there. Reynaud withdrew his resignation. Gamelin kept his job. In London, Churchill succeeded Neville Chamberlain in Downing Street.

Instead of Belgium, the key battlefield turned out to be the supposedly impenetrable wooded highlands of the Ardennes on France's eastern frontier where German tanks bypassed the Maginot Line. French and British forces deployed to the north were cut off as the Germans took Sedan and drove into France, free to turn either towards Paris or to the Channel coast. Mandel insisted that what was needed was 'an implacable will never to give in'. But Reynaud was a weathervane. At one moment, he pledged to fight on; then he told Churchill the battle was lost. Flying to Paris to confer with his counterpart, the British leader became aware of just how deep defeatism ran.

Not only was France's army suffering a massive defeat, the political class was also bankrupt. Daladier, Herriot and the other former prime ministers were tarred with the brush of failure. Blum had too many enemies and Mandel lacked solid parliamentary backing; both were unacceptable to some of the French because they were Jews. Finally, on 19–20 May, Reynaud sacked Gamelin and dropped Daladier, taking over the Defence Ministry himself, bringing back Pétain and Weygand and promoting Mandel to the Interior Ministry. Weygand, who had mouthed eulogies about the army the previous year, now called the war 'sheer madness' since 'we have gone to war with a 1918 army against a German Army of 1939', without adequate reserves and with an erroneous strategy. Churchill might insist from London on the need to continue the struggle, but the vast majority of the French were looking for a way to end the disaster that had broken on their heads. At the front, the historian Marc Bloch recorded in his great book *L'Étrange défaite* (*Strange Defeat*) the 'shakiness' of the army and the 'tide of despair' that overcame officers, and communicated itself to their troops as millions of refugees fled south from the advancing enemy.[2]

II
Battlefront

Having returned to the front from Paris after being vetoed by Daladier from the War Cabinet secretariat, de Gaulle found himself vindicated by the turn of events, and yet more solitary than ever. For Pétain, Weygand and those around them, defeat meant the end of the struggle. For de Gaulle, the campaign was lost, but, as he wrote to the Prime Minister, France could still win another war. Before that vision could take shape, Colonel Motors had to prove himself in battle.

On 11 May, he took command of the Fourth Armoured Division outside the city of Laon, 150 kilometres north-east of the capital on a defensive line running between the Rivers Aisne and Somme. Its mission was to delay the German advance while France's Sixth Army moved from the Maginot Line to block the German path to Paris. Pétain and Weygand agreed that if the Aisne–Somme line was lost the war was over.

As he prepared to plunge back into war a quarter of a century after Verdun, de Gaulle did not forget the difficulties facing his wife. Since the house at Colombey did not have a telephone, correspondence was his only way of maintaining contact. To 'my dear little darling wife', he wrote: 'I had rather hoped to have received a letter from you today. Anyway, I think that you will have received mine.' Another letter warned that 'real war' was starting, though he thought Colombey should be safe because it was not on the main route of a German advance on Paris. Still, he advised Yvonne to 'be very careful to take shelter by day if there is an alert and to turn out the lights at night'.

He was anxious that Philippe, who was in Paris, should not show off pointlessly if there was fighting in the city. He added that he had good expectations of Élisabeth's prospects in her baccalaureate examination, and attached a letter from her. He also wrote to his sister and brother-in-law to ask them to correspond frequently with Yvonne to 'distract and encourage her'. 'She is very much alone and quite worried,' he added. 'All the more so since, as you know, she does not let her feelings show. Do not lose sight of my children.'

On 15 May he changed his mind about Colombey and suggested that Yvonne arrange an escape route; she moved west to stay with her sister near Orléans, driven there by the owner of the village garage. A week later was her fortieth birthday, and her husband sent her his 'most tender wishes' after four days of 'long and hard' fighting. He hoped Anne was getting used to her new surroundings, and advised his wife that he was dispatching a collection of his papers and letters to her. Later in the month, he asked her to arrange for their silver to be sent from Colombey to her new abode because of the danger of looting. 'A thousand tendernesses to my dear little wife,' he signed off.[3]

*

Though most of the French army put up little resistance to the Germans, and its high command was overtaken by events on the battlefield, some units did stand their ground, showing the potential strength of France's big tank force. In the opening stage of the western campaign, French armoured vehicles had demonstrated their worth in the battle of Hannut in Belgium, though mistakes by Gamelin's high command let the invaders through. French infantry backed by armoured forces including thirty-two-ton Char B1 tanks fought for three days for the town of Stonne, near Sedan, which changed hands seventeen times.

On his sector of the front, de Gaulle imposed a ruthless command style. He replaced his chief of staff, whom he considered insufficiently energetic and resolute. He held no staff conferences. His orders were abrupt. If an officer raised a query, he snapped back: 'One does not question a divisional commander.' He was constantly on the move in his black Talbot car, joining columns of tanks or driving up to a ridge to get a better view. He snatched sleep when and where he could, in an armchair, on a camp bed, and, on one occasion, in the bed of a local couple who moved out for the night to make room for him.

On 17 May he launched an attack against a German position near a road junction at the small town of Montcornet and the adjoining village of Lislet, where the 1st Panzer Division had its headquarters. Before going into battle, in leather jacket and peaked helmet, he asked the chaplain of his unit to say a mass for himself and Anne. His habitual fearlessness was evident to all – though, some years later, he would remark of another soldier that this was the result of overcoming one's feelings rather than an innate lack of fear. He insisted on walking into the middle of a battlefield near Laon to see if tanks which had sunk into soft ground could be dragged out. A major on his staff recalled him standing upright during the fighting – 'Everybody admired him and our courage returned.' The major asked, 'What did he owe his bravery to? I think to his greatest quality: mastery of himself.' On 21 May he left his car to walk into a small wood, which was attacked by dive bombers. But he emerged and got into his Talbot to overtake a tank column.

He had some eighty-five tanks at his disposal, fifty of them light vehicles. Some had not been tested, and were manned by inexperienced one-man crews who had to drive the vehicles, aim the gun, fire it and try to keep in line with the division. They lacked maps. Their radios could send only coded messages for fear of enemy interception. On the other hand, the Germans had powerful anti-tank weapons, coordinated infantry, good radio communications and dive bombers.

De Gaulle's timing was fortuitous since the invaders had stopped to carry out maintenance work and to let the tank crews get some sleep. The German divisional commander had been injured when a lorry ran over his leg while he slept in the open. The French were successful in their first encounter with an enemy convoy, but their heavy tanks ran out of fuel as they advanced across sugar-beet fields to Montcornet and the light vehicles went the wrong way. The supporting infantry was so demoralised that it took the sound of the French tanks for a German advance, and so did not join in the attack.

German anti-tank guns positioned on a hill pummelled the French vehicles. Lislet was soon on fire. The light French tanks also ran short of petrol and had to turn back. Then the infantry finally arrived, and the refuelled French tanks took Montcornet. Stukas dived out of the clear summer sky while German reinforcements forced the French to pull back. De Gaulle wrote of his division as being 'lost children' beyond the defensive line on the Aisne. 'Stop this massacre,' one account has him shouting as he ordered the retreat. Twenty-three of the eighty-five French tanks were destroyed. Between twenty-five and thirty French soldiers were lost, but the Germans suffered a hundred casualties and as many men taken prisoner.

The German Panzer chief, Field Marshal Ewald von Kleist, said later that the French attack caused his forces no danger. The Wehrmacht sector commander, Heinz Guderian, recalled that he was irritated, even worried, by this sudden display of armoured resistance. De Gaulle kept Reynaud informed by telephone.

After receiving seventy new tanks, de Gaulle, once again in leather jacket but this time with helmet and goggles, ordered an advance on 19 May to try to secure two river bridges. French air support did not materialise because of confusion over the timing of the attack, and Stukas still dominated the sky. The French tanks once again ran out of fuel. Lack of radios meant they could not communicate with one another. Most of the infantry did not show up and one unit which did join the battle arrived in civilian buses. Yet the French succeeded in taking one bridge, and de Gaulle appealed for more forces to continue the fight. But the Luftwaffe intervened again and, after twenty-four hours, he was forced to order a retreat.

In the middle of the fighting, he set out the argument on which he would base his action thereafter. For all its reverses, France would emerge victorious in the end, he insisted in a broadcast on a local radio station. The Germans had taken the initial advantage only because they understood that tanks and aircraft were the principal factors in the battle, he argued. 'Well, our success of tomorrow and our victory – yes, our victory – will come to us one day from our armoured divisions and our attack air force.'

Though achieving little beyond displaying his readiness to fight, de Gaulle emerged satisfied from his first tank battles. 'I write to you at the end of a long and hard fight which went very well for me,' he told his wife. 'If the general atmosphere is bad, it is excellent for your husband.' Two days later, he was promoted to the temporary rank of brigadier general with effect from 1 June. Laon had fallen, meanwhile, and de Gaulle's Fourth Armoured Division moved two hundred kilometres west to join British forces seeking to stop the Germans on the Somme while the evacuation began from Dunkirk.

As he prepared for battle, he gave further displays of his lack of nerves. When officers around him took shelter at the approach of dive bombers, he admonished them with a cry of 'Behave, gentlemen!' As he and a group of British officers came under artillery fire and the Frenchman refused to take shelter, a British general exclaimed: 'The bloody man will get us killed.' 'What did he say?' de Gaulle asked. 'The general thinks it would be prudent to fall back,' his interpreter translated. De Gaulle walked off slowly, raising his shoulders. 'A bit of a show-off,' a fellow French officer thought.

After a brief engagement at Crécy-sur-Seine, de Gaulle's division staged two successful attacks on an enemy pocket near Abbeville which gained eight kilometres and took several hundred prisoners. Its commander was mentioned in dispatches. He set up his field headquarters in a château, his tank knocking down the gate on its way in. According to the owner, when his officers tried to get some rest, their commander called out: 'One does not sleep on the eve of battle.' Still his own mind ranged beyond the immediate task at hand. 'The greatest and most immediate danger may come from the Muslim band which goes from Tangiers to India,' he told the divisional chaplain. 'If this band comes under the authority of Russian Communism or, what would be worse, that of China, we are done for,' he added.

He continued his solitary habits, eating and drinking his coffee alone and keeping his officers at a distance. As one noted, he had no need of others since he was convinced that his judgement was the best. Rough and sarcastic, he greeted news of reverses with contempt for the messenger. He made no allowances for the weaknesses of others, even in extreme circumstances, and saw no need to reach out to those around him. Taxed with aloofness by the chaplain, he responded: 'One does not speak in an operating theatre or on the bridge of a boat. And, what I have to say as chief to the men and tanks of the division in the middle of battle demands the silence of reflection. Solitude, silence, reflection, you know better than I, without them what would the word of God be and mean? All those who have done something worthwhile and lasting have been solitary and silent.'

As in the engagements around Laon, German anti-tank guns proved highly effective. The invaders' superior forces held Abbeville, and then broke through the French lines. When the British headed home from Dunkirk and Belgium began surrender negotiations, France found herself alone. The key question, to de Gaulle's mind, was whether the government would ensure the independence and future of the state or whether it 'would give everything up in the panic of the collapse'.

His division is estimated to have lost 30–45 per cent of its vehicles in its various encounters, and to have inflicted human losses on the Germans five times as great as those it suffered. It had not engaged in a battle with the Panzers, having faced anti-tank weapons, infantry and dive bombers. But de Gaulle had shown that French tank units could take the fight to the enemy, and had established himself as a leader on the battlefield. Both were vital to the next stage in his progress towards assuming the role he had seen for himself for the past quarter of a century.[4]

PART THREE
ONE MAN'S COMBAT

8

'FRANCE HAS NOT LOST THE WAR'

I
Flayed alive

If all successful leaders are, to varying degrees, magicians and actors, the three who led the Western resistance to Nazi Germany were in a special class as star performers, employing spoken words as a major weapon – Churchill in his great wartime speeches, Franklin Roosevelt in addresses to the nation and his radio fireside chats, Charles de Gaulle in his use of an extreme command of the French language to set out a grand vision that would have been hyperbole coming from anybody else. It was the Frenchman who kept his magic going the longest and conjured most from least.

In June 1940, he was a man in serious need – in need of a British plane to fly him out of Bordeaux, in need of the BBC to broadcast to his own country, in need of allies who would enable him to realise his vision. As he wrote later, he had 'not the shadow of a force, not an organisation. In France, nothing behind me, and no fame. Abroad, no credit or justification.' In addition, he had rebelled against the framework within which he had spent his adult life. But, he added, he was so solitary that he 'had to reach the heights and never come down again'. That was the pattern of the second half of his life, in which he would embrace reverses and difficulties as the spur to action like the mythical hero he imagined himself to be.[1]

The saga of Charles de Gaulle's war at the head of the Free French movement revolved around two poles – his quest to become the undisputed champion of France and his edgy relationship with the Allies. To achieve the first, he depended on the help of the British and, to a lesser degree, the Americans. But he had to ensure that this assistance did not reduce his status: 'I am too poor to be able to bow,' he told Churchill. The result was a series of monumental clashes, in which the General repeatedly went to the brink. Meeting him in September 1940, the diplomat Hervé Alphand detected 'no desire to please, no concern for nuances, no spirit of negotiation. The only manoeuvre he seemed to know and use was that of the tank that forges ahead.' De Gaulle himself told his spokesman, Maurice Schumann, that intransigence was the one weapon he had, and one which served his campaign to establish leadership of the French. 'He had to be rude to the British to prove to French eyes that he was not a British puppet,' Churchill observed. 'He certainly carried out this policy with perseverance.'

Observing how well-brought-up British officials shrank from a row, he decided to attack as if leading a military charge. Initially, his offensive approach brought a cold shoulder from his hosts, he noted: 'No meetings, no correspondence, no visit nor lunches. The telephone did not ring. Those British whom we met by chance were sombre and impenetrable.' Then a formal discussion would be organised, followed by détente, with favourable mentions in the press and a result that was 'very much what we had proposed in the first place'. As for his relationship with the Prime Minister, he observed: 'When I am right, I get angry. Churchill gets angry when he is wrong. We are angry at each other much of the time.'

This scratchy relationship was in keeping with his long-standing distrust of *la perfide Albion*. The Resistance leader Pierre Brossolette remarked that one had to remind him regularly that Germany was the number one enemy, since his natural inclination was to accord Britain that role. The retreat from Fashoda had marked him as a boy, and he now feared that his hosts wanted to prevent France being restored to its rightful status and glory. Nor could he exclude the possibility that military reverses might force London into a compromise peace with Germany which would perpetuate the subjugation of his nation and enable the British to grab parts of its Empire. On top of this, his personal position was still at risk since the British continued to explore the possibility of what Churchill called 'a kind of collusive conspiracy' that would see members of the Pétain government moving to North Africa to act independently from there.

While Roosevelt would dismiss the General as an unbalanced crypto-dictator who took himself for Joan of Arc, Churchill swung between extremes, admiring his 'massive strength' and hailing him as 'perhaps the last survivor of a warrior race', but then threatening to have him clapped in chains. In 1942, when the writer and politician Harold Nicolson said that, for all the problems he caused, the General was a great man, the Prime Minister responded: 'A great man? Why, he's selfish, he's arrogant, he thinks he's the centre of the universe . . . You're right, he's a great man!'

One thing he was not was the impassive, imperturbable figure he appeared to be. The British Prime Minister noted that he seemed to have a 'remarkable capacity for feeling pain'. In a telling pen portrait of the General in 1940, Lady Spears, the novelist Mary Borden who ran a Free French hospital, wrote of him assuming his country's dishonour 'as Christ assumed the sins of the world. In those days, he was as flayed alive, and the slightest contact made him want to snap. The uneasiness that I felt when I was with him certainly came from the pain and the rage that were burning in him . . . When he spoke for France and in the name of France he was expressing a fact that he desperately yearned to have accepted as true, defying the whole world to disbelieve him.'

But there was more to it than the pain he felt at the debacle in France. The future British Prime Minister Harold Macmillan, who dealt with de Gaulle during the war in North Africa, detected a 'terrible mixture of inferiority complex and spiritual pride . . . He would immensely like to be liked, and the smallest act of courtesy or special kindness touches him with deep emotion.' Recalling a meeting with the General in London in 1942, Christian Pineau, an early leader of the internal resistance to the Germans, wrote of how, as he left to return to France, his host gave him 'an almost affectionate look, but he did not say a word which had a personal character to it. It was as if he was ashamed of being human.' That was the key. De Gaulle had always been extremely protective of his privacy, letting his guard down only with Anne, who could not speak. Now that he was the Constable, he could not allow himself to be seen as an ordinary human being. As a result, he came to be viewed by many as a man lacking in humanity, an arrogant autocrat in a world of his own.[2]

That he emerged triumphant from the war years was a tribute to his strategic vision, tactical skill, sheer pig-headedness and ability to channel his strong emotions in constructive directions for both himself and his cause. It was a performance which catapulted him on to the world stage, and ensured that, for most of the three decades between his flight to London and his death, he would be a unique global player.

II
The Free French

The first volunteers to join de Gaulle were a motley band who resembled medieval knights pledging themselves to a baron who had put himself forward to the rank of Constable of the kingdom. De Gaulle described them as being bound together by a taste for risk and adventure, scorn for the spineless, national pride sharpened by the suffering of their nation and 'an overwhelming confidence in the strength and cunning of their own plot'. He demanded unquestioning allegiance as a matter of course. 'With him, it is take it or leave it, serving the Resistance and national honour, uncompromisingly demanding,' wrote one. 'With him, we would have to get used to breathing the rarefied air of the summits.'

Those who called on the General in June 1940 found him inexpressibly remote, intensely reserved, apparently lacking in humour or concern for others, a man from another era who belonged in a suit of armour and helmet. His height made an immediate impact as he stood bolt upright in uniform and jodhpurs. The future Nobel Prize winner François Jacob described the impression he made as 'gothic'. Albin Chalandon, who would become a minister under the Fifth Republic, was struck by the extremely piercing and deep look in his eyes, but also by the way in which his mind seemed to be elsewhere – 'he was impenetrable'. 'His features evoked, at first, a mediaeval drawing,' recalled a journalist, Pierre Maillaud, who went to see the General the day after his first broadcast. 'There was in his eyes an abstract fire, capable of suddenly flaring up . . . a nobleness and reserve, a superficial shyness and a singular pride, the pride of the soldier and the pride of the man "who has read all the books".'

Another journalist, Yves Morvan, who took the wartime name of Jean Marin, saw in his eyes the sadness 'of those who know that history is tragic and who discover that suddenly they are in charge of making it'. One unconvinced early visitor, Robert Mengin, felt unease at the host's self-importance; he thought the General belonged in the ranks of puffed-up officers who believed that they were never mistaken.[3]

De Gaulle wrote to Churchill on 23 June to propose the formation of a French National Committee to continue the war alongside the British. This was agreed and promptly announced. The committee's object was defined as being 'to maintain the independence of France, to honour her alliances and to contribute to the war effort of the Allies'. It undertook to account for its actions to the representatives of the French people when they could 'assemble in conditions compatible with liberty, dignity and security'. But it had no constitutional foundation; the Pétain administration was still the legal government, and was not at war with Britain. France's parliamentarians offered no support to the Free French.

So the committee did not have the same status as governments-in-exile in London or other European countries which had been invaded. As Charles Corbin, the French ambassador to London, told the Foreign Office, British backing might make it appear to many French people as no more independent than the administration in Bordeaux. But de Gaulle did not hesitate. As he put it in his memoirs, 'it was for me to take the country's fate upon myself'. His argument, and that of the British, was that France no longer had an independent government capable of upholding its interests. Typically, he took an absolutist point of view; there was no middle ground between him and the administration in Bordeaux. That made life difficult for those who did not back Pétain but did not support the General either, but he always believed in imposing hard choices on those around him.

With the help of Spears, the committee set up in four rooms in St Stephen's House on Victoria Embankment, a dusty, run-down building where Sir Edward had a private office. De Gaulle occupied a triangular room looking out on to the Thames, with maps of France and the world pinned to the walls. The furnishings were summary, a few wooden desks, school benches and a coat hanger. The General's aide, de Courcel, described by one French visitor as 'tall, fair-haired, rosy cheeked and very polite', worked in an adjoining room to the General, as did his secretary, Élisabeth de Méribel. The offices closed for an hour and a half at lunchtime. All expenses had to be approved in advance by de Gaulle. A cask of red wine was installed to cater for Frenchmen who rallied to the cause.

René Cassin, a dignified fifty-five-year-old jurist with a white beard, remembered that, when he arrived at the end of June, de Gaulle had only three or four officers with him. In the following weeks, the numbers grew and the staff spread through a dozen rooms. René Pleven, who had helped draft the Franco-British unity declaration on 16 June, was an early recruit, as was the journalist Maurice Schumann, who became a frequent broadcaster on the BBC. Others came from further afield, sometimes by circuitous routes from the Soviet Union or North Africa. De Gaulle sent a terse message to Gaston Palewski, Reynaud's former aide who was with the air force in Tunisia: 'Come and join me immediately.' He did, and was given the job of overseeing political relations with France before returning to combat in Ethiopia – and then joining de Gaulle again as head of his civilian office.

The Free French leader made a point of talking to the young men at his headquarters, sometimes inviting recent arrivals from France to lunch to ask them about conditions across the Channel. With them all, he played the role of a teacher who not only imparted theoretical learning but backed it up with action. Several were surprised by the limpness of his handshake, but they contrasted his straightforward attitude to the pomposity of French generals they had encountered before. Despite the differences in background of those around him, he transmitted what one called 'a mental cohesion' born of their common rejection of the armistice and their crusade for France waged from a foreign land. But he was still a superior man alone; his first biographer, Philippe Barrès, recalled him remarking, 'I look down on those who serve me. As for those who contradict me, I can't put up with them.'[4]

At the end of June, the Free French gained their most eminent recruit in Vice Admiral Émile Muselier, who arrived dirty and dishevelled after escaping from France via Gibraltar with some naval craft. These he equipped with flags emblazoned with the Cross of Lorraine, originally a form of Byzantine cross, giving the Free French their emblem. De Gaulle appointed him commander of the Free French navy and, in effect, number two in the movement. A tribunal in France sentenced the admiral to death and confiscation of his property.[5]

In his memoirs, de Gaulle pays tribute to the kindness and generosity of British people, recalling the support he received when he appeared in public. He was touched by the way in which women sent in jewels and even their wedding rings to provide funds. An early recruit, Pierre Julitte, recalled how, when he stepped out for lunch with the General, men stood to attention and raised their hats. However, he was far from uniting the French in London. A Socialist group regarded him as a latter-day Boulanger. The political thinker and writer Raymond Aron spoke for those who were alienated by the way in which 'he transformed the [Free French] into a personal affair' and exasperated by the 'ferocity of the small Gaullist circle which made him lose his sense of proportion'. Jean Monnet, the best-connected French figure in London and who believed in resistance, did not trust the General as a political leader and thought action should be organised in North Africa. On 24 June de Gaulle wrote to him as 'my dear friend' to say that it would be absurd if they fell out with one another, because they both had the same objective. 'Come and see me, wherever you wish,' he added in his softest tone. 'We will quickly agree.' But the former banker soon left London on a mission to organise arms purchases for Britain in Washington.

De Gaulle devoted the best part of a page of his memoirs to listing the figures who were in London but who declined to join him. They included the celebrated writer André Maurois, who went to the United States, as did the former Secretary-General of the French Foreign Ministry, Alexis Léger (the poet Saint-John Perse). Ambassador Corbin, who resigned on the day the armistice was signed, left for South America. Many of his staff went home, some trying to dissuade French soldiers in Britain from joining the General before they departed. It was said that members of the remaining

French community crossed to the other side of the road when they saw known Gaullists approaching.

As a result, the Free French committee fell far short of expectations while the General's aloof personality restricted his appeal to evacuated troops housed in London exhibition halls. Only a tenth of the two thousand men at White City signed up. Some preferred to join the British forces or asked to be repatriated. A British government report estimated that, at most, the Free French had 4,000 soldiers, many in medical care, 1,000 sailors and 150 airmen.[6]

In France, the armistice with Germany came into effect on 25 June. Cafés, cinemas, halls and shops (except for food stores) closed while memorial services were held for the dead of both wars and a one-minute silence was declared at 11 a.m. 'Tomorrow, a new life will begin for France,' the Interior Minister promised.

Three days later, after the senior French figures in North Africa had turned down an offer from de Gaulle to serve under them if they would join the resistance to the Pétain administration, the British formally recognised him as 'Leader of all Free Frenchmen, wherever they may be, who rally to him in support of the Allied Cause'. Churchill told him, 'You stand alone. So what? I recognise you alone.' On the BBC, the General declared: 'I take under my authority all the French who remain in British territories or who come there.'

De Gaulle's promotion to the rank of general was cancelled by the high command in Bordeaux, and a message was delivered to him via the London embassy telling him to return to France. He wrote back to Weygand urging him to put himself at the head of resistance to the Germans, and pledging to follow him if he did so. The letter was returned several weeks later with a note on it saying that de Gaulle should go through the proper channels. On 30 June, another message instructed him to present himself for court martial in Toulouse. When he did not turn up, he was sentenced to four years in jail and fined one hundred francs for treason, desertion and helping the enemy. After Weygand appealed on the grounds that the sentence was too lenient, it was increased to the death penalty. The Free French leader was also condemned to national degradation and confiscation of his assets. De Gaulle issued a statement saying he regarded the verdict as null and void. 'They and I will have it out after the victory,' he added. When Cassin asked him on what basis he justified their movement, his simple answer was 'We are France.'*[7]

III
Magnificent demeanour

In later years, de Gaulle was quoted by one of his early followers, Colonel Rémy, as admitting that the armistice was inevitable in the circumstances, and remarking that France had to have two strings to its bow, Pétain and de Gaulle, so long as they both served the national interest. Rémy had a cause to argue at the time – he was lobbying for the rehabilitation of the Victor of Verdun. Still, the Marshal and the General could, indeed, be seen as representing the dichotomy between France's conservative and radical natures that together made up the nation, one man standing for tradition, the other for change, the one-time pupil the country's sword, the one-time mentor its shield.

Less than three weeks after he crossed to London, the sword-bearer faced a jolting challenge from his British ally. Obsessed with preventing France's fleet from falling into German hands, Churchill decided action was needed to neutralise it. Ships still in British ports were boarded, but that left the bulk of the navy stationed at the Mers-el-Kébir base outside the Algerian city of Oran.

In the early hours of 3 July 1940, a destroyer, HMS *Foxhound*, approached the harbour with a message for the French commander there, Admiral Gensoul, demanding that his ships 'continue the fight' or go to the West Indies where they could be decommissioned and perhaps be entrusted to American hands. If these 'fair offers' were refused, the message warned, the French must sink their ships within six hours, failing which a British fleet of twenty-seven warships sailing from Gibraltar would 'use whatever force may be necessary to prevent your ships falling into German or Italian hands'.

*Consulted in 1963 about the way his personal army dossier should be classified at the Armed Forces Ministry, de Gaulle said that the record of his condemnation in 1940 should not be included in it since the proceedings were null and void (*Lettres, Complément*, p. 426).

Churchill and de Gaulle both thought Gensoul would accept the demand once he saw that London meant what it said. A parallel operation to neutralise French naval vessels in Alexandria was carried out peacefully. But Gensoul rejected the demand and added that 'French warships will defend themselves by force'. Darlan was in the Massif Central at the time and difficult to contact but, when told what was going on, he ordered all French naval vessels in the Mediterranean to steam to Mers-el-Kébir to join Gensoul. 'You will reply to force with force,' he instructed Gensoul.

'Have opened fire on French ships,' the British task force telegraphed to London just before 6 p.m. A ten-minute bombardment was followed by attacks from the air. The battleship *Bretagne* blew up. Two other big ships were badly damaged and had to be beached. A second attack was launched on 6 July. In all, the French navy lost 1,285 dead, with 351 wounded. Darlan and Laval wanted the rest of the fleet to sail against the British, but were overruled by Pétain and Baudouin, heading off a full-scale Anglo-French sea war. Relations with London were severed. There was an outcry in France and recruiting of Free French sailors in Britain dropped off sharply.

It was a crucial moment for de Gaulle. His first reaction was an outburst to the First Lord of the Admiralty, but, meeting him that evening, Spears found 'his calm . . . very striking, the objectivity of his views astonishing'. He recognised that the attack was no doubt inevitable from the British point of view. With what Spears called 'magnificent dignity', the General added that he now had to make up his mind whether to continue to work with Britain or to retire from public life and go to live as a private citizen in Canada. He wanted to think about it overnight, he concluded.

In the morning, de Gaulle told Spears he had decided that continuing to fight alongside the British represented the only chance for France to survive as a great nation, even if it opened him up to the hatred of his countrymen. Two decades later, he told a government minister that, had he been in Churchill's place, he would have done the same thing. At the time, speaking on the BBC, he said that all French people felt grief and anger at the sinking of ships at Mers-el-Kébir, but argued that it was better for them to have been sunk than to have been manned by German crews to attack the British. 'No Frenchman worthy of the name can for a moment doubt that a British defeat would seal for ever his country's bondage,' he added. 'Our two great peoples are still linked together. Either they will both succumb, or they will triumph side by side.'

In his memoirs, Churchill recalled that de Gaulle was 'magnificent in his demeanour'. It was, as Spears wrote, 'a brave thing to say to a France overwhelmed with sorrow and resentment, whose ears were filled with vituperation'. But de Gaulle was not only applying the logic of his diagnosis of France's best long-term interests. He was also playing a cool political game. To have denounced the British would have brought him no dividend. On the other hand, to express understanding at what had been done could bring only gratitude from the government on which he depended. It was the first of a number of wartime decisions in which, while never abandoning his vision, the General would draw tactical advantage from adversity.[8]

IV
'Maréchal, nous voilà!'

Two days before the attack on its fleet, the Pétain administration moved from Bordeaux to the spa town of Vichy in central France. The parliamentary deputies who had not left for North Africa with Mandel and Daladier met in the casino there on 9–10 July to confer full powers on the Marshal and approve a new constitution. Though President Lebrun had not formally resigned, the National Assembly and Senate voted by 624 to 4 for Pétain to become head of state with legislative and executive powers. Laval warned that, if they did not do so, the Germans would occupy the whole country. Having done its job, parliament was dissolved until the Victor of Verdun saw fit to reconvene it, which was never to be.

For the next four years, the traditional political geography of France was turned on its head. The collaborationist capital lay in the isolated region of the Auvergne; the power centre of Paris was far away across the demarcation line that divided the country. The Marshal moved into the third floor of the Hôtel du Parc and went for daily constitutionals by the River Allier, even when snow fell. His appetite was good, and he took red wine with meals. Laval became his deputy and preferred successor. Weygand, who told Laval that he was 'worse than a dog; you roll in shit', stayed in charge of the army and Darlan of the navy, each of them potential rivals to the Auvergnat. Baudouin remained Foreign Minister.

The Marshal's one-time military aide, Bernard Serrigny, initially found the old man 'too feeble for the task at hand' with only a vague idea of how he planned to deal with the Germans. But then he perked up, speaking more than usual and taking decisions quickly. Most of those around him hoped to keep the Germans at arm's length and justify the armistice. Initially, the Vichy administration showed some spirit in declining to bow to a demand from Berlin to put airfields, ports and railways in North Africa at the Wehrmacht's disposal. It maintained diplomatic links with the United States and Canada. A message from Pétain proposed a meeting with representatives of de Gaulle in Lisbon, but drew no response from the General.

In Asia, the French governor, Georges Catroux, was cashiered by Vichy for giving in to Japanese demands and cutting off supplies to China without consulting the government in France; his ability to resist Tokyo had been undermined by the refusal of the still neutral United States to supply 120 fighters and anti-aircraft guns for which France had already paid. Pétain told him to come home; instead, Catroux flew to London and joined the Free French. His successor tried to hold back the Japanese, but they gained the upper hand in two days of fighting that cost eight hundred French lives. After Vichy recognised its 'pre-eminent position' in the Far East, Tokyo took control of airports and major harbours and forced the French to cede territory in Laos and Cambodia to the Thais. Vietnamese resisters, including the Communist Ho Chi Minh, sought refuge in south-west China and began to gear up for guerrilla warfare. But, though 740,000 square kilometres of Indochina remained under the tricolour flag, France's Asian colonies became a Japanese satellite, compared by de Gaulle to a great crippled ship in the fog which he could not reach.

At home, the new administration was not drawn entirely from conservative circles. The Marshal's first Cabinet included two Socialists, a Radical and a senior member of the trade union federation, the CGT. The Radical Socialist leader, Édouard Herriot, appealed to the Cabinet to rally round the Marshal, 'united in the veneration which his name inspires in all', and to 'take care to avoid disturbing the unity established under his authority'. Still, the dynamic of the national revolution declared at Vichy was to rebuild France in expiation for the sins of the Third Republic. The poet Paul Claudel noted in his diary that 'after sixty years France has been freed from the yoke of the Radical and anti-Catholic party (teachers, lawyers, Jews and Free Masons)'.

The Vichy judicial authorities mounted a case that sought to fix responsibility for France's plight on the politicians of the old Republic, but the long-delayed trial turned into a fiasco when it was held in the town of Riom at the beginning of 1942. Daladier and Blum demonstrated the extent of military spending by their governments, and the Socialists pointed out that cuts in expenditure had been by administrations that contained Pétain and Laval. Gamelin refused to recognise the court and did not utter a word. The Germans eventually ordered the hearings to end, and Blum and Daladier were taken to Buchenwald concentration camp where they were held for the rest of the war.

That the principal political manager of the collaborationist regime should be Pierre Laval, one of the ultimate operators of the 1930s, was ironic, as Weygand noted; but such ironies are not rare in history. However, the swarthy Auvergnat was hardly a typical Third Republic grandee. Son of an innkeeper, he was self-made and had remained independent of the big political groupings. His habitual white tie often decorated with food stains, he stood apart from the Parisian elite. His pacificism went back to before the First World War, and he had become strongly anti-Communist when struggling against the party as mayor of the Paris suburb of Aubervilliers. Alongside his parliamentary career, he did well as a businessman, in particular by buying up provincial newspapers at low prices – one of his presses printed official transit passes.

His aim was to achieve 'state collaboration' between France and Germany to give France a measure of protection and enable it to benefit from a Nazi victory. In pursuit of that, he developed a relationship with Germany's new ambassador in Paris, Otto Abetz, a thickset former drawing teacher with a pudgy face who married the secretary of one of France's more corrupt journalists, Jean Luchaire, and who thought France should be reduced to a satellite through diplomatic and political means rather than by armed force. There was a fatal flaw at the heart of Laval's policy. Hitler was interested only in France's collaboration; he was not going to give the defeated nation anything. Vichy would be left to administer its territory, but only so long as it did what Berlin wanted.

The new regime urged the French to rally in defence of traditional values under the banner of *Travail, Famille, Patrie* (Work, Family, Fatherland). As defined by one of its ideologues, René Gillouin, it aimed to be 'national, authoritarian, hierarchical and social'. The family was its centrepiece. Women were encouraged to concentrate on their role as homemakers. Though some of the most ardent French Fascists left the spa town for occupied Paris in disgust because they thought the Pétain regime was too soft, democratic principles were suspended and a repressive legal framework created. The executive and its provincial prefects ran the regime. Appointed bodies replaced elected legislatures. Professions were controlled. Youth movements were launched to whip up support. Anti-clerical measures were replaced by a close identification with the Catholic Church. Streets called after republican icons such as Jaurès and Zola were renamed. Leading politicians from the Third Republic were arrested, among them Paul Reynaud, who wore a bandage round his head after a serious car accident in which Hélène de Portes had been killed when a suitcase shot forward and broke her neck.

Companies in the unoccupied zone rallied in the expectation that the new government would be business-friendly and undo the remaining legacy of the Popular Front. Industrial production was organised by committees which favoured the big players in what became, in effect, trusts. French firms collaborated with their German counterparts, supplying the Reich war machine. Technocrats and planners hoped to create a new and more efficient economic order, jousting with those who idealised rural France.

The regime soon began to play to the anti-Semitic strand in French life, which had taken centre stage in the Dreyfus affair and flared up in often violent hostility to Blum. Jews were excluded from state employment and jobs in enterprises that received government money. Subsequent legislation barred them from all professions, confiscated their assets – and prohibited them from possessing radios and telephones. Posters advised: 'In 1803, the trade directory contained

3 people called Lévy. In 1940, the telephone book has 496.' The Justice Minister, Raphaël Alibert, who had been behind the short-lived arrest of 'the Jew' Mandel in Bordeaux, played a leading role. A commission began to revoke naturalisations granted to foreigners since 1927, mainly of Jews. A decree authorised prefects to intern Jews while legislation against racism in the media was repealed.

Pétain intervened at one point to tell Alibert to exempt from the effects of the legislation Jewish veterans of the First World War and anybody judged to have rendered exceptional service to the state, together with his own Jewish friends. The Marshal may not have been a committed anti-Semite, but, as a biographer has remarked, he was not anti-anti-Semitic, and was certainly highly hostile to Freemasons linked with Jews in being blamed for contributing to defeat. 'A Jew is never responsible for his origins,' the old man said. 'A Free Mason is always responsible for his choice.' A list of 170,000 suspected Masons was drawn up – although there were in fact only 45,000 members of lodges in France at the outbreak of war. Legislation barred them from public service jobs.

The Marshal was the glue that held the regime together. He was acclaimed wherever he went by crowds chanting '*Maréchal, nous voilà!*' (Marshal, here we are!) as he acknowledged acclaim with a paternal smile and a gentle wave of the hand. Millions of cards bearing his image were printed. Edicts began: 'We, Philippe Pétain, Marshal of France, head of the French state, decree that . . .' In an ode for Christmas 1940, Claudel called on France to 'listen to this old man who bends over you and speaks to you like a father', and whose 'reasonable voice' offered truth that was like gold.

Though the issue of collaboration, whether active or passive, remains a highly emotive matter in France, the fact was that, in the summer of 1940, most people in the unoccupied zone accepted the armistice. Those who had to live under German occupation in the northern half of the country were brought to a more bitter awareness of what defeat meant, though plenty were ready to compromise with the new state of affairs and get on with their lives. For both, the Third Republic had done little in its final years to give it a purchase on their loyalty. No wonder that so many shrugged and looked after their own interests as best they could. The simplistic division of France into clear camps of resisters and collaborators is misleading. Despite some early resisters and some zealots in Vichy and Paris, relatively few people were committed either way. Most of the French belonged to a silent majority. The quest for survival and a quiet life, with a passive acceptance of what had happened and the hope that others would bring liberation, was the leitmotif.

An exchange between an early Resistance leader, Henri Frenay, and his mother, the daughter of a military officer, spoke of the split which, in its way, perpetuated divisions within families seen at the time of the Dreyfus affair. When Frenay said he was going to continue the fight against the Germans, she told her son that he would be harming his country. 'I love you tenderly, you know, because my children are my life,' she went on. 'But the fatherland is greater than maternal love. I will go to the police to denounce you to stop you doing wrong.' Her son responded that, while he respected her conscience, he asked her to respect his. 'If you do what you have said, it will be useless to call me to your deathbed, I won't come,' he added, kissing her and leaving home. They did not meet again till the Liberation in 1944. She had not denounced him.[9]

V
'How solitary I feel'

On Bastille Day, 14 July 1940, de Gaulle issued the proclamation that went down in history alongside his broadcast of 18 June, with which it became amalgamated in the Gaullist mythology.

> To all the French
>
> France has lost a battle, but France has not lost the war. Some authorities gathered by chance, giving way to panic and forgetting honour, may have surrendered, delivering the country into bondage. Yet nothing is lost!
>
> That is why I call upon all Frenchmen, wherever they may be, to join me in action, in sacrifice, in hope.

The General spent the rest of the summer on the twin tasks of establishing and expanding the remit of his movement in Britain and trying to win over territories in France's Empire. He received a material boost when Britain agreed to pay European personnel of the Free French at its own basic military rates, with different arrangements for 'non-European and native troops'. Monthly payments to the movement ran at around £20,000. The General did not take a salary from this, but was paid out of a pool of funds donated by private individuals, which the British estimated to total £150,000.

On 7 August, de Gaulle went to the Prime Minister's country residence at Chequers to sign a formal agreement with the British government on the status of the Free French movement and its forces, negotiated by Cassin with intense attention to detail and nuance. The document was satisfactory as far as it went in recognising the right of the Free French to run their own affairs and in affirming de Gaulle's authority. It guaranteed Treasury funding on a loan basis, making the French borrowers, not suppliants for handouts. The money was repaid in due course.

An exchange of letters with Churchill was less pleasing. Not excluding the possibility that London might reach a compromise peace with Berlin and seize some of France's imperial possessions, de Gaulle asked for a guarantee of the re-establishment of the frontiers of both metropolitan France and its colonies. Churchill replied that his government was determined to 'secure the full restoration of the independence and greatness of France'. But he made no commitment on frontiers, though adding that 'we will do our best'. This was hardly reassuring for the perennially suspicious Frenchman, who wrote that he hoped 'events will one day enable the British government to consider these questions with less reserve'.

There was another source of friction with the British after the Free French created its own intelligence service under a young army captain, André Dewavrin, who took the cover name of Passy, from the Metro station near his Paris home. A cool, precise figure, he got his recruits from amongst French soldiers in camps in Britain and sent the first agents to France during the summer. He fought running battles with other members of the Free French – as de Gaulle told Churchill, the Free French were, by their nature, somewhat difficult people who all too easily rebelled against authority.

Passy's enemies accused him of creating a secret police operation, complete with torture cells where, in his Mayfair headquarters in Duke Street, members of the movement he considered unreliable were interrogated. His principal investigator, Roger Wybot, was said to have had suspects beaten up, deprived of food and made to sit for long periods under bright lights. This would not be the last time that de Gaulle would be accused of harbouring strong-arm supporters, though how much he knew of what they did is unclear. Loyalties were sometimes uncertain among the French, and, like their leader, some of the General's followers were haunted by the fear that the British secret service was trying to infiltrate their movement.

This concern made Passy intent on keeping his outfit separate from Britain's MI6 and Special Operations Executive (SOE), using a different code which could cause delays in processing information from France, sometimes meaning that German ships or trains that were the targets of RAF raids had moved on by the time the news was acted upon. Relations between the British and French intelligence services were often strained, with the British worried about security lapses. When the Socialist politician Jules Moch met de Gaulle after reaching London in 1943 and was told that he would be working for Passy, he asked where this would be. 'Shsh,' the General replied; the location was secret. But when Moch gave a taxi driver the address at 18 Duke Street, he received the response 'Ah, yes, the French secret service.'

Despite such tensions, senior British figures and London society remained friendly. George VI visited the Free French forces. Queen Elizabeth was particularly warm, making a broadcast in French to the women of France. A member of the aristocracy turned one of her houses into a hotel for the Gaullists. The Petit Club Français opened in Saint James's Place. The jazz quintet of the Hot Club de Paris, which had found itself in London in June 1940, stayed to play in Britain, but minus its most talented member, Django Reinhardt, who preferred to return home. *The Times* reported de Gaulle's radio speeches at length. The BBC provided facilities for a regular programme, *Les français parlent aux français,* which became the main means of communicating with France. There was also help for non-Gaullists: Reuters news agency in Fleet Street housed a newspaper called *France*, edited by one of the General's leading critics, the Socialist Charles Gombault.

Churchill nagged government departments to give assistance, and made a lyrical speech in the Commons about the veneration that would be shown in France to the Constable and his companions when the war was won. The military standing of the movement was boosted by the adhesion of General Catroux from Indochina. Some of the British may have envisaged the pipe-smoking commander as an alternative or co-equal to de Gaulle, but Catroux never challenged for the leadership.[10]

After being rebuffed by France's proconsuls in North Africa, de Gaulle looked to West Africa for support, sending Pleven and other emissaries to lobby on the spot. They criss-crossed the colonies in a British seaplane, by canoe and on foot. Edgard de Larminat, an energetic colonel, was named High Commissioner for West Africa, and promoted to the rank of general. On 26 August 1940, the highly regarded black governor of Chad, Félix Éboué, who had developed economic relations with the British in Nigeria, came out for the Free French, an event hailed by de Gaulle as 'capital'. Chad, he declared, had 'shown the path of duty and given the signal for the recovery of the whole of the French Empire'.

A former student of the General's father in Paris, Captain Philippe Leclerc de Hauteclocque (always known as Leclerc), who had arrived in London with head wounds, flew to the Gold Coast with another early recruit to resistance, Hettier de Boislambert. At the head of twenty volunteers, they made their way to Cameroon where Leclerc took charge of the colony. In French Congo, the Vichy governor, described as a comic-opera general, was easily displaced. The territory of Ubangi-Shari (later the Central African Republic) followed in what became known as the 'Three Glorious Days' of 26–28 August. The governor of Gabon announced that he would join the Free French, too, but the local bishop and a naval officer reversed the decision. However, the movement did gain the adhesion of a key figure in north-east Africa – the French administrator of the Suez Canal Company.

The movement now had solid achievements to its name, with four significant African territories behind it, offering a strategic contribution to the Allied cause in the shape of air and land routes to Egypt, Sudan and

Libya, protection for the Belgian Congo, and South Atlantic naval bases. Britain bought coffee, cotton, rubber, palm seeds and oil, wood and sesame seeds at a favourable exchange rate from African colonies that rallied to the cause. Less prosaically, the freebooting, romantic aspect of the missions undertaken by de Larminat, de Boislambert, Leclerc and their colleagues gave off a heady flavour, reminiscent of the élan celebrated by Colonel de Grandmaison in de Gaulle's youth a quarter of a century after it had been extinguished on the Marne.[11]

*

The Free French successes in West Africa whetted the General's taste for a more spectacular operation. His target was the Senegalese capital of Dakar with its key naval base. He told his staff officers that he intended to make the city the capital of the French Empire at war. Capture of the base would offer the British protection for convoys sailing round Africa; equally, if the Germans moved in, the threat from their submarines would increase. A subsidiary advantage was that large stocks of Belgian and Polish state gold, which had been sent to Paris for safe-keeping in 1940, had been transferred to Senegal and could be recovered if the attack succeeded. Such was Dakar's importance that Vichy sent an accomplished soldier, Pierre Boisson, a one-legged Verdun veteran, to defend it.

Churchill was enthusiastic, imagining that the expedition, code-named Operation Menace, would be in the nature of a festival in which the Free French would be welcomed ashore.* He agreed to contribute an eight-thousand-man force and a naval flotilla. At the end of August, de Gaulle took the train to Liverpool with Spears and a former monk, Thierry d'Argenlieu, a naval captain who was to become one of his most faithful followers. His luggage included a mosquito net, a tent and a sun hat. They embarked on a Dutch ship, *Westerland*, which sailed south with the British fleet. The operation was meant to be highly secret; to disguise his absence from London, the General recorded

*Speaking to the Information Minister, Alain Peyrefitte, in 1962, de Gaulle would claim, unconvincingly, that the idea was Churchill's (Peyrefitte, I, p. 146).

several speeches to be broadcast while he was away. However, security was lax as Free French officers gossiped about what was to come, and a crate filled with leaflets to be dropped on Dakar burst open at a London station, showering them over the platform.

At sea, Spears depicted the General as in rare relaxed form, sitting in the mess listening to jokes from his staff. 'I saw de Gaulle laugh as I never did again,' he recalled. The General wore a beret instead of his kepi, in a throwback to the headgear of the unit he had commanded in Trier, and showed off his ability to read backwards. He unveiled to Spears a scheme to land a mass of motorcyclists and armoured cars in northern or western France which would race around the country causing maximum disruption; they might, he added, 'stop long enough in Vichy to capture or hang most of the government'.

His good humour was helped by news that Tahiti and more French possessions in India had come out for the Free French, while New Caledonia was on the verge of doing so. Though he worried about his family, he was confident about the outcome of the Battle of Britain. He and Spears chatted as they sat in wicker armchairs set up for them on the deck. One photograph shows the Englishman in shorts, the General in long trousers, both wearing white solar topees. In one conversation, he said he would withdraw from public life when the war ended. 'No, *mon Général*,' the Englishman replied, 'you have condemned yourself to a life sentence from which there is no reprieve.'

Relaxed the General might be, but he was in for a nasty surprise when news arrived that three French cruisers had sailed out of Toulon and reached Dakar, joining France's most modern warship, *Richelieu*, which had sailed to the base in June from Mers-el-Kébir; though it was still under construction and had been damaged by a British air attack, it could serve as a powerful gun battery. The War Cabinet in London proposed shifting the operation to elsewhere in West Africa 'unless General de Gaulle has any strong objections'. He certainly did. Operation Menace went ahead.

It turned into a disaster. Advance information about local conditions was extremely poor. Fog blanketed the harbour and communication between the ships was weak. Leaflets dropped from the air disintegrated in the humidity. Pro-Vichy officials and officers put up strong resistance; the crews of the ships which had just arrived from North Africa were strongly anti-British after Mers-el-Kébir. The crews of two small Free French planes that landed from *Ark Royal* were detained; one of the fliers had on him a list of sympathisers in the city which was seized by the authorities who arrested the Free French supporters. An unarmed party from *Westerland* led by Thierry d'Argenlieu entered the harbour with a message for Boisson. An order was sent to arrest them, but they returned to their boats and sailed off; as they did so, a junior naval officer opened up with a machine gun, wounding d'Argenlieu. A subsequent landing on a beach outside the main harbour was turned back, with heavy losses.

The defenders shelled the attacking ships from forts along the shoreline while *Richelieu*'s guns stopped the attacking vessels getting within firing range of the main base. Still, the British bombardment killed two thousand people, half of them civilians. Both sides suffered naval losses. Two British battleships and two smaller ships were damaged, as were two Vichy destroyers and two of the defenders' submarines. *Richelieu* was hit by a shell. Recognising failure, on 25 September the British and Free French called off the attack. De Gaulle said it was producing a battle between Frenchmen 'which I do not want' – as though this had not already happened.

Alert to the need for an explanation to the British press, he sent an account of the battle to London which minimised the debacle and blamed the defenders for the French casualties. He told Admiral Muselier that broadcasts from London must refer to the attackers who had died at Dakar as 'martyrs for French independence'. He refused a suggestion of an exchange of a captured Free French soldier for a Vichy trooper taken by the Gaullists, since this would constitute recognition of the right of the Pétainists to arrest his men. Another statement asserted, with no evidence, that the Germans had forced the defenders to fight. France's recovery was a match in several sets, de Gaulle added. 'In rallying twelve million men in the Empire, the Free French won the first. In forcing Vichy to fight at Dakar, the Germans won the second. The game continues. We will see what follows.'

The shock of failure was plain. De Gaulle had handed the Pétain regime a stick with which to beat him as a would-be leader ready to set Frenchmen to fight one another in league with the British who had bombarded his countrymen at Mers-el-Kébir. Weygand castigated him for being naive, getting men killed needlessly and drawing the British into 'a sorry adventure'. British and American newspapers were highly critical. Roosevelt, who had been keen on the expedition when informed of it originally by Churchill, blamed the fiasco squarely on the Free French leader.

'If you only knew how solitary I feel,' de Gaulle told an officer wounded in the battle. In his memoirs, he wrote of the 'cruel' days that followed and likened himself to a man whose house was shaken by an earth tremor that sent tiles crashing down on his head. According to Jean-Raymond Tournoux, the assiduous historian of de Gaulle, the General made a most unusual confession to René Pleven a few days later: 'I thought of, yes I thought of, blowing my brains out.' Pleven issued a denial that de Gaulle had really had any such intention, and said he thought 'he wanted me to feel the horror of the trial he had been through'. Geoffroy de Courcel's wife believed she remembered her husband saying that the Free French leader was 'on the brink of suicide'. Much later, de Gaulle told a government minister, Philippe Dechartre, that the idea of suicide had crossed his mind at the time. 'After Dakar, he was never entirely happy again,' Maurice Schumann felt.

Still, the man who mattered most to de Gaulle expressed no reservations. Churchill told parliament the General's conduct and bearing had increased his confidence in him. De Courcel recalled that de Gaulle soon recovered his zest for action and made plans for further operations. 'My faithful followers remain faithful and I have great hopes for the future,' he wrote to his wife.[12]

Landing in Cameroon, he waded through a crowd gathered at the port of Douala, his first *bain de foule*. When he took a small African child by the hand, its mother embraced him so warmly that she almost knocked off his sun hat. Then he headed for Chad, insisting on travelling in an ancient French plane rather than accepting a British offer of a new aircraft. There were storms, and engine trouble forced the plane to turn back. After another take-off, an engine conked out, obliging the pilot to land in marshes by Lake Chad where the General and his companions spent the night inside the aircraft. In the morning, a rescue party arrived with two small horses. Carried to dry land on the back of a native, de Gaulle mounted one of the animals; his feet touched the ground.

In the Chad capital of N'Djamena, he discussed with Governor Éboué a plan for a Free French military column to march north through the Sahara region of Fezzan and Italian Libya to the Mediterranean. He also met General Catroux, who flew in from London. Though he was de Gaulle's hierarchical successor, the former Governor of Indochina snapped to attention and saluted, calling out: 'At your orders, *mon Général*.' Later, Catroux told Éboué, 'de Gaulle is France and I put myself under his orders because I was at the orders of France'. When the General toasted him at dinner, Catroux raised his glass to 'the Constable of France'.

On 27 October, the last of the Vichy forces in Gabon capitulated to a Free French unit under Leclerc and Pierre-Marie Koenig that had crossed from Cameroon. The Governor committed suicide. This success did not erase Dakar, but, as de Gaulle wrote to his wife, 'No storm lasts indefinitely.' Apart from the military successes, the African tour had shown him the enthusiasm of crowds. For colonial supporters, he wrote, he incarnated their hopes and the destiny of France while, for foreigners, he represented an invincible nation. That, he added, 'imposed on me an attitude that could never change', which guided his conduct but was 'a heavy yoke'. He had, he added, become a 'living legend'.[13]

VI
Rabbit and stoat

While de Gaulle was in Africa, an unexpected visitor from France turned up in London in late October 1940. Louis Rougier was a French-Canadian philosophy professor at Besançon in east France. Through a contact at Vichy, he had had an informal conversation with Pétain during which the Marshal approved of a mission to London, where the professor claimed to know people. He was to offer a middle path between de Gaulle's radical resistance and the state collaboration of Laval, who was not told what was going on.

Reaching London, Rougier met Churchill, who had just warned in a broadcast that Germany and Italy wanted to dismember France and its Empire 'like a fowl: to one a leg, to another a wing'. De Gaulle was not informed of the visit. The professor suggested agreements under which Vichy would undertake not to hand over the fleet or naval bases to the Germans if Britain would relax its naval blockade of France. In the colonies, the status quo would stand. The British would stop being rude about the Marshal. The Prime Minister made no commitment, but was sufficiently intrigued to agree to a second session. However, news then arrived in London that Pétain had met Hitler.

The encounter followed a summons for Laval to see the Führer, who was on his way to meet Franco in an unsuccessful attempt to get Spain to enter the war, at the railway station of Montoire-sur-le-Loir on the demarcation line between the two zones of France. Laval said he hoped with all his heart for the defeat of Britain. Hitler made plain that the treatment France would receive depended on its readiness to join in a common front against Britain. He added that he would like to see the Marshal on his return journey.

German and French flags were flying at the small station when Pétain arrived by road on 24 October. Hitler left his personal train to greet the Marshal with a long handshake, photographed by the Germans. He helped the old soldier to climb the steps into his carriage for two hours of talks during which the Vichy leader said Britain was the prime cause of France's defeat. A statement announced that the two men had agreed on collaboration.

The Germans wired the photograph of the Hitler–Pétain handshake around the world. When shown it, Churchill flew into a rage, and, at his second meeting with Rougier, shouted that the Marshal had signed a peace treaty with the Nazis and that he would send the RAF to bomb Vichy. After the collaborationist administration started to receive disturbing reports of popular concern about the meeting, Pétain attempted damage limitation with a broadcast on 30 October in which he insisted that France remained sovereign and that the policy being followed was his. But he also added, 'in the framework of the active construction of the new European order, I enter today on the path of collaboration'.

The Rougier mission evaporated though the professor claimed on his return to Vichy that an agreement had been reached. This was denied by a British White Paper. Still de Gaulle could not be sure of the constant nature of his ally. Anglo-Vichy contacts were maintained in Madrid and Geneva. George VI sent a message to Pétain saying nothing of substance but keeping a channel open. For the Foreign Office Halifax said it did not matter whether Vichy or the Free French controlled France's colonies so long as they remained 'healthily anti-German and anti-Italian'. Churchill dispatched a letter urging Weygand to raise the flag of revolt, which Weygand predictably declined to do, and sent another to the Marshal at the end of the year. The Third Republic veteran Pierre-Étienne Flandin, who joined the government, said he did so because he thought there was a secret understanding with Britain, which may have reflected the hopes of wishful-thinking moderates at Vichy, though Pierre Dupuy, the Canadian chargé d'affaires, reported that, in a conversation, the Marshal said a British victory was 'much to be desired'.

At the end of the year, Berlin showed the limits of the handshake at Montoire by refusing to free French prisoners of war or to ease passage across the demarcation line. A meeting between Laval and Hermann Goering did not improve matters. Given the Marshal's fumbling incompetence as his periods of lucidity diminished, the attempts to find a space between Germany and Britain were bound to prove fruitless, particularly when Vichy was faced with two such determined players as Hitler and Churchill, with de Gaulle hovering behind the Prime Minister. As Spears put it, the collaborationist regime conjured up the image of 'a rabbit while it is being chased round its cage by a stoat' – or two.

From Africa, where he had an official residence known popularly as 'de Gaulle's cabin' and the use of the powerful radio transmitter at Brazzaville, the General condemned Montoire as 'one more step on the path of treason'. When Churchill eventually told him about the Rougier visit, he replied with slightly condescending reasonableness that he understood London's desire to handle Vichy tactfully, so long as it did not make further concessions to Germany. The key element was that he could still count on the Prime Minister, who responded to a suggestion that the General should be reined in by saying that he was 'not going to "card" his friends'.

From Brazzaville, the General declared that, since the Vichy regime was unconstitutional, a 'new power has to assume the responsibility to direct the French war effort. Events impose that sacred duty on me; I will not fail.' Éboué was appointed Governor-General of French Equatorial Africa, and de Gaulle announced the establishment of a Council for the Defence of the Empire, with Catroux, Cassin and Muselier among the members. He did not inform the British of this in advance, which irritated Churchill. Britain did not recognise the council until the end of the year, and then mainly in military terms.

For Armistice Day 1940 de Gaulle adopted Foch's motto 'One is only beaten when one admits defeat.' Several thousand people marched to the Tomb of the Unknown Soldier at the Place de l'Étoile in Paris in the first popular demonstration in occupied France since the defeat. Wreaths were laid at the statue of Joan of Arc on the rue de Rivoli, beneath a plaque to British dead of the First World War, and under the statue of Clemenceau at the foot of the Champs-Élysées. Though the marchers were not, for the most part, Gaullists, a wreath placed by a Free French emissary from London under the effigy of 'the Tiger' had a large visiting card in the General's name; police quickly removed it. Students paraded carrying two fishing rods each – the combination of the number *deux* and a word for rods, *gaules*, speaking for itself. The demonstrations were broken up after clashing with Fascist groups. Hundreds were arrested. During that night's performance of Corneille's classic play *Le Cid*, at the Comédie-Française, with Jean-Louis Barrault in the title role, patriotic passages were loudly applauded.

Despite Dakar, de Gaulle was increasingly confident. He estimated that his movement had 20,000 men in the colonies, and intended to consolidate its position with attacks on the Italians to the north. He told Churchill it was 'a territorial military, economic and moral entity whose leadership . . . has duties and, as a result, national and international rights'. Seeking better relations with the US, he offered Washington the use of air and naval bases on French territory in Central America, the Caribbean and West Africa, but Washington did not reply.

In similar wording to that proclaimed for Pétain at Vichy, decrees now began 'In the name of the French Empire, we, General de Gaulle, chief of the Free France'. The Free French declared all laws passed in the homeland since the armistice null and void. An Order of the Liberation was created. In his memoirs, de Gaulle noted the 'heart-lifting' nature of what had been achieved, and quoted Chateaubriand about the way in which he might be able to 'lead the French on by way of dreams'.[14]

9

FAMILY TIME

While de Gaulle had been moving on to the stage of history, he had more personal concerns. He had no idea of the fate of his wife and children. Spears thought the General was tortured by the uncertainty, and wondered to Churchill whether the Germans might use them as hostages if they were captured. The Prime Minister authorised a seaplane to go to search for Yvonne, Philippe, Élisabeth and Anne; it crashed in fog with the loss of all its crew.[1]

On 17 June 1940, Yvonne's sister, Suzanne, had driven her and Philippe from their temporary home in Brittany to Brest to see if they could get a boat to take them all to a safer haven. Suzanne was a novice driver and the car broke down on the way. Eventually, they arrived in the port city where they borrowed money from an aunt to buy them passages on a ship. But, not knowing where Charles was, where should they head? Bordeaux? Marseille? North Africa?*

Yvonne was in a terrible predicament. Philippe recalled her asking, 'Where can we go? How can we cope with a handicapped child who cannot walk for a hundred metres, who is unbearable in a vehicle or a train and who bothers everybody?' Then she decided to head for Britain and see what came next. Her husband had been to London several times, she knew, so he might be there. At the docks she was told about a Polish ship they might be able to board. They drove back to the seaside village of Carantec where they had been staying to pick up the rest

*The personal details in the following account are drawn from Philippe de Gaulle's recollections in *De Gaulle, Mon Père*, Chapter 11.

of the family, and, the following day, set off for Brest again after lunch. The crush on the road was such that it took four hours to cover the seventy kilometres, smoke rising from the radiator, the suspension threatening to give way.

When they reached the harbour, the Polish vessel was pulling out, fortuitously for them since it was subsequently torpedoed by a German submarine and most of those on board were lost. British troops were boarding another ship moored at the dock, manned by Flemish-speaking sailors, bound for Falmouth. Though her sister tried to dissuade her from making such a risky journey, Yvonne insisted. According to her son, she said: 'We're in God's hands. We're going!' The de Gaulles and Anne's carer, Marguerite Potel, climbed the gangplank, their only possessions a few jewels which Yvonne carried in her handbag, Philippe's academic diplomas and Anne's medicine. They slept head to toe in a single cabin. Yvonne told the children to say their prayers.

Their boat crossed the Channel as de Gaulle was making his 18 June broadcast. After landing in Cornwall, they booked in to a bed-and-breakfast whose owner said they could stay for only forty-eight hours, payable in advance. Going for a walk, Philippe bought a copy of the *Daily Mirror*. On an inside page he saw a small news item reporting his father's speech. Hurrying to the nearest police station, he identified himself in his rudimentary English. After initial incomprehension and disbelief, the police agreed to follow up his inquiries.

Just before dinner that evening, a constable arrived at the B&B to say that they should travel to London in the morning. According to a biography of Madame de Gaulle, she spoke to her husband by telephone that evening. 'Ah! You're here! Good!' he said. 'My dear, take the first train to London. I'll be waiting for you.' Instead, they were met at the London station by a bowler-hatted Foreign Office functionary wearing a white gardenia in his buttonhole for purposes of recognition.[2]

They were taken to the Rubens Hotel, a conventional middle-class establishment situated between Buckingham Palace and Victoria Station. Because of Anne's condition, they were moved quickly from reception to a first-floor suite. De Gaulle soon arrived, embracing them – it was one of the rare occasions on which Philippe saw his father kiss his mother.

The General, who entrusted the handwritten original of his 18 June speech to his wife for safe-keeping, moved into the hotel. He walked to and from his office in uniform with highly polished brown boots, white gloves in his left hand, smoking as he went. When he did not have an engagement, he dined in the evening with his eighteen-year-old son in the ground-floor dining room. Yvonne and her daughters ate in their room. Though their English was poor, father and son listened with the other guests to the news on the wireless, rising to their feet when the national anthem was played.

Philippe recalled that his father sometimes fell into prolonged silences, and that his mood changed with the days. To begin with, he was morose and hardly spoke, lighting a cigarette as soon as he had finished the last mouthful of food. But, a few days later, he began to strike a more hopeful note. 'Don't worry, old boy,' he said on his return from broadcasting at the BBC on 22 June, 'we're going to come out of this.' On other occasions, he predicted that the war would last for several years, and that, if the Germans crossed the Channel, they would be defeated because they could not bring sufficient equipment with them. 'We will win,' he added. 'Perhaps not straight away, but we will win . . . We will have done what we could. Nobody can reproach us.'

Finding the Rubens Hotel too expensive for the six of them, the de Gaulles moved to a five-room brick and half-timbered house at Petts Wood in Kent. It was furnished, with a small garden; according to Philippe, the rent was £70 a month. As well as Marguerite Potel, they had the services of a cook from southern France. In London, the manager of Cartier, the renowned French jeweller, put his Bentley at the General's disposal.

The house, it turned out, was badly located, being close to the main theatre of the Battle of Britain in the skies above Kent. A building at the end of the road was hit by a bomb, and the de Gaulles sheltered under the stairs during air raids since there was no cellar. Yvonne told the owner they would have to move because of this – 'my little Anne is terrified,' she added. A neighbour was a journalist for the *Daily Herald* who noted the General's comings and goings until he discovered her profession and took evasive action to avoid being seen.

In July, de Gaulle moved his office to number 4, Carlton Gardens, a seven-year-old block between Pall Mall and St James's Park. Ironically, it stood on the site of the home of the Francophobe nineteenth-century Prime Minister Lord Palmerston, in a cul-de-sac to which access was by Waterloo Place. The building was unremarkable though surrounded by elegant classical mansions looking out over the park. Financial circumstances were eased when the British secret service absconded with francs to the value of £13 million from a bank in France and brought them to London for the Free French.

In his new accommodation, de Gaulle had a spacious room with a heavy wooden door and a chandelier. Four armchairs were ranged around his wooden desk in front of a classical fireplace. Maps hung on the walls. The royal photographer, Cecil Beaton, was called to take a dramatic image of the Free French leader standing behind his desk, half in the shade as sunlight fell behind him, every inch the man of destiny. In 1993, Queen Elizabeth II would unveil a statue of the uniformed General opposite the building, his right hand outstretched in appeal.[3]

That autumn, de Gaulle learned of the death of his mother; she had passed away three months earlier in Brittany. The German censor had changed the name in the death notice in the local newspaper to her maiden name and her grave bore only a number. But local people knew who she was, and a crowd turned out for the funeral. A unit from the *gendarmerie*, which came under military jurisdiction, presented arms at the graveside. When a relation thanked the commander, he replied: 'We rendered the honours to the mother of General de Gaulle because we are part of the French army.' A great-niece put small stones on the grave; returning a few days later, she found they had been removed as souvenirs by people making pilgrimages to the site. A young man took a photograph of the tomb and carried it with him to London; in this manner the General learned of Jeanne's death.[4]

In November 1940, Yvonne, the children, the carer and the cook moved far out of range of the Luftwaffe, to Ellsmere on the Welsh border. Their new home was a complex of three brick bungalows standing in front of a pond. Lighting was provided by oil lamps, heating by wood fires, but the countryside offered perfect peace, with the nearest neighbour 500 metres away. Charles made the eight-hour train journey there once a month. His first visit was to celebrate his fiftieth birthday in

November, for which the cook and Yvonne found extra provisions. Philippe gave Yvonne a little Kodak camera to take pictures of himself and his father.

In London, the General moved between various hotels, settling finally on the Connaught in Mayfair where he took rooms on the top floor, which were paid for weekly, and where a Frenchman called to give him English lessons. His linguistic progress was limited and, though he liked to be able to start a conversation with the British with a few phrases in English, he was happier to revert to French. He left the hotel at 9 a.m. for Carlton Gardens, sometimes returning at 1 p.m. for lunch and enjoying what he termed its 'island specialities', such as roast beef and Yorkshire pudding, and barley broth and smoked salmon. Alternatively, he patronised the Savoy, the Ritz, the Cavalry Club and the Royal Automobile Club, where Spears had taken him on his first day in London after leaving Bordeaux. Sometimes, he ate at the smart Écu de France restaurant, though he told his wife off after she had procured two ducks for a dinner from the owners, regarding such a breach of rationing regulations as unacceptable. He drank red Burgundy and finished his lunches with cognac and a cigar. He opened an account at the venerable wine merchants Berry Bros & Rudd, in St James's, and continued to smoke heavily, Players and then Craven A filter tips because he disliked getting tobacco on his lips. When his wife tried to get him to stop, he told her, 'Yes, yes, understood, Yvonne, we'll see.'

Transport difficulties meant that the General was unable to spend Christmas 1940 with his family, so Spears and his wife invited him to celebrate it with them at their home nearer to London. After dinner, he spoke at length with their son, Michael, an Oxford undergraduate. Lady Spears recalled that 'he relaxed and grew gentler as he talked about my son's studies and about the young people of England. And when he left for London, Michael . . . said to me "I should like to serve under General de Gaulle's orders."'

When the Blitz ceased the following year, the de Gaulle family moved back south to a three-storey Tudor-style manor outside Berkhamsted in Hertfordshire, where de Gaulle visited them when he could, going for walks in nearby woods and across the heather-covered slopes of the surrounding park. He gave way to British pressure to pose for a set of publicity photographs of him and his wife sitting by a goldfish pond, walking down steps outside the house or talking beside two ornamental stone elephants in the garden. In his plain uniform, the General towers over Yvonne, who wears a polka-dot dress and sensible flat shoes and at one point reaches out to straighten the Cross of Lorraine pin on her husband's tunic. Other photographs showed her at the kitchen stove and making jam.

Finally, in September 1942, a more convenient location was found in north London, in Frognal, Hampstead, where the de Gaulles rented a red-brick house with a dozen rooms on three floors. It came with a Scottish cook who recalled how patient the General was with Anne, trying to spend an hour a day with 'our very little one'. The cook told nuns who subsequently occupied the building that Yvonne wore black dresses in mourning for France, and laid a black tablecloth for the same reason.

The General had a small, wood-panelled study next to the large drawing room looking out on to a sizeable garden. He walked each morning to mass at a nearby Catholic church established by Royalists fleeing the French Revolution at the end of the eighteenth century. The house in Colombey, meanwhile, had been taken over by the Germans, but the furniture was moved out before they arrived and was kept under a false name by a local storage firm.[5]

In London, Élisabeth boarded at a Catholic school and then went to Oxford. Philippe joined the Free French naval school at Portsmouth. His father followed his progress closely and took great pride in his appearance in a photograph of the naval college's march past on Joan of Arc Day in July 1941, 'superb in the front rank'. In 1942, Philippe was put in command of a small Free French naval craft. 'However small it may be, it is important and a piece of French territory,' the General wrote to him. 'I am sure you will command it as you should, that is to say with decisiveness, courage and care.' In early 1943, after his son had seen action at sea, de Gaulle wrote to express his 'admiration and also satisfaction', signing himself 'Your very affectionate papa'.

Madame de Gaulle followed the progress of the war through the BBC and newspapers. For much of the time she was on her own, and Free French staff were ordered not to offer her any assistance. Always a keen knitter, she learned to use a sewing machine. She kept chickens to ensure that Anne had fresh eggs, and served up rabbit, which the British rejected, fearing that they were actually eating cat. Though she could show irritation when the house was not in perfect order or when an unexpected visitor called, she retained her habitual calm. Philippe recalled that she acted as though what had happened to them was normal, a destiny to be accepted without question or complaint.

In his letters, Charles acknowledged his failure to write to her often enough, but also bemoaned the shortage of correspondence from her. 'I want to know everything about you and *les Babies*!' he told her from Africa in the autumn of 1940. Expressions of affection were always evident, along with the recognition of how important her companionship was to him, and how inseparable she was from his role in life. 'I send you all my deepest tenderness,' he wrote before departing on another trip in March 1941. 'I embrace you with all my heart . . . my dear little beloved wife, and also my friend, my companion so courageous and good, through a tumultuous life.' Two months later, he began a letter written on her birthday with 'I love you and, in the hard mission I have given myself, I think very, very, very often of you.'[6]

10

ALLIES AT ODDS

I
The admiral is arrested

On his return to London from Africa at the end of 1940, de Gaulle found the British 'tense and melancholic', proud of the victory in the Battle of Britain but concerned about the continuing German aerial blitz on major cities, the impact of submarine warfare on shipping, rationing and shortages, America's absence from the war and the Soviet–German alliance. They were, he recalled in his memoirs, 'at the blackest part of the tunnel', and had more pressing priorities than helping the Free French. As for himself, his return to Carlton Gardens meant plunging into the minutiae of administration, surrounded by petty staff rivalries. His mood soon soured. He shouted at some of his staff and treated others with scorn. 'It was a very painful period for the General's collaborators, a particularly disagreeable period of gestation,' Passy wrote.

While in Africa, he had found it necessary to send Admiral Muselier, his number two, a curt message taking him to task for causing disarray among the Free French staff by his 'uncontrolled criticism' and lack of self-control and discipline. Passy recalled the 'turbulence and absurd personal quarrels' at Carlton Gardens. The disarray and disorder shocked Reynaud's former aide, Gaston Palewski, who had become director of political affairs, making the most of his excellent English perfected during his studies at Oxford; his skill as a mimic, particularly of Laval, was used to mock Vichy politicians on the Free French broadcasts on the BBC.

Rising above everyday concerns, de Gaulle lunched with Churchill on 13 December, giving his view that the war was the result of perennial German militarism and the nature of the German people, rather than Nazi ideology. 'We fought the last war against the Hohenzollerns and German militarism; we crushed them both; and then came Hitler – *et toujours le militarisme allemand*,' he observed. 'So there is something to be said for those who blame the Germans as a whole.' It was an analysis he would express again in a speech at the Oxford Union the following year in which he refused to draw a distinction between the Germans and Hitler's regime.

As the General and the Prime Minister lunched, there was a sudden power shift at Vichy where conditions had deteriorated after a poor harvest, aggravated by the absence of farm workers in German prisoner-of-war camps. On 13 December, Laval's enemies got Pétain to sack him and have him arrested. His protector, the German ambassador in Paris, Otto Abetz, hurried down to the Auvergne with an SS guard but was unable to get the Marshal to change his mind about dropping the Auvergnat. Darlan became the old man's chief lieutenant and travelled to Germany to assure Hitler that Vichy wanted to pursue cooperation. At the lunch with Churchill, de Gaulle said that, while most people in unoccupied France did not want war with Britain, Darlan and the fleet might seek revenge for Mers-el-Kébir. A note from Churchill in February 1941 described the admiral as 'dangerous, bitter . . . an ambitious crook', who was all the more of a threat because he did not attract the 'odium which attaches to Laval'. The Prime Minister added that Darlan's rise meant 'an end should be put to cold-shouldering of General de Gaulle and the Free French movement, who are the only people who have done anything for us and to whom we have made very solemn engagements'.[1]

At the end of the month, de Gaulle took the long train journey to Shropshire to welcome in the New Year with his family. Before leaving London, he recorded a broadcast to France calling on people to stay at home on 1 January as a mark of protest; this was widely followed. As the de Gaulles celebrated the advent of 1941, a drama erupted in London when Muselier was arrested on 1 January outside his flat by a British naval officer and two detectives. He was taken to Scotland Yard and then on to an unheated cell at Pentonville. On the basis of letters which had come into British hands, he was accused of having passed plans for the Dakar operation to Vichy through the Brazilian embassy in London. He was also alleged to be plotting to hand a big French submarine to the Pétain regime, and to have received £2,000 for sabotaging the recruitment of sailors to the Free French. Shown the documents, Churchill exploded, and ordered Muselier's arrest.

On 2 January, Eden telephoned the General to ask him to return to London, but without saying why. When de Gaulle arrived, the Foreign Secretary showed him the letters implicating Muselier. The Free French leader was shocked by the allegations and by the British action in arresting his military number two and locking him up without making further investigations.

Muselier and de Gaulle were the antithesis of one another. Eight years older than his superior, the fifty-eight-year-old Muselier was a voluble, headstrong Mediterranean character. Of average height and with a full black moustache, he belonged to the Radical Socialist milieu of the Third Republic (his leftist connections led to him being dubbed the 'Red Admiral') from which de Gaulle stood aloof. The Free French leader would allege later that he took drugs; John Colville referred to him as 'very loose-living'. Some of the General's strongest supporters could not stand him; Cassin recalled that, at their first meeting, Muselier said his navy did not want the jurist to take on ministerial responsibilities because he was Jewish and 'the fleet is made up of Bretons'. Passy remembered the General describing Muselier as 'an unbearable busybody who always involves himself in things that have nothing to do with him'. But nobody could imagine him as a traitor.

Concluding that the letters were forgeries, de Gaulle delivered an impassioned defence of Muselier to Eden and Cadogan. The British agreed that it was a frame-up, but it took four days before Muselier was shown the documents and released. Two Englishmen who worked with the Free French and had a grudge against the admiral were found to be responsible; de Gaulle believed, wrongly, that the letters had been planted by the intelligence service. Churchill apologised, and the British fell over themselves to try to placate Muselier's feelings, the Prime Minister inviting him to lunch and the King granting him an audience.

The episode caused a deterioration in relations between de Gaulle and Muselier since the admiral did not think his chief had acted fast enough to clear his name. The *affaire Muselier* did nothing for de Gaulle's temper either. He ordered that all British women working for the Free French should be banished in case they were secret agents. When his staff pointed out that this would bring work to a halt, he calmed down, but nonetheless replaced them, bit by bit, with French recruits. He exploded regularly to Passy about British intelligence, and accused his subordinate of not being up to the job. He told his press chief to issue a statement making clear that he took responsibility only for BBC broadcasts by his spokesman, Schumann, thereby disowning other Free French programmes. The press chief said he would follow the order, but then resign. De Gaulle withdrew it.

At the time, he was too good a tactician not to exploit the embarrassment the British felt about their mistake over Muselier, which made them more pliable. They were, he wrote to his wife, 'valiant and solid allies, but very tiring'. It was a verdict many of his allies would have applied to him that summer as the first major crisis of the Anglo-Free French erupted.[2]

II

Back to the Levant

The cause of the dispute was the region to which de Gaulle had been posted early in his career. The General had hoped that the Vichy authorities in the French mandates in Lebanon and Syria would rally to him. On the spot, Catroux tried to muster backing. But Vichy sent out a tough soldier, General Dentz, as High Commissioner for the Levant, and he instituted a crackdown on Free French supporters. To make matters worse, the British commander in the theatre, Archibald Wavell, preferred to leave Syria and Lebanon alone and cooperate with the Vichy regime there while he got on with the war against the Italians and Germans in North Africa.

De Gaulle set out for the Middle East in mid-March 1941. Before leaving Britain, he spent the weekend with Churchill at Chequers, where he remarked over dinner that the Germans were inferior beings and that the idea of a world war gave them vertigo. At dawn on the Sunday, the Prime Minister woke him to tell him that the US Congress had passed the Lend-Lease Bill to send supplies to Britain without requiring payment. Churchill was, de Gaulle recalled, 'literally dancing with joy'.

Arriving in Egypt on 1 April 1941, the General spoke of capturing Damascus and Beirut with Free French forces, which included his future Defence Minister, Pierre Messmer – Messmer recalled him spotting a woman with a sword and remarking, 'Women are put on earth to give life, not death.' He clashed with the British over a testy dinner in Jerusalem, sweeping out and going to his hotel room where he delivered an hour-long monologue on the importance of not accepting defeat to a young lieutenant on Catroux's staff. He subsequently engaged the young man, François Coulet, as his aide-de-camp when de Courcel left for the battlefront.

De Gaulle's plan of conquest required transport assistance and tank backup from his ally, but Wavell had no vehicles to spare. It was a trying time for the British. On 6 April, Germany invaded Yugoslavia and Greece. Forces under Rommel, which had been sent to bail out the Italians in North Africa, scored spectacular successes against the British in Libya. Meanwhile, King Farouk of Egypt appealed to Germany to 'lift the British yoke', raising a potential threat to the vital Suez Canal link. Though Churchill remained supportive, de Gaulle's continual pushing of his own agenda in Lebanon and Syria was an irritant Wavell did not need. The strain on the taciturn British commander grew when a nationalist revolt broke out in Iraq, the rebels assuming power in Baghdad and, like Farouk, appealing to Germany for help. The rising was put down, but Darlan complicated the regional situation by offering Hitler the use of French airfields in Syria as a sign of his collaborationist faith. The Luftwaffe sent in a small unit.

At Churchill's instigation, Wavell was ordered to lend all possible assistance to a Free French invasion of Syria. The British commander remained far from enthusiastic and dragged his feet – from 20 May, he had to deal with the German attack on Crete as well as preparing a counter-attack to bar Rommel's advance. But, given the Prime Minister's determination, he had to comply. Churchill warned him that, if he did not go along, 'arrangements will be made to meet any wish you may express to be relieved of your command'. De Gaulle responded with a note in English to the Prime Minister starting 'Thank you' and ending 'You will win the war.'

Edward Spears, who had been posted to the Middle East, found himself playing a liaison role with de Gaulle once again, but he now rebelled against the demands of the man he had accompanied out of France a year earlier. He took exception to de Gaulle's insistence that France alone would determine Syria's political future, and to his refusal to make commitments on granting self-determination. In a letter to Churchill complaining that the Free French had become a heavy handicap, Spears coined a phrase, often attributed to the Prime Minister, that the cross to be borne was the Cross of Lorraine.[3]

On 8 June, the Syrian campaign began. The battle with the Germans did not materialise since Berlin had already withdrawn its air force unit – Hitler did not think Syria could be held and wanted as few distractions as possible from the German invasion of the Soviet Union two weeks later. So the conflict pitted the Vichy forces against the combined British–Free French. If one of his officers did not want to lead his troops against fellow countrymen, de Gaulle allowed him to pass his responsibilities to somebody who did not have the same reservations – but subsequently disbarred him from battle command. Pétain sent the defenders a message denouncing de Gaulle's forces for serving under a dissident flag and not hesitating to shed the blood of their brothers defending the nation's sovereignty. As at Dakar, Vichy troops had no hesitation in firing at Free French units which advanced with white flags seeking peaceful agreements.

The defenders did well to begin with, but then suffered reverses as British reinforcements arrived. Damascus fell without a struggle on 21 June, de Gaulle arriving in the city two days later. By the beginning of July, Vichy forces faced complete defeat. Dentz sued for a ceasefire.

Victory, however, did nothing to improve relations between de Gaulle and the British. The General had a low opinion of his allies and an even lower view of their commander, Maitland 'Jumbo' Wilson. Matters grew far worse when the British opened negotiations with Dentz without involving the Free French, while de Gaulle made a unilateral announcement on the political future of Syria and Lebanon, foreseeing independence only if they undertook to ally with France. On 14 July 1941, Bastille Day, he heard 'with astonishment' the terms of an armistice concluded by the British and Dentz. It did not mention the Free French; nor were they invited to sign. He exploded to Spears about a British plot to establish leadership in the region, supported by a 'Prime Minister whose ambiguous promises and calculated emotions disguised his intentions'. Vichy soldiers in Syria were allowed to return to France without being approached by the Free French, dashing de Gaulle's hopes of recruiting them to bolster his movement in the Levant. For him, British conduct was even worse than he had feared.

The General went to Cairo on 21 July to meet the British Secretary of State for the Middle East, Oliver Lyttelton, who described him as like a man who had not slept and would not listen to any arguments. The climate was further worsened when the Free French found the British flag flying over positions they expected to occupy in Syria; in the case of one fortress, de Gaulle warned that, if the British did not leave, his forces would open fire – it was duly evacuated. He read Lyttelton a declaration saying that, from 24 July, French forces in the region would no longer come under British command and would answer only to the French Imperial Council. The British minister replied that this amounted to an ultimatum which would break the Anglo-Free French alliance. If the British wished to regard it as an ultimatum, they were free to do so, the Frenchman replied.

Having thumped the table, de Gaulle fell back on a more reasoned approach when the two men met again that evening. This led to an agreement which formally recognised France's historic rights in the Levant and provided for non-interference by Britain. The Free French would get Vichy military equipment and be able to enlist its soldiers – though Dentz kept his army out of the way of the Free French, who were able to recruit only six thousand of his men. Despite the agreement, which gave him most of what he wanted, the General continued to complain about the 'usurpation of French rights by the British'.[4]

At the end of July, he set off for a month-long tour of Beirut and Damascus to establish local governments. The outcome was patchy, and left Arab nationalists discontented. A Francophile appointed to head the administration in Syria enjoyed only moderate popular backing. In Lebanon, Dentz's appointee stayed in office. Free French–British relations deteriorated even more sharply after that. Claude Auchinleck, Britain's new commander-in-chief in the Middle East, told John Colville that he thought the General was 'mad and consumed by personal ambition'. Britain's mission in Brazzaville sent London a list of hostile statements by de Gaulle. The man who mattered most, Churchill, was changing his mind, alienated by the way in which de Gaulle cast aspersions on British forces in the Middle East.

The General aggravated the situation by an interview with the correspondent of the *Chicago Daily News* that spoke of an implicit arrangement between Berlin and London in which each made use of Vichy. Britain, he charged, feared the French fleet. He added salt to the wound by referring to his offer of naval bases to the US, and saying that, unlike London in its first aid agreement with Washington, 'I have not asked for any destroyers in return.'

Even de Gaulle realised that he had gone too far. Instructions were sent to Pleven, who was in Washington, to prevent publication of the interview. When that failed, a statement was issued denying that de Gaulle had spoken of offering America bases or had said Britain feared the French fleet. He told Pleven all he had said was that Vichy did not represent the real France and that his movement had an important strategic position in West Africa. He ordered the journalist to be expelled from Free French territory – and then cancelled this instruction.

Churchill told Lyttelton that the General had gone off his head and would be discarded. Colville recorded the Prime Minister accusing him of caring little for Britain's fortunes in the war. A month later Lyttelton noted, 'the P.M. is sick to death of him'. Eden, one of the strongest supporters of the Free French, wrote that 'it may well be we shall find that de Gaulle is crazy'. Shown a cable from him, the Foreign Secretary responded: 'I hate *all* Frenchmen.'

Churchill's close aide, Desmond Morton, told him that Free French headquarters were 'getting nearly as tired as we are of their chief's ungovernable temper and lack of balanced judgement', adding that Muselier enjoyed some backing among the Free French as an alternative.

Knowing nothing of this, as he flew back to London at the end of August, de Gaulle regaled a travelling companion with criticisms of the British and said he intended to 'put his foot in it' when he arrived.

Churchill issued draconian instructions – 'No one is to see General de Gaulle. No English authority is to have any contact with him when he arrives . . . If the occasion demands, it may be conveyed to him that a most serious situation has arisen with which the Prime Minister is dealing in person.' A request by the Free French leader to broadcast on the BBC was refused. The press was told not to report his return. When de Gaulle sought a meeting, Churchill said he did not think this would serve any useful purpose until he received an explanation of the *Chicago Daily News* report.

De Gaulle's tactic was to blame the messenger. He wrote to Downing Street that the journalist had invented most of the interview and added that he had a very good impression of his personal relations with Lyttelton, a statement which might have taken the minister aback. Churchill agreed to see him on 12 September, but instructed the Foreign Office to draw up a list of complaints against the Free French – it was lengthy. He also carefully choreographed the meeting at Downing Street, telling Colville that he would rise and bow slightly but not shake hands, while indicating to the General the chair in which he should sit on the other side of the big table in the Cabinet Room. He would not speak in French but would converse through Colville as interpreter.

Churchill went through this rigmarole when de Gaulle came into the room. 'General de Gaulle, I have asked you to come here this afternoon,' he began. Colville translated, '*Mon Général, je vous ai invité à venir cet après-midi.*' Churchill broke in to say: 'I didn't say *Mon Général,* and I did not say I had invited him.'

After a little more from Churchill, de Gaulle began to speak, also correcting the translation. So the secretary left the room and called in a linguist from the Foreign Office. When he arrived, the two leaders had been sitting looking at one another silently for several minutes. After a short time, the interpreter emerged red in the face, protesting that they must be mad: both had told him he could not speak French properly so they would have to manage without him.

The official British record of the conversation, presumably dictated by the Prime Minister, has Churchill complaining that he felt he was no longer dealing with a friend, and invoking the 'accumulation' of hostile statements by the General. De Gaulle's account says his host began by accusing him of Anglophobia. To this, he replied that it could not be seriously maintained that he was an enemy of Great Britain.

They then skirmished over Syria, and Churchill pressed for new men to join the Free French Council. The British version says the General gave broad agreement to this, though pointing to the danger of bringing 'political factors into play'. The Prime Minister warned that some British figures suspected that his visitor had 'become hostile and had moved towards certain fascist views which would not be helpful to collaboration in the common cause'. Rejecting the charge of authoritarianism, de Gaulle said he 'begged the Prime Minister to understand that the Free French were necessarily somewhat difficult people: else they would not be where they were. If this difficult character sometimes coloured their attitude towards their great ally . . . [Churchill] could rest assured that their entire loyalty to Great Britain remained unimpaired.' It was just the kind of statement designed to melt his host's anger.

Outside, Colville tried to eavesdrop, but the double doors defeated him. He decided it was his duty to burst in – 'perhaps they had strangled each other'. Just then, Churchill rang the bell for him. Entering, Colville found the two men sitting side by side, 'with an amiable expression on their faces', smoking cigars and speaking in French.[5]

III
Revolt

On the face of it, de Gaulle had emerged well enough from the first major confrontation with his ally. But he faced a crisis within the Free French as plotters met secretly at the Savoy Hotel. They included Muselier, who had a stormy meeting with the General on his return to London. As well as their consciousness of growing personal rivalry, the admiral's supporters felt de Gaulle was becoming too autocratic and developing Fascist tendencies.

This raised a question that would hover over the General to the end of his life, with many on the Left retaining the distrust of a military leader and seeing him as a soldier-dictator. In fact, de Gaulle showed himself a democrat, albeit preferring referendums to parliamentary elections, and held the realistic view that dictators always ended up badly. But his manner was that of an autocrat who brooked no opposition. His stress on nationalism, authoritarian leadership and a taste for action appeared to put him in the same category as Bonaparte, Boulanger and Europe's Fascist leaders. His insistence that the Third Republic and its legislature had 'abdicated' in 1940 and should be replaced by a 'new France' could all too easily be seen during the war as an excuse for a future dictatorship. As always, he was a complex study. Was he a democrat, the Resistance leader Jean Moulin would ask himself? 'I do not know.'

The Muselier camp had plenty of pointers to invoke. De Gaulle had dropped the republican motto of *Liberté, égalité, fraternité* – as the Vichy regime did – as too politically charged, replacing it with *Honneur et Patrie* (Honour and Fatherland). Many of those who rallied to his cause in the early years came from the Right, often from the extreme groups such as *Action française.* While de Gaulle rejected anti-Semitism and judged people on their abilities, some of those around him brought with them hostility to Jews. An early Free French publication blamed the defeat of 1940 on the perverse sentiments of recently nationalised citizens 'with a dubious past'. The General's chief of staff in 1940 refused to allow Georges Boris, a former close aide to Léon Blum, to see de Gaulle on the grounds that the Free French did not need Jews or Socialists; but when the Free French leader heard of this, he banged the table and shouted 'we will never be too many' and went on to give Boris a series of jobs.

After their Downing Street meeting, Churchill decided de Gaulle should be put 'in commission', by which he meant surrounding him with a group of others who would control him. The Admiralty backed Muselier. The conspirators got a sympathetic hearing from Lord Bessborough, a former Governor General of Canada who headed the Foreign Office department looking after French refugees. Desmond Morton from Downing Street kept in touch with them as they evolved their plan to reduce the General to the status of a figurehead, while Muselier became the effective boss. In two letters to de Gaulle, the sailor demanded to be appointed President or Vice-President of the movement, with close collaborators in senior positions.

De Gaulle pre-empted the attack by drawing up plans for a committee, from which Muselier and his co-conspirators would be excluded. The admiral denounced this as 'a comedy' and said he would run the fleet independently. De Gaulle met Churchill to tell him of his plans, and sent Muselier a strongly worded ultimatum on 23 September giving him a day to get back into line. Failing that, he warned, 'I will take all the necessary measures to ensure that you will be rendered harmless and that your conduct will be publicly known, that is to say stigmatised.' Muselier put himself under the protection of the Admiralty.

By now, Colville recorded, the Prime Minister was 'heartily sick of the Free French'; still, he sent British mediators to find a solution. This led to what the General called an 'eminently satisfactory' meeting. Muselier, however, said they could not work together. So the two Frenchmen were taken to the Foreign Office where they sat in separate rooms with Cadogan shuttling between them. The First Lord of the Admiralty told Muselier to 'knuckle under' while Eden prevailed upon de Gaulle to abandon his accusations against Muselier and confirm him as head of the Free French navy.

On 25 September 1941, de Gaulle announced a new committee, including Pleven, Cassin and Catroux – and Muselier. Churchill's hopes of reining in the General were dashed; all the members reported to him and he had complete authority to issue decrees. The Prime Minister's verdict on the episode was: 'All we have done is to compel Muselier and co. to submit themselves to de Gaulle. It is evident that this business will require the closest watching, and that our weight in the immediate future must be thrown more heavily against de Gaulle than I had hoped would be necessary.' Once again, the General's skill at brutal politics had won out, but at the cost of forfeiting the complete backing he had enjoyed from Churchill in his first year in London. Soon he was to have to get to grips with a far more hostile ally in the fight to win the war and restore France's greatness.[6]

IV
The so-called Free French

De Gaulle had recognised the power of the United States in his writings in the 1930s, and greeted news of the Japanese attack on Pearl Harbor on 7 December 1941 by predicting that 'the war is finished since the outcome is known from now on. In this industrial war nothing will be able to resist.' America's entry into the war meant Britain would no longer be a major element, he noted; what counted now were relations between Washington and Moscow. Speaking to Passy, with whom he heard the news on the radio after a walk in the woods near his home at Berkhamsted, he added his fear that, after the defeat of Germany, there would be another great war between the United States and the Soviet Union which the Americans risked losing if they did not prepare in time.

He recognised that Churchill's main priority was to maintain friendship with America. From now on, he judged, 'the British will do nothing without Roosevelt's agreement'. This was a particular problem for the General since the US attitude towards him and his movement was, at best, dismissive, and often deeply hostile. Matters were aggravated by Roosevelt's assumption that Washington had the right to determine the fate of France after the war; the President thought of imposing an American military governorship and toyed with the notion of splitting off the General's birthplace of Flanders from the rest of the country and combining it with French-speaking Belgium as a new post-war entity to be called Wallonia.

There were profound differences in the mindsets of the General and the New Dealers in Washington. Seeking to fashion a new world order along American lines, they wanted to sweep away European empires. 'Anything must be better than to live under French colonial rule,' Roosevelt told his son, Elliott; after a century of French rule, the people of Indochina were worse off than before the Europeans arrived, he added. For de Gaulle, on the other hand, the Empire was an essential component of French greatness and the colonies were needed as wartime bases. For Roosevelt, history had no importance in fashioning current policy; for de Gaulle, it was omnipresent. The General's taste for lofty rhetoric contrasted with the President's use of catchy phrases. The gulf between the politician who gave fireside chats on the radio and the soldier who always seemed to be making a grand declaration from on high was simply too great to be bridged, even if either man had wished to do so.

Though Blum wrote to Roosevelt to urge him to work with de Gaulle, most of the prominent French figures in Washington were hostile, as was the State Department. The influential commentator Walter Lippmann was supportive but the widely heard radio analyst Gram Swing blasted de Gaulle as a right-wing Catholic monarchist. Strange as it might seem to those in London who had to put up with his outbursts, the General was widely viewed in Washington as a British puppet. The upshot was that, though adroit diplomacy by René Pleven led to the Free French being made eligible to receive Lend-Lease, de Gaulle continued to be seen by Roosevelt as 'just another French general' and a 'well-nigh intolerable figure'. His offer to the US of naval facilities in West Africa received no response, the US continued to recognise Vichy and the Free French were reduced to operating in the US out of the office of the representative of the Patou perfume firm.[7]

*

On Christmas Eve 1941, Admiral Muselier led a small force of ships and marines to attack the islands of Saint-Pierre et Miquelon off Canada. They met no resistance. The British supported the expedition because it would mean the capture of a powerful radio transmitter that might be used to inform German submarines of cargo ship movements across the Atlantic. Canada was also in favour. But the State Department was outraged; it had just reached an agreement with Vichy to maintain the status quo in French possessions in the western hemisphere. The legalistic Secretary of State, Cordell Hull, denounced the 'arbitrary action', referring to the 'so-called Free French' – a phrase that brought him letters addressed to the 'so-called Secretary of State' at the 'so-called State Department'.

Muselier had not wanted to go ahead with the expedition without US agreement, but de Gaulle ordered him to proceed. When a quick vote showed 90 per cent of the inhabitants of the islands in favour of the

Free French, the General hailed it as having 'thrown a stone into a frogs' swamp'. In a memorandum for Washington, he argued that it had been carried out 'to re-establish the independence and greatness of France that is necessary for the equilibrium of the world'.

Hull and de Gaulle's opponents had their revenge a few days later when the pact providing for the creation of the United Nations was signed in Washington by twenty-six nations, which pledged to uphold the principles of the Atlantic Charter drawn up by Roosevelt and Churchill and to use their full resources against the Axis. The Free French were excluded on the grounds that they did not constitute a government. Churchill tried to get them admitted, but Hull was adamant. De Gaulle reflected how strange it was 'that, as soon as America entered the war, the Free French were eliminated from the Allied conferences in spite of the military effort which they were making'.[8]

*

There was good news at the beginning of March when Leclerc's desert column forging nearly a thousand kilometres north from Chad took the Italian-held oasis of Koufra in Libya. De Gaulle hailed this as 'the first decisive step towards victory' and declared that his movement intended 'to march with its allies under the formal condition that its allies march with it'. Leclerc vowed that he would not lay down arms until the French flag flew once more over Paris and Strasbourg. De Gaulle now felt able to make concessions on Saint-Pierre et Miquelon where American and Canadian personnel took over the radio station and the Free French ships departed. 'Our concessions would be only over appearances,' he told Muselier. 'The realities would be with us. It is, in short, a matter of saving face for Cordell Hull and the State Department.'[9]

That did nothing to improve relations between the General and his number two. At a tense meeting, Muselier charged de Gaulle with having withheld information on his discussion with Churchill about the expedition, producing a copy of the minutes as evidence. He followed this by announcing that he was resigning from the National Committee. De Gaulle accepted the offer, saying that the admiral's continued presence would work against the cohesion of the group.

Archives de Gaulle, Paris, France/Giraudon/The Bridgeman Art Library

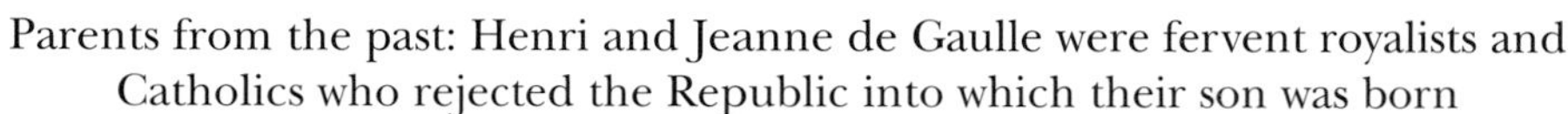

Parents from the past: Henri and Jeanne de Gaulle were fervent royalists and Catholics who rejected the Republic into which their son was born

Archives de Gaulle, Paris, France/Giraudon/The Bridgeman Art Library

A baby of his time: de Gaulle grew up in a society full of questions, and waiting for war

Archives de Gaulle, Paris, France/Giraudon/The Bridgeman Art Library

The perfect officer: de Gaulle passing out from Saint-Cyr

The perfect bride: Yvonne photographed before the wedding

Archives de Gaulle, Paris, France/The Bridgeman Art Library

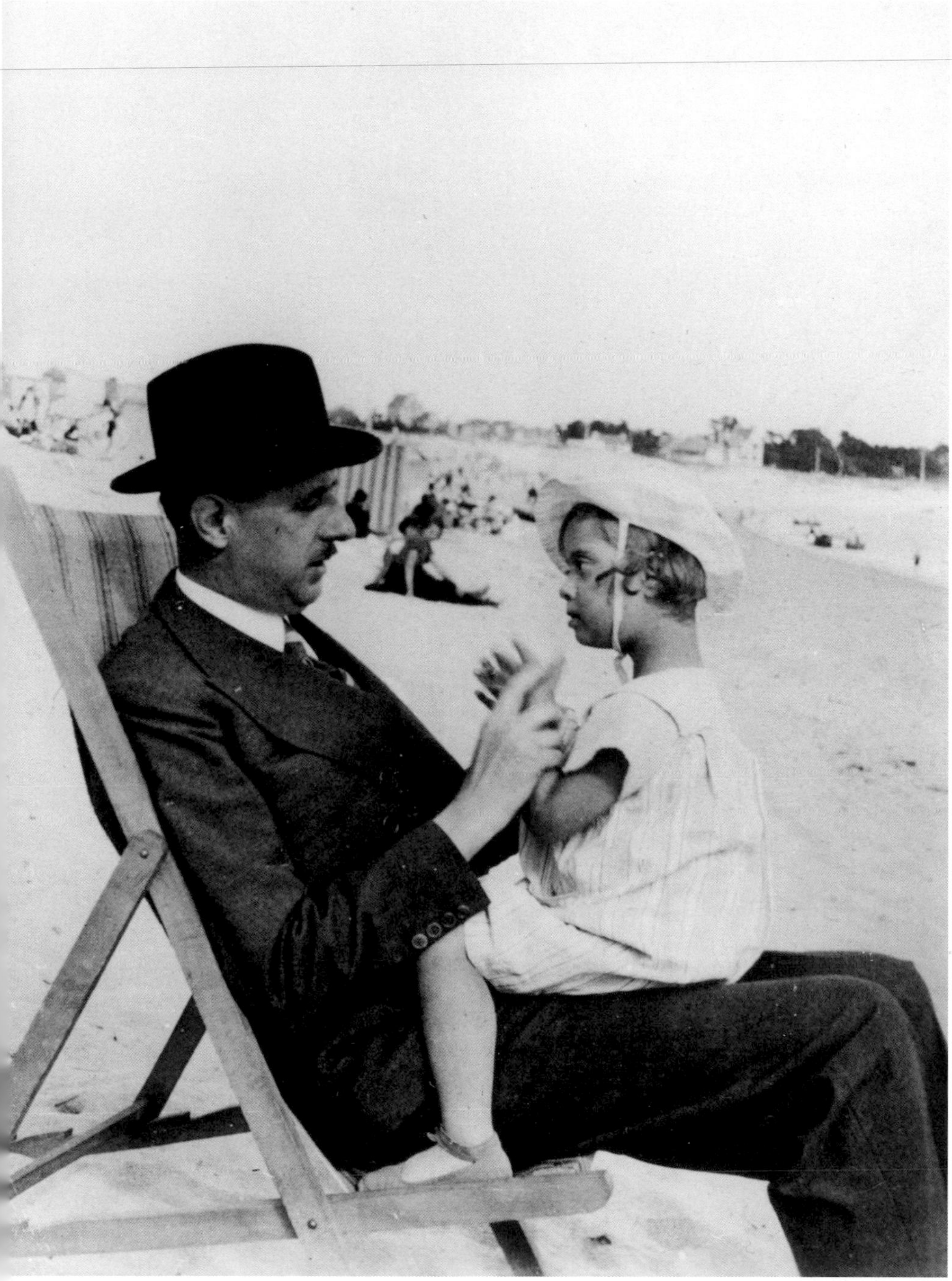

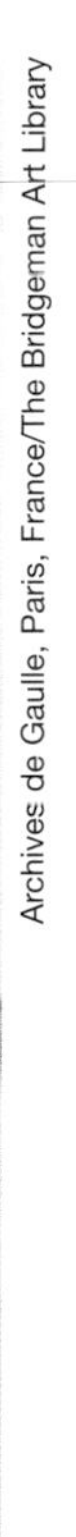

'She made me what I am': de Gaulle with his second daughter, Anne, who suffered from Down's syndrome

Hulton-Deutsch Collection/Corbis

Moment of destiny: de Gaulle broadcasts on the BBC in 1940

Mary Evans Picture Library

A TOUS LES FRANÇAIS
La France a perdu une bataille!
Mais la France n'a pas perdu la guerre!
Des gouvernants de rencontre ont pu capituler, cédant à la panique, oubliant l'honneur, livrant le pays à la servitude. Cependant, rien n'est perdu!
Rien n'est perdu, parce que cette guerre est une guerre mondiale. Dans l'univers libre, des forces immenses n'ont pas encore donné. Un jour, ces forces écraseront l'ennemi. Il faut que la France, ce jour-la, soit présente à la victoire. Alors, elle retrouvera sa liberté et sa grandeur. Tel est mon but, mon seul but!
Voilà pourquoi je convie tous les Francais, où qu'ils se trouvent, à s'unir à moi dans l'action, dans le sacrifice et dans l'espérance.
Notre patrie est en péril de mort.
Luttons tous pour la sauver!
VIVE LA FRANCE !
C. de Gaulle.
GÉNÉRAL DE GAULLE
QUARTIER-GÉNÉRAL,
4, CARLTON GARDENS,
LONDON, S.W.1.

Defiance: the poster proclaiming that France had lost a battle but not the war

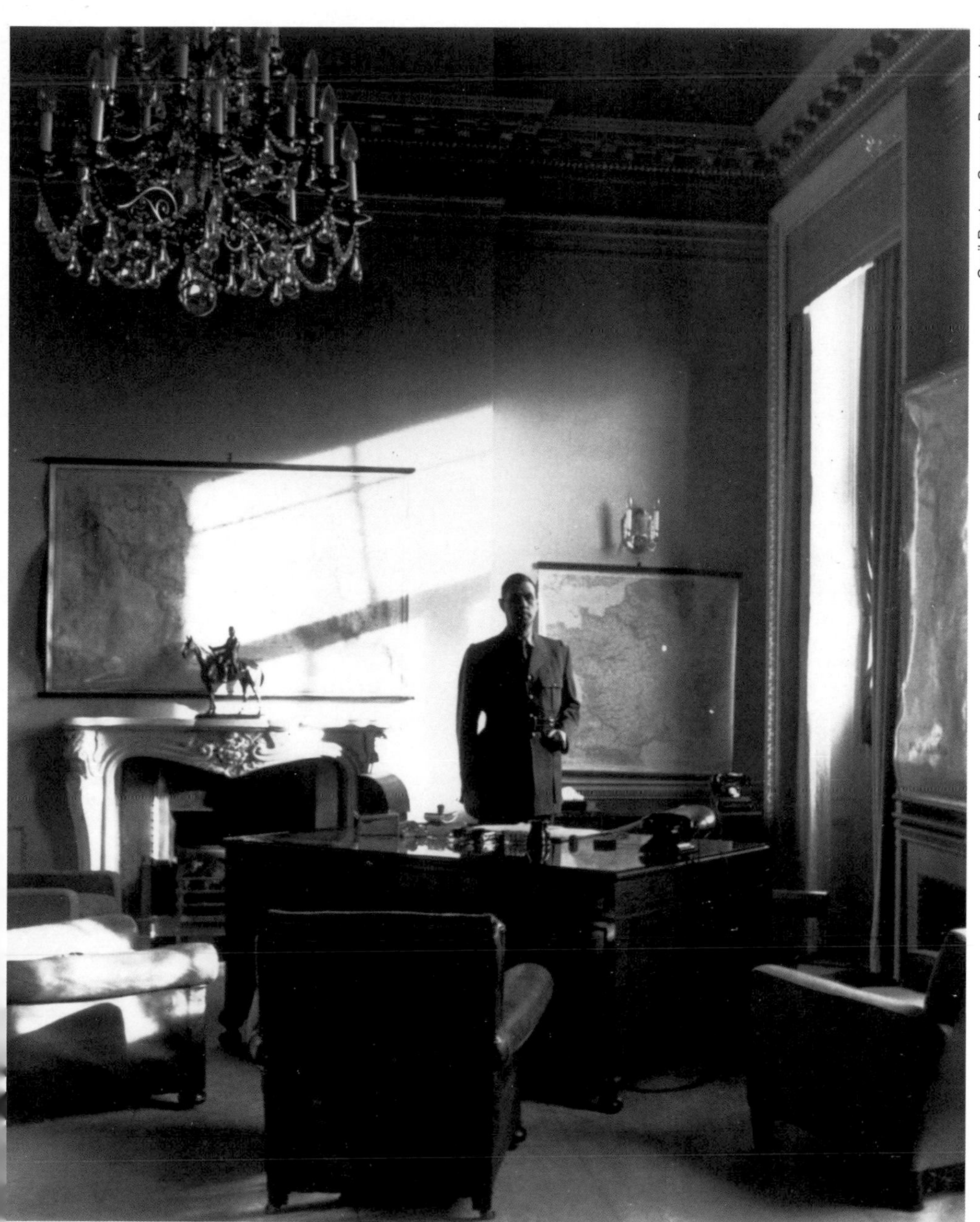

A man alone: the Free French leader in his London office pictured by Cecil Beaton

At home: Charles and Yvonne at their home in Hertfordshire

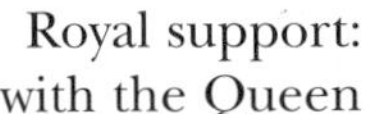

Royal support: with the Queen

AFP/Getty Images

Wholehearted collaboration: Pétain meets Hitler

As time goes by: de Gaulle and his rival, Giraud, agree to shake hands for Roosevelt at the Casablanca summit

Corbis

Mary Evans/De Agostini Editore

Liberation: the General leads the triumphal march down the Champs-Élysées in August 1944

Time and Life Pictures/Getty Images

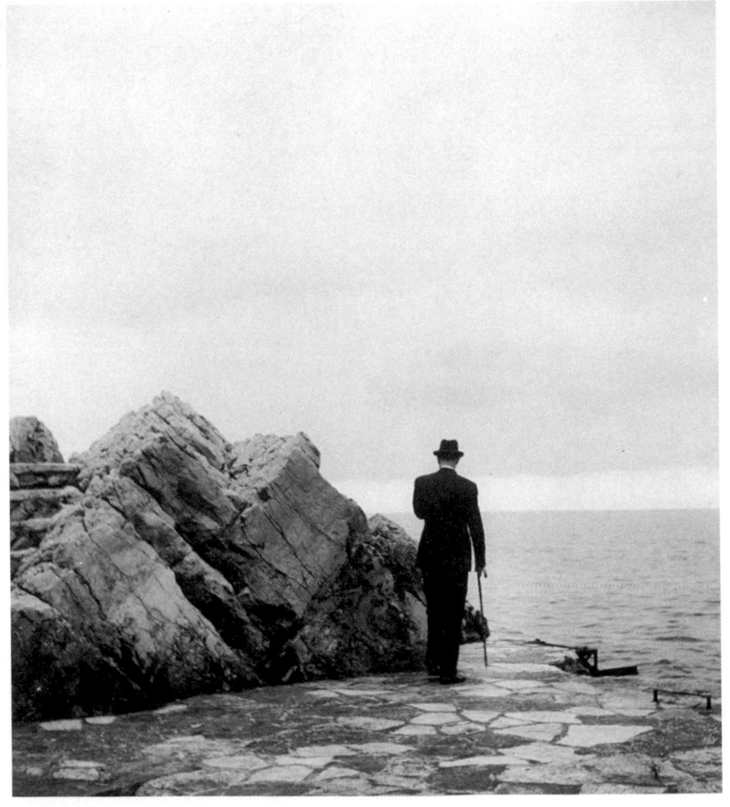

Turning his back: de Gaulle in the south of France just before he resigned the premiership in 1946

The Free French naval commander in the Pacific, Admiral Philippe Auboyneau, was called to London as a replacement, but Muselier then insisted that he would retain control of the ships. There was a violent public confrontation at Free French naval headquarters after de Gaulle sought to assert his authority there. The First Lord of the Admiralty, A. V. Alexander, rallied the War Cabinet behind a demand for Muselier's reinstatement, failing which 'we should have to take the necessary action ourselves to make it effective'.

Anthony Eden, who had become Foreign Secretary in late 1940, called in de Gaulle to warn him that his conduct could have serious consequences. The General objected that Muselier was 'no longer young and was a tired man who indulged in drugs. He was morally unbalanced.' The Foreign Secretary gave de Gaulle forty-eight hours to think the matter over. In what Pleven described as 'a very excited state', the Free French leader called a meeting of the committee which told Muselier to take a month's rest. When he refused, he was put under house arrest by the Gaullists.

The General then staged a tactical withdrawal to his home at Berkhamsted, surprising his wife by his unannounced appearance. She recalled to their son that his father appeared to be a man who had arrived at a crossroads of his life, waiting to see what would ensue but determined not to give in. If the British persisted, he was ready to quit London. 'We will soon be in Africa,' he told her.

Matters were further complicated for de Gaulle by the onset of a malaria attack caused by his failure to take preventive medicine on his African trips. He lay in bed, immobile and deathly pale. Two doctors were called. They judged that his condition had been aggravated by heavy smoking, lack of exercise and nervous strain. After a couple of days, he recovered.

His mixture of firmness and tactical retreat, a technique he would use in the years ahead, won the day. Eden concluded that, if Britain continued to back Muselier, de Gaulle would throw in his hand. That was enough for the War Cabinet, which saw the admiral as a brake on the General, not a successor. The British gave way and de Gaulle returned to London. The British still hoped that the French number two would be found 'suitable employment', but he went too far by calling on the

Free French navy to go on strike against the General. At the end of June 1942, a decree signed by de Gaulle announced that he had been put on the retirement list.

Even if the General had won, the affair had shown dissension in the Free French ranks and some wavering by the British, so it was probably no coincidence that de Gaulle followed his victory by making his strongest public embrace of democracy to date. In an answer to those who accused him of being a dictator in the making, he told a press conference: 'Democracy is the government of the people by the people, and national sovereignty is the people exercising its sovereignty without constraint.'

During the crisis, he also drew up a testament in which he criticised the British for unacceptable infringement of French sovereignty in the Muselier case and 'a series of other pressures and abuses of the same sort (for example what has happened in Syria) which I have been able to repel only with great difficulty and which exhaust my confidence in the sincerity of the British as allies'. France had already understood how he intended to serve her, he went on. If confrontation with the British forced him to abandon his mission, it would be because of his duty to his nation. 'She will choose her path accordingly,' he concluded. 'Men come and go, France continues.'[10]

V

'You are not France!'

There was more good military news in May–June from Libya where Free French troops under General Koenig scored a notable single-handed success in holding back Axis forces at Bir Hakeim, allowing British troops in the area to escape from the Germans. This feat sent Free French morale soaring; in his memoirs, de Gaulle wrote that 'when, at Bir Hakeim, a ray of revived glory came to caress the bloody forehead of its soldiers, the world recognised France'. On the evening he received the news, he went from Carlton Gardens to a nearby chapel to sing the Magnificat.

Walking through the streets of London that night with Maurice Schumann, he was accosted by two French prostitutes who recognised him. One took a photograph of the General from her bag and asked him to sign it. Schumann worried that she might pin it to the wall of her bedroom and use it as an excuse to charge high rates. But de Gaulle asked the woman her name and, learning that she and her companion were married to Englishmen, signed a dedication to them for having 'worked for the entente cordiale'. Getting back to the Connaught, he sang a celebratory verse and, in his memoirs, recalled his heart beating with emotion as he felt tears of pride and of joy.

*

On 14 July, the Free French took on a new name – Fighting France – to encompass the Resistance inside their country, which had some 30,000 active members at this point, about half the number of forces under de Gaulle outside the mainland. But the movement's relations with its allies remained as fraught as ever. In a note to leading Free French delegates in the Empire, de Gaulle wrote of the 'pernickety attitude of our British and American allies towards the French problem and the Free French'. He accused one of his representatives across the Atlantic, Étienne Boegner, of working against him in league with the State Department. At a meeting in London, he exploded when Boegner said he thought the President would welcome a visit. 'That Roosevelt!' he cried. 'Let him invite me if he wants to see me.'

Seeking to develop relations with Moscow, de Gaulle sent an emissary to the Soviet Union, met the Foreign Minister, Molotov, when he visited Britain, and dispatched French pilots to the Eastern Front, where they flew five thousand sorties in Soviet Yak fighters and claimed to have shot down 268 German aircraft. To the US diplomat Averell Harriman he remarked that, after the war, France would not be able to depend on Britain and America 'and therefore French policy should be tied to Soviet policy'. At his stormy meeting with Boegner, he said the Russians were 'the only ones who understand. It is with them that I will rebuild France and Europe.' He asked the Soviet ambassador to his movement, Alexander Bogomolov, if Moscow would play host in case he needed to leave London. But, though the Kremlin said it would recognise the National Committee as 'the only body entitled to organise [French] citizens' participation in the war and to represent French interests in the USSR', Stalin had a low opinion of the Free French and continued to regard France as a nation which had to pay for its performance in 1940.[11]

Fresh trouble broke out with the British after they launched an operation against the French territory of Madagascar in May 1942, without informing Carlton Gardens – de Gaulle learned of the attack when telephoned by a news agency at 3 a.m. The British then made matters worse by trying to negotiate with the Vichy authorities on the island. The General told the French committee he would dissolve the movement in protest; he advised its members to enrol in the Canadian army. Word of this reached Churchill who tried to telephone, but de Gaulle was said to be unavailable. He ordered the Foreign Affairs Commissioner, Maurice Dejean, to have nothing to do with the Foreign Office, and refused a request from Eden to meet. After two days, however, he considered that he had put up enough of a show and condescended to talk to the Prime Minister. Everything was settled. 'After all,' the General remarked, 'it's better to see those English pigs in Diego Suarez than those pigs of Germans.'

There was also an embarrassing spat in New Caledonia, where de Gaulle's emissary, the monk-sailor Thierry d'Argenlieu, who had accompanied him on the Dakar expedition, tried to impose his authority by having the popular governor arrested and sent to New Zealand. This provoked a general strike. In the end, American troops, who had been allowed to use the territory as a base, declared martial law to calm things down until another Free French envoy arrived.

But it was in the Levant that major trouble erupted once more. Relations worsened between Catroux, the senior representative in the area, and Edward Spears, who had been appointed Britain's minister for the region. Their wives were also on bad terms. On a trip to the area in August 1942, the General came out with a stream of anti-British statements. In a message to his office in London, he accused Britain of wanting to use its money, supplies, forces and propaganda to dominate the Levant at France's expense. Spears, he added, was throwing oil on the fire. Eden had to be warned that, without a change in British policy, he did not see how cooperation could go on.

When de Gaulle returned to London in late September, he and Churchill had a heated discussion during which the General said the 'very serious situation' in the Levant called into question collaboration between France and Britain. 'Between General de Gaulle and England,' the Prime Minister interjected, and then exploded: 'You claim to be France! You are not France! I do not recognise you as France!' He then spoke of 'the great difficulty' he had in working with the Free French leader. 'General de Gaulle had shown marked hostility towards us,' the British account has Churchill saying. 'Wherever he went there was trouble. The situation was now critical. This made him sad, since he admired the General's personality and record. But he could not regard him as a comrade or a friend. He seemed to wish to strengthen his position with the French by adopting brusque methods with us. He tried the same tactics with the Americans. This was a serious situation.'

'This was very sad,' de Gaulle replied, by this account. 'His position in France depended simply on the fact that he had wanted to go on fighting with us . . . But just because of this, and because of the importance of maintaining the alliance after the war, the French people must receive the impression that Fighting France were regarded as real allies and not as creatures of the British.' That did nothing to stop the Prime Minister, who said de Gaulle 'had not helped us at all. Instead of waging war with Germany, he had waged war with England. This was a great mistake. He had not shown the slightest desire to assist us, and he himself had been the main obstacle to effective collaboration.' The General responded that he would take the consequences. The meeting ended.*

The next day, de Gaulle told the National Committee he was ready to resign if it thought his presence at its head was detrimental to French interests. The offer was unanimously rejected. The British showed their displeasure by refusing to allow cables to be sent from Carlton Gardens to Fighting France representatives in Africa, the Middle East and the Pacific. The Foreign Office put pressure on Dejean, who envisaged concessions. But de Gaulle would have none of that. Dejean resigned, and

*The French version of the meeting simply notes that Churchill 'brought into question the personality of the General' (*Lettres, Complément*, p. 354).

Pleven took over the foreign affairs and colonial portfolio pending the arrival of an experienced diplomat, René Massigli.

As so often, a combination of the General's inflexibility and the difficulty Churchill had in maintaining his anger led to a temporary resolution. After eleven days, the British relented and resumed transmissions to the movement's delegates abroad. The Foreign Office opened negotiations for an agreement on Madagascar. Churchill sent congratulations on the sinking of two German ships by a Fighting France submarine off Norway, as well as thanks for participation of troops in the victory over Rommel at El Alamein.

In October, the General tried to explain himself to Roosevelt with a lengthy letter in which he sought to dispel concern about his lack of electoral legitimacy by writing that the Free French movement saw itself as only a provisional authority, to be replaced when a proper government could be voted in. He noted that not even Vichy had accused his movement of aiming to impose a dictatorship. After the 'odious' exercise in personal power by Pétain, who could imagine that the experience could be repeated in France? he asked. Harking back to June 1940, he put to Roosevelt the rhetorical question of whether he should have remained silent when the government to which he belonged decided on a ceasefire. The letter brought no softening of Washington's hostility. Far from responding, Roosevelt was set on facing the General with a challenge which would determine whether he could achieve the status to which he had aspired since flying out of Bordeaux two years earlier.

11

AT THE SUMMIT

I
Two generals and an admiral

Before daybreak on 8 November 1942, seven hundred ships landed 100,000 Allied troops in Vichy-held Morocco and Algeria in Operation Torch. The Americans were in charge, with the British playing a supporting role and Fighting France nowhere. The United States had begun the fightback against the Japanese in the Pacific the previous summer, but this was the first time its troops had intervened in the European–North African theatre.

The attack on the Axis's 'soft underbelly', as Churchill termed it, had been a key element in British strategy as the chief of the Imperial General Staff, Alan Brooke, waged a bitter campaign against the American plan for a cross-Channel landing in 1942, which he saw, rightly, as risking disaster. After Roosevelt fell in with the British proposal, Churchill and Brooke agreed that the US should command the operation; the Prime Minister assured the President that he would be 'your lieutenant'. In his first field command, Dwight Eisenhower took control. The Germans had expected any Allied attack in the region to be directed against one of the large Mediterranean islands, and had not reinforced the Vichy defenders.

Torch and the simultaneous victory of British forces in the desert battle of El Alamein greatly boosted Allied morale. On 19–20 November, the Red Army unleashed a massive counter-offensive at Stalingrad. Final victory would come the following February. 'We are striking back,' Roosevelt told visitors when informed of the Torch landings at his retreat of Shangri-La (later Camp David). Churchill's popularity soared above 90 per cent. 'There is a long road still to tread,' the Prime Minister remarked, 'but the end is sure.'

Not only were there no Fighting France soldiers among those who landed on the North African beaches, Roosevelt had also vetoed a suggestion from Churchill that de Gaulle should be told of the operation in advance. This was not simply spite; the London French had shown themselves extremely leaky at the time of Dakar. The Americans also believed that Gaullist participation would stiffen the resistance of Vichy commanders on the spot. However, Pleven heard of the plan at a reception given by the Czechoslovak government-in-exile in London, which had been tipped off. By the time he got to Carlton Gardens, de Gaulle had gone home and his colleague did not bother him. Instead, an aide woke him at 6 a.m. to inform him. Pulling on his dressing gown on top of his white pyjamas, de Gaulle exploded. 'I hope the Vichy folk throw them into the sea,' he cried. 'One does not break into France.'

Still, as over Mers-el-Kébir, the General soon calmed down, and had a constructive luncheon meeting with Churchill at Chequers. In a BBC broadcast, he said that the Allies did not have territorial designs on North Africa and called on Vichy troops to ally with them. The possibilities that Torch opened up for him were worth a diplomatic approach. The southern shore of the Mediterranean was much closer to France than the colonies where the Free French had established themselves. If he could move there, he would be back on French territory, and that much closer to achieving his ultimate goal. But he knew this was not something the Americans intended to facilitate, so he had to plan his strategy carefully rather than flying off the handle.[1]

*

Washington's first choice as its French partner in North Africa was Maxime Weygand, who had been sacked by Pétain under German pressure. But the former commander-in-chief said he was too old to become a rebel. So the American choice to head the new order in Algiers fell on General Henri Giraud, who was given the codename King Pin. The very model of an officer, the handsome, straight-backed soldier with a handlebar moustache stood almost as tall as de Gaulle and was described by Jean Monnet as having the eyes of a Siamese cat. Like de Gaulle, he had been given up for dead in the First World War. He had commanded armies in northern France in 1940 before being captured and sent to a prison camp in a German castle on a rocky promontory.

More successful than de Gaulle in his First World War escape bids, the sixty-three-year-old Giraud slid down a rope strengthened with wire which his wife had sent him hidden in food tins. He used false papers to cross to France and went to see Pétain in Vichy where he was contacted by the Americans. Moving on to Eisenhower's temporary headquarters in Gibraltar, he called on the US commander who found him 'a gallant if bedraggled figure'. Giraud thought he was going to be put in overall charge of the landings. When told that his role was simply to go to Algiers to rally French forces there, he replied in his usual abrupt manner that he could not accept a subordinate role. The conversation went on till midnight, with each soldier repeating the same arguments.

In the morning, however, King Pin agreed to go along with the American proposal. Still, his limitations soon became apparent. He was contemptuous of politics, and Eisenhower found him lacking administrative and organisational skills. He was reluctant to be cast as a turncoat by fellow officers who remained loyal to Vichy. The American commander described him to Washington as a man who 'wants to be a big shot, a bright and shining light, and the acclaimed saviour of France', but who procrastinated in the hope that it would all soon be over and 'he could go as a knight in white armour and be the big hero to lead France to VICTORY'. But he proved 'a terrible blow to our expectations; he was completely ignored'.

Giraud was not the only miscalculation by the Americans. Vichy forces put up strong resistance, motivated in part by memories of Mers-el-Kébir. Some of the defenders were troops from Syria that the British had allowed to be repatriated after the fighting there. In addition, as Eisenhower reported: 'The name of Marshal Pétain is something to conjure with here.' As Allied losses mounted, and several warships were sunk or badly damaged, the Americans turned to a more dubious but powerful figure, Admiral François Darlan, described by Eisenhower as the only man who had 'an obvious right to assume the

Marshal's mantle in North Africa'. As a US naval envoy told Gaston Palewski: 'Giraud found himself in front of a wall to which Darlan alone had the keys.'[2]

Darlan had emerged as Pétain's number two after the eclipse of Laval, implementing repressive, anti-Semitic measures and cooperating with the Germans in the Middle East and Africa, where he granted permission for U-boats to use the base at Dakar to attack Atlantic shipping. But he faced growing internal opposition in the murky world of Vichy politics. Critics alleged that he was connected to a shadowy financial ring known as the *Synarchie* – this invention was taken seriously by the deeply anti-Masonic Pétain. The Germans, led by Abetz, preferred Laval, and had the Auvergnat reinstated in April 1942. That made the admiral receptive to approaches from the Americans. As it happened, at the time of Torch he was visiting Algiers to see his son, who was gravely ill with polio. Whether the visit was coincidence or part of a plan by the admiral remains uncertain: the latter seems more likely. Darlan met Robert Murphy, the US diplomat in charge of the preparations for Torch in Algiers, and an understanding emerged.

The US–British alliance with Stalin had shown how little the principles of the Atlantic Charter meant when practical considerations prevailed. At a bad-tempered meeting with Fighting France representatives in November, Roosevelt said he was prepared to ally with anybody if that was necessary to win the war; today it was Darlan, and, tomorrow, why not Laval if he offered the Allies Paris? Writing to Churchill, he called Darlan, Giraud and de Gaulle prima donnas and insisted that anything they did in North Africa was subject to Eisenhower's approval. Stalin, who had to accept that Torch would delay the opening of a second front in France for which he had been pressing, sent the President a message in which he quoted a Russian proverb about needing to be ready to use 'even the Devil himself and his grandma'.

Not all those around Roosevelt were as blasé as him. Cordell Hull, War Secretary Henry Stimson and Navy Secretary Frank Knox felt repugnance at working with Darlan. In France the readiness of the Allies to collaborate with such a prominent member of the Vichy hierarchy caused dismay among the Resistance. De Gaulle protested to the

White House, but got no reply. Eden was critical; the Fighting France leader recalled that, at the end of one meeting on the subject, the Foreign Secretary was on the verge of tears.

But Churchill went along in the name of Allied solidarity, though, to counter US influence in the region, he took the precautionary political step of appointing a rising young minister, Harold Macmillan, to join Eisenhower's command, reporting directly to Downing Street. According to de Gaulle, the Prime Minister sought to reassure him by arguing that 'Giraud has been liquidated politically. In due course, Darlan will be impossible. You will remain as the only one. Don't get into a confrontation with the Americans. Be patient! They will come to you because there is no alternative.' 'Perhaps,' the General replied. 'But how much crockery will you have broken by then? You allow the Americans to take the leadership of the conflict. Rather, it is for you to exercise it, at least in the moral sphere. Do so! European opinion will back you.' The General's memoirs recall that Churchill shifted in his chair, apparently struck by what he had heard.

On 13 November 1942 Eisenhower, who had flown to Algiers from Gibraltar, reached an agreement with Darlan who got Vichy forces to stop fighting after suffering 3,000 dead or wounded (about the same as the Allies' losses) along with the loss of 21 ships and 135 of their 168 military planes. Riding high, Darlan established his mastery over Giraud. He signed an agreement with the Americans granting them control of all military installations in North Africa. A French 'Imperial Federation' was proclaimed, with him as High Commissioner. He resumed the repressive methods he had pursued in Vichy. Free French supporters were harassed. Anti-Semitism was rife; Eisenhower recalled being told of a rumour that he and Roosevelt were both Jewish and that the aim of Torch was to turn North Africa over to Jewish rule.[3]

*

Torch brought a dramatic reaction from Hitler that underlined the distinction between Vichy and de Gaulle's crusade to keep alive the flame of independence and sovereignty. In June, Laval had gone further than before on the path of collaboration by expressing publicly his hope that Germany would win the war. On 7 November, the day before Torch, Hitler raised the prospect of a German–French treaty binding the two countries to fight together. Three days later, he summoned Laval to his residence at Berchtesgaden. The Frenchman took a cyanide pill with him in case he was arrested. But, he told the Cabinet on his return, his host was amiable, saying he wanted to maintain the collaborationist regime to save Germany the task of running the whole of France. As a sign of friendship, the flowers in Laval's room were in his country's national colours.

On 11 November, the twenty-fourth anniversary of the end of the First World War, Hitler showed how hollow his assurances to Laval had been, sending the Wehrmacht across the demarcation line into unoccupied territory and breaking the armistice. Italian troops did the same on the south-eastern frontier. Pétain recorded a broadcast saying these were 'the darkest days of my life'. It was transmitted every fifteen minutes until, after an hour, the Germans turned up at the radio station and confiscated the disc. Only one Vichy commander refused to accept the occupation, General de Lattre de Tassigny, who happened to have been, like Leclerc, a pupil of Henri de Gaulle in Paris. He was arrested and sentenced to ten years in prison.

In the following days, Laval took executive power and German troops moved on the naval base at Toulon, where the admiral in charge ordered 250,000 tonnes of shipping to be scuttled, including three modern battleships and eight cruisers. Weygand was arrested and taken to Germany. Pétain's aide, Bernard Serrigny, pressed the Victor of Verdun to fly to North Africa but he refused. 'He believes that Germany will be defeated; he has repeated this to me for the last six months, and yet he throws himself into Hitler's arms,' Serrigny noted.[4]

*

In London, de Gaulle needed to maintain his sangfroid as Churchill shifted into aggressive mode against him, perhaps prompted by his awareness of the moral shoddiness of the Darlan deal. The Prime Minister told Eden that the admiral had done more than de Gaulle for Britain in not handing the French fleet to the Germans. A Free French plan to broadcast a message from internal Resistance leaders was quashed. De Gaulle's speeches on the BBC were held up after Churchill sent a message to Roosevelt asking whether they should be transmitted. At a closed parliamentary session, the Prime Minister spoke of his friendly personal relations with the Fighting France leader, but added: 'I could not recommend you to base all your hopes and confidence on him, and still less to assume at this stage that it is our duty to place, so far as we have the power, the destiny of France in his hands.'

The General reacted by telling the Soviet embassy in London that the Americans might install Fascist sympathisers in Italy, and perhaps even appoint Goering in Germany. As he left, according to the Soviet ambassador Ivan Maisky, 'de Gaulle walked to the door. Then he came back and looked me straight in the eye and said in a low voice, "With all my heart, I hope you get to Berlin before the Americans."'[5]

In December, de Gaulle sent an emissary, General François d'Astier de la Vigerie, to Algiers to meet Darlan. The visit went badly. The Americans, who had been told in advance, forgot about it and did not inform the admiral. When the two Frenchmen met, they stormed at one another, and d'Astier de la Vigerie was asked to fly out; he left $38,000 with Gaullist supporters in Algiers.

Darlan's position was, in fact, more fragile than it may have appeared. Though the admiral professed loyalty to Pétain, his association with Torch undercut his appeal to Vichyites. Algiers was a political hothouse; Eisenhower lamented at the 'petty intrigue and the necessity of dealing with little, selfish, conceited worms that call themselves men'. Local Gaullist leaders, including two future ministers, Louis Joxe and René Capitant, established relations with the Resistance across the Mediterranean. The pretender to the French throne, the Comte de Paris, popped up in North Africa, where he contracted a violent fever. Reports of coups and assassination attempts flew; Madame Darlan was said to have told her husband he risked losing his life.

Moscow began to have second thoughts about Darlan and, more important, Roosevelt was taking notice of the rising criticism of the US relationship with him. His supporters had lost ground in the mid-term congressional elections, including nine state governorships. The State

Department warned of a storm of protest at the way a 'semi-Fascist' government had been installed in the first major territory liberated by US forces. As criticism rose, Roosevelt told Eisenhower that, while he backed the use of Darlan for the time being, 'it is impossible to keep a collaborator of Hitler and one whom we believe to be a Fascist in civil power any longer than is strictly necessary'. He ordered the release of all political prisoners in Morocco and Algeria, and envisaged naming American and British delegates to supervise the local administration. He also invited de Gaulle to visit Washington at the end of the year.

The resolution of this treacly affair came not from Washington or London but from Fernand Bonnier de la Chapelle, a young French Royalist from a patriotic group in Algiers, who had been trained by the British in the use of firearms. On Christmas Eve, he entered Darlan's office and shot him in the stomach. The admiral died two hours later. While Roosevelt called the assassination 'cold-blooded murder', Churchill drew the realistic conclusion that it 'relieved the Allies of an embarrassment'. There was no direct link between the killing and de Gaulle, but some of the dollars taken to Algiers by the General's emissary were found on Bonnier de la Chapelle. De Gaulle regarded Darlan as a traitor and later called the murder an execution. The assassin was swiftly tried and shot. Gaullist supporters were arrested; some sent to detention in the Sahara. Louis Joxe recalled that, when he was held, he was accused of being an enemy agent, to which he asked 'Which enemy?'

De Gaulle's trip to Washington was abruptly cancelled. Roosevelt's favourite diplomat, Sumner Welles, told the Free French representative that Washington disapproved of the way the General had sent messages to Giraud proposing discussions. The American wanted to maintain full control of French affairs, with King Pin as their man after Darlan's death. However, Giraud continued to show himself to be a poor politician while his masters fumbled badly. Collaborationist officials were kept on. Local Resistance fighters were detained. As Governor of Algeria, the Americans and Giraud appointed Maurice Peyrouton, a former Vichy Interior Minister who had signed the death sentence for de Gaulle and implemented anti-Jewish measures but who had then fallen out with Laval and gone to live in Argentina. The food situation in North Africa deteriorated and the US advance east along the coast got bogged down in bad weather.

Writing to his delegate in the United States, de Gaulle judged that Giraud had shown 'extreme political clumsiness'. In his New Year broadcast from London, he insisted on the need to establish 'a provisional and enlarged central authority, having as its basis national union, as its inspiration the spirit of war and liberation, and as its laws those of the Republic, until the nation should have made known its will'. He blamed the confusion in French Africa on the lack of such an authority and the failure to give Fighting France official representation. Increasingly, he appealed to democratic tradition, which now became a central element in his political philosophy.[6]

II
A handshake is just a handshake

In mid-January 1943, Roosevelt and Churchill met in the Anfa suburb of Casablanca in Morocco to review the progress of the war outlook, plan for the invasion of Sicily and Italy and get agreement between the two French generals. Giraud was on hand, but de Gaulle refused to attend a meeting to discuss France organised by foreign powers on French soil. 'You've got to get your problem child down here,' the President told Churchill at dinner on the first night of the summit. 'De Gaulle is on his high horse,' the Prime Minister replied. 'Refuses to come down here. Refuses point blank. I can't move him from London . . . Jeanne d'Arc complex.' To which the President responded that he had produced Giraud as the groom, now it was up to the Prime Minister to fetch the bride for a shotgun wedding.

Churchill duly sent a summons to London but de Gaulle still refused to go to Anfa. His mood had been boosted by several pieces of good news. The Fighting France motorised column led by Leclerc was continuing its progress through Libya towards Tunisia. The island of La Réunion rallied to his cause. The East African territory of Djibouti had been taken while a Gaullist administration was being installed in Madagascar, now that the British had handed it over. Replying to

Churchill, de Gaulle pointed out that Giraud had not replied to his suggestions of meetings and insisted that, if they were to get together, it must be in a French place free of Allied control. If he was being invited to the summit to be put forward as the British candidate in a beauty contest with Giraud, the result would be 'an unseemly, even dangerous, show', he objected. 'This, I should think, is the end of the Free French movement,' Cadogan wrote in his diary. If Churchill had to choose between de Gaulle and Giraud, the diplomat reasoned, he would back the latter simply to maintain the relationship with Roosevelt.

The President envisaged creating a Committee for the Liberation of France headed by Giraud, with de Gaulle as a member alongside a civilian, probably Jean Monnet. When he met Roosevelt, Giraud reacted enthusiastically. But he did not impress the American President. 'I am afraid we are leaning on a very slender reed,' Roosevelt judged. 'He's a dud as an administrator. He'll be a dud as a leader.'

To get de Gaulle to knuckle under, Roosevelt suggested to Churchill that he threaten to withdraw British financing for Fighting France. 'W.S.C. beamed,' the President wrote to his cousin, Margaret Suckley. 'Good idea – no come – no pay!' A second message to London spelled out that the invitation to Casablanca was from the President, as well as the Prime Minister. If the General did not change his mind, Britain would have to 'review' its attitude to the Free French and 'endeavor to get on as well as we can without you', it added.[7]

The War Cabinet, which on several occasions showed itself less than ready to go along with Churchill's blandishments of the President over the Free French, toned down the warning. De Gaulle still played hard to get but, in the end, agreed to make the trip. He knew that, if he continued to refuse to go to Casablanca, Giraud would have the advantage of being on the spot with American backing, and, for all his weakness, might become a real rival. So it was time to be somewhat reasonable.

Still, there was trouble from the moment de Gaulle arrived. When he saw that the windows of his car were covered with mud, he assumed that his hosts wanted to conceal him from the local people, not knowing that this had been done for security reasons to Roosevelt's car as well. The intrusive presence of armed US guards on French soil grated. At lunch with Giraud, he refused to sit at table until French soldiers replaced the American sentries, and exploded that it was 'odious that they should finally get together behind barbed wire manned by foreigners'. When Giraud addressed him as 'Gaulle', he replied sharply 'Call me *mon Général.*' Giraud gave an account of his escape from captivity which was greeted with applause; in the ensuing silence, de Gaulle was heard to say 'And now, General, suppose you tell us how you came to be taken prisoner.'[8]

Their conversation showed how far apart they were. Giraud refused to condemn Pétain and put up a quasi-defence of the Darlan deal. Fighting France should work under him alongside former Vichyites and officials he had inherited from Darlan, he added. At a tête-à-tête with Churchill, de Gaulle said the proposed arrangements 'might seem adequate at the level of American sergeant-majors' but could not be taken seriously. Neither the US nor Britain could presume to decide the attribution of powers in France's Empire, he insisted, proposing that he should form a war government in Algiers which would become the government of the French Republic when appropriate. It would appoint Giraud to a military role provided he condemned Vichy, called the armistice null and void and identified himself with the Republic and France's independence in the world.

Late at night, de Gaulle and Roosevelt had their first encounter. The President had just been at dinner with Churchill and the Sultan of Morocco, to whom he denounced European empires and looked forward to the post-war involvement of American business in North Africa. (It had been an uncomfortable evening for the Prime Minister on two counts – the President's anti-imperial remarks and the absence of alcohol.) At Roosevelt's villa, armed American secret service men were reported to have been hidden behind drapery round the gallery above the living room. The President's closest aide, Harry Hopkins, who wrote that de Gaulle was 'cold and austere', found the whole set-up an 'unbelievably funny' scene that could not have been bettered by Gilbert and Sullivan. Roosevelt, wearing a white suit, was emollient, and spoke in French. Half lying on a sofa, he gestured to the General to sit beside him. 'I am sure that we will be able to assist your great country in re-establishing its destiny,' he began.

The Frenchman grunted.

'And I assure you, it will be an honour for my country to participate in the undertaking,' Roosevelt went on.

'Nice of you to say so,' de Gaulle replied in a low voice.

The President stressed the importance of French unity and advanced the argument that none of the various groups could claim sole legitimacy. De Gaulle, for instance, had never been elected. To that, the General responded that Joan of Arc had drawn her legitimacy from taking action and refusing to lose hope.

Roosevelt said he thought the US and Britain should hold North Africa in a trusteeship until the war ended. According to the US record, he compared France to 'a little child unable to look out and fend for itself' and said that in such a case a court would appoint a trustee. He could hardly have done more to antagonise his visitor, but de Gaulle restrained himself, realising that nothing was to be gained from a showdown at that point. As he wrote in his memoirs, both men saw virtue in maintaining 'a certain degree of imprecision on the matter of France'.

According to the US record, the General left the session 'with some show of cordiality'. The Free French leader told an aide that he had just met 'a great statesman. I think we understood one another well.' Macmillan reported that Roosevelt had been impressed. Churchill's doctor noted in his diary, without citing a source, that the President had been attracted by 'a spiritual look' he detected in the other man's eyes. But Elliott Roosevelt recorded his father as saying that de Gaulle was determined to establish a dictatorship in France. 'There is no man in whom I have less confidence,' the President added. He also invented a story that de Gaulle had compared himself to Joan of Arc, the First World War 'Tiger' Georges Clemenceau and other great figures of French history. The Fighting France chief was not amused when word of this reached him.[9]

That night, the General summed up his feelings in another of the testaments he drew up at crucial moments, as he had done during the crisis over Admiral Muselier. Addressed to a member of the Casablanca garrison who had been his student at Saint-Cyr, he wrote that it was 'quite possible that the blindness and anger of the Americans and the English may put me in such a situation that our activity becomes impossible. I would rather that than a capitulation. In the extreme hypothesis of a break, there is no doubt that Washington and London will account for things in their own way, that is to say by heaping blame on me. In that event, I should have little means of informing France and the Empire. That is why I am writing you this letter and asking you to make it as public as possible if things go completely wrong . . . The good Frenchmen of North Africa will thus be able to see that I have not betrayed them.'[10]

Mail from the United States for Roosevelt's delegation brought bundles of press clippings critical of his North African policy. Eisenhower feared that anti-Giraud French would group against the Allied presence in North Africa. The American diplomat Robert Murphy, who had been at Vichy before making the political preparations for Torch, drew up proposals to ditch de Gaulle, but the much more influential Hopkins grew sympathetic to him. The President changed tack to the extent of saying that the two generals could be granted equal footing, with a future consultative assembly choosing between them. However he had no illusions: 'De Gaulle will oppose it, obviously,' he noted.

In the morning, the General got a roasting from Churchill which he described as their roughest session of the war. The Prime Minister, who does not mention the encounter in his memoirs, had fortified himself with a bottle of white wine at breakfast. He said he would denounce de Gaulle publicly as the man who had prevented agreement, and would turn the British public against him. Churchill was 'free to dishonour himself', the Frenchman replied. To satisfy America at any price, the British leader was embracing a cause unacceptable for France, he added. As he walked down the path from his villa, the Prime Minister told his doctor: 'His country has given up fighting, he himself is a refugee, and if we turn him down he's finished. But look at him! Look at him! He might be Stalin, with 200 divisions behind his words. Perhaps the last survivor of a warrior race.'[11]

At the same time, Roosevelt received Giraud at his villa nearby. The President handed over a memorandum providing for King Pin to be recognised as responsible for managing 'French interests in the military, economic, financial and ethical spheres'. He told his visitor the US would assure French forces of military supplies as a matter of priority, and help him achieve their unity. The President was in a hurry. A press conference was scheduled for an hour later, and he needed a statement on the French front.

Having given Giraud the bait, Roosevelt insisted he must sit down with de Gaulle to discuss the creation of a three-man committee with the French second-in-command from 1940, General Georges, who was highly regarded by Churchill. When Roosevelt mentioned de Gaulle's name, Giraud broke in: 'That man! He is a self-seeker!' according to Elliott Roosevelt's account. He called the Fighting France chief 'a bad general' but Roosevelt persisted and he gave way. 'It is understood, *Monsieur le Président*,' he said. 'It is understood.' Walking out, he found de Gaulle waiting in the hallway to go in to see FDR.

The General said Giraud should serve under him. Roosevelt expressed sorrow at the lack of understanding between the two soldiers. 'Leave me be,' the visitor replied. 'There will be a communiqué, even if it is not yours.'

Churchill arrived at the Roosevelt villa, and spoke to Giraud before entering the main room. Hopkins went into the hall to fetch Giraud. De Gaulle looked 'somewhat bewildered', the President's fixer recalled. Waving his finger, Churchill bellowed in improvised French: '*Mon Général, il ne faut pas obstacler la guerre!*'

All charm, Roosevelt turned to de Gaulle to ask if he would agree to be photographed with him, the Prime Minister and Giraud. 'Naturally, because I have the greatest esteem for this fine soldier,' de Gaulle replied, by his own account.

'Will you go as far as to shake hands with General Giraud in our presence and in front of the cameras?' Roosevelt inquired. 'I shall do that for you,' came the response – in English.

The two Frenchmen looked stiffly at each other, and circled, in Elliott Roosevelt's words, like two dogs. As Roosevelt beamed, they exchanged a brief handshake. 'We have agreed,' de Gaulle said, now in French, 'we have agreed that we will do our best to work out a satisfactory plan of action.' He paused, then uttered the hardest word – 'together.' Giraud nodded. 'Come on,' Roosevelt cried, 'pictures!'

At the press conference, the two tall generals shook hands for the cameras on the lawn outside the President's villa watched by Roosevelt and Churchill. Giraud was pictured full face, the index finger of his right hand pointing to the ground, while de Gaulle stood in profile, a cigarette in his left hand by his side. They kept as far away from one another as possible. Since some of the photographers failed to capture the scene the first time round, they did a second take.

De Gaulle dismissed the show of unity as ridiculous, and Churchill remarked in his memoirs that the photograph 'cannot be viewed . . . without a laugh'. But Roosevelt looked greatly relieved, smiling broadly as he watched, and then turned to other matters, announcing to reporters that the Allies would follow a policy of unconditional surrender towards their foes. A statement by the two French generals said simply: 'We have met. We have talked. We have registered our entire agreement on the end to be achieved which is the liberation of France . . . This end will be attained by a union in war of all Frenchmen.'

III
'The Monster of Hampstead'

'What we want and what France wants is not an agreement between two generals,' de Gaulle told a press conference after returning to London. 'That is meaningless . . . The stakes are infinitely higher: a union of France's empire for the liberation of France and the realisation of the goals set by France herself.' What followed the summit only served to deepen his suspicions of the motives of his allies, to reinforce his intransigence and accentuate his lack of any sense of proportion when French interests were at stake. His supporter in Algiers, Louis Joxe, wrote of him at this time as 'proud, haughty, vain, arrogant . . . Reserved, suspicious, grudge-bearing, indeed hard, wounding, and sometimes vindictive . . . often indifferent and remote'.

At first, the General thought his conversations with Roosevelt had brought home to the President what Fighting France really was. But the Americans were still intent on imposing Giraud while, at dinner with Roosevelt in Marrakech after Anfa, Churchill returned to a familiar analogy, saying the General was a Joan of Arc and that the British were trying to find some bishops to burn him. He wrote to King George VI that he had more confidence in Giraud than in de Gaulle and saw no future for Fighting France so long as the General remained at its head.

Anglo-American obstructionism grew as spring approached. A ban instituted by Churchill on de Gaulle leaving Britain prevented him visiting the Middle East. '*Alors, je suis prisonnier,*' the General remarked. When he asked Churchill if the British intended to exile him to the Isle of Man, the Prime Minister cried: 'No, for you it will be the Tower of London.' He told Charles Peake, the Foreign Office official in charge of relations with Fighting France: 'I hold you responsible that the Monster of Hampstead does not escape.'

Washington accused Fighting France of using funds derived from Lend-Lease to bribe French sailors who called at US ports to desert and join it. At a dinner with Eden in Washington, Roosevelt trotted out his notion of the new country of Wallonia made up of north-east France, Belgium and Luxembourg. The Americans briefed the press that de Gaulle was a dictatorial figure surrounded by extreme right-wingers while Giraud was a simple soldier who would protect democracy – Muselier popped up in Algiers to assist Giraud. Roosevelt sent Monnet there to make his favoured French general a more acceptable political figure. Visiting London, the Catholic Archbishop of New York, Francis Spellman, urged de Gaulle to work with Giraud and show Christian charity by forgiving officials who had served Vichy. It would, this political man of the church added, be unfortunate if the Americans were obliged to do without him when France was liberated.

De Gaulle was not swayed. Taking a military approach to politics, he ran a brilliant offensive campaign in the months after the Anfa summit, combining forceful frontal attacks, guerrilla thrusts and sudden expressions of sweet reasonableness. He remained behind the lines in London rather than venturing into the uncertain waters of Algiers. But, on the ground in North Africa, local councils came out for him; when Allied troops entered the town of Sfax in Tunisia, the welcoming crowd shouted '*Vive de Gaulle!*' French regiments joined

Fighting France. On May Day, Gaullists and Communists marched side by side in Algiers shouting, 'We want de Gaulle.' Above all, the General now had a trump card that would defeat Giraud and enable him to face down Roosevelt.[12]

12

RESISTANCE AND COLLABORATION

I
Intelligence

On 17 July 1940 the Free French movement sent its first agent across the Channel, a young man called Jacques Mansion who had been wounded during the fighting and whose papers were in order so that he could move about freely. He was soon followed by two others. Their mission was to collect information about conditions in France and to bring it back to London. They had no radio transmitters, and two of them took carrier pigeons which they abandoned for fear of being too conspicuous. They, and those who followed, made the journey by sea, counting on the connivance of port authorities in the far west of France. To disguise their purpose, their vessels were equipped with fishing gear and powered by sails, since fishermen in the area had no fuel to drive their motors. The British naturally wanted to use members of the Free French for intelligence purposes through the Special Operations Executive (SOE) set up by Churchill to 'set Europe alight'. But, then and in future, de Gaulle was intent on preventing his hosts trespassing on his reserved domain.

While Mansion and his colleagues operated individually or in tiny groups, Passy picked Gilbert Renault, a former *Action française* sympathiser and unsuccessful film producer who had followed a circuitous route to London, to set up a full network of agents in France. The day before he returned to France, Renault, who took the codename Rémy, went with the intelligence chief to see de Gaulle at the Connaught. The General stood with his back to an open fire, serene and seemingly in good humour as he smoked a cigar. He waved his guests to armchairs. As he stirred his cup, de Gaulle fell silent, as if in a dream. Then he suddenly said, 'So you are going back.'

'Yes, *mon Général.*'

'Well, you are going to be caught.'

'I hope not, *mon Général.*'

'But yes,' de Gaulle said good-naturedly. 'One always gets caught in that line of work.'

Rémy made his way to a château owned by a friend on the Vichy side of the demarcation line in the Dordogne which he used as his headquarters. He recruited agents among port officials, merchant-shipping captains and railway station managers in western France whose information about the movement of German troops and supplies could be used to guide British air and sea attacks, keep tabs on the enemy's heavy warships stationed at Brest and furnish details of German coastal defences. The ring was given a name which reflected traditionalist, religious sentiments, the *Confrérie Notre-Dame* (the Brotherhood of Our Lady).

Passy's intelligence-gathering operation evolved into what became known as the *Bureau Central de Renseignements et d'Action* (Central Bureau for Intelligence and Operations) (BCRA) with divisions for information, action, counter-espionage, politics and escape. On the British side, the SOE had its own intelligence operation in France, based on a network called Alliance set up by a brilliant former member of the far right-wing *Cagoule* movement, Georges Loustaunau-Lacau. Daladier had him imprisoned as a conspirator early in the war, but he escaped from a military hospital in the occupied zone in August 1940, and went to Vichy to put together a new version of an anti-Communist unit he had headed in the army. Pétain put him in charge of a veterans' association which he used to form his own resistance movement as he became disillusioned with the collaborationist regime.

Loustaunau and de Gaulle did not get on – the Free French leader admitted the other man's intelligence but thought he lacked 'weight and judgement', while the other man compared the General to a lift that never stopped at the right floor. Another bone of contention between them was Loustaunau's cooperation with the British who funded his group through Switzerland. In 1942, the Alliance chief was arrested by the French police and subsequently sent to the concentration camp at Mauthausen, which he survived. His ring continued to operate under his associate Marie-Madeleine Méric, the only woman who headed a Resistance intelligence outfit. It lost 303 of its members to execution while 520 were deported to Germany.[1]

II
The underground

When Rémy and Loustaunau began their intelligence operations, the Resistance barely existed. A few individuals had distributed pamphlets denouncing the armistice, but theirs were isolated voices. Though one of its members, Charles Tillon, immediately raised a flag of refusal, the Communist Party was gagged by the Nazi–Soviet pact for the first two years of the war. In 1939 its leader, Maurice Thorez, who went to Moscow, denounced French support for Poland as imperialist aid for 'the oppressors of the people'. Everything changed in June 1941 when the Wehrmacht rolled into Russia and Moscow proclaimed an armed struggle against the occupiers. Adopting united-front tactics to draw in non-Communists, the Party's *Front National* (National Front) movement eventually grew into the largest Resistance group in France, with an action branch known as the *Francs-tireurs partisans* (FTP) (Partisan irregular snipers).

Non-Communist groups which sprang up in the Vichy zone had a varied political membership. Several were headed by men who hailed from the far right. Some limited their aim to fighting the occupying power or the Pétainist administration. Others looked further ahead to a national revolution. The unifying element was a refusal to admit defeat.

Libération-sud, created in July 1941 with Socialist support, was headed by an aristocrat, Emmanuel d'Astier de la Vigerie, who had begun as an anti-Semitic monarchist but moved to the Left and hoped to bring together Socialists, Communists and trade unionists. In November 1941, another non-Communist group, *Combat*, was founded in Lyon under Henri Frenay, a former officer who came from the Right but had grown disillusioned with the Vichy regime; its newspaper, which bore the unit's name, was edited by the novelist Albert Camus. Another group based in Lyon, *Franc-tireur* (Sniper), had a similarly wide appeal, drawing members from the far left and far right, Communists and *Action française*. Lyon became the focal point for the growing force of partisans known as *L'Armée des Ombres* (the Army of the Shadows).

Resistance groups in the occupied zone were smaller and more fragmented as they sought to evade the attention of German security. One early ring formed by anthropologists and ethnologists at the Musée de l'Homme in Paris was uncovered in February 1941, and most of its members executed. The Socialist Christian Pineau launched *Libération-nord* which linked with d'Astier's group. *Combat* spread across the demarcation line, though many of its members were shot after being betrayed in early 1942. Other groups were created at the Sorbonne and by industrialists who wanted to see a British victory. Charles Tillon continued his campaign, while another PCF member, Auguste Lecœur, organised a strike by miners in northern France in May 1941.

Sabotage became a prime Resistance activity, notably in the '*bataille du rail*' to destroy tracks and disrupt enemy traffic. In 1942–3, units stormed several factories and a big power plant as well as a German artillery depot in Grenoble. Collaborationists were attacked and raids were mounted to free captured fighters. Resistance newspapers, usually consisting of four small pages, blossomed – one count put their number at more than a thousand, the biggest with circulations of more than 100,000 and, in one case, 450,000 by 1944. In the autumn of 1942, the first edition of a Resistance literary review, *Les Lettres françaises*, appeared and, the following year, a song broadcast from London, '*Ami, entends-tu?*' ('Friend, do you hear?') was adapted as a rallying anthem, '*Le Chant des Partisans*'.

From August 1941, hit-and-run assassinations of occupation troops began; they aroused controversy, then and afterwards, as to their effectiveness and cost, as the Germans stepped up reprisal executions. In October 1941, fifty people were shot at a camp near Bordeaux and forty-seven in the western town of Chateaubriand in retaliation for attacks on Germans and prominent collaborators. The next day, de Gaulle advised against further assassinations by the Resistance. While it was 'absolutely normal and absolutely justified' that Germans should be killed by French people, he warned that it was too easy for the enemy to massacre French fighting men in return. It was not advice likely to be followed by those on the ground. For them, de Gaulle was a voice on the radio not a front-line commander. 'We took our first steps without him,' Christian Pineau recalled. 'He was not living in national territory and was not sharing our dangers.'[2]

III
Jean Moulin

In September 1941, the former civil servant Jean Moulin, who had tried to cut his throat when the Germans invaded France (he wore a scarf thereafter to hide the scar), arrived in London via Portugal, claiming to be the delegate of three Resistance movements. This was untrue; he had had some contacts with Resistance leaders, but represented nobody. He was, however, a rare recruit from the senior ranks of the French administration and a man of undoubted talent. He also quickly became a Gaullist believer. In January 1942, he was parachuted into Provence with the mission of uniting the Resistance under de Gaulle's umbrella, a set of orders and 250,000 francs.

Moulin, a secretive man who excelled at playing several roles at once, had been chief of staff to the Aviation Minister, Pierre Cot, during the Popular Front government, and helped to organise the smuggling of arms to the Republicans in the Spanish civil war, which brought him into contact with Soviet agents. He then became France's youngest prefect in the Aveyron department before being promoted to the same post in Chartres in 1939. Though he lost his job, he was allowed to move around, and got in touch with an underground Communist cell in Paris before crossing to the Vichy zone and then heading to London.

Moulin's real political loyalties remain a matter of debate. If he was not a covert Communist, he was certainly close to members of the PCF. But he saw de Gaulle as the rallying point which the Resistance required, around whom he wanted to group the pre-war political parties, creating a broad-based movement which would pay ultimate allegiance to the General. Returning to the Vichy zone, Moulin lived a double life as a retired prefect outside Avignon and as a Resistance organiser in Lyon under the codenames 'Rex' and 'Max', working to bring the disparate groups together in what became known as the *Armée secrète* (Secret Army).

After Moulin's visit to Britain, a string of other Resistance figures made the same journey; there was also support from further afield, including backers organised by the ethnologist Jacques Soustelle in Latin America and the academic Georges Gorse in Egypt. In October 1942, Frenay and d'Astier sailed from Bordeaux for a meeting of Resistance chiefs in London with de Gaulle (but without Moulin) at which the two men led the opposition to the former prefect, whose powers they resented. The General made his intentions quite plain. At the end of one discussion, he said simply: 'I shall give orders.' When Frenay said that, while they would follow orders as soldiers, they remained free citizens in other respects, the General replied: 'Well, France will choose between you and me.'

De Gaulle's desire to establish a traditional form of authority over the Resistance groups was evident in the appointment of a general, Charles Delestraint, who had shared his enthusiasm for armoured warfare in the 1930s, to head the *Armée secrète,* which was to be apolitical. Moulin would preside over a committee bringing together the three main Resistance groups, with which other units were required to affiliate. The seeds of a battle between the General and the Resistance were thus sown from the start and there were soon violent quarrels between Frenay and Delestraint. But, for the moment, a form of unity was necessary to fight the occupiers.

While de Gaulle's wife and children had reached safety in Britain, twenty or so relations fought in France, either in the army before the defeat or in the Resistance. Madeleine de Gaulle, wife of the General's brother Pierre, belonged to one of the earliest networks in Paris as well as sheltering partisans in Normandy. Arrested by the Gestapo in November 1941, she was subsequently released and escaped on foot across the Pyrenees to Spain with six children, one the adopted daughter of an executed Resistance fighter. Her husband was among several members of the family active in the Resistance who were dispatched to camps in Germany but survived; the General's niece, Geneviève, was sent to Ravensbrück concentration camp, where Himmler ordered her to be kept alive in case she might be useful as a bargaining counter with the Allies. De Gaulle's sister Marie-Agnès, and her Belgian engineer husband, Alfred Cailliau, were deported to Germany, while their paralysed brother, Jacques, was rescued from German detention by a priest and carried across the Swiss border.[3]

IV
The politics of resistance

In London, de Gaulle had a formidable weapon in the form of BBC broadcasts which were used to pass coded messages to the Resistance as well as maintaining a drumbeat of propaganda against Vichy and the Germans. The medium suited its star perfectly, his voice delivered over the air wave as if he was a mystical force soaring above temporal constraints. His oratorical style improved steadily as he gained in assurance and lost the slight hesitation noticed by some listeners at the start.

A formal programme, *Honneur et Patrie* (Honour and Fatherland), was accompanied by the lighter *Les Français parlent aux Français* (the French speak to the French). As well as journalists and spokespeople, writers who contributed scripts ranged from leading literary figures such as Georges Bernanos and the philosopher Jacques Maritain to the great comic wordsmith Pierre Dac. Vichy figures showed the audience rising from 300,000 at the start of 1941 to ten times that during the following year. After tuning in to the broadcasts, listeners did well to spin the dial on their radio sets before turning off lest they be incriminated in the case of a raid.

The General's own broadcasts meant that his voice became well known, the sound of a public persona whose messages repeated the call to resistance and refusal to accept defeat. In response, Vichy launched a wave of propaganda campaigns against 'General Micro'. Posters showed him as a barrage balloon floating from a boat occupied by Churchill which was pierced by a Vichy soldier's bayonet at Dakar. Another, adorned with hook-nosed Jewish predators, identified a sexual illness, *dingaullitte* – a play on his name and *dingue*, French slang for madness.[4]

De Gaulle would reflect that he had been obliged to accept support wherever it came from to maintain his role as the embodiment of France. Had he picked and chosen among his followers, he added, he would have reduced himself to the leader of a party in exile. This meant rejecting the advice of a prominent Resistance figure, the Socialist Pierre Brossolette, who argued that he should create a movement with a left-wing bias which would replace the old parties of the Third Republic and revolutionise French politics. Despite his contempt for the system to which he attributed a significant part of France's weakness in 1940, the General preferred Moulin's strategy of working with the existing political movements; he believed that, by incarnating the nation, he could dominate them. Working with the non-collaborationist parties which had won seats at the last peacetime election would provide a counter to Roosevelt's accusation that he was a dictator in the making, and provide him with a degree of the legitimacy he claimed for himself.

In January 1943, the various movements agreed to come under the broad umbrella organisation set up by Moulin in the *Mouvements unis de la résistance* (United Resistance Movements) (MUR) which became the *Conseil National de la Résistance* (National Council of the Resistance) (CNR) at a meeting of its leaders in a flat in Paris the following May. This did not mean Moulin's presidency of the internal Resistance was easily accepted – there was a running debate between the former prefect and Brossolette – but the need for a central figure was clear, and de Gaulle was the only person who could fill that role. Emmanuel d'Astier de la Vigerie took to referring to him as 'the Symbol'. 'Most of us were prepared to recognise his authority,' Pineau recalled after a stormy session with the General in London. 'For we needed a flag, if not a guide.'

The main political conundrum de Gaulle faced, during and immediately after the war, was how he should deal with the Communists, the largest element in the Resistance, whose appeal was enhanced by the progress made by the Red Army against the Germans on the Eastern Front. De Gaulle wrote to a Communist trade union leader, Léon Jouhaux, seeking cooperation, and Rémy had talks with a Communist Resistance leader, Pierre Villon, which established contact even if the two men were far apart. The subservience of the Communist Party (PCF) to Moscow meant that it was difficult to count on its leaders, but, if de Gaulle was to pursue his goal of national unity, he had to work with it if it would work with him.

A working relationship with the PCF could also serve the General's goal of forging a relationship with Moscow to balance his dependence on the material support of Britain and act as a counter to Roosevelt. The Free French had been to see the Soviet ambassador in London, Ivan Maisky. Following the dispatch of French pilots to the USSR, the General sent a small military mission to Moscow as well as offering to move troops from North Africa to the Caucasus, an idea the British vetoed. When Vichy broke off relations with the Kremlin, Maisky transferred recognition to the Gaullist movement. There was, in truth, little de Gaulle could offer Moscow, and Stalin had a low opinion of France. This did not deter the General. At a meeting with the Soviet ambassador in neutral Ankara in August 1941, the Free French representative, Gérard Jouve, handed over a message from his leader saying France and the USSR were both continental powers and so did not necessarily have the same war aims as the essentially maritime USA and Britain.

Such long-term thinking was always a hallmark of de Gaulle's approach, but, set against political parties such as the Communists and Socialists, Gaullism was still quite inchoate as a philosophy, apart from its core nationalism and its increasing embrace of democracy. It was not until 24 June 1943 that the General used the word Gaullism for the first time, in a letter in which he put it in inverted commas as referring to those who 'back me with passion'. Gaullism at that point consisted mainly of a series of pronouncements from the leader that hardly amounted to a platform on which a country could be run. A Vichy report of 1943 was not entirely mistaken in reporting that many people saw it as 'a sort of anti-German thought, more than a policy or a programme'. The General's experience was quite limited. The depth of his backing was unknown. While he had deeply committed followers around him and talked of 'an entirely new France guided by entirely new men', his broad-tent approach meant that it was difficult to evolve a detailed ideology for fear of alienating one section or other of his supporters.

So the question arose of whether the highly disciplined Communists would use him as a figurehead and then brush him aside as they staged a takeover. Pierre Villon envisaged a popular uprising that would make de Gaulle redundant. The united-front tactics of the Party's *Front National* in working with non-Communists, including Catholic groups, aroused suspicions that it was trying to infiltrate them. Henri Frenay asked whether de Gaulle was to play the role taken by the moderate Alexander Kerensky in the Russian Revolution before the victory of the Bolsheviks.[5]

V
Collaboration

The Nazis regarded France as a rich source of money and resources as their wartime expansion strained the German economy. By 1943, annual state payments from France to the Reich had risen to the equivalent of 31 per cent of the pre-war gross national product, and contributed 9 per cent of the Reich's GDP. The occupiers requisitioned food, and modern industrial machinery. Renault and Citroën supplied 30,000 vehicles a year. French factories turned out weapons valued at thirty-one billion francs between 1940 and 1943, and delivered 2,517 military aircraft during the war. Railway rolling stock was sent to Germany or commandeered by the occupation forces, accentuating the dislocation of the economy.

After 1942, the pillage of French resources spread to its population. Vichy traded three workers for every prisoner of war freed by the victors, a scheme that developed into the *Service du Travail Obligatoire* (Obligatory Labour Service) (STO) which conscripted labour for Germany and greatly boosted the number of young men who evaded it by joining the Resistance in the *maquis*. It has been calculated that, in all, 4.5 million French people went to work in Germany.

France had another importance for the Nazis. It would be the battlefield for the Allied counter-offensive, whenever and wherever that came. In 1942, Hitler ordered the construction of the Atlantic Wall, a series of coastal fortresses from Dunkirk to the Spanish border designed to guard against attack. After his eclipse in North Africa, Rommel was rehabilitated to oversee the preparations, which involved further use of French labour to build up the defences and also provided contracts for French collaborative businesses.

While France did not suffer as badly as countries overrun by the Nazis in eastern Europe, food was often scarce. As queues lengthened, inflation soared and barter became common. The black market thrived. Social life was restricted by regulations, curfews and the danger of arousing suspicion. Georges Simenon told his publisher to produce an advertisement suggesting people stay at home and spend the winter rereading all his books. Colette's advice that the best way of surviving was to stay in bed was not entirely a joke, and, along with the pro-family rhetoric of Vichy, may have been a factor in the growth of fertility during the war, despite the gloom and uncertainty; among the babies were an estimated 50–80,000 born from liaisons between German soldiers and French women.

The rich and powerful, and those who adapted their wits to the new situation, escaped relatively unscathed, although Jews were always at risk – the wife of Baron Philippe de Rothschild was deported to Ravensbrück while her husband escaped to join the Free French. A brittle form of high society life continued in Paris where swastika flags replaced the tricolours on the rue de Rivoli, official buildings and big hotels. The occupiers took control of top-class restaurants, ensuring that their favourite haunts received enough coal to keep them heated. In his diary, the German officer and writer Ernst Jünger compared diners at the Tour d'Argent restaurant overlooking Notre-Dame to 'gargoyles, seeing below them, with a kind of diabolical satisfaction, the grey oceans of roof tops under which the starving tried to keep body and soul together. In such times, eating well and copiously gives a feeling of power.'

French artists, entertainers and writers faced the choice of continuing to work, which inevitably brought them into contact with the new authorities, or retreating into silence. Most found a modus vivendi. 'Will I be understood if I say that the Occupation was, at the same time, intolerable and that we accommodated ourselves to it very well?' asked Jean-Paul Sartre. The playwright, actor and wit Sacha Guitry was to be seen at Abetz's embassy on the rue de Lille on the Left Bank in Paris, while the choreographer Serge Lifar received German top brass at the Opera. French writers called on Goebbels. The popular singer Tino Rossi gave two gala performances in the context of a German-approved exhibition on the building of a new Europe. Maurice Chevalier and Édith Piaf performed at prisoner-of-war camps in Germany. Leading French actors, artists and musicians were fêted in the Reich. Both the fashion queen Coco Chanel and the celebrated actress Arletty had affairs with German officers while living at the Ritz. The owner of the newspaper *Le Matin* held dinners with flowers arranged on the table in the shape of a swastika.

The cinema flourished under the aegis of the Continental Film Company set up at Goebbels' behest to make entertaining productions to divert the population. Its work was often technically brilliant but, of necessity, addressed the state of the country only indirectly, if at all. Most films were what has been dubbed 'a cinema of silence'. Some of France's leading figures preferred to spend the war in Hollywood, while the actor Jean Gabin joined the Free French and was decorated twice for valour fighting in North Africa.

Though industrialists headed by the boss of the electricity company in the Rhône and Jura regions organised a group which sabotaged a big power station, most businessmen went along with the occupation. In January 1941, thirty-five representatives of banks, industry and commerce joined technocratic ministers from Vichy at a dinner with a German general to lay plans for economic collaboration. When the Resistance tried to get Michelin tyre firm managers to sabotage plants supplying the Germans, they were told that this would be 'indecent and useless'. After Allied bombings of his factories, Louis Renault was obsessive about getting the production lines going again.[6]

Repression grew steadily. In Paris, the occupation authorities used gangsters to track down and kill opponents. In Vichy in 1942, the government recognised a militia, the *Service d'Ordre Légionnaire* (SOL), headed by a First World War veteran, Joseph Darnand, who had not initially joined the collaborationist effort but whose ardent anti-Communism led him to do so after war broke out between Germany and the USSR. In 1943, Laval asked him to create the *Milice* (Militia) as a paramilitary force which worked increasingly with the Germans in combating the Resistance.

The greatest violence, and the greatest stain on wartime France, was the fate of its Jewish population, numbering some 330,000, of whom 190,000 were French citizens. Anti-Semitism had been a theme of the Right for decades. The Jews, many of them first-generation immigrants from eastern Europe, had no protectors. Anti-Jewish legislation was promulgated by Vichy from August 1940. In March 1941, the Pétain regime established a General Commissariat for Jewish Questions, headed by a prominent anti-Semitic parliamentarian, Xavier Vallat. He proved too moderate for the SS and was replaced by the more extreme Louis Darquier de Pellepoix, who combined racial obsession with dissembling self-promotion.

In the northern zone the pro-German press began to talk at the beginning of 1942 of 'a final reckoning for the Jews', who were ordered to wear Star of David patches made of gold-coloured cloth, for which they were charged two clothing coupons. They were banned from working and excluded from public places. Jewish veterans of the First World War were among the persecuted.

Round-ups started in May 1941 and gathered pace in 1942 when 5,800 women, 4,000 children and 3,000 men were taken from their homes. The operation was planned with the Gestapo and SS by Darquier de Pellepoix and René Bousquet, Secretary-General of the French national police. In agreement with Laval, Bousquet ordered that children be included. He got French police to do the work, in part to reassure the Germans that his men could be trusted. About 7,500 of those detained were herded into the Paris cycling stadium, the Vél d'Hiv, where they were held for five days in stifling summer heat. There was one water tap and no lavatories. Then they were moved to camps outside Paris before being taken to Auschwitz. Laval expressed satisfaction at having got rid of such 'dregs' of society.

As a reward, the Germans gave Bousquet additional arms for his police with which to fight the Resistance. In August 1942, deportations of Jews from Vichy France began. French police and the SS worked together on round-ups in Marseille, classified as 'moral cleansing'. In all, some 75,000 Jews would be deported from France in terrible conditions to concentration camps in eastern Europe. Only 3 per cent returned alive.[7]

*

Morality and human lives apart, by 1942 the bankruptcy of Laval's state-to-state collaboration became clear. The grand plans of the Vichy technocrats made little headway. Some nationalists resented subjection to the Germans; the *Croix de Feu* leader Colonel de La Rocque got in touch with British Intelligence. *Attentisme* – that is, waiting for the Allies to arrive – became common among civil servants, some of whom began to play a double game, as in the case of the future President François Mitterrand. Having escaped from a German detention camp, he took a job in the Vichy department for prisoners of war but also became involved with the Resistance. In the autumn of 1942, he was in contact with the *Combat* network while also meeting Pétain, who decorated him. He established links with Giraud and, at the end of 1943, crossed to London and then to Algiers where he met de Gaulle. The two men did not get on.

French Fascists who found Vichy too soft gravitated to Paris where they formed political parties, and published magazines. The former Communist Jacques Doriot spewed out pro-Nazi propaganda on Radio Paris. The one-time Socialist Marcel Déat, who had briefly been Aviation Minister in the 1930s before making waves with his 1939 article 'Why Die for Danzig?', founded the biggest collaborationist party, the *Rassemblement National Populaire* (National Popular Rally) (RNP). Déat and Doriot, the first short with a thick moustache, the second taller, corpulent and wearing round spectacles, created the *Légion des volontaires français* (Legion of French Volunteers) to fight alongside the Wehrmacht in the Soviet Union. Membership of their movements was limited; the RNP probably never had more than 20,000 members. However, collaborationist newspapers and magazines reached a larger public. Déat's had a circulation of 130,000 and the violently anti-Semitic *Je Suis partout* (I am everywhere) reached 300,000 in 1944. Its editor, Robert Brasillach, a brilliant manipulator of the French language, called for the death of leftist politicians and the summary execution of members of the Resistance. For such arch collaborators, France needed a populist revolution of the far right to enable it to take its proper place in a new Europe alongside Germany. 'If necessary, France will cover itself with concentration camps and execution squads will work round the clock,' wrote Déat. 'The birth of a new regime is carried out with forceps and in pain.'

However, Hitler saw no need to enlist France as an ally. He did not intend to make the country a slave state or to exterminate its inhabitants, but had no interest in a meaningful alliance. Absolute German supremacy was what the Führer wanted. The collaborators had, at best, minor supporting roles. As that hard reality set in, they grew ever more extreme. Some really believed in a German victory. They had committed themselves so deeply and so publicly that they could not turn back, caught inexorably in their engagement with evil.

That facilitated de Gaulle's task. When the Germans retreated, as he was sure they would, the collaborationist house of cards would collapse. This made it important to solidify the Gaullist links with the Resistance. In February 1943, Moulin and General Delestraint visited London where they had lengthy talks with the General and his staff as well as with British military figures. Moulin was confirmed as the head of the Council of the Resistance, which was to act 'with de Gaulle in the fight he leads to set the country free and to give the power of decision back to Frenchmen'. The General's advice not to kill Germans was discarded. In his memoirs, he described the ceremony at his home in Hampstead in which he presented Moulin with the Cross of the Liberation as the most moving of any in which he participated.[8]

13

BLITZKRIEG

I

'France is a great power'

For all the hopes America entrusted in him, Giraud could not cope with the challenge de Gaulle mounted in the summer of 1943. As an orthodox commander, King Pin depended on static defence in the form of American support and the local establishment in Algiers, which was, however, poorly coordinated and weakened by its association with Vichy. What he now faced was a political rerun of the Panzer surge of 1940, except that this time the offensive was directed by a Frenchman.

De Gaulle, on the other hand, was in his element, helped by the way in which the course of the war was proving he had been right in 1940. The Germans had surrendered at Stalingrad. As well as Torch, there had been the Allied victory at El Alamein, and preparations were being made to invade Sicily. In the Pacific, Japan was in retreat. America's industrial machine was pumping out tanks, aircraft and guns. France's armed forces had made a mark during the campaign in Tunisia, which had seen the re-emergence of a skilled soldier, Algerian-born Alphonse Juin, who had been held as a prisoner by the Germans in 1940–41 and had then returned to serve Vichy as commander in North Africa. After Torch, he switched sides. De Gaulle did not hold his service for the Marshal against him. A contemporary at Saint-Cyr, Juin was one of the very few people whom he addressed by the second person singular *tu*. The long-time post-war Gaullist Olivier Guichard thought that Juin was the person outside his family with whom de Gaulle came closest to intimacy.[1]

Giraud was prompted by his American-sponsored tutor, Monnet, to make a speech denouncing the armistice, stressing French sovereignty and praising democracy. When his rightist supporters protested, he replied: 'I don't believe a word of what I said; that was only politics.' He also told the visiting American diplomat Averell Harriman that, after defeating Germany, the Western allies must drive back Soviet forces. Harriman regarded this as preposterous. Giraud came under added pressure when the Fighting France leader made a speech insisting that France faced only two choices – 'the cross of Lorraine for almost all, the old Marshal for some'. His committee sought national unity, which required a strong central authority with majority support among the French based on just laws, he said. On the other hand, he added, his rival had been 'elected' by civil servants faithful to Pétain who maintained a repressive regime.

Monnet denounced this as 'Hitlerian' and, in a private note, called the General 'an enemy of the French people and its freedoms; an enemy of European reconstruction in peace and order'. This meant that 'he must be destroyed in the interests of the French, the Allies and peace', the banker-diplomat added. Still, he knew that Giraud could not be imposed as sole leader and joined the British Minister for North Africa Harold Macmillan in putting forward a proposal for a committee with the two generals as co-chairmen. Each would name two representatives, with three other members brought in from outside. Giraud agreed and Catroux and Macmillan flew to Britain to seal the accord with the Fighting France leader. That was followed by a fresh expression of support from the Resistance Council, which called for a provisional government in Algiers presided over by de Gaulle with Giraud as military chief. 'Whatever the outcome of negotiations, General de Gaulle will remain the only chief of the French Resistance,' concluded a statement adopted by a clandestine meeting in Paris.

At the end of May, it was time for the General to leave London for the front line. Before departing, he wrote a two-paragraph letter to Churchill who was meeting Roosevelt in Washington; he expressed no thanks for British help, though he did say that he was more certain than ever that his host would be 'the man of the days of glory as you have been the man of the worst moments'. What he did not know was that, at the Anglo-American summit, Roosevelt was suggesting that Britain should 'eliminate de Gaulle as a political force', perhaps by posting him as Governor of Madagascar, while a new committee including Herriot and the anti-Gaullist diplomat Alexis Léger might reach an accord with Giraud. The Prime Minister sent a message to London envisaging ending backing for de Gaulle. A Sunday night Cabinet meeting turned this down, and Churchill advised Roosevelt that he had to bow to the decision. Nonetheless, he cabled his colleagues about the 'dangers to the Anglo-American unity inherent in your championship of de Gaulle . . . a Frenchman who is a bitter foe of Britain and may well bring civil war upon France'.

Before leaving London on 30 May 1943, de Gaulle had a meeting with Eden at which the Foreign Secretary asked him what he thought of the British.

'Nobody's more friendly than your people,' the General replied. 'I do not always think the same of your policy.'

'Do you know that, of all the European allies, you have caused us the most difficulties?' Eden asked in a friendly tone.

'I don't doubt that,' de Gaulle replied with a smile. 'France is a great power.'[2]

II
Algiers

Shortly before midnight on 30 May 1943, Charles de Gaulle emerged from his aircraft, decorated with Fighting France colours, at the smaller of the two Algiers airports. He concluded that it had been chosen by Giraud to prevent a crowd welcoming him. Waiting at the bottom of the steps, his rival greeted him with 'Hello, Gaulle', a salutation he had used at Anfa to the General's annoyance at the dropping of the quasi-aristocratic 'de'. On the drive into town, de Gaulle asked whom Giraud intended to name to the new committee. At the mention of Jean Monnet, the General remarked, 'Yes, the little financier in the pay of England.' Giraud added the name of General Georges, the deputy army commander in 1940, to which de Gaulle replied that his war record was 'rather rotten'.

His first gesture was to lay a wreath in the form of a Cross of Lorraine at the war memorial in the centre of the city. A throng of people, swollen by members of the Resistance who had been alerted, cheered. The General made a short address and then broke into the national anthem, joined by those around him. It was the kind of scene which was to be repeated again and again by a man who, whatever his personal shyness, knew how to play a crowd to perfection.

Meeting Monnet, he spoke very critically of the Americans and the British. Afterwards, Monnet told Macmillan that it was difficult to know 'if the General was a dangerous demagogue, a madman or both'. At the first formal meeting of the two camps on 31 May in a *lycée* overlooking Algiers, de Gaulle insisted that, as military commander, Giraud must be under civilian control. Senior Pétainist officials in Africa must be replaced, he added. Not getting agreement from Giraud or Monnet, he picked up his papers and strode from the room. That night Giraud wrote a letter accusing him of wanting to create a Nazi-style dictatorship in France, and called in Muselier to take charge of law and order. At the same time, the Governor General of Algeria, Marcel Peyrouton, sent de Gaulle his resignation, which was promptly accepted. When Giraud learned of this, he reacted with such fury that Harold Macmillan thought he had lost his wits.

As rumours of a putsch by pro-Giraud forces flew around Algiers, de Gaulle had a sticky lunch with Churchill, who was visiting. Still, he took another step forward when a new body, the *Comité français de la Libération nationale* (French Committee of National Liberation), was announced on 4 June. This brought together the existing organisation in Algiers and the internal Resistance. The two generals were joint Presidents. The non-Gaullist camp was represented by General Georges and Monnet, who were balanced by the diplomat René Massigli and André Philip, a Socialist who had been a leader of the Resistance in northern France. The Gaullist Louis Joxe was its Secretary-General.

The General summoned from London Pleven, André Diethelm, Mandel's former chief of staff, and Jacques Soustelle, who had become a leading figure in Fighting France. To show his displeasure with the pressures on him, he boycotted a session of the committee on 10 June. His suspicions could only be heightened when the *Observer* newspaper in London published an unsigned statement drawn up by Churchill stating that French opinion did not support de Gaulle and that the Allies were getting tired of him. Macmillan was more accommodating, even trying a touch of levity when he told de Gaulle that he was so obstinate he might have been a Scot; to which the General replied that his great-grandmother had been from Scotland.

The British minister also invited de Gaulle to accompany him on an expedition to the ancient Carthaginian trading post of Tipasa. While Macmillan swam naked in the Mediterranean, the Constable sat on a rock in uniform. They discussed politics, religion, history, philosophy and Roman and Greek literature, and had supper in an inn. Macmillan recalled the General as 'attractive and yet impossible'. It was a rare moment of relaxation for somebody who never let up until victory – if then. To his wife de Gaulle wrote: 'You cannot imagine the atmosphere of lies and false news in which our good allies and their good friends here (even those who fired on them in the past) are trying to drown me. One has to have a solid heart and keep France in front of one's eyes not to let everything slip.'[3]

*

The General established his office in a villa, Les Glycines, in the suburb of El-Biar on the heights overlooking Algiers. Palewski, Soustelle and General Pierre Billotte were his closest collaborators. It was a crowded place and the Fighting France leader worked in the sitting room in which the temperature rose above 100 degrees Fahrenheit. The wallpaper was blue and gold, the curtains thick, and the paintings of imaginary desert scenes in North Africa. Some of the staff slept on camp beds; one compared it to 'a junk shop'.

In July, Yvonne flew to Algiers to join her husband in their new home, a large Moorish building known as Les Oliviers, close to Les Glycines. In his memoirs, de Gaulle recalled how saddened he and his wife were by Anne's condition; they had powdered milk flown in for her. He tried to devote his evenings to writing his frequent speeches, but often had to receive French and foreign visitors. Food supplies were short. At the weekends, the family sometimes drove out to stay at a small house in the

Kabylie region between the sea and the Atlas Mountains. To begin with, Yvonne felt quite isolated, but then her other daughter, Élisabeth, arrived, working in the office which collated foreign press stories. They acquired a pet okapi which they called Lorraine. Despite the summer heat, *Madame la Générale* remained true to her northern French notion of decorum, wearing severe black clothes and a matching hat while the other women appeared in light dresses.[4]

Her husband was still tense, worrying about plots but intent on pursuing his own course. After dinner one night, he remarked to Pleven and Joxe that, during the Hundred Years War, 'treason was everywhere and reached to the steps to the throne, but Joan of Arc remained Joan of Arc. She did not compromise herself in these Monnet-style committees.' Still, when the full Algiers committee was appointed, the extent of de Gaulle's success became apparent. It included six supporters, among them Pleven, who was responsible for colonies, an important post given the location of most of Fighting France's support.

René Massigli retained Foreign Affairs and André Philip ran the department dealing with mainland France. At Giraud's request, the finance portfolio went to a former Vichy official, Maurice Couve de Murville, who had gone to Algiers to work with him, but who moved steadily towards the Fighting France leader. As time went on, a string of other figures with government experience from the 1930s rallied round the General. A former Third Republic minister, the Radical Socialist Henri Queuille, chaired interministerial commissions, using political skills learned under the old regime to smooth over differences. Though still keeping his distance, Monnet rallied, and sought to get supplies from the Americans.

Henri Frenay and Emmanuel d'Astier crossed from France to represent the Resistance. Pierre Mendès France, the Popular Front Deputy Finance Minister who had escaped from detention under Vichy to London and joined the Fighting France air force, arrived to help manage economic affairs. When his name was put to de Gaulle, the General blurted out, 'Yet another Jew!' In an interview with Jean Lacouture in June 1980, Mendès commented that 'Anti-Semitism was foreign to him. But he was sensitive to balance and to public opinion; and above all in North Africa public opinion was less innocent than he.'

Algiers was, in some ways, an inferior base to London. It offered no access to British leaders or BBC studios from which to broadcast. Flying agents into France was more difficult than from RAF aerodromes. North Africa's Vichy links had been strong. Though France lay across the Mediterranean, the main invasion battleground in the homeland would be far away in Normandy. But it was French territory and thus a more suitable base on which to rebuild the apparatus of the state.

There were, however, two serious setbacks when both the leaders de Gaulle had picked for the Secret Army were arrested within twelve days of one another. On 9 June, the Gestapo caught General Delestraint; he was imprisoned in camps in Germany and executed as the war ended. A month earlier, Moulin had sent a message to de Gaulle saying that Vichy and the Germans knew everything about his identity and activities. On 21 June, he was arrested outside Lyon and died under torture; whether he was betrayed or caught by German detective work remains a matter of controversy.* As de Gaulle noted in his memoirs, Moulin's death tempted others to play a more individual role, bringing the threat of a split between Resistance groups.

The dead man's deputy had been sent across the Channel only a short time before, and lacked Moulin's authority. De Gaulle dispatched Émile Bollaert, another former prefect who had refused to swear allegiance to Vichy, as his new representative in metropolitan France, but he was caught by the Gestapo and sent to Buchenwald concentration camp. Pierre Brossolette was also detained, and died jumping from a high window of the Gestapo building in Paris. After this period of uncertainty, one of Moulin's close associates, Georges Bidault, a prominent Christian Democrat journalist who was also a member of the Communist-led united front, emerged to hold the Resistance together under the Gaullist umbrella – American attempts to buy support for Giraud with payments made through Switzerland did not get far.

Despite internal problems and losses of leading figures, the Resistance was steadily strengthened by the growing expectation of Allied victory, the imposition of forced labour in Germany and

*One theory is that the Gestapo followed one of Moulin's colleagues who had been arrested and tortured before being freed to lead them to him. Others posit betrayal either by a member of his immediate ring or by the Communists.

increasingly vicious repression. According to a British estimate, the partisans now numbered 150,000, though only 35,000 were properly armed. A US report noted they were 'capable of creating a considerable degree of disruption in the interior of France and of facilitating Allied operations directly as well as indirectly'.[5]

*

Pressing his advantage, de Gaulle insisted that Giraud had to choose between his political and military posts. Gaullist supporters noted that refugees from France, liberals and Jews were refusing to serve under officers who had followed Vichy. De Gaulle received tumultuous welcomes on visits to Morocco and Tunisia. In mid-June, he overawed Eisenhower, walking out at the end of a meeting with the American and Giraud.

Yet the Free French leader remained on a knife edge, and engaged in what was to become a familiar display of histrionics about resigning. One night, returning to his room at 1 a.m., the Fighting France military chief of staff, Pierre Billotte, found a note from de Gaulle attached to his pillow with a safety pin, summoning him. De Gaulle, who had been reading in his dressing gown, gave Billotte a letter to be typed up which contained his resignation from the committee in Algiers on the grounds that he could not work with those who took their orders from the Americans. Billotte left the room with the letter and tore it up. A week later, de Gaulle went through the same process with Catroux, who also refused to take the threat seriously.

One reason for his concern was a further deterioration in relations with the Americans. Blowing up over the General's refusal to work with Governor Boisson in Dakar, Roosevelt threatened to send troops and warships to West Africa to keep out the Fighting France forces. When the Allies invaded Sicily and then Italy, de Gaulle was not informed in advance. Nor was he told when the Italians sought an armistice. Churchill planted another piece in the *Observer*, warning that those who had shown the most sympathy and tolerance for the General could take no more; he must understand that this was his last chance and that American patience was exhausted. Payments to the Fighting France committee in London were suspended. The Prime Minister thought Catroux would make a good replacement and accused de Gaulle of Fascist, dictatorial tendencies.[6]

On the other hand, de Gaulle's position in Algiers strengthened steadily. Despite Giraud's position as commander-in-chief, the General got himself appointed to head a group that oversaw the organisation of French forces. Boisson resigned. French Guiana and Caribbean territories backed the Gaullist cause. Eisenhower decided that de Gaulle was more likely than Giraud to rally support among the French. In another of his recurrent mood swings, Churchill acknowledged that, given the balance of forces in Algiers, it would not be a good thing to get rid of the man of 18 June.

When Giraud returned to Algiers from a trip to the USA at the end of July, he was unable to prevent a restructuring of the national committee under which the two generals remained joint chairpersons but with de Gaulle presiding. The signature on documents of the one-time King Pin became a formality. On 26 August, the committee was recognised by the USA, Britain and the USSR. Giraud aggravated matters by organising a rising in Corsica off his own bat, to which de Gaulle responded with a triumphal visit to the island.

The committee's hierarchy was altered once more to create a single chairmanship, which the General assumed. In his memoirs, Giraud acknowledged: 'I let myself be beaten without a fight . . . On the political level, I was unbelievably incompetent, clumsy and weak.' Macmillan judged that 'never in the whole history of politics has any man frittered away so large a capital in so short a time'. Churchill reacted badly, writing to Roosevelt to suggest a 'complete reserve' towards de Gaulle as a fresh Levantine row broke out after elections in Syria and Lebanon gave majorities to pro-independence politicians.[7]

The result in Syria was no surprise, but the French had hoped that their links with the Christian population of Lebanon would produce a more palatable result. After the Lebanese winners voted through constitutional changes, the French general representing the Algiers committee had their leaders arrested and the Lebanese President deprived of his office. French marines then attacked a group of students approaching the British legation to talk to Spears, who was out. Ten of the protesters were hurt. Eden instructed Macmillan to tell the Algiers committee the repression was 'intolerable'.

Catroux was sent to try to calm things down, but de Gaulle backed the general in charge, who was said to be lucid for only three hours a day. Richard Casey, who had replaced Oliver Lyttelton as Britain's minister in the region, suggested British forces should assure order by occupying the whole country. Eden told him that, if the French did not back down, he should fly to Beirut and threaten to declare martial law. Faced with this ultimatum, the Algiers committee voted to recall its delegate in Lebanon, release the detainees and reinstate the President. Spying a fresh British plot to weaken France, de Gaulle was among three members who voted against this. But he felt he had to give way to new colleagues from the Resistance who valued good relations with London. Though there was no doubt who was in ultimate charge, the leader needed to show some sensitivity to differing shades of opinion if he was to epitomise the national struggle.

III
Sailing on

In the second half of 1943, what the historian Serge Berstein has called 'a virtual republic' was built up in Algiers, ready for the day when it could move to metropolitan France. Boisson and the former Vichy Governor, Peyrouton, were arrested at the end of the year, together with the pre-war Prime Minister, Pierre-Étienne Flandin, who had worked briefly at Vichy. The Algiers committee proclaimed itself the 'sole French central authority' and began to publish its gazette, the *Journal officiel de la République française.*

A reshuffle showed that, whatever his feelings about the Third Republic, de Gaulle wanted to recruit some of its politicians to maintain continuity with the 1930s. Six representatives of the non-Communist parties got posts. Queuille became vice-chair of the committee, replacing de Gaulle when he was absent; the former Third Republic minister's approach was highly unGaullist – he believed that 'politics is not the art of settling problems but of shutting up those who pose them'. Mendès France took charge of economic and financial affairs.

The other four political representatives were two Socialists, a moderate and a Christian Democrat. There were five Resistance figures, including Frenay and Emmanuel d'Astier, and five others, including Monnet, Massigli and Catroux. De Gaulle's desire to add a senior Catholic churchman was thwarted by lack of approval from the Vatican.

An examination of laws passed since June 1940 was launched to decide which would be annulled after the Liberation. A Provisional Consultative Assembly was appointed, including 52 representatives of the Resistance, 20 of the old parliament and 12 of the general councils of the Empire. A Socialist, Félix Gouin, one of the handful of members of the National Assembly who refused to vote powers to Pétain in 1940, became the body's President. There was one female deputy, Lucie Aubrac, from Moulin's network in Lyon. However, a plan for an elected parliament after the Liberation laid down that women would get the vote at last.

Though the assembly was the scene of lively debates on post-war France, de Gaulle's memoirs paint a picture of a political world populated by dreamers, Communists intent on expanding their influence and politicians thinking of their post-war careers. He recalled wondering if 'among all those who spoke of revolution, I was, in fact, the only revolutionary'. He told the committee's representative in Moscow, Roger Garreau, that, though 'entirely favourable' to Communist participation in his administration, he would not give in to the Party's attempt to dictate which posts its representatives would hold.

He also banned the PCF leader, Maurice Thorez, who was in Moscow, from visiting North Africa because of the fuss this would cause and because he had deserted the army in 1940 and so would have to be tried if he set foot on French territory. Though the General did not know this, Stalin had instructed the French Communists to pursue a 'left bloc' line appropriate for France; they should not defy de Gaulle, and should cultivate Socialists and moderate progressives. Two Communists joined the administration in March 1944.[8]

However, the first tripartite summit between Stalin, Roosevelt and Churchill in Tehran at the end of 1943 showed the hill de Gaulle still had to climb. At the meeting, the American and British leaders finally gave a date for the invasion of Normandy – May 1944 – but the committee in Algiers was not to be involved in the planning of the operation in the country it claimed to represent. Stalin took a particularly harsh line. While Roosevelt maintained his dismissive attitude, remarking that nobody aged over forty should be allowed to take part in a future French government, the Soviet dictator said France should not hold its Empire or any strategic positions after the conflict. As for de Gaulle, Stalin said the trouble with him was that he behaved as if he was head of a great state. Fighting France was not given a seat on the Allied Control Commission for Italy though it sent 15,000 troops to fight there in November 1943; the number would rise to 115,000 by the following May.

After the summit, Roosevelt further irritated de Gaulle by instructing Eisenhower to stop the trials of Boisson, Flandin and Peyrouton. Three days later, the President backed down, but then proposed that France be administered by an Anglo-American force under a US commander between Liberation and the holding of elections. Writing to his son, de Gaulle noted that the foreigners were piling up problems under his feet, but 'the final result is certain'. Philippe was serving on a frigate at the time operating in the Atlantic and Arctic, and his father wished that 'God look after you!' '*Au revoir*, my dear little Philippe,' his letter ended. 'I embrace you tenderly. Your very affectionate father.'[9]

IV
'No authority in France other than yours'

On 30 December 1943, Eisenhower went to see de Gaulle in his office at Les Glycines before leaving North Africa for London to plan the invasion of France. Despite the tensions between the French leader and Roosevelt, the two generals had developed real respect for one another. De Gaulle said he was pleased to know that a man like Eisenhower was to command the operation that was 'vital for my country', and advised him to ensure that French troops were present when the Allies entered Paris. Eisenhower replied that he would do so. The American then referred to their differences as he pursued policies laid down by his government, before saying, 'I admit that I was unjust to you and I had to tell you so.'

'You are a man,' de Gaulle responded in English.

'I am prepared to make a declaration stating the confidence I have derived from our contacts, acknowledging my injustice with regard to you,' Eisenhower replied. 'I must tell you that as far as facts are concerned I shall acknowledge no authority in France other than yours.'[10]

But Washington remained intent on sending in military governors of its own after the landings in Normandy under a system known as Allied Military Government for Occupied Territories (AMGOT). The 'O' word could only be a red rag to de Gaulle; he had entered the fight against German occupation eighteen months before the United States, and was not going to accept the Americans putting his country in the same category as Germany or Italy. But Washington persevered with its scheme, and, though Churchill had stood up for France at Tehran, he was in a bad mood with de Gaulle when they met in Marrakech after the summit. For his part, de Gaulle was 'very difficult and unhelpful', Duff Cooper, who had replaced Macmillan as Britain's representative in Algiers, recorded in his diary. The General declined an invitation to spend the night at the Prime Minister's villa, saying that he would only sleep in a French bed.[11]

As so often during this period, bad relations with his allies were balanced by improvements in de Gaulle's position in Algiers. At the end of 1943, the General received the support of another major military figure, Jean-Marie de Lattre de Tassigny, who had been sentenced to ten years' imprisonment for having refused to accept the occupation of Vichy territory by the Germans, but escaped by using a saw smuggled into his cell to cut the window bars and scaling two walls. After a period in hiding, he made his way to Algiers. 'You haven't aged,' de Gaulle said when they met. 'And you, you've grown,' came the reply.[12]

To consolidate his committee's position in Africa, de Gaulle flew to Brazzaville to open a conference of French colonies in Africa in January 1944. The idea was to lay down guidelines for their post-war evolution, but the result was uninspiring. Independence was not on the cards, though some decentralisation was envisaged. On the other hand, Catroux unveiled plans for political reform in Algeria, giving greater rights to some Muslims, which enraged the settlers but led de Gaulle to declare that 'those who imagine that . . . the status quo can be prolonged and that Algeria can remain the Algeria we learnt about at school are profoundly mistaken'.[13]

V
Radicalisation

In metropolitan France, the struggle between Vichy and the Resistance was sharpening as partisan activity grew and a series of dramatic events in late 1943 pushed the collaborationist regime in a more radical direction. Pétain still enjoyed warm welcomes on tours of major cities but his mind was unravelling: visiting Lyon, he asked as he walked in front of a welcoming parade 'Who am I? Where am I? What am I doing?' Still, the Victor of Verdun was sufficiently alert to be increasingly unhappy with Laval and what was happening as Germany's economic pressure on France grew, Corsica was liberated, and the Allies advanced in Italy.

The old man sent emissaries to talk to de Gaulle, Giraud and the British. He instructed one of these to tell the generals in Algiers that he proposed to meet them at the Arc de Triomphe at the Liberation and to transfer his authority to them. His offer to the British was to put himself in their hands – he would go anywhere except North Africa and seek a compromise peace to enable him to mend fences with the Fighting France leader. The British were not interested. Macmillan advised that the only reason to take the Marshal out of France would be 'to execute him as an arch traitor'.

On 27 September, an anti-Laval group at Vichy unveiled the draft of a new constitution under which a Regency Council would take over if Pétain died or stepped down. Laval was not among its members. On 26 October, the Marshal told the politican he had to go, which he refused to do. On 12 November, Pétain prepared a radio speech, saying that he embodied French legitimacy which should return on his death to the National Assembly. Laval did not object since he thought he would be able to manipulate parliament. But the Germans were horrified; they had seen Marshal Badoglio take over from Mussolini in Italy and side with the Allies and feared the same happening in France. So their soldiers occupied the radio station to stop the broadcast. Pétain told his long-time aide, Bernard Serrigny, that he considered himself a prisoner, and would act accordingly.

Abetz travelled to Vichy with a letter from Berlin which stated that the Reich had to approve any changes to legislation, and that the Cabinet must be reshuffled under Laval. As usual, Pétain caved in. Cecil von Renthe-Fink, a tall Prussian aristocrat who advocated the creation of a European confederacy under German leadership with a single currency and a central bank in Berlin, was sent to mind the Marshal.[14]

*

At the beginning of 1944, the head of the collaborationist *Milice*, Joseph Darnand, was appointed Secretary-General for Order; the police chief René Bousquet, who had organised the round-up of Jews in Paris in 1942, was ousted after insisting on investigating the murder of a newspaper owner in Toulouse carried out by *miliciens*. Darnand, who had taken an oath of loyalty to Hitler and held an officer's rank in the SS, expanded his paramilitary force to 35,000 men and personally presided over the repression from his headquarters in a prison which contained 1,200 inmates.

Summary courts judged members of the Resistance. Suspects were shot out of hand. The Germans took a growing role in the fight. Special units attacked Resistance groups in northern France, the Jura and the south-west, with mass shooting of hostages; in one case, eighty-six men, women and children were killed after a train carrying SS men was sabotaged. An important Alpine base on the Plateau des Glières in Savoy was assaulted by Vichy forces and then by German troops and planes; 150 *maquisards* were killed, some after being captured and tortured.

In Algiers, too, the mood hardened. Resistance figures called for 'the rapid trial of traitors'. A statement on 14 February said that civil servants who followed Vichy orders were guilty of 'cowardice and punishable servility'. Behind this lay the prospect of Resistance fighters taking retribution into their own hands, leading to reprisals and counter-reprisals which would produce a breakdown of law and order.

On 11 March 1944, an example was made of a one-time Vichy Interior Minister, Pierre Pucheu. A former banker and industrialist who had lost his job when Laval returned to power, he had crossed to North Africa with what he thought was a safe conduct from Giraud, intending to enlist in the forces fighting the Axis. Though Giraud sent him to an out-of-the-way military garrison, he was discovered, arrested and put on trial. The Communists were after his head for his alleged involvement in handing over hostages, mainly from their party, to the Germans for the mass execution at Chateaubriand in 1941.

It turned into a show trial. Passy left one session feeling revolted by the proceedings during which judges slept and the evidence was insubstantial. Giraud did not appear as a witness for the defence as the accused had requested. Still, the original charge could not be sustained, and Pucheu was instead tried for his role in the creation of special security squads that executed members of the Resistance. Convicted, he was sentenced to death. De Gaulle was said to have spent a sleepless night in considering an appeal for clemency; he was not in good physical shape, suffering a recurrence of malaria for which his doctor prescribed soft-boiled eggs at breakfast.

Some of those around de Gaulle thought such trials and sentences should wait until after the Liberation, but the General concluded that reasons of state meant that the verdict should be carried out. 'I owe this to France,' he said as he wrote his decision on the appeal document. In addition, he did not want to alienate the Communists.

The execution was in keeping with the leftwards tilt pressed for by the Resistance. A charter published by its committee stipulated the equality of all citizens, 'the eviction from management of France's economy of the great economic and financial feudal forces', a minimum wage, full social security, nationalisation of big companies, worker participation in management and enhanced rights for inhabitants of colonies. Thus the General found himself at the head of a movement which aimed to revive and enlarge the spirit of the Popular Front of 1936. He told the Consultative Assembly in Algiers that, after Liberation, France would wish 'the end of an economic regime in which the great sources of riches escape from the nation, where the main production and distribution activities are beyond its control and where the management of firms excludes the participation of workers' organisations on which, however, they depend'.

What he sought was an economy that would bring together the whole population incarnating his rejection of bourgeois liberalism and the power of money. Looking back on the war years in the 1960s, he would blame the scale of wartime collaboration on the way that the French put 'their little houses, their little gardens, their little shop, their little workshop, their little farm, their little collection of books or state bonds' above the nation, compared to the Free French who had no material assets to lose. De Gaulle thus brought together the Left of the pre-war era with the distrust of capitalism inherited from his parents as they had looked back to an earlier and supposedly less exploitative France. That fitted naturally with his aim of national unity once his country had been freed. Now, the vital thing was to seize the moment as the Allies prepared to land in France. Having achieved so much, it was time for the General to move on to the next stage of his ascent – and to go through another bruising confrontation with the allies he continued to need.[15]

14

GOING HOME

I
Provisional government

By April 1944, de Gaulle and his colleagues had put in place the structure of the Republic they intended to install after the Liberation of France. Seventeen 'general secretaries' were to run the administration, with a network of regional commissioners and prefects below them. Communist Party members or sympathisers were present at all levels. Inside France, where living conditions deteriorated as coal, sugar and other foodstuffs became increasingly rare, the General's chief delegate, Alexandre Parodi, a career civil servant who had refused to serve Vichy and joined the Resistance, exerted the central authority lacking since Moulin's death.

Internal military affairs were delegated to the twenty-nine-year-old Jacques Delmas, who subsequently added his Resistance pseudonym of Chaban to his name. In theory, all Resistance units were included in the *Forces françaises de l'intérieur* (FFI) which came under the command of the victor of Bir Hakeim, General Koenig, based in London. In fact, many partisan groups went their own way, applying local brands of 'immediate action'. Sabotage of railway lines cut traffic by 37 per cent in April 1944. Partisans assembled nearly four thousand men in an isolated region of the Massif Central. In the Lot department, they occupied the town of Carjac for two days. In strongholds in the Limousin, Brittany, the Lot, the Ain and parts of Savoie, they ruled the roost. Police closed their eyes. Overconfidence produced some disasters, notably on the Alpine Plateau des Glières.[1]

Resistance activity was accompanied by summary punishment of collaborators. As early as 1941, the Free French radio in London had urged French people to carry out their own 'terror' in opposition to that of the Germans and Vichy. The united Resistance movements urged that the period before the 'insurrection' and the Liberation should see 'an intensification of the execution of traitors'. In March, a prominent partisan leader, Philippe Vianney, published an article saying there was 'a clear duty to kill . . . without pity or remorse' all Germans, French traitors, those who had helped the occupation forces, *miliciens* and police who had aided in the arrest of patriots.

In May 1944, a message from the National Resistance Council declared that the committee in Algiers was 'the legitimate government of France'. But Roosevelt was adamant that the Fighting French should be excluded from the Normandy landing, though there were talks about post-invasion arrangements in France. At the President's urging, the French in London were forbidden to send messages using their own codes. In response, de Gaulle instructed the French ambassador, Pierre Viénot, and Koenig to halt all negotiations on post-invasion arrangements, and refused to receive Duff Cooper in Algiers. In a speech in Tunis, he referred pointedly to 'dear and powerful Russia, our permanent ally'. As usual, he won the argument with London, and the French codes were allowed once more. The General then went to Italy to inspect troops participating in the advance on Rome, which provided the French under Juin with their biggest military role since 1940.[2]

Despite his repeated clashes with de Gaulle, Churchill observed that it was difficult to envisage the invasion of France without some French involvement. On 3 June, the National Committee in Algiers proclaimed that it was now the provisional government of the French Republic, and its President flew to London the next day in response to an invitation from Churchill who sent him his converted bomber for the journey. He brought 140 people with him. The British laid on every facility. The General was driven into London from the airfield in a Daimler from the royal fleet. While he stayed in his old haunt of the Connaught hotel, members of his staff were put up at Claridge's where, despite the strict rationing in Britain, they were served sumptuous breakfasts, and were ferried around in a fleet of limousines. There was a temporary alarm over a lawsuit brought against de Gaulle and his movement by a Frenchman called Dufour, who had worked as a British agent and had been arrested by Passy's secret service whom he accused of having tortured him; the matter was dealt with by a payment of £1,000 to the complainant.[3]

II
Overlord

From London, de Gaulle went to lunch with Churchill in his private train parked near Portsmouth. The Prime Minister finally told him the date for the landing: 6 June. The French leader reacted calmly. They agreed that de Gaulle would broadcast to the French people and that two hundred special liaison agents would help the troops after they came ashore. Of the provisional government's forces only Leclerc's armoured division was to go to Normandy, but some time after the main landing. In his memoirs, the General noted 'how short France's sword was at the moment when the Allies launched themselves on the assault on Europe, never on such a grave occasion has our country been reduced to such relatively limited forces'.[4]

The lunch went awry when Churchill tried to discuss post-invasion politics in France and urged his visitor to seek an invitation to see Roosevelt. The General was unbending on both, and the atmosphere round the table became 'deplorable', according to the diplomat Pierson Dixon. Things got worse when the powerful Labour minister Ernest Bevin said that his party would be hurt if the French would not have political talks with the British. Bevin's term was translated to de Gaulle as '*blessés*'.

'*Blessés!*' the General shot back, '*vous dites que* vous *seriez blessés!*' ('Hurt! You say that *you* would be hurt!') Had it not occurred to the British that the French were also *blessés*? Had they no thought for French feelings? Bevin asked for a translation but Churchill interrupted to repeat his recommendation that the General should go to Washington to try to mend fences. De Gaulle asked why he should 'lodge my candidacy for power in France with Roosevelt. The French government exists. In that area, I have nothing to ask of the United States of America any more than of Great Britain.'

Raising the question of special franc notes that the US was proposing to distribute in France, he remarked scornfully 'go and wage war with your false money'. After some further inconclusive exchanges, Churchill told the General that he should know that each time Britain had to 'decide between Europe and the open sea, it is always the open sea that we shall choose. Every time I have to decide between you and Roosevelt, I shall always choose Roosevelt.'

Nonetheless, the two men ended by toasting one another, Churchill raising his glass 'to de Gaulle who never accepted defeat' while his guest drank 'to England, to victory, to Europe'. In his memoirs, de Gaulle recalled Bevin coming up to him after the meal and saying in a voice loud enough to be heard by everybody present: 'The Prime Minister told you that, in any circumstances, he will take the side of the President of the United States. You should know that he was speaking for himself and not in the name of the British Cabinet.'

The two leaders went to see Eisenhower at his headquarters in a cabin in the New Forest. The Supreme Commander had been anxious to avoid a repetition of the political mess into which he had been pitched in North Africa after the Torch landings. He wanted to prepare the ground with 'properly accredited French authorities', assuming that they would be representatives of the National Committee, a view also taken by the State Department and the Foreign Office. 'The need for prompt action cannot be overstated,' Eisenhower told Washington, 'since we will desire to turn over to French control at the earliest possible date those areas not essential to military operations.'

But the White House demurred, pointing out that the Senate would have to approve any civilian accord with a foreign administration. Roosevelt decreed that Eisenhower should have the freedom to deal with groups in France other than a provisional government Washington did not recognise. A text to be read out on the radio and distributed in leaflets named Eisenhower as ultimate authority for France and omitted any mention of Fighting France, the Resistance or de Gaulle.

Shown this, de Gaulle exploded. Eisenhower said the leaflets might be modified – a diplomatic lie since they had already been printed.

The Frenchman's anger increased when he learned that he was expected to speak immediately after the US commander on the radio, giving the impression of endorsing what had just been said. He declared that he would not speak at all, and withdrew the cooperation of French liaison agents. That set off an epic confrontation played out as the Allied force headed across the Channel.[5]

Returning to London, Churchill harangued the Cabinet about de Gaulle's misdeeds. In his diary, Cadogan noted that 'Roosevelt, P.M. and – it must be admitted, de G. – all behave like girls approaching the age of puberty. Nothing to be done . . . We always start by putting ourselves in the wrong. Then de G. puts himself *more* in the wrong.' While the General dined with his son, to whom he confided 'it's for tonight' as the advance detachment of parachutists began to drop on Normandy, Eden called in Viénot. The ambassador denied that the Fighting France chief was refusing to make a broadcast but confirmed that there would be no liaison help for 'an occupation' of France. Going on to the Connaught, Viénot was treated to a tirade from de Gaulle, who described Churchill as a gangster and said he denied the British the right to know whether he would speak to France. The unhappy Viénot returned to Whitehall to tell Eden that the General would broadcast at a time of his own choosing.

The Foreign Secretary was at number 10 Downing Street with Churchill at 1 a.m. on 6 June, just three hours before Eisenhower unleashed his invasion force which amounted to 156,000 men on the first day, 177 of them French marines. The Prime Minister was still incandescent with the French leader – some accounts say he had drunk even more than usual. To Viénot, he accused de Gaulle of 'treason at the height of battle' and of putting no value on the lives of British and American soldiers. Viénot stood up several times, threatening to walk out at such language. When he did finally go, the Prime Minister did not rise or hold out his hand. 'You have been unjust; you have said untrue and violent things that you will regret,' the ambassador told him. 'What I wish to say to you on this historic night is that in spite of everything France thanks you.' He recorded that Churchill looked astonished and deeply moved.

De Gaulle had calmed down by the time the diplomat got back to the Connaught at 2 a.m. Viénot detected both 'a shade of regret at having gone too far and an arrogant satisfaction'. The General instructed him to arrange a dinner with Eden and Duff Cooper in order to seek an understanding on security and economics. He confirmed that he would speak on the BBC so long as this was some hours after Eisenhower. He also agreed to supply the liaison agents. Back in Downing Street, however, Churchill was still enraged. From his bed, he dictated an instruction that de Gaulle was to be flown to Algiers 'in chains if necessary' and a letter to the General ordering him out of Britain. The aide who received the instruction ignored it. Eden had the letter burned.[6]

From the BBC studios that afternoon, de Gaulle declared that 'the supreme Battle of France has begun'. The duty of the sons of France was to fight the enemy with all the means at their disposal, he added. Paying no heed to American plans to administer his country, he went on to say that 'the orders given by the French government and by the French leaders it has named for that purpose must be followed precisely'. Though Churchill remained resentful, saying that neither he nor Washington intended to let de Gaulle become master of France, Viénot and the Foreign Office began talks to find common ground.

Showing continuing bad temper, the Prime Minister did not ask de Gaulle to accompany him when he visited Normandy on 12 June, but chose as his travelling companion Field Marshal Smuts of South Africa, who had once suggested that France's best course after the war would be to join the British Commonwealth. Nor did the Prime Minister attend a dinner Eden gave for de Gaulle. He also raised last-minute objections, without success, about de Gaulle's intention to visit France. In Washington, the War Secretary, Henry Stimson, added to the anti-de Gaulle sentiment when he compared the General's opposition to the issuing of special franc notes by the US forces to a stab in the back. The more he considered the situation, the more convinced he was of the danger the Frenchman represented, he told Roosevelt.[7]

III
'A kind of stupor'

On 14 June, as the Allied force in France rose towards its total of 600,000 men, de Gaulle crossed the Channel in a French destroyer,

Combattante, with Palewski, Viénot, Koenig, Admiral Thierry d'Argenlieu and a few others. He might have been expected to be jubilant, but he appeared gloomy, silent, as he stepped ashore on the beach at Courseulles-sur-Mer surrounded by a Canadian regiment which was landing in a floating harbour. He told his son later that he was almost stupefied by the emotion he felt. When Viénot broke the silence by remarking that it was four years to the day since the Germans had entered Paris, the General replied: 'Well, they made a mistake.'

Muffled in a long, thick coat, he went to see Eisenhower and then paid a visit to the British commander, Bernard Montgomery, who had been advised by Churchill not to greet the visitor on the beach. Driving inland in a British jeep with a French flag attached to the windscreen, de Gaulle stopped to talk to local people, most of them elderly. 'They cried out with joy,' one of his companions, General Béthouart, recalled. After they had passed through a village, the local priest rode after them on a horse. He told de Gaulle that he had heard the appeal of 18 June, had helped members of the Resistance and had sheltered parachutists, 'and you have passed through my village without even shaking my hand!' The General got out of the jeep to take the *curé* in his arms, telling him, 'I do not shake your hand, I embrace you.' A little further on, two gendarmes dismounted from their bicycles and saluted the tall man with two general's stars on his kepi. When de Gaulle told them who he was, they were so astonished that they let their bicycles fall to the ground. He asked them to ride back to Bayeux, the first town to have been liberated, to tell people he was coming.

When he arrived in mid-afternoon, the Mayor and Municipal Council were waiting with a hero's welcome in streets hung with tricolour flags. 'At the sight of General de Gaulle, a kind of stupor took hold of the inhabitants who broke out into cheers or dissolved into tears,' the Constable recorded in his memoirs. 'Coming out of their houses, they made me a procession amid extraordinary emotion. The children surrounded me. The women smiled and sobbed. The men held out their hands. Thus we went, all together, overcome and fraternal, feeling joy, pride and national hope rising from the depth of the abyss.'

The French leader visited the town's subprefecture, where the portrait of Pétain had been taken down only an hour earlier. In the square outside the castle, the General told the crowd that, for the first time for four years, it was 'hearing a French leader say in front of it that the enemy is the enemy, that the duty is to fight it, that France, too, will win victory. In truth, is that not the "national revolution"?'

The band played 'La Marseillaise' and the General and the visitors drove off for a tour of the neighbouring region. Everywhere, he was acclaimed. In the town of Isigny, which had been badly damaged in the fighting, corpses were still being pulled from ruined buildings. A dense crowd surrounded the General's jeep as he stopped at the war memorial to make another short speech. Before he boarded the destroyer to return to England, de Gaulle appointed François Coulet, his aide-de-camp who accompanied him on the visit, to stay behind to take charge of civilian administration in the region. 'Don't do politics – they [the French] don't want it,' he told the young man. Another trusted figure, Colonel de Chevigné, was to supervise military matters. Then the General sailed to England by night, awarding the Croix de Guerre to the *Combattante.* It was sunk by the Germans soon afterwards.

It had been a crucial day. As in Africa, de Gaulle had shown that, whatever distance he maintained in personal relationships, he could work a crowd to perfection. The popular reaction would be used to give the lie to Roosevelt's insistence that he was not a representative figure. By appointing Coulet, he had taken a practical step to establish that post-war France would be ruled by the French. In a letter to his son, he described the visit as 'very comforting'. Relations with Churchill warmed after de Gaulle wrote to the Prime Minister to, as he put it, 'pour balm on the wounds he had inflicted on himself'. In his reply, the British leader stressed his own feelings for France, and his 'intense pain' at the differences that had arisen. He could only hope that this was not the last chance of putting things right, he concluded.[8]

15

LIBERATION

I

'President of some French committee or other'

De Gaulle flew back to Algiers on 16 June. At the end of the month, Viénot told him that he and Eden were close to agreement on recognition of the provisional government and French sovereignty with the removal of any supervision by Eisenhower. De Gaulle then visited Rome where he saw the Pope and the new Italian government. At the beginning of July he finally went to Washington.

In visibly poor health, Roosevelt greeted his visitor in French, '*si content de vous voir*' (so pleased to see you'). The President, whom de Gaulle described to Palewski as 'a patrician', made a grandiloquent speech about France at a lunch in the General's honour, and gave his guest a photograph of himself inscribed to his 'friend', but to his wife and grandson he referred to his visitor as 'President of some French committee or other' and an 'egotist'. On arrival at Washington airport in torrid summer heat, de Gaulle received the seventeen-gun salute given to senior military leaders, not the twenty-one blasts accorded to a head of government or state.

The Americans did not bother to keep an official record of the discussions. One anecdote had it that, when tea was served, Roosevelt remarked to Admiral Leahy, his chief of staff and former ambassador to the Pétain regime, that Vichy water would be more appropriate for him. De Gaulle presented his host with a fully operational model submarine which he had had specifically built after learning that Roosevelt collected model ships; the President gave it to his grandson.

The visit was, as the French representative in New York, Raoul Aglion, put it, 'devoid of trust on both sides'. The two men spoke at, rather than to, each other. De Gaulle found his host's world view grandiose, foreseeing 'a permanent system of intervention' which would relegate Western Europe to a secondary role. Objecting to this, he insisted that the region was essential for the strength of the West. Of the main nations of Europe France was 'the only one which has been, is and always will be your ally,' he added. How could it revive if excluded from great world decisions? he asked, adding that this would consign it to the 'psychology of the defeated'.

The talks left de Gaulle convinced that America was 'already trying to rule the world'. Britain would always accede to its wishes, he told Aglion. So France had to count on itself. When he said as much to his host, the President replied: 'We will do what we can. But it is true that, to serve France, nobody can replace the French people.'

Even Roosevelt could not refuse to admit the value of de Gaulle in rallying support in France for the Allied armies. Eisenhower was firmly of this opinion and, despite the row over the banknotes, Stimson took the realistic view that the US must recognise the provisional government. At a press conference at the end of de Gaulle's visit, the President changed tack to the extent of agreeing that the provisional government in Algiers could be granted 'temporary de facto authority for the civil administration of France'.

Before leaving Washington, de Gaulle visited the hospital where the US First World War commander, General Pershing, was dying. The old soldier asked after his companion-in-arms, Pétain. 'I haven't seen him for a long time,' his visitor replied.

He went on to an enthusiastic reception in New York, where Mayor Fiorella La Guardia escorted him round the city, and the main commentators in the US press were supportive. After a triumphal visit to Canada, it was time to focus on the last round of his war to 'bring back to France independence, the Empire and the sword'.[1]

II
Tragedies

That, as always, could only be achieved by France's allies and they were facing stiff resistance from German forces fighting from defensive positions in towns and villages and among the hedgerows of Normandy. The town of Saint-Lô, a German submarine base, and the city of Caen, on the route to Cherbourg, were the scene of particularly violent encounters. German casualties for the battle of Normandy totalled 240,000, with 200,000 men taken prisoner, while Allied casualties were 225,000.

The fighting took a heavy toll on French civilians. This was nothing new. One inventory of Allied attacks on France throughout the war numbered 1,570 places hit from the air, killing 67,078 people and destroying 90,000 buildings. The official civilian death toll in Normandy is registered at 20,000, more than suffered by the invading British forces and almost as many as registered by the Americans, though some historians have put it at 50,000 to include those who died subsequently from wounds. Most of the deaths were caused by Allied bombing; Saint-Lô was attacked eight times in two weeks and 90 per cent of its houses destroyed; Le Havre and Saint-Malo were devastated from the air. On top of this, the Germans massacred hundreds of civilians, including eighty partisans detained in Caen prison who were summarily shot on the day of the landing. There were also killings of civilians, raping and pillaging by the Allied forces. Overall, this meant that France suffered more civilian deaths than military losses during the war.[2]

Numbers and air supremacy told in the end and the Wehrmacht was shaken by the attempted assassination of Hitler on 20 July. Still, it was not until 1 August that the Allies broke out from Avranches on the Bay of Mont Saint-Michel and forged south, west and east. The French Second Armoured Division (*la 2ème DB*) under Leclerc crossed the Channel and joined in the headlong advance through Normandy to Alençon and Chartres, opening the way to Paris. De Gaulle's son was in a regiment of marines incorporated into the division.

Seven thousand Resistance fighters gathered in the Morbihan department in Brittany. Another three to four thousand climbed on to the rugged uplands of the Vercors in east France. Communists in the north of the country decided that the time had come to unleash their insurrection. In the centre and south-west, partisans took over Limoges, Toulouse and Annonay and extended their influence over whole departments. Though they could play only a subsidiary role, they undoubtedly contributed to the Allied advances, harrying the retreating enemy troops and sabotaging their supply lines; the American general George Patton remarked that the Resistance had done 'better than expected, less than advertised'.[3]

New 'republics' proclaimed by local groups of partisans sprouted. In some places, criminals grabbed the opportunity to loot. Maurice Bourgès-Maunoury, the provisional government's delegate in southern France, approved two bank raids to get cash. There were vengeance killings and summary trials. In Toulouse, Limoges and Montpellier, Jacques Baumel, a Resistance fighter and future Gaullist minister, witnessed 'atrocities comparable to the killings in the Spanish civil war'. The numbers of those slain in the process and earlier in the war are subject to wildly different estimations. In 1951, the Interior Ministry provided a figure of 9,673 for all summary executions by the Resistance during the war, 4,439 of them during or after the Liberation. An official committee on the war opted for 12,000. In 1959, the revisionist historian Robert Aron arrived at a figure of 20,000 for 1944 and 30–40,000 for the war as a whole, a figure contested by other experts but seized on by those who prefer to depict the Liberation as the occasion for an outbreak of mass lawlessness.[4]

The *attentistes* became 'eleventh-hour resisters'. Many policemen came out for the Resistance. As the situation grew desperate for them, the *Milice* and the occupation forces became ever more violent, showing no quarter. In the Vercors, where the partisans were cut off and did not receive expected arms drops or bombing support, 650 were killed and local villages ravaged. On its way from Bordeaux to Normandy, the SS Panzer Reich tank division slaughtered 642 people in the Limousin village of Oradour-sur-Glane, 240 of them women and children burned alive in the church. The division then put down a rising in the town of Tulle, hanging 97 men, while members of the *Milice* picked out 149 hostages to be sent to death camps.

At one town in the Loire Valley, the Germans shot dead 124 people, including 44 children; in another massacre, 305 were executed and 732 deported, 405 to their deaths. Even as they retreated, Nazi troops searched out Jews for liquidation. A *Milice* leader, who carried in his wallet a piece of skin taken from a Jew adorned with the Star of David, had 80 Jews rounded up and the men buried alive under bags of cement in a well. On 28 June, partisans disguised in blue *Milice* uniforms got into the building where the Vichy Propaganda Minister, Philippe Henriot, was sleeping and murdered him in his bed. In retaliation, members of the *Milice* took Georges Mandel, who had been handed over to them by the Germans, into the forest of Fontainebleau and killed him. Other *miliciens*, pretending to be partisans, led the Popular Front Education Minister, Jean Zay, from the prison where he was held in Riom, shot him, stripped the body, tore off his wedding ring and flung the corpse into a quarry.

Le Maréchal, who was reported to have reacted to news of D Day by singing 'It's a long way to Tipperary', denounced the repression to his minder, Renthe-Fink, and wrote to Laval to attack the *Milice* for imposing 'an atmosphere of police terror unknown in this country until now'. But he was a prisoner of the Germans, who had moved him out of Vichy to what amounted to house arrest in a château in the northern Auvergne, and his words carried no weight with the victors of 1940 or with the *miliciens* who professed loyalty to him.

In early August, Laval went to Paris with a plan to revive the Third Republic. He got backing from eighty-seven mayors and had talks with the regional prefects. A passer-by who saw him being driven through the capital described 'his face ravaged, almost unrecognisable'. The Hôtel Matignon, which he used as a base, had no electricity. While Gestapo agents patrolled the courtyard, Laval bundled up his papers by the light of two candles and an oil lamp. He persuaded Abetz to let him travel to the lunatic asylum in eastern France where the stalwart of the old regime, Édouard Herriot, was being detained, and bring him back to Paris to ask him to resume his place as President of the National Assembly. He also sought to get in touch with the American intelligence service in Switzerland.

Herriot refused his advance, and the Germans ordered him to join other collaborators in moving to eastern France before the Allies reached Paris. Before they left, a lunch was organised for Laval, Herriot, their wives, Laval's daughter and son-in-law, and Abetz. Herriot was invited to join the journey to Belfort in the Jura. He declined, and was driven back to his asylum, from where he was later deported to Germany. Though the

Radical veteran had rejected the scheme, the fact that he had lunched with Laval was a major stroke against him in de Gaulle's eyes.

The situation became even more desperate for the Vichy remnants when the Allies landed in Provence in Operation Dragoon, took Toulon and advanced up the Rhône Valley amid heightened Resistance activity. Fighting France contributed an armoured division under de Lattre de Tassigny, commandos and a battleship to the southern operation. Ordered by Abetz to get a move on, Laval shook hands with the staff at Matignon one evening and told them, 'There is no French government any more. I am a prisoner like the others.' He complained that an aide whom he had sent to buy cigarettes had not returned. By the light of a torch he led his wife to their car, kissed his daughter and son-in-law, got into the back seat and then got out to kiss his daughter again. Two German guards sat in front as the car drove out of Paris.

In Vichy, the Germans told Pétain, who had returned from his château to the Hôtel du Parc, to pack his bags to join the exodus. The old man protested; his doctor advised him to join the *maquis* and prepared a case for him containing a torch, binoculars, string, a knife, maps, a missal and a book of writings by Rabelais. The Marshal told the Germans he would not leave, but the Germans reread their ultimatum to him. He caved in once more, and prepared for the journey east.[5]

III
Paris

At 8 a.m. on 20 August, the two soldiers whose destinies had been entwined for thirty-six years each went their own way. Watched by a few people in the rain, Pétain walked to his car outside the Hôtel du Parc, raising his hat in farewell. A statement he left behind read: 'Of all the principles which I taught, of all the things which I have freely said, I withdraw nothing.' At the same time, de Gaulle landed outside Saint-Lô, his return from North Africa having been delayed when a Flying Fortress sent by the Americans crash-landed and damaged its undercarriage on arrival in Algiers; he suspected a plot to try to hold up his arrival in France. He was greeted by delirious crowds as he was driven through Normandy and Brittany. Church bells rang. Windows were decked with tricolour flags; streets were garlanded with flowers. 'The contrast was striking between the ardour of the people's spirits and the material ravages,' he recalled in his memoirs. He made a side trip to visit the cemetery where his mother had been buried in 1940.[6]

Relations with the Allies were still tense. There was yet another row with Britain over Syria and Lebanon, and an argument about who should be responsible for distributing arms to the police in France. De Gaulle objected at not being consulted over the Allied destruction of ships at Toulon, Sète and Marseille. A trip Churchill made to Corsica without telling the French in advance caused further offence – de Gaulle told the military governor of the island to ignore the visitor.[7]

The main issue was Paris. Eisenhower did not want to attack the city, knowing of Hitler's order that it should be defended to destruction and fearing a prolonged urban battle. Nor did he want to divert supplies to the partisans in the capital. His objective was to press the advance eastwards towards Germany with all possible speed. He hoped that, if it was encircled, the city would fall to the Allies without a fight. But the Resistance forced the pace with a rising that began on 15 August, the day that a final convoy of more than two thousand prisoners left for Buchenwald. Railway workers, led by the Communists, went on strike. The city's bus and underground transport systems followed. The 20,000 police stayed away from work after the Germans disarmed their colleagues in the suburb of Saint-Denis. The Wehrmacht laid explosives in strategic points and prepared to destroy the city.

De Gaulle put Eisenhower's tactics and Laval's manoeuvres together to come up with a conspiracy theory alleging that it was all an American plot to block him. The only possible evidence for this seems to have been the alleged involvement of an intermediary the Americans used to keep in touch with Laval. Given Eisenhower's genuine military reasoning and the way the Germans scuppered Laval's plan, this can only be seen as the fruit of suspiciousness bordering on paranoia bequeathed by four years of solitary struggle.[8]

As well as the dispute with Eisenhower over Paris, de Gaulle faced the problem of ensuring that the Resistance did not move from insurrection in Paris towards forming a revolutionary government. In a message to his senior representative in France, Alexandre Parodi, he said that the partisans should operate on military lines with command systems under the authority of the state he was about to re-establish. In his memoirs, he invoked the danger of being confronted by a 'populist government which would encircle my head with laurels, ask me to take a position which it would designate for me and pull all the strings . . . until the day when the dictatorship of proletariat was established'. This was, in fact, unlikely, for the reasons we have seen, above all Stalin's cautious mood. But he still needed to assert control.

*

On 18 August, a general strike was declared in Paris. The unified Resistance command, the *Forces françaises de l'intérieur* (FFI), headed by the Communist Henri Rol-Tanguy, told Parisians to mobilise. The City Hall, public buildings, railway stations, telephone exchanges and electricity stations were occupied; at the huge Hôtel de Ville, the bust of Pétain was replaced by a portrait of de Gaulle decorated with a tricolour ribbon and champagne was fetched from a neighbouring restaurant under fire from German troops on the banks of the Seine. Barricades went up in the streets. Trees were cut down to block boulevards. The Germans blew up the main flour mill on the Seine, threatening bread supplies. Resistance fighters were executed. The opposing forces were equally matched, an estimated 15,000 armed Resistance fighters against 17,000 Germans. The Wehrmacht had stronger weapons, including ten tanks, but the French had popular support.

A temporary ceasefire was negotiated on 20 August by the Swedish Consul-General, Raoul Nordling, between the German commander General Dietrich von Choltitz, Parodi, the Gaullist military delegate Jacques Chaban-Delmas, and members of the Resistance Council. The PCF denounced this as 'a manoeuvre of the enemy'. Parodi warned of a complete rupture between Gaullists and the Communist National Front. A meeting of the Resistance Council grew so heated that proceedings were suspended. Then Parodi and Chaban-Delmas agreed to resume hostilities against the Germans.

In a message to Eisenhower, de Gaulle stressed the danger of 'serious trouble' unless the city was liberated as soon as possible with French troops leading the way. On 22 August, he received a letter from Leclerc proposing to advance on Paris with his armoured division even if the Allied Supreme Command had not ordered him to do so. At the same time, a Communist envoy met Eisenhower's staff to urge the Allies to attack the capital. Leclerc's move was agreed and the Second Armoured Division rolled through the flat countryside of the Beauce region while, in Paris, Parodi presided over a meeting of ministerial secretaries-general appointed by the provisional government at the Hôtel Matignon. De Gaulle left Le Mans to drive to Chartres through towns where he was acclaimed as the liberator. At Le Mans, a man stood in front of his car shouting '*Vive le Maréchal!*' – 'How can you expect them to keep their bearings?' the General asked an aide.

Leclerc's division covered the 240 kilometres to Paris in less than forty hours, despite stiff German resistance round the town of Trappes. On the evening of 24 August, a few tanks crossed the Pont de Sèvres over the Seine, south-west of the capital. Surrounded by welcoming crowds, they stopped where they were. Meanwhile, the main column was still eight kilometres from the main southern gateway into the city, the Porte d'Orléans. The overall field commander, General Omar Bradley, ordered the US 4th Division to join the attack, raising the prospect that French troops would not be alone in liberating the city. That was enough to spur on Leclerc. Cane in hand as he walked through the streets of a southern suburb, he took aside a captain, Raymond Dronne, who had been with him in Chad in 1940–41, and told him, 'Head immediately for Paris. Do not let yourself be stopped. Go fast. Arrive this evening. By any route you want. Infiltrate.'

Dronne's small detachment of tanks and half-tracks entered the capital by side streets and crossed the Seine at the Pont d'Austerlitz, rolling along the quays on the right bank of the river to the Hôtel de Ville. The bells of nearby Notre-Dame began to peal. Other churches took up the refrain; soon the city was awash with jubilation. A brigade led by General Billotte reached the suburb of Antony and fought its way into the city through heavy German resistance. Waiting at Rambouillet, de Gaulle considered what he would say when he reached Paris; a doctor was called to attend to the sore throat he had developed from all his speech-making on the way from Normandy.

The Communist newspaper *L'Humanité*, able to print after years of clandestine roneotyped editions, covered its front page with five decks of headlines in different fonts:

To each Parisian, his Hun

Consolidate the barricades! United combat!

FIGHT LIKE LIONS

Arm yourselves and disarm the enemy

To arms! To arms! To arms!

Billotte sent a message through Nordling to von Choltitz in the Hôtel Meurice on the rue de Rivoli, urging him to give up immediately. After his headquarters had come under attack, the German commander decided to comply, and signed the surrender at the police prefecture on the Île de la Cité in mid-afternoon. Paris did not burn as Hitler had wished.

When de Gaulle set out from Rambouillet for the capital, he refused to drive in an armour-plated limousine which Laval had used, preferring an open vehicle from which he could salute the throngs along the roadside. He also countermanded the presence of four armoured cars which had been due to accompany him. To have acknowledged the need for protection would have sullied the mystical embrace between him and the French people. At one point, a woman who seemed hypnotised by the sight of him ran forward with a child in her arms and forced his car to stop.

In Paris, the General went first to Montparnasse Station where he was welcomed by Leclerc and Chaban-Delmas, whose youth surprised him. Philippe de Gaulle was also there and the General told him to join him, but Leclerc said Philippe had been assigned to a unit which was to dislodge the Germans from the parliament. De Gaulle kissed his son on the cheeks, and watched as he headed off on his mission.

The General drove on to the War Ministry in an eighteenth-century building in the rue Saint-Dominique, the government building in which he had worked before leaving the city on the night of 10 June 1940. On the way, his cortège had to divert when a firefight broke out along their route. De Gaulle's choice of destination showed that he was picking up the threads of 1940. In his memoirs, he wrote that nothing had been changed – 'Not a piece of furniture, not a curtain had been moved. The telephone was in the same place on the table with exactly the same names on the call buttons.' Whether this was strictly true may be doubted, but it was important symbolically. The General needed to be able to put the period since the capitulation into a time capsule. As he put it: 'Nothing was missing except the State. It was up to me to restore it.'

After calling at the police prefecture, where a young woman in a white dress presented him with a bouquet of flowers, he walked through dense crowds to the Hôtel de Ville where he made one of his most evocative speeches, to proclaim 'the emotion which seizes us all, men and women, who are here, at home, in Paris that stood up to liberate itself and that knew how to do this with its own hands'.

'These are minutes which go beyond each of our poor lives,' he declared. 'Paris! Outraged Paris! Broken Paris! Martyred Paris! But liberated Paris! Liberated by itself, liberated by its people with the help of the French armies, with the support and the help of all France, of the France that fights, of the only France, of the real France, of the eternal France! Well! Since the enemy which held Paris has capitulated into our hands, France returns to Paris, to her home. She returns bloody, but quite resolute. She returns there enlightened by the immense lesson, but more certain than ever of her duties and of her rights.'

He did acknowledge 'the help of our dear and admirable Allies' but his stress was on the French vanguard that had entered Paris, on the French army that had taken part in the southern invasion, on 'our brave and dear Forces of the Interior'. To achieve final victory, he insisted that national unity was essential. 'We, who have lived the greatest hours of our History, we have nothing else to wish than to show ourselves, up to the end, worthy of France,' he concluded.

When the Resistance chief, Georges Bidault, tearfully urged him to proclaim the Republic, the General replied that it had been incarnated by the Free French movement and its successors. Vichy had always been null and void. He was now the Prime Minister of a republican government. So 'why should I proclaim it?' he asked. Then he went to the window looking down at the crowd below and raised both his arms in a vast Gallic version of Churchill's V for victory sign; it would become a familiar element of his speeches, his great height turning him into a monument. The Gaullist narrative had been set in stone.[9]

*

The situation in the city was still extremely unstable when de Gaulle staged a triumphal walk down the Champs-Élysées on 26 August, a Saturday. He towered above those around him, making gestures that seemed to be asking the crowd to come together in a wave beside him. Parodi was in the front row, severe in a three-piece suit and bow-tie. Bidault walked a few steps behind the General, flapping his hands.

The crowds lining the wide avenue erupted in joy as the tanks of Leclerc's division rolled down from the Arc de Triomphe. It was a great popular consecration of the mission on which the Constable had embarked four years earlier. France, he declared, had regained its glorious place in the world; now it was time for work and for the restoration of order. Yet fighting continued in the city. Snipers – mainly members of the *Milice* – were shooting from the rooftops of the Hôtel de Crillon on the Place de la Concorde and along the rue de Rivoli. 'The tanks massed in the square are firing back at the hotel,' reported a radio correspondent. 'Smoke rising . . . the tanks were all lined up facing the hotel and they gave it a tremendous salvo.'

The General boarded an open car to drive on to Notre-Dame, followed by the French tanks on to which people climbed. As he arrived at the cathedral, more shots broke out and people in the open space before the church flung themselves to the ground. Armed partisans returned fire. Showing his customary disregard for danger, de Gaulle marched through the church, his shoulders thrown back while bullets ricocheted off the pillars behind which people sheltered, women cuddling children in their arms. During the service, he stood erect between the stout figure of Parodi and a bespectacled Franciscan brother in dark cassock and white rope belt. The cathedral was darkened by lack of electricity and without the presence of the Cardinal of Paris, excluded for having presided over the funeral of the assassinated collaborator Henriot.

When the service ended, shooting was still going on but the General took no notice as he walked out into the sunlight. It was never clear who the snipers were. Some reports spoke of four Germans in grey flannel trousers and white singlets being caught. Another version has it that the noise which set off the return fire was from pigeons flapping their wings, and that the shots were all fired by overexcited partisans. In a letter to his wife, de Gaulle suggested that 'certain elements' – i.e. Communists – had seized on the occasion to flex their muscles.[10]

Isolated German detachments still had to be winkled out – one, holed up in the Senate by the Luxembourg Gardens, only surrendered after a Sherman tank manned by French troops fired into the building at point-blank range. In the northern suburb of Le Bourget, Leclerc's troops fought sharp engagements. On the night of 26 August, the Wehrmacht launched a bombardment of the city that killed 50 people, injured 400 and turned the night red with the flames from burning houses. Electricity was cut off – in the War Ministry, de Gaulle's aide-de-camp took the only oil lamp available to the General. Carrying it, he called on his staff late at night; he looked tired and very much alone, his newly recruited secretary Claude Mauriac, son of the writer François Mauriac, noted in his diary.

Amid these great events, de Gaulle looked ahead to his domestic arrangements, writing to his wife, who was in Algiers, that, when she joined him in Paris, they would move into an *hôtel particulier* with a garden in the Bois de Boulogne. He signed off '*ton pauvre mari*'. In a letter taken to Paris by General Juin, Yvonne told her 'dear darling Charles' that she shared his emotions and his triumph. Their house had been filled with flowers and telegrams, she told him. 'Of course we were a bit staggered on Saturday evening when we heard the story of events at Notre-Dame on the London radio,' she added. 'As soon as possible I would like to join you with your *Babies.* The climate is starting to oppress us; these days the humidity has been atrocious. . . . everybody is very fidgety, there are departures, false departures, lots of trouble, always at each other's throats!'[11]

*

Paris had not become a second Stalingrad but, in all, the Resistance lost some 3,000 dead and 7,000 hurt in the fighting in the city. Leclerc's division suffered 130 killed and 319 wounded. The German death toll was put at 2,800. Visiting Paris, Eisenhower recorded that he found the 'exuberant greetings of the liberated population a bit embarrassing'. De Gaulle requested food, supplies, military equipment and the temporary loan of American troops to help establish order. The Supreme Commander's mind went back to North Africa where neither Darlan nor Giraud had asked for US troops to sustain the local authority. 'There seemed a touch of the sardonic in the picture of France's symbol of liberation having to ask for Allied forces to establish and maintain a similar position in the heart of the freed capital,' he added in his memoirs. He could not spare any men but sent two divisions to march through the city on their way to the front.[12]

De Gaulle had emerged remarkably intact from the crucible of the war years, his natural steel tempered by events, and showing an extraordinary ability to face down far more powerful chieftains in Washington and London. Now, returning victorious to his realm three decades after his first meditations on what it took to be a great leader, he had to look the nation he identified with straight in the eye. His character was clearly formed, but his credit was not unlimited. The next quarter of a century would test whether France was ready to fall in with him or whether the nature of the country was not what he demanded, making him a man who, however much he achieved, would never be able to realise his ultimate dream.

PART FOUR
FROM VICTORY TO DEFEAT

16

WITCHES' BREW

I
The problems of peace

Charles de Gaulle liked to call himself the only true revolutionary among France's leaders. His conduct after the Liberation hardly bore out that claim. He knew what he wanted – to restore his country's greatness – and what he did not want – a return to the pre-war system of 'parties, intrigues, combinations'. On the first count, he achieved only partial success. On the second, his record was remarkably cautious and ended in failure.

The image most often employed by his supporters was that of a giant surrounded by dwarves. But it was Gulliver de Gaulle who let himself be tied down by Lilliputians. He did not intervene to stop them fashioning ropes which he would not break as he held back from seeking the dictatorship Roosevelt feared. In part, this was the result of his observation that twentieth-century authoritarian regimes ended badly and his belief that the French people would not tolerate a dictator. But it was also a sign of his own uncertainty in the face of political realities.[1]

By accepting the backing of the established parties while in London and Algiers, the unelected General had been able to absorb a degree of their democratic legitimacy, and nobody objected to his becoming Prime Minister after the Liberation. But he could never appreciate the real attachment leaders like Blum or Herriot had for movements to which they had belonged all their adult lives. Nor, as a supreme individualist, could he sympathise with the idea of democracy as communal action in which participants gave and took for the common benefit. The dysfunction between the General and France's political world would continue through the rest of his life, starting with their different conceptions of the source of legitimacy.

The party leaders insisted that democracy meant that the legislature, emanating from the people through parliamentary elections, must rule supreme. Their feelings were all the stronger given the Pétain experience. On the other hand, the General put his faith in a direct democratic link between voters and the executive, that is to say, himself. Intermediary bodies, be they the National Assembly, trade unions or professional organisations, had their place, but they were not to stand in the way of the mystical contact he sought with the people of France. His conviction, nurtured over three decades, had been strengthened by the war years in which his claim to be France underpinned his high-stakes poker game with the Allies. He was certain that events had proved him right, and that he must continue on his course. When anybody suggested that he might be wrong, he replied: 'They told me that in 1940, in 1941, in 1942 . . . But I had chosen a different policy – and I stuck to it.'[2]

The historic figure who had seized his moment on 18 June was not going to truckle with politicians who negotiated over long lunches, cut deals with lobbies and promised to divert state funds to their voters. Since eternal France was above petty matters, so must he be if he was to remain the 'intact' man hailed by Mandel in 1940, relying on the prestige he had accumulated to govern France from on high. Posters showed him looking out like a proud father over Resistance fighters marching behind the iconic revolutionary symbol of Marianne, bare-breasted and waving a tricolour flag, while the leading actor Jean-Louis Barrault recited a lyrical 'Ode to de Gaulle' by the poet Paul Claudel in his presence at the Comédie-française – the writer tried to explain away his similar accolade to Pétain in 1940 as having been prompted by the Marshal's decision to drop Laval.

Had the General allowed a Gaullist party to be organised to support him, he might have pulled off his gamble by remaining aloof while enjoying the support of a movement that could face down other parliamentary groups and form the necessary alliances. But he refused any such notion as contrary to his historic mission. 'I don't want to be the chief of a [parliamentary] majority,' he remarked. That, however, was just what was needed to rule the country, and his stance condemned the 'man of the storms' to increasing isolation, a great figure without whom the country would come to feel it could survive as it strove to get back to normal.[3]

*

In his memoirs, de Gaulle described France in 1944 as a nation 'ruined, decimated, torn apart'. There were still 75,000 Nazi soldiers holding out in bastions scattered through the north and west of the country. More than two million French people were held in Germany as prisoners of war or under the Vichy scheme as labourers.

The combination of the German invasion, the activities of the *Milice* and the Resistance, Allied bombing and the deaths and destruction of the advance after D Day meant that most of France's departments had been affected by the war, far more than in 1914–18. A quarter of the housing stock had been knocked down or damaged. The government estimated that it would take the equivalent of three times the 1939 national income to restore the country to its pre-war state. Half the railway track was out of service, and more than a third of stations. Many roads were cut, as were 7,500 bridges. Lorries had been requisitioned by the Reich or rendered useless by the fighting. Petrol and electricity supplies were scarce. The only big port left undamaged was Bordeaux, which was cut off by German units holding out at the mouth of the Gironde River. Telephone communications were sporadic – in the autumn of 1944, there were good links between Paris and only a third of the departments. Coal output was half the 1939 level, and what coal there was went mainly to industry, leaving people without fuel – a woman was shot dead by guards after being found stealing wood from the garden of de Gaulle's office in the rue Saint-Dominique.

Many people were weak and badly nourished. A million families were homeless. Rations in Paris in 1944 provided less than half the necessary calorie intake, rising to 75 per cent the following summer. Long queues were familiar elements in everyday life. The black market was estimated to involve four million suppliers and intermediaries. In Béziers in the south, a quarter of the factory labour force was reported to be away from work at any one time searching for food. A 'banquet' for the Agriculture Minister consisted of grated carrots with one slice of sausage, an inedible stew and what was described as 'some very uncertain cheese'. (On the other hand, the Chief of the Imperial Staff, Alan Brooke, recorded being offered a dinner by General Juin consisting of soup, pâté de foie gras, lobster, chicken, ice cream, soufflé and fruit, accompanied by Chablis, Burgundy, Sauternes and Champagne.)

Shortages spurred inflation; retail prices were four times those of 1939. After a 50 per cent jump in 1944, salaries rose much more slowly. The trade deficit increased. The government's receipts covered only a third of its spending in 1944. The state debt was four times that of 1939 while there were five times as many banknotes in circulation as the administration fell back on the old device of printing money, which only exacerbated inflation.

National production in 1944 was 38 per cent of the 1938–9 level. Much modern equipment had been shipped to Germany. Big companies such as Renault were besmirched by collaboration. There was a serious shortage of farm machinery and fertilisers. The Germans had taken away 700,000 horses. The wheat harvest of 1944–5 was half that of pre-war years. Boosting industrial and farm output became an obsession; de Gaulle took a different productivist tack by calling on the French to breed 'twelve million bouncing babies' in ten years.

In his memoirs he recalled that, when he took a long view, he saw blue skies ahead, but when he looked at the immediate prospects he was like Macbeth peering into the witches' cauldron. What made things serious, he thought, was the way in which the material difficulties came on top of the deep weakening of France, which he blamed not only on the immediate past but also on the way in which economic and social problems had been allowed to accumulate during the interwar years. A poll in the summer of 1944 showed that 60 per cent of those questioned thought there was a danger of an outbreak of 'public passions'. Big demonstrations and strikes erupted in Nantes, Le Creusot, Laon and Lyon. Protesters marched under the banner 'Our kids are hungry'. In Normandy, bakeries were pillaged. In Tours, a crowd attacked the prefecture to protest at rationing. Receiving France's ambassador to the Vatican, Jacques Maritan, in the summer of 1945, de Gaulle remarked that, a year earlier, the French had been miserable but now they were just dissatisfied – 'that's progress'.[4]

*

The General's natural distaste for ostentation or luxury fitted well with the national mood. So did his refusal to make the most of his position. When he gave a Saturday evening reception for the administration, he paid the costs himself. Rather than occupying a grand official residence in central Paris, he moved to a white villa surrounded by chestnut trees on the edge of the Bois de Boulogne on the western outskirts of the capital. At the weekend, he was driven to a nearby forest to take long walks.

The house, which was owned by the city of Paris, had been set aside by the Germans as a future residence for Goering. The ever-modest Yvonne de Gaulle said it was 'a degree above what I would have liked'. The General installed wartime mementoes including Hitler's sword, which Leclerc had brought back from Germany, and a model of the French submarine the *Surcouf*. His secretary, Claude Mauriac, went to Brittany to recover the belongings de Gaulle had stashed there in June 1940.

As Prime Minister, he kept his office in the rue Saint-Dominique and did not move into Matignon or the Élysée presidential palace because he did not want to be seen to be presuming on his position under a future constitution. Also, as he noted in his memoirs, he felt that the cost of using the palace would have been shocking at a time of national misery. For the same reasons, he did not use the presidential retreat at Rambouillet.

Their daughters joined Charles and Yvonne at their new home, while the General kept a close watch on the military career of his son, who was taking part in the fighting in eastern France where he was decorated by Leclerc with the Croix de Guerre. In one letter, in

December, de Gaulle asked Philippe to confirm that he had received a new pair of boots, twenty pairs of woollen socks, a flask of rum and cigars and cigarettes which had been sent to him. He assured the young man that his luggage had arrived safely from London, that his clothes had been cleaned and that the appropriate military stripes had been sewn on.

Though he could not avoid the ceremonials that went with his job, de Gaulle appeared ill at ease on social occasions, tall and unbending. He would retreat to a corner of the room and commune with his close associates before emerging for a round of farewells. After one dinner, Duff Cooper wrote in his diary that it should have been a gala evening, 'but gala is not a word included in the vocabulary of General de Gaulle'. Cabinet meetings were run on military lines with admonitions from a commander who allowed no dissent. Georges Bidault, who left some of his sessions with the General visibly furious, complained, 'If you only knew how he treats us, his ministers.' As François Mauriac noted: 'In front of him, you feel like a complete idiot. He does not see you. One does not exist in his eyes as a distinct person. He judges what you say *in abstracto* without linking it to who one is or what one knows.'[5]

II
Order

De Gaulle remarked that the problem with the last head of state of the Third Republic, Albert Lebrun, was that neither was he a chief nor did he preside over a state. His own concern was to be the first and to achieve the restoration of the second. France, he told his staff, was 'a nation which has been gravely ill for a long time, without diplomacy, without hierarchy . . . and entirely empty of men of government'.

To help him in his task, he put together a team at the rue Saint-Dominique which combined associates from London with new faces. The debonair Gaston Palewski became chief of staff, showing an unshakeable faith in his boss but notoriously disorganised in his paperwork. A former Fighting France airman, Claude Guy, was appointed aide-de-camp. Claude Mauriac dealt with a flood of correspondence from the public, including a package of knitted woollen socks with unusually long feet sent by women in Australia. Jacques Soustelle, the anthropologist who joined Fighting France in Latin America before moving to Europe, took care of 'special services'. René Brouillet, who was close to Resistance leader Georges Bidault, dealt with political parties. A literary academic, Georges Pompidou, who had written to one of the General's recruiting agents saying that he felt France needed everybody ready to help it, assisted on education policy and worked with Brouillet. Except for three secretaries, the staff were all male.[6]

The first people the General called in to talk to him the day after the celebrations of the liberation of Paris were writers, including the dashing novelist André Malraux who had fought in the Resistance. Over lunch with François Mauriac, who had also belonged to an underground network, he inquired about vacant seats in the Académie-Française. The following day, 28 August, de Gaulle was ready for politics. He summoned the chiefs of the Resistance. After they were lined up in his office, he referred briefly to the sacrifices they had made for France. Then he switched to a matter-of-fact tone to make clear that their role was over. Unless they joined the regular army, they and their companions should go back to civilian life. That was it. The Constable had spoken on behalf of his master, the French state. For him, the Resistance was finished.

Two weeks later, de Gaulle met a larger group of partisans in the Palais de Chaillot across the Seine. François Mauriac recalled that they had expected an emotional event, but de Gaulle talked at length about the national and international situation in what the writer's son described as a 'cold and sober speech . . . rigorous and lucid'. His attitude, stated again at a press conference in the autumn, was uncompromising. No latitude would be accorded to any organisation that tried to involve itself in the administration of the country or the exercise of justice independently of the state, whose authority was paramount. All fighting forces must be integrated into the regular army.

'We didn't know what to do with our handkerchiefs,' François Mauriac wrote after the Chaillot meeting. 'Remaking the state, remaking the army, waging war, forcing the Allies' hand so that France would be present alongside them in occupied Germany and at its capitulation, that alone counted,' he added. 'For the rest, let the dead bury their dead.' Claude Mauriac recalled the General telling him that, while the Resistance was anti-Nazi and anti-Fascist, it was 'in no way national'. So it did not have the legitimacy which he claimed for himself.

For some, this was all too much. The Communist Pierre Villon said he could never have imagined such ingratitude. A passionate pamphlet written by the partisan leader Philippe Vianney depicted de Gaulle as playing on the national desire for peace and order to 'pick up from the Pétain government'. This bitter charge epitomised the feelings of those who had believed the Liberation would bring political and social revolution, who had seen the fight against the Germans as more than a simple military combat, and who still hoped that moral values incarnated by the Resistance would flower after victory.

But, when non-Communist Resistance leaders broke with the PCF, the General declined to give them any sign of recognition. Nor did he do anything to help a new party, the *Union démocratique et socialiste de la Résistance* (UDSR), which included wartime Gaullists such as Pleven, Soustelle and Baumel. However much this hurt the feelings of the former partisans, the public was with him. An opinion poll reported that only 12 per cent of those questioned favoured a new political movement based on the Resistance. France was ready for peace, and wanted to put the war years behind it.

The Communist Party leadership played along, though some regional Party chiefs, notably in the Limousin in central France, operated independently of Paris. When de Gaulle proposed the dissolution of militia forces set up to help with the Liberation, the PCF bosses accepted without demur. The General compared them to 'reeds painted in iron'. 'One does not make a revolution without revolutionaries,' he went on before adding, inevitably: 'There is only one revolutionary in France: that's me.'[7]

However, there was nothing at all revolutionary about the government the General formed on 9 September 1944. Jules Jeanneney, the President of the pre-war Senate who had abstained in the vote of powers to Pétain in 1940, became its second-ranking member as Minister of State. Wartime associates of the General, such as Tixier (Interior), Pleven (Colonies), Catroux (North Africa), Diethelm (War) and Capitant (Education), were outnumbered by representatives of the main political parties, including the Communists and a new Christian Democrat group, the *Mouvement Républicain Populaire* (Popular Republican Movement) (MRP), whose leader, Bidault, became Foreign Minister and was kept on a tight leash. He received a stream of injunctions from the head of the government telling him how to deal with the Americans and the British, and, when he got married to a member of the Foreign Ministry, the General had him called back to his office as he left the church to remind him where his duty lay. The strain led the minister to start drinking too much; he became known in diplomatic circles in Paris as 'In Bido Veritas'.[8]

To assert his authority and re-establish the control of Paris over the fragmented country, de Gaulle embarked on a tour of major provincial cities in mid-September 1944. In uniform, with a Cross of Lorraine pin on his tunic, he alarmed his staff by his lack of concern for security arrangements and his readiness to leave the official cortège to wade through crowds. When a prefect commented on the danger he was running, the General replied: 'To avoid assassination attempts, a little authority is enough. And to get this authority – which I am not sure you possess – it is enough to exhibit it.'

In Lyon, the Prime Minister was pleased to see that things appeared to be in hand. But he had to read the riot act to the authorities in Marseille where the Communists were strong. He was unimpressed by a ragged march past there that included young women in flimsy dresses sitting on a tank. In Bordeaux, where he raised no objection to the continued employment of the senior Vichy civil servant Maurice Papon who had authorised the deportation of Jews, there was an awkward moment when a partisan leader arrived for a meeting with six men, and had to be persuaded to send them out to wait in the street.

Toulouse was the most troublesome stop. Resistance forces in the area were acting autonomously under the leadership of a chief who had taken the wartime pseudonym of Ravanel and had been promoted to the rank of colonel. De Gaulle gave the reception committee of

Resistance leaders short shrift, inquiring of them: 'What is your army rank?' as if their service in the Resistance counted for nothing. When Ravanel presented himself by pseudonym and rank, the General replied: 'No, Lieutenant Asher.'

The situation in Toulouse was complicated by the presence of a British officer, Colonel George Starr, who had arranged supplies to the wartime underground in south-west France and commanded a unit of seven hundred armed men. When the Commissioner of the Republic in the city, Pierre Bertaux, asked Starr to lunch with the General, de Gaulle told him to cancel the invitation and ordered Starr to leave the city. Starr objected that he took his orders from the Allied Forces Headquarters. His standing in the region was such that de Gaulle gave way for the moment, even shaking the colonel's hand. Soon afterwards, however, Starr was made to quit Toulouse, though the Prime Minister agreed that he should be awarded the Légion d'honneur and the Croix de Guerre for his services to France.

The campaign to spread order was popular; the IFOP polling organisation reported 63 per cent in favour of what de Gaulle was doing, with 24 per cent against and 13 per cent of don't knows. The General tempered his stern message with a vision of hope, talking of building 'a purer, more fraternal France . . . rejecting all that could corrupt us, hinder us'. Most of France's middle class saw the General as a reassuring figure who would block the Communists from gaining power, but he remained sharply critical of the bourgeoisie, which he said had backed Vichy 'because it wanted no interruption in its dinner parties'. The role played by the working class in the Resistance ruled out any idea of keeping it in the subservient position it had occupied before the war, he believed. To turn the page back to the old regime would be to open the door to Communism, so social and economic renovation was essential.[9]

The coal industry in northern France was nationalised at the end of 1944, followed by all energy companies. In quick succession, plans were rolled out for state control of credit institutions, the Bank of France and the four big retail banks, the merchant navy, the main aircraft manufacturers and airlines, and Renault. In some places, local workers and unions took matters into their own hands – in Marseille, fifteen big firms were requisitioned and run by the workforce. Factory committees were established across the country. Trade unions expanded fast. A new social security system was introduced to cover 80 per cent of medical costs. Though employers set up an association to defend their interests, there was little opposition; de Gaulle concluded that the bosses had expected much worse treatment.

Such change did not come without cost, however. Inflation rose further. The budget for 1945 showed a 55 per cent deficit. In November 1944 prices were blocked, but this deterred production and boosted the black market. The tough-minded Economics Minister, Pierre Mendès France, wanted fresh price controls and monetary reform, but his colleagues feared the popular reaction and the Finance Ministry, headed by a northern banker and Resistance leader, Aimé Lepercq, preferred to float a large public loan of the kind traditionally used to bail out the state.

The differences between the Economics and Finance Ministries faced de Gaulle with his first ministerial crisis after Lepercq was killed in a road accident and Pleven succeeded him. In January 1945, Mendès France submitted an eighteen-page resignation letter. The Prime Minister called him and Pleven to his home in Neuilly on a Sunday. Mendès delivered a three-hour lecture whose length did not charm the head of government. Nor did the way in which he made repeated radio broadcasts pushing his ideas without making any mention of the Prime Minister. However, de Gaulle did not want to lose one of his most capable ministers, a man known for his integrity. So he got Mendès to withdraw his resignation.

Given the Economics Minister's temperament, a fresh clash was inevitable. In March 1945, he called for a tax on capital and the blockage of bank accounts. Again, he had little support in the government, so he again submitted his resignation. This time, de Gaulle accepted it, realising that he had to come down on one side or the other in the quarrel. The two ministries were united under the more supple Pleven. Inflation continued its upward course as did the budget deficit; almost half of state spending was going to the military as the army swelled from 560,000 men in September 1944 to one million at the end of the year.

The decision not to back Mendès France has been depicted as a sign of weakness on the General's part, a failure to support a man who was as uncompromising as himself and who might have mastered the inflation that characterised the post-war years. In his memoirs, the General wrote that he was not unconvinced by the arguments advanced by Mendès. But 'the country was ill and wounded' so he thought it better not to risk 'dangerous convulsions' and upset economic activity. Certainly, most French people and a large majority in the government were in no mood to accept hair-shirt economics, much preferring the soothing Doctor Pleven, with his sweet if corrupting medicine, to Surgeon Mendès wielding his scalpel.[10]

III
The purge

The Pétain regime had evaporated as if it had never been. Nobody spoke out for collaboration or defended the Marshal's national revolution. His relations acted as if he did not exist. De Gaulle denied the Vichy experience any legitimacy, arguing that the Republic had been transferred abroad for a time, embodied in his person.

Still, the collaborators had to pay, or at least some of them did. The pressure for a thorough purge was particularly strong from the Communists who, exaggerating hugely, claimed that 75,000 of their members had been shot by Germans and Vichy – *le parti des 75,000 fusillés.* The most common image from the time is of women who had slept with Germans having their hair cropped and being paraded through the streets, sometimes daubed with tar, stripped to the waist and painted with swastikas; the number punished in this way totalled at least 20,000.

Harsh as their treatment was, others suffered much worse. In Paris, some prostitutes who had entertained Germans were kicked to death. In half a dozen cities, there were riots to force tribunals to condemn collaborators to death. In others, mobs grabbed the accused and executed them. In random cases reported at the time, a member of the *Milice* was tortured and had his ears cut off before being beaten to death with a pickaxe as he crouched in his grave; a woman was stripped naked, made to sit on the point of a bayonet, severely mutilated and then thrown into a bathtub full of petrol which was set alight; another woman was rubbed with stinging nettles, put into a tub of boiling water, whipped with a belt, burned with cigarettes and a red-hot iron and hung up by her arms before being killed.

The need to bring the purge under the Justice Ministry became a priority for de Gaulle. After Paris gained control of the process during the autumn, 126,000 people were detained on allegations of collaboration in the capital. Hundreds of suspects were packed into the Vél d'Hiv, which had been used to hold Jews after the 1942 round-up. About half of all those held were subsequently released without punishment. Four per cent of trials ended in death penalties, but most were *in absentia*; only 767 were actually executed. De Gaulle commuted 998 of the 1,554 death sentences submitted to him, including all those of women. Twenty-three per cent of those tried were condemned to national degradation and 16 per cent were sent to prison or otherwise detained.

The right-wing prophet Charles Maurras got both degradation and life imprisonment; he called it the 'revenge of Dreyfus'. Robert Brasillach, editor of the violently anti-Semitic collaborationist journal, *Je suis partout*, was sentenced to death, setting off a wave of appeals from writers and intellectuals. As Brasillach waited in his cell in chains and with the light burning day and night, Claude Mauriac organised a petition for a reprieve on the grounds that the country did not need further divisions and that the condemned man was 'a thinking head even if he thought wrongly'. But de Gaulle refused to commute the sentence; Albert Camus lamented: 'They have made a martyr of him; as if France requires more martyrs.'

Famous figures who were condemned included the actress Arletty who had lived with a German officer in the Ritz: in her defence she declared that 'my heart is French but my pussy is international'. She was held initially in a camp in the Paris suburb of Drancy which had been used as an assembly point for Jews being shipped to their deaths; then she was put into the Fresnes jail in the capital, where another detainee was the celebrated operetta star Tino Rossi who was noted for his singing at mass. After 120 days in prison, the actress was put under house arrest for two years and banned from working for another three years. A group of partisans hustled her good friend the flamboyant Sacha Guitry out of his home in yellow pyjamas, green pumps and a panama hat. Held for sixty days, he was quizzed as to why he had met Goering. 'Out of curiosity,' he replied, adding that the same would have applied to Stalin. The examining magistrate ran press advertisements asking for any accusations against him to be lodged with the authorities. When none were received, Guitry was freed. Coco Chanel was also detained briefly, and then found it wise to flee to Switzerland.

Some business figures were punished. Louis Renault, for one, died in prison after being sentenced for collaboration. But most got off. Though some of their companies were confiscated or lined up for state ownership, it was estimated that less than 2 per cent of profits made under the occupation were recovered. There was a definite class pattern to the punishments. Poor, defenceless people were convicted more often than richer citizens who could employ legal means or use contacts to escape. Some collaborators fled abroad. Others went into hiding. Judges presided over cases of wartime conduct even if they had held their posts under Vichy. Civil servants generally escaped lightly, typified by the case of Maurice Papon in Bordeaux; de Gaulle's crusade for order needed the services of such men, some of whom had established pre-emptive contacts with the Resistance in the later years of the fighting which could be summoned in their defence.[11]

The case and future career of the well-connected collaborationist police chief René Bousquet, who had been hailed by Himmler as 'a precious collaborator', were the most shocking. He was not tried until 1949 and was sentenced to only five years of national degradation, which was immediately lifted on the grounds that, after being sacked in Vichy, he had participated in the Resistance. He then held senior positions at a major bank and at a big newspaper in Toulouse. In 1957, he was reinstated as a holder of the Légion d'honneur. After being amnestied the following year, he ran unsuccessfully for the National Assembly and developed a friendship with the anti-Gaullist politician François Mitterrand, as well as with a number of other prominent figures. When legal proceedings concerning his wartime activities were launched in the mid-1980s, the dossier was sidelined by being sent to a court that no longer existed. In 1991, he was finally charged with crimes against humanity but was murdered by a deranged gunman just before the trial was due to start.

17

FOREIGN AFFAIRS

I
The search for status

The General accorded high priority to the presence of 100,000 French troops in the Allied forces pressing towards Germany, despite the financial pressure this added to the already strained budget. The Americans, Russians and British had no great need of the forces of de Lattre de Tassigny and Leclerc to defeat the Third Reich, while Eisenhower sometimes found the First French Army difficult to fit into the command structure. There was also a problem in the touchy relations between the two leading French generals, with Leclerc resenting the way de Lattre de Tassigny had treated him in North Africa, and telling de Gaulle that he preferred to operate as part of the US 3rd Army rather than serving under his compatriot. But, for the Prime Minister, their presence was an essential part of France's national revival, and he could draw comfort from their impressive performance as they drove through southern Germany to the Danube, taking Hitler's retreat of Berchtesgaden and crossing into Austria.[1]

De Gaulle remained intensely suspicious of the Allies, whom he accused of malevolence towards France and of wanting to return it to its 'malleable and convenient' pre-war state. In fact, the Allies were supportive. The Americans relinquished their plan for a military government and did not distribute their 'false francs'. When hc visited the General in Paris in August, Eisenhower regarded it as 'a kind of recognition of him as the provisional President of France' – he gave the French state, as personified by de Gaulle, a Cadillac as a token of esteem. The provisional government was recognised by the United States in October 1944, rapidly followed by the Soviet Union and Britain. Lobbying by Churchill and Eden led the Big Three to agree to grant France a permanent seat in the United Nations Security Council, a future occupation zone in Germany and a place on the Allied Council of Foreign Ministers for Europe; the British realised that they would need a strong France to help them confront the USSR in Europe, particularly since Roosevelt was talking of withdrawing troops from the continent after a couple of years.[2]

But, as the British ambassador Duff Cooper put it, de Gaulle seemed to seek out real or imagined insults to which to take offence wherever possible. At a lunch in his ministerial offices in the rue Saint-Dominique on 31 August 1944, he said the Americans and British would only leave France when they were thrown out. Five days later at another lunch with his son, Colonel Passy and others, he spoke of a secret agreement between the United States and the Wehrmacht to allow the Americans into Germany to avoid a Soviet occupation. 'The Allies are betraying us,' he exclaimed. 'They are betraying Europe, the bastards. But they'll pay for it to me.' Nor were relations helped when he instructed Bidault to wield France's veto on the European Council and raised difficulties about attending the San Francisco conference to establish the United Nations. As if to annoy the General further, Roosevelt wrote him a letter urging him to include Giraud in the government.[3]

On Armistice Day 1944 there was a more friendly public occasion when Churchill received a hero's welcome as he paraded down the Champs-Élysées to loud cheers from dense crowds. The British leader spoke in his idiosyncratic French and took delight in wallowing in the gold bath in his suite at the Quai d'Orsay, which had been installed for Goering. When he laid a wreath at the statue of Clemenceau at the foot of the Champs-Élysées, de Gaulle had the march '*Père la Victoire*' (Father Victory) played and told his visitor in English, 'For you'.

The visit marked the first official public appearance of Yvonne de Gaulle, who had flown in from Algiers to join her husband; she was photographed with Churchill's wife watching their husbands parade. Dressed in black, her mouth half open, she wore an expression of happiness and pride. The two leaders then travelled through thick snow to inspect the forward French positions in the Jura. Alan Brooke recorded that de Gaulle was 'most affable and pleasant' and Duff Cooper described the talks as being conducted in 'the happiest of humours'. What the British did not know was that, before the visit, de Gaulle had expressed concern about an excessive display of popular affection for Churchill, and instructed that, during his time in Paris, 'no démarche, no demonstration, no presence of any kind can be carried out on the French side without my agreement'.

When Churchill raised the subject of a Franco-British alliance, de Gaulle showed interest only if it would lead the two nations 'to create the peace together' independently of the US and the USSR. The idea of a separation from Washington was unpalatable to the British leader, who quickly back-pedalled to offer only 'an alliance in principle', and that conditional on Roosevelt's approval. The matter was dropped.[4]

Having got nowhere with Britain, it was time for de Gaulle to try the Soviet card which he had been nurturing for much of the war, pursuing his long-held ambition of developing relations with Moscow to balance Britain and America. He saw the USSR as sharing with France the vocation of a continental European power, and accepted that the Kremlin would be the arbiter of east Europe after the defeat of Germany. In November 1944, Stalin agreed to a visit by de Gaulle, whose aim was to get the Kremlin to sign a friendship treaty with France. He travelled via Cairo and Tehran where he met King Farouk and the young Shah, then flew to Baku to board a tsarist-era train for Moscow, stopping at Stalingrad to present a sword of honour to the devastated city.

The importance the General attached to the trip was shown by the twenty-four pages devoted to it in his memoirs. However, Stalin did not seem very interested. He judged other countries by their military and economic strength, and France weighed only lightly. The first meeting between the two men began with a long silence. Then, rather than opening up on global politics, Stalin said he supposed that de Gaulle wanted the Communist leader, Maurice Thorez, who had spent the war in the Soviet Union, to return to France. 'I wouldn't shoot him if I were you,' he added. 'He's a good Frenchman.'

Stalin and the Foreign Minister, Molotov, pressed their visitor to recognise the Lublin Committee which the Soviet Union had set up to run Poland, in preference to the Polish government-in-exile in London. That, the American ambassador Averell Harriman warned the Frenchman, would cause problems with Washington. De Gaulle limited himself to posting a liaison officer to the Lublin group.

The chilly atmosphere was echoed by the delegation's living quarters in the French embassy, which was without heating in the Moscow winter. Stalin told Harriman he found de Gaulle 'an awkward and stubborn man'. Later, he remarked to Roosevelt that he did not think de Gaulle was a very complicated person, and considered that the Frenchman lacked realism in claiming the same rights for France as those of the other three Allies. In his toasts at a final banquet, he raised his glass to Roosevelt and Churchill, but not to de Gaulle.

After the banquet, the General sat through one of the habitual late-night films in the Kremlin, a documentary about the war on the Eastern Front; each time a German soldier fell, Stalin gripped his thigh, leaving him quite bruised. De Gaulle left before a second film started. In the early hours, he was summoned back to the Kremlin where Stalin had sat up drinking. He was presented with a draft of the treaty put forward by the Soviet side at the start of the meetings without taking any notice of amendments negotiated subsequently. 'France has been insulted,' de Gaulle replied, refusing to accept the text.

His bluff called, Stalin produced the revised draft which was signed at dawn by Bidault and Molotov with Stalin and de Gaulle looking on. Afterwards, the dictator offered a meal, and, in a typically sinister aside, told the Russian interpreter that he knew too much and would have to be sent to Siberia. As de Gaulle left the room, he turned to take a last look at his host. Stalin sat alone at the table, eating. The French delegation left by train later that morning. De Gaulle elected not to give his host an ashtray he had brought him as a present.

The pact did not amount to much. But, for the General, what counted was that he had visited Moscow as well as Washington and had been able to talk as the leader of a resurgent power. He had also agreed to the return of Maurice Thorez from Moscow to France and the dropping of the desertion charges against him. Returning home, the General wrote to his son that his visit had had satisfactory results which he hoped would be developed. But Stalin's attitude at tripartite summits in 1945 would show how dismissive his view of France remained. In his world of realpolitik, the visit had not heightened the General's status.[5]

With the Americans, there was a sharp confrontation when Eisenhower ordered French troops to evacuate Strasbourg so as to form a more cohesive front after the Germans launched their last offensive in the Battle of the Bulge at the end of 1944. In November, de Gaulle had been in the city during the final stage of its liberation from the Germans, standing unperturbed as enemy shells fell around him. He again visited the Alsatian capital at Christmas, and believed that the city, which had greeted the French forces with great enthusiasm, could not be allowed to be reoccupied by the Germans. It also had a highly symbolic importance, given Leclerc's oath at the Koufra oasis in 1941 to raise the flag of France over Strasbourg. At a Cabinet session, the Prime Minister said the French army must fight to the last man to prevent the city falling into enemy hands again. Meeting Eisenhower and Brooke, he warned that abandoning Strasbourg would bring down his government: 'It will be our Stalingrad,' he added. Churchill, who flew over to see the Supreme Allied Commander, backed the French. Eisenhower desisted.[6]

Evidence that France was still not the power it had been came with its absence from the two major summits of 1945 that confirmed the shape of post-war Europe, at Yalta in January and Potsdam in July. Both conferences discussed major matters involving France without bothering to consult the government in Paris, for instance on the agreement to grant France an occupation zone in Germany or to include it among the five powers which would invite others to attend the founding conference of the United Nations, thus giving it a permanent seat on the Security Council. Less positively, Potsdam brought a decision to divide Vietnam into British and Chinese spheres of influence; de Gaulle immediately ordered his companion from the Dakar expedition, Admiral Thierry d'Argenlieu, and Leclerc, to Saigon as High Commissioner and military commander respectively, and drew up instructions on reasserting French authority.

Yalta has acquired a particular place in French demonology as the time when the Big Three carved up Europe over the heads of the countries concerned. Two decades later, de Gaulle would still be inveighing against it as a major source of the troubles of the world. In fact, much of the dissection had been done at the previous tripartite summit in Tehran at the end of 1943 or was shaped by events on the ground, notably the advance of the Red Army through eastern and central Europe. What really rankled about the summit in the Crimea was that France had not been invited to sit alongside the USA, the USSR and Britain, though Churchill went out of his way to defend its interests during the discussions – assistance de Gaulle never acknowledged. Such an open demonstration of France's unequal status could simply not be accepted, then or subsequently.

To show his displeasure, the General refused a suggestion from Roosevelt that they meet in Algiers on his way home from the Crimea. His reasoning was that he saw no point in the encounter since the Big Three had made their decisions at Yalta without France's presence, and that he could not countenance an invitation from a foreign leader to a meeting on French soil. His stance earned him criticism in the French press. Bidault was unhappy but de Gaulle ignored him. Furious, Roosevelt dictated a highly insulting message to the French leader. The diplomat Charles 'Chip' Bohlen tried to get it toned down, though he told the President that he agreed de Gaulle was 'one of the biggest sons of bitches who ever straddled a pot'. Amused by the expression, Roosevelt approved a new and more diplomatic draft. But, reporting to Congress, he remarked on 'a certain prima donna' whose star-like caprices meant he missed a useful meeting.

Nonetheless when Roosevelt died on 13 April 1945, de Gaulle nonetheless declared a week of national mourning in France and wrote to his successor Harry Truman of his 'immense emotion and profound sadness', calling the late President a man who had left a model and a message for the world. 'From his first to his last day, he was the friend of France. France admired and loved him.' That summer, when he crossed the Atlantic to see the new President, he travelled to Roosevelt's home at Hyde Park in Upper New York State to pay his respects at the grave. Still, standing up to Washington was essential if de Gaulle was to maintain his fundamental argument that he represented an undefeated nation. Given Roosevelt's view of France and of de Gaulle, their quarrel was inevitable. Though it is difficult to see the two men enjoying a weekend together, it was not personal but a matter of state, and so would persist on both sides.[7]

Soon after succeeding Roosevelt, Truman received a pertinent memorandum from his Secretary of State, Edward Stettinius, which said the best interests of the United States would be served by making every effort 'to assist France, morally as well as physically, to regain her strength and her influence'. But the note added that an obsession with restoring prestige after the debacle of 1940 led the French 'from time to time to put forward requests which are out of all proportion to their present strength and have in certain cases . . . showed unreasonable suspicions of American aims and motives'. Washington should take this into account and treat France 'in terms of her potential power rather than her present strength', it concluded.

But de Gaulle saw little evidence of support from across the Atlantic, his government complaining about insufficient supplies of food and goods. He made a point of tripping up a congressional delegation for not having gone through the full accreditation process with the Quai d'Orsay; until this was done, he declined to see the visitors. When Bidault called at the White House and expressed France's desire to participate in the final assault on Japan, Truman replied that any forces sent to the Far East would have to be under US command.

On the European battlefield, the clash over Strasbourg was repeated when, at de Gaulle's urging, French troops under de Lattre de Tassigny raced to capture Karlsruhe, where the Prime Minister visited them and told them to continue to Stuttgart. This they did. When the Americans arrived to take over from them, as laid down in the plan of campaign, de Gaulle told them not to budge. His pursuit of French interests compromised Allied coordination, and led Truman to threaten to cut off supplies. The General retreated, ordering only a token force to stay behind while the main French force resumed its advance to the south. 'The roses of glory cannot be without thorns,' he noted in his memoirs. But the irritation he was causing posed a distinct risk to Franco-American relations; 'I don't like the son of a bitch,' Truman told his staff. [8]

There was an unexpected episode at this time when Heinrich Himmler sent de Gaulle a message as the Red Army advanced on Berlin, urging him to reach an understanding with Germany. The SS chief proposed to free the General's brother Pierre, a prisoner in Germany, in return for a safe conduct for himself to the Spanish border. 'No follow-up,' the General wrote on it. In another message, Himmler warned that the US and Britain would treat France as a satellite while the Soviets would impose their law on France and liquidate him. 'Enter into relations without delay with the men who, in the Reich, still have power and want to lead their country in a new direction,' he added. 'If you surmount the spirit of vengeance, if you grasp the occasion that History offers you today, you will be the greatest man of all time.' In his memoirs, de Gaulle wrote that, 'flattery aside', there was some truth in Himmler's insight. But he did not respond.[9]

On 4 May 1945, after an unconditional surrender had been signed with the British and Americans at Allied headquarters in Reims, a fuller ceremony was held in Berlin with the Soviets. At the second occasion, which de Lattre de Tassigny attended, the French presence had not been provided for and a small tricolour flag had to be pieced together – the first version got the colours in the wrong arrangement but this was rectified in time. Seeing the French commander, Marshal Keitel, the head of the Wehrmacht high command, who had been at the signature of the armistice in 1940, snorted, 'Ah, the French are here too? That's all that was missing.'

De Gaulle had achieved his aim of ensuring France's presence at the time of victory. 'Honour! Honour, for always to our armies and their chiefs!' he declared in a radio address to mark the day. 'Honour to our people, whom terrible trials have not reduced or made to bend. Honour to the United Nations who mixed their blood with our blood, their sufferings with our sufferings, their hopes with our hopes, and who today triumph with us. Ah ! Long live France!'[10]

By the end of 1944, an opinion poll reported that 64 per cent of French people thought that their country had already regained the rank of a Great Power. The results of Gaullist foreign policy certainly seemed impressive. For the Prime Minister, keeping the Germans down was paramount. He wanted to see the defeated enemy split into regional administrations without a central authority of the kind which had, within living memory, launched three wars against his country. France, he insisted, must control the east bank of the Rhine, where he had served as a young officer, including the city of Cologne. It should also have access to coal from the Ruhr and Saarland basins to alleviate its energy shortage. In addition, he wanted two million German labourers to be sent to France to help with reconstruction. His demands were such that Lucius Clay, who administered western Germany for the Allies, was led to remark, 'sometimes, I wonder who conquered Germany, who pays the bills and why'. He achieved some success, notably in exerting French influence over the Saarland, though Cologne remained in the British zone and France got only a small number of German workers. But his problem was that the dictates of the Cold War meant that the US and Britain increasingly favoured building up western Germany as a counter to the Soviets.[11]

There was a fresh confrontation with Washington on the territory of the other defeated Axis power in June 1945, when Paris sent units into the French-speaking Italian border region of the Val d'Aosta against US wishes, and their commander threatened to open fire on American forces if they blocked him. When pressed to order a withdrawal, de Gaulle told the American ambassador to France, Jefferson Caffery, that this would be a humiliation. Truman, who detected 'injured dignity' in the Frenchman, recalled in his memoirs that his feelings about him had become 'less and less friendly'. When the War Secretary, Henry Stimson, said he considered de Gaulle a psychopath, the President agreed with him. 'The French are using our guns, are they not?' he asked. On hearing that they were, Truman decided to stop arms shipments immediately. In a private message to the General, he said he found 'almost unbelievable' the threat that French troops bearing American weapons could fight US troops so soon after they had contributed to the Liberation of France. Faced with the prospect of suspension of arms supplies, de Gaulle again reined himself in, agreeing to withdraw from most French positions. He still claimed victory.[12]

II
Vietnam – the 'big game'

Washington was also unprepared to help France in the Far East, given the anti-colonial stance inherited from Roosevelt. In his memoirs, the

General wrote of an American 'veto' on a French presence in the Pacific; the truth was that the collapse of Vichy rule in Indochina left Paris with little or no role to play. In the spring of 1945, Japanese troops had attacked French positions across Vietnam. The governor, Admiral Decoux, a Vichy holdover, refused to submit, and was arrested by the Japanese along with the army chief. The American command based in China refused to provide assistance. Some 13,000 French troops were killed or taken prisoner, and all Frenchmen of adult age were interned in concentration camps. Almost five thousand soldiers managed to retreat to south-west China but four thousand others died on the way.

At the urging of the Japanese, the figurehead emperor of Vietnam, Bao Dai, declared an end to France's sixty years of colonisation. As well as resenting the American position, de Gaulle scented British duplicity and hypocrisy in support of China's designs on the French territories. He ordered a force to be put together to restore colonial rule, but had trouble getting it to Indochina. Instead, as Japan's hold weakened, it was the Communist guerrillas of the Viet Minh, under Ho Chi Minh and the military commander, General Giap, who took the initiative, forming the People's Liberation Committee and a Liberation Army that moved into the countryside of the northern region of Tonkin with the backing of the US intelligence service, the OSS, which saw them as a progressive ally. A State Department policy paper in June 1945 judged that France would need to assent to a greater degree of self-government if the population was to be reconciled to its rule, but that Paris showed little intention of going this way.

De Gaulle recalled in his memoirs that news of the dropping of two atomic bombs on Japan on 6 and 9 August 1945 left him with 'a despair at seeing the appearance of a weapon that might destroy the human race'. But, as Constable of France, he was also keen to exploit the situation in the national interest. 'We have got a big slice to recover, a big game to play,' he told his High Commissioner, d'Argenlieu. 'Over to you! Move ahead.'

He did not react when Bao Dai wrote to him on 18 August pleading for the independence of Vietnam. Eight days later, the emperor abdicated, noting 'the mighty democratic impulse which is developing in the North of Our Realm'. Asked about Indochina at a press conference at the end of the month, the General said France intended to reassert its sovereignty and install an administration headed by d'Argenlieu which would include representatives of the native population as well as of the French settlers.

After Japan's surrender in September, at which Leclerc represented France, the Viet Minh declared a Democratic Republic of Vietnam. Its proclamation quoted from the Declaration of the Rights of Man and of the Citizen, a fundamental document of the French Revolution, and listed seventeen ways in which the French had 'violated our Fatherland and oppressed our fellow citizens' – ranging from the refusal of democratic liberty to forcing opium and alcohol on the Vietnamese. 'They have built more prisons than schools,' it charged. 'They have mercilessly slain our patriots; they have drowned our uprisings in rivers of blood.' When the Japanese had moved into Indochina in 1940, it added in a passage that could only have provoked particular irritation in de Gaulle, 'the French imperialists went down on their bended knees and handed over our country to them'.

Though the new administration in Hanoi broke off relations with Paris, a French envoy, Jean Sainteny, opened talks with Ho. Still, the French had little role to play as the Viet Minh extended its control of villages and small towns, while the British held nominal sway in the south. A hundred thousand Chinese nationalist forces moved across the border, ejecting the few remaining colonial officials from their buildings and seeking to install a puppet government they had brought with them. France's position improved when the British in Saigon facilitated the entry of its soldiers into the city, though they had to be protected from local people by surrendered Japanese troops pressed into service.

D'Argenlieu set out to enlist the support of the southern Vietnamese elite to balance the Viet Minh, but a southern Communist leader, Tran Van Giau, gained steadily in influence in the Saigon region, operating largely independently of Ho in Hanoi. In the autumn, 450 French and Eurasian women were massacred by mobs incited by the Communists. Indochina was, clearly, not proving as 'accessible' as the Prime Minister had hoped, and Washington remained favourable to the nationalists. For de Gaulle, on the other hand, the preservation of France's Empire was essential. As at the Brazzaville conference of 1944, there was vague talk of moving towards internal rule, but only in a system dominated by France. Independence was not on his agenda.[13]

III

Old quarrels and a new test

As for Britain, the bonhomie of Churchill's visit to Paris in November 1944 soon evaporated. For all his support of France at Yalta, his backing for de Gaulle over Strasbourg and the British help in Saigon, Churchill swung into anti-de Gaulle mode at the beginning of 1945. In January, he told Eden that he could not think of 'anything more unpleasant and impossible than having this menacing and hostile man in our midst, always trying to make himself a reputation in France by claiming a position far above what France occupies, and making faces at the Allies who are doing the work'.

A week later, he remarked to the Foreign Secretary that de Gaulle was 'a great danger for peace and for Great Britain'. Churchill also came to believe that the General's hold on power was not as strong as it appeared. During the crisis over the Val d'Aosta, he told Truman that, if Washington had made public the pressure it was putting on Paris, de Gaulle would have been overthrown, an opinion which found its way to the French leader and produced a typically scornful reaction. Churchill's cable went on: 'After five long years of experience, I am convinced [de Gaulle] is the worst enemy of France in her troubles' and 'one of the greatest dangers to European peace. No one has more need than Britain of French friendship, but I am sure that in the long run no understanding will be reached with General de Gaulle.'[14]

His prickliness towards the British led to a particularly unpleasant, if characteristic, incident during victory celebrations on the Champs-Élysées when the Free French ambulance unit which Lady Spears had helped to run passed the reviewing stand. The vehicles bore British and French flags, and as they passed a group of wounded French soldiers, a cry went up '*Voilà Spears. Vive Spears!*' ('There's Spears! Long live Spears!') De Gaulle turned to General Koenig and ordered that the ambulance unit was to be disbanded forthwith and its British member sent home. In protest, French officers being treated by the unit returned their medals to the War Ministry in Paris. As Lady Spears wrote, it was 'a pitiable business when a great man suddenly becomes small'.[15]

Syria and Lebanon emerged once more as flash points as pro-independence, anti-French agitation grew. The result was an Anglo-French crisis which so enraged de Gaulle that he subsequently told his secretary that Britain's conduct constituted 'an infamy that should never be forgotten'. To deal with the nationalist unrest, he sent in three battalions of soldiers on two warships. Duff Cooper expressed his government's disapproval, confirming the General's conviction that London was trying to push France out of the Levant, a conviction further reinforced when Britain, too, sent in army units to strengthen its positions.

Demonstrations against French citizens broke out in Damascus in May 1945. On the night of the 20th, the French general in command ordered his troops to fire on the crowd while an aircraft dropped bombs. The death toll reached a thousand. As street fighting continued, the French ambassador in London was warned that Britain could not remain passive if the situation continued as it was. On the 31st, Churchill sent de Gaulle a message saying that he had ordered the British commander in Syria to intervene to stop further bloodshed. He asked the French to call a ceasefire and pull their soldiers back into their garrisons. Unfortunately, Eden read the message out to the House of Commons before it reached the General in Paris.

The French Cabinet unanimously backed de Gaulle, who told a press conference in Paris that he did not think the damage done in Damascus had been very great – 'only several hundred people killed or injured'. But the British went ahead and restored order, backed by Truman, who told White House staff: 'Those French ought to be taken out and castrated.' In messages to Bidault, the General raged against the British, and deplored the lack of firmness of French representatives in the region who were trying to work out a formula for both countries to withdraw forces. Summoning Duff Cooper, de Gaulle told him, by his own account: 'I recognise that we are not in a position to wage war against you. But you have outraged France and betrayed the West. That cannot be forgotten.'[16]

He managed to discern a connection between British intervention in the Levant and even more bloody events that followed in North Africa. France was facing the start of a rise in nationalism in the Maghreb, encouraged by the creation of the Arab League in Cairo. The end of the war brought hopes of democratisation and independence, particularly given the presence of large numbers of young men from North Africa in the French forces in Europe who might be thought deserving of some kind of political reward. There was movement towards an understanding in Morocco when the Sultan of Rabat visited Paris in June 1945, but in Tunisia calls for autonomy by the nationalist Habib Bourguiba were rejected.

Algeria was the key, for both the French and the North Africans, a country for which France felt a special attachment given the large number of Europeans living there and one which had played an important role for de Gaulle in 1943. At the beginning of 1945 a conference of Algerian nationalists called for independence, and on 1 May violent demonstrations broke out in Algiers and the port city of Oran; police fire killed four people. The main pro-independence leader, Hadj Messali, was deported to Brazzaville.

On VE Day, 8 May, fresh demonstrations were held in the town of Sétif in the Constantine region. Marchers shouted 'Free Messali! Independent Algeria!' Algerians killed 102 people of French origin over two days. The French commanders ordered the artillery and the air force into action. Local inhabitants were massacred by troops from French West Africa, who were joined by German and Italian prisoners of war pressed into service. The death toll remains the subject of controversy, but was probably around eight thousand.

The governor of Algeria, Yves Chataigneau, who favoured a moderate line, was in Paris at the time and the decision to open fire appears to have been taken on the spot by the senior civil servant and three French generals in charge of military affairs in Algeria. De Gaulle's responsibility has proved impossible to establish, but the repression fitted with his general approach. He had told a military commander in 1944 that North Africa 'should not be allowed to slip between our fingers'; an Algerian historian, Mahfoud Kaddache, reported that the Prime Minister had earlier sent Chataigneau a telegram ordering 'all necessary measures to suppress the anti-French actions of agitators'. In his memoirs, the General devoted just three lines to the episode, noting merely that the 'start of an insurrection which took place in the Constantine region and was synchronised with the Syrian riots of the month of May was smothered by governor-general Chataigneau.'*[17]

*One reason for his reticence may have been that, when his memoirs were published, France was gripped by the Algerian crisis and he did not wish to give any hostages to fortune.

18

PÉTAIN AND LAVAL

I
Sigmaringen

After he had been taken by the Germans to Belfort in eastern France in August 1944, Marshal Pétain gave up his salary as head of state and drew only his military pension. The gesture mattered to him. For his part, Laval said he would not participate in any administration, and refused a summons from Hitler to meet him in Germany. Instead the trip was made by Darnand, Déat and Fernand de Brinon, the hawk-nosed former Vichy representative in Paris. The Führer told them his flying bombs would turn the tide of the war, and insisted that a new government must be created, with the Marshal's approval.

Pétain caved in once again. He gave de Brinon, whose Jewish wife had been classified as an honorary Aryan, a statement that could be interpreted as granting him a free hand. Forming a government, the former journalist handed Darnand responsibility for defence and Déat for law and order. It was all a tragic farce. When American troops approached Belfort in September, the collaborators were taken across the border into Germany to a fortress on a rocky outcrop overlooking the upper Danube in the small town of Sigmaringen. Other Nazi sympathisers joined them, including the writer and doctor Louis-Ferdinand Céline, whose brilliance with words was matched by his virulent anti-Semitism and nihilism.

The original castle had burned down in the 1850s and had been rebuilt in grandiose style, its huge rooms crammed with suits of armour, paintings, hunting trophies and massive furniture. The corridors were vast and draughty, the lift big enough to house a motor car. The eighty-eight-year-old Marshal was allocated quarters on the seventh floor. Laval was below him. A newspaper was produced and a radio station set up.

There was a great deal of bad blood among the refugees; Pétain asked to be allowed to leave but his request was refused. As the Marshal and his regime went through its death throes, 7,500 Frenchmen who had signed up to fight for the Nazis were joined at a camp in Germany by two thousand members of the *Milice* and, after swearing loyalty to Hitler, were sent to fight the Red Army on the Vistula. Some were said subsequently to have taken part in the defence of Berlin.

Pétain was intent on returning home to try to clear his name. In a petition to Hitler, he noted, 'I can answer for my actions only in France. At my age the only thing one fears is not having done one's full duty: I wish to do mine.' Asked at a lunch what he would do if the Marshal returned to France, de Gaulle replied: 'What do you expect me to do with him? I'll assign him a residence somewhere in the Midi and I'll wait for death to come and take him.' An opinion poll found that 58 per cent of those questioned thought the old soldier should not be tried. At lunch with his son and members of his staff, de Gaulle added that he had 'seen Pétain die – it was in 1925'.[1]

II
The Marshal goes on trial

A decree of November 1944 had set up a High Court to try Vichy ministers, senior military men and officials. The first case ended with the jailing of Admiral Jean-Pierre Esteva, the Vichy resident governor in Tunisia who had allowed German troops to land there after Operation Torch. He was followed in the dock by General Dentz, who had fought the Free French in Syria and who was condemned to death. De Gaulle commuted the sentence. In March 1945, the court decided to try Pétain. The following month, having been allowed by the Germans to go to Switzerland, the Marshal crossed into France. General Koenig met him at the frontier, refusing to shake the old man's hand. As his train headed for Paris, it was pelted with stones by local people in the Jura. After arriving, Pétain was held in a fort in the suburb of

Montrouge in a small cell furnished only with a bed, a cupboard and a bedside table.

At 1 p.m. on 23 July 1945, he entered the court room at the Palais de Justice by the Seine in the centre of Paris, wearing a simple blue uniform adorned only with the country's highest military honour, the Médaille Militaire. In his left hand he held his kepi, which he put on a table in front of him as he sat down. The city was suffering from a heatwave, with stormy skies. The court was packed; some of the journalists in the press gallery had to sit on each other's knees.

It was not an event de Gaulle had particularly wanted. He would probably have preferred his one-time mentor, to whom he referred as '*Le Maréchal*', never as 'Pétain', to have remained in Switzerland and to have been tried in his absence. The General looked gloomy when the Justice Minister, Pierre-Henri Teitgen, reported to him on the trial. 'Do your duty, do your duty,' he said while taking care that General Juin, who had served Vichy faithfully until 1942, went on a lengthy foreign mission so that he could not be called as a witness.

The public attitude to Pétain had hardened as evidence mounted of Vichy's conduct and as workers returning from forced labour in Germany told of their bad treatment. By the time the trial opened, emotions were running high – the proceedings had to be suspended several times because of shouting matches between lawyers and outcries from the galleries. The jurors, who were allowed to intervene in the hearings, included Resistance figures and politicians with axes to grind. The defence argued that the court was not competent to try the case since the constitution of 1875 stipulated that the head of state could only be tried by the Senate. There was also the awkward fact that the principal judge, Paul Mongibeaux, and his two assistants had served under the collaborationist regime and taken an oath of allegiance to the Marshal. For that matter, the prosecutor, André Mornet, had applied unsuccessfully to do the same job at the Vichy trial of Third Republic politicians in Riom.

After Mongibeaux and the other judges decided that the court was competent, the charge sheet was read, accusing Pétain of treason and of having plotted against the Republic for many years. It did not mention the persecution of the Jews, the *Milice* or the sending of Frenchmen to do forced labour in Germany. Such aspects of Vichy rule were best passed over in the interests of not arousing controversy that would have disturbed the post-Liberation consensus and the maintenance of public order, while French participation in atrocities such as the round-up of 1942 at the Vel d'Hiv was brushed under the carpet for many years in line with the General's cold-blooded insistence on painting out of history anything that could hinder his resurrection of the state. His principal quarrel with his one-time patron remained the signature of the armistice of 1940 rather than what followed.

Pétain's most active defence lawyer, the tall, thin Jacques Isorni, had helped him to prepare a statement which the old man had memorised, though he also copied it out in letters large enough for him to read without his spectacles. Standing to speak in a voice which grew increasingly firm, he insisted that he had sacrificed himself and his prestige for the good of the nation to prepare for the liberation of a country that was 'sad but alive'. The armistice had contributed to the Allied victory by keeping the Germans away from the Mediterranean coast and safeguarding France's Empire, he said. He concluded by expressing readiness to bear the full burden if found guilty; a Marshal of France asked pardon from no one. Considering the proceedings, Claude Mauriac found it hard to disentangle the strands of guilt, innocence, senility, powerlessness, faults and crimes in the trial. 'Was there a deliberate crime, organised treason? In all honesty, I do not believe so,' he added in his diary.

After his statement, the old soldier said little else, cupping his hand over his ear to hear better and sometimes dozing off as a procession of witnesses from the political world replayed the drama of 1940. Reynaud was the most long-winded, Daladier the most forceful, and Blum, who had just returned from a German concentration camp, the most persuasive. Herriot, who wore a slipper because of gout, was reminded by Isorni of how he had called on ministers to rally round the Marshal in July 1940. While the Radical leader veered between prevarication and bombastic self-justification, Pétain went to sleep.

Weygand saluted the Marshal as he walked to the stand. In an extremely lengthy deposition, he drew a distinction between the armistice and a capitulation. He argued that, if France had fought on, the Wehrmacht might have marched through France to Spain, taking

Gibraltar and occupying North Africa. He also claimed that the first talk of seeking an armistice had come from Reynaud and Lebrun. After the former Premier rose to deny this, the argument became so violent that Mongibeaux suspended the proceedings.

On 3 August, Pierre Laval gave evidence. The sixty-two-year-old politician had fled from Germany to Spain, only to be sent by Franco to Austria where the Americans delivered him to the French. Brought to court from his prison in the Paris suburbs, Laval cut a poor figure initially. His suit was creased, his white tie discoloured, his moustache stained with nicotine, his dark hair plastered on his scalp. He carried a black hat in one hand and a briefcase under his arm, and, at first, seemed to have difficulty speaking. Though the newspaper *France-Soir* ran a cartoon showing everybody holding their noses when he appeared, the former lawyer was soon in his element, sparring with opponents and correcting Mongibeaux on facts in his Auvergnat accent with its rolling 'rs'. At times, he feigned not to understand what was going on, as one journalist put it 'like a village idiot speaking to local magistrates for the first time'. When he asked for water and a bottle of Vichy was brought, there was laughter. As Claude Mauriac put it: 'Though destined for the execution stake, this man did not fail to be touching.'

'Deal with me according to your conscience,' the Marshal said in his final statement. 'Mine brings me no reproach since during a life that is already long, and, having arrived at the threshold of death, I state that I have no ambition other than to serve France.' The jurors repaired to a buffet set up in a side room where they ate and drank well, arguing into the night about the sentence. In the end, by 14 votes to 13, the Vichy leader was condemned under an article of the criminal code that meant the death penalty – the key vote came from a Communist. He was also sentenced to national indignity. Then a proposal that the penalty should not be carried out was adopted. Though the jurors did not know this, de Gaulle had decided to commute the death sentence.

The verdict was announced at 4 a.m.; Pétain was summoned after celebrating mass and making his confession. The Prime Minister provided his own aircraft to fly him to a prison fortress in the Pyrenees where the Vichy regime had held Third Republic politicians. Three months later, he was moved to a desolate island off the coast of western France, where he was allocated two rooms in a fort and cared for himself in all ways except for cutting his toenails, an art he had forgotten when attended by a pedicure specialist at Vichy. He remained on the Île d'Yeu until he died in July 1951 at the age of ninety-five, growing increasingly depressed, physically infirm and mentally senile. In a verdict written fifteen years later, de Gaulle judged that his life had been 'successively banal, then glorious, then deplorable, but never mediocre'.[2]

III
The death of Laval

In a string of trials that followed, major collaborators were sentenced to death, starting with the former head of the *Milice*, Joseph Darnand, who was shot after a brief hearing. His colleague and rival, Marcel Déat, was sentenced to death, but he escaped to Italy, hiding in a convent where he died in 1955. The newspaperman Jean Luchaire, who had become Information Minister in the last-gasp collaborationist regime in Germany, also fled to Italy, but was less fortunate: he was caught and brought back to France, where he was tried and executed. Fernand de Brinon was repatriated from Germany, found guilty of war crimes and shot. Louis-Ferdinand Céline, who managed to get to Denmark, was sentenced to one year's imprisonment and national disgrace in his absence, but then amnestied, enabling him to return to France in 1951 and to resume his writing career until his death ten years later.

The only collaborator de Gaulle met in person was the wartime Governor in Indochina, Admiral Decoux. The General gave him a glacial welcome, and listened in silence as Decoux argued that the best way of keeping Indochina under French rule had been by maintaining a presence there. 'Why did you have to keep singing the Marshal's praises as you did and shouting all the time *Vive le Maréchal?*' de Gaulle asked. The admiral was acquitted of any crimes.

The biggest trial was that of Laval. When the proceedings opened on 5 October 1945, the former lawyer brought out the familiar claim that Vichy's actions had limited the damage done to France. Where had ultimate responsibility lain? he asked. Obviously with Pétain, whose death sentence had been commuted by de Gaulle. The implications were plain: the Auvergnat could not be executed if the Marshal was spared. That was to overlook the very different status of the two men, particularly in the General's eyes.

Wearing a dark grey chalk-stripe suit and white scarf and looking haggard, the former Premier took issue with the obviously biased jurors and judges. The time given to the defence was so abbreviated that he and his lawyers boycotted the hearings. When he asked to be allowed to return to court, the principal judge hissed to an attendant: 'He's pissing me off. We've got to finish.' A death sentence was pronounced after four days.

Approached by the defence, Reynaud and Blum both expressed regret at the way the trial had been conducted. The Socialist, to whom Laval's wife had addressed herself for help, wrote to the General saying that a man could not be executed after such a pantomime. The defence asked for a retrial. De Gaulle received Laval's main lawyer, Jacques Isorni, and his colleagues as well as consulting the Justice Minister, who blamed Laval for the disruption of the trial, though he added that a new hearing was possible. There was strong political pressure from the Communists to go ahead. Laval's lawyers were told that the execution would proceed.

At dawn on 15 October 1945, a few hours before Laval was due to be shot, the prosecutor, the Paris Prefect of Police, Charles Luizet, his assistant, Edgard Pisani, and a doctor went to the prison in the Paris suburb of Fresnes. There they found that the former premier had swallowed the cyanide pill he had carried with him since the previous year. Laval's stomach was pumped and he was taken back to his cell, vomiting and shouting.

Luizet and Pisani went to see de Gaulle. Standing before a tapestry, the General wagged his head from side to side 'like a worried eagle', according to Pisani. He asked: 'Have the last rites been pronounced?' Luizet said they had. 'Then he no longer belongs to us,' said the Prime Minister coldly, his eyes half shut. 'Let the firing squad do its duty.'

Laval's shoes were removed and he was taken to a mound behind the jail and strapped to the execution post. 'You wanted this show, you'll have it to the end,' he shouted at the watching judges who hid behind a prison van. He was not allowed to give the firing squad, who wore British tin helmets, the order to shoot; as they did so, he cried '*Vive la France!*' 'Pierre Laval . . . died bravely,' de Gaulle recorded in his memoirs.[3]

19

'NEST OF INTRIGUES'

I
Getting on with business

De Gaulle always had trouble accepting the politicisation of government. He preferred the idea of an administration consisting of loyal followers who were not subject to external party discipline or affected by electoral considerations. When municipal elections were held in April 1945, he circulated a note to ministers saying that, while it was praiseworthy for them to be candidates, they 'should abstain from speaking in public in constituencies where they stand'. He ran Cabinet meetings like a military exercise. Ministers were not allowed to take notes or to light a cigarette before the General had done so. They could not question him and were instructed to forget their party allegiances.[1]

Having refused to found a party of his own, the General showed sympathy for the *Mouvement républicain populaire* (MRP), which was close to the ideas of the liberal Catholic group he had been associated with before the war. It rejected the Marxism and anti-clericalism of the Left and embodied the values of moderate members of the Resistance. It also, pleasingly, called itself a movement rather than a party. De Gaulle's wartime spokesman, Maurice Schumann, was a prominent member, and the General urged Pleven to join it, advice he did not follow.

More broadly, however, there could be little prospect of the French leader fitting in with the political groups that survived from the Third Republic or their desire to resume the parliamentary game. As early as December 1944, he told an aide in an aside at a party for the children of his staff around two Christmas trees on the rue Saint-Dominique that he would go to the next debate in the National Assembly: 'but I won't speak. That doesn't interest me.' Commenting on the quality of his ministers, he remarked to Claude Mauriac that France had not given him the men he needed.

Though he stood forth as the representative of the nation on occasions such as the final victory over Germany with its mass singing of the national anthem and cries of '*Vive de Gaulle!*' in the provisional legislature, public criticism of the Prime Minister was rising. Legislators complained that the government was taking no notice of them. In March 1945, Claude Mauriac noted in his diary that it was now 'the thing to do to denigrate Charles de Gaulle, to say that it was worth distrusting him, that he had shown incompetence in government matters . . . In political circles, an ironic tone was adopted as if, really, it was not right to take this military man seriously.'[2]

The climate remained touchy as the General approached a key issue of the constitutional form to be adopted for post-war France. It had been agreed in Algiers that a constituent assembly would be elected to decide on the political system. The question was whether the National Assembly was to rule supreme, exercising the will of the people, or was there to be a strong presidency, ensuring executive leadership? In the first case, it was likely that the Left would dominate, led by the Communists. The second-ranking member of the government, Jules Jeanneney, warned the General that such a body would abrogate power to itself and become 'omnipotent and ungovernable'. De Gaulle favoured a return to the original shape of the Third Republic with a strong president who would avoid the weaknesses of the pre-war years. But this would be seen by many as a precursor to dictatorship by the Man of 18 June, and might provoke action by the Left.[3]

As so often at such crucial moments, de Gaulle retired to consider his options. After three days at home, he called a Cabinet meeting on 9 July 1945. He opened the proceedings by saying he had decided against a return to the past and favoured the election of a constituent assembly. But, with Jeanneney's warning in mind, he proposed that this election should be accompanied by a referendum on a proposal that its life should be limited to seven months and its powers restricted. It would vote on laws and the budget, ratify treaties and elect the Prime Minister;

but it would not be able to take the initiative on spending measures, would have no say on the choice of ministers and would not be able to overthrow the government.

Having issued that challenge to the powers of the legislature and the political parties, de Gaulle returned to his favourite theatre: global affairs. In August, he flew to Washington for seven hours of discussions with Truman. His memoirs betray a somewhat condescending view of the President, but he noted that he and Truman never exchanged acid words. At their last meeting, the host hung a decoration round the General's neck and presented France with a DC4 airliner, but he would not think the visit worth mentioning in his memoirs.

The Washington talks were followed by another triumphal visit to New York during which Mayor La Guardia again did the full honours: a cartoon of the two men was captioned 'The Great Asparagus Kisses the Little Flower'. The black contralto Marian Anderson sang 'La Marseillaise' at a night-time ceremony in Central Park. De Gaulle embraced babies and made a ticker-tape walk down Broadway. After New York, there was a successful stay in Chicago, marred only by the way in which a delay in the arrival of the French plane led the reception committee to drink too much and some of the welcoming speeches rambled. Canada followed, with warm welcomes in Montreal and Ottawa. Then it was time to return to France, to continue the debate on the new constitution and to try to get to grips with the budget gap.[4]

There was also the sensitive issue of the treatment of prisoners of war and workers returning from Germany. Some of the repatriation ceremonies saw protests at the lack of aid they received. De Gaulle felt for these war victims and had his staff send some deserving cases gifts of money, insisting that these must remain anonymous. But in his memoirs he accused outsiders of infiltrating the welcome-home occasions, dressed in German prison uniforms. Their aim, he added, was to provoke a police response to discredit the government. Though he did not name them, the Communists were clearly in his sights. Receiving leaders of the movement that claimed to represent the returnees, he told them that what they were doing was unacceptable. His guests took three minutes to confer, and then promised that the demonstrations would cease.[5]

The cost of assistance to more than a million men coming home without jobs and sometimes in poor physical condition further widened the budget deficit. New taxation was inevitable. The government decided to levy it on the assets of the rich and on profits made during the occupation. The Left said that the rate was not high enough, the Right that it would harm the revival of business, but the legislation was passed with a large majority. It was the last time that the bulk of parliamentarians in the main parties all followed the government.

The impending referendum polarised politics. The Communists came out against the limitation of the authority of the legislature and the Socialists declared that nothing should hamper the power of parliament. In reply, de Gaulle insisted on the need for the government not to be hobbled. He hoped to gain support from Léon Blum, who, in a much-noted book written in captivity in Germany, had concluded that parliamentary government was not the only or the purest form of democracy and opted for an American-style presidential system with a separation of powers. But, on his return to France, the former Premier insisted on the need to prevent one-man rule, and for a strong parliament to deal with 'the case of de Gaulle'. He declined to become a Minister of State on health grounds – he was in fact in good condition – and because of his desire to spend all his time rebuilding his party.

'My refusal distresses you,' he told de Gaulle when they met. At which the General, who had received him with considerable warmth, went glacial and replied: 'It doesn't distress me, it hampers me.' Blum's refusal, followed by a similar attitude taken by Herriot and the conservative Louis Marin, was proof enough for the General that party leaders put sectarian concerns above the national interest.[6]

II
Trench warfare

A total of 19.2 million people out of the enfranchised electorate of 25 .7 million went to the polls on 21 October 1945 in metropolitan France and the North African possessions to vote on the referendum and for members of the proposed new assembly. The occasion was notable as the first national ballot in which women could take part – Yvonne de Gaulle, in black hat, black coat and black gloves, did so in the 16th *arrondissement* of Paris.

The establishment of the Constituent Assembly received 96 per cent approval and 66 per cent backed the limitations placed upon its powers and duration proposed by de Gaulle. This vindicated his insistence on consulting the people directly. But the simultaneous election for the assembly produced a result which boded ill for him, and conferred a legitimacy on the parties which he himself lacked.[7]

The Communists took 26 per cent of the vote, the MRP 24.9 per cent and the Socialists 23.8 per cent. Moderates won 13.3 per cent. Though there was some fluidity over party affiliations, the official parliamentary list drawn up a little while later showed the PCF with 161 of the 586 assembly seats, the MRP and Socialists with around 150 each. With only 9.3 per cent of the vote and twenty-eight seats, the once dominant Radical Socialists were humbled for representing the old politics; half their usual voters were estimated to have gone against the party line and voted 'yes' in the referendum.

The country now had three major political formations with a clear delineation between the Left and the MRP. The PCF had earned the dividend of its strong organisation, its Resistance record and the national appetite for economic and social reform. Its membership rose from around 400,000 in 1944 to 900,000 by 1946; its support for the government was, as Palewski remarked, that of a rope for a hanged man. The Socialists had re-established themselves. An influx at the Liberation increased their membership to 354,000 by 1946. The key question was the degree of cooperation between the two parties of the Left, which enjoyed a near-majority of seats in the body that would draw up France's new constitution.

The new political player, the MRP, attracted votes from a wide spectrum of centrists and liberal Catholics. It declared itself 'the party of loyalty' – implicitly to de Gaulle – and its first president was Maurice Schumann. But it had no wish to be counted as the General's political army and some leading MRP figures, such as Bidault and the Liberation-era Justice Minister, François de Menthon, suffered from the Prime Minister's overbearing manner. Having attracted nearly 5 million voters and enrolled 200,000 members, its parliamentarians wanted to play their legislative role to the full, which meant that they would not find de Gaulle's vision of executive supremacy very attractive.

Faced with this double-edged result, the General was in two minds. He felt that the referendum represented a national vote of confidence in him, but the assembly portended trouble. He mused about resigning as he fell into a familiar spell of melancholy. The people, he feared, no longer felt they needed him now that the nation was heading for calmer waters. During the Remembrance Day ceremony on 11 November 1945, which Churchill attended, he received a warm reception from the crowd. Yet he picked up the sentiment from politicians and officials around him that the nature of power was about to undergo a change. 'If I kept the leadership, it could only be on a transitory basis,' he wrote in his memoirs. 'But I still owed France and the French something: to leave as a morally intact man.'

In keeping with parliamentary practice, he submitted the resignation of his government to the Constituent Assembly when it met in the Palais Bourbon. For the occasion he discarded his uniform in favour of a civilian suit made for him by a fashionable tailor on the rue Royale; Yvonne thought it made him appear slimmer.

The legislature, presided over by a veteran of Algiers, Félix Gouin, went out of its way to demonstrate its authority by delaying approval of the government for a week. Critical passages in the opening speech by the parliamentary doyen, a Radical Socialist, were applauded while his praise for the General evoked little reaction. De Gaulle remembered the proceedings as 'mediocre'. Having made their point, the deputies voted unanimously for him to continue as Prime Minister, with a single abstention, that of Clemenceau's son. An opinion poll reported that 80 per cent of those questioned expressed satisfaction with this. A motion passed by the assembly declared that Charles de Gaulle 'was well worthy of the fatherland'. It was, he recalled, prompted by 'reverence for my past action, and not at all a promise for the future'. Indeed, he characterised what followed as 'a nest of intrigues'.

The formation of the government provoked a crisis as the PCF demanded a major ministerial post as a matter of right. The General insisted that he alone would decide on appointments. The Socialists raised the stakes by declaring that they would not join a government in which the Communists were not represented. As newspapers speculated about whether the General would walk out, his staff prepared to move his archives from his office. Palewski shuttled between the rue Saint-Dominique and the villa in Neuilly. Claude Mauriac noted that one of the staff, whom he does not name, spoke nostalgically of the great days of Fighting France, 'of dependable men, arms, false papers'.

De Gaulle went on the radio to state that he would not give the Communists any of the three 'levers' of the government – foreign affairs, the interior or defence. He followed this up with a letter to Gouin, asking if the legislature really wanted to remove his mandate only a few days after giving him overwhelming backing. He spoke of going to Canada as a private citizen if he was forced out; there he would fish and Yvonne would cook the catch.

The showdown came in a debate in the Assembly on 19 November. To ensure security, troops encircled the building and police blocked surrounding streets. Inside the Palais Bourbon, the Communist parliamentary leader, Jacques Duclos, a short, round man with a fierce tongue, denounced the General for insulting the 'party of 75,000 shot' and said de Gaulle was demeaning himself in clinging to power. But the Socialists did not want to see him fall and tabled a supportive motion with the MRP which carried the day. There was a price to pay. Another successful Socialist motion instructed the Prime Minister to form a government with an equitable distribution of seats among the three main groupings. He could choose which jobs went to which parties, but the politicians had not given way on asserting parliamentary power.

Leaders of the Communists, Socialists and MRP called at de Gaulle's office after noon on 20 November. From an adjoining room, Claude Mauriac heard raised voices and uneasy laughter followed by silences broken by the General. At the end of a tête-à-tête with André Philip, the Socialist who had tabled the assembly motion forcing him to name a tripartite government, Mauriac heard the General say in a violent tone: 'I've had enough.'

However, he fell into line. The Communist Maurice Thorez, the Socialist Vincent Auriol and the MRP Francisque Gay became Ministers of State, along with the moderate Louis Jacquinot. There were four Socialist ministers and as many from the MRP and the PCF plus one Radical, and Pleven, Soustelle and Malraux from de Gaulle's supporters. In his memoirs, the General insisted that he had succeeded in restricting the PCF to 'economic' ministries. But this was achieved only by subterfuge: de Gaulle took overall responsibility for defence, and the job of handling armaments, which went to the PCF stalwart Charles Tillon, was technically classified as an 'economic' portfolio.[8]

III
'Im-pos-si-ble to go-ver-n'

The parliamentary sniping continued as the government pushed through a highly ambitious economic and administrative programme. Bank nationalisations were pursued. The state took over production and distribution of electricity and gas. A decree – parliament was not consulted – established a national planning authority under Jean Monnet. From its offices in a classic old Parisian building with high windows a hundred metres from de Gaulle's headquarters, it set out to modernise the country's economy and infrastructure to make up for its pre-1940 backwardness, the destruction of the war and the German plundering of industry.

A national scientific research organisation, the CNRS, was given the job of improving university work and making France internationally competitive. A finishing school for civil servants, the École Nationale d'Administration (ENA), was opened in the 7th arrondissement of Paris. The brainchild of the Gaullist official Michel Debré, it was designed to provide a class of top administrators to build a new France. To give the country a great newspaper which would be respected by foreign governments, funds were provided to create *Le Monde*, under the austere, dedicated Hubert Beuve-Méry. De Gaulle claimed to have dreamed up the newspaper's title though the editor said it was his idea.

Abroad, yet another row broke out with Britain over the withdrawal of troops from the Levant, which de Gaulle saw as a fresh move by London to gain ascendancy in the region; while British forces would fall back to Baghdad, Amman and Jerusalem, the French would be far away in Algiers, Tunisia or Marseille. He also took strong objection to his country's exclusion from a meeting of Allied foreign ministers in Moscow; its subject, the conclusion of peace treaties in east Europe and the Baltic, did not concern France since it had not been at war there, but this did nothing to improve his temper. Had he not been de Gaulle, his anger might have been assuaged by a decision of the US to grant France a credit of $550 million to finance imports. Instead he wrote darkly in his memoirs of the Allies waiting for a change of leadership in Paris.

Despite American help, the economy remained in dire straits. The franc was devalued. Bread rationing returned. In a parliamentary speech at the end of December 1945, de Gaulle insisted on the need to reduce the budget deficit, increase production and balance prices and wages. The government had managed to achieve an initial economic recovery, he claimed, with little evidence to show for it.

The Communist Jacques Duclos kept up his attacks from the Left, Herriot waged a typically subtle, half-spoken campaign against the General and the Socialists fought the government to get better pay increases for the striking civil servants, who constituted an important section of their electorate. De Gaulle remained intransigent. If things were not going well, it was the fault of others. Exploding to Claude Mauriac, he shouted that his ministers, the parliamentarians and the journalists were all cowards.

At the turn of the year, his refusal to accept a Socialist call for reductions in military spending set off a fresh crisis. On the morning of 1 January 1946, de Gaulle was woken at home by a call from a minister saying that he had to drive to the parliament building. Never an enthusiast for early mornings, or for being rushed by others, the General refused, and telephoned the main proponent of the cuts on military spending, the Socialist André Philip, to say that, if he persisted, the government would ask for a vote of confidence. Philip replied that this was the third such threat in a week by the Prime Minister. 'It's too serious a question to be dealt with from bed before you shave and without having consulted any member of the government,' he added. De Gaulle hung up.

Later that day he was driven into Paris for a parliamentary debate which, according to his future son-in-law, Alain de Boissieu, who watched the proceedings, was marked by 'a circle of hatred closing in on General de Gaulle'. The Prime Minister insisted that the government should have sole executive responsibility. If the legislature refused it the means to govern, it would step down. Then, taking a broader approach, he told the chamber: 'We have started to reconstruct the Republic. We will continue to do so. Whatever you do, I think I can say in all conscience, and without doubt, this is the last time I will speak in this hemicycle; I think I can say to you in all conscience that if you act without taking into account the lessons of our political history of the last fifty years and in particular of what happened in 1940, if you do not take account of the absolute necessity for authority, dignity and the responsibility of the government, you will go to a situation in which, one day or another, I predict to you, you will bitterly regret having taken the path that you will have taken.'

Still, he compromised to get the military budget voted through by pledging to introduce a proposal for army reform within six weeks. Little attention was paid to the 'last time' reference in his speech, but he recalled in his memoirs that, when he left the Palais Bourbon on the evening of 1 January, he had made up his mind to resign. As well as the political infighting, the framing of the new constitution was heading in a direction of which he could not approve, with parliament likely to become all-powerful. When he asked to be informed about the work of the commission, the MRP rapporteur told him it was none of his business since he had not been elected by the people. His aide from Algiers, Louis Joxe, recorded how wounded the General was by this incident. 'From day to day, I saw the shadow of sadness grow on his face,' Joxe added.

Even worse, the commission proposed that the President of the Republic should be elected by the National Assembly, should not preside over meetings of the Cabinet or the National Defence Council, and should not have the right to commute death sentences – in addition, discussions were being held on whether he should name the Prime Minister.[9]

Characteristically, the General temporarily withdrew from the front line. On 5 January 1946, after attending the marriage of his daughter

Élisabeth to Major de Boissieu of his military staff, he set off for a week at a villa at Eden Roc on the Riviera. He was accompanied by Yvonne, his younger brother Pierre, who resembled him so closely that guards at official buildings sometimes saluted him, and his brother-in-law, Jacques Vendroux, who had been elected to the Assembly for Calais on the MRP ticket. Auriol conducted government business while he was away.

Before leaving he told his new son-in-law that he was ready to step down immediately. Apart from anything else, the fifty-five-year-old General was extremely tired, having hardly had a break during the five and a half years since the start of the war. He meditated on his next move as he walked along the rocky inlets of the Mediterranean coast in a dark suit and homburg, chain-smoking as he went. He visited local beauty spots, and devoted a press conference with local journalists to the joys of tourism in the region. In his memoirs he wrote that, in the winter sun, he decided to 'leave in silence, without accusing anybody either in public or in private, accepting no post . . . and without saying anything about what I would do afterwards'.

On 13 January, after a last visit to Cap d'Antibes, the General and his party drove to the local station in a big Cadillac, the gift from the US administration after the Liberation. As their special train headed north, he asked his companions what they thought he should do. His brother advised him not to resign, but to hold new elections; Vendroux said he should step down and leave the parties to make a mess of things so that he would be recalled.

Wishing to enter Paris as discreetly as possible, de Gaulle left his train at a siding outside the capital. The Socialist Transport Minister, Jules Moch, drove to greet him, clambering down from the road to the railway track. Emerging from the train, the Prime Minister climbed up the metal ladder behind Moch, and asked him to get into the car which had come to fetch him, adding, 'I've something to tell you.'

On the way into the city, speaking slowly and precisely, he told Moch it was 'im-pos-si-ble to go-ver-n wi-th the par-ties.' He did not wish to be criticised every day by men whose only claim to office was that they had been elected in some little corner of France. 'As I cannot govern as I wish, that is to say with full powers rather than letting myself be bound and my power dismembered, I am going.' Then he moved into the mythology of greatness in adding: 'One cannot imagine Joan of Arc, married, mother of a family and, who knows, cheated on by her husband.' He instructed Moch to pass the news only to Blum, who reacted by saying that the decision was logical, but badly timed. 'It will hit the country, but it won't knock it down,' the Socialist leader judged.[10]

In the following week, de Gaulle disclosed his decision to Malraux, who had become Information Minister, to Palewski and Pompidou from his staff, and to two MRP ministers. But he did not tell Bidault, having become so estranged by the Foreign Minister's perceived softness towards the Allies that he made it clear he did not wish the former Resistance chief to succeed him. There was a last passage of arms in parliament with Herriot which, while minor in substance, illustrated the state of relations between de Gaulle and the politicians. In a parliamentary question time, the Radical Socialist queried a government decision to confirm the award of decorations by Giraud to some of the French troops who had fought against the Torch landing; he called this an insult to the Allies and a glorification of a battle that had harmed France. In his defence of the decision, the Prime Minister remarked in a reference to Herriot's lunch with Laval and Abetz just before the Liberation of Paris: 'For myself, I never had anything to do with Vichy or with the enemy, except at gunpoint.'[11]

On Sunday 20 January, de Gaulle called a Cabinet meeting in a room in the rue Saint-Dominique which was adorned with pikes, shields and suits of armour. He arrived just after noon, in uniform, his back straighter than ever, his features drawn. He shook the hands of ministers and, before anybody sat down, told them: 'The exclusive regime of the political parties has reappeared. I disapprove of it. But, short of establishing by force a dictatorship which I do not want and which, doubtless, would turn out badly, I do not have the means of preventing this. I therefore have to retire.' He said he would send a letter to Gouin to inform the President of the Constituent Assembly of his decision. The ministers, he wrote in his memoirs, seemed 'more saddened than surprised'.

A fuller account by the Agriculture Minister, François Tanguy-Prigent, had de Gaulle saying he had decided to step down because he considered that his mission of reform and national renewal was finished. If he had enjoyed unanimous support in the legislature, he would have stayed, but parties which sat in the government attacked his administration. 'I do not wish to participate in party struggles,' he went on. Adding that he did not want any kind of demonstration on his behalf, he walked out saying, 'I am leaving for the country.'

Behind him, Moch said good could come out of the General's departure since parliament would be able to express itself free from the 'suffocating' effect of his personality. Thorez recognised the 'grandeur' of the departure but said the PCF would continue to work with the Christian Democrats for economic and foreign policy reasons – in other words to placate Washington.

De Gaulle intended to make a radio address that night – in contradiction of his subsequent statement in his memoirs that he had decided to leave in silence. But he was dissuaded by Auriol, whom he designated as interim head of government. Various versions exist of the speech it is said de Gaulle would have made. In one he warned that the party system was a 'fearsome anachronism'. Another, which may have been the work of faithful followers rather than of the General himself, declared that the prospect was for 'the state [to become] more despised, the government more powerless, the country more divided and the people poorer'. In terms redolent of 18 June 1940, it called on a gathering of all the French to save the nation, in particular 'you my old companions of the Free French forces, and you the fighters of the interior'.

In a later interview with the journalist Jean-Raymond Tournoux, de Gaulle reflected that he could have called in the army under Leclerc and banished parliament. In reality, the prospect of a coup in 1946 was highly dubious. Whether the army would have followed him is far from certain and opposition from the Left would have doomed France to civil war. In any case, de Gaulle noted that 'dictatorships have only been possible in history in countries which want to rise, not in those which want to go to sleep'.

Some years later, speaking to his nephew, de Gaulle called his resignation an error. Yet, given the way that French politics had evolved since the Liberation, and his own character, it was inevitable. In *Le fil de l'épée* he had written of the effort required to exert leadership at the top:

'The constant strain is hard to bear . . . Here one finds the real motives for retirement that are hard to explain.' In this case, the course of events since the Liberation made his departure all too easy to understand. Nor could anybody think that he would be content to return to the 'joys of relaxation, familiarity and friendship' he mentioned in his book. The question was what he would do next.[12]

20

'THAT WILL TEACH THEM'

I
'Shambles and mediocrity'

The twelve years between de Gaulle's resignation in 1946 and his return to power in 1958 are often depicted as a period during which he removed himself from public life to become 'the hermit of Colombey'. He himself wrote of solitude being his friend, and of wrapping himself in 'silence and serenity'. The eminent American *New York Times* journalist Cyrus Sulzberger, who saw him from time to time at this point in his life, described him as living in a 'self-imposed exile from politics'. Nothing could be further from the truth. If '*le désert*' has become the accepted term for these dozen years, it was a desert filled with political oases during which the former Premier was far from a recluse.

In his memoirs, de Gaulle wrote of the French people 'withdrawing into sadness' at his departure. Many of the letters he received did indeed express grief: 'We still love you,' one read. 'Why did you go? We are like orphans.' According to Jean-Raymond Tournoux, a great collector of unsourced remarks made by the General to visitors, he said the French would return to 'their vomiting' and 'go to the dogs', sliding towards the precipice before calling on him to save the situation, only for the 'shambles' to begin again if he turned his back on them for a second time.

But the summons to return to office did not come. A poll showed that, while 40 per cent of those questioned said they did not take pleasure in his departure, only 27 per cent wanted him back. Meanwhile, the parties concentrated on forming a new government under Gouin.

When presented with the proposal that he head the administration, the Socialist was said to have wailed: 'Succeed de Gaulle? Me? Impossible', and to have burst into tears. He still took the job and Auriol was elected to replace him as President of the Constituent Assembly and putative President of the Republic once a constitution came into effect. Thorez and Francisque Gay of the MRP continued as Ministers of State while the Socialist André Philip became Finance Minister. The Constituent Assembly overwhelmingly approved the government.

Despite reservations by the MRP, the legislature adopted a draft constitution which enshrined parliamentary power. As Duclos put it for the Left: 'Say what you want, we will do as we wish; we have the absolute majority.' Having greatly extended state power over the economy, France seemed on the brink of installing a political regime which would meet the Communist desire for a popular assembly to run the country.[1]

*

De Gaulle's house at Colombey-les-Deux-Églises was still being repaired and redecorated after being damaged by the retreating Germans. So he rented from the state a former hunting lodge built in the time of Louis XIV overlooking the large park at Marly outside Paris. His aide-de-camp, Claude Guy, signed a three-month lease for the house for 15,000 francs. Charles and Yvonne moved in with Anne and Marguerite Potel, the homely woman who looked after her.

The two-storey white house with a brick chimney and a gravel driveway was smaller than the one the de Gaulles had occupied in the Bois de Boulogne. The couple thought Anne would be as happy as possible there, and Yvonne felt more at home than in Neuilly. Still, the decorations were shabby and the facilities quite basic, with only rudimentary heating. A small orchard behind the house contained only a few twisted pear trees. On the first evening in the house, Yvonne searched for crockery and saucepans while her husband decided which room to use as his office and settled down to read a biography of Disraeli by André Maurois. The Cadillac Eisenhower had given France was parked in a former stable with broken-down walls. A goat was tethered outside; in the evening, the General took grass to feed it. He refused to use his position to gain additional food ration coupons, and supplies were sometimes tight. The de Gaulles bought their vegetables from a local who charged only the official prices, a miracle given the prevalence of the black market.

The General walked through the woods in the park, wearing a grey hat, singing as he went and returning with mud on his shoes. Night birds sang from the bare trees round the villa, which was guarded by three or four policemen. The former Premier wrote a poem in memory of soldiers, sailors, airmen and partisans who had died for Fighting France; it concluded:

Your example is the reason for our pride today,
Your glory will always accompany our hope.

In early February, Claude Mauriac moved in, taking an upstairs bedroom and handling de Gaulle's correspondence. On his first day, he noted a surprising sense of intimacy. Yvonne sat in the drawing room, leafing through magazines. Cooking smells hung in the air. When the General asked his secretary what the public was saying about him, Mauriac gave a careful reply. De Gaulle remarked: 'What a good thing I left. They're waiting for explanations, but . . . pfff.' When Mauriac added that things were going from bad to worse, the General said: 'All the better. That will teach them.'

'The country needs a chief,' he told his secretary some days later, dismissing the Gouin ministry as 'a brasserie government'. He contemptuously rejected a ministerial suggestion that his military rank should be raised to the status of marshal. His two stars had been enough for the war years, he wrote back; to change it now would be 'strange and even ridiculous'. On a loftier plane, he exclaimed: 'One does not decorate France.'

Mauriac noted that the General was sleeping badly, and seemed nervous and tired. On 15 February, Mauriac's father called for an hour-long meeting which began with a diatribe by the General against the British and Churchill, followed by ruminations on the state of France which, he said, faced three possibilities – the continuation of 'shambles and mediocrity', the Communists taking power, which would mean war as it would bring a Russian presence that the Americans and British would not accept – 'or my return'. Bidault was 'unfortunate . . . a poor little Christian Democrat' unable to resist the British. The Prime Minister was 'old father Gouin'. The Socialists were 'jealous, cuckolds, failures'. The General's vituperation took the younger Mauriac aback – 'impossible not to see in this a weak spot in a great spirit,' he wrote.

In letters to members of his family and admirers, the word de Gaulle used most frequently of the politicians in Paris was *bassesse,* a contemptuous expression denoting lowness, meanness, vulgarity and servility. Writing to his nephew François, he said that each day brought fresh justification of his decision to quit. To his faithful follower Michel Debré he called himself 'a sort of physical treasure' which should be 'pulled from the mud'. But all his self-belief could not keep reality at bay. Surprised by the lack of people coming to take a look at his new home, he sent a bodyguard to see if the police had set up barriers on the drive through the park from the main road; there were none. When he went out to the cinema in Paris on 1 April, he attracted little attention. It was time to act before he was relegated to history.[2]

II

'I will return if . . .'

In the spring of 1946, de Gaulle re-established contact with wartime companions, starting with the underground organiser Colonel Rémy, and then the intelligence chief Passy, who had broken his leg skiing and who was fetched in the General's Cadillac. Gaston Palewski followed, as did another wartime supporter, André Diethelm, who had served at the Armed Forces Ministry in 1944. In April, a Paris newspaper published a story based on leaks from visitors to Marly entitled 'I will return if . . .'

At the end of the month, he wrote to his wartime companion Leclerc declaring: 'The future is ours.' He would have need of the general one day, he added. But the immediate imperative was to lie low while waiting for the moment to set out on a fundamentally different course. 'In short, "we others", and you in particular, must play a tight game,' he went on. 'The stakes reach well beyond our own desires and even, I do not hesitate to write, beyond our own ideas. I embrace you, my dear friend.' The PS advised 'Burn this letter.'[3]

*

The referendum on 5 May 1946 rejected the constitution drawn up by the assembly by 10.58 million votes to 9.45 million. De Gaulle jubilated: 'I have spent my life being beaten to start with and then triumphing,' he told a visitor. For all its strength in the legislature, the Left could not muster a majority in the country. The gathering Cold War held back the advance of the PCF. A Socialist leader, André Le Troquer, recalled Thorez's desertion at the start of the war and added that putting the Communist leader in power would be to serve Russia's cause. France was anchoring itself increasingly in the Western camp, with Washington drawing comfort from the presence of the MRP in the government. At the end of May, a transatlantic mission by Blum and Monnet got a $650 million credit and liquidation of France's war debts. Seventy-five American cargo ships were earmarked to carry supplies. In return, French trade barriers on American goods were lifted.

De Gaulle turned down an invitation from Gouin to attend the celebrations for the first anniversary of the victory over Germany on 7 May with the lordly explanation to his secretary that he did not want to overshadow his successor. Instead, he was driven west from Paris on 11 May to the Vendée to pay homage at Clemenceau's tomb, and make a brief speech about national themes. He looked pale and emotional. There were shouts from the crowd urging him to take power.

On 25–26 May, he spent his last weekend at Marly before moving back to Colombey. Leaving the hunting lodge, Claude Mauriac picked a daisy from the lawn in front of the house and put it in his buttonhole. As the two aides drove into Paris, Claude Guy told him that de Gaulle was sure the parties would ask him to form a government but that he would refuse again and again until he got their 'unconditional surrender'.[4]

La Boisserie had been restored with a three-storey tower added; the

General established his study on its ground floor, his desk looking out at the rolling fields and a forest in the distance. The patch of grass and two trees which had stood in front of the house were replaced with a stone terrace. Receiving Claude Mauriac and Claude Guy on a Saturday at the beginning of June, the General insisted that a 'popular ocean' still remained faithful to him, but acknowledged that 'the people are difficult to know, difficult to handle. They want to be directed but do not wish to give their consent to those who wish to direct them. They want to be taken in hand, but refuse to give themselves up. They hate weakness but they do not intend to give way to force.' When one of his aides mentioned a decision by the government, their boss replied in an aggressive, nasty tone, 'What government?' The others laughed in what Mauriac recalled as 'a somewhat servile manner'.

The General's estimation of his own status was certainly high. When his secretary raised the prospect of him becoming a member of the Académie-Française, he replied: 'The King of France does not belong to the Academy, nor does Napoléon.' He spoke to his staff of the revival of monarchical figures, among whom he included Stalin, Tito in Yugoslavia, Chiang Kai-shek in China and Perón in Argentina. As for the United States, Americans, he said, were gnashing their teeth at the disappearance of the regal Roosevelt. The implication for France was plain. The Constable would ascend to the throne by means of a referendum to give him the patina of democracy.[5]

III
The arbiter of Bayeux

On 16 June 1946, wearing military uniform, his hair slicked back, the would-be republican monarch returned to the Norman towns and villages he had visited on his one-day voyage to France two years earlier. The occasion was a calculated snub to the government's anniversary celebration of his 18 June broadcast, which he had told Gouin he would not attend 'because of the circumstances in which we find ourselves'. He took with him an impressive delegation including Malraux, Koenig and Maurice Schumann. The climax came in the emblematic town of Bayeux with one of his most important speeches that laid out the political creed he would follow for the rest of his life, based on ideas he had nurtured since his twenties.

Once the Constituent Assembly had been elected, he said, adopting regal style, 'we' had left the stage. This had been to avoid jeopardising the status he had acquired and in order not to interfere with the work of the legislators. But he noted that no constitution had been agreed and the rivalry between the parties continuously threw everything into question, overshadowing the higher interests of the nation. It was vital for the future of the country and democracy that France's institutions guarded against this danger in order to preserve the standing of the law, the coherence of government, the efficiency of the administration and the prestige and authority of the state. For disorder within the state inevitably caused popular disaffection with a nation's institutions, at which point 'it takes just one event for the threat of dictatorship to rear its head'. Dictatorships, he argued, always ended in disaster. So the new French democratic institutions should be able to compensate for 'the effects of our perpetual political effervescence'.

'The position, the independence, and indeed the very existence of our nation and our French Union are well and truly at stake,' he warned. The legislative, executive and judicial authorities must be 'clearly separated and powerfully balanced'. There must be a second chamber chosen by local government councils and with representatives of economic, family and intellectual organisations which would rein in the National Assembly and link France with its Empire. A 'national arbiter' must stand above immediate politics, with executive power. Though the government would be responsible to parliament, this head of state would pick the Prime Minister and members of the government in accord with the general interest, promulgate laws, issue decrees, preside over Cabinet meetings and have the power to dissolve the legislature and call elections 'at times of serious confusion'.

Opinion polls showed a fair degree of support for his thinking. One survey reported 50 per cent in favour of the election of the President of the Republic by universal suffrage, while another showed 46 per cent wanting the head of state to play an active political role. On 18 June, de Gaulle went to the Resistance shrine of Mont-Valérien outside Paris where he was surrounded by a crowd roaring support, to which he reacted by flinging up his arms in the now familiar V shape; he said later, with only a touch of irony, that he had been afraid of being carried bodily to the Élysée Palace.[6]

The Communists accused him of seeking 'a plebiscitary dictatorship' and predicted that former Pétainists would rally behind him. Blum drew the comparison with a royal pretender to the throne. The MRP could not go along with much of what he advocated, for instance the right of the head of state to dissolve parliament, but it did not want to repel Gaullists by being too critical, so it tied itself in knots and earned the General's contempt.[7]

A new constitutional draft approved by the Constituent Assembly accorded greater power to the President of the Republic than in the previous version, but, in retaining parliament at the apex of the system, was far from what the General envisaged. He duly condemned it in a speech; when MRP leaders travelled to Colombey to try to get him to change his mind, he sent them packing. The text was approved by a referendum on 11 October by 9 million votes to 7.8 million. Only 67 per cent of those entitled to vote took part, so the new system had the support of 36 per cent of the total electorate.

The first general election held under the new constitution, on 10 November 1946, made the PCF the biggest party with 29 per cent of the vote and 183 parliamentary seats. The MRP did well but the Socialists slumped to 18 per cent of the vote. Despite this, Blum was called on to form a government as a short-term compromise to straddle the hostility between the PCF and MRP. At seventy-four, he appeared to many as a kind of lay saint. He received an overwhelming vote of confidence from the assembly but the strains between the Communists and Christian Democrats were such that he decided to form a government made up only of Socialists.

On 16 January 1947 the new regime got its first president, the tubby, bespectacled Vincent Auriol, who was elected in a ceremony at Versailles with 452 votes against 242 for the MRP candidate. Herriot succeeded him as President of the National Assembly. Since the Radicals had opposed the constitution, Herriot's election to preside over its principal legislature was a further sign of the incoherence de Gaulle denounced.

After five weeks, Blum resigned, and Auriol asked another veteran

Socialist, the tufty-bearded Paul Ramadier, to form a new administration. The Prime Minister had been decorated for his service in the battle of Verdun and had joined the Resistance after refusing to vote full powers to Pétain. Of peasant stock, he slept little, thought a lot, received evening visitors in his carpet slippers and was happy to dine on goat's cheese. He went for an extreme broad-tent approach, appointing not only representatives of the three main parties but also Radicals and Independents, among them the strongly anti-Communist François Mitterrand of the UDSR, who became Minister for Ex-Servicemen. The PCF got the Defence Ministry, along with three other seats, while outside government it wielded the formidable strength of the CGT, the union federation.[8]

As well as problems at home, Blum and Ramadier confronted trouble in France's colonies. A rebellion that began in March 1947 spread across one-third of the Indian Ocean island of Madagascar, killing some 550 French people and 1,900 native inhabitants. An 18,000-strong force of paratroopers and Foreign Legionnaires brutally suppressed the insurrection; the official death toll reached 89,000. Thousands more were imprisoned. Twenty of the alleged leaders of the revolt were executed. A 300,000-member local political movement which had dominated elections on the island in January 1947 was dissolved.

In Vietnam, a united front dominated by the Viet Minh swept the board at elections in January 1946. Ho Chi Minh was proclaimed President of the Democratic Republic based in Hanoi. He and the French emissary, Jean Sainteny, reached an accord providing for Vietnam to become a free state with its own government within a French Union. The Viet Minh leader flew to Paris to finalise the agreement, which allowed France to keep 15,000 troops in the country.

De Gaulle had no doubt about the policy France should follow. Three days after stepping down, he had written to the High Commissioner, Thierry d'Argenlieu, calling on him and Leclerc to continue to try to recover Vietnam for France. D'Argenlieu cold-shouldered the Viet Minh, recognising the independence of South Vietnam, without authorisation from Paris. In France, Ho got precious little from politicians more concerned about the battle over the new constitution and their own futures. On his return home in October, the Viet Minh called together a constituent assembly to elect a government. Independent politicians were arrested. Ho was voted in as head of the government and Giap became Defence Minister. French troops continued to be stationed in Hanoi.

The following month, the Vietnamese assembly approved a constitution for a Democratic Republic which made no mention of any link with France. D'Argenlieu cut off the southern territory of Cochin China from the Viet Minh while, in the north, the French tried to control trade in the main port of Haiphong. Street fighting erupted there in late November, and a French cruiser opened fire, killing an estimated six thousand people. After heavy fighting in Haiphong, Hanoi, Hue and other cities, Ho called for a general uprising. The Viet Minh blew up the Hanoi power station. Mobs massacred French civilians. Sainteny was badly hurt when a mine planted in his car detonated. Superior firepower won the day for the French in urban areas and along the main highways as the Viet Minh retreated into guerrilla warfare. The first Vietnam War had begun.[9]

21

'GUIDE FOR THE NATION'

I

'One does not come here to laugh'

The winter of 1946–7 at Colombey justified its depiction by its most celebrated inhabitant as a place of grey skies, frost, fog and rain – that is, a suitable place for a great man to sit in solitude and ponder, free from the distractions and creature comforts of the capital. The climate, and lack of central heating, fitted in with de Gaulle's vision of himself as living out a tough, austere existence in which he would triumph over everything thrown at him. In his memoirs, he writes with delectation of the 'melancholy' countryside of the Haute-Marne department, the 'sad' horizons, and the simple villages where 'nothing changed'. When Louis Joxe and his wife called at La Boisserie, de Gaulle told Madame Joxe: 'You see, madam, this is not a gay place . . . one does not come here to laugh.' Taking another visitor by the arm, he opened the windows as rain fell and the wind blew. 'Ah! They speak of *douce France*,' he said. 'Here it is, *douce France*.'[1]

Since his appointment to the rank of general had not been confirmed in 1940, he and Yvonne had only a colonel's retirement pay on which to live, and finances could be tight; though, as a matter of pride, the General did not apply for reimbursement of medical costs from the social security system. One visitor noticed that, when de Gaulle remarked on the absence of a piece of family silver, Yvonne murmured 'And on what do you think we live, my dear?' At times, he portrayed himself in the unlikely role of a henpecked husband, saying that his wife, whom he called 'Maman', blamed him for everything. At others, he lapsed into self-pity: 'Let me put logs on the fire,' he said at one point. 'It's all there is left for me to do.'

He installed souvenirs from the war in the house – Rommel's ultimatum to Koenig to surrender at the Battle of Bir Hakeim in 1942 hung on one wall and a collection of Free French emblems lay on a huge V-shaped piece of velvet. The de Gaulles kept a cat which sat on Charles' knees. A telephone had been installed on a table under the stairs where the firewood was stored, but the General preferred to leave it to others to answer when it rang. Two newspapers were delivered each morning, a day after they had appeared in Paris. After lunch, the Constable listened to the radio news, commenting sardonically on the doings of the politicians in Paris, and the state of the world. Yvonne knitted placidly beside him – it was said that every baby in Colombey had a garment from her – or got on with her frequent letter writing. At 5 p.m., there was tea with biscuits. In the evening, the General played patience at a card table by the window, sticking his thumb between his teeth as he decided what to do next – it was alleged that he cheated since he hated not to win.*

There were two servants at La Boisserie, and the General had the services of his aide-de-camp, Gaston de Bonneval, a colonel from the Foreign Legion who had been with him since 1945 and who was the principal butt of de Gaulle's outbursts of irritation when things went wrong. Still the couple persisted in their frugal ways. The cuffs and collars of the General's shirts were turned so that he could continue to wear them for as long as possible. Food was generally simple, prepared by the cook, Augustine. De Gaulle's favourite dish was grilled pigs' ears, which were served for Sunday lunch. He also liked beef stews, cabbage dishes, tripe, pigs' trotters and soup. There was meat from rabbits kept in hutches in the garden, and from chickens in a pen in the grounds – the General did not like the idea of eating them, however; when one was killed and cooked, Yvonne would pretend she had bought it in a neighbouring town.

*The English writer Ursula Bloom alleged that de Gaulle cheated at ping-pong – insisting on keeping the score and announcing arbitrarily that he was in the lead. The present author has found no evidence that the General ever played the game, though, given his height, he would have enjoyed a considerable serving advantage (information from Richard Lambert).

Meals were eaten early, and finished quickly. Yvonne practised good home economics – the stew for dinner one night would give a broth to be consumed at lunch the next day and then meat balls the following evening. De Gaulle drank beer with his meals when he and his wife were alone, with a brandy and cigar after lunch. When there was company, a sweet aperitif was served and wine was poured in small glasses.

The General went for frequent walks in the two-hectare garden with its tall trees and distant views, but did not leave the grounds till November 1946, when he paid a visit to a paralysed farmer. Then he ventured regularly into the forest of Dhuits across from the house, striding along the leaf-strewn and frequently muddy paths between its thickly planted trees, marking his way with his cane. His movements were followed by a police agent sent to the village to report on what he was doing: the farmer apparently suffered badly from the cold of winter and lack of food.

For three or four hours a day the General worked on his war memoirs, drawing on the contents of three hundred boxes of documents, which were classified by two assistants. He wrote in sloping script with his black fountain pen in his study in the new tower built in a hexagonal shape, the outline of France. He smoked Navy Cut cigarettes as he worked, endlessly refashioning his text before passing the pages to his daughter Élisabeth, the only person who could read his handwriting; she typed them up on her portable. 'At last I can write in peace!' he remarked. He read out drafts to his family when they took coffee, sometimes making changes in the light of their comments.

The village was very much a part of traditional France. There was no industry and the agricultural seasons dominated the year. The couple attended mass each Sunday, sitting in the tenth row of the modest church flanked on each side by a stained-glass window depicting Joan of Arc and Saint Louis. Madame de Gaulle bought cakes from the village baker to take home afterwards. At New Year, the local firemen called to sell a calendar to raise funds. At Easter, the children of Colombey came to collect painted eggs. All year round, villagers brought milk.

Yvonne passed her driving test; the Cadillac was replaced with a more modest grey Citroën. From time to time she drove to the nearest big town, Troyes, to buy the pigs' ears the General so liked from the Fuin *charcuterie* and to pick up warm woollen socks for him from a factory outlet there. Further improvements were carried out to the house and grounds, and de Gaulle selected a burial plot just outside the garden so that people would be able to get to it without disturbing future inhabitants of La Boisserie. Philippe became engaged. There were occasional visits to family members in northern France – an unusual photograph taken during one shows the General roaring with laughter – and a trip to the wedding of his niece, Geneviève, in Geneva. It was all very peaceful and ordered, redolent of traditional upper-middle-class life, from the way in which the couple addressed one another (*vous*) to the careful pouring of wine – when the General remarked to a visitor that he had heard he was a drinker, the man replied, 'Not in your home.'

But such a life was, for all its pleasures, also increasingly frustrating for a man who retained his desire for action and his driving sense of destiny. Yvonne discouraged him when he mused on staging a new 18 June: 'My poor friend, nobody would follow you,' she said, according to Claude Guy. To which the General threw out his arms and replied: 'Leave me alone, Yvonne! I am big enough to know what I have to do!' He conferred with wartime aides and with Malraux, and made a protracted visit to Paris in February 1947, staying in a suite rented for him by Colonel Rémy in the Hôtel La Pérouse by the Arc de Triomphe. As an indication of the distance he put between himself and the new regime, he turned down invitations from President Auriol to two lunches for foreign visitors at the Élysée. What was needed, he told Claude Mauriac, was a *rassemblement* (rally or union) to bring the French people together.[2]

II
The rally

On 30 March, the General travelled to Normandy for a gathering of Resistance fighters on the towering cliffs by the hamlet of Bruneval. Facing 50,000 people from a platform decorated with a tricolour flag and a giant Cross of Lorraine, he told them: 'Times are too difficult, life too uncertain, the world too hard to enable one to vegetate for too long in the darkness.' The time was coming to set aside 'sterile games' and reform the political system, he added, after which 'the immense mass of the French will rally to France'. Cries of 'De Gaulle to power!' rose from the crowd.

The same day, Ramadier addressed a rally; there was 'no supreme saviour, no Caesar', he told those assembled. That night, he slipped out of Matignon by a side door and was driven to Colombey. He arrived as de Gaulle was getting ready for bed. The servant called up that there was somebody to see him. Who? asked de Gaulle. 'He says he's the Prime Minister,' came the reply.

Ramadier wanted to get an idea of the General's intentions and to warn him that he was now considered as a politician and opposition leader; therefore he would not get military honours or broadcasting time or be escorted by prefects when he appeared in public at non-official – that is to say, political – occasions. Fifteen years later, de Gaulle recalled replying that he had had sufficient honours in his life, that he had no need of prefects. As for the radio, he reminded the visitor of how he had used it in the war – 'when we didn't hear much from you' – but said he would do without it now. 'I will remain the guide for the nation,' he added. 'I serve only France.' Coffee was provided – the politician reported that it was of poor quality. Then de Gaulle walked the Prime Minister to the door, assuring him that he would not be a Boulanger. Ramadier told Auriol the conversation had been courteous, even cordial, and that de Gaulle had been moving. The President of the Republic responded that he would not play the role of Hindenberg opening the door to a dictator.

The following weekend, de Gaulle travelled to Strasbourg for a commemoration of American soldiers who died liberating Alsace. In a speech from the balcony of the city hall on 7 April, he told a large crowd that the Republic had to be 'brought out of its tomb' by a movement of the French people. Working within the framework of the law, it would reach across differences of opinion to rescue and reform the state. As he finished, he flung up his long arms while the crowd sang the national anthem followed by shouts of '*De Gaulle au pouvoir!*' A week later, on 14 April, the General announced the launch of the Rally of the French people (*Rassemblement du Peuple Français*) (RPF). The country had three choices, its posters declared – the Communists, the parties which were 'burning France's cards', or the 'rally of the mass of French people'.[3]

Groups were set up to cater for families, students, ex-servicemen and civil servants as the movement preached familiar themes of national greatness and independence and the need for a new political system with a powerful head of state. Banging the table in front of him at a press conference in Paris, de Gaulle said that his aim was to bring together those whose only concern was the nation, and to overcome by democratic means the 'paralysis and disorder' caused by class warfare and party rivalries. Afterwards, he compared his task to that of 1940 in combating 'blindness and abdication'.

The RPF advanced the idea of an association between capital and labour, championed by left-wing Gaullists René Capitant and Louis Vallon. But it also moderated the statist economic policy over which de Gaulle had presided in 1944–5, placing greater emphasis on individual enterprise to appeal to small business people and the self-employed. As for colonial issues, the General remained firm in his insistence that France's overseas territories must remain under the control of Paris even if a degree of self-government was allowed. 'The RPF is like the *métro*,' André Malraux remarked of the movement's diverse appeal. De Gaulle said privately that it consisted of 'one-third good folk, one-third idiots and one-third collaborators', and remarked that 'if there's a cuckold, a pederast or a crook somewhere, I'll find him in the RPF'. By 1 May, the movement claimed to have received 810,000 membership applications, an exaggeration but still an indication of its impact. Kept off state radio, the General undertook a round of provincial tours, sometimes flying in an aircraft decorated with the Cross of Lorraine. In uniform, he attracted enthusiastic crowds of up to 100,000 people in Bordeaux, Lille and Rennes.

For all the big-tent approach, the primary appeal was to the Right, sharpened by constant warnings that the USSR was preparing an invasion, and the General's observation that the distance separating the Red Army from the French border was equivalent to only two days' stages in the Tour de France. His denunciations of the regime reflected the distinction drawn by anti-republican thinkers of his youth between those who happened to be occupying the seats of power and the 'real

France' which endured through changes of government and regime, and which he epitomised. He joked to his staff that his letters should no longer be headed as originating from Colombey but just from 'somewhere in France' since he would be everywhere.[4]

The mounting economic troubles facing the Ramadier administration gave him reason for hope that the regime might be weakened. Inflation rose and output fell. The bread ration was reduced to two hundred grams a day. There was a poor harvest and shortages of coal. Strikes bloomed. The black market flourished and rumours spread of armed action by extremist groups. A 'wheat crusade' was launched to try to boost production by Auriol and leaders of the Catholic, Protestant and Jewish faiths.

The tripartite system of government broke down after the Communists attacked repression in the colonies and became more and more critical of social and economic policy. In May 1947, the Prime Minister dismissed the PCF ministers who expected to be called back to join a new government. Their departure may be seen as the true birth of the Fourth Republic, as Socialists, Radicals and Independents sought to govern through a 'Third Force' in the centre-left of French politics, dominated by a small cast of individuals who swapped government posts or held on through thick and thin. France's links with the United States strengthened further, notably through the assistance granted under the Marshall Aid programme. Between April 1948 and January 1952, this amounted to $2.6 billion, 20 per cent of the total sent to West Europe and almost half the budget spent on national reconstruction. The money funded the planning run by Monnet which was the key element in modernising the economy. Meanwhile, the colonial war in Vietnam could be conveniently transformed into a contribution to the anti-Communist cause, and plans for cooperation across the Rhine fitted in with Washington's desire to build up West Germany.[5]

III
'France is here!'

For all the General's rhetoric, the RPF came increasingly to resemble a partisan political party as it organised mass meetings for municipal elections in October 1947. Forty-one National Assembly deputies who backed de Gaulle formed a parliamentary group. Neophyte organisers were given advice on how to arrange public meetings – they were told to beware of drunks and to make sure of the electricity supply, and warned against setting up branches in cafés or bars since this would suggest levity. There were sharp physical clashes with Communists which raised morale but threatened to give the RPF a violent reputation and played into the hands of those who accused its leader of Fascist leanings.

Times were tough; the General's faithful aide, Olivier Guichard, who operated in western France, recalled that he had to beg local prefects to let him have petrol for his political journeys. Another RPF militant, twenty-year-old Brigitte Friang, ran short of gas when driving with a male companion to a rally in eastern France. She had the idea of calling at La Boisserie to ask de Gaulle's aide-de-camp for coupons to buy fuel. When they arrived, at night, the General took her companion into his study. The young woman, who had fought in the Resistance, was left alone with Yvonne. It was evident to her that her hostess could not understand how she had allowed herself to be out at night with a man in a car. 'She trembled for my virtue,' Friang recalled. 'She remarked to the General that saving France was a good thing, but it was unacceptable to do this by taking out young women at night on the road.'

De Gaulle adopted the wartime term of 'companion' for those who worked for him; Malraux moved up a tone by speaking of 'the companions of greatness'. The movement was run on military lines with orders transmitted from the top and the equivalent of a regimental commander in each region. The leader showed a taste for micro-management, getting involved in detailed decisions he could well have left to others. He chose the movement's governing council from among his 'companions', many from the wartime days and none from his parliamentary supporters.

The RPF set up its headquarters in a rented three-storey building dating from 1900 on the rue de Solférino on the Left Bank of the Seine near the National Assembly. The offices were furnished simply with chairs and desks bought from department stores. The atmosphere, the Gaullist Jacques Baumel recalled, was one of 'Franciscan austerity'. Three secretaries typed documents and speeches on Imperial typewriters imported from London which produced large type to accommodate de Gaulle's poor eyesight. If the General had work for them at Colombey, the secretaries were installed in the dining room there. They were overawed by their boss, and one recalled that, at lunch, she never took dessert for fear of delaying the resumption of work. Noticing this, de Gaulle told her: 'Listen, Mademoiselle, there's one thing I know, that girls adore desserts. So I will serve them myself.' Which he promptly did.

In mid-week, de Gaulle was driven to Paris to preside at sessions of the movement's governing council with the colonels of the RPF – its Secretary-General Jacques Soustelle, Guichard, Christian Fouchet, Pierre Lefranc and Roger Frey, plus the future Gaullist *éminence grise* for Africa, Jacques Foccart. The General occupied an office on the first floor where he sat at a wooden desk with his back to the windows giving on to the wide street.* Large maps of France and the world were housed in frames sticking out from the wall beside him. The parquet floor was bare of carpets. A wooden model of a tank and a statuette of people on the Isle of Sein off Finistère, which had rallied to him early in the war, stood on the bookcase. On the other side of the room, by the fireplace, was a large radio set that had been taken from a German-occupied building opposite in 1944 by earlier tenants of number 5. The high doors were padded in dark red leather.

When the RPF high command had gathered round a big oval table in the ground-floor conference room, the aide-de-camp announced 'The General' as the Man of 18 June walked in from his office above and shook hands with each of them. Then he took his place at the midpoint of the table, Soustelle at his right, and Malraux, who maintained a more luxurious propaganda office near the Opéra, at his left.

De Gaulle dominated meetings with his reviews of the political situation, his denunciations of the regime and his calls for the country to wake up. When somebody spoke of action by the government, he exclaimed: 'I couldn't care less about the government. France is here!' The country was being chloroformed and undergoing euthanasia, he thundered. Members of the political establishment had grown used to living in palaces with liveried servants, but that was not the Republic –

*Today the French Socialist Party has its headquarters in a far grander building opposite.

'the Republic is the people'. 'How many times do I have to tell you that we are different from the others,' he would cry. 'Do you think you are in the Radical Party?'As Malraux put it, 'The RPF is the Resistance. The Third Force is Vichy. Communism is the enemy.'

Plunging wholeheartedly into the campaign for municipal elections in October 1947, the RPF dramatised the ills gripping the country and the historic nature of the poll, seeking to belittle its opponents; when Ramadier asked, quite sensibly, for a weekly report to the Cabinet on food supply and the state of the transport systems, the General snorted to a visitor: 'So we go from 18 June to concern ourselves with herrings.' Yvonne wondered if Soviet paratroopers would land near Colombey.

Her husband's barnstorming of the country reached a climax with a mass meeting at the Paris suburban racecourse of Vincennes on 5 October. Opponents scattered nails on roads leading to the rally. The organisers put the crowd at half a million; even if that was an exaggeration, it was a massive turn-out. The atmosphere was that of a huge popular festival as people ate and drank at stands while a band played military airs. Entertainment was provided by music-hall acts and regional dance troupes. Amid a deep rumble from the crowd, de Gaulle stepped out on to a massive white rostrum over which flew tricolour flags and Cross of Lorraine banners. He appeared almost superhuman as he surveyed the multitude, like a prophet appearing at the prow of a great ship. Silence suddenly fell.

'Do you agree with me?' he cried.

'Yes! Yes!' the crowd shouted back.

Tracing an oratorical path familiar to the post-war years, he denounced the 'abyss' into which the parties had led the nation as each devoted itself to 'cooking its little soup, on its little fire in its little corner'. He would show the way to salvation, he pledged. 'Fortune has never betrayed a France that stands together,' he intoned, raising his arms in a concluding salute. René Serre, a former boxer who had joined the RPF security service, detected 'the ardour of a neophyte at his first religious experience, mixed with the modesty of a woman who is going to give herself for the first time and knows it. One felt that the General could have done as he wished with the crowd.'[6]

22

TRIUMPHS AND TRAGEDIES

I
Making the frogs croak

The outcome of the municipal election of 1947 was all de Gaulle could have hoped for. The RPF captured 38 per cent of the vote in major cities, taking control of thirteen of the twenty-five biggest urban centres, including Strasbourg, Rennes, Nancy and Bordeaux, where Chaban-Delmas, who was referred to in RPF documents by his Resistance title of General, became mayor. The movement won a majority on the Paris city council, of which de Gaulle's brother Pierre became the president.

In smaller towns, the RPF won 21 per cent of the vote on its own and another 13 per cent in joint lists. Most victories were at the expense of the centre-right, but it captured Lille from the Socialists and Marseille from the Communists. While the Communists maintained a 30 per cent score and the Socialists held on, the MRP slumped to 10 per cent of the vote. Radicals and moderate centrists were also hurt.

The movement's reach across social classes gave substance to its claim to be leading a rally of the entire French people. Civil servants made up the single biggest group of its electorate, followed by industrial workers and shopkeepers and artisans. It could not, however, claim to be a perfect mirror of the nation. It attracted considerably more men than women, and enjoyed greater support in cities than in the countryside. It was strongest in the north and in Alsace-Lorraine.

'The success of the *Rassemblement* is a triumph,' the General wrote to his son. 'The frogs are croaking in desperation.' He called for a general election as Ramadier resigned and Blum was called on once more to try to save the day. In a speech to the National Assembly, the old Socialist warned that the Republic faced a double danger – 'On the one hand, international Communism has openly declared war on French democracy. On the other, a party has been formed in France whose object, and perhaps its only objective, is to remove fundamental rights.' As he took office, France underwent an outburst of labour militancy. Strikers cut off railway services to and from Paris. Jules Moch, the Transport Minister, turned the Esplanade des Invalides in Paris into a giant parking lot for buses and lorries to take people to the provinces and got the Interior Minister to send in police to ensure that food supplies passed through the pickets.[1]

Blum soon gave way to the Christian Democrat Robert Schuman who put together a working majority of the MRP, Radicals and Socialists. A lifelong bachelor who would become a leading figure of the Fourth Republic, the new Premier had been born to an Alsatian father in Luxembourg in 1886, which led to both Jacques Duclos and de Gaulle referring to him as a 'Boche', a pejorative term for a German. He had held a junior post in Reynaud's government of 1940 and was among the members of parliament who voted power to Pétain; this earned him an automatic sentence of 'national indignity' after the war, which was then annulled. The essence of reason, Schuman listened patiently and spoke in a low, measured tone. He was memorably described by the political journalist Jacques Fauvet of *Le Monde* as being like an old-fashioned pharmacist counting out his pills when he addressed the National Assembly. 'His audience did not grow impatient; it fell asleep,' Fauvet added. The General dismissed him as 'a man as fitted to resist events of the gravity of those we must face today as I am to become pope'. But he was not without wit. When the hard-drinking Bidault remarked that Schuman was 'a motor running on low gas', the Prime Minister replied, 'Not everybody can have a spirit motor.'[2]

Though the railway pickets were cleared, an increasingly violent labour conflict ripped through the coal mines of northern France at the end of 1947. The army was sent in and opened fire, killing some strikers. On 1 December, electricity supplies were cut in Paris by stoppages at power stations; again troops went into action. Two days later, sabotage to the track derailed an express train, killing twenty-one passengers. On 4 December, three people died in fighting between strikers and security forces. Strikes hit a range of other industries. Communists in Marseille attacked the city hall and the main law courts, injuring the new mayor. Now Interior Minister, Moch applied heavy repression in major cities. Army reserves were called up. Amid the violence, the National Assembly held a stormy six-day debate that ended with the approval of a motion in favour of 'republican defence' to guarantee freedom to work. Sensing how opinion was moving, the Communist CGT trade union federation agreed to end the strikes while non-Communist workers set up a separate labour group, *Force Ouvrière*, with US encouragement.

Moch's tough tactics undermined de Gaulle's charge that the Third Force could not defend the Republic, and the General sounded less combative at the end of 1947 and beginning of 1948. This was not purely the result of political developments; there was also a personal reason – a double tragedy – for his relative inaction.

II
Two deaths and a wedding

On 28 November 1947, Leclerc, who had just been named Inspector General of French forces in North Africa, was killed with eleven other passengers when his plane crashed during a sandstorm in southern Algeria. The soldier who had undertaken the first daring Free French expedition in West Africa and had then led the Liberation of Paris had always been among those de Gaulle most prized, for his obstinacy as well as his determination and courage. He had played a major role in affirming his country's military presence in the final stages of the defeat of Germany in 1944–5, even if he and the General had then fallen out over his conclusion that Vietnam should be granted independence.

De Gaulle seems to have regarded the younger man as a son, and as the man most fitted to succeed him if he managed to return to power. In a note after his companion's death, he proclaimed the 'Leclerc epic' as one of the finest pages of France's history. To his widow he wrote of his 'immense sorrow', adding in unusually emotional terms, 'I loved your husband, who was not only the companion of the worst and the greatest days, but also a sure friend in whom no feeling, no act, no gesture, no word was marked by even a shadow of mediocrity . . . We never ceased to be profoundly linked one to the other.' Eleven years later, one of de Gaulle's aides at the Élysée heard him murmur during a difficult period, 'Ah, if only I still had Leclerc!'

According to the RPF official Louis Terrenoire, de Gaulle wrote the instructions for his own funeral during the weekend after Leclerc died, dating it for the day after he went to pay his respects to the soldier's remains in Les Invalides. He wanted an austere occasion. The inscription on the tomb was to read simply 'Charles de Gaulle (1890 . . .)'. The ceremony should be equally simple. No officials should participate, only the army, in modest fashion with no music or fanfares. There should be no speeches, though 'the men and women of France, and of other countries of the world, may, if they so wish, honour my memory by accompanying my body to its final resting place. But I want it to be carried in silence. No posthumous honours should be offered.'

Leclerc's death had another effect, according to Jean Lacouture's biography of the General. This quotes an unnamed source as saying that the General had told him that it was now more important for him to preserve his health for the sake of the nation, so he gave up smoking. Philippe de Gaulle, however, recalled that his father announced the decision six days earlier after a birthday party at Colombey. Whatever the truth, he was irritable for a time, sucking little sweets and chewing gum to make up for the lack of nicotine. He wondered to his son if he had made a mistake, and whether he needed tobacco to make his brain function. But he kept to his pledge, though in 1959 his aide-de-camp noted how the General pressed him to smoke a cigar on a car journey in order to have the pleasure of breathing in the smoke. Years later, he told a visitor who lamented his inability to stop smoking that his recipe had been very simple: 'I told my wife and all around me that I would stop. After that, it was simple: I obviously could not smoke again.'[3]

Ten weeks after Leclerc's death, his beloved daughter Anne caught pneumonia and had increasing difficulty breathing. On the night of 2–3 February 1948, de Gaulle telephoned the Prefect of the Haute-Marne department, Pierre-Henry Rix. 'My dear Prefect,' he said, 'please excuse me, it is a poor anguished father who is calling for help: my child is dying. Send me a good doctor quickly.' Rix undertook to wake up an excellent specialist in Troyes and send him to Colombey. 'Thank you,' de Gaulle said. 'Be quick . . . My God!'

The specialist found Anne's heart was weak. A penicillin injection and oxygen did no good. As de Gaulle wrote to his other daughter, she 'went on growing weaker and choking'. At 10.30 p.m. on Friday 6 February, Anne died in her father's arms.

'She died . . . with her Mother and Madame Michignau [her new carer] beside her while the doctor gave her an injection *in extremis*,' de Gaulle wrote to Élisabeth. 'The priest hurried in to give the blessing. Her soul was freed. But the disappearance of our little girl without hope caused us immense suffering. May little Anne protect us from on high and protect, first of all, you, my very dear daughter Élisabeth.'

The body was placed in an open coffin at La Boisserie. The General sat beside it as village people called to commiserate over the weekend. Marguerite Potel, who had looked after Anne for years, came to see her face for the last time. Snow fell as she was buried in the Colombey churchyard in a simple stone tomb covered with flowers. The General asked that in due course his body and that of his wife be buried beside her. The only people invited to the ceremony were immediate kin, a few close acquaintances and the village people. The Dominican priest, Father Théry, recalled that the General stood by the tomb in his jacket, head uncovered, his face in his hands. 'I knelt and said my prayers,' the priest went on. 'When I stood up, he took two steps towards me and, literally, fell on my shoulder. Maybe we were ridiculous: Don Quixote in tears supported by Sancho Panza.' After the body had been lowered into the earth, de Gaulle remained for a time by the grave with Yvonne. Then he put his hand on his wife's arm and, as they turned to leave, murmured to her, 'She's like others now.'

In the following weeks, he took to writing regular affectionate letters to his other daughter; she and her husband were in a colonial military posting in Brazzaville. He addressed her as 'my dear little daughter Élisabeth' and noted the 'emptiness caused by your distance from us'. 'I embrace you from the bottom of my heart,' he signed off. On 10 September 1949, he wrote to her 'for no particular reason, simply to say that I love you greatly'.

Fourteen months after the death, he wrote to another relation to say that 'little Anne' protected him from the heavens. Visiting Toulouse in 1959 as President of the Republic, he and Yvonne asked especially to see the four-year-old daughter of the Prefect, Odile, who had suffered a similar handicap from birth. When she was brought into the big room in the prefecture reserved for Heads of State, they greeted her affectionately and spoke about Anne.

'Their emotion was profound,' the Prefect, Jean Morin, recalled. 'For them we were a kind of double . . . I can still hear Madame de Gaulle murmuring "one has to be brave. God wished it to be so and we have to accept it."' On the last day of their visit, Yvonne, who usually shrank from physical contact, kissed Madame Morin on the cathedral steps after mass. Four years later, when Morin left the Élysée after being presented with the Légion d'honneur by the General, he and his wife found a large package on the back seat of their car – it contained a Breton doll with a message from the de Gaulles: 'For Odile who could not take part in this little party.'[4]

*

On 30 December 1947, there had been a happier family occasion when Philippe married Henriette de Montalembert de Cers. At the wedding in a château in eastern France, the groom wore naval uniform, the bride an elaborate dress with a huge train. Philippe recounted that the first time his future wife met his father she was so terrified that she dared not speak. But the General found her appealingly straightforward and, according to Philippe, was 'not immune to her physical aspect'. Relations with Yvonne were less easy since, as her son put it, 'my mother often had the state of mind that daughters-in-law sometimes reproach in their mothers-in-law'. In November 1948, just in time for the General's fifty-eighth birthday, Henriette gave birth to a boy whom the General hailed as a 'magnificent' baby. He was christened Charles.

The couple were posted to naval bases in North Africa and Brittany. At other times, Philippe was at sea, so father and son saw little of one another. But de Gaulle wrote frequently, following his son's career closely; he suggested avenues through which he might seek promotion and reported that he had asked high-level contacts to review his son's position. Addressing Philippe as 'old boy', he reproached him for not writing often enough. More frequent correspondence, he added, would not only answer his concern for his son but also 'be right'. In one letter, he reported that Yvonne had a number of worries and missed her children 'in an ugly time which haunts her continually because she is Madame Charles de Gaulle'. He enclosed cheques to help with the family expenses. When Henriette was pregnant with their second child, he said that, if it was a girl, he and Yvonne would like her to be called Anne. The baby was a boy, named Yves, followed by a third son, Pierre.

The General's letters to his son included an acid running commentary on the 'spineless' French regime, but were also full of expressions of joy at his three 'magnificent' grandsons. The 'noble and audacious' Charles was a particular source of pleasure. After Henriette and the boys had visited Colombey in 1952, the General noted that the four-year-old had made himself well known in the village 'by his deeds and words'. He must not be allowed to fall behind in his education, he wrote to Philippe, who was posted to Oran in Algeria at the time, and must follow 'the best classes in the best schools whatever the difficulties'. At the end of 1953, de Gaulle took pride in the boy coming top of his class though he was its youngest member.[5]

III
Back to the battle

Returning to the political fray, de Gaulle plunged into the campaign for the elections for the upper house of parliament. He insisted 'I am still France', but did not renounce contact with the mainstream political leaders, receiving Robert Schuman at Colombey and having talks with Pleven, who wanted to promote an understanding between the RPF and the Third Force. He imagined a Soviet attack with 'Cossacks reaching Brest' – his supporters prepared plans to evacuate him and his family from Colombey if an invasion came. It was noted that the only firearm at La Boisserie was a machine gun stowed in a wooden box: 'Those things go off on their own,' de Gaulle remarked. 'You can count on me to leave it alone. Give me a tank instead.' In an interview at the end of the year, he spoke of the need for constitutional change, the importance of France remaining master of Indochina, the United Kingdom as a perennial enemy, and associated his denunciation of Britain for seeking to block French efforts in Europe with 'the French Socialists, Léon Blum and the Jews'.[6]

Though the RPF claimed to have a million supporters, finance was a constant problem. To gather funds, the movement sold special stamps for fifty francs which sympathisers then sent to the General's home. De Gaulle set Claude Mauriac and his military aide, Colonel Bonneval, to count the stamps in the village hall. They got through 1,300 letters in the first morning; when five sacks containing 70,000 envelopes arrived, the work was transferred to RPF headquarters in Paris. In six months, 116 million francs were raised.[7]

At his house, de Gaulle supervised improvements in the garden where flower beds were laid out and cherry and plum trees planted. He listened to the songs of the French entertainer Bourvil with pleasure. He also expressed interest in the forthcoming Olympic Games and the world title fight of the French boxer Marcel Cerdan; he thought the Frenchman would lose because he had been seen in the United States with too many ravishing women; this was a serious matter for the General, Mauriac reflected, because 'French boxing involved France'. (In fact, Cerdan, Édith Piaf's lover, won the title but subsequently lost it before dying in a plane crash.)

The General seemed to his secretary to have aged considerably. He acknowledged that he found it increasingly difficult to write speeches, which often kept him up into the early hours. The difficulty was threefold, he explained: 'First because I am no longer carried forward by events. Secondly because I am getting older. And then because, it must be said, it consists in repeating the same thing, and that becomes tedious.' Still, he maintained a heavy schedule of trips round the country, usually in his Citroën, the luggage on a roof rack covered with a black tarpaulin. On one journey, the car was stopped by a level-crossing barrier. The railway attendant looked in through the passenger window and recognised the figure sitting in the back. She immediately raised the barrier and the driver took the Citroën across the track. Seconds later, the train hurtled by. 'Well, well,' the General remarked to his travelling companions.

Charles, Yvonne and the small group with them sometimes picnicked in the countryside, de Gaulle sitting on a folding chair. Or they stopped, unannounced, at restaurants, the General reading the menu with care as the owners installed a bowl of flowers on the table and local people came to see the eminent visitor. There was often a problem over the bill; when the owner refused to accept payment, de Gaulle sent one of his staff to leave the cost of the meal as a tip.

He preferred to stay in private houses of supporters rather than in hotels, provoking worried telephone calls from his hosts to the RPF's provincial delegates to find out if he liked a bolster or two pillows, what kind of bedside reading was appropriate and whether Madame de Gaulle fancied lamb for dinner. Finding a sufficiently long bed was often a problem. Pierre Lefranc, who had joined the Free French and became one of de Gaulle's aides, recalled that the hosts were usually Resistance veterans; there were few invitations to châteaux whose owners retained a soft spot for Pétain. The General's choice of lodgings was prompted in part by his sense of economy and his desire not to be surrounded by other guests at hotels, but it also enabled him to meet ordinary people and discuss local affairs with them, giving him a grasp of grassroots feelings to go with his lofty visions.[8]

The simplicity of the couple's private life contrasted with the huge congresses staged by the RPF. These took on the air of quasi-religious occasions at which the throng venerated the leader. The first was held in April 1948, in Marseille; the General, who appeared tired, spoke from a boat moored off the quay, and some of the crowd fell into the water. Such rallies made it all too easy for the Communists to depict the Gaullist enterprise as a Fascist undertaking and for others to view the

General as an aspirant dictator, an impression bolstered by the movement's strong-arm security service and the presence in its ranks of one-time followers of the pre-war far-right leader, Colonel de La Rocque. However deep the General's attachment to democracy, he always attracted people with less respect than him for legality and a taste for direct action. From the intellectual Left, Jean-Paul Sartre compared him to Pétain and Hitler, while Hubert Beuve-Méry of *Le Monde* commented, 'The movement he has conjured up around himself unarguably operates in a pre-fascist atmosphere.'[9]

In September 1948, a merry-go-round of governments led to Auriol calling on the veteran Radical Henri Queuille to form an administration which included Socialists, Radicals, the MRP and Independents. Originally a doctor from the deeply rural Corrèze department in central France who had joined de Gaulle in Algiers, the new Premier had held ten ministerial posts before the war and two after it, being famous for his remark about politics being a matter of avoiding problems rather than solving them. De Gaulle dismissed his government as 'a rotten plank', its members 'swimming in dirty water'. In conversations at the time, he called mainstream politicians puppets, dwarves, clowns, show-offs, and waverers who had no balls and were playing at masquerades. As for the French people, he said the only thing they could do was to make demands which rendered them impossible to govern.

Queuille sought to calm things down, postponing by six months cantonal elections which could have provided the RPF with a fresh platform. But the confrontation between the two outsider parties, the RPF and the PCF, did not abate. When the General spoke in Grenoble, the Communists arranged demonstrations to denounce him as an aspirant dictator who had sold out to the United States, pardoned Pétain and betrayed the partisans on the Vercors. Admiral Muselier was brought out of obscurity to attack him. As RPF and Communist security men clashed in the Alpine city, shots were fired and cars were set alight. One person was killed and more than a dozen seriously hurt. The police were notable by their absence. In another clash at the southern port of La Seyne, near Toulon, Gaullist 'gorilla' security guards threw Communist opponents, including two parliamentary deputies, into the sea. In a conversation after lunch at Colombey, Yvonne said she thought the violence would cost the movement votes, but de Gaulle replied that it was the fault of the weakness of the state, and publicly pinned responsibility on Moch as Interior Minister. Still, he issued an internal 'instruction' to the RPF to centralise the movement's security forces to avoid local groups becoming too militant.

Elections for the upper house of the legislature, the Council of the Republic, in November 1948 appeared to be another triumph for the RPF which claimed 123 of the 320 seats. De Gaulle took particular satisfaction in the MRP's loss of 50 of its 78 seats; the Christian Democrats, he said, deserved 'the Nobel Prize for Treason'. But many RPF deputies were fair-weather friends, who campaigned in the first round of voting as Gaullists but then negotiated for the support of other parties in the run-off second round and, subsequently, for places on parliamentary committees. In the end, only fifty-six were admitted to the Gaullist group in the council, which took the name of Democratic and Social Action. 'The RPF is fraying,' Auriol noted in his journal, adding that the General had no sense of political realities.

When cantonal elections were finally held the following March, the RPF staged an intensive grassroots campaign, even sending Pierre Lefranc to canvass in Queuille's bastion in the Corrèze where he won just 5 per cent. With 32 per cent of the vote nationally, the movement's overall performance was, again, respectable but still showed no progress on the initial breakthrough at the municipal level the previous autumn. De Gaulle's pessimism, not to mention the strong-arm tactics of the RPF security forces, went down badly with a country which, according to opinion polls, wanted peace and a quiet life.

Moch had forced the CGT to back off, and Washington had shown itself ready to help defend Western Europe. The economy appeared to be improving, and the government shied away from addressing structural problems that could have caused disruption. Rationing of bread, milk, fats, chocolate and textiles was lifted. Marshall Plan aid was flowing in, and the International Monetary Fund extended large loans. Monnet's planning authority was getting to work. At the Foreign Ministry, Robert Schuman pursued West European cooperation. The press was squared with a generous law on journalists' tax-free expenses. Against all the evidence, the Minister for the Colonies declared that the army had won in Vietnam, and the government signed a conditional independence agreement with the exiled Emperor Bao Dai.

Two crises in central Europe – the Soviet blockade of Berlin that led to the airlift to supply the city and the Communist coup in Prague – pushed the PCF further into its corner as it was instructed by Moscow to radicalise its opposition. All in all, France preferred the medicine of the 'good doctor Queuille' to the jeremiads about impending war and disaster on which de Gaulle traded. The number of people who told pollsters they wanted the General to return to office dropped from 40 to 28 per cent in a year. Queuille's government became the longest-serving administration of the Fourth Republic.[10]

As its electoral score stagnated, the RPF began to run into trouble. As well as recurrent financial strains, there were internal rivalries. Provincial RPF committees resented the central direction from the rue de Solférino. There was criticism of the heavy-handed, secretive style of the Secretary-General, Soustelle, who gained the nickname of the 'big tomcat' from his habit of listening to people with his fists clenched against his cheeks, his eyes half shut – he was in frequent conflict with colleagues, especially Malraux.

The head of the parliamentary group resigned after a by-election dispute. Four RPF deputies warned the General of 'ambitious, impatient elements'. A major row erupted between the leader and Colonel Rémy when the wartime underground chief proposed rehabilitating Pétain: de Gaulle responded with a sharp statement that ended their ten-year-old relationship. Businessmen who had initially been attracted by de Gaulle's persona were worried by his capital–labour partnership policies, not that these drew much enthusiasm from workers. Radical Socialists who had allied with the movement for tactical reasons were alienated when it came out in support of church schools.

Grander Gaullist policies were showing distinct signs of incoherence. While the General was stridently anti-Communist, he also opposed France's involvement in the growing network of Western defence organisations that led to the formation of NATO in 1949. Nor did he like the political and economic cooperation embodied in the Council of Europe and then in the European Coal and Steel

Community negotiated by Robert Schuman. France's reliance on American aid made a mockery of his dream of seeing his country standing between East and West; in an interview, he spoke of 'rebuilding a true France, not a France of the Marshall Plan'. His insistence on the need to keep France's main neighbour weak and divided became untenable as Washington backed the development of West Germany as a bastion against Communism, and allowed France to hold on to the Saar and its coal only as the quid pro quo for Paris going along with its European policy.[11]

Above all, the basic dilemma of de Gaulle's political course since 1944 was increasingly evident. He rejected the idea of a *coup d'état* and wanted to pursue a legal path to power. But he was equally resolute in his desire to change the regime which politicians commanding the majority of the popular vote were set on preserving. As Malraux put it, he had led his troops to the Rubicon but only to fish.

In the autumn of 1949, a row with the Socialists over wage controls led Queuille to resign. Bidault, described by Chaban-Delmas as 'that little man, always with his back arched, always living on his nerves, cutting and jerky, lacking the physical means to live up to his immense ambition', formed a government that held on for ten months. It had to face increasingly strident parliamentary attacks from the Communists headed by Duclos, who became the Party's main voice after Thorez suffered a stroke and went to the Soviet Union for treatment. The clashes became so violent that fist fights broke out on the floor of the National Assembly and police had to be called to lead PCF deputies from the chamber.

When Bidault's Cabinet collapsed in June 1950, de Gaulle's wartime companion René Pleven formed his first government. The tall Breton proved adept at making political deals and conjuring up compromises. But he provoked the General's ire with a proposal for a European Defence Community of France, West Germany, Italy and the Benelux countries designed to contain the German rearmament on which Washington insisted. De Gaulle said he would even lead a rally of conscientious objectors to kill the project, which he saw as national abdication.

There were also serious imperial problems. Protests swept the Ivory Coast – thirteen people died in the repression – and, in Indochina, the

Viet Minh staged a series of successful attacks in the autumn of 1950 that threatened Hanoi. De Lattre was sent out as High Commissioner and commander-in-chief. By throwing in all available troops and bringing heavy artillery and air power to bear, he stopped the offensive, though he suffered a personal tragedy when his son was killed in action. But the cost of the war was a major drain on the already strained state finances as inflation rose once more. On top of this, a scandal erupted over currency profiteering on the Indochinese piaster alleged to involve leading political and military figures.

Passing his sixtieth birthday in November 1950, de Gaulle remained in an apocalyptic mood. He saw the war in Korea, where France contributed troops, and the setbacks in Vietnam as precursors to a much wider war in which Soviet forces would invade France. Atomic weapons would be used, and there would be famine and deportations. Political leaders would be hanged because 'the Communists are hard people', he warned. But the Americans were also 'brutes', he wrote to Pompidou. His campaign message for legislative elections to be held in June 1951 concluded:

> For France to be France,
> Liquidate separatism;
> Get rid of the partisans.*
> Bring together the French people under a just and strong state.[12]

The election did everything to reinforce his contempt for mainstream politics, as the Third Force leaders imposed a voting system that divided France into 103 national constituencies in which parties could make agreements on local lists whose composition varied from place to place. Thus, in one department, Socialists and Radicals might unite to maximise their mutual advantage against the MRP; in another, the MRP and Radicals might join forces against the Socialists. The RPF and the Communists, who would not make arrangements with anybody, were thus marginalised.

Some Gaullists believed the RPF should play along by concluding

*A reference to the Communists, not the wartime Resistance.

local agreements with other parties. De Gaulle rejected any such policy – when Jacques Chaban-Delmas, the most dashing of the Gaullists who was a good tennis and rugby player as well as an ambitious politician, argued for local alliances in his region of Bordeaux, he responded that the Resistance general thought France could be run between two sets of tennis. But de Gaulle's writ proved fallible. Chaban had maintained his double membership of the RPF and the Radical Socialists to build up a political barony in Bordeaux where he won the mayor's office in 1947. Herriot, motivated by a combination of anti-Gaullism and a desire to block the ascension of a younger rival, had him expelled from the Radical ranks in March 1951. Unfazed, Chaban immediately opened negotiations with the local MRP.

Similar scenarios unfolded in Brittany and Burgundy, where a former Vichy civil servant and ambassador turned Gaullist loyalist, Léon Noël, was given a dispensation to form a list to oppose the formidable local cleric-politician, Chanoine Kir, who lent his name to the aperitif of white wine and blackcurrant liqueur. In all, there were agreements in a dozen constituencies. Even de Gaulle compromised; on a campaign visit to Algiers, he yielded to pressure to integrate the RPF list with one led by colonial notables.

The final stages of the campaign did not find the General in good form. His speeches were stale or beside the point. When the results came in on the night of 17 June, it was apparent how effective the electoral system had proved. With 52 per cent of the vote, the Third Force parties took 396 of the 627 National Assembly seats. In contrast, the 48 per cent won by the RPF and PCF brought them 220 deputies; it was estimated that, with a fairer system, they would have won an additional 71 and 26 respectively, which would have given the two rejectionist groups an overall majority.

Still, helped by its piecemeal alliances, the RPF was the biggest party in the legislature with 120 seats, 20 more than the PCF – Chaban and Soustelle thought the Gaullists could have taken 200 had they agreed to accords across the country. De Gaulle handed Soustelle, who had been elected in Lyon, 'the capital and very delicate mission' of presiding over the RPF group in the National Assembly; his place at the rue de

Solférino was taken by Louis Terrenoire, a former Christian Democrat who was the epitome of loyalty and more self-effacing than the anthropologist veteran of the Free French. Since the General regarded the movement as a whole as being more important than its parliamentary presence, it was difficult to see this as anything other than a demotion for Soustelle.

De Gaulle told Jean-Raymond Tournoux that the result had been a victory for those who wanted to let France go to sleep. This was not an option he could have envisaged, he added, but 'how can one bring together a country with 265 different cheeses?' Still, at a press conference after the election, he declared that all French people had been or would be Gaullists. Yet nearly 80 per cent of the electorate had preferred either the Communists or the Third Force to him. Voters had now been given four chances to rally to him since 1947 but had done so in diminishing numbers. The General found a scapegoat – the bourgeoisie had got over the great fear of Communism, 'so they naturally returned to their little concerns, the defence of their little interests, their little quarrels'. 'The great shudder of national fear has passed,' he added.[13]

This did not stop him claiming that, as the 'French' group which had attracted most votes – he presumably regarded the PCF as 'non-French' – the RPF should be called on to form a government dedicated to constitutional reform. President Auriol did not respond, and spent a month trying to find an alternative. He ended up with Pleven. The Premier's party, the UDSR, was among the smallest in parliament, but he manoeuvred skilfully to get approval of laws that placated Catholics on religious schools, raised wages and committed France to Robert Schuman's plan for European economic cooperation. However, as 1951 ended, his government was defeated in an economic debate and Pleven resigned.

Auriol now proposed that the RPF, as leader of the biggest group in the National Assembly, should consider forming a government. The proposal was put to Soustelle, who thought there was little chance of any positive result, but felt that going through the motions would boost the movement's confidence, extend his range of high-level contacts, provide access to the press and radio and enable him to take a look at secret dossiers to get an idea of the real state of the nation. He went to Colombey in early January to seek the General's approval. He found his leader 'serious and worried' as they talked late into the night – in a letter to his son and daughter-in-law at the time, de Gaulle wrote of living a life 'fairly filled with worries and melancholy'.

'There is no question of you becoming Prime Minister,' he told his visitor. 'The parties would be against it. Or it would mean entering into an unacceptable scheme.' Soustelle replied that there was no question of taking office, but laid out the advantages of exploiting Auriol's approach. The matter would, in any case, be reviewed by the RPF's council, he added. According to Jean-Raymond Tournoux's account of the conversation, de Gaulle merely responded in lofty fashion that, if his name came up in the conversation, Soustelle should tell Auriol that, were the President to be concerned about national or international events and felt it useful to contact him, an approach would not be refused.

Soustelle considered that he had been given a green light, and went to talk to Auriol. Emerging from the Élysée as Prime Minister-designate, he spoke to reporters of his party's programme and ambitions; he did not mention de Gaulle by name. Taking an office in the rue de Varenne, not far from the Hôtel Matignon and RPF headquarters, he met Pleven, Bidault, Schuman, Queuille, Moch, Mitterrand and Mendès France while bombarding the media with statements. After he saw Reynaud, a press story appeared saying that a government of national union was being considered – hearing of this, de Gaulle spoke in such harsh terms by telephone from Colombey that Soustelle hung up.

By the time the RPF council gathered for its weekly meeting in mid-January, the General was ready to launch an offensive against the follower who was assuming a life of his own. When de Gaulle took his place in the middle of the table in the ground-floor conference room, the seat opposite, Soustelle's, was empty. The RPF chief mocked the absent parliamentary leader for his radio appearances and for trying to do a deal with Auriol. It was all a circus and led nowhere, he rumbled on. If anybody wanted to know what Gaullism stood for, they had only to listen to de Gaulle himself. Then he turned sarcastic, saying he was impatient for the new Premier to arrive so that he could be told what job he was to be offered – Deputy Minister of the Arts, perhaps, or of Physical Education. Could they start their meeting while the Prime Minister was forming his government? he asked acidly.

Malraux passed a note to his neighbour: 'Is he jealous?'

Then Soustelle arrived and began to brief the meeting. De Gaulle broke in explosively.

'You are all the same,' he cried. 'Having a red carpet unrolled under your feet, that is enough to get you to walk in whatever direction it leads.'

Soustelle grew pale.

'Prime Minister, where have you got to in your consultations?' de Gaulle asked.

'*Mon Général*, I told the President of the Republic that I could not succeed.'

When his boss accused him of wasting time, Soustelle said he had drawn up a statement. The General ordered him to read it out. It said that the dispute over the electoral system had to be settled, and called on the other party leaders to examine the nature of the majority which had emerged from the general election.

'That's idiotic,' de Gaulle objected. 'What does it mean?'

He stood up, said a collective *au revoir* and left without shaking anybody's hand. According to the council member Christian Fouchet, tears ran down Soustelle's cheeks as he remained motionless at the table.

De Gaulle climbed the curving stairs to his office where he sat at his desk and regained his calm, before calling for Fouchet to join him. 'Well, you've seen them,' he remarked contemptously when the RPF delegate arrived.

In March, Pompidou and Terrenoire took Soustelle to Colombey to try to build bridges, but the result was another tongue-lashing. When Soustelle offered to step down, the General said his role was to be attacked from both sides. In his memoirs, Soustelle put it all down to the older man's 'jealousy' towards him. In May, he resigned from the presidency of the RPF group with a letter to de Gaulle in which he said he had failed in his task – he told Pompidou that he could not continue the 'miserable life' which had become his lot.

The episode was, in part, personal – de Gaulle felt the need to slap down Soustelle, as would be the case with others in the years to come. But the General was also having considerable difficulty in coming to terms with the situation in which the RPF found itself. Many of the movement's elected members were unwilling to join him in his magnificent solitude. Since he would not launch a personal bid for power, they saw no alternative to cooperating with what he dismissed as the 'odious' regime whose only goal, he told his son, was to keep him out of power. When de Gaulle asked an RPF deputy what he would have been without him, the man replied, 'A minister, *mon Général*.'[14]

Once the Soustelle initiative had collapsed, France was plunged into a fresh round of Cabinet-making involving the Radical Edgar Faure, who lost four kilos while keeping his administration afloat for all of five weeks. Reynaud then launched an abortive effort to form a government of national unity including the RPF to save the currency and institute constitutional reform – de Gaulle rejected this out of hand. Finally, in March 1952, the President of the Republic found his best candidate in a former Minister of Public Works, Antoine Pinay, a modest-looking provincial conservative from the Auvergne with a neat moustache whose trademark was his little round hat with an upturned brim. As a young senator, he had voted powers to Pétain in 1940 and had been appointed to the Vichy national council in 1942, though he never attended that body and worked in the Resistance, insisting later that by remaining mayor of his home town of Saint-Chamond he had been able to get food supplies for the inhabitants and protect Jewish families.

Pinay was the incarnation of the bourgeois France the General so abhorred. But some of the RPF's new representatives found him appealing, and twenty-seven voted for the installation of his government, which pledged to defend the franc, cut state spending and reduce prices. Then, forty-one RPF deputies sent de Gaulle a joint letter refusing to guarantee that they would follow voting instructions from the party leadership, opening the way for them to support Pinay's government. 'I did not carry out 18 June to bear Mr Pinay to power,' de Gaulle growled, comparing the new Premier to Giraud. He called the RPF deputies who backed Pinay 'a handful of crazy men'. When one said he was sorry to have separated from the General but considered Pinay's investiture to be in the national interest, the General listened with clenched teeth and replied, according to Jean-Raymond Tournoux: 'Christ was betrayed, too!' Still, he could see that the prim, conservative Pinay might enable the orthodox Right to stage its comeback from the shadow of Vichy, presiding over economic improvements and low unemployment as France went into the period of expansion known as 'the thirty glorious years'.[15]

That meant he had to counter-attack. At an RPF council meeting in the Paris suburb of Saint-Maur, the General sat in a sweltering hall surrounded by delegates in short sleeves. Formally dressed, his hands clasped on his knees, he listened as he was criticised from the platform by parliamentarians who claimed the right to unheard-of freedom of choice. When loyalists barracked, he rose to tell them to follow his example and remain silent. Then Malraux took the stage to launch an attack on 'our adversaries', unleashing a torrent of applause, and de Gaulle rose once again to insist that the movement must not compromise with the political system; he received an ovation. By a vote of 478–137, the meeting backed tight parliamentary discipline. That led twenty-six deputies to leave the RPF and set up a group of their own which was joined by nineteen others in the following months.

The General now focused his attention on a campaign against the European Defence Community, for which the treaty had been signed in May 1952. France, he argued, had to keep its own independent army rather than seeing it melded into a joint military force for a Europe which did not exist. But RPF parliamentarians flirted increasingly with the idea of entering government, and Chaban-Delmas overcame internal opposition to muster the support of eighty-one RPF deputies for the Radical René Mayer, who succeeded Pinay as Prime Minister in January 1953, on condition that he agreed to conduct a study of constitutional reform and to reopen negotiations on European defence in a way that would protect the French army. The days of the RPF as a pure expression of Gaullist faith were clearly numbered, and the General had other causes for concern.

At the end of 1952, he underwent an operation for cataracts. Six weeks later, his eye was still half closed. It was a sign of ageing that he greatly resented, and his mood was bitter. He disliked having to wear the thick, black-rimmed spectacles prescribed for him, and only did so in public when essential. After the operation, he had to protect himself against the cold and wind and was told to stop his walks at Colombey, an instruction he only partially respected. 'I don't wish my worst enemy to suffer as I have suffered,' he remarked. There was also an unfortunate incident when he gave a lunch at the Hôtel La Pérouse at which he and his guests were poisoned by vol-au-vent that induced vomiting and kidney pains.[16]

Municipal elections in early 1953 brought fresh evidence of the decline of the *Rassemblement*, which attracted only 10.6 per cent of the vote, hardly more than a third of those won by the Communists and behind the Radicals and MRP. Sixty per cent of the seats it had taken at the breakthrough poll of 1947 were lost. Now that the public was no longer afraid of a Communist takeover, it had 'returned to its usual vomiting', de Gaulle wrote to his son. He became so disenchanted with his own creation that he asked the faithful Jacques Foccart: 'When are you going to stop bothering me with *your* RPF?'

In May, he freed the movement's deputies to do as they wished; Pompidou told Claude Mauriac, who had resigned as the General's secretary, of the bitterness felt by loyal deputies at the way in which he had abandoned them. Soustelle, writing at a time when he had gone into violent opposition to the General, called the RPF legislators 'lost children in the political jungle'. Visiting the rue de Solférino the day after de Gaulle's announcement, Mauriac found it virtually abandoned and like 'a ship adrift which the rats have left'. While demanding the unswerving loyalty of others, the General never hesitated to close the door on them when it suited him. He was not bereft of human sentiments, to be sure, but was not going to let his mission be compromised by concern for the feelings of others.

In some ways, the RPF had been a mistake, badly timed and ill suited to the realities of post-war France, poorly organised and too prone to extreme behaviour. In his memoirs, de Gaulle devotes less than a page to it. For all the weaknesses of the system, the political class contained skilful men such as Ramadier, Auriol, Pleven, Pinay, Moch and Schuman. Simply inveighing against them as nincompoops while waiting for the trumpet blasts from Colombey and the rue de Solférino to bring down the walls of the Republic was not enough. The General was not at home with everyday politics, and, by his nature, would not compromise with fair-weather friends. Despite his assertion that all French people were or would become Gaullists, the RPF had not been able to build on its initial breakthrough or to exploit the failings of the ministerial merry-go-round or supplant the Communists as the biggest vote-winners.

Still, the experiment served several purposes. It kept the Gaullist flame alive, and its cohort of followers would prove invaluable in the future. De Gaulle's provincial trips brought him into contact with ordinary French people – he once remarked that he had not carried money on him since 1940 and did not know the price of anything. He had also learned that, if he was going to follow the democratic route back to power, he would need a well-structured movement which would play an unambiguous parliamentary role.[17]

Having let the RPF go, the General spoke of staging a new 18 June inside France with a hard core of followers whom he would call *Les Vigilants.* The catastrophic defeat of French forces by the Viet Minh at Dien Bien Phu in May 1954 might provoke the kind of conditions on which he counted to usher him back to power; not only had the engagement cost the French army 2,300 men killed, 5,200 wounded and 11,000 captured, but it had lost a pitched battle at the hands of a native army which had shown itself capable of beating the cream of France's soldiery.

The following month, de Gaulle set up a dramatic appearance for the tenth anniversary of D Day at the Tomb of the Unknown Soldier at the Arc de Triomphe to test the waters. He inspected a guard of honour and saluted the 10,000 spectators from an open car, but the occasion was not a great success. The crowd was smaller than he had expected; 'the people are not much in evidence,' he murmured to Guichard as he got into his car to leave. Nor did his intransigence appeal to a significant number of his followers. Sixty-two RPF deputies voted for the next government, headed by the conservative Joseph

Laniel, and five became ministers; de Gaulle cut off contact with his old companions Fouchet and Chaban-Delmas when they took Cabinet posts. He was alone once again.[18]

PART FIVE
THE ROAD BACK

23

BIDING HIS TIME

I
Not so strong

In the summer of 1954, France finally got a head of government whom de Gaulle respected, in the person of his one-time Economics Minister Pierre Mendès France, brought to power as a result of the deteriorating situation in Indochina. Taking office on the iconic date of 18 June, the Radical Mendès broke with the chair-swapping tradition by including only four ministers who had belonged to the previous administration. Gaullists who rejected the General's isolationism figured prominently. General Koenig, who de Gaulle said 'thought with his kepi', became Defence Minister and the second-ranking member of the government; Chaban-Delmas was Minister of Public Works, Transport and Tourism; and Fouchet was Minister for Moroccan and Tunisian Affairs. Soustelle became Governor General of Algeria. Only Chaban formally consulted the General before taking the job. However, the new Premier's espousal of the plan to create a European army led to the departure of Koenig and Chaban after a couple of months though the Mayor of Bordeaux returned almost immediately to the Public Works Ministry, only to leave once again shortly afterwards.

Mendès devoted himself to getting on with business rather than indulging in jousting between parties. Chaban-Delmas noted the 'sober, effective and rapid' nature of Cabinet sessions. A month after taking office, the government signed a peace agreement in Geneva under which France withdrew from Indochina at the end of six and a half years of war which cost it 3,000 billion francs and 75,000 dead. It had been a huge defeat, and shaming for national pride, but the country had grown heartily sick of the fight to hold on to its faraway colony and Mendès was seen by all but imperial diehards as a miracle worker simply for having ended the struggle. Ten days after the Geneva accord, he flew to Tunisia, accompanied by Fouchet and Marshal Juin, for negotiations that led to an agreement to grant independence in 1956.

Despite their differences over the European army, de Gaulle hailed the patriotism and devotion to the public good shown by Mendès, and the two men met for seventy-five minutes in October in the General's rooms at the Hôtel La Pérouse. Both were courteous, with the Prime Minister showing deference to his host, but de Gaulle noted that his visitor was 'not even determined to try' to introduce essential constitutional reform.[1]

At the end of 1954, de Gaulle paid another ringing tribute to Mendès in a speech to followers at the Vél d'Hiv, but by then the Prime Minister was running into increasing visceral political opposition. Though he gave the green light to the development of a national nuclear strike force, the withdrawal from Indochina and the agreement on Tunisian independence made it easy for the Right to portray PMF, as he became known, as a man who did not stand up for France's interests. Europeans in Algeria suspected him of preparing to make concessions to nationalists there. There was intrigue among police officials who had been sacked, and the far right waged a virulent campaign drawing on anti-Semitism reminiscent of the insults flung two decades earlier at Blum. The young deputy Jean-Marie Le Pen spoke of his 'patriotic, almost physical repulsion' for the Premier. A future mercenary, Bob Denard, was sentenced to fourteen years in jail for plotting to kill him.

Beetroot farmers in northern France revolted against the abolition of a system under which a third of their crop was bought by the state and turned into low-quality alcohol. When Mendès decided to let the European defence plan drop after it was defeated in parliament, he alienated the MRP which was also anxious to stop the Prime Minister attracting its centrist voters to a broad non-Communist reform movement. The waters were further muddied by allegations that the Prime Minister's real name was Cerf and that he had changed it because he had something to hide, and that François Mitterrand, the Interior

Minister and third-ranking member of the government, had leaked military secrets to the Communists. The struggle to keep the government together and maintain a parliamentary majority while fighting on so many fronts was both physically and psychologically exhausting. Nor was Mendès helped by his own unbending personality, his lack of political finesse and his Gaullien insistence that he was correct, not to mention his calls for his fellow citizens to drink milk rather than wine.

At the end of February 1955, the government fell after being defeated in a National Assembly debate on North Africa. Though it agreed with plans drawn up by Mendès France for reforms in Algeria, the MRP voted against him. 'Tonight or never,' the former minister Pierre-Henri Teitgen cried as the vote approached. The beaten Premier remarked on the strange nature of the majority which had unseated him, 'made up of men who want reforms but vote against the government which applies them, and men who want to return to a policy of repression'. Speaking to the chamber, he vowed that the process he had started over the previous eight months would not stop. 'Men come and go, national necessities remain,' he added in Gaullian terms.[2]

The Radical Edgar Faure formed a new administration with Pinay as Foreign Minister, Koenig at Defence and a rising politician from Strasbourg, Pierre Pflimlin, at Finance. Faure's ability to resolve disputes and his political skills, which earned him the nickname 'weathercock',* enabled the government to last for almost a year.

*

There was a new source of comfort for the General when the first volume of his war memoirs appeared in October 1954. One hundred thousand copies were sold in five weeks – in all, sales of the complete work would reach two million. The General sent the first four dedicated copies to the Pope, the Comte de Paris, the President of the Republic and Her Majesty Queen Elizabeth II. *Paris Match* serialised the book and did a photo story on the General at Colombey, the reporters taking Yvonne up for a ride in their helicopter. The earnings

*He responded that it was the wind which changed.

went largely towards funding a foundation for children with Down's syndrome which the de Gaulles set up in memory of Anne and whose finances were handled by Georges Pompidou. The General also gave seven hundred francs to the village council to beautify a patch of wasteland in Colombey that had been used as a dumping ground for farm machinery.

Written in a sweeping but profound style, the book drew on the author's deep knowledge of the French language and its literary traditions. His endless reworking and editing saved it from containing too many grandiloquent passages, and there were trenchant pen portraits of world figures, notably of Stalin in the account of his trip to Moscow in 1944. As in the war memoirs of his sparring partner, Churchill, events were sometimes treated in cavalier fashion to suit the General's purpose and to place himself in history, building up the case for his unelected legitimacy as the once and future saviour of the nation. It was, he told his archivist, not a work of history but 'the evidence of a man, so fallible and incomplete'. Since the book was a message to the French people, he saw little point in having it translated, but it did appear in English the following year.

As the narrative reaches London after the fall of France, a second character emerges at the front of the stage alongside the 'I' of the author. This is the third-person 'de Gaulle', a historic figure who takes up the national standard when opponents or allies of France are to be confronted. Given the particularly vaulting nature of the status he claimed, the book was a relentless tale of destiny fulfilled, of obstacles overcome and of undying devotion to the cause of France. In the political context of the mid-1950s, he certainly needed to reassert his claim to history.

*

France seemed able to get on without either of its potential strongmen. A poll reported that only 1 per cent of those questioned saw the General returning as Prime Minister. The ultra-loyal Michel Debré sat in the upper house of parliament and kept up a stream of invective against the system through his bulletin, *Le courrier de la colère* (*The Courier of Anger*), gaining the nickname 'Michou la colère' ('Angry Mike'). But other key followers had scattered to jobs elsewhere – Pompidou with the Rothschild bank, Guichard at the Atomic Energy Commission, Palewski into the diplomatic service.

The Faure government benefited from economic reform and from a general rise in prosperity in Western Europe. The Prime Minister attended a four-power conference in Geneva at which he sensed that Molotov was particularly anxious to get on well with France. Negotiations for Tunisian independence were brought to a successful conclusion, and the nationalist leader, Habib Bourguiba, returned to take charge of his country. Meanwhile, Auriol handed over to a new head of state, René Coty, a lightweight centrist who had been among those who had voted full powers to Pétain in 1940. De Gaulle characterised him as 'an unknown without any features and reassuring for the bourgeois who want to sleep'. It took thirteen ballots of the electoral college at Versailles to reach a decision – this was the first such event covered by television and so the entire nation could witness the difficulty the Republic had in reaching coherent outcomes.

The General's mood was further weighed down by having to undergo a second eye operation; he wrote to his niece, Véronique, that he was 'a poor man who is losing his sight, who would have lost it entirely by now had it not been for surgery'. When he received Tournoux for an interview at Colombey, he wore heavy dark glasses, which he took off occasionally to rub his scarred eye sockets. 'I do not want to appear in public,' he said. 'I don't see any more. I am an old man. I will go. France . . . will bury us all.'

Between mood swings he predicted to the journalist that the regime would have to cede France's possessions in the Sahara, and then lose Alsace-Lorraine – 'we'll only keep the Auvergne because nobody will want it,' he added. Then he switched to an optimistic note about France; it was 'young, alive, vigorous', he said, with spreading prosperity. But, he added, 'that is why I do not have much chance of returning to power . . . except if these imbeciles go on with their idiotic policy.' As evening fell, he sat in the growing dusk without turning on the electric lights, lamenting: 'You see, one thinks oneself strong, brave, invincible, and then, when your head or your eyes are opened . . .'

As during difficult times in the past, he went into temporary retreat, pondering his options and marshalling his forces before returning to the fray. He put tens of thousands of kilometres between himself and the political world of Paris by visiting Africa. His wife and Guichard, who was as tall as the General, accompanied him, Yvonne knitting as she sat beside her husband in the Dakota aircraft given by Truman in 1945. In Chad he received a royal welcome and a local imam told him he was like the rain arriving after a drought. These journeys included several all-night flights during which the sixty-five-year-old General sat up in his seat talking to his companions rather than retiring to his bunk. When, at 3 a.m. on one long flight, his wife said she was going to lie down he replied: 'Yvonne, you're not going to sleep, are you? They're going to serve us onion soup.'

Returning to Paris, reinvigorated by his reception on his travels, de Gaulle saw visitors on Wednesdays at his office in the rue de Solférino; callers ranged from Albert Camus to the populist politician Pierre Poujade. Across town, his 'barons', including Malraux, Soustelle, Michelet, Debré, Pompidou, Chaban-Delmas, Guichard and Palewski, kept the flame of the Gaullist Round Table alive by meeting, also each Wednesday, to discuss politics over lunch at a club near the Arc de Triomphe.

At Colombey, the grounds had been remodelled again, with a large bed of red, white and blue flowers laid in the shape of the Cross of Lorraine, and another to resemble a giant general's star. Receiving visitors in his hexagonal study, lit by a single lamp on the desk in front of him, the General continued to foresee catastrophe as he had done two decades earlier. In conversations with close aides, he flirted with the idea of staging a coup backed by the army but never committed himself to direct action. As so often, he juggled with different ideas, not letting others know where his preference lay – and probably not having determined this himself. He was increasingly sure that his forecast of crisis and catastrophe was going to be borne out, but he had had enough of the political game for the time being.

At a press conference in Paris in June 1955, he announced that he would not involve himself in public affairs henceforth. In September, he suspended all the RPF's activities. In each case, things were not quite what they seemed. Though he was no longer leading a national movement, his political contacts and conversations continued. As for the RPF, its parliamentary members formed two successive groups which kept up the networks forged since 1947. Being a Gaullist without de Gaulle's active leadership was a tricky task, but it was one which the men he had marginalised for having compromised with the Fourth Republic were ready to perform; they were no less faithful to the cause even if they believed that burrowing into the system from within was more effective than single-minded opposition.[3]

II
Algeria

At his press conference in June, the General had predicted that the epicentre of the shock which would hit France would be North Africa. In November 1954, encouraged by the Viet Minh victory in the Far East, the National Liberation Front (FLN) in Algeria staged bomb attacks and killed French civilians in the Aurès Mountains, marking the start of its organised assault on colonial rule. Paris reacted by sending in reinforcements to track down the guerrillas. 'The only negotiation is war,' Mitterrand declared, insisting 'Algeria is France', a sentiment echoed by Mendès France.

For most people in metropolitan France, and more so for the million *pieds-noirs** inhabitants of European origin across the Mediterranean, the territory was not a colony but had become an integral part of the nation after its conquest more than a century earlier. Stretching over 2.4 million square kilometres between Tunisia and Morocco and reaching down into the Sahara to the borders of Niger and Mali, it was almost four times the size of metropolitan France. The minority population of foreign origin, including 140,000 Jews, regarded it as home – 80 per cent of them had been born there. The fiction that Algeria was a part of France that just happened to be on the other side of the Mediterranean was maintained; even its school history textbooks began 'Our ancestors,

*Literally 'black feet', a name given to early French settlers by native inhabitants because of the shoes they wore.

the Gauls . . .' The French Algerian lobby was powerful in Paris, working through National Assembly deputies and with friends in high places.

A few *pieds-noirs* were extremely rich, including a trio of prominent tycoons – the shipowner Laurent Schiaffino, said to be the wealthiest man in the territory, the entrepreneur Henri Borgeaud who farmed some of the best land, which produced four million litres of wine a year, as well as owning the biggest-selling brand of cigarettes, and Georges Blanchette, whose alfalfa crop accounted for a fifth of Algeria's foreign exchange earnings. All three were involved in politics; Schiaffino and Borgeaud, both of them members of the legislative upper house in Paris, were conservatives, while Blanchette backed a more liberal approach, though his workers were among the worst-paid.

But most of the population of European origin, who came from other Mediterranean countries as well as from France, were ordinary workers, shopkeepers and civil servants. The poor Europeans kept together in suburbs like Bab-el-Oued in Algiers. In the countryside, the *bled*, some lorded it over their native workers; others tried to create a joint community in which, however, the French always remained on top. Though some individuals such as Schiaffino were cold and reclusive, the *pieds-noirs* were generally known for their exuberance and their love of the sun. To their compatriots across the sea they were a somewhat exotic breed, more North African than French, and their country was a land known mainly through films such as the 1937 classic *Pépé le Moko*. The novels of Albert Camus, *L'Étranger* and *La Peste*, explored the human condition in the context of sun-baked North Africa while the mythology of Beau Geste spun romance and films around the Foreign Legion and its Sahara base of Sidi-Bel-Abbès, prompting Édith Piaf's classic song '*Mon légionnaire*'. The psychological gap between the *pied-noir* leaders and de Gaulle, with his dour northern background and sense of propriety, would be an intangible but important element in the playing-out of the Algerian drama in the years ahead.

When they were depicted as a minority, the settlers replied that they were part of the fifty-five-million-strong population of France stretching 'from Dunkirk to Tamanrasset [in the Sahara]'. But, in Algeria itself, they were outnumbered nine to one by the non-Europeans though they controlled 90 per cent of the territory's wealth. Of the nine million natives, some 70 per cent were Arabs and the rest were mainly Berbers living in the rugged mountains of the Kabylie and Aurès regions, and 600,000 nomads in a million square kilometres of the Sahara. In villages some 55,000 native self-defence militiamen, known as *harkis,* joined the French to guard against nationalist guerrillas. But the attractions of urban life and employment drew millions of Muslims from the countryside to the main cities, where they crowded into *bidonvilles* (slums). In Algiers, the Casbah, a maze of narrow streets in which one could jump from rooftop to rooftop, had a population density of 100,000 to the square kilometre.[4]

The army, which became increasingly powerful as the war against the FLN intensified, backed 'integration' of Algeria's thirteen departments with metropolitan France so long as the balance with the rapidly growing native population was maintained in favour of the French. This did not answer the question of how the majority population was to be treated; they were French subjects but did not enjoy the rights of French citizens. Any proposals from the national government for reform and greater rights for the Muslims were regarded with extreme suspicion by the *pieds-noirs.* They blamed the FLN violence on lax government policy, and viewed the agreement being worked out for Tunisian independence as evidence of the readiness of Paris to sell out. When Faure argued that refusing reforms fed anti-French agitation, a deputy from Algiers replied that 'announcement of reforms gives the agitators their greatest hope'. Some army officers saw the fight against the nationalists as part of a wider war against revolutionaries and Communists which had been lost in Indochina, a defeat they blamed on lack of resolve at home and repetition of which they were determined to avoid.

Algeria became an international matter of concern when it was brought up for debate at the United Nations. Foreign opinion, including that in America, was turning against what was seen as a dirty colonial war. It was, however, a crisis over an agreement aimed at giving Morocco full independence in place of the existing halfway-house arrangement that led Faure to call a general election in December 1955. The Left did well – shrugging off questions raised by Nikita Khrushchev's denunciation of Stalin earlier in the year, the Communists took 25 per cent of the votes and 150 seats, an increase of 47. It was a disaster for the Gaullists who won only 4.4 per cent and 21 seats, a sixth of their score of 1951. The Socialist Guy Mollet formed a government with the tacit support of the PCF under the banner of a Republican Front. Mendès France and Chaban were Ministers of State, and Mitterrand Justice Minister. Félix Houphouët-Boigny from the Ivory Coast, who had participated in national politics since being elected to the post-war Constituent Assembly, became France's first African Cabinet member, serving as Minister Delegate to Mollet.

The big shock for the political elite was the electoral success of a right-wing grassroots movement headed by Pierre Poujade, a shopkeeper from south-western France whose movement gathered support from small retailers, artisans and others as it inveighed against the 'thieving' state, the 'brothel' of parliament with its 'rubbishy, pederast' deputies, price controls, big industry, foreigners, intellectuals and the granting of independence to French possessions. The *Union de Défense des Commerçants et Artisans* (Union for the Defence of Shopkeepers and Artisans) trumpeted extreme nationalism and championed 'the good little people of France', and 'the humble housewife'. Mendès France was a particular target for having ceded Indochina and for being Jewish – the only thing French about him was the second part of his surname, Poujade said.

Before the election, the party was generally dismissed as a fringe expression of bad temper; de Gaulle called it 'simply one of the signs of endemic revolt generated by the . . . incapacity of the regime'. But it won 2.5 million votes, or 12 per cent of the total, slightly more than the Radicals or the MRP. Replacing the Gaullists as the main non-Communist foe of the Fourth Republic, and drawing on discontented voters who had previously backed the RPF, it held fifty-five seats in the National Assembly it abhorred.[5]

Mollet, a former teacher and member of the Resistance who was arrested three times by the Gestapo, had sat in the National Assembly since 1945. An accomplished party bureaucrat, he represented the left wing of the Socialist party but had an edgy relationship with the Communists. His position as Premier was fragile from the outset. He was in open disagreement over economic policy with Mendès France, who went to Colombey to discuss the situation with de Gaulle; the two men agreed to disagree – the General continued to focus on constitutional change, but Mendès regarded Algeria as the main problem.

Before taking office, Mollet had spoken of opening negotiations with the FLN. In March 1956, parliament gave him special powers to deal with Algeria; the aim was to achieve a ceasefire from a position of military strength. The shadow of Dien Bien Phu hung heavily over French politics. The length of military service was extended to twenty-seven months and troop numbers across the Mediterranean rose steadily.

The Prime Minister proposed to replace Soustelle with de Gaulle's wartime colleague General Catroux, who had drawn up plans to devolve a degree of power a dozen years earlier. That sparked an explosion among the *pieds-noirs*, already concerned about the government's intentions. At the suggestion of Mendès, Mollet decided to fly to Algiers to install Catroux in person. He expected a triumphant reception; instead, he was pelted with rotten tomatoes and stones amid cries of 'Mollet to the gallows' and 'Throw Catroux in the sea.' The police did not intervene. Troops had to escort the Prime Minister to the government residence.

Catroux had already decided not to take the job, and the Socialist Robert Lacoste was named in his place with the title of Minister Resident. He put the death toll since 1954 at 25,609, 5,933 as a result of terrorism. Of the 19,676 who had died as a result of military action, 17,784 were non-European. The army's use of torture had been revealed from 1951 by courageous journalists such as Claude Bourdet, but politicians in Paris with theoretical authority over the security operation across the Mediterranean could not control what went on. In seeking a military victory over the FLN, they ceded to the army, and preferred not to know the details of the increasingly dirty war.[6]

In May, Mendès France resigned in protest at the hard-line Algerian policy. This did nothing to deter the thickset, combative Lacoste. He tried to reduce the gulf between the two communities in Algeria, but the nationalists had no interest in that and the settlers had shown their muscle with their hostile reception of Mollet. So the military option prevailed.

Tension increased in June 1956 with the guillotining of two members of the FLN, one for killing a gamekeeper, the other for an ambush in which eight *pieds-noirs*, including a seven-year-old girl, died.

In retaliation for the executions, squads controlled by Saadi Yacef, the head of the FLN network in Algiers, shot forty-nine civilians. Two months later, a house said to have been occupied by nationalist terrorists was blown up by a *pied-noir* 'self-defence' group: seventy Muslims died. Secret contacts with France in Rome were broken off after an FLN conference restructured the movement politically and voted to pursue violence as the way to achieve independence. The French then kidnapped the nationalist leader, Ahmed Ben Bella, after illegally intercepting his aircraft on its way from Morocco to Tunis. He was jailed in Paris. The operation was prepared by the military in Lacoste's absence, but the Minister Resident did not countermand it when informed of the action.

III
Suez and the Battle of Algiers

It was elsewhere in North Africa that international attention focused on France. In July 1956, a desire to stem Arab nationalism prompted the Mollet government to join the British and Israelis in attacking Egypt after the nationalisation of the Suez Canal by the Egyptian leader Gamal Abdel Nasser. The operation was a military success but ended in diplomatic disaster when American opposition and the threat of intervention by Moscow brought it to an abrupt end.

De Gaulle saw the episode as yet further evidence of the regime's weakness; when questioned, he said that if he had been in office he would have broadcast an immediate warning to the Egyptian leader that two divisions of French paratroopers were being dispatched. They would have taken Cairo within two hours, he added, 'and no force in the world would have stopped them'. He also depicted the Suez debacle as yet another example of the error of depending on London, remarking, 'you have to be a socialist to believe in the military virtues of the British'. He would have been even more cutting had he known that Mollet secretly proposed a Franco-British political and economic union, which Anthony Eden's government turned down.[7]

No sooner had the French been humiliated over Suez than the crisis in Algiers turned even more murderous, as the FLN boss Saadi Yacef launched a series of bombings carried out by young women who left explosives in places frequented by Europeans, including a milk bar, a cafeteria, a restaurant and a nightclub. The mayor of an Algiers suburb, a leader of 'ultra' settler conservatives, was shot. A bomb went off at the cemetery just before his funeral. *Pieds-noirs* ran amok, killing four Muslims and injuring fifty. Under Yacef's instructions, the Casbah was transformed into an armed camp – the FLN leader had been born there, one of fourteen children of a baker, and knew its narrow, winding streets well. His artisans constructed a network of tunnels, explosives factories and hiding places, and he moved to and fro disguised by the veil and long dress of a Muslim woman.

At a loss as to how to cope with the escalating crisis, Lacoste handed over responsibility for suppressing the revolt to the paratroop general Jacques Massu, a tough, craggy Suez veteran with a formidable record which included service in Leclerc's Free French forces in the desert. He had fought in Indochina and been among troops deployed by Jules Moch to put down Communist-led strikes. A committed Gaullist, Massu was a proud professional soldier with little interest in politics who believed in following his orders successfully, whatever the cost. But he did not underestimate the scale of the challenge he had been handed. 'We're in for piles of shit,' he told his chief of staff, Yves Godard.

Godard was a more intellectual figure who had run a 'dirty tricks' unit for the French counter-intelligence service and fought in Indochina. He elaborated a systematic plan to defeat Yacef and his guerrillas, recruiting informers and moving forward block by block as the Battle of Algiers unfurled. Paratroop reinforcements were called in. A curfew was imposed and the Casbah was sealed off. A general strike called by the FLN was defeated by strong-arm methods, including ripping the grilles off shops which closed and forcibly trucking in workers.

Torture was stepped up, including the application of electric shocks and near-drowning. When a leading FLN figure who had been arrested died in custody, the official version was that he had hanged himself with strips torn from his shirt; he was almost certainly killed by his captors. Independent reports put the number of people who 'disappeared' at three thousand, mainly Algerians, but also including a few French sympathisers. A Communist, Henri Alleg, blew the lid off the official secrecy with a book recounting how he had been tortured and the Secretary-General of Lacoste's office tried to resign in protest at army methods. A respected officer, General Jacques de la Bollardière, who took part in the Battle of Algiers, published a letter in the news magazine *L'Express* warning of the danger to the army of relinquishing moral values for a short-term victory. He was sentenced to sixty days' 'fortress arrest'.

In the summer, the French army gained the upper hand. Yacef was cornered and gave himself up to a unit led by Godard. He was sentenced to death three times but not executed, and was later amnestied. A group of his leading associates was blown up when an army bomb detonated a cache of explosives. By the autumn, the Battle of Algiers was over. Massu had won. But the cost was a further widening of the division between the French and the Algerians, the corruption of the army through the use of torture and illegal methods and the strengthening of the devotion to the cause of *Algérie française* (French Algeria) of men like Godard. For the *pieds-noirs*, the paratroopers in their camouflage uniforms were the heroes, in sharp contrast to the pusillanimous politicians in Paris. A seed had been sown which would germinate and grow into bitter fruit in the years ahead.[8]

De Gaulle forecast that none of the parties would be able to save Algeria; its eventual loss would, like that of Indochina, stem from the weakness of the regime as a whole. Interviewed by Tournoux in November 1956, he pointed to the growth in pan-Arab feeling and said the Arabs were 'clever politicians . . . as clever as beggars' even if 'one has never seen Arabs build roads, dams, factories. After all, perhaps they don't need roads, dams, factories.' Would France lose its territories in West Africa next? the journalist asked. 'The problem is not the same,' the General replied. 'The blacks are good fellows. They are not motivated by the same passion, the same hatred as the Arabs.'[9]

24

'I WILL SEE'

I
'I will be better understood in fifty years'

Even if he fell into occasional bouts of gloom and self-pity and worried about his eyesight, de Gaulle's mental faculties were as sharp as ever and his memory remained extraordinary; he amazed a French officer posted to NATO, Pierre Gallois, to whom he spoke about nuclear strategy one night in an impromptu exposé that lasted until 3 a.m. In the late summer of 1956, he made another trip far from France, travelling on a liner from Marseille to the Pacific with his wife, Guichard, Foccard, his aide de Bonneval and, unusually, a journalist, Jean Mauriac of the Agence France-Presse (AFP), the son of François and brother of his former secretary, Claude.

In the Coco Islands, the General was photographed standing in military uniform under a palm tree with Yvonne beside him – he hated the shot, which he said made them look as if they were in a décor at a booth at a country fair, with none of the dignity he wanted to project. In Tahiti, he was caught by a violent storm that flooded the room in which he was eating – he continued the meal with his feet in the water. On the boat, the General was the master on board; at one meal, he ordered the steward to serve Mauriac with soup after the reporter had waved it aside – one did not turn down the food offered by one's host. On another day, the journalist was flirting with a young Australian woman in his cabin when de Bonneval burst in and told him he was compromising the General by his behaviour. One morning, Mauriac had a highly unusual glimpse of de Gaulle standing at the door of his cabin in his pyjamas gazing at the sea.[1]

Back in France, de Gaulle told Cyrus Sulzberger of the *New York Times*: 'Great circumstances bring forth great men. Only during crises do nations throw up giants.' As for himself, he remarked: 'I will be better understood in fifty years. Ah, if I was dead, how everything would be simpler.' He wrote to his son that 'the situation will only hatch with a catastrophe (general revolt in Africa)'. Suez and the troubles in Algeria were provoking reactions he had not witnessed for ten years, particularly in the army, he added. 'We will see. I will see,' he concluded.

Marshal Juin wrote to urge another 18 June. An outing to the ceremonies at the Mont-Valérien memorial that day produced an outpouring of popular enthusiasm for the General. The publication of the second volume of his memoirs reinforced his historic status, and an article in the weekly magazine *Carrefour* suggested that the moment had come for him to resume office. Speaking again to Sulzberger, the General said a 'certain degree of chaos' would be needed to pave the way for his return, and forecast that blood would be shed. When a dozen young parliamentarians, including the future President Valéry Giscard d'Estaing, told Coty he should deal with the next crisis by calling on de Gaulle, the head of state replied: 'It's my place he needs.'[2]

II
Political roundabout

While the General watched and waited, the Mollet government was far from inactive. In Europe, France was a major player in the negotiation and signature of the Treaty of Rome establishing the six-nation European Common Market in March 1957. It was also among the founders of the European atomic agency, Euratom. The Minister for Overseas Territories, Gaston Defferre, completed a reform of France's relations with its African dominions which gave them a form of internal autonomy under a government council headed initially by a French official but then by a local. At a conference in Bamako, attended by Mitterrand and Mendès France, Houphouët-Boigny called for the 'right to independence' of Francophone territories which would enter into a federal relationship with Paris. Léopold Senghor of Senegal urged the divided African colonies to unite while the militant Sékou-Touré from

Guinea said a new form of association with France should be negotiated once the Africans had come together.

In June 1957, the government was brought down by internal tensions, a spiralling trade deficit and high inflation, plus the failure to end the revolt in Algeria despite the dispatch of reinforcements. The next Cabinet, headed by the Radical Maurice Bourgès-Maunoury, who had fought in the Resistance and held eight previous ministerial posts, was also unable to get to grips with the quagmire across the Mediterranean. Lacoste remained in charge on the spot and another hardliner from the Socialist ranks, Max Lejeune, became Minister for the Sahara. In Paris, police staged a demonstration on 13 March outside parliament that ended in violence. De Gaulle marked his distance from the administration by asking the Prime Minister not to attend the 18 June anniversary ceremonies at Mont-Valérien despite his Resistance record.

When Bourgès-Maunoury fell after five months, five weeks were spent trying to construct a new majority. This ended when another Radical, Félix Gaillard, moved into Matignon. At thirty-seven, the reserved technocrat was the youngest Prime Minister of the Third and Fourth Republics. Chaban-Delmas became Defence Minister; in a letter, de Gaulle wrote that he did not object to him taking the post, but said that most of the national responsibility of the job had been abrogated by France's membership of the NATO unified command. Gaillard oversaw a devaluation, spending cuts and tax increases, but the trade results remained poor and inflation raged. However, the new Premier took one step of which the General did approve with an order to press ahead with France's nuclear weapons programme begun during the Mendès France government.

A Gaullist cell began to operate in Algiers under two RPF veterans, Lucien Neuwirth, who had joined the Resistance at sixteen and made a political career in Saint-Étienne, and Léon Delbecque, a tough political operator with a fine head of black hair, clear blue eyes and broad shoulders who shared Paris–Lille links with de Gaulle. In charge of 'psychological operations' in Algeria, Delbecque's main job was to muster support for the General. Lacoste complained to Chaban about the two men's activities, but the minister insisted that they were acting independently of him; their Paris controller was Jacques Foccart, who had built up substantial business interests in Africa.

A fresh crisis broke out in North Africa when a French air attack killed sixty-nine people in a Tunisian frontier village, near which sixteen French soldiers had died in an FLN ambush a month earlier. The Tunisian President Habib Bourguiba demanded the withdrawal of French troops from their base at Bizerta in his country. Paris accepted a mediation effort by America and Britain, but the settler lobby warned that this would lead to foreign interference in Algeria. The mission was headed by the US diplomat Robert Murphy, who had been a major backer of Giraud during the war. That, the General judged, demonstrated its lack of seriousness. In April 1958, the Gaillard administration was defeated in the National Assembly. After another protracted round of negotiations, Coty asked the Alsatian Pierre Pflimlin to try to form an administration. In all, eighty-eight of the 358 days since the fall of the Mollet government were spent on putting together governments.[3]

*

De Gaulle, who had broken his arm in a fall, kept above the fray, disguising his intentions. To some visitors he insisted that he was not wanted any more, but then, on a visit to Brittany, he remarked to his brother-in-law that the Algerian imbroglio would force 'the best of the French' to call on him. His only public statement, running to nine lines in September, maintained the useful suspense. It said that remarks attributed to him by visitors to Colombey were their responsibility. 'When General de Gaulle considers it useful to make known what he thinks, one knows that he will do it himself, and publicly,' it added. 'That is the case, in particular, on the subject of Algeria.'[4]

In private, he noted that the gulf between the French and the Muslims was widening by the day. He seemed to make a gesture towards the liberals by receiving the Tunisian ambassador before he left France after being recalled in protest at the French attack; Madame de Gaulle made cheese sandwiches for the envoy and Olivier Guichard to eat on the drive back to Paris, remarking to de Gaulle's aide that, aware of the ambassador's religion, she had been careful not to include ham.

The General assured Delbecque there was 'no question of de Gaulle giving up anything whatsoever', but he spoke to Maurice Schumann of self-determination for Algeria and told another caller that independence was the only solution. The only uncertainty was how this would come about, he informed the heir to the Moroccan throne. When the Socialist André Philip raised the question of the *pieds-noirs*, de Gaulle was dismissive: 'Come on, don't be naïve. They just bawl. As for the military, I'll wait while they devour one another. Then I'll deal with the remainder by giving them promotions and decorations.' As he debated with himself, the General remarked to Terrenoire that 'if I have a plan, I'll be careful not to make it known'.[5]

III
'Little Plum'

In his memoirs, Pflimlin, known as 'Little Plum', recalled that, on being asked to form a government in May 1958, he found the 'decomposition' of the Fourth Republic worse than he had realised. Familiar economic problems persisted; Jean Monnet made a fresh trip to Washington to raise a $274 million loan and France's poor trading record meant that the economy was ringed with protectionist measures and currency controls; a tough decision would lie ahead when the free trade provisions of the Common Market went into effect in the following year. The ballooning budget deficit fuelled inflation which politicians tended to regard as inevitable given the electoral pain that would be incurred by any serious attempt to eliminate it.

Still, France was not in terrible shape. Growth was strong and employment levels high. Infrastructure was being modernised. French companies had become world technological leaders in sectors such as aviation and cars. A new generation of more modern-minded technocrats had emerged, more open to foreign (mainly American) influences and ready to assume leadership in politics, business and the civil service. Relations with Washington had recovered from the Suez disaster. French food and wine dominated world gastronomy. Paris was a global cultural and artistic centre. Jean-Paul Sartre and Simone de Beauvoir held court in Saint-Germain-des-Prés. In the cinema, God created woman in the shape of Brigitte Bardot, and the New Wave was launched.

But, like the Third Republic before it, the regime had forfeited popular support and was seen as the playground for self-absorbed politicians whose prime concern was to swap jobs. As the commentator Pierre Emmanuel noted of members of the younger generation, 'though they are most competent and full of initiative in their fields . . . they have not succeeded in changing the obsolete part of the existing French structures'. Governments appeared unable to rely on two bastions of the Republic, the police and the military. Pressure from the settlers in Algeria rose with the establishment of a 'vigilance committee' and a demonstration of 30,000 settlers and friendly non-Europeans on 26 April to demand military rule; 'I have Algeria in my hand now,' Delbecque cabled Chaban afterwards. Seeing the threat to his own position, Lacoste ordered the Gaullist to go back to metropolitan France, but he soon returned to Algiers.

Six hundred thousand posters calling for the return of de Gaulle were now plastered on walls across France, but the General was evasive when Neuwirth delivered an appeal for him to act. At Easter his nephew, Bernard, thought he was showing his age. He compared himself to the central character in the 1957 Goncourt literary-prize-winning novel, *La Loi*, a disabused old Italian village chieftain (also, no doubt seeing parallels, he recommended Hemingway's *The Old Man and the Sea* as a masterpiece). He had difficulty walking and getting up from his chair, reaching out for his stick with a shaking hand. 'It's done for,' he told his visitor. 'This country will never pick itself up . . . Just one chance, Bernard, have children, it's the only service your generation can still render to the country.' An associate of Mendès France, Simon Nora, remarked on leaving La Boisserie that what he had heard from his host was enough to make him want to go into a Trappist monastery. 'I won't advise you otherwise,' de Gaulle replied.[6]

*

It was not long, however, before what Jean Lacouture termed the General's 'power libido' kicked in, after de Gaulle displayed a recurrent pattern of gloom which acted as the precursor to intense, decisive action. In a bravura performance in the spring of 1958, he mixed force, nerve, fear, bluff, charm and a readiness to make concessions in his second great historic performance in defence of the nation. His strategy was simple, but extremely hard to execute as he insisted on taking a legal route back to office, but let those in authority imagine him heading a military coup, thus frightening the establishment into acquiescence.

For many on the Left, the way in which he outmanoeuvred the Fourth Republic constituted the original sin of the new regime he would usher in. Mitterrand characterised it as the start of a permanent *coup d'état* akin to Napoleon III's power grab in 1851 which had established an autocracy with army backing, or to Bonaparte's 17th Brumaire overthrow of the post-revolutionary Directory in 1799. The editor of *Le Monde*, Hubert Beuve-Méry, judged, rather, that the regime committed suicide; the cartoonist Tim depicted Marianne dropping the guillotine blade on her own head. For the historian Jacques Julliard it was a case of euthanasia; for the political scientist René Rémond a combination of circumstances; for the Christian Democrat Robert Buron the regime established in 1946 simply disappeared little by little, like Lewis Carroll's Cheshire Cat, with a mocking smile as it went.[7]

Personal ambition apart, the General's key purpose was to remould the Republic to raise France above the travails of the system which had ruled since the victory over Germany. He saw himself as uniquely fitted to achieve that aim, the man of 1940 who enjoyed what he called 'somewhat mythic' status. Even more than eighteen years earlier, the character he had forged since the First World War enabled him to master events and live up to his own evaluation of himself as he charted his second coming. The way in which he achieved his goal needs to be related day by day to demonstrate how he played his cards, never losing sight of his long-term objective, but showing himself an expert at political poker, justifying his remark to Delbecque when it was all over: 'Admit it, I played well.'[8]

25

SAVING THE SHIP

I
'I am ready'

At the beginning of May 1958, a fresh demonstration outside the National Assembly by right-wing police symbolised the ebbing control of the government. There were recurrent reports of plots to overthrow the Republic; one account listed thirteen such conspiracies. The Left feared a repetition of the violent anti-parliamentary demonstrations in 1934, while the Right trembled at the thought of a Popular Front government dominated by the Communists.

Shuttling between metropolitan France and Algiers, Léon Delbecque built up support for de Gaulle, working with a tough officer, Colonel Thomazo, known as 'Leather Nose' for the strap on his face which hid a war wound. The wartime group the Companions of the Liberation named the General as the only man who could rally the people of France and restore the nation's prestige. At the rue de Solférino, the chubby-faced Olivier Guichard ran the Gaullist machine, and kept up contacts with politicians who might be ready to help. Jacques Foccart, whom the General regarded so highly that he always referred to him as 'Monsieur Foccart', maintained discreet links with confederates in France and Africa. Soustelle headed a Union for the Safeguarding and Renewal of French Algeria (USRAF) which attracted the membership of eminent academics, military men, religious figures and others who believed that Algeria's best future lay in continued rule by France. At army headquarters, an assistant chief of staff, General Petit, was in touch with Foccart and Debré.

6 May. An emissary from Coty met Guichard and Foccart. The next day, Guichard went to Colombey where de Gaulle said that, since the President had taken the first step, matters were proceeding in a suitable fashion.

8 May. Pflimlin formed a government made up of five Christian Democrats, nine centrists and four Independents. Lacoste was recalled. Before leaving Algiers, he threw fresh fuel on the fire by telling a group of officers that the government in Paris was preparing a new Dien Bien Phu. The new Prime Minister had caused concern among the *pieds-noirs* by publishing an article in which, while vowing not to abandon Algeria, he talked of the need to win hearts and minds and said that, when the time was ripe, he would offer negotiations for a ceasefire.[1]

9–10 May. De Gaulle sent a message to Coty saying he did not intend to go to the Élysée for talks and would not present himself in person for approval by the National Assembly. It could all be done in writing, he insisted in an aloof manner. Then he waited, giving instructions that Debré and Foccart were to keep quiet and that Soustelle was not to be put in the picture. When the pro-Gaullist daily newspaper *Paris-Presse* polled twenty-four leading politicians, only one was unequivocally in favour of his return: the head of a farmers' party.

The French military reported that the FLN had lost 15,000 men since the beginning of the year. The army commander in Algeria, Raoul Salan, was a careful, calculating man with little charisma. Known as 'the Mandarin' for his manner and from his time in Indochina, he had been among the Vichy defenders of Dakar in 1940 and was no Gaullist. *Pied-noir* extremists did not trust him. He had been the target of an assassination attempt when a bazooka round was fired at his office. He was out of the room at that time and the rocket killed another officer. Debré was questioned about possible involvement in the plot, but no proceedings were taken against him.

Salan's strategy consisted of consolidating control over inhabited areas, district by district, using force, aid, collaboration with the native authorities and 'psychological warfare' designed to win over the local population. Despite his caution, he joined his fellow generals in Algeria in writing a joint letter to Coty warning that the army would have a 'desperate reaction' to any surrender to the FLN. The military, which de Gaulle had always insisted must be the servant of the Republic, was seeking to influence government policy.[2]

11 May. The FLN cranked up the tension by announcing that, in retaliation for the execution of some of its prisoners held by the French, it had killed three soldiers taken captive two years earlier. The Sunday edition of the main settler newspaper, *L'Écho d'Alger*, published an open letter to de Gaulle from its director, Alain de Sérigny, calling on him to break his silence. Though he said nothing, the military hero of the settlers, Massu, was thinking along the same lines: he lamented the incapacity of the politicians in Paris, and thought that only the General could lead events in the right direction. The last time the two men had met, in West Africa five years earlier, the veteran of the Free French and Vietnam had told the General that, if he could help him one day, he would.[3]

13 May. In Algiers, de Sérigny, once a fervent Pétainist, wrote that Pflimlin could not be allowed to form a government since his programme could lead to *l'abandon*, an evocative term much in vogue among adherents of continuing French rule. A general strike was called.

In the afternoon, the Pflimlin administration faced the National Assembly for the first time. The Prime Minister-designate called for institutional reform to strengthen the executive and stated that negotiations with the FLN would only be possible after a French victory. His government, he pledged, would never allow the links between Algeria and France to be broken.

Pflimlin's assurance had no effect in Algiers where the strike closed down public buildings, shops, factories, transport, cinemas, cafés and restaurants. At 5 p.m., tens of thousands of *pieds-noirs* (some accounts put the number at 100,000) gathered at the war memorial in the centre of the city to honour the three soldiers killed by the FLN and to reject the new government. A student leader, Pierre Lagaillarde, a tall, intense figure with a brooding look who might have stepped out of a medieval religious painting had he not been wearing a paratrooper's uniform, jumped on to the plinth and asked in a stentorian voice: 'Are you going to let *Algérie française* be sold down the river? Will you allow traitors to govern us?' After Salan had laid a wreath, Lagaillarde led a mob in an attack on the main government building while the rest of the crowd watched from outside.

Riot police retreated after firing a few cans of tear gas. Paratroopers let the demonstrators commandeer a lorry with which to break down the gates. They rampaged through the building, sacking the premises and flinging furniture, typewriters and a blizzard of official papers from the windows. The crowd outside applauded Lagaillarde wildly when he appeared on an upper balcony. Sheltering under a desk, Lacoste's deputy called his former boss in Paris asking for instructions; he was told that under no circumstances should the troops fire on the crowd, which they had already decided against.

Massu arrived in a furious temper. While the mob booed Salan as a suspected compromiser, it cheered the paratroop general who went to the balcony to call for 'a Government of Public Safety under General de Gaulle'.

Gaillard, still nominally in office in Paris, had agreed, along with Pflimlin, to give civil and military powers to Salan. But 'the Mandarin' clearly did not control events, so the outgoing Premier said Massu should take charge. The one-time Free French fighter thus became chairman of the Public Safety Committee. Lagaillarde was among the first to join it. Delbecque was vice-chairman. General Petit arrived by air to promote de Gaulle's cause.

Massu telephoned Lacoste who was in the National Assembly with Gaillard beside him. He asked if he should order his paratroopers to fire on the crowd. Lacoste put his hand across the mouthpiece and turned to Gaillard. The answer was no. 'I don't know if they would have obeyed,' Massu said and hung up.

As news of the events in Algiers spread through the legislature, the Left spoke of forming an administration of 'republican defence'. The Communist Secretary-General, Waldeck Rochet, called for Massu to be dismissed and declared an outlaw. Telephone and transport links with Algeria were cut.

Demonstrators in Algiers next took over the radio station. The Public Safety Committee formally called on de Gaulle to assume power. Coty, constitutionally the head of the armed forces, issued a statement insisting that the army follow government orders. It was not broadcast in Algeria where officers were plotting an airborne landing in France.[4]

14 May. In his winding-up speech in the Assembly in the early hours, Pflimlin got loud applause when he referred to events in Algeria as an 'insurrection'. His administration was supported by a majority of deputies who voted but the number of abstainers, among them the Communists, meant that the new Prime Minister lacked overall backing. At 3.30, Pflimlin held a two-hour Cabinet meeting. His government had Mollet as Vice-Premier, Pleven as Foreign Minister and Edgar Faure as Finance Minister. After a delay, Jules Moch took the Interior Ministry. The government formally assumed office at 6 a.m. As ministers made their way home to snatch some sleep, de Gaulle left Colombey in his Citroën 15CV. It was Wednesday, the day he usually went to the capital. He had an appointment with a prince of the Bonaparte family which he did not intend to break.

For all their immediate success, the rebels in Algiers lacked a political leader; the natural candidate, Soustelle, was forbidden to leave France. The Public Safety Committee ballooned to forty-five members, including de Sérigny and 'Leather Nose' Thomazo. The Gaullist Lucien Neuwirth took charge of the information department. Massu was exhausted and lost his voice after all his exhortations. As his wife treated his throat, he croaked: 'I am going to the end of this tunnel whatever happens, until General de Gaulle gives us his hand.'

But the General was intent on keeping his options open till the right moment arrived. After the imminent 'explosion', the military would try to set up a dictatorship, he believed. This would provoke resistance and the prospect of civil war. The sole escape would be through a figure of national authority, and 'that authority could only be mine,' he recalled in his memoirs ten years later.

Arriving from Colombey at the rue de Solférino, he found a letter from the pro-*Algérie française* Bidault pledging loyalty. De Gaulle told a visitor from the Companions of the Liberation that he saw no reason why they should not send a delegation to Coty to put their case for his return. The *Parisien libéré* ran a front-page banner headline reading 'Only one solution: de Gaulle'. But most of the press backed Pflimlin. Moch judged later that strong action would have nipped the revolt in the bud, but the Premier preferred not to exacerbate the crisis.

Public Safety Committees sprouted in major Algerian cities and generals took over regional government posts. The Place du Forum was still the scene of mass demonstrations. Some of the crowd waved banners emblazoned with the Cross of Lorraine, or with their company logos, including that of British Petroleum. In an address from the balcony of the government building, Salan declared military victory to be the only solution. When he ended with 'Long live France! Long live Algeria!' Delbecque, standing behind him, hissed: 'Call out, Long live de Gaulle!' The legal government's representative in Algiers complied. (According to some accounts Delbecque jabbed his fingers into the general's back – Salan may have imagined it was a pistol.)

Guichard telephoned Colombey with the news – the call was tapped by the Interior Ministry. Debré, Chaban-Delmas and Soustelle were put under surveillance.

At 6 p.m., de Gaulle finally issued a statement: it was just ten lines long. He noted the inevitable consequences of the degradation of the state on the nation and the army. 'For twelve years, France, grappling with problems too tough for the party regime to handle, has been on a disastrous path,' he added. 'Formerly, the country, from its depths, put its confidence in me to lead it to salvation. Today, facing the challenges rising once more, let it know that I am ready to assume the powers of the Republic.'

The statement was a superb example of the way he placed himself above events, and used his position for maximum tactical advantage. The lack of any specific reference to Algeria enabled him to avoid either condemning or supporting the rebels, but to remain the arbiter above the fray. In Algiers, Delbecque read de Gaulle's statement to the crowd in the centre of the city. As the news spread, 30,000 members of the native population marched to the main square behind tricolour flags in support of de Gaulle, they and the settlers mingling in a demonstration that, for a moment, brought the two camps together in the hope of a solution which would satisfy them both. Madame Massu broadcast an appeal to 'all women of goodwill' to keep alive 'the flame of joy'.[5]

15 May. 'De Gaulle drops the mask . . . Down with military dictatorship,' read the front-page headline in big bold type in *L'Humanité*. The conservative *Figaro* took issue with the General's statement for its lack of precision and said that it deeply troubled public opinion. The greatest risk, its editorial added, would be to mobilise one part of the nation against the other, and thus to facilitate a *coup d'état*. *Le Monde* was moving cautiously but unmistakably towards the General, declaring that he might rally a majority behind a real national government.

At an MRP congress in the Breton town of Dinard, Robert Buron, who had worked in the Mendès France administration, was loudly applauded when he called for the party to back de Gaulle. But the American ambassador to France, Amory Houghton, told Washington that French contacts with whom he had spoken considered the General's return to office would sharpen divisions between Right and Left and favour Communist designs to create a Popular Front. Most thought that street violence would spread throughout France in the coming days.

An officer from Massu's staff called Vitasse flew to Pau and Toulouse to brief army detachments on what was going on in Algiers. From Toulouse, he reported to Algiers that the local commander was ready to lead an operation on the mainland. In a telephone conversation with one of his deputies who was in Algiers, the army chief of staff, Paul Ély, said that Salan's cry of '*Vive de Gaulle!*' went 'in the right direction'. When he was handed the transcript of the telephone tap, Pflimlin exploded: 'They're all treacherous and disloyal!'[6]

II
Belonging to nobody and to everybody

16 May. In Algiers, another 'fraternisation' demonstration was organised in support of integration: army lorries went into the countryside to fetch native people, who had never experienced such friendship. Some Muslim women even removed their veils for the occasion. Lucien Neuwirth, who had taken control at Radio Alger and was putting out a stream of broadcasts in favour of the General, warned Salan that if he back-pedalled, army unity would be shattered. Salan replied: 'We are in the same boat. Trust in me.'

In protest at government policy, Ély submitted his resignation, which was accepted the following day. A National Association for the Appeal to General de Gaulle in the Respect of Republican Legality was created, its title reflecting the careful balancing act the General was maintaining. In the National Assembly, the Communists voted for Pflimlin when he asked for emergency powers for three months. Mollet responded to the statement from Colombey by asking the General if he recognised the sole legitimacy of the government, whether he disapproved of those behind the Public Safety Committee in Algeria and whether, if he was called on to form an administration, he would present himself to the Assembly with a programme of government, and, if defeated in a parliamentary vote, would give way. It might have seemed that the Socialist leader was throwing down the gauntlet; in fact, he was recognising the General's legitimacy as a figure with whom a dialogue could be opened.

Hiding under a rug on the back seat of a Renault Dauphine, Soustelle was driven from his home in the 16th *arrondissement* undetected by the ten police agents posted outside. On the other side of Paris, he switched to a Buick driven by Pierre de Bénouville, a former RPF deputy and supporter of *Algérie française*, who transported him to Switzerland from where he took a private plane to Algeria, the trip funded by the aircraft manufacturer Marcel Dassault.[7]

17 May. Fighter aircraft flew over Colombey in the formation of the Cross of Lorraine; from his garden de Gaulle raised his arms in salute to them. Soustelle arrived in Algiers, where the crowd acclaimed the former Governor General. Appearing with Delbecque at a rally in the Place du Forum, he paid tribute to Muslim women who had burned their veils 'in a symbolic gesture of emancipation'. Wearing his trademark rimless dark glasses, the rotund politician and the granite-faced

Massu were filmed laughing together. But Salan gave him a cool reception and sent him on a tour of provincial towns. Still, the one-time RPF Secretary-General remained the potential political leader of the revolt; 'At last we have a chief,' demonstrators shouted.

19 May. De Gaulle, who had taken pains to reassure the Americans of his democratic intentions through discreet emissaries, called a press conference in Paris at the Hôtel d'Orsay, a faded building by the Seine with a grand staircase leading to the large salon chosen for the occasion. Light from heavy chandeliers was reflected from long mirrors on either side of the stage. Heavy purple drapes hung behind the table where the General spoke. The heat was such that some of the audience tried to open the windows, but an attendant sprang forward to insist that they should be kept shut and that the curtains should remain closed. Tiers of cameramen and photographers were arranged on either side of the stage, their spotlights further raising the temperature. The British author Graham Greene was present, standing behind the scribbling journalists.

The state broadcasting service did not cover the event live. Coty told Pflimlin that he feared de Gaulle's press conference would unleash mass demonstrations, and suggested that the members of the government should go to the Interior Ministry opposite the Élysée where they could be guarded; the Prime Minister rejected the idea, seeing it as evidence of the 'unreal atmosphere' reigning at the presidential palace. Still, Moch deployed a big police force near the Hôtel d'Orsay; in his memoirs, de Gaulle described the rows of armoured vehicles on both banks of the Seine as 'pathetic'.

In a dark double-breasted suit, the General appeared significantly older than many journalists remembered him. He had put on weight and gained a pot belly. He stooped slightly. His face seemed sallow and grey. His hair was streaked with white. He used his heavy black spectacles as a prop, removing them with a flourish as if to signify that he did not need them. His voice was softer than it had been though it sometimes rose to a higher pitch as he made a point.

He was in fine form, ironic, dismissive of political parties as a whole while expressing his 'esteem' for Mollet and referring to 'my friend'

Lacoste, and remaining vague and evasive about the generals in Algiers. He presented himself as a solitary figure who 'could perhaps be useful' because he stood apart from the political parties and could draw on the moral capital he had acquired from his activities in the past. 'I am a man who belongs to nobody and who belongs to everybody,' he went on. The crisis across the Mediterranean, he suggested, might be the 'start of a sort of resurrection'. As to the authority he sought, all he would say was that he wanted 'delegated power'. When the prominent commentator Maurice Duverger asked him if he did not risk putting public freedom in danger, de Gaulle replied, 'Have I done that? On the contrary I re-established freedoms when they had disappeared. Do you think that at the age of sixty-seven I am going to start a career as a dictator?'

'Now I will return to my village and remain there at the disposal of the country,' he told his audience in the manner of Cincinnatus, before walking out in front of his Praetorian Guard of Guichard, Foccart and the one-time RPF organiser Pierre Lefranc. That he repeatedly returned home to Colombey, rather than staying in his Paris hotel, was symbolically important. In so doing, he showed himself as the great man of history, separating himself physically from the political maelstrom, imposing his personal rhythm on events from his retreat in the country. France now had three power centres – Paris, Algiers and the small village in the Haute-Marne.

The reaction from the Left and from liberals in Paris to the General's performance was hostile. Mendès France and Mitterrand took severe exception to his refusal to condemn the rebels. However, after his hostility to the RPF, that important weathervane François Mauriac was won back to Gaullism. In Algiers, there was disappointment that de Gaulle had been so opaque, but he had had a kind word for Lacoste and the critical reaction of politicians on the Left contributed to the belief that he was still, at heart, sympathetic to the insurrection.[8]

20–25 May. At La Boisserie, the General was host to his daughter-in-law and three grandsons for a spring holiday. On 22 May, he was visited by Pinay, to whom he pledged to do nothing that might incite street violence and to adopt constitutional methods. An emissary from Salan told him of the 'enormous hope' he represented. Pompidou agreed to return to his service. Compared to Debré or Malraux, the solid, calculating banker was no *illuminé*; if he signed up to the project, that was one more brick in place.

In Algiers, the crowd in the Place du Forum chanted for the army to take power and Salan abandoned his usual caution to declare: 'We are all united now and will march together up the Champs-Élysées and be decked with flowers.'

In Corsica, paratroopers sympathetic to the rebels, and joined by comrades from Algiers, took control of the island in a swift move orchestrated by a right-wing deputy, Pascal Arrighi, and 'Leather Nose' Thomazo, who became military governor. Moch tried to send in riot police, but Pflimlin vetoed the idea since only six hundred men could be spared. When a force was eventually sent, it was quickly neutralised.

There was resistance in Bastia, but this soon crumbled. One of de Gaulle's cousins ensured that the coup was allied with the General's cause. The affair was peaceful – asked if there had been any deaths, Arrighi replied: 'It wasn't an election.' Corsica had been the first territory to be liberated in the Allied advance in 1943: was it now to play the same role in the army's liberation of France from the Fourth Republic? As if it made any difference, the National Assembly stood on its dignity and lifted Arrighi's parliamentary immunity.

In Paris, Henri Tournet, a friend of Foccart, delivered a reassuring message to the American ambassador: if he regained power, de Gaulle would keep France in the Atlantic Alliance, pursue European cooperation and adopt a 'liberal policy in Algeria which would aim for autonomy in association with France but would not exclude independence'. Though Eisenhower initially hoped that Pflimlin would survive, and preferred Pinay or Pleven as a potential successor, Washington came round to the General.[9]

III
Shaping destiny

26 May. De Gaulle went through an extraordinary performance for a man who was still legally a private citizen. In the morning, he called the

Prefect of the Haute-Marne department to La Boisserie. That afternoon, the Prefect arrived at Matignon with a message from the General. It said that direct contact was necessary between the government and him to examine ways of avoiding a deterioration of the situation awaiting the establishment of 'authorities capable of assuring the unity and independence of the country'.

A senior prefect called at Matignon with a suggestion that de Gaulle should be kidnapped and taken to a house in a forest where he would be obliged by 'appropriate means' to sign a statement disavowing the rebels in Algiers and Ajaccio. According to Michel de Poniatowski, a member of the Prime Minister's staff, the prefect, who was not named, proposed using electrodes on the General if he resisted. Pflimlin rejected the proposal.

He called in Mollet, who had also received the letter from Colombey. They agreed that they had to meet the General or face a military putsch. They proposed to take Moch with them, but the Interior Minister refused to go and the Socialist parliamentary group voted strongly against any rapprochement with the General.

The possibility of an attempted military coup in mainland France was becoming an increasing threat as army officers worked on a plan which took as its codename the word de Gaulle had used at his press conference: *Résurrection* replaced the original codename *Grenade.* The CIA in Algiers helped to tip off the government.

The idea was that paratroopers would land at two Parisian airfields and march on the Champs-Élysées and the National Assembly, raising a mass demonstration to force Pflimlin to resign and opening the way for a government of public safety under de Gaulle. One of the generals in Algiers, Edmond Jouhaud, added that, with the complicity of the police, the troops would occupy Matignon, the Assembly, the Foreign Ministry, the Paris City Hall, telephone and broadcasting headquarters and the Eiffel Tower. Massu wrote later that the generals had been given the green light by Foccart, Lefranc and an assistant to Debré. It would, he improbably claimed, have been neither a military coup nor a rebellion. From a very different standpoint, Maurice Duverger wrote in *Le Monde* that the Fourth Republic had lost touch with the people and he appealed for the General to be called to office 'before the nation is completely torn apart, before it becomes the hostage of one camp or another'.

The tension was heightened by a fresh incident involving French troops stationed in Tunisia, which led to a massive demonstration in Tunis. Pleven and General Gambiez, the French commander in Tunisia, called on Pflimlin to tell him that France had either to take military action or open talks with Bourguiba, who was threatening to bring the issue to the United Nations. The Prime Minister felt too weak to do either and the matter was left hanging in the air.

Late at night, Pflimlin left Matignon secretly, going through the kitchen and down a back staircase while an aide distracted waiting journalists and then parked his car across the street to stop anyone following the Prime Minister who was taken the short distance to the Defence Ministry in an unmarked car driven by a policeman in civilian dress. At the ministry, he was led to a side entrance and transferred into the Citroën 4CV belonging to Poniatowski who drove him across the Seine and up the Champs-Élysées, where they were surrounded by cars from which *Algérie française* banners flew as crowds on the pavement shouted '*Vive de Gaulle!*'

Arriving at the home of another official, Pflimlin changed into yet another vehicle and set off for Saint-Cloud, the suburb where Bonaparte had launched his coup against the post-revolutionary Directory and where Napoleon III had proclaimed himself emperor. On the way, the car broke down. A policeman approached but did not recognise the Premier. The vehicle was restarted. Eventually, at 12.15 a.m., Pflimlin reached the rendezvous at the home of the warden of the one-time royal domain of Saint-Cloud.[10]

27 May. During their 105-minute conversation after midnight, de Gaulle assured the Prime Minister that, if there was a military coup, he would retire to Colombey. 'I will not take power in a tumult of generals,' he added. Still he refused to condemn the rebels. 'These people want things to change,' he went on. 'They think the regime is bad and I cannot say they are wrong.' He found the politician 'calm and dignified'. Pflimlin recalled that de Gaulle seemed to be weighing him up, distrustful and a little dismissive, ironic and watchful.

The Prime Minister reacted angrily when the General implied that his main motive was to hang on to office. He stressed that he could not agree to a transfer of power without the accord of those who had given him his mandate. 'The system is speaking through your mouth,' de Gaulle shot back. The meeting ended without agreement at 2 a.m. As he left, Pflimlin insisted that it must remain secret. The General gave no such undertaking before being driven back the three hundred kilometres to Colombey.

As Jean Lacouture has observed, de Gaulle was no longer simply the man of destiny; he was now a man shaping destiny. He had probably received word that the plotters planned to launch Operation Resurrection in the coming days. A military message reported by Tournoux says he was 'in complete agreement' though with exactly what is not stated. Be that as it may, he preferred to gain power legally, and did not want the army to move until he had exhausted his options.

At noon, seven hours after arriving back at Colombey, de Gaulle issued a statement claiming that he had begun 'the regular process necessary for the establishment of a republican government capable of assuring the unity and independence of the country'. He called for public order and for the troops to remain under their military leaders, in whom he expressed confidence. A military message was duly relayed to Algiers ordering the postponement of Operation Resurrection.

Poniatowski handed the text of the message to Pflimlin as he came out of a meeting with the President of the Senate, Gaston Monnerville. Having asked de Gaulle to keep their early-morning meeting secret, the Prime Minister was shocked. He asked his aide to telephone Colombey to stop the publication of the statement. Poniatowski returned to say it was too late. Pflimlin had not told Coty of the encounter and hurried to the Élysée Palace to make amends. He proposed to issue a denial, but Coty advised him not to make matters worse by reacting publicly.

The Interior Ministry intercepted a message from the General to Salan, asking for a rundown of the forces at his command and telling the commander in Algeria to await orders as to his intentions. Having put the legal government on the back foot, he was now, in effect, assuming command of the army. 'Technically, it was a magnificent piece of political work,' Poniatowki wrote in his memoirs, 'carried out without any means or legality at his disposal and without making any moral compromise.'

In parliament, Pflimlin confirmed the early-morning conversation and spoke of the disagreement between him and the General. He won a large majority for a constitutional bill to strengthen the executive, but this was now irrelevant. Three ministers resigned. At a Cabinet meeting at 2 a.m., Pleven pointed out that the government was unable to send its Minister for Algeria to Algiers, that the Defence Minister did not control the army and that the loyalty of the police was breaking down. 'We claim to exercise power,' he added, 'but we do not have it.' Pflimlin said he was going to step down.

De Gaulle was driven back to Paris for another secret midnight meeting at Saint-Cloud, this time with the presidents of the two houses of parliament. Gaston Monnerville of the Senate appeared understanding, but the General ran into the sharp hostility of the Assembly Speaker, André Le Troquer, a Socialist who had held the defence portfolio in the wartime committee in Algiers and had walked down the Champs-Élysées with de Gaulle in August 1944. Moch wrote later that his fellow Socialists thought that Coty would be forced to resign and that Le Troquer would become acting head of state as a result – he had already started considering possible prime ministers he might appoint. Socialist deputies shared Le Troquer's hostility. They voted 102–3 against supporting de Gaulle if he tried to form a government. Since the Communists would also oppose him, this meant that he would not command a majority in the Assembly, opening the way to a military coup and civil war.[11]

28 May. In the early hours, Pflimlin told Coty he was ready to resign. Salan's chief of staff, André Dulac, flew to France and was driven to Colombey, where the General quizzed him about the balance of power in Algiers. Dulac said his boss was manoeuvring between the Public Safety Committee and a few neo-Fascist paratroop commanders. De Gaulle asked what the army would do if the Socialists barred his route. Dulac laid out the details of Operation Resurrection.

According to the visitor's memoirs, de Gaulle asked when Salan and Massu would arrive in metropolitan France if the operation was launched. In the first wave, Dulac replied. The General explained that he would not want to take power immediately since that would make him the creature of a military coup. He would wait for a few days to be called in as an arbiter to prevent the country tearing itself apart. As he saw Dulac out, de Gaulle told him: 'We've got to save the ship. Tell Salan that what he has done and what he will do is for the good of France.'

Replying to a letter from Auriol, de Gaulle underlined the threat facing France because of the attitude of the Socialists. His proposal to form a government by legal means was being blocked by the opposition of parliamentarians, he noted. That risked creating anarchy and civil war, and the responsibility would lie with those who 'with a sectarianism incomprehensible to me, would have prevented me from saving the Republic once again'. As for himself – 'I would have nothing else left, to my death, except to remain in sorrow.'

A military message to Algiers informed the commanders there that a representative of de Gaulle insisted Resurrection should be launched, but another said it was difficult to establish the General's point of view. Massu was told scare stories about the Interior Minister stockpiling machine pistols and grenades in the Paris suburbs and asking Duclos about raising a Communist militia – the PCF was said to be arming fighters trained in Russia with weapons and Molotov cocktails.

There was panic buying from shops and stories of paratrooper landings. Lagaillarde flew to the capital – the command in Algiers sent instructions to the military in France to keep him under control. Reports spread of paratroop officers in civilian clothes arriving in Paris carrying suitcases filled with arms, and of a plan to kidnap the Interior Minister, who strengthened protection for the Élysée, the National Assembly and broadcasting stations.

The Communist-led CGT union federation called a general strike in metropolitan France, and left-wing parties organised demonstrations – an estimated 200,000 people took part in a march in Paris headed by Mendès France, Waldeck Rochet, Mitterrand and Daladier. Participants shouted 'Hang Massu' and 'De Gaulle to the museum', but they had no solution to offer. The Communists presented a fundamental problem. They had the support of a quarter of the electorate, 150 seats in the National Assembly, a mass of dedicated and well-organised supporters across the country and the backing of an influential body of intellectuals.

The PCF's inclusion was essential for any new Popular Front, but it was a pariah for other parties – Mollet remarked that its true allegiance was to Moscow. For the Socialists, the choice boiled down to whether to lie down with the Communist lion or accept that de Gaulle was not another Franco and follow him like lambs. Since they could not resolve that dilemma, they were doomed to impotence as the Fourth Republic went into its death throes.[12]

29 May. At the end of the morning, the chief of the air force, General Nicot, went to the rue de Solférino where Debré, Guichard, Foccart, Papon and Lefranc were waiting. According to Nicot, after they had agreed that there would be no alternative to seeking the support of the armed forces if the politicians opposed de Gaulle, Lefranc telephoned Colombey, and told the others 'the General agrees that the operation should be launched without delay'. Lefranc later denied this but Nicot insisted on his version and invoked confirmation from another senior military figure. A message from military headquarters in Paris cited by General Jouhaud in his memoirs talked of de Gaulle's complete agreement with Resurrection. Six Dakotas took off to ferry troops to south-west France for the operation, scheduled for 30 May.

In a letter to his son that day, de Gaulle wrote that 'according to my information, action is imminent from south to north . . . It is infinitely probable that nothing more will be done under this regime which cannot even wish for anything.' Signing off 'My dear old son, I embrace you with all my heart. Your mother does the same', he regretted that the stay at La Boisserie of Henriette and his grandsons had been disturbed by events, 'but how happy your mother and I were to have seen them!'

A message from Coty read to parliament said France was on the brink of civil war, so he was 'turning towards the most illustrious of Frenchmen, towards the man who, in the darkest years of our history, was our chief for the reconquest of freedom and who refused dictatorship in order to re-establish the Republic. I ask General de Gaulle to confer with the head of state and to examine with him what, in the framework of Republican legality, is necessary for the immediate formation of a government of national safety and what can be done, in a fairly short time, for a deep reform of our institutions.'

As the hostile President of the Assembly, Le Troquer, read the text, Communist deputies sat down in protest rather than standing, as was the rule for presidential statements. When the Speaker finished, right-wing deputies cheered loudly while the Left sang 'La Marseillaise' and shouted 'Fascism will not pass'.

At 4 p.m. de Gaulle left Colombey by road for Paris. On the way, his Citroën outdistanced its police escort, Moch called for a vehicle that could go as fast as de Gaulle's. When it caught up – by one account when the Constable stopped to relieve himself at the roadside – the General summoned the inspector from the police car and said, 'Very good. Only M. le Troquer is still trying to trip me up now. But I will be designated as Prime Minister, and then voted in.'[13]

A military message to Algiers passed on de Gaulle's insistence that any army intervention must be avoided. So 'the action planned for 30 May is annulled,' it added. 'Will be resumed during the week in case of difficulty for *le Grand Charles*.'

Arriving in Paris at 7.26 p.m., the General went straight to the Élysée. According to de Gaulle's memoirs, Coty overflowed with emotion as he asked him to form a government. At the President's request, the General agreed to address parliament and to reduce the period for which he wanted special powers from one year to six months. He issued a statement saying that he would propose a referendum to separate the executive and the legislature. His aim would be 'to restore national unity, re-establish order in the state and raise the public authorities to the heights of their duties'. The statement showed that he, rather than the President of the Republic, was in charge. Then he drove back to Colombey, once more putting a physical distance between himself and the political world in the capital as his supporters celebrated in the streets and the CGT called another strike, which attracted only minimal backing.[14]

IV
I've won

30 May. Knowing he needed the support of the Socialists, de Gaulle received Mollet and Auriol. The former was won over. 'He is a great man, a very great man,' he told colleagues. 'He is not the man he once was, or the man he is depicted as being. He is a lot better. But he has aged. He must be helped. He has a big chance of succeeding if parliament has the intelligence to vote him into office unanimously. The Algerian problem will take on another aspect. This is really a chance that should not be missed.'

In Algiers, 300,000 people joined an evening demonstration lit by flaming torches, some waving military banners. 'Will you go through with this to the end?' Soustelle thundered from the balcony overlooking the Place du Forum. 'Will you fight every attempt at compromise and surrender?' The crowd roared back its agreement. 'May your answers reach the ears of those who need to hear them,' Soustelle shouted through the hot night air.'[15]

31 May. Wearing a casual suit and yellow shoes, de Gaulle received non-Communist Party leaders and political veterans at the Hôtel La Pérouse, among them Daladier, Pinay and Mollet. He charmed some and sidelined others. Replying to a query from Ramadier as to whether his government would contain any figures linked to the rebels in Algiers, de Gaulle shot back, 'Do you see me presiding over the Committee of Public Safety?' When Pflimlin said he did not want to join the new administration, the General replied: 'You cannot say no to de Gaulle.'

The only open critic was Mitterrand, who warned that France was entering an era of Latin American-style military coups. De Gaulle put himself forward as the only solution, he went on, 'but you are mortal'. The General interrupted: 'I see where you are heading. You wish for my death. I'm ready . . . You are a politician, M. Mitterrand. That's all right. They are needed. But in certain circumstances, political men should know how to raise themselves to the level of statesmen.'

Despite Mollet's endorsement, the Socialist parliamentary group was split. It voted to back the General, but only by 77 votes to 74. Still, that gave the Premier-designate his parliamentary majority. He had achieved a legal return to power and headed off the very real threat of a military operation and civil war. It was an extraordinary victory.[16]

1 June. In the afternoon, the General was driven to the National Assembly through a violent storm to ask the legislature to vote him into office and grant full powers for six months. He also announced a referendum on constitutional reform. It was the first time he had been inside the Palais Bourbon since his passage of arms at the beginning of 1946 with Herriot, who had died in 1957. He sat alone on the bench at the front of the chamber as he waited to be called to speak. Unusually, he carried a text of his speech with him.

In his memoirs, de Gaulle recalled that the deputies were overcome with curiosity and were 'in the end, sympathetic'. Other observers found them cooler towards him, giving only 'timid applause'. In his brief speech, he mentioned the danger of civil war, and pledged that his government would bring 'unity, integrity and independence'. Then he left the crowded chamber, handing over to Mollet, who had been named as Deputy Prime Minister.

His staff, headed by Pompidou, sounded out ministers for the new administration, sustaining themselves with sandwiches as they telephoned from a small room at the Hôtel La Pérouse, next to that of the General. The composition of his government was designed to reassure the country and ensure maximum support. There were senior posts for leaders of all major parties except the Communists.

Only three ministries went to out-and-out Gaullists – Debré (Justice), Malraux (Information and Culture) and Michelet (Veterans). The Socialists were said to have vetoed the inclusion of Soustelle, who was, however, brought in as Minister of Information in July. Chaban and others who had compromised with the Fourth Republic were excluded. Mollet and Pflimlin became Ministers of State. So did Houphouët-Boigny, the veteran Louis Jacquinot, who had been Poincaré's chief of staff, and Pinay, who also took the Finance Ministry. News of the appointment of these figures from the Fourth Republic was greeted with consternation in Algiers while the ultra-loyalist Debré stigmatised the Ministers of State as 'the black Houphouët, the wily Pflimlin, the backwoods Mollet, the idiot Pinay'.

Putting competence above party loyalty, the General chose civil servants for several leading posts. The Quai d'Orsay went to the wiry, highly experienced ambassador in Bonn, Maurice Couve de Murville. An impassive, reserved servant of the state who epitomised the Protestant upper class and appeared to conform more to the stereotype of a

British official than to that of a Frenchman, the golf-playing Foreign Minister would be the faithful executor of de Gaulle's policy for ten years. His appointment showed that, when de Gaulle thought he had found the right person for a job, he was ready to overlook past conduct. Couve, who was recommended to the General by Pompidou, had held a senior post at the Finance Ministry in Vichy and then switched to support Giraud in Algiers before ending up in the Gaullist camp. But he was a perfectly disciplined diplomat, and that was what counted most now. Another civil servant, Pierre Guillaumat, previously in charge of the atomic research agency, took responsibility for the armed forces, though he came under de Gaulle who held the Ministry of Defence. Pierre Sudreau, who had been deported to the Buchenwald concentration camp after fighting in the Resistance and then became France's youngest prefect, was put in charge of economic reconstruction.

Alongside the government, de Gaulle set up a personal staff which acted as a parallel administration planning the new order. Loyalists were among its twenty members, but, again, there was also a heavy dose of civil servants. As chief of staff, Pompidou showed himself to be the consummate manager, mixing efficiency with good humour and acting as a virtual Deputy Premier.

The Assembly approved the administration by 329 votes to 224. If this was not the overwhelming backing the General might have hoped for, it was more than enough. Most of the political establishment fell into line. The opposition consisted of 147 Communists, 49 Socialists including Gaston Defferre, and 18 Radicals, among them Mendès France, who appeared deeply troubled as he said that he could not approve the new administration since the Assembly's hand had been forced by insurrection and the threat of a military coup. Mitterrand cast his negative vote after a stinging speech in which he said that, whereas de Gaulle's action in 1940 had been in the service of national honour, he now had as partners 'force and sedition'.[17]

2 June. Pierre Lefranc made a scouting mission to Matignon. He found 'complete silence. Nothing moved. I had the impression that ears were listening behind each door, that eyes were looking through each keyhole. I was the invader. Did I eat children?' Pflimlin's aide, Jean

Lecanuet, received him in an empty office. There were no dossiers or papers on the desk. Lefranc saw a pair of eyes following him from behind a curtain; it was the outgoing Premier's chief of staff, Poniatowski.

The National Assembly gave large majorities to bills for institutional reform and special powers as the ranks of Gaullist supporters swelled. Where he had been stiff and formal the previous day, de Gaulle was now relaxed, charming many deputies with his assurance of the 'pleasure and honour' he felt on being with them. 'Albert, I've won,' he told the night porter at La Pérouse when he returned to his hotel for the last time.[18]

3 June. The National Assembly broke up for the summer without fixing a date for a new session. Salan flew to Paris to call on the new Prime Minister. The two men talked across one another. Salan objected when de Gaulle said that the Minister of State, Jacquinot, and the Socialist Minister for the Sahara, Max Lejeune, would accompany him when he visited Algeria. Those two men, Salan felt, represented the old system. 'But no,' de Gaulle replied in a joshing tone, 'these gentlemen will accompany me and all will be well.'[19]

*

The Fourth Republic had only as long to live as it took the General to submit his constitutional proposals and get to grips with Algeria. There were echoes of 1940 in the way that France, with its politicians at sixes and sevens, turned to a providential soldier as its saviour. But de Gaulle in 1958 was very different from Pétain eighteen years earlier. Nor had France been beaten by an external enemy; the task was not to make the best of sudden defeat but to deal with an internal crisis. Some of those who backed the General may have thought that, once this had been surmounted, things would return to normal, enabling them to pick up the reins of power once more. That was a profoundly mistaken reading which failed to recognise the extent to which the events of May and early June had revolutionised not only French politics but the way the country was going to evolve.

De Gaulle's return to office had been very much a personal performance in keeping with the prime actor's solitary stance. By remaining intransigent and utterly self-confident in his powers of manoeuvre, the General had ensured that his star was born for the second time, as he had dreamed for twelve years. Nearly two decades after stepping on to the front stage of history, the Constable had a unique opportunity to incarnate France for a second time and to bring it back from the brink of disaster. It was not an opportunity such a highly realistic dreamer was going to let slip again.

26

FIRST IN FRANCE

I
Making a new Republic

Despite the criticisms enunciated by the Communists, Mitterrand and Mendès France, most people agreed with the political editor of *Le Monde*, Jacques Fauvet, that de Gaulle was the only rampart between the Republic and Fascism. The suspension of parliament for six months gave him vital breathing space and avoided the danger of a rerun of the post-war Constituent Assembly. The presence in the government of political leaders like Mollet and Pflimlin denoted a consensus. But he needed to act quickly given the volatile nature of the situation in Algeria and the heterogeneous composition of his government.[1]

Under de Gaulle's supervision, Debré was given the job of elaborating the new institutions. Looking enviously at the authority enjoyed by cabinets in Britain, he aimed to provide France with a 'government able to govern'. But there was a key element that did not apply across the Channel – de Gaulle. As he had made plain since his speech at Bayeux twelve years earlier, he aspired to be the supreme arbiter of the nation standing above parties and politics, a President of the Republic with ultimate power, however he chose to exercise it. So the framers of the constitution for the Fifth Republic had to evolve a system which would create a strong presidency with powers for its occupant to intervene when he saw fit, but which would also provide for an effective government to handle day-to-day matters and a legislature which, while less powerful than before, would represent the electorate.

The outcome was a clear separation of the executive and the legislature, with the first greatly strengthened against the second. The President was defined as the guarantor of national independence and territorial integrity. He would appoint the Prime Minister. Article 16 of the new constitution allowed him to take special powers when 'the institutions of the Republic, the independence of the nation, the integrity of its territory or the execution of its international commitment are gravely and immediately threatened and the regular functioning of the constitutional public authority is interrupted'. Another article permitted him to hold referendums on any bill dealing with the organisation of government or ratifying a treaty. As the constitutionalist Georges Vedel put it, he would be 'an umpire who touches the ball'. He was to be elected for a seven-year term by an electoral college made up of members of parliament, of departmental councils, of the assemblies of French overseas territories and of local councils – this would amount to a body of some 80,000. Since its membership would contain a majority of men and women from rural and small-town France, the President would be elected 'by the representatives of grain and chestnut', in Vedel's words.

Parliament would consider legislation put to it by the executive but would have little power to initiate action, let alone propose spending measures. It could examine government plans only when invited to do so. The government would be able to push through legislation without amendments, notably on budgetary matters. Deputies would not be allowed to advance bills which would have the main effect of raising government spending. The result of these stipulations was that, in the first eight years of the new regime, the National Assembly voted through more than 500 bills but 450 were from the government. A Constitutional Council would ensure that laws were in accordance with the constitution and that elections were properly conducted. The head of state and each of the speakers of the two legislatures named three of its nine members. The Council reflected de Gaulle's desire to place the constitution above partisan politics as the core of the new order.[2]

A tour of Africa at the end of August convinced him of the need to create a federal system within which France's colonial territories would have the right to vote for independence. The desire for autonomy he experienced on his trip could not be denied, but, in private, he took a jaundiced view of the proposed community. 'It's bollocks,' he told the journalist Jean Mauriac. 'Those people, no sooner will they have got in than they'll have one idea: to get out.'[3]

On 4 September, the anniversary of the proclamation of the Third Republic, de Gaulle presented the constitution to the public in a ceremony at the symbolic site of the Place de la République in Paris where the forces of the Left had marched at the end of May. The crowd was carefully controlled to weed out opponents, and three thousand police guarded the square. Wearing a civilian three-piece suit, the General told the throng that France had just avoided irremediable harm. The constitution, he went on, would enable the country to be ruled effectively by those it chose to lead it. When he called for a 'yes' vote in the referendum to be held on the proposals, the crowd answered with cries of '*Oui*'. 'Thank you,' de Gaulle murmured, his voice magnified over the loudspeakers. Then he threw up his arms in his familiar V gesture, fists clenched, before joining in the national anthem and plunging into the crowd, shrugging off his security guards for one of the *bains de foule* (crowd baths) that were becoming a feature of his contact with the public. Not that he had the day to himself. The Communists organised a counter-demonstration and fighting broke out between police and protesters.[4]

The Socialists came out in support of the constitution at a special congress; a splinter group that opposed the changes went off to found a new group of its own. The Radicals approved by 57 per cent, but Mendès France and his allies remained hostile. The MRP was in favour, as were Edgar Faure, René Pleven, Marshal Juin, Jean Monnet and the pretender to the throne. The Communists constituted the bulk of the opposition, joined by the CGT union federation and the teachers' union, along with Left Bank intellectuals headed by Jean-Paul Sartre, who wrote scornfully of the French as 'frogs who want a king'. On the Right, a ragbag of opponents melded Poujadists, remnant Pétainists and Catholic diehards who refused to accept the definition of France as a lay state.

The referendum campaign was extremely one-sided as the Gaullists threw everything into the crusade for the constitution and to ensure a high turnout. The only significant media resources available to the opposition were the Communist press and the big Radical Socialist daily newspaper of Toulouse, *La Dépêche du Midi,* where the wartime collaborationist police chief René Bousquet was on the board. The country was placarded with posters urging a 'yes' vote. Envelopes sent out containing ballot papers and the text of the constitution also had a copy of de Gaulle's case in favour, but nothing from the other side. Tax collectors were told to act with 'very special tact and discernment' during the campaign; prosecutions for non-payment were deferred 'because of political circumstances'.

As Information Minister, Soustelle appointed loyalists to senior posts at the state broadcasting network, and made sure news programmes were heavily biased in favour of the proposal. Pounding at the anti-Communist theme, Gaullist stickers posed a choice between 'Oui' or 'Nyet', and made the equation 'FLN + Communists = Assassins'. The General delivered a final broadcast just before the vote; the opposition was not permitted to do the same. At *Le Monde,* Pierre Viansson-Ponté judged that it was the biggest propaganda operation seen in France in the twentieth century. 'Conceived in sin, the Fifth Republic was going to be born in lies,' he added.

The contrast was striking between the simple choice presented to the electorate of a vote of 'yes' or 'no' and the complexity of the ninety-two articles couched in juridical language and thrown together at great speed. Despite being its midwife, Debré described the text as the worst-drafted of France's constitutions. Half those who voted told pollsters they had not read any of it. They did not need to. There was only one question: did they want de Gaulle back?

The General was greatly helped by the lack of an alternative. Nobody defended the Fourth Republic. The Left's campaign was directed against the way in which de Gaulle had returned to power, not against the need for change. Lurking in the background was the probability that a 'no' victory would lead the army to unleash Operation Resurrection. On 29 September, the constitution was approved by 78.25 per cent of those who voted in a record turnout of 84.9 per cent of the electorate. The 'no' vote of 4.6 million was well below the 5.45 million won by the PCF alone in 1956; estimates of the number of Communists who voted 'yes' went as high as 1.9 million. Speaking for the Paris intelligentsia, Simone de Beauvoir reacted by bursting into tears: 'I can feel death in my heart,' she wrote. 'An enormous collective suicide.'[5]

In Algeria, where Muslim women voted for the first time and the army oversaw the campaign, the positive vote was 96 per cent. There was backing from the rest of French Africa. Only Guinea opted for independence; Paris cut off not only all assistance, but also the country's telephone system.

II
Winning the day

The referendum was the first of three steps needed to take France into a fresh epoch. Next came elections for a new National Assembly in November for which the Gaullists created a new party, *L'Union pour la Nouvelle République* (Union for the New Republic) (UNR), a catch-all grouping of veterans of the rue de Solférino, fervent supporters of *Algérie française,* hard-line military men, left-wing Gaullists, liberals and technocrats. Soustelle's hopes of leading it were dashed by his colleagues; instead, the stalwart Roger Frey became Secretary-General. Wanting to remain aloof, de Gaulle ordered that the UNR was not to use his name, an instruction widely ignored as the electoral tide of the referendum led centre-right candidates to clamber on to his bandwagon. But, in contrast to the RPF experience, he was adamant in wishing to appear above everyday electoral politics.

The new party took 188 seats in the 537-member legislature, and had the support of many of the 132 moderate and right-wing deputies in the *Centre National des Indépendants et Paysans* (National Centre of Independents and Peasants) (CNIP). Chaban-Delmas was elected President of the National Assembly – the General would have liked to see Reynaud in the post, but the Gaullists preferred the Mayor of Bordeaux.

The Left was routed in parliament. The PCF held only ten Assembly seats and the Socialists forty. The Poujadists were eliminated. In all, 344 of the 475 deputies who stood for re-election were beaten, among them Edgar Faure, Defferre, Duclos and Mitterrand. It was said that de Gaulle had wanted the boundaries of Mendès France's constituency in Normandy to be drawn so as to ensure his election since he valued the presence of such an opponent in the legislature; but the local UNR organisation and adversaries of the former Premier banded together to bring about his defeat.

In terms of parliamentary seats, the result was misleading since the UNR and its conservative allies won two-thirds of the metropolitan parliamentary seats with just 37.5 per cent of the vote. The centrist parties and non-Communist Left had one percentage point more from the electorate, but only 29 per cent of the deputies. The Gaullists actually received 50,000 fewer votes than the RPF in 1951 and, with 17.5 per cent of the poll, could hardly claim to be a national majority party, with their significant dependence on regional barons such as Chaban-Delmas and Delbecque in the north.

Though Soustelle would have loved to become Prime Minister, there was no question of him getting the position. De Gaulle's feelings towards the one-time Secretary-General of the RPF were evident when the FLN staged an assassination attempt against him; at the next Cabinet meeting, all the Prime Minister had to say to the 'big tomcat' was 'Please don't do that again.' The only realistic candidate for Matignon was Debré. The industrious Premier, who came from a prominent family known for its attachment to the Republic, could be more Gaullist than de Gaulle. An adherent of French rule in Algeria, his loyalty, intellectual capacity, hard work and pugnacious intensity made him the ideal man to deal with aspects of government with which the General did not wish to concern himself, while he accepted the concentration of power on the Élysée.

With the constitution adopted and a pliant Assembly in place, the path was now open for the apex of the arch of the new Republic to be put in place. On 13 December, de Gaulle formally lodged his candidature for the presidency. Eight days later, he was elected with 78.5 per cent of the votes against a Communist senator and a representative of a centre-left group set up in opposition in the summer.

III
Looking abroad

While the referendum, the elections and Algeria occupied the front stage, de Gaulle set out to restore France's international stature. He received his British counterpart, Harold Macmillan, the man he had declined to join for a naked swim in the Mediterranean during their time together in Algeria in the Second World War. According to the General, Macmillan depicted the Common Market as akin to Napoleon's policy of shutting Britain out of Europe, and pressed for the creation of a European free trade area wider than the six-nation grouping. France's five partners were interested in the idea but de Gaulle wanted to consolidate the existing market under the leadership of Paris.[6]

At a five-hour meeting with US Secretary of State, John Foster Dulles, de Gaulle said he wanted France to be able to decide on the use of any nuclear weapons deployed within NATO. But he got a sharp reminder of his country's subordinate position in the alliance when he invited the American NATO commander, General Lauris Norstad, to brief him on its deployments in France at a session attended by senior officers. Everything went well until de Gaulle asked about the location of nuclear weapons and their targets. Norstad said he could only speak about this if they were alone. After the others left the room, he then said that, to his great regret, he was unable to reply. Enraged, de Gaulle shot back: 'This is the last time a French leader is going to hear such a response!'

The rebuff did not stop de Gaulle sending a secret memorandum to Eisenhower and Macmillan calling for NATO to become a global policeman run by a triumvirate of the United States, Britain and France. It was not an original notion – the General had first put it to the President at a dinner in Paris in 1952. The Americans rejected the idea. Such a geographical extension would be difficult to implement and Washington could not discriminate against its other transatlantic allies, they argued. De Gaulle had probably not expected agreement; it was a marker for the future. Still, Eisenhower took a positive view of the new administration in Paris. A message of congratulations he sent on 2 June, drafted by Dulles, expressed 'my sympathetic understanding in the great tasks which you are about to undertake'. In a note later that month, he said of de Gaulle that the 'Western world should do anything possible to support him, assuming that he continues along the lines that he has chosen'.[7]

On 14 September the West German Chancellor, Konrad Adenauer, was driven through the gates of La Boisserie to spend the night there. It was the only time de Gaulle invited a foreign statesman to Colombey. He told his son that he had had to make an effort to receive a German after all that the successive Reichs had done to France. But there were fears of hostile demonstrations if the Chancellor went to Paris and, having recognised the need for reconciliation across the Rhine, the General was certainly aware of the impact his gesture would make as he offered the visitor what he termed 'the modest honours of La Boisserie'.

At first, according to Philippe de Gaulle, the two men were somewhat guarded with one another. Then the atmosphere thawed. They both came from another age dating back to before the First World War – at eighty-two, Adenauer was fourteen years older than the General. De Gaulle's links with Germany went back to his adolescence. The Rhineland from which Adenauer came was, for him, the most accessible region of the country, the closest to France. In a note in 1959, he referred to the Chancellor as 'this good German'. However, the General's stock was not high across the Rhine where politicians had been in the habit of talking to Schuman, Monnet and the MRP, and where the press tended to paint him as an autocrat, recalling his rejection of European integration that their government placed at the core of its policies, including favouring British involvement in Europe.

Bonn also wanted to strengthen the alliance with Washington while, as had been the case since 1941, de Gaulle thought American influence should be reined in. His support for the post-war eastern frontiers was not likely to please Bonn, either. As for reunification, he saw how the divided nation served French interests. When an American ambassador commented that the separation of West and East Germany would one day prove a threat to world peace, he shot back, 'So would a united Germany.'* He was also in the process of

*As François Mauriac put it, 'I love Germany so much that I hope there will always be two of them.'

cancelling a secret agreement between Paris and Bonn that gave the Germans and Italians access to French nuclear technology in return for a cash contribution to the isotope separation plant at Pierrelatte in the Rhône Valley – de Gaulle had no intention of sharing French secrets with any other country.

Despite the wide range of differences, the two elderly statesmen believed they had a historic mission, that of bringing their two countries together. 'We both understood Europe would not be built without our understanding,' the General told his son. For him, there was a natural fit between France's political weight and Germany's industrial strength, while the vital thing for Adenauer was that de Gaulle had committed himself to the continued participation of France in the development of the European community, with West Germany as its preferred partner. Thus the idea of a unified Europe led by a politically strong France and an economically powerful Germany was established within the walls of La Boisserie – by one man who had been wounded three times fighting the Germans and had refused to admit their victory of 1940, and another who had been Mayor of Cologne while de Gaulle had been a prisoner of war and who had been elected as the first post-war Chancellor at the head of the Christian Democrats.

When Adenauer left, the two men embraced on the doorstep. However, there were limits to how far de Gaulle was prepared to go; he did not mention to Adenauer the proposal for NATO to come under French, British and US leadership which he sent to Eisenhower and Macmillan the next day. They met again on 26 November in the Rhineland wine town of Bad Kreuznach for a further friendly discussion of bilateral, European and world affairs. The Frenchman stood firmly behind West Germany in a crisis that month when the Soviet Union sought to extend its influence over Berlin. But his effort to get Bonn to come out against the British plan for a wider free trade area was blocked by the Economics Minister, Ludwig Erhard, who was in favour of exploring the idea further. Still, the essential plank of West Europe cooperation had been laid; France and Germany now recognised that, as de Gaulle put it, they had 'to walk hand in hand'.[8]

IV
The plan

Europe was also an element in a major battle over France's economy that developed after a leading French economist, Jacques Rueff, sent the Finance Ministry a note in June 1958 proposing a radical change of direction from the laxist approach of Fourth Republic governments. The sixty-two-year-old Rueff, a man of robust opinions about the need for strong monetary measures and a resilient currency, had advised Poincaré and governments during the 1930s – he was dismissed as Deputy Governor of the Bank of France by Vichy because he was Jewish. A believer in free markets, he proposed a concerted attack on inflation by limiting government spending and borrowing, increasing taxes, strengthening the franc and dismantling protectionist barriers so as to participate fully in Common Market trade liberalisation due to go into effect in 1959.

Pompidou and the economics adviser at Matignon, Roger Goetze, backed him. The General was often depicted as having only a passing interest in economic affairs, but he saw Goetze every morning, and the aide recalled him listening at length before coming up with a lucid analysis, accepting necessary proposals even if they were politically dangerous – 'Well, M. Goetze,' he would remark, 'the French will shout. So what?'

A committee formed to deliberate economic policy under Rueff met in secret during the autumn, facing the hostility of the employers' association, the *Patronat*, and of the Bank of France. At the Finance Ministry, Pinay favoured a softer approach and wanted to retain the last word on policy; he launched a successful state loan, but this was only a stopgap. In early November, Rueff presented Pompidou with his recommendations over lunch at the restaurant at the Hôtel La Pérouse. Pinay was also given a copy. The following day, de Gaulle himself was informed.

He liked big ideas such as those put forward by Rueff, and knew the importance of a sound economy to accompany his political project. If he was to restore national prestige, he could not allow his government to go cap in hand to Washington for loans or to shelter behind trade barriers that would demonstrate weakness in the face of resurgent

German industry. The idea of creating a strong, freely convertible franc after the temporary tactical retreat of a devaluation was extremely appealing. It would win Bonn's support. So long as he enjoyed an electoral honeymoon, the General could afford to inflict some pain to contribute to national resurrection. With a budget deficit running at 1,200 billion francs a year, he had little choice. When Goetze told him the plan had a 75 per cent chance of success, de Gaulle replied: 'Leave the other 25 per cent to me; that will be de Gaulle's personal contribution to financial recovery.'

Rueff's most extreme plans for cuts in spending were softened somewhat, given the need to continue to subsidise Algeria and the General's insistence on maintaining military expenditure. But the draft measures included painful cuts in farm subsidies and even in military pensions, together with rises in tobacco and alcohol taxes and increased prices for energy, transport and postal services. Protectionist measures were done away with, propelling the nation of Colbertism into the world of modern commerce. A 17.5 per cent devaluation was to be accompanied by the creation of a 'heavy franc' equivalent to one hundred old francs.

The opponents rallied in the days before Christmas. In Cabinet, according to Couve de Murville, only Debré, himself and de Gaulle were in favour. Pinay told Goetze he would resign; it took the man from Matignon an hour to dissuade him, and to get him to attend a special ministerial meeting on Boxing Day. That session, to which Rueff was invited, lasted from 3 p.m. until after midnight. As the debate raged, leaks about the devaluation led to an outflow of money from France estimated by Goetze at a billion old francs an hour. The next morning, the Socialist Education Minister André Boulloche resigned in protest at the anti-social nature of the programme; Mollet wanted to do the same but was persuaded by de Gaulle to stay on until the new Republic was proclaimed. Pinay again threatened to quit. When Goetze told de Gaulle of this, he replied: 'Don't accept a centime's difference from the original plan.'

At the start of a Cabinet meeting that afternoon, the General declared that, if the Rueff programme was not implemented, he would be the one who would resign. Opposition collapsed. The meeting lasted for all of fifteen minutes. Pinay agreed to go along – by an irony of history, the package would often be referred to subsequently as the 'Pinay plan'. De Gaulle went on television to announce the measures. He linked the changes to the need for a great national effort to restore France's stature. Sacrifices were needed to escape from mediocrity, he told the nation.[9]

V
Pursuing greatness

With the political and economic boards cleared, it was time to take the ultimate step. At noon on 8 January 1959, wearing a tailcoat, the General was driven to the Élysée where Coty greeted him at the top of the steps leading up from the courtyard. In a ceremony inside the palace, Charles de Gaulle was proclaimed President of the Republic. 'The first among Frenchmen is now the first person in France,' Coty declared. In a brief response, de Gaulle spoke of his duty to uphold and, if necessary, impose the national interest. Then the two men went to a lunch attended by only their closest aides, including Pompidou – though he had decided to return to banking, he retained a personal link with the de Gaulles by managing the finances of the Anne de Gaulle Foundation.

Then the General and the last head of state of the Fourth Republic were driven to lay a wreath at the Tomb of the Unknown Soldier at the Arc de Triomphe. After this, it was intended that the General should see Coty to his car and be driven alone behind him down the Champs-Élysées. Instead, de Gaulle murmured '*Au revoir, Monsieur Coty*' and plunged into the crowd. He was his own man, owing nothing to his predecessor. When he did get into his car, to accompany him he chose not one of the dignitaries of state gathered at the Arc de Triomphe but Pompidou. In his memoirs, he depicted himself on his return to the Élysée as being on 'the horizon of a great enterprise'. It would not be as exultant or heroic as in 1940, he went on, but, despite the temptations of mediocrity, he had to pursue greatness.[10]

PART SIX
REPUBLICAN MONARCH

27

THE SOVEREIGN, HIS COURT AND HIS PEOPLE

I
The ironies of power

In a broadcast to the nation on 28 December 1958, de Gaulle referred to himself as 'the Guide of France and Head of the Republican State'. Despite his dozen years out of power, he spoke of enjoying a legitimacy stretching back to 1940. 'Basically, the Republic is me,' he would tell Guy Mollet. His political pre-eminence was echoed in the way he towered above those around him, but, in keeping with the weight of his position, he was now heavier and slower, his paunch more protuberant, his nose more bulbous, his eyes more hooded, his face more elephantine.

His accession to the summit had been cloaked in irony. The man who had always inveighed against political parties was now the idol of the biggest group in parliament. His parliamentary majority depended on the CNIP conservatives, many of whom reflected the bourgeois attitudes he despised, and he retained their standard-bearer, Pinay. A prophet of change, de Gaulle had been chosen as head of state by an electoral college made up mainly of moderates from the old regime. He had drawn on the activism of Gaullist proponents of *Algérie française*, but had given them scant pickings. A believer in the primacy of the state, he allied himself economically with a man of the market. An advocate of social progress and equality, he had accepted measures that would hurt the poor most. A fervent champion of national sovereignty, he had taken the European option.

Such contradictions did not matter though some would have their effect subsequently. For now, the Man of 18 June was back with a vengeance. The balance of authority between the new head of state and the head of government was evident from the manner in which the choice of ministers was imposed from on high. Though Mollet and Pflimlin did not feature in the Cabinet, Debré had to accept the continued presence as Ministers of State of Houphouët-Boigny and Pinay, whom he had so disparaged. The third Minister of State, Robert Lecourt, came from the MRP, which also furnished the ministers of Labour, Public Works and Transport. There were several conservative Independents, including the rising young star, Valéry Giscard d'Estaing, as Junior Finance Minister. Among seven civil servants turned ministers, Couve de Murville retained the Quai d'Orsay and Guillaumat the armed forces portfolio.

As in the administration of the previous summer, the Gaullist faithful were not given many top jobs. Malraux stayed at the Culture Ministry. Soustelle, who saw himself as number two in the government and was believed to have his eyes on the Interior Ministry, was fobbed off with a post that combined responsibility for overseas territories and the Sahara with atomic research – France's test ground was in the desert.

The electoral glow would be slightly dimmed at municipal elections in March which saw a recovery in the Communist vote and the failure of the UNR to gain major urban targets such as Lyon, Marseille and Saint-Étienne. The following month, elections for the Senate returned most of the outgoing members and gave the centre left 40 per cent of the seats. Among those who joined the upper house were Fourth Republic stalwarts such as Mitterrand, Defferre, Duclos and Edgar Faure, making its ornate chamber in the Palais du Luxembourg a bastion of persistent if largely impotent dissent from the new regime in which its President, Gaston Monnerville, a native of French Guiana, took an increasingly critical view of the General. But this was marginal, and opinion polls showed that the public were happy with the passage of events since the rebellion in Algiers. Not only had the regime changed radically, but France had acquired a new star with a new way of performing as champion of the nation.

II
The mysteries of office

In *Le fil de l'épée*, de Gaulle had written of the way in which a true leader isolates himself from others, renouncing 'the joys of relaxation, familiarity and friendship'. Always in control, he operates free from the limitations of collective decision-making, working in his own time and his own way. 'One does not telephone de Gaulle,' Couve de Murville told an American Secretary of State. When a hot line was installed between the Élysée and the White House, the General insisted on an hour's notice of any call so that he could prepare himself – rather undermining the point of the system. On the national and international stage he was not only the supreme actor-manager but also wrote the plot and the lines. Even if, like many stars, he still had passages of doubt and periods of gloom, he relished the moments of high drama, and drew strength from them as he exalted what the political scientist Alfred Grosser termed 'national messianism'.[1]

His performance combined the oracular mystery of a long-gone monarchical age with the techniques of modern communications. Like a tribal leader of old, he had his own emblem in the Cross of Lorraine and a powerful story of battles fought and won. But he was also the first French politician to master the medium of television, using *le petit écran* to penetrate homes across the country. His appearances became huge events, and he knew how to milk them for all they were worth, with his mobile facial expressions, his gesticulations and his mining of the recesses of the French language for the precise word he needed to announce a policy change or vilify opponents in the rhetorical equivalent of the tank attacks he had championed in the 1930s.

His press conferences became what Pierre Viansson-Ponté of *Le Monde* described as 'high masses' and 'the absolute weapon of the regime'. Flunkeys in tailcoats and white ties held open the red velvet curtains for the General to appear in a grand salon of the Élysée. Rows of ministers sat below the presidential dais in what was known as 'the bus'. Malraux had a tendency to fall asleep. Newspaper proprietors were known to grab the invitations from their journalists for the glory of attending. Questions were handed out in advance to provide the starting point for a presidential monologue. If a subject on which the General wished to expound seemed to have been forgotten, he would raise it himself. In the evening, the Élysée distributed an official text in which the General might have corrected his own words. Nothing was to be left to chance; control was everything.

Trips to the provinces provided a third means of contact with the people. No one cared much if the remarks he made on such journeys were Delphic, banal or made no sense at all – it was enough that the oracle had spoken. Members of the crowds that awaited him grasped his hand as if he was bringing a magical response to their problems, while the great ship de Gaulle emerged from the *bains de foule* with buttons torn, a sleeve ripped, military kepi tipped over, his eyes filled with adrenalin even if the police had arrested men with knives, pistols and hypodermic syringes on his path.[2]

His opponents could not agree on how to characterise him, though most saw him as a born-again Bonapartist or a latter-day Caesar. For the weekly *Le Canard enchaîné*, France was back to the days of the Sun King, Louis XIV; it called its weekly account of goings-on at the Élysée *La Cour* (The Court). Mitterrand continued to inveigh against the permanent *coup d'état* while Mendès France refused to be reconciled with the regime brought to power by the events of 1958. The acute left-wing commentator Giles Martinet depicted the President as a 'liberal monarch with Stalinist tendencies . . . like him, a brutal realist'. Supporters saw him as a saviour or, in more homely fashion, as a wise uncle who stuck to old-fashioned traditions and could be stern, but who had the good of the family at heart. All were right, and that is where de Gaulle's uniqueness lies.[3]

III
The palace

De Gaulle did not consider the Élysée Palace in the 8th *arrondissement* of Paris an entirely suitable place from which to rule. In 1960, he complained to luncheon guests that it was full of 'unpleasant ghosts' such as Louis XV's mistress Madame de Pompadour, and President Félix Faure who had expired there in the arms of his own mistress in 1899. It was located in 'a district of money, the well-off and luxury shops', he went on. 'Nothing here recalls our great glories or the French people.' Though the General did not mention this, it was also the place where Napoleon had signed his second abdication after Waterloo, which was then used as a billet by British and Russian troops. But in his memoirs he noted that moving to Versailles would have been excessive, and that the châteaux at Rambouillet and Compiègne were too far from the capital to serve as a permanent residence, while Vincennes, with its military associations, was being restored. So the new Republic had to do the best it could with the palace behind high walls on the rue du Faubourg Saint-Honoré.[4]

De Gaulle presided over the nation from an antique desk inlaid with gilded ornaments and figures in a stately first-floor salon. On it stood a lamp, a leather paper holder and a blotting-paper pad – the General wrote with his customary fountain pen. In the morning, five dossiers in different-coloured folders awaited him; when he had dealt with a memorandum, it was stamped with the emblem of a small Cross of Lorraine in a circle. Sometimes there would be books he wanted to consult, but no piles of documents; they were dealt with in order and dispatched to staff or ministries. Beside him was a large globe on a wooden stand; behind was a marble fireplace with golden candlesticks and an antique clock on the mantelpiece. Alongside were paintings of scantily clad Muses, an inheritance from Napoleon III's wife, the Empress Eugénie. On the side walls were long mirrors. The ceiling bore plaster nymphs from the days of Madame de Pompadour. A huge chandelier hung in the centre of the room. The General and his visitors sat on wooden armchairs with upholstered seats.

There were three bell pushes on the desk to summon his aide-de-camp, the Secretary-General of the Élysée and the director of his personal staff. In the evening, the President received each of them for twenty minutes' briefing and debriefing, and to go over the programme for the following day. On Fridays, he fixed his schedule of appointments for the coming week. Punctuality was insisted upon; de Gaulle became irate if kept waiting for only a few minutes.

As well as political meetings with his staff and ministers, he undertook an unceasing round of ceremonies and receptions: over one New Year, seventeen in a single day. The enormous Salle des Grandes Fêtes at the

Élysée, with its great crystal chandeliers, tapestries, gilded wainscoting and ornate columned doorways was the setting for innumerable state receptions and presidential press conferences. Banquets assembled two hundred guests, but the General allowed them to last for just one hour. The porcelain was the finest Sèvres; the tablecloths were inlaid with gilded fleurs-de-lis. Food was classic French. As well as dishes taken from Escoffier, the chef accepted recipes picked up by Yvonne de Gaulle from women's magazines. The President wolfed his food and, when he had finished a dish, the waiters removed the plates from all the tables even if the guests were still eating. Smaller lunches, usually held three times a week, were more relaxed, with a glass of Muscat wine before the meal, which de Gaulle might serve himself, and a few remarks from the host in honour of his guests.

At the Gaullist court, everybody knew his place and kept to it, exhibiting due deference. Visiting the President's office with John F. Kennedy, the Secretary of State Dean Rusk was taken aback when Debré and Couve de Murville came in and clicked their heels, for all the world like military cadets in front of a superior officer. Some of the barons around the monarch could draw on two decades of service to him; they knew how to cope with his changing moods, how to interpret his more Delphic utterances. Beyond them was an array of experts whom he would summon at will, sometimes for no evident purpose. There was even an unofficial court jester in the shape of a comedian, Henri Tisot, who resembled the President and delivered a perfect imitation of him. 'I must try to match up to the national parrot,' de Gaulle remarked before one press conference.

It was a very masculine world. De Gaulle did not consider women to be cut out for political positions, and feared that their presence would interfere with the smooth working of his administrative machine. Nor did he set much store by their opinions. After the wife of his Minister of State, Louis Jacquinot, joined the conversation at some length during a lunch, the General remarked to him: 'My dear friend, we agree: men should remain bachelors.' On a rare occasion when Yvonne de Gaulle ventured a political opinion, he told her 'get back to your saucepans'.[5]

Still, he was devoted to his wife, always wanting her by his side when he travelled and fretting when she was not present. She in turn worried constantly about her husband, considering that security at the Élysée was insufficient, fearful that he might catch cold at Colombey. When they travelled, she packed pills in case he suffered from pain from his war wounds. At presidential shoots at Rambouillet – de Gaulle did not join in the slaughter of pheasants, but arrived to watch proceedings at the end – she took with her phials of anti-viper serum in the event of snakes in the grass. 'With the General,' one of her staff recalled, 'she really behaved like a nurse.'[6]

Her conservative ways and outlook earned her the nickname '*Tante Yvonne*' as she kept an eye on female visitors' décolletages and made it plain that divorced people were not welcome at the Élysée. One report had it that, when the name of one particular male divorcee was mentioned during a telephone discussion from Colombey about a government reshuffle, Yvonne stopped her knitting; this was enough to disqualify the candidate. She asked the owner of a dress shop opposite the palace to lower his shutters in order that the mannequins in the window should not distract the palace guards. At lunch with de Gaulle's scientific adviser, a mathematician, she asked him if there were 'young girls' in the university where he taught. 'Indeed, Madame,' he replied. 'There are even young girls who do maths with great success.' 'But, *Monsieur le Professeur*,' she went on, 'these young girls who attend your university, can they be married afterwards?'

Small and invariably dressed in dark clothes, she was described by the British ambassador's wife as 'a charming, natural, simple woman with a pretty smile, no chic or allure, but most agreeable'. Yvonne was as unassuming as her husband was high-profile, staying in the background in public and going on solitary outings to favourite shops, such as the Bon Marché department store on the Left Bank, or the grander Fauchon grocery in the Place de la Madeleine near the palace. On the evidence of several members of staff she was not popular within the palace, known for listening to rumours and advising her husband to take action as a result. He generally followed her counsel if only because he had too many other things to do to quibble with her – he did put up a fight to save the job of the head gardener who had got on the wrong side of his wife, but eventually gave way. Few of the women on her personal staff lasted long.

The couple's daily routine in their five-room apartment on the first floor of the palace was precisely organised, though the distance from the kitchens meant that food was usually lukewarm when it arrived. Some of their rooms looked out on to a street, and the curtains were kept constantly closed. Others gave on to the garden in which the General liked to stroll, pausing to look at the ducks in the small pool.

Between 7.30 and 8 a.m., the General's valet would enter the room where they slept in twin beds – the General's was 2.2 metres long – and open the shutters, calling out 'Good morning, *mon Général*'. Then he would tell his master about the weather before the couple put on their dressing gowns and went for breakfast in Yvonne's office next door – the General took tea and rusks. The newspapers would be brought. They often managed to irritate the General. A valet recalled seeing Madame de Gaulle surreptitiously putting those which were particularly critical of her husband into the wastepaper basket; the President must have noticed, but said nothing.

The previous night, his valet would have selected one of his dozen suits for him to wear in the morning – his wife sometimes dissented and a change was made. Four of the shirts she bought from the luxury haberdasher Charvet in the Place Vendôme were laid out for him to choose from. Once a month, a barber from the Left Bank crossed the Seine, put on his white smock and trimmed the General's sparse hair as he recounted the latest gossip. At the end of the session, de Gaulle paid him personally, having got the cash from an aide-de-camp; he had not carried money since 1940.

After listening to the radio news, de Gaulle arrived in his office at 9.30. An aide-de-camp brought him a folder containing overnight telegrams and messages, and replies to questions he had put to his staff and ministers. If there was not a formal luncheon, he returned to his quarters to eat, watching the television news and reading the first edition of *Le Monde* attentively – he wrote corrections of what he regarded as mistakes on the pages.

In the afternoon, the General liked to leave his work for half an hour to take tea with his wife in her office. They spoke little; it seemed more of an occasion for him to reflect. After he had finished his tea, he played patience while she knitted or wrote letters. He would sometimes sit in an armchair with his eyes closed, perfectly still. Then, getting to his feet, he would tell his valet, 'Let's go.'

When there was not an official dinner, he left his desk to reach his private apartment in time for the eight o'clock television news, carrying documents with him in a briefcase. After supper, he read classical French texts or thrillers, or watched television with his wife, mainly popular plays and films; the General was fond of James Bond films and Steve McQueen westerns as well as the comedies of the French duo Bourvil and Louis de Funès. Greeting the latter at a reception one day, de Gaulle addressed him as 'Master' and, when the comic looked surprised, said to those around him: 'So, isn't he a master at his art?'

In their private apartment the de Gaulles were as frugal as ever, telling aides to turn the lights out when they left rooms. After Yvonne learned that the Republican Guards were entitled to as many baguettes as they wanted, she instituted a ration of half a loaf a day. Though he relished the bouillabaisse prepared by the chef, the General was also content with tinned sardines. He wrote his letters by hand; they were put into ordinary envelopes which secretaries posted on their way home. His wife opened her own mail. When she telephoned, she never gave her name, but expected her voice to be recognised. If a couturier lent her a gown for a state occasion, she made sure it was returned immediately afterwards.

The General would express surprise at the number of official cars parked in the gravel courtyard, wondering why junior officials could not use the Metro instead. Drawing a strict line between their personal and official positions, the de Gaulles paid the telephone and electricity bills in their apartment. When a question from a journalist led him to realise that, as an author, he should have been paying social security, the General wrote out a cheque for a million old francs. His wife explained to a minister that they did not invite their grandchildren to the Élysée for fear that they might break something which belonged to the state. On another occasion, she expressed regret to a visitor that the children had been unable to go on a winter sports holiday because they had left it too late and could not get seats on the train; the idea of pulling rank in a personal matter was alien to them both.[7]

Despite his wife's constant concern about his physical wellbeing, the General's health remained good for his age. He had treatment in the early years of his presidency to ease his breathing – the temporary result, as one of the doctors present recalled, was to make his nose even more enormous than usual. The other duty of the medical staff who followed him on his tours was to carry lozenges against the colds and sore throats to which he was prone. His main physical problem was his eyesight, which required him to wear spectacles with thick lenses. He regarded them as a sign of physical decline which he did not wish to show. But, when he dispensed with them on public occasions, he depended on those around him to guide him. He could not see the size of crowds listening to him on provincial tours and, uncertain with the aim of his fork at mealtimes, occasionally spilled food down his shirt. At official functions he was sometimes unable to make out the features of those about to be presented to him. On one visit to Africa, he greeted a national leader who was also a priest and was wearing long robes as 'Madame'.

All this made him more aware of his advancing years as he moved towards his seventieth birthday in 1960. When Eisenhower's granddaughter was intrigued by the thickness of the lenses in his spectacles on a trip to the United States in 1959, the General told her: 'I am an old man, many people have been angry with me, I am almost blind. But I still have to follow my path.' To Pleven, he classified himself as 'the man of 1940' and said he was twenty years too old. He told his doctor he had returned to power ten years too late.[8]

The de Gaulles spent as many weekends as possible at Colombey. On 11 November, the anniversary of Armistice Day, a tricolour flag was raised over their house. 'I went there to think,' the General wrote in his memoirs. 'There I wrote the speeches which were a painful and perpetual task. There I read some of the books I was sent. There, looking at the horizon or the immense sky, I restored my serenity.' The couple attended mass at the small village church each Sunday, and the General was driven fifteen kilometres to a home for retired clergy for confession. Their children and grandchildren, and Jacques Vendroux and his family, were regular visitors, not least on holiday breaks: 'The family harmony was precious to me,' de Gaulle recalled. 'The presidency is temporary,' his wife remarked to Nixon, 'but the family is permanent.' The outside world was kept beyond the stone walls and railings surrounding the property.

The General attended to the three-hectare grounds with their flower beds set in the pattern of the Cross of Lorraine. The big fir trees were dying and had to be replaced. He had a tennis court built and for the grandchildren, clock golf was installed and a small green rubber swimming pool, mounted on struts. The young ones also played with a sheep which their grandfather refused to have slaughtered, finally giving it to a village lucky draw (after which it no doubt suffered the fate from which he had originally saved it).[9]

IV
The President's men

De Gaulle's staff numbered forty-five, headed by his aide from June 1940, Geoffroy de Courcel, as Secretary-General at the presidency. This was more than three times the number who had worked with Auriol and Coty, but the nature of the presidency had changed radically as the General took the French tradition of centralised authority to new levels. Staff members were expected to dedicate themselves entirely to the service of the state as represented by the President, to be extremely discreet and self-effacing and to avoid journalists. The secrecy de Gaulle had always prized was the order of the day, both for its own sake and to help him stage sudden surprise moves to galvanise public opinion or rout opponents. The devotion to service expected of the Élysée entourage had something Jesuitical about it, appropriate for a man with de Gaulle's upbringing.

The civil servant René Brouillet, who had worked with him after the war, became *chef de cabinet* after Pompidou decided to return to work at the Rothschild bank. Jacques Foccart was the *éminence grise* for Africa. The ever-dependable Olivier Guichard and Pierre Lefranc were on hand to undertake whatever task the General gave them. Albin Chalandon, a loyalist from the days in London, kept the UNR party under control, and Louis Terrenoire, the former Secretary-General of the RPF, headed the Gaullist group in the National Assembly. This core of faithful followers was joined by figures from the former regime, apolitical officials and advisers like Jacques Rueff.

Because of the status of their master, the staff at the Élysée often enjoyed greater authority than ministers, who sometimes learned of decisions affecting their sector through news broadcasts. Chaban-Delmas defined the President's 'reserved domain' as including foreign affairs, defence, Algeria and the Sahara, and the Franco-African community. But this understates the General's authority, which extended to any field or subject in which he chose to interest himself. As he made clear, ministers were there to implement his instructions. The government emanated from him. Decisions were not taken 'by' Cabinet sessions, he stated in a note, but 'in' them. The President of the Republic determined the outcome.

As de Gaulle focused on Algeria and raising France's international status in his early years in the presidency, Debré enjoyed a certain degree of freedom in shaping domestic policy on issues such as state aid for religious schools and reform of the hospital system, holding discussions of his own at Matignon outside the power nexus of the Élysée. But this changed in the 1960s with the President's assertion of his overarching powers, reflected in the growth of interministerial meetings held at the presidential palace that short-circuited regular government business. Debré's vision of a British-style system of a strong government resting on a parliamentary majority gave way to the Gaullist reality of a single source of power embodied in the President who, as the General would put it in 1964, was alone in holding the authority of the state granted to him by the people to exercise over ministers, civil and military affairs and justice.[10]

All the same, he tolerated significant disagreements among ministers so long as they remained loyal to him. His long-time follower Edmond Michelet supported independence for Algeria while Jacques Soustelle spoke for the *pieds-noirs.* Gaullists could point to the fact that there were only three prime ministers between 1958 and the General's retirement in 1969 as a sign of stability, compared to twenty-one under the Fourth Republic – but the finance, agriculture and justice portfolios all changed hands five times in eleven years, and there were eight education ministers. As for the Gaullist UNR party, it had seven secretaries-general over the same period.

For the most part, however, unanimity reigned at the weekly Cabinet sessions held in the presidential palace on Wednesday mornings. At

9.45, the ministers gathered round a long oval table covered with green baize while de Gaulle conferred with the Prime Minister in his office above. At ten o'clock, the two men walked down to join the meeting, the General going around the table to shake the hands of each of the other two dozen present before taking his place in the centre. Malraux was always seated on his right; the Culture Minister said little, but, when he did speak, de Gaulle paid particular attention.

Very occasionally there were round-table sessions in which the President called on each participant to give his opinion (with one exception only, it was always a man's) without any further debate. More often, de Gaulle called on ministers to deliver a report in turn on their specific field of responsibility, and then announced his verdict on outstanding issues, which was to be implemented, again without further discussion. Though he would sometimes launch into monologues on a subject that preoccupied him, he usually spoke relatively little in Cabinet. He did not need to. As Pinay remembered: 'He behaved like a man who dominated the members of the government. Nobody dared to stand up to him.' From time to time, he would direct a jibe at one or other of the ministers, but there was none of the small talk with which many presidents and prime ministers of the two previous republics had lightened the atmosphere.

On the very rare occasion when a minister presumed to dissent, he got short shrift. The most striking revolt came from Pinay at the end of 1959. The idol of middle-class France, who annoyed de Gaulle by addressing him as '*Monsieur le Président*' rather than '*mon Général*', was a firm believer in the Atlantic Alliance and a potential threat as an alternative national saviour. When he objected at a Cabinet meeting to a speech in which the President called for a change in NATO so as to reduce US supremacy, de Gaulle inquired: 'Is the Finance Minister interested in foreign policy questions?' Yes, foreign policy interested him, the Finance Minister replied, explaining his pro-American stance and complaining about the way in which decisions on major issues were taken without the Cabinet being consulted. 'Thank you, Monsieur Pinay,' de Gaulle cut in. 'Gentlemen, the session is over.' He stood and left the room without shaking the hands of the ministers, as he usually did. Soon afterwards, Pinay was replaced.[11]

Just as ministers had to know their place, so the role of parliament and its parties was reduced as was only to be expected from a man with de Gaulle's view of the legislatures of the last two republics. Many bills were framed in broad terms, leaving it to officials to shape their implementation. Budgetary discussions were cut back and the 'blocked vote' system used to force through laws without giving deputies a chance to debate detailed points. The government controlled the National Assembly programme, sidelining many draft bills by ruling that they infringed a ban on legislation that increased state spending. De Gaulle's use of referendums, speeches and televised addresses further diminished the influence of the parliament. Major issues, such as Algeria, were rarely debated in the Palais Bourbon. Rising to the top of a parliamentary party was no longer the passport to ministerial office; bright and ambitious graduates of the ENA, the administrative finishing school, found the path to advancement through the civil service or state companies. The government was full of unelected officials. Few of de Gaulle's staff had ever been anywhere near the hustings.

The UNR, the movement set up to support the General, was a broad coalition with no coherent ideology or programme beyond the continuing rule of the man to whom it was devoted. Its members became known as de Gaulle's 'walking shoes' (*godillots*). UNR chiefs were imposed by Matignon and the Élysée, and its election candidates selected by Gaullist bigwigs. It was also different from its rivals in that it aspired to dominate the National Assembly on its own with no need for the coalitions that had been essential to form administrations under the Third and Fourth Republics.

For all the hauteur de Gaulle demonstrated, past experience reinforced his taste for secrecy, guile, ambiguity and duplicity. He was at one and the same time the most straightforward of politicians in his ultimate aims, and among the most tricky in the way he proceeded towards them, an Olympian who adopted wily, crab-like tactics. He excelled at pursuing two courses simultaneously, only making his intentions clear when he judged the moment right – or when he had made up his mind. He got ministers to carry out secret missions in areas outside their official competence, and kept Debré in the dark about his policy on Algeria.[12]

There was nothing untoward about this. He had now become more than the Constable, enjoying instead the prerogatives of a king. Sitting by the fire with Eisenhower, both in their dressing gowns, after a formal banquet at the château of Rambouillet, de Gaulle recalled that Roosevelt thought he took himself for Joan of Arc. 'He was wrong,' he went on. 'I simply took myself for General de Gaulle.' Though he had been elected by a restricted college of dignitaries, there could be no doubt of the popular backing he enjoyed. He had triumphed at the referendum that legitimised the new order, and his supporters had a majority in the popularly elected lower house of parliament. Those around him were in his thrall. His adversaries – the Communists, Mendès France and Mitterrand – were marginalised. Now he had to get to grips with the crisis across the Mediterranean which had done so much to propel him to power.[13]

28

ALGERIA

I
'I have understood you'

De Gaulle's memoirs present a picture of a man who knew what he was doing from the start when it came to Algeria. Receiving the journalist Jean-Raymond Tournoux in 1962, he said that he had never wavered. That has to be doubted. As his ruminations before 13 May showed, he was in several minds at the time. In 1958 he had remarked to Edgar Faure that the most common mistake made by statesmen was to believe that, at any given moment, there was a solution for each problem. At some periods, there were problems that had no solution; this was the case for Algeria when he resumed office, he added.[1]

While rejecting integration between France and Algeria, which he said would bring eighty Muslim deputies into the National Assembly if the two communities were put on an equal footing, de Gaulle feared that complete independence would lead to disaster and mass killings. His hope was for a form of self-determination under which Algeria would maintain close cooperative links with metropolitan France. But this depended on the emergence of a 'third force' of moderate Muslims and *pieds-noirs,* and the increasingly visceral struggle ruled that out. The logic of the Gaullist enterprise meant that there could be little doubt of the final outcome; Algeria was, at best, a running sore, at worst, a cancer in the French state, and, since the General's prime objective was to restore the greatness of that state, he would have to apply surgery. The question was how.

France could not be seen to have suffered another military defeat after the trauma of Indochina. So the General had to step up the war against nationalists of the FLN and their *Armée de Libération Nationale* (ALN) to try to gain the superior position at the negotiating table when the time came for talks. But increased action by the army would be only a preparation for ultimate withdrawal. That was a bitter pill for a man who boasted that he never gave up anything – when Chaban-Delmas spoke to him in 1961 of the suffering of the Europeans in Algeria, he got up from his desk and thundered: 'And de Gaulle? You think he was created and put in this world to give up Algeria? You think he doesn't suffer, de Gaulle?'[2]

To emerge on top and with his new regime intact, he would need all his genius for ambiguity, duplicity and improvisation, his ability to impose abrupt changes of policy and his capacity for rallying popular support to succeed in finding his way to a solution. He knew that if he failed, his greater ambition of restoring France and installing a new form of government would be put in grave danger, not just from the threat of a putsch led by the generals and colonels in Algeria, but also from a disappointed majority of citizens who had been ready to welcome him back to office. The prospect of failure in such a massive enterprise was one he could not entertain.

On 4 June 1958, as Prime Minister, de Gaulle flew to Algiers, his Caravelle airliner accompanied by fighters flying in a Cross of Lorraine pattern. As he stepped from the plane, the waiting spectators cheered and wept with excitement. 'One could feel an electric current running through the crowd,' a reporter wrote. 'Amid all the cruel doubt, here was a man they thought they could really trust.' Ticker-tape rained down as he was driven to the Palais d'Été government headquarters, standing in the back of an open Citroën DS limousine. Meeting the granite-faced victor of the Battle of Algiers there, he bantered: 'Ah, Massu, still as bloody thick?'* To which the soldier replied, 'Still as bloody thick, and still as Gaullist as ever.'

As Salan had predicted, there was a problem with the two men de Gaulle had brought with him – Minister of State Louis Jacquinot and the Minister for the Sahara, Max Lejeune, who were seen in Algiers as holdovers from the despised Fourth Republic. At the airport, they

*'*Ah, Massu, toujours aussi con?*'

struggled to find seats in the procession of cars driving into the city. While the General walked ahead of them to the balcony overlooking the Place du Forum to make his speech, members of the Public Safety Committee shouted 'Socialist pederasts!' at the two politicians, and hustled them into a side room, by some accounts a lavatory.

De Gaulle continued imperturbably on his way, accompanied by Soustelle and General Ély, the army chief of staff who had resigned the previous month but had since returned to his post. 'Our great cry of joy and hope had been heard,' Salan declared to the throng of *pieds-noirs* and Muslims in the square below, which erupted into three minutes of deafening cheers. Then the Prime Minister, in plain uniform without medals, raised his arms in his familiar V gesture and shouted '*Je vous ai compris!*' The first three words were covered by the noise of the crowd but the fourth sounded loud and clear.

The words were meaningless in themselves; there was no indication of what de Gaulle had 'understood'.* But the crowd interpreted them to mean that he was on its side; he had understood their cause and would back their struggle to retain control of Algeria. For them, he was truly their saviour on a white horse, and the rebellion of 13 May had succeeded, symbolised by the Public Safety Committee filing out on to the balcony when de Gaulle finished speaking to sing 'La Marseillaise' with him and those below. His words may also have saved his life: a fifty-year-old antiques dealer and former Pétainist had positioned himself in a building opposite the balcony from which the General spoke, armed with a rifle with which he intended to kill the Prime Minister. But when he heard 'I have understood you', he took his finger off the trigger.

Had his listeners in Algiers paid more attention to the rest of what the General said, they might have been less comforted, even more so if they had known of his remarks before his return to power about the inevitability of Algerian independence. 'In the whole of Algeria, there is

*There was a historical echo. When Reynaud asked to be allowed to explore an armistice with Germany in June 1940, Churchill had used the verb *comprendre* to signify that he understood the plight in which France found itself. Appeasers presented that as British acceptance of the French request. Now, eighteen years on, de Gaulle played on the same ambiguity – he meant the verb in the Churchillian sense, but adherents of *Algérie française* took it in the same way as had the proponents of peace in 1940 (see p. 21).

only one class of inhabitant, there are only Frenchmen in the full sense, with the same rights and the same duties,' he insisted in his speech. Nor was his offer of 'reconciliation' to the FLN what the *pieds-noirs* had in mind.

The gulf between the cold, rational man of the north and the emotional settlers was evident from the start, even if his four key words submerged everything else. He was exasperated by their cries of 'Soustelle! Soustelle!' when he visited the cities of Oran and Constantine, and was heard to mutter 'Oh, shut up' at the noise from the streets. When the Public Safety Committee asked to be recognised, he replied that he was in charge of Algerian affairs, and told Salan, as Delegate General, to re-establish regular government authority (just as he had done with the Resistance in 1944). There was also a reminder of the FLN's ability to strike when its men attacked the police station in the city of Bône on 6 June.

None of this made any difference in the euphoria surrounding the trip which was only increased when de Gaulle cried '*Vive l'Algérie française*' on one occasion. He said later that the phrase escaped him in the pressure of events, or argued unconvincingly that 'one speaks of French Canada or French Switzerland' – his collected papers include the whole speech but not the two emotive words, suggesting that he added them on the spur of the moment.

Opinion in metropolitan France at the time was divided – a poll showed 52 per cent of those questioned favouring integration while 41 per cent thought Algeria should become independent. But the cause of *Algérie française* had high-profile supporters such as Soustelle and Bidault and, from the election of November 1958, the support also of most members of the large independent conservative group in the National Assembly which gave the General his parliamentary majority. Debré saw the war against the FLN as a contribution to the defence of the West. While left-wingers argued for an end to colonialism, the sentimental hold of French Algeria remained strong; in the media and on the far right backers of continued French rule kept up a constant clamouring for people to stand by their brethren across the sea, along with dire warnings of what Arab rule would bring.

But when he returned to Paris after his three-day trip, de Gaulle told

Pierre Lefranc that those who thought France could remain master across the Mediterranean were dreaming, because of the 9:1 population ratio. There had been Muslim demonstrators in the crowds that welcomed him, but the gulf between the two communities was evident – when one of de Gaulle's representatives asked leaders of the European community for names of Muslims who could sit on joint bodies, they mentioned a single civil servant and said that otherwise they knew of nobody. 'Believe me, I am the first to regret it, but the proportion of Europeans is too small,' de Gaulle told Lefranc.

Still, the trip had achieved its immediate aims. The General had established his primacy over the rebels of May. The Public Safety Committee had been relegated. At least part of the native population had welcomed him, putting the nationalists on the back foot. But there was no guarantee that these achievements would last. If he moved towards a settlement, the ultras might well take to the streets once more, his rule might come into question and the 'fraternal' spirit evident in the streets of Algiers might evaporate, propelling the majority of Muslims into the arms of the FLN. Most important, although the army appeared loyal, it had changed. Defeat in Indochina and its experience in Algeria had given it a political complexion that made it a very different instrument from the 'greatest thing' de Gaulle had joined as a young man. Its extremist officers saw themselves as fighting the mirror image of a war of national liberation to sustain French rule. Others dreamed of sweeping away democracy; when asked which leader he admired, one colonel replied, 'Franco'.[3]

II
Clearing the decks

At the beginning of July 1958, de Gaulle made a second visit to Algeria, accompanied this time by Mollet. Refusing to receive the Public Safety Committee, he announced plans for social and economic development and greater access for Muslims to civil service jobs. The *pieds-noirs* had several reasons for disquiet. As Minister of Information, their champion, Soustelle, had no responsibility for Algerian policy. The General's readiness to allow colonies in Africa to opt for independence could be a harbinger of what lay ahead. After Jacquinot and Lejeune, he had brought with him the man who had been pelted with rotten tomatoes in 1956. As a result, his welcome was a good deal less warm than it had been on his first trip though he made sure that troops from Algeria were given pride of place in the Bastille Day parade in Paris on 14 July and that Salan and Massu were suitably decorated.

On a third trip to Algeria at the beginning of October, the General appealed to the FLN to stop 'a fratricidal struggle . . . We must cooperate; so stop this absurd combat . . . The prisons will then empty. A future will open up for everybody and particularly for yourselves.' That caused members of the Public Safety Committee to walk off the platform. The Prime Minister, as he still was, offered the creation of 400,000 jobs, industrialisation and use of oil revenue to develop the territory, new homes for a million people, land distribution, parity of salaries between Algeria and metropolitan France, improved transport and health services, and allocation of 10 per cent of French civil service posts to Algerians. It did not sound like a plan from a man who was preparing to pull out. But, at the same time, he spoke of Algeria and France as separate entities. His intentions were as difficult to read as ever, perhaps even for himself.

On his behalf, General Ély conducted a purge of the army, forcing some extremist officers to retire and breaking up groups formed during the spring revolt. Soldiers were ordered not to take part in any political organisation ahead of the November poll for the National Assembly. Despite this, the voting in Algeria was closely controlled by the military. With the FLN calling for abstention, the sixty-seven deputies returned to the National Assembly were all *Algérie française* supporters, including forty-five Muslims. The nationalist boycott meant that 36 per cent of registered voters did not cast a ballot.

Pursuing secret channels, de Gaulle sent the newly appointed Minister for Youth and Sports, the mountaineer Maurice Herzog, on monthly trips to Algeria during which, under cover of ministerial duties, he gathered information on opinions among Europeans and Algerians. Lucien Neuwirth established contact with the FLN, while Pompidou, working unofficially from his banking position, laid the ground for talks with the newly constituted Provisional Government of the Algerian Republic (GPRA) grouping disparate independence movements under its banner in exile.

At a press conference on 23 October, de Gaulle made a nuanced suggestion of some form of negotiation if the ALN would lay down arms. Rooms were booked at the Hôtel de Crillon on the Place de la Concorde for the GPRA chief, Ferhat Abbas, an adroit negotiator with an Alsatian wife. But the initiative came to nothing. In part this was due to divisions within the FLN. But de Gaulle's air of superiority, expressed in his language at the press conference, did nothing to help either. He referred to his willingness to see '*une paix des braves*' under which the nationalists would stop fighting. It was as far as he could go politically, but was not much of an offer for a movement which saw force as the means to achieve independence. The FLN was not ready to admit defeat and rejected preconditions to negotiations.[4]

The General had been planning since the autumn to move Salan so that he could put in his own men. During a visit to Algeria in December, he proposed to transfer him to Paris as Inspector General of National Defence. But, shortly after Salan agreed to this, the post was abolished in an army reorganisation. Instead, he was named Military Governor of Paris, a ceremonial post. The following year, he resigned, a bitter man whose resentment would have an effect before very long.[5]

To supervise military affairs in Algeria, de Gaulle appointed a pipe-smoking air force general, Maurice Challe, who had transmitted the Luftwaffe order of battle to the British ahead of D Day and had backed de Gaulle's return to power. Paul Delouvrier, a tall, serious-looking forty-four-year-old civil servant, who had fought in the Resistance and then worked as an economics expert with Monnet, was sent in as Delegate General for civilian affairs. When he protested that he was not big enough for the job, the General replied: 'You'll grow.' In a sign of the primacy of the state, when the two men arrived in Algiers Delouvrier walked a few steps ahead of the uniformed Challe. He made the reassuring statement: 'France stays', but, after an initial tour of the territory, told de Gaulle that Algeria would become independent.

The General's own policy remained incoherent. His minister Robert Buron called him a 'prince of ambiguity', but he may simply not have known where he should head. Despite his olive branch to the FLN, to junior officers who crowded around him during his December visit he referred to himself as 'de Gaulle who has never given up on anything'. As one of those present recalled, the officers returned to their posts convinced that he would never abandon Algeria.

At the General's urging, the army jettisoned Salan's cautious strategy, and took the fight to the enemy in its mountain strongholds in the Kabylie using helicopters as the key to victory. The offensive brought the nationalists to a very low ebb, reducing their strength to an estimated eight thousand active *fellagha* fighters in Algeria – another 10,000 were across the border in Tunisia and Morocco but were cut off when the frontiers were sealed. Militarily, France seemed on the brink of victory. The FLN was buffeted by internal feuds and the loss of several leaders in the fighting. Psych-ops units led by the veteran of the Battle of Algiers, the strongly pro-French Algeria Colonel Yves Godard, conducted successful disinformation operations, provoking a major purge in one of the main Kabylie bases.

The French herded a million Muslims into 'regroupment' camps. Their native militia, the *harkis*, was expanded to 250,000 men. Abuse of civilians in the *bled* and use of torture by the army increased. But, in an inversion of the slogan of 1940, however many battles the French won, they could not clinch the war. International opinion was alienated by their methods, and there was a growing lobby at the United Nations to discuss what Paris regarded as an internal matter.

On the ground, the FLN hit back with savage reprisals, including the massacre of more than a hundred people in one village, Melouza, which had put itself under the French colours. The way in which ALN fighters used knives to slit their victims' throats was a particular source of horror, the word for it, *égorgement*, carrying an emotive force which was played on, at times, by de Gaulle. Though he was pleased at the success of Challe's offensive and hoped that the busier the army was in fighting the less it would meddle in politics, he did not appreciate that field officers who sympathised with *Algérie française* had a genuine rationalisation of their mission to maintain French rule. If they were to get villagers to rally behind them, they had to offer the prospect that they would remain to extend protection to them. As Soustelle wrote, the decisive question put by village elders was: 'Are you going or staying? If the village raises the French flag, if this or that head of family agrees to become mayor, if we send our boys and girls to school, if we hand out arms for self-defence, if we refuse grain, mutton and money to the *fellagha* . . . will you, the army, be there to defend us from reprisals? Or will you abandon us so that one day, as at Melouza, we will be butchered?'[6]

In the spring of 1959, it was time for de Gaulle to try a new initiative after the flop of the *paix des braves.* Though Debré remained wedded to the cause of French Algeria, four ministers favoured a new effort to solve the problem, among them the technocrats Pierre Sudreau and Jean-Marcel Jeanneney. At the General's instruction, Delouvrier opened secret contacts with FLN political leaders, and Pompidou made a trip to Algiers ostensibly in his role as a banker but during which he met Muslims linked to the GPRA.

At the same time, in an interview with Pierre Laffont, the editor of the main newspaper in the Algerian port city of Oran, de Gaulle said there was no cause to recognise the FLN since it did not represent Algeria, or even Muslims. Nor was there any need to speak of integration since France and Algeria were already integrated. His words were greeted enthusiastically by the *pieds-noirs,* but, as usual, they did not remark on passages of the interview which were less to their taste, for instance when the General noted that those who shouted loudest for integration wanted to be given back 'Papa's Algeria', 'but Papa's Algeria is dead, and, if one does not understand that, one will die with it'.[7]

That summer, on his first break since he had begun his return to office the previous June, de Gaulle took with him to Colombey a memorandum written by Bernard Tricot, the senior civil servant on his staff dealing with Algeria. This argued that the idea that Algeria had to remain entirely French was evaporating, and that the heavy economic cost of the war could not be ignored. Nor could the international dimension, with the prospect that the United States might vote against France at the United Nations in the autumn.

On 26 August, the General called a Cabinet meeting to canvass ministerial views. A rare account of the secret proceedings came from

Soustelle, written later when he did not feel bound by any restrictions. According to this, the government was fairly equally divided between those who wanted to maintain the status quo and those who saw a need for movement. Debré launched into a lengthy statement of which the principal conclusion was that the Algerian people should be allowed to determine their future democratically. Given the electoral demography, that was not good for the integrationist cause. Soustelle thought the Prime Minister had been influenced by prior conversation with the General, his loyalty to his leader overcoming his *Algérie française* convictions. In his memoirs, de Gaulle noted the way in which his Premier 'adopted each of my initiatives with complete loyalty . . . but suffered in the process and did not hide it'.

De Gaulle ended the session by saying, 'We have to march forward or die. I chose to march, but that does not mean we will not also die.' The most outspoken voice around the Cabinet table had been Jeanneney, the Industry Minister, who used the word 'independence'. Afterwards, he asked Debré if he had gone too far. 'No. You were the closest to him in your thoughts,' the Prime Minister replied.[8]

The next day, the President travelled once more to Algeria to sound out the army. He put forward the idea of allowing the Algerians to choose their own future after a long period of pacification, and told Massu he was growing fed up with the *pieds-noirs*. The victor of the Battle of Algiers was not convinced. According to his chief of staff, the small, nervy *Algérie française* militant, Colonel Argoud, he remarked afterwards that de Gaulle was not eternal. The growing opposition led the President's doctor to wonder if three venomous scorpions he found in the General's bathroom had got there by chance.

Ignoring Massu's objections, de Gaulle moved steadily forward on the path he had been following in his own mind since reading Tricot's memorandum. 'The Algerians will make their own destiny,' he said in one speech. Then, at the headquarters of an operation in the Kabylie region, he told a group including Challe and Delouvrier that the era of administration by Europeans was over, so 'we must act in Algeria only for Algeria and with Algeria in such a way that the world understands'.[9]

This recognition of the international dimension of the struggle increased as the UN General Assembly loomed. Though he maintained the tradition that France declined to take part in a discussion of what it regarded as an internal issue, the President wanted to minimise the negative votes. He promised a rethinking of policy when the UN Secretary-General, Dag Hammarskjöld, whom he did not like, called at the Élysée. This was followed by the transfer of Ben Bella and most of his fellow prisoners from their jail outside Paris to the more congenial surroundings of the island of Aix off the west coast of France, where Napoleon had been held before sailing to Saint-Helena. (One of the FLN prisoners refused to go because he could not stand Ben Bella and preferred to stay in his solitary cell.) On 2 September, during a visit to Paris by Eisenhower, de Gaulle told the American President of his plan to opt for self-determination. He also noted that France needed a peaceful Algeria in order for oil companies to be able to continue operations in the Sahara. The US abstained at the UN vote. The motion by African states which put France and the FLN on the same footing failed to get the two-thirds majority needed to become binding.[10]

III
Goodbye

At 8 p.m. on 16 September 1959, the General spoke on television and radio to announce that Algeria would be invited to vote on a choice between three alternatives. The first, secession, was a recipe for disaster, leading to misery, political chaos, 'generalised throat cutting' and, before long, a warlike Communist dictatorship, he said. Full Frenchification (*francisation complète*) would mean equal rights with access for Algerians, as an integral part of the French population, to all public sector jobs. Put that way, it was not a prospect to charm the *pieds-noirs*, for all their theoretical talk of integration, and might not appeal to many people in metropolitan France either. So there was the third path, 'the government of Algeria by the Algerians, supported by the help of France and in a tight union with her for the economy, education, defence, foreign relations' in a federal regime which would guarantee the rights of the different communities.[11]

In twenty minutes, de Gaulle in effect waved farewell to French Algeria, though he referred to the 'twelve departments' which would vote, to denote that France intended to retain the Sahara with its energy resources and atomic testing site. In private, he still considered the FLN incapable of running the country, and, as Challe's centurions descended on the ALN in their helicopter raids, he could not give up the idea that military success could force the nationalists to compromise and allow him to negotiate as a victor. The reaction in metropolitan France to his address was overwhelmingly positive; polls showed a steadily increasing desire to get out of Algeria. After a delay of a week, the GPRA welcomed the recognition of the right of Algerians to decide their own destiny and said it was ready to talk – though it maintained the unacceptable condition of being the sole representative of the non-European population. The ultras across the sea were, naturally, horrified. The student leader of May 1958, Pierre Lagaillarde, who had become a lawyer and had been elected to the National Assembly, detected 'the liquidation of French Algeria'. The colonels like Argoud, who had sensed the way the wind was blowing from de Gaulle's visit in August, were now confirmed in their conviction that they had been betrayed.

Nine UNR deputies, including Delbecque, quit the party while eighteen of the seventy members of its central committee abstained on a motion backing the General. Fifty-one of the seventy-one deputies from Algeria left the parliamentary majority. A *Rassemblement pour l'Algérie française* (Rally for French Algeria) was created on both sides of the Mediterranean, joined by Bidault, Roger Duchet, leader of the CNIP conservative group in the National Assembly, and four UNR deputies, including two leaders of the previous year's coup in Corsica, Pascal Arrighi and 'Leather Nose' Thomazo. Eleven associations opposing self-determination called for a censure motion against the government. Soustelle, whom de Gaulle had refused to see before his speech, stayed in the government for the time being, but did not hide his antagonism.

The political opposition was soon seen off. The government had a majority of 441 to 23 in a parliamentary vote on Algeria. One of its most persistent critics, Mitterrand, had been temporarily eclipsed by a murky affair in which he claimed to have been the target of an assassination attempt by *Algérie française* extremists close to the Paris Observatory, but which his opponents said was a put-up job designed to bolster his reputation. The first UNR national congress, in Bordeaux in November, was tightly controlled by Chaban-Delmas, Terrenoire, who headed the National Assembly group, and the party boss, Albin Chalandon. Soustelle made an eloquent *Algérie française* speech, but the final resolution backed the General's policy. In the following weeks, de Gaulle, Debré and Couve de Murville all spoke of the government's readiness to talk about a ceasefire with the ALN, but the GPRA said the Algerian leaders held on the island of Aix would be its delegates to any negotiations. De Gaulle replied that he found this 'almost insulting' and that his offer was only to the fighting men.

*

Amid all this, a tragedy in his family occurred just before Christmas when de Gaulle's brother, Pierre, collapsed with a stroke while visiting the Élysée – he had apparently been overcome after telling Foccart about difficulties he was experiencing in organising France's participation in the World's Fair to be held in Montreal. A doctor was immediately called as he was laid on a Louis XV couch, his head hanging over one arm, his feet on the ground. He had no pulse. The President, who had not known that his lookalike sibling was in the palace, was alerted. He sat in an armchair, one hand on his brother's left knee. 'Under the sway of huge emotion, mixed with anxiety, the General was totally silent,' an official recalled. His valet, who brought a pillow and blanket, remembered him as looking 'so sad, so lost'.

Suddenly Pierre came round, but his face was paralysed and he had no movement in one of his arms. Then he recovered and said: 'Oh Charles, like Félix Faure' – a reference to the President who died of a heart attack in the palace while making love to his mistress. 'Now, Pierre, what's happened to you?' de Gaulle responded.

Pierre died on 26 December. When his valet offered his condolences, de Gaulle, his eyes moistening, pressed his hand and said, 'He was a brother I loved a lot.' Two years later, in a letter to Louis Jacquinot, whose brother had just died, de Gaulle wrote, 'To lose a brother is not only to lose somebody one loves, but to see something of one's own youth rubbed out, in short, something of oneself.' The burial took place in a village in Normandy. Despite heavy, cold rain, de Gaulle stood by the tomb for fifteen minutes, the drops running down his neck and back. One of his nieces tried to hold an umbrella over his head, but she was not tall enough.[12]

IV
The barricades

The General went for a short holiday at the end of the year in the Var department of the south, staying in an abbey that had been converted into a hotel and stopping to picnic by the roadside on the drive back to Paris. He returned to more tension over Algeria where his change of course made his opponents in North Africa even more determined. Their most zealous members saw him as a traitor who had to be neutralised along with the regime he had created. This chimed with the extreme right-wing strand of anti-democratic thinking apparent in the settler community throughout the century. Some of their leaders were unreconstructed Vichyites or Poujadists; Algeria had never been Gaullist territory. Fascism, high-church Catholicism and anti-Semitism all had their adepts in a population that did not know quite what it was, but knew all too well what it feared. The climate was heightened by a new wave of FLN atrocities against Europeans.

Delouvrier, who was walking with two sticks after a serious car crash, sought to calm the fears of the *pieds-noirs* by issuing figures showing that those of their number killed, wounded or kidnapped had declined sharply since June 1958, but the victims for December 1959 nonetheless totalled more than 250. There was also the matter of the impending trial of paratroop officers accused of having killed a young Communist in Algeria. Lagaillarde gathered together his co-conspirators of May 1958 and began to obtain weapons.

Another veteran of 1958, Joseph Ortiz, headed a *Front national français* (French National Front – FNF), whose members wore khaki shirts, and armbands decorated with the Celtic cross, a symbol of Fascist movements. The owner of the Bar du Forum by the city's main government offices, 'Monsieur Jo', was a plump, swarthy, beetle-browed populist agitator of Spanish origin with a taste for flashy suits. After meetings with Colonel Jean Gardes of the army's department for propaganda and psychological warfare, he came to believe that the FNF could count on the support of the paratroopers if it took action.

Ortiz, who could not stand Lagaillarde, was said to be involved with the underworld and in running brothels catering for the soldiers. When Bidault visited Algiers in the middle of December to inveigh against de Gaulle's policy, the FNF fielded 1,500 men as a security force. Ortiz warned the *pieds-noirs* that, if de Gaulle had his way, their only choice would be between 'the suitcase and the coffin' – leaving Algeria or being killed by the nationalists. He was helped by an incendiary orator, Dr Jean-Claude Pérez, a tall man with a ready smile whose practice in the suburb of Bab-el-Oued gave him a ready-made audience among the poor Europeans living there. A twenty-five-year-old medical graduate, Jean-Jacques Susini, provided the ideological arguments for the group. A slight, unimpressive figure with burning eyes, Susini had stood successfully for election as the president of the students' association as 'the army candidate'.

Delouvrier wanted to arrest Ortiz, but Massu dissuaded him, aware of the effect it would have had on the Europeans. A 1,200-man 'shock' unit set up by 'Leather Nose' Thomazo, whose members slept with their weapons under their beds, was also left to its own devices. Massu was the key figure. He was trusted by the army and the *pieds-noirs*, but was also loyal to Paris and had Gaullist loyalties stretching back to the Free French days. However, he was finding it increasingly difficult to conceal his movement away from the man he had followed for two decades.

On 18 January 1960, Massu dropped a series of bombs in an interview with the West German newspaper *Süddeutsche Zeitung* – the journalist involved was a former paratrooper. It reported him as saying that part of the army regretted having called de Gaulle back to power, did not understand his policy and was disappointed that he had become 'a man of the Left'. Settlers were being encouraged to form paramilitary units which the military would arm, he added.

Massu was immediately summoned to Paris, where he was stripped of his responsibilities in Algeria and sidelined with a posting to Metz – the city in which de Gaulle had served in the late 1930s. The sentence was delivered by Pierre Guillaumat as Armed Forces Minister. It was not until 23 January that the President agreed to see his hitherto faithful follower. Aides in the adjoining room heard raised voices during their twenty-minute encounter; there was one report of a wristwatch being broken by a blow. When Massu left, the chief of de Gaulle's military staff made a sympathetic gesture to him, but the departing man brushed past him violently. According to his son-in-law, de Gaulle thought the whole affair had been whipped up by opponents of a settlement.

After leaving the presidential palace, Massu telephoned Argoud to reverse an order he had given his chief of staff the previous day to do nothing. Argoud, whose dislike for de Gaulle dated back to his days in the Vichy forces, needed no urging; he must have heard that the General referred to him as 'that little colonel, what's he called? *Ragoût* [stew]?' At a meeting at the Élysée on 22 January, the President told generals from Algeria they understood nothing, and were not carrying out his orders. When he asked the air force chief in North Africa, Edmond Jouhaud, if he was correct, the *pied-noir* general replied 'No, *mon Général*, you are not.'

A general strike was called in Algeria. Lagaillarde established armed positions in the university. Ortiz mobilised his shock force. On 24 January, police threw tear gas at the rebels behind their barricades. The ensuing gun battle killed fourteen members of the security forces and eight demonstrators. Some two hundred people were wounded. 'The hour has come to bring down the regime,' the ideologue Susini declared. 'The revolution will start from Algiers and reach Paris.'[13]

De Gaulle was at Colombey, but returned immediately to Paris after being informed of developments. Working late in his office at the Élysée, an official, Jacques Narbonne, suddenly found the General behind him. 'His arms were dangling and he seemed fairly demoralised,' Narbonne told the historian Michel Tauriac. 'I had never seen him like that.'

'My poor Narbonne, what a business! What a business!' the President said, looking completely dejected.

Narbonne urged him to see the crisis through.

'Yes, of course we have to hold on,' de Gaulle sighed. 'But we will always have to start over again.' Then he turned and walked back to his office. He was in an emotional mood for another reason: his brother Pierre had just been buried.

At a Cabinet meeting, he insisted that the challenge to the new Republic had to be put down. The question was whether to order the army to open fire on the rebels, which would show firmness but might further inflame the situation. Sudreau, Michelet and Buron were for tough measures. Malraux proposed dropping tear gas bombs on the rebels. 'And why not the atom bomb?' asked Soustelle who argued that the *pieds-noirs* had backed Lagaillarde and Ortiz out of desperation at being abandoned by France. As de Gaulle threw him a frosty look, the minister said it was awful to talk of using violence 'against French people who want to remain French'. There was no way he would back such a policy, he added. Instead, he proposed establishing contact with the leaders of the rising.

'You want to negotiate with the insurgents?' Malraux asked.

'We're negotiating with the FLN,' Soustelle shot back.

After de Gaulle had denounced the rebels as 'stupid and criminal', a decision was taken to replace the parachute division in Algiers, which was in sympathy with the rebels, with more reliable units, and for Debré to fly to Algiers with instructions to put down the revolt and punish those responsible. Arriving at 1 a.m. on 26 January, the Premier went into a meeting with the rebels at which Argoud told him that neither Europeans nor Muslims had confidence in de Gaulle. The General should reverse his support for self-determination, he added. If there was no change, the only outcome would be a junta of colonels. Leaving the room, Argoud's gesture to fellow officers outside signified that he had told the politicians from Paris where to get off. Challe took no part in the discussion. He seemed an ill, broken man, shot through with rheumatism, letting events take their course, in no physical or mental condition to stand up to his turbulent subordinates.[14]

In Paris, the President received his old comrade Marshal Juin, who had been brought up in North Africa and had boycotted the last Armistice Day celebrations to show his sympathy with the French Algerian cause. He said that de Gaulle did not have the right to order the rebels to be shot at. 'The right that I do not have is to allow the state to be humbled,' de Gaulle responded. Then he took his head in his hands and said in a bruised voice: 'Our tragedy is our age. I am an old man; I am going to die.' Pulling himself together, he shot out: 'I will not capitulate; I will not give in to the riot.'

Rumours flew of the creation of a shadow government by extremists in Paris. Members of the presidential military staff were told to carry handguns. A group of ministers made plans to move the government to Belgium if there was a military takeover in the capital. Summoning Massu's successor, General Jean Crépin, de Gaulle told him: 'The Europeans do not want the Arabs to make a choice [but] the Muslims do not want to be Bretons. If the army collapses, it is Algeria, it is France which collapse.' He instructed Delouvrier and Challe, who was wearing slippers because of a foot complaint, to move to an air force base outside Algiers, from where the Delegate General broadcast emotional appeals to the people of Algeria, the first time any official from Paris had spoken to the *pieds-noirs* in such language. He 'saluted' the rebels, and said they would mourn the dead together, adding a personal note that he had left his wife and children in the city, and asking them to look after his youngest son – 'I want him to grow up as a symbol of the unswerving attachment of Algeria to France.'[15]

After the initial shock, time was now working in the General's favour. Apart from freeing some prisoners from the city jail, the rebels did not know what to do. Despite Argoud's talk of a junta, the army did not live up to Ortiz's hopes. There was no support from the Muslims. The decisive moment came with a television address by de Gaulle on 29 January, the first of several occasions on which he used his rhetorical power to undermine a revolt across the sea. Wearing military uniform, he established a personal and historical link with his audience with his words 'Well, my dear and old country, here we are again facing a heavy test.'

Insisting that self-determination was the only way ahead, he called on the army to reject even passive association with the insurrection and instructed it to re-establish order. If the state bowed before the challenge it faced, 'France would be no more than a poor, broken toy floating on an ocean of uncertainty,' he warned.

Within fifteen minutes of his image fading from the television screen, forty army units in Algeria had declared their loyalty. Lagaillarde and his two hundred companions were persuaded to leave their stronghold; the leader was flown to prison in Paris, but his followers were allowed to enroll in a special unit in the regular army – 105 did so. Slipping out of town in disguise, Ortiz made his way to the Balearic Islands. For the first time in the long crisis over Algeria, Paris had gained the upper hand, greatly aided by the weakness of the extremists. The only dissenting voice in Cabinet was that of Soustelle who said that the barricades were a call for help from France by the settlers who felt abandoned. 'Are we going to reply to that call with repression?' he asked.[16]

*

According to Louis Terrenoire, who saw him the morning after the broadcast, de Gaulle's face was drawn, but he was resolute and full of energy. Delouvrier was confirmed in his post, although it had been offered to Sudreau, who turned it down. Challe was told he was being moved to a command in Germany. Soustelle was sacked at a two-minute meeting during which he regretted that he had not been able to remain until the twentieth anniversary of his joining the Free French. Another *Algérie française* politician, the former ambassador Bernard Cornut-Gentille, was dropped as Minister for Posts, Telegraphs and Telecommunications. Soustelle and Bidault were banned from Algeria. Guillaumat was replaced as Armed Forces Minister by Pierre Messmer, the veteran of Bir Hakeim who had been serving in Algeria as a volunteer. De Gaulle informed him of his appointment at a dawn meeting, telling him to go home and shut himself away 'because I now have to convince the Prime Minister'. Terrenoire became Information Minister.

By 441 votes to 75, the National Assembly granted the President the power to rule by decree for a year. Trade unions held a symbolic one-hour strike to back the government. A poll by the IFOP organisation gave the President a 75 per cent approval rating; only 17 per cent of those questioned opposed his conduct. There was a further boost when the country's first atom bomb test was conducted successfully in the Sahara on 13 February – 'Hurrah for France,' de Gaulle exclaimed. However, his Algerian policy was still a matter of a hope and a prayer – the hope that, if the Muslim majority was given the right to determine its future, it would not wish to separate itself completely from France, and the prayer that the army would remain loyal.[17]

V
At the end of his tether

In early March 1960, de Gaulle set out for a 'tour of the military canteens' in Algeria, his large frame visible in the perspex bubble of an Alouette helicopter as he flew around inspecting the progress of operations. He told the troops to 'crush the enemy' and 'push pacification to the end'. But his envoys, including Pompidou and Michelet, were working simultaneously to open a channel of negotiations with that same enemy. Progress was achingly slow. On his return to Paris, the President fell into one of his periodic moods of depression tinged with determination. 'I could fall,' he told General Ély: 'I do not like wearing glasses. Facing the sun, I see nothing . . . I am at the end of my tether . . . I see nothing any more. In Colombey I will go and walk in the forest. In the Élysée I am a prisoner. But I will not give up!'[18]

There was an apparent breakthrough when contact was established with one of the nationalist leaders in the field, Si Salah, which led to an extraordinary encounter on the night of 10 June 1960. Si Salah, together with his military and political advisers, was driven in secret to a side door of the Élysée and taken to the presidential office. The Algerians saluted de Gaulle; he responded with a gesture, but did not shake their hands. Bernard Tricot and a military aide sat on either side of de Gaulle. An aide-de-camp, who had stumbled on the scene by chance, stood behind the half-closed door with another officer, revolvers at the ready in case the visitors attacked their boss who had insisted that they should not be searched beforehand.

The meeting produced nothing of substance, but Si Salah said it had given him confidence in the French leader. De Gaulle hoped they could meet again. He did not shake the visitors' hands even as they left but looked forward to the day when he would be able to do so, once peace was restored. Walking down to the palace gardens on their way out, Tricot asked the Algerians if they were satisfied. Yes, they said, they had received 'a great guarantee'.

Four days later, de Gaulle recorded a broadcast in which he spoke of 'the transformation of Algerian Algeria into a prosperous, brotherly country'. In reply, the GPRA said it would send a delegation led by Ferhat Abbas to meet him. But the negotiating process ran into the ground. FLN hardliners disapproved of Si Salah's initiative and one of the delegates who had gone to the Élysée was liquidated. Si Salah himself was put under house arrest by the nationalists in September – and would die in action the following year. Talks for a proposed Abbas–de Gaulle meeting broke down, too, primarily because of continuing French reservations about recognising the FLN as the sole negotiating party and de Gaulle's insistence on an agreement to end the fighting as a preliminary to discussion. Debré's representative at the talks at Melun, outside Paris, refused to shake the Algerians' hands, and Terrenoire recorded that the other principal French negotiator 'did not seem to me very attached to the General's policy'.[19]

De Gaulle remarked at a press conference that 'one does not have talks unless one has left the knives in the cloakroom', while the FLN stepped up its activity and Abbas declared that 'independence is not offered; it has to be seized'. Under a new military commander, Houari Boumédiène, the nationalists increased attacks on settlers and the GPRA increased the pressure on France in international bodies. Lagaillarde was released by a military tribunal and, with Ortiz's sidekick Susini, went to plot in Spain.

In metropolitan France, the crisis was polarising society. Publications that dared to write about torture by the French army were censored; a book on the subject, *Gangrène*, was banned. Some opponents of the war began to assist the FLN. A manifesto by writers and professors declared that desertion was justified. Jean-Paul Sartre was among the signatories, and judicial proceedings approved by Debré were started for his arrest before de Gaulle leaned on the Chief Prosecutor to drop them, taking Malraux's advice that a prosecution would turn the philosopher into a latter-day Zola with his modern version of *J'accuse*. 'One does not imprison Voltaire,' the General added.

29

RAISING THE GAME

I
The summit that never was

While Algeria was his most dramatic continuing challenge, de Gaulle also had his eye on the international scene as he sought to give his country the global role he believed it deserved. For him, France's external status was intimately linked with the ability of its people to be at their best; when the country was run down, he thought the French divided into warring clans and became intolerant and jealous, but when it lived up to their expectations, they exhibited bravery, generosity, dash, curiosity, invention and an ability to deal with extreme challenges. In addition, great glory for the nation might help rally the people behind him in a way that would paper over the division on Algeria.[1]

As a starting point, he insisted that France must enjoy complete independence in decision-making and in deploying its resources as it aimed for a multipolar world in which it would be the third major player alongside the United States and Soviet Union. Despite tepid support in the opinion polls, he insisted on the development of the nuclear *force de frappe* which, while far smaller than the superpower arsenals, would deter an aggressor and thus eliminate any dependence on the US protective umbrella; it would be a badge of France's Great Power status, just as imperial possessions had been in his youth. He took pride in France's ability to repay debts to the US and Canada on the back of its economic revival. Having established himself as a critic of NATO's integrated military structure, he announced that France's fleet in the Mediterranean would act independently in case of war. Though adopting a stern line when the USSR put pressure on the West over Berlin, he pursued his wartime policy of seeking better relations with Moscow. In Western Europe, the General's aim was to ensure that Paris exercised political leadership, helped by the division of Germany and absence of Britain. Though he championed the nation state and rejected supranationality among the six Common Market nations, he recognised that the collaboration started by Jean Monnet and Robert Schuman could serve his purpose in strengthening Europe in the face of American power, and, after his meeting with Adenauer at Colombey in 1958, saw Franco-German cooperation as the key element.

There were serious questions in all this. However much its own defences developed, France, like other NATO countries, remained ultimately dependent on the American nuclear umbrella as a deterrent to the Soviet Union. The cost of building a *force de frappe* created a budgetary strain for Paris that could only be resolved by shifting spending from conventional forces, thus restricting its ability to project its power in limited conflicts. Among the Common Market Six, the Netherlands and Belgium had no wish to be led by France and preferred to promote a supranational system. West Germany did not want to alienate America, and did not share the General's opposition to Britain. But, for de Gaulle, such matters had little importance; France had to be made great again so that it could truly be France once more.

Establishing his position as a world leader, he invited Eisenhower to pay a state visit to Paris in the autumn of 1959; it was a friendly occasion but produced nothing of substance though the American President was amazed at the size of the crowds which greeted him. The following March, Nikita Khrushchev spent ten days in France during which de Gaulle announced with pride that France had carried out two more atomic explosions in the Sahara, only to get the reply from the Soviet leader: 'If France had a hundred thermo-nuclear bombs, we would not be worried. But if Germany had just one, that would change the world situation.'

The talks at Rambouillet produced no give on either side. Khrushchev warned that, if the Americans started a nuclear conflict, Moscow would destroy Western Europe and the United States. 'If the USSR and the USA start an atomic war, one already knows who would be the winner,' de Gaulle replied, 'China.' 'That's true,' Khrushchev responded.

'Monsieur K' summed up de Gaulle as 'one of the most intelligent statesmen in the world, at least among bourgeois leaders', while the General found the Russian a 'cunning, intelligent self-made man'. He emerged from the talks convinced that the Kremlin would not make war – the Soviet leader was 'too old and too fat', he told aides, adding his continuing belief that the Russians belonged with Europe. 'The Russian Communists are traitors to the white race,' Tournoux quoted him as saying in private. 'One day, they will line up again with Europe.'

There was a lighter moment when de Gaulle took his visitor out in a rowing boat on the lake in the park. The two men sat shoulder to shoulder, Debré opposite them while an aide-de-camp manned the oars. Khrushchev began to sing 'The Volga Boat Song' and de Gaulle joined in. As the boat returned to shore, the aide-de-camp made a mistake and the General nearly fell into the water, only regaining his balance by holding on to Khrushchev's neck.[2]

The talks opened the way for a four-power summit in Paris, a considerable feather in the General's diplomatic cap at a time of renewed tension over Berlin, where Moscow was trying to isolate the western half of the city marooned in the middle of its East German satellite. Ahead of the summit, de Gaulle made a visit to London that combined discussions on world affairs with ceremonial occasions in which he paid eloquent tribute to Britain's resistance during the Second World War and lauded the 'exceptional links of friendship and esteem' between the two nations. Later in the month, he flew to Canada, where he celebrated the country's historic association with France and expressed his belief in peaceful co-existence with the USSR, before going on to the United States.

Speaking to the National Press Club in Washington, he held out the prospect that the summit might bring progress on disarmament, the German question and aid to poor countries. He made a wide-ranging and well-received address to both houses of Congress where he again put the accent on disarmament, saying that, if there was no agreement, France would be obliged to develop a nuclear force and would be followed by others. Showing himself to the American public, he went on to New York, San Francisco and New Orleans before flying to France's Caribbean possessions.[3]

When the summit convened in Paris on 15 May 1960, de Gaulle could be content at the way he had enhanced France's international standing. Alone among the participants, he had held talks with the other three leaders. He had also presided over a preliminary meeting in the French capital bringing together Eisenhower, Macmillan and Adenauer – on Berlin, de Gaulle pleased the West Germans by taking a firm line in contrast to the greater readiness of the Americans and British to negotiate with Moscow.

But everything went wrong before there was time for any substantive discussions. Two weeks earlier, an American U2 spy plane piloted by Gary Powers had been shot down over the Soviet Union. The State Department said it was an ordinary aircraft which had gone astray, but Eisenhower was forced to admit the truth after Khrushchev produced photographs Powers had taken of military facilities. The affair undercut Khrushchev's decision to seek better relations with the United States based on his assessment of Eisenhower as a man with whom he could do business, and forced him to adopt a tough stance to protect his back from Soviet hardliners opposed to détente. He told de Gaulle he would only attend the conference if he received an apology and assurances that U2 flights would be stopped and those responsible punished. Eisenhower refused to comply. De Gaulle asked Khrushchev if he still wanted to go ahead with the meeting; he said he did, but read the General a lengthy statement demanding that America express regrets.

The four men, with their staffs, met in a large high-ceilinged chamber beside de Gaulle's office on the first floor of the Élysée overlooking the palace gardens. Khrushchev was accompanied by the glowering Defence Minister Marshal Malinovsky, who wore fifty-four rows of decorations, including the American Legion of Merit. The Western leaders shook hands, but Eisenhower refrained from doing so with Khrushchev. De Gaulle said he would ask the US President to speak first as the only other head of state present, but the Soviet leader insisted on reading out a statement. The General looked at Eisenhower, raising his eyebrows quizzically. The US President inclined his head, and the Russian was allowed to begin. His hands trembling with emotion, his voice rose steadily in volume as he denounced the Americans.

'The acoustics in this room are excellent,' the General broke in. 'We can all hear [Khrushchev]; there is no reason for him to raise his voice.' When the Soviet interpreter went pale and stumbled over his words, de Gaulle told his own interpreter to do the job. Khrushchev stopped, cast an angry look at the Frenchman over the top of his spectacles and continued in a quieter tone, speaking for forty-five minutes in all.

After he finished, de Gaulle observed that he, too, had been spied on from the sky.

'By your American allies?' Khrushchev asked.

'No,' the General replied. 'By you.'

Soviet satellites passed overhead eighteen times a day, he added, crossing his arms and looking down the table. They had taken photographs of the moon, he went on, so why should they not be doing the same with France? Khrushchev raised his palms above his head and exclaimed: 'God be my witness, my hands are clean. You do not believe I would do such a thing.' De Gaulle expressed his scepticism. Khrushchev became even more agitated; Eisenhower grew pink with anger; Macmillan was increasingly ill at ease. As for de Gaulle, he seemed to be bored by the whole thing.

Eventually, Eisenhower intervened, seeking to justify the U2 flights before saying he had ordered them to stop. Khrushchev continued to insist on an apology. De Gaulle took him to task for having agreed to come to the summit but then preventing any progress. Soon afterwards, the Soviet delegation walked out. The General went round the table to take Eisenhower by the arm, telling him: 'I want you to know that I will be with you to the end.' Getting into his car to drive back to the US embassy, Eisenhower turned to an aide and said: 'That de Gaulle, he is somebody.'

Macmillan, who was almost in tears according to several accounts, asked the other Western leaders to agree that he should visit the Soviet embassy to try to find a way out. When he did so that night, he got nowhere. De Gaulle arranged a fresh meeting at the Élysée the following morning, but Khrushchev did not appear, preferring to hold a press conference to denounce the United States once more. In response to an inquiry from the French President, he said he would not join the others until he had received the apology he sought. The summit collapsed. The climax to the General's Great Power diplomacy had been a fiasco but he had come out of it as a cool, collected leader who would not give in to bluster or be overwhelmed by the negative turn of events. The British ambassador, Gladwyn Jebb, told his wife he had appeared 'very calm, Olympian, slightly annoyed by Khrushchev's vulgarity'.[4]

II
'Why strive?'

De Gaulle also faced problems at home as big trade union demonstrations called for wage rises and the main farmers' association demanded a special parliamentary session to vote its members emergency aid; a majority of deputies favoured the request but de Gaulle turned it down on the grounds that he would not give in to a single interest group. A large minority of 207 deputies voted against the government on a censure motion, which was accepted by the Senate. On 1 October, supporters of French Algeria staged a demonstration at the Arc de Triomphe that included six members of the Académie-Française, among them Juin, as well as the rising rabble-rouser of the Right, Jean-Marie Le Pen, and the widows of Marshals Leclerc and de Lattre de Tassigny; de Gaulle reacted to the presence of the two ladies by quoting a verse from Thucydides to the effect that, while widows had both glory and sorrow, their glory would be all the greater if they were less noisy.[5]

Meanwhile, fourteen African countries declared their independence in line with the provisions extended to them by Paris. Among them were Senegal and Ivory Coast, whose leaders had been seen as epitomising the spread of French culture south of the Sahara. The General accepted this as inevitable, his rhetoric turning it into a victory for France in adopting decolonisation. But the regional community which he had envisaged perpetuating France's position in its former colonies proved considerably weaker than he had hoped. His critics on the Right accused him of having sold out the country's overseas birthright for no great advantage. Walking in the Élysée gardens one evening, he asked his aide, Flohic, if France did not seem to him to be 'a country which is finished'. 'So why strive to hold on?' he added.

As the year moved towards an end, he fell into fresh lamentations about his age, and compared the grind of trying to find a solution to the Algerian crisis with the 'uplifting' days in London during the war. When visitors wished him a happy birthday, he growled, 'Do you enjoy seeing me grow old?' He recited poems about nights filled with doubt and anguish. His great fear was that he would be unable to complete the task he had set himself, that he would lose control without realising it, and that nobody would dare to tell him. Then he reflected that a man, like a nation, was bound to go through times of hopelessness and 'the trait of a man of will is not to let himself be discouraged'. In keeping with that sentiment, it was time to spring back on Algeria.[6]

III
An Algerian republic

In a television address on 4 November 1960, de Gaulle spoke of an Algerian republic. The two words were not in the original text shown to Debré, but were inserted later by the General in front of the cameras. The Prime Minister was informed too late to stop it. When he protested, de Gaulle responded: 'Anyway, that's how it will end.'

Looking to 'an Algeria which will be emancipated, where responsibility will lie in the hands of Algerians', he told his audience on both sides of the Mediterranean that this Algeria would have its own government and laws. A group of *Algérie française* extremists set off fifteen explosive charges in a single night in Paris and drew up a plan to kidnap the President; word of the plot leaked to the police and it was abandoned.

A Ministry for Algeria was set up under the solid figure of Louis Joxe, the General's follower since 1943. Its task was to conduct negotiations, reporting to the Élysée and bypassing Matignon. Delouvrier left Algeria after being abused by settlers at the 11 November ceremonies; he was replaced by a prefect from France, Jean Morin, the man with whose handicapped daughter de Gaulle had sympathised in Toulouse the previous year. Exhausted and discouraged by the hostility he faced, General Crépin quit, too, and was succeeded by Fernand Gambiez, a small, bald, professorial-looking pioneer of parachute tactics.

In an interview with the newspaper editor from Oran, Pierre Laffont, the President said the reality was that everything separated the majority population of Algeria from the French. The Muslims wanted to govern themselves, and, as Chief of State, he had to build his policy on such facts. France could, of course, continue the war, he added, but that led nowhere given the way in which the Muslim population would increase in the next five or ten years. Not that his opinion of the FLN was any higher. 'Those men really think they are capable of ruling Algeria on their own,' he said. 'But Ferhat Abbas is incapable of doing so. Does he imagine that the one million French people will not react? It will be a bloodbath . . . Let them [the Muslims] die for all I care.' As for the *Algérie française* leaders, he dismissed them as 'the revenge of Pétainism'.

On 9 December, the President made his last visit to Algiers, accompanied by Joxe, Messmer, Terrenoire and General Ély. Avoiding the main urban *pied-noir* strongholds, he landed in the rain at a town in an agricultural region outside Oran, to be met by a hostile crowd. At the front were a group of Muslims. Flanked by his four bodyguards, the General walked towards the demonstrators. According to Terrenoire's account, the native group changed their shout from '*Algérie française*' to '*Vive de Gaulle*', but other reports have the crowd continuing to barrack him with shouting and whistling.

The trip coincided with fighting in Algiers between Europeans, Muslims and the police forces; the death toll reached one hundred. It also saw four separate assassination plots. One was by a pilot who planned to crash his single-seater plane into the General's helicopter but could not identify it from the surrounding aircraft. Another was to have been carried out by a member of the riot police who stood within a few yards of de Gaulle, but who was told by co-conspirators at the last moment to abandon the plan. A third was aborted when the lieutenant who was to have carried out the killing could not start his car and was then diverted by a clash between Muslims and men from his unit.

The other bid to kill de Gaulle was staged by a poor Jewish employee of a haulage company who, with a group of like-minded *pieds-noirs*, set up an ambush at the entrance of the town of Orléansville. The Israeli secret service, which had agents in the Jewish community in Algeria, tipped off the French. Once informed, Delegate General Morin begged de Gaulle to agree to change the route as they drove towards the town in an open-topped car. 'You don't have to ask me anything,' the General replied. 'You are the man responsible for the maintenance of order. You decide.' Morin shouted an instruction to the driver, and the convoy turned off along a mountain road, avoiding the main entrance to Orléansville and arriving safely at the prefecture where yet more hostile crowds were awaiting them. De Gaulle's doctors were alarmed when they found traces of blood where he had been sitting in his car; subsequent tests showed that it was a digestive haemorrhage, but his medical staff were happy to get him home. In the aeroplane, he told Terrenoire that an arrangement with the FLN had to be worked out. 'Laboriously we are moving towards the solution,' he said at the next Cabinet meeting.

Events were forcing his hand, but he had to appear to be on top of them. As he had told Laffont, a leader must never admit that a solution had been imposed on him – 'One must never say that one is beaten, because, if one says so, one is. One decides on solutions, one chooses them, one decides them. They are not imposed on one.'[7]

30

THE CRUCIBLE

I
Talks, putsch and terror

By the nature of their jobs, all government leaders face tests on different fronts at the same time. From 1958 to 1960, de Gaulle had juggled with constitutional change, economic policy, international relations and Algeria. In the following two years, the scale and scope of the challenges he faced ratcheted up in a manner quite enough to submerge a man entering his seventies. The major themes overlapped in an intricate pattern and the way in which he orchestrated his policies to make himself the sole master of the game was an object lesson in political tactics, even if eventual outcomes were less positive than he might have hoped. Having won back power in 1958, it was in 1961–2 that the Constable truly came into his own, setting patterns that persist to this day.

When the proposal for self-determination for Algeria was put to a referendum on 8 January 1961, 75 per cent of those who voted were in favour. At 23.5 per cent, the abstention rate was higher than in previous ballots, giving the General the support of 56 per cent of the total registered electorate. The issue was more divisive than the foundation of the new Republic, and a significant section of the electorate may have preferred not to give backing to either self-determination or *Algérie française.* The proposal had the support of most of the mainstream political parties, though Communist opposition to the regime meant that the PCF refused to come out for a 'yes' vote despite its calls for independence. In Algeria, 42 per cent of voters stayed away from the polls in line with an FLN instruction; 40 per cent said 'yes' and 18 per cent 'no'.

Building on the result, de Gaulle dispatched Pompidou and an accomplished diplomat, Bruno de Leusse, to meet GPRA representatives secretly in Switzerland in February. The nationalists saw the fact that de Gaulle had sent his trusted former aide as a positive sign. But there were major differences, and Pompidou reacted to a diatribe against French rule by one of the Algerians by remaining silent for three minutes before de Leusse interjected with a pleasantry to get the conversation going again. The French maintained their insistence that a ceasefire had to precede full negotiations, and that other Algerian groups had to be included in the peace process. De Gaulle warned that, if the talks broke down, Paris would establish a separate zone for the *pieds-noirs* and retain its military bases; in private he spoke of it as a 'French Israel'. There were also disagreements about the status of the Sahara. Still, both sides wanted to talk, so agreement was reached to open full negotiations on 7 April in the Alpine city of Évian, which the Algerians would be able to reach easily and safely from nearby Geneva.[1]

For the diehards across the sea, the January referendum brought the harsh realisation that a majority of their compatriots in metropolitan France was ready to let them go. Their reaction was to fall back on violence. An extremist group, the *Organisation de l'Armée Secrète* (OAS) (Secret Army Organisation), was set up to hit back at the FLN and its sympathisers. Antoine Argoud, the fervently pro-*Algérie française* officer, and Joseph Broizat, another colonel who had been on Massu's staff, plotted a putsch. They had already been to see their former chief to try to persuade him to join them; he did not agree but said he would meet them again. Meanwhile, the recently retired *pied-noir* general Edmond Jouhaud contacted army chiefs in Algeria who he thought might be sympathetic.

The conspiracy was joined by Salan, who had left the army after being humiliated following his removal from Algeria. He had initially gone back to live in North Africa, nurturing links with Ortiz's group, but then got into trouble with the government by issuing a statement to a meeting of Indochina veterans in which he argued that 'it is not within the power of any authority to decide on the relinquishing of a part of the territory where France exercises sovereignty'. He was banned from

Algeria. In response, he held a press conference in Paris at which he denounced de Gaulle and offered himself as leader of *Algérie française.* He then took a train to south-west France, and was driven by taxi to Spain where he enjoyed the help of Franco's brother-in-law, Serrano Suñer, and conferred with Lagaillarde and Susini.

Argoud and Broizat won over several officers in metropolitan France in a series of meetings, some in the military school in Paris where de Gaulle had once lectured. But they wanted a figurehead with stars on his kepi. Salan did not inspire confidence. As an airman, Jouhaud was not known to the soldiers. Another supportive general, André Zeller, was a dim figure. So they went back to see Massu in January. He asked them whether they would kill de Gaulle if they had the opportunity. 'Without hesitation,' they replied. Massu looked at them without saying anything, which they took to be a good sign. At a further meeting in March, he told them that what they were planning was mad.[2]

Maurice Challe, Salan's successor as commander in Algeria, who had been moved to a European command after the week of the barricades, had retired from the army on 1 January, an unhappy man who thought he had been badly done by. This made him the general the colonels were seeking. Seeing Argoud and Broizat on 30 March, he said he would join them so long as he could be the boss and decide when action would be taken.

The conspirators' resolve was hardened by a press conference de Gaulle gave on 11 April at which he advanced dry economic reasons for leaving Algeria which 'costs us more than it brings us'. As for the prospect of the United States or the Soviet Union taking France's place in North Africa, he remarked, 'I wish them the best of luck.' The plotters found his 'shopkeeper's approach' shocking.

Most of them gathered in Algiers on 20 April, though Argoud was not present. The following evening, the police and army headquarters in the city were informed of unusual movements by paratroopers. Driving out to the road leading into the city, the commander, General Gambiez, saw a column of lorries carrying paratroopers in camouflage uniforms. He ordered them to stop; they took no notice. When he got back to the centre of the city, Gambiez was arrested by the insurgents together with the Delegate General, Jean Morin, and the Minister of

Public Works, Robert Buron, who had just arrived to open a technical college. By dawn, the rebels controlled the city's main administrative buildings.

De Gaulle had been host to the visiting President Senghor of Senegal at the Comédie-Française as the plotters swung into action; extremists had thought of planting a bomb in his box at the theatre, but were unable to put their scheme into practice. So the General returned to the Élysée unscathed, and was awakened at 2.30 a.m. with news of events in Algeria. He gave instructions that Joxe, as Minister for Algeria, should fly immediately across the Mediterranean with the new armed forces chief of staff, General Olié. When the minister went to the presidential palace for instructions as to what to do when he got to Algeria, de Gaulle appeared in yellow pyjamas and said simply '*Au revoir, Joxe.*' From Washington, Kennedy offered any help that was needed. The suggestion annoyed the General, who did not think he required assistance and regarded the putsch as an entirely internal matter. But it showed how wide of the mark the putschists were in hoping for American backing, a forlorn prospect apparently based on Challe's links with NATO commanders.

At a Cabinet session that afternoon, the President was dismissive of the putsch – 'You know what is grave in this affair?' he said. 'That it is not serious.' When Malraux and Frey spoke of mobilising civilians in defence of the Republic, he smiled. Two weeks later, de Gaulle told Reynaud that what characterised the rebels was their foolishness. All the same, French troops were ordered to move from bases in West Germany to defend Paris, and the President assumed emergency powers under Article 16 of the constitution. As he had done during the wartime crisis over Admiral Muselier in London, he drew up his political will and gave it to his doctor, telling him to hand it back the following Wednesday if, as he expected, the rebels had collapsed by then.

Salan flew from Spain to Algiers with his ideological sidekick, Susini. Argoud also arrived, though the generals shunted him off to Oran to stop him interfering with their show. Challe, who did not get on with Salan, broadcast an appeal but only to the army. The putchists made no attempt to rouse the civilian European population, which made it all the easier to depict them as a group of disgruntled old soldiers and deprived them of the street support seen in the week of the barricades. This annoyed the *pied-noir* Jouhaud and created a further rift with Salan. That was not the only problem for the rebels. Some key units refused to join them, including the army corps in Oran. Most senior officers waited to see what would happen. The navy remained loyal to Paris, and the air force flew planes back to France to keep them safe. The plotters had no cash reserves to draw on. In metropolitan France, there was broad condemnation, and almost all the press was hostile.

The decisive moment came at 8 p.m. on 23 April, when de Gaulle, in military uniform, deployed his rhetorical powers in one of his finest performances. As in the past, he used the drama of events to conjure up a moment of high theatre that united him and the nation. He was overwhelming, a man speaking from another sphere on prime-time television and radio. His words, his cadences, his gestures and his expression swatted the rebels aside as he spoke for France, his fists laid on the desk in front of him, 'like Colts', as Jean Lacouture noted.

'An insurrectional power has set up in Algeria on the basis of a military pronunciamiento,' he said. 'This power has a face: a quartet of retired generals. It also has a reality: a group of partisan, ambitious and frenetic officers. This group and this quartet have an immediate and limited savoir-faire. But they only see and understand the world as deformed by their frenzy. Their undertaking leads straight to a national disaster.' Everything that had been achieved since 1958 would be put at risk, the President warned. He followed this with an order that everything – 'I repeat everything' – must be done to stop them, and added: 'I forbid every French person and, first of all, every soldier, to carry out any of their orders.'

The General's language merits a moment's pause in this narrative. As so often with de Gaulle, translation is inadequate. The word I have rendered as 'quartet' – *quarteron* – is more pejorative than when applied to a group of four, particularly when delivered with all the disdain de Gaulle could muster. The retired status of the generals added to this. The opening 'pronunciamiento' relegated the putsch to the level of a Latin American comic opera. The 'partisan, ambitious and frenetic officers' put the colonels in their place. The order to 'every French person' established the link between the sovereign and the people to come together for the sake of the nation, consecrating de Gaulle's role as the embodiment of France.

Officers in Algeria who had been waiting to see what would happen rallied to the regime. The conscripts did likewise – the way in which they listened to de Gaulle's speech on their transistor radios was an important element in this. Debré dramatised the situation by appearing on television at midnight asking people to go to airports to prevent paratroopers from Algeria landing. Chaban-Delmas told de Gaulle that, if he was Challe, he would have already sent troops to Paris. 'Yes,' the General replied, 'Fidel Castro would be here, but not Challe.'

The courtyard of the Interior Ministry, close to the Élysée, was filled with an excited crowd of politicians, civil servants, journalists, actors, young people who had crossed the Seine from Saint-Germain-des-Prés – and a priest in his cassock wearing a police cap. Malraux joined them briefly, his forelock even more askew than usual. A group of Communists demanded to be given weapons. Inside the ministry, officials kept an open telephone line to radar stations on the Mediterranean coast for news of any planes flying north from Algeria. Hearing the din across the road in the presidential palace, de Gaulle dismissed the demonstration as a masquerade. No invasion force materialised. When two journalists drove out to Orly to see how many people had followed the Prime Minister's exhortation, they found themselves alone. An instruction from the Interior Ministry that refuse trucks should be parked on the runways to stop planes landing was not carried out because it had not been delivered in the proper written form.

In Algiers, loyalist forces which took the radio station broadcast an announcement that order and legality would be restored. When Salan and his three co-conspirators appeared on the balcony overlooking the Place du Forum, government agents cut off the electricity, and they could not make themselves heard. Zeller changed into civilian clothes and fled. The paratroopers marched back to their base camp singing Édith Piaf's '*Je ne regrette rien*'. Challe gave himself up; so did Zeller a few days later. Salan and Jouhaud fled in a truck to a military camp and went underground.

Having won, de Gaulle cracked down with a vengeance. A special military tribunal was created outside the justice system in keeping with the

General's growing exasperation at what he saw as the failure of courts to serve the Republic adequately. It sentenced Challe and Zeller each to fifteen years' imprisonment. Suspect groups were dissolved and their members arrested. There was a purge in the army. Left-wing critics suffered, too – *L'Humanité* was seized. Polls showed 84 per cent backing for the General and 78 per cent in favour of the opening of negotiations with the FLN. The political way ahead was now clear, but it would only be completed amid the bullets and bombs of assassins.[3]

*

After a number of delays, the Évian talks opened on 20 May 1961. Joxe headed the French delegation, working in close collaboration with Tricot from the Élysée. The GPRA delegation travelled each day by helicopter from Switzerland for the sessions at the Park Hotel beside Lake Geneva. It was led by Belkacem Krim, who had fought in the French army during the Second World War and joined the Algerian underground in 1946, rising to command one of the main base areas before becoming the GPRA's Foreign Minister. He was ill-shaven and spoke in halting French.[4]

On the eve of the talks, the OAS launched a wave of terror in Algeria, which took more than a hundred lives, almost all Muslim, on the single day of 19 May. The Secret Army also assassinated the Mayor of Évian to express its opposition to the talks being held in his city. For its part, the nationalist Army of Liberation slayed eleven gendarmes in an ambush in the *bled* while fourteen Muslims in the French forces killed four soldiers and four co-religionists before deserting. This pattern of talks and extremist violence would last for more than a year as the growing futility of its campaign spurred the OAS into ever more desperate terror.

The Secret Army, which enjoyed inside information from accomplices in the administration on both sides of the Mediterranean, brought together a familiar cast, with Salan and Jouhaud as its figureheads. The former, who appeared on an OAS poster in his three-star general's uniform with an enormous display of medals on his chest, dodged between hiding places, while the latter shaved his hair and grew a moustache. The ultra colonels joined the terrorists along with Susini and Dr Pérez, the orator from poor white Algiers. The most dangerous figure was Roger Degueldre, a charismatic, strongly built former paratroop lieutenant with a hatchet face and small, bright eyes. Lying about his nationality to get into the Foreign Legion, he had fought with distinction in Indochina where he was wounded at Dien Bien Phu; Massu presented him with the Medal for Valour for his exploits. Alienated by French policy, Degueldre deserted in 1960 and built up a five-hundred-man 'Delta Commando' force made up of small operational units which included other deserters. They were well armed, determined and had no respect for human life. A sympathiser let them use his luxury villa in a suburb of Algiers as their headquarters.

Degueldre began his trail of terror with the fatal stabbing of a liberal lawyer in his office. Then two Delta commandos tracked down a senior police officer and killed him with a paratroop dagger. Degueldre and his men had extensive contacts in the administration as was shown when they were tipped off about an impending raid on their villa after police had been told of their presence by a civil servant who lived nearby. They escaped in time, and some returned a few days later to shoot the official dead.

The OAS turned the poor white district of Bab-el-Oued in Algiers into a virtual no-go area for the police and regular army. For funds it had cash stolen from government safes during the putsch, and demanded 'contributions' from the European population, fining those who defied its order not to go to France on holiday. Its gunmen raided banks, building up a sizeable treasury that disappeared mysteriously when the organisation was finally destroyed. Extending its operations to metropolitan France, it set off a plastic explosives charge that derailed a passenger train running between Strasbourg and Paris, killing eighteen and injuring seventy.

The political aims of the terrorists ranged far and wide. Salan envisaged an apartheid-style society on South African lines. Susini saw the OAS acting like the Jewish Haganah paramilitary force in Palestine; it would somehow gain the backing of Muslims and eventually spread its rule to France. Pérez presented the fight in Algeria as the last struggle of white Christianity. Degueldre told a fellow OAS member: 'Only violence will make us heard. The generals and colonels didn't want it . . .

They failed. That proves they were wrong. Now, one must strike. Blow for blow. Unleash war on the authorities. Kill the traitors. It's the only solution remaining to us.'[5]

II
Kennedy, Britain and Europe

This unfolding of the drama in Algeria coincided with de Gaulle's involvement on another of the stages on which France's greatest star performed at this period. In May 1961, President Kennedy made a high-profile visit to Paris which brought out huge crowds and included a particularly glitzy reception in the Hall of Mirrors at Versailles. Eisenhower had told his successor that the General's attitude jeopardised the Western alliance, but Kennedy liked the French leader's strong resistance to Soviet efforts to put pressure on West Berlin, particularly during the crisis over the building of the wall dividing the city in 1961. He also approved of his support for self-determination in Algeria, calling him 'a great captain of the western world'.

The French-speaking First Lady, Jacqueline Kennedy, was a great hit, and the General fell for her charm. Greeting the couple at the airport, he made the unusual gesture of speaking in English, asking, 'Have you made a good aerial voyage?' At a banquet, he praised Kennedy's energy, drive, intelligence and courage. Matching the charm offensive, Kennedy quoted passages from de Gaulle's memoirs and presented him with a letter George Washington had sent to Lafayette.

Both men could draw political capital from the trip – Kennedy by demonstrating his popularity in Europe after the failed US-backed attempt to invade Cuba at the Bay of Pigs the previous month, and de Gaulle by showing that, despite Franco-American differences, he could still act as the elder statesman to the young President. However, the visit produced little of substance; Kennedy called in at Paris on his way to a more important meeting with Khrushchev in Vienna. The final communiqué was 'even more laconic and useless than is customary,' wrote the *New York Times* columnist Cyrus Sulzberger, though he added that the two men had agreed implicitly that 'Paris would be treated by Washington on the same degree of intimacy as London'.

The Americans refused to help France develop a missile delivery system for its nuclear weapons, and Kennedy was not swayed by his host's warning that Indochina would be 'a bottomless military and political quagmire'; he simply asked de Gaulle not to state this openly. If they agreed on the need to stand up to the USSR over Berlin and the use of US troops to keep open the road to the western part of the city, de Gaulle took a harder line than Kennedy, rejecting the idea of talks with the Soviets. While he thought Khrushchev would not dare to go to war, he wanted to head off any entente between Washington and Moscow that might isolate France. They were also at loggerheads over the US-backed United Nations intervention in the Congo, which was falling apart after Belgium's withdrawal from its former colony; de Gaulle refused to contribute soldiers or money to this, and, at a press conference, denounced the UN for 'its global incoherence'.

Despite all his warm words in public, the General considered Kennedy a novice. For his part, Kennedy thought that the older man cared only for the 'selfish' interests of France and, echoing Churchill's wartime feelings, concluded that he 'seemed to prefer tension instead of intimacy in his relations with the United States as a matter of pride and independence'. 'Rather quickly, the Kennedy administration reached a point where we simply did not care what de Gaulle thought except on those matters over which he had a veto,' the Secretary of State, Dean Rusk,* recalled. 'We learned to proceed without him.' When he again visited Europe in 1963, Kennedy did not go to France.[6]

*

On his third stage, Europe, de Gaulle fought not only the threat of America asserting influence through its 'Trojan Horse' across the Channel but also any increase in the powers of the Common Market Commission, headed by the German Walter Hallstein, whom he saw as seeking to erect a counter-power in Brussels that would undermine French national sovereignty. He was dismissive of France's partners.

*Rusk made an unusual comparison in his memoirs where he wrote that talking to J. Edgar Hoover was 'like talking to de Gaulle, he was untouchable' (Rusk, p. 492).

Speaking to Rusk, he said his own country was 'the heart and soul of European culture' and dismissed Belgium, the Netherlands, Luxembourg and Italy contemptuously. West Germany's economic power had to be respected, he acknowledged, 'but Germany must be kept in its place'. As for the British, they were not Europeans. In similar vein, Jean-Raymond Tournoux recorded him as dismissing Belgium with 'Two provinces do not make a nation' and West Germany as 'a country that does not know where it is going' – and the vassal of Washington.[7]

His approach ran into the determined opposition of two formidable figures, Paul-Henri Spaak of Belgium and Josef Luns of the Netherlands. The first had been a central figure in the construction of Europe since the end of the war, presiding over the Assembly of the Coal and Steel Community in 1952–3 and drawing up the report which formed the basis of the Common Market; he was a strong defender of the Brussels Commission, declaring at one point, 'The Europe of tomorrow must be a supranational Europe.' The Dutchman, who referred to himself to journalists as 'the Wizard of the Hague' and had a taste for red socks, wanted to prevent France and Germany dominating Europe; an Atlanticist, he served as his country's Foreign Minister from 1952 to 1971. One of the rare statesmen tall enough literally to look de Gaulle in the eye, he was known for his refusal to be cowed by the French. On one occasion, Couve de Murville found him and a British negotiator conversing over drinks before a dinner in Brussels. With what he may have thought passed for humour, the Frenchman remarked that the Dutch had always been 'lackeys' of the British. 'Yes,' Luns replied,' I suppose you could say that in the sense that you could talk of you French as always having been the raw material of their victories.'[8]

On 31 July 1961, Britain announced that it was applying for Common Market membership. Now that the Six had made a clear success of their enterprise, the Macmillan government wanted to be part of it. The European Free Trade Association (EFTA), which the United Kingdom had joined after shunning the Treaty of Rome, had brought limited results, and was clearly inferior to the Brussels-based grouping. Britain's economy needed a shot in the arm; 1960 had brought the worst balance of payments deficit for a decade, and there was a sterling crisis the following year. Washington was keen on the idea of London becoming the leader of an Atlanticist Europe. Though Hugh Gaitskell of the opposition Labour Party warned of 'the end of a thousand years of history' and spoke emotionally of ties with the Commonwealth, Macmillan claimed a wider vision of strengthening the West and contributing to world peace at a time of recurrent crises with Moscow.[9]

The British move could only reawaken all de Gaulle's old suspicions of the island. In a broadcast and a press conference, he noted that the UK had 'very special and very original' traditions and added that its trading system was 'obviously incompatible with the Six'. If it joined, he foresaw that 'a colossal Atlantic community would emerge under American dependence and control which would soon swallow up the European community'.

Given attitudes among France's partners, he could not reject the bid to start talks, so he launched a flanking movement. His long-time associate Christian Fouchet, who presided over an intergovernmental European commission, proposed the creation of a Union of States which would welcome new members ready to accept the same responsibilities as the Six. This union would forge common foreign and defence policies, but would be run by heads of state or government, and decisions would have to be unanimous. The Dutch and Belgians refused to support the idea pending the outcome of British entry talks that opened in September. The West Germans watched nervously from the sidelines.[10]

III
'How clumsy!'

In Évian, the discussions on Algeria soon identified two break points: the future of the million square kilometres of the Sahara, where France wanted to safeguard its oil and nuclear testing rights, and the status of the *pieds-noirs* after independence. The differences were large enough to lead de Gaulle to order a suspension of negotiations, and to threaten again that, if there was no progress, France might opt for a territorial division. Matters were complicated by a confrontation with Tunisia, whose President, Habib Bourguiba, had acted as a go-between with the FLN.

Expecting something in return, he asserted his country's right to land around the big French base at Bizerta, which contained oil deposits. On 5 July, he demanded that France pull its troops out of the base. Thirteen days later, Tunisian forces tried to occupy the zone. Paris sent in paratroopers, killing more than seven hundred Tunisians.

Despite this, Franco-Algerian talks resumed on 20 July in a château near Évian, but saw no significant progress. De Gaulle fell into a protracted bad temper – not only was his Algerian initiative going badly but he was facing labour problems in France. There was tension with Debré who did not relish being kept out of the negotiations. Flohic found his chief 'emptied'. The General told Joxe that he feared physical collapse, adding, 'There are two solutions: my resignation or my death.'

The FLN was also going through a difficult phase, which led to a reorganisation in which Ferhat Abbas, seen as the leading proponent of negotiations, was replaced by the more radical Ben Youssef Ben Khedda. Belkacem Krim had to argue hard to justify continuing talks with the French. The FLN military commander Houari Boumédiène, a proponent of the hard-line approach, gained in strength. But, despite this, neither side was ready to break off the talks, and de Gaulle indicated a readiness to be more flexible on the Sahara. He also sought to calm domestic criticism of his authoritarian ways by announcing an end to the special powers under Article 16, opening the way for the National Assembly to resume its legislative role.[11]

On 7 September 1961, Bidault wrote the briefest of notes to OAS colleagues. It read simply 'With confidence'. The following night, de Gaulle left Paris for Colombey at eight o'clock with his wife in a black Citroën DS 21, accompanied by three escort vehicles. An aide-de-camp, Colonel Teissère, was in the front passenger seat. An hour and a half later, as the convoy was driving at 110 kilometres an hour through Pont-de-Seine, near Nogent-sur-Seine, a huge sheet of flame from a gas container exploded across the road. The car was propelled to the left. The driver, a policeman called Francis Marroux, put his foot down and took the car clear, stopping five hundred metres further on.

'How clumsy!' the President growled as he got out. Assured that the rest of the convoy was unharmed, he instructed his aide-de-camp: '*Teissère, en route.*' When Terrenoire later congratulated him on his escape, he replied, 'Obviously a human being notes with relief what he has escaped from, but from a historic point of view, perhaps it would have been worth more than dying in bed or by accident. It is also true that the political consequences would have been weighty and that, from the point of view of the public interest, it was better that this attempt failed.'

A binoculars case was found at the scene, and the man who had set off the blast was caught with the glasses. He gave the names of two OAS members; one was arrested, the other escaped. The organiser was identified by his codename, 'Germain', but could not be tracked down. Despite his sangfroid, the General went along with a suggestion that henceforth he should travel between Paris and Colombey by air, taking off from and landing at military bases.[12]

The latest assassination attempt made de Gaulle even more anxious to see progress in the negotiations on Algeria, but the FLN decided it was time to put on a show of strength in Paris where 30,000 members of the Algerian community in the capital were mobilised to demonstrate on its behalf in October 1961. The police, under the control of the wartime collaborator Maurice Papon, reacted savagely. The screams of tortured Algerians were heard by people living next to commissariats. Bodies bearing the marks of severe beatings were fished from the Seine. The total number killed has not been established but some reports put it at a hundred or more while an expert investigation came up with a figure of between thirty and fifty. When Buron and Sudreau raised the subject of police brutality in Cabinet, de Gaulle spoke of policemen wanting revenge for colleagues killed by the FLN and of their exasperation at delays by the courts in convicting Algerian terrorists. Putting their numbers at 400,000, he added that the presence of Algerian workers in France would have to be re-examined after a settlement. He exploded to Peyrefitte about the pain withdrawal from Algeria would cause to 'me who was brought up in the religion of the flag, of French Algeria, of the army as guarantor of the empire'.[13]

He also had to face the fact that the OAS was not going to go away. In an interview with the American news agency UPI, published on 3 November 1961, Soustelle, who was living in self-exile, called it 'the expression of the resistance of the people who do not wish to die'. A group of deputies, including the one-time Poujadist and paratrooper Jean-Marie Le Pen, put down a motion in the National Assembly for its recognition as a legal organisation; though this failed to be passed, the audience cheered Salan's name at a rally in Paris addressed by Bidault, Lacoste and Lejeune. The following month, the General's former Foreign Minister announced plans to form a new organisation. Using the same name as the wartime *Conseil National de la Résistance* (National Council of the Resistance – CNR), it appointed Salan its commander-in-chief to conduct 'the fight against the abandonment of Algeria, Gaullist dictatorship and international Communism'. Bidault assumed overall leadership, Argoud took charge of operations in metropolitan France and Soustelle of activities elsewhere.

IV
Endgame

As the British team negotiating entry into the Common Market, led by the Lord Privy Seal, Edward Heath, worked its way through meetings in Brussels and more than fifty visits to Common Market capitals, de Gaulle travelled to Macmillan's country home at Birch Grove in East Sussex in November 1961. The General had suggested the location, in an apparent effort to create a relaxed atmosphere for a discussion of Britain's Common Market bid. He was on his best behaviour. Heath found him 'quietly spoken, reserved' though bearing 'the marks of the heavy burden he carried and the decisions he had to take'. Heavy security in the grounds led the gamekeeper to complain that the pheasants were being disturbed; there were also difficulties over the stock of blood that travelled everywhere with the General – since there was no room for it in the refrigerator, which was stuffed with food, a special cold store had to be installed in the house's squash court.

Despite the polite nature of the meeting, de Gaulle maintained his basic belief that UK entry would change the way the Common Market operated in ways unacceptable to France. That conviction could only be strengthened by the way in which the British sought to safeguard trading relationship with Commonwealth countries and appeared unready to accept the farm policies planned by the Six which de Gaulle regarded as essential for the modernisation of French agriculture. After dinner at Birch Grove, the General took Heath aside and asked him: 'What is all this about? Is it serious or a game?' The Lord Privy Seal replied that Britain was serious. 'And the Empire and the Commonwealth?' de Gaulle asked. Heath tried to explain that he hoped the former British and French colonies would be able to work together more effectively, but de Gaulle said he remained 'puzzled about it all'.[14]

Back in Paris, the President lamented the state of his nation. At a Cabinet meeting on 19 December 1961, he said France was 'ill; it is still ill from the events of 1940; it is ill from Vichy; it is ill from Algeria, ill from communism, ill from political parties that are no more than clubs that do not know how to raise themselves above themselves'. There was a growing feeling, as expressed by Pinay to American diplomats, that the General had no clear policy on Algeria. On his provincial visits, the crowds were less friendly than in the past. Military tribunals set up to try rebel soldiers were under attack for their summary nature. Some senior officers who had resisted the putsch were troubled by what was happening. 'I chose discipline but I feel the shame of abandonment,' General de Pouilly, who had withstood Argoud's solicitation during the putsch, told the judges at Challe's trial.[15]

Information extracted under torture from a Secret Army courier who had been picked up in the autumn enabled the authorities to smash parts of the network and arrest Degueldre's number two. But virtual civil war gripped Algiers, with OAS assassins slaughtering policemen and the security forces blowing up six cafés known to be haunts of the extremists. Night life closed down. Cinemas were deserted. Fear of bombs, bullets and knives kept people at home. Despite an appeal by the Delegate General for police reinforcements, the OAS and FLN were left to fight it out between themselves.

This led a former radio producer called Lucien Bitterlin to recruit undercover operatives known as *barbouzes* (false beards). Some of them were borderline legal, but, with their local contacts, they gathered a good deal of information, and became a target for Degueldre who led two dozen members of his commando to attack their headquarters on New Year's Eve as the *barbouzes* celebrated inside. The building was demolished with rockets and machine-gun fire, but only one occupant was killed. A month later, however, an OAS booby trap set in a crate delivered to the new headquarters of Bitterlin's men killed nineteen. It was time for the 'false beards' to be disbanded while the campaign against the Secret Army was taken over by a more professional force.[16]

A hundred experienced policemen under Michel Haq, Director of the Criminal Police, moved into Algeria and, drawing on information gathered by the *barbouzes,* made six hundred arrests. As twenty-five of Bitterlin's men waited in a hotel to be taken to metropolitan France, the Deltas struck, staging a siege that lasted for two days; the lack of local police intervention showed how unreliable, or frightened, they were. When four *barbouzes* managed to get into a car to take a wounded comrade to hospital, it was shot up and crashed into a wall. Civilians surrounded the vehicle, prevented the men inside from getting out and set fire to it, burning them alive.

In Paris, an OAS bomb attack on the Quai d'Orsay in January caused one death and eleven injuries. Prominent journalists, including Hubert Beuve-Méry of *Le Monde,* Françoise Giroux of *L'Express* and the Gaullist Michel Droit, were targets, though none was hurt. Another bomb aimed at Malraux's flat blinded the five-year-old daughter of a friend of his. At Gaullist headquarters at 5 rue de Solférino, members of the *Service d'Action Civique* (Civic Action Service) strongarm force kept watch through the night, sleeping on army cots with their revolvers, automatic pistols and an American M1 carbine.[17]

On 8 February 10,000 demonstrators attended a rally at the Bastille to denounce the Secret Army. Strong police forces, deployed by Papon, waded into the crowd with heavy truncheons, driving some down the staircase of the Charonne Métro station, where the gates had been closed. Nine people, including three women and a young child, were crushed to death. The government blamed 'Communist provocation' but a document found subsequently in OAS files spoke of a group of thirty of its men being sent in to cause trouble, some with truncheons. 'The outcome is known,' the document added. 'Cost of this operation: 90,000 francs.' The funeral of the victims saw a mass turnout against both the brutality of Gaullist repression and OAS terror. The General remained unmoved; he did not mention Charonne in his memoirs. He wanted to hush up the whole matter to avoid further controversy that might impede his plans. While recognising that a judicial investigation could not be avoided, he said it should not have immediate consequences, blaming the tragedy on 'a certain trade union and Christian set', meaning the CGT and left-wing religious groups that opposed torture.[18]

On 10 February Robert Buron, the MRP Minister for Public Works who had been detained during the putsch in Algiers, left his office by a side door, wrapping a scarf round his spade beard and putting on an unaccustomed hat in an attempt at disguise. His wife drove him in the family 4CV car to the motorway south of Paris. Near Orly airport, he was picked up by two police inspectors in a Peugeot 404 which headed south-east to the subprefecture of Chalon-sur-Saône, where he was lodged. The next day, his police guards took him eastwards towards the Alps. On the way, they were passed by a DS with a pair of skis on the roof, as if its occupants were off for a spot of winter sports. Inside the Citroën were Joxe and Jean de Broglie, a prominent independent conservative who had taken over from Lejeune as Secretary of State for the Sahara.

The three ministers finished their journey at a mountain chalet, Le Yéti, where talks resumed with the FLN. The chalet's isolation was inconvenient for the Algerians, who still went to sleep in Switzerland, but was regarded as offering safety from an OAS attack. Hoping for a quick breakthrough, de Gaulle told the negotiators not to dwell on details and to be flexible – 'there is the possible and the impossible,' he advised. Compromises were reached after he insisted on a speedy resolution, even though this meant concessions on the French side over the Sahara and military bases. On 19 February, the two delegations agreed on a text and, for the first time, shook hands.[19]

A Cabinet meeting two days later heard a lengthy report from Joxe. The President asked everybody round the table to give their opinion. There were only three discordant voices: Pierre Guillaumat, the former Armed Forces Minister who was now Minister Delegate to Debré; Raymond Triboulet, the ex-serviceman minister who was close to the Prime Minister; and the sole representative of the Muslim community, Nafissa Sid Cara, Deputy Minister for Social Affairs, who spoke with tears in her eyes of the fate awaiting Muslims who had not rallied to the

FLN. De Gaulle asked her if she did not think that the great majority of Muslims were in favour of independence. Couve de Murville forecast that an independent Algeria would become a revolutionary, totalitarian regime with which cooperation would be difficult, but he remained a partisan of self-determination. Malraux said that the independence of Algeria would represent a certain form of liberation for France – 'There lies the true victory, the victory in depth,' he declared in typically lyrical terms. 'Today is not Dien Bien Phu.'

Then it was Debré's turn. The tightly wound Prime Minister, whose sympathy for French Algeria was known and who had been excluded from negotiations, said Malraux's use of the word 'victory' surprised him; he understood it as meaning 'a victory over ourselves'. He spoke at length about how his hopes that Algeria would be led to political maturity by France had been undermined by the division between the communities, the revolt of the Muslim world and external forces. Everybody should remember, he concluded, de Gaulle's belief that what came first was France. The President ended the session by saying that, though an outcome had been reached, 'an outcome is always only a beginning'. It had been indispensable in getting France out of a situation which had brought it so many ills. France had to move fast and inflict the rigours of the law on those who continued to rebel against the state.[20]

On 7 March, the French and Algerian delegations met for what was meant to be a short final meeting in the Hôtel du Parc at Évian. However, plenty of differences remained, and tense discussions dragged on while the OAS staged more than a hundred operations, including the burning of Oran prison and the killing of six European and Muslim leaders at a social centre. Finally, on 18 March, a French official appeared at a hotel window and waved a handkerchief to signal to a reporter from *Le Monde* that an accord had at last been reached. Debré made his reservations known to the General in writing; de Gaulle replied that the ninety-three-page agreement was not perfect, but that there was no going back at this stage. At eight o'clock that night, he went on television to announce 'the good-sense solution' to conclude a ceasefire in Algeria, which was to take effect in twenty-four hours.[21]

The Évian agreement provided for Algerians to vote on 1 July in answer to a single question asking if they wanted their country to become an independent state cooperating with France on conditions laid down in the accord. The French in Algeria would be able to have dual nationality for three years and would be represented in Algerian assemblies. French people wanting to leave Algeria could take their assets or the proceeds of the sale of their belongings with them. In the Sahara, French companies would enjoy preferential treatment in the allocation of energy licences. France would keep a renewable fifteen-year lease on its naval and air base at Mers-el-Kébir, and retain a military position in the Sahara for five years, as well as three airfields on Algerian territory. Algeria would remain in the franc currency zone, and Paris undertook to maintain its financial aid at the existing level.

Ahmed Ben Bella and his imprisoned companions were freed, and flown to Switzerland. A moderate FLN figure, Abderrahmane Farès, who had been held in a French jail partly for his own safety, was also released and took the chair of the Provisional Authority, which would oversee the application of the agreement in Algeria and which included three Europeans alongside five FLN representatives. International reaction was highly positive. Congratulations arrived from Kennedy, Macmillan and Franco – and from the singer Josephine Baker, who was living in the Dordogne.

The OAS response came on 20 March when two Foreign Legion deserters fired four mortar shells into a Muslim crowd in Bab-el-Oued, killing twenty-four and injuring sixty-nine. The Secret Army declared the suburb an 'insurrectional zone' prohibited to 'the occupation forces' – that is to say the French army. Six soldiers were killed and nineteen wounded when they refused to allow themselves to be disarmed. The ensuing battle led to twenty-seven more deaths, mostly civilians but also seven soldiers. Eighty people were wounded. When he heard the news, de Gaulle told Joxe the OAS must be crushed. 'There must be no let-up. All methods must be used. We have to attack. We have to impose our will.' Security forces surrounded Bab-el-Oued.

The OAS called on the European population to march from the war memorial in the centre of Algiers to Bab-el-Oued. At 3 p.m. on 26 March, as the unarmed crowd surged down the big thoroughfare of the rue d'Isly, shots broke out. Nobody knew where they originated, though it could have been from an army unit posted along the route which consisted mainly of Muslims who had come over to the French side. Forty-six Europeans died and 121 were injured. It was just the kind of event the Secret Army dreamed of, for it enabled it to blame the Gaullist authorities and to win over doubters among the *pieds-noirs.* De Gaulle noted that the response of the forces of order had been inevitable. In the following days, thirty-four Muslims were killed in the 'Arab hunt' in the suburbs of Algiers; native maids stopped going to work in European districts for fear of being massacred in the street.

On the night of the shooting on the rue d'Isly, de Gaulle announced the holding of a referendum in metropolitan France to approve the agreement reached at Évian. That would settle the Algerian problem for France, he told the government. Then in typically Sibylline terms, he added: 'Now other problems present themselves to the head of state. He has responsibility towards himself, towards the government and towards parliament. Today I will not tell you yet what response I intend to give to myself.'[22]

On 7 April, the day before the referendum in metropolitan France, Degueldre was arrested following information given to the police by a captured Foreign Legion deserter. Pérez and four others hid behind a false wall when the squad arrived, but the Delta chief did not conceal himself, apparently believing in his invulnerability. He was taken to France for trial, sentenced to death and executed.

The referendum gave 90 per cent backing to the Évian agreement. At 24.4 per cent, the abstention rate was swelled both by people who were uncomfortable with the outcome but did not want to cast a ballot that might encourage the OAS and by those on the Left who could not oppose independence but objected to the General's use of referendums as a means of rallying support. De Gaulle had gone through many contortions since arousing the crowd in the Place du Forum with his 'I have understood you' speech. From the start, he had understood the difficulty France would have in holding on to Algeria. For a time, he had hoped for military victory and a compromise solution. But the first proved beyond the army's grasp and the second was always a chimera given the FLN's attitude and the absence of a 'third force'. Then the generals' putsch and, more important, the OAS, had added a further deadly element. While foreseeing a sombre future for an independent Algeria, he had grown increasingly exasperated with the *pieds-noirs*; having started by calling them 'imbeciles', he now insisted that they were 'not French. They do not think like us.' Then he thundered that they were 'all accomplices of the OAS'.

It is difficult to see de Gaulle's handling of the crisis as anything more than the manoeuvres of an extremely skilled politician operating on his own with a mixture of guile and ruthlessness to find an escape route from the challenge that had brought down a republic. According to Malraux, he dated the start of his break with the French people to the early months of 1962 – the way in which Algeria forced him to descend from his Olympian perch to enter the political arena sowed the seeds of a divorce that would become reality half a dozen years later. But he saved France from civil war. As Reynaud judged, the Algerian crisis 'did not end in favourable conditions, but in the only conditions that were possible'.[23]

V
Changing the guard

De Gaulle opened the first Cabinet meeting after voters had approved the Évian accord by asking Debré to speak. The Prime Minister read out his resignation. Terrenoire's notes report that he had tears in his eyes. In a letter, the President paid tribute to the way in which he had shouldered 'an extremely heavy task' for three and a half years, but agreed it was time for him to take his leave.[24]

The choice of his successor said much about how the President saw the Premier's job. Georges Pompidou had none of the Resistance credentials of other Gaullist veterans. He had never run for any kind of election. He was chosen for his managerial skills, and because de Gaulle valued his ability to handle domestic and economic affairs. From now on, the Prime Minister would be akin to a chief of staff, able to accommodate the changing humours of his boss, anticipating his needs and ensuring that the machinery of government functioned smoothly. The President told the Information Minister, Alain Peyrefitte, with whom he had regular conversations after Cabinet meetings, never to refer to Pompidou as the head of the government – that was the General's role. The Premier was the first among ministers, no more than that.

*

The son of schoolteachers from the village of Montboudif in the Auvergne, Pompidou had been brought up in the south-western cathedral town of Albi before working his way through some of France's best educational establishments to become a teacher, too. Having joined de Gaulle's staff in 1944, he headed the General's private office during the RPF era, also looking after the finances of the charitable foundation established in memory of Anne while pursuing his career at the Rothschild bank. He presented an unusually strange mixture of calculation and conviviality; the top of his face, with hooded eyes, denoted the first while the bottom, with fleshy cheeks and a gourmet's mouth, suggested the second, accentuated by the cigarette seemingly pasted to his lower lip, the smoke obliging him to screw up his left eye and giving him a quizzical look. His work at the bank supported a comfortable, worldly way of life, with a Porsche, holidays at Saint- Tropez, a country house outside the capital and a flat overlooking the Seine on the Île Saint-Louis in Paris where he and his tall, elegant wife, Claude, entertained artists, writers, musicians and fashion designers. As Prime Minister, he made a point of spending his weekends away from Matignon, noting that, in the First World War, Marshal Joffre slept a lot and won the battle of the Marne as a result. But fellow ministers remarked that, when he left for his country home on Saturdays, his car was packed with dossiers.

In his memoirs, the General described Pompidou as a man who looked at things from a practical, prudent point of view; that is, an ideal lieutenant who would provide ballast for the President's lofty ambitions. Pompidou saw himself as a transitional figure. After taking office, he told Peyrefitte that he would be a 'reflection' of de Gaulle. 'I have no political life of my own, no voters, no clientèle,' he went on. 'I don't even have any ideas of my own in political matters. I have only the General's ideas.' Still, there were echoes in him of the ambitious Radical

Socialists of the Third Republic who had 'mounted' to Paris from the faraway provinces to achieve power and wealth. He was in no hurry but his ambition would grow over the years. Though he read his first speech to the National Assembly from a text and was ill at ease, Mitterrand detected 'an unusual force' in the enigmatic figure who stepped from the shadows at the General's behest.[25]

To extend the government's support, Pompidou got the General to appoint five MRP ministers, including the Free French spokesman Maurice Schumann and the former Premier, Pierre Pflimlin. The rising star of the independent conservatives, Valéry Giscard d'Estaing, who had been promoted as Finance Minister at the beginning of the year, joined Pompidou in pressing for economic modernisation that sought to develop companies which could compete internationally. But the wily Edgar Faure turned down the job of Education Minister, fearing trouble ahead as the end of the war in Algeria freed the parties to oppose the General, and Europe became a new battlefield.

VI
Europe

In April 1962, nine days after the referendum on Algeria, talks on the Fouchet Plan for Europe collapsed at a meeting of foreign ministers in Paris. De Gaulle put this down to the 'negativism' of Luns and Spaak, and wavering by Italy. At a Cabinet meeting, Couve de Murville said France would blame the breakdown on the British and 'make them pay in blocking their membership of the Common Market'. At a press conference in the Élysée on 15 May, de Gaulle launched a major attack on the European front. The continent, he insisted, must be founded on nation-states. Anything else was a matter of 'myths, fictions and show'. Political integration would lead to American domination. Indeed, he added, this might be the goal of some of his opponents.

In the middle of his peroration, he referred to the national languages of the great classical authors of Europe being replaced by 'Esperanto or Volapük', the latter word a term invented for a mixture of English and German by a nineteenth-century writer. It was a typically brilliant soundbite, fishing a forgotten reference from his enormous memory, with the requisite menacing overtones. Headlines reproduced it and television viewers watching the evening news as they ate their supper in the Berry or the Gers could only wonder what sinister-sounding force was about to be launched upon them.

Pierre Pflimlin, who had attended the press conference, left with his face burning 'almost violet' at the General's attacks on European integration, according to Peyrefitte. That evening, 'Little Plum' met the four other MRP ministers. They decided that they had to resign. Pflimlin telephoned Pompidou with the news; the Prime Minister was privately annoyed that de Gaulle had not told him what he was going to say about Europe, believing that he could have suggested language that would not have so offended the Christian Democrats.

On the telephone to Pflimlin after midnight, de Gaulle minimised the weight of what he had said, his voice soft, almost supplicating. He asked the five MRP representatives to attend a Cabinet meeting later that day. They declined; there was a subtext to this – under the constitution, the deadline for ministers to hand over their parliamentary seats to their substitutes fell the following day. The General asked Pflimlin to come alone to the Élysée at 9 a.m. The former Premier set his alarm clock wrongly and arrived thirty minutes late. De Gaulle told him the resignations were 'excessive'. Pflimlin said there was no going back. As the President accompanied him to the door, Pflimlin said he hoped he still ranked in de Gaulle's esteem. All he got in return was '*Au revoir*', delivered in a strange, high-pitched voice as they shook hands. At the next Cabinet session, the General accused the MRP ministers of 'abandoning' their positions, hammering home the word to make clear he meant this in the sense of a soldier deserting.[26]

There was also trouble over Europe from the independent conservatives, most of whose deputies withdrew their backing from the administration, leaving a rump group of loyalists led by Giscard d'Estaing under the name of Independent Republicans. Nearly three hundred deputies, a clear majority of the Assembly, put their names to a declaration critical of the administration's Common Market policies. But there was no give from de Gaulle when he played weekend host to Macmillan in June at the château of Champs-sur-Marne, east of Paris, which the General favoured for meetings with foreign leaders because it was a cheaper venue than other state residences in the region.

What Edward Heath called the Dance of the Seven Veils over British entry was not going well; there was deadlock on the issue of preferential tariffs for Commonwealth countries, and de Gaulle spied a broader British plot. 'Having been unable, from outside, to prevent the Community from being born, they now planned to paralyse it from within,' he wrote in his memoirs, perpetuating the distrust of Britain he had felt since his boyhood shock at the Fashoda Incident of 1898. His suspicions of British–American links were heightened when Kennedy and his Defense Secretary, Robert McNamara, described France's nuclear policy as 'unfriendly' and stressed the interdependence of the alliance. As the General said at a press conference, he wanted to see Europe built 'beyond the United States'. Instead, Kennedy proposed a multilateral military force (MLF) based on a united Europe – but with continuing US control of nuclear arms. The idea found support in West Germany and non-Gaullist Europe, but was plainly unacceptable to Paris.

Such factors suggest that de Gaulle was never going to agree to British membership given the gulf between him and basic positions taken by the Macmillan government. He was helped by the mind-numbing details of the Brussels negotiations that enabled the French team to spin out the talks and bog them down in minutiae while the British were reluctant to confront him head-on by forming a united front with the Dutch and Belgians and supporters in West Germany. A tougher, starker – more Gaullist – approach from London could have put the President on the spot. But the UK allowed de Gaulle to rule the roost, and counted on his goodwill. Once again, his opponents made life easier for him than it might have been. With his popularity among the French riding high at 70 per cent, he had only to hold on and wait till the moment was ripe to pounce.[27]

*

The approval of the Évian accord was followed by the capture of Salan who had dyed his hair and moustache. But the killing went on across the Mediterranean. The FLN attacked bars which had been used by Secret Army personnel, killing seventeen people and injuring thirty-five. The remnants of the OAS hit back with the usual ferocity, claiming fifty-six Muslim lives and injuring thirty-five in a single day in May. The European extremists then embarked on a campaign to destroy all they could, burning schools, hospitals, buildings at the University of Algiers, the city's town hall and the oil refinery in Oran. In their final paroxysm, they wanted to take Algeria back to the condition in which it had been before the French arrived in 1830. Finally, even the surviving ultra leaders in Algeria had had enough. In mid-June, Susini reached a ceasefire agreement with the provisional authority set up by the peace agreement, and the exodus of *pieds-noirs* began to grow.

Even then, the extremist 'Resistance Committee' in exile did not give up. It condemned de Gaulle to death for high treason. There were rumours of an air attack on Colombey that led to the banning of any flights within a twenty-kilometre radius. A fighter aircraft at a nearby base was kept on permanent alert. An anti-aircraft battery was placed around La Boisserie – one of de Gaulle's grandchildren noticed a gun when walking in the woods with the General whose poor eyesight meant that he had not seen it. De Gaulle instructed that the artillery should be concealed with bales of straw.

Then there was the matter of the two generals who had sided with the OAS. The *pied-noir* Jouhaud was sentenced to death but, at a subsequent hearing, his superior, Salan, was given life imprisonment thanks to a brilliant defence by Jean-Louis Tixier-Vignancour, a one-time Vichyite and far right-wing deputy. De Gaulle saw the Salan verdict as a slap in the face, and an example of cowardice by the judiciary – or connivance with his enemies. His fury led him to send a note to Pompidou and the Justice Minister, Jean Foyer, demanding legislation to facilitate action against those responsible for crimes against state security. Publications that were thought to side with the OAS, including the daily newspaper *L'Aurore*, should be banned and there should be provision for the forced retirement of magistrates on the grounds of age, the seventy-one-year-old President added.

He also insisted that Jouhaud's execution should go ahead. Pompidou and Foyer, who ignored the call for new legislation, argued that this was impossible. They pointed out that Jouhaud had been Salan's subordinate in the Secret Army, and had tried several times to limit attacks on Algerians. He had not signed orders that led to massacres, and was generally regarded as a political child – de Gaulle had called him a fool. But the General would not budge. When Pompidou said that, as head of the government, he would not allow the execution, de Gaulle told him 'So you will have to go.' The Premier replied 'I am ready', adding that four of his ministers would also resign. On the Friday before the execution, as Jouhaud waited in his best blue suit, defence lawyers came up with a clever legal ploy, which Foyer accepted. De Gaulle spent an extremely bad-tempered weekend at Colombey, seeing himself as standing alone while everybody else betrayed France.

Jouhaud complicated things by writing a statement calling on the remnant OAS to give up its struggle. De Gaulle was advised that its publication would be valuable in bringing greater calm to Algeria. 'So be it,' he replied. The execution was postponed. Joining Challe and Zeller in prison, Jouhaud was said to have remarked, 'I am coming back from a long journey.' But it took the President five months to sign the clemency document.[28]

*

On 1 July, the Évian settlement received 99.72 per cent backing in a referendum in Algeria. Two days later, France recognised the new independent state. The struggle had been so long and savage that it was bound to leave a bitter heritage. The new regime in Algeria was dominated by hardliners under Ben Bella. It limited citizenship to the Muslim population, and allowed killings of Europeans which, in the Oran region alone, were put at five to six thousand. At a Cabinet meeting in the spring, de Gaulle had been asked whether French army units which remained in bases in Algeria would protect the *pieds-noirs*. 'There is no question of that,' he replied dryly. 'After self-determination, the maintenance of public order will be for the Algerian government, and no longer for us. The French will have to get on with this government . . . Napoleon said, "In love the only victory is flight." In decolonisation, the only victory is to leave', though he added, 'We may be asked to return.'

He was not keen on the idea of a wave of *pieds-noirs* moving to metropolitan France, suggesting to ministers that they might be directed to the overseas territories of French Guiana or New Caledonia. But in the end a million crossed the Mediterranean, choosing the 'suitcase' for fear of ending up in the 'coffin', their plight aggravated by the way in which, despite the Évian accord, they were only allowed two cases each for their belongings while their homes and assets were requisitioned. Most went to southern France. The iconic Foreign Legion base at Sidi-Bel-Abbès was abandoned, and the troops transferred to a headquarters outside Marseille. Some OAS members who had gained a taste for illegal enrichment established underworld gangs in France, carrying out, among other raids, a major bank robbery in Nice.

Some departing Europeans were comfortably off, but many were poor and disoriented in their new surroundings, forming a pool of anti-Gaullist discontent, particularly in cities along the Mediterranean coast. Two decades later, they would be an important electoral base for the far right National Front led by the pro-*Algérie française* demagogue Jean-Marie Le Pen, playing to sentiment directed against North African workers who continued to be a mainstay of cheap labour in France despite de Gaulle's remark about re-examining their position once a settlement was reached.

Much more perilous was the outlook for Muslims who had worked with the French, in particular, members of the *harki* militia. At Évian, the French had accepted FLN undertakings that there would be no reprisals, motivated by a desire not to let the fate of the *harkis* stand in the way of an agreement. The only way to protect them would have been mass emigration to metropolitan France, but a proposal to this effect was rejected by a committee presided over by de Gaulle. The slaughter of the *harkis* began as soon as Algeria achieved independence. How many died remains uncertain – an inquiry by Jean Lacouture for *Le Monde* in late 1962 came out with the figure of 10,000; other sources speak of 30,000 to 80,000. There was a 150,000 gap between the number of *harkis* registered before independence and those who reached France.

The Algerian government sent some of them, with their children aged over twelve, to the border with Tunisia to explode mines planted there by the French, killing themselves in the process. In other cases, men were reported to have been boiled alive or emasculated. Those *harkis* who managed to get out of Algeria found themselves crammed into unsanitary camps in Provence, treated by the French state as the detritus of a struggle people wanted to forget. To this day, they agitate for proper recognition of their past services but Paris, mindful of relations with Algiers, prefers to ignore them, just as the majority of French people prefer to forget about the long, poisonous struggle across the Mediterranean.[29]

31

FULL HOUSE

I

'This time, it was close'

On 22 August 1962, after a Cabinet meeting, de Gaulle left Paris by road for the airbase at Villacoublay to fly to Colombey. His wife was with him as was his son-in-law, Alain de Boissieu, who, with the aide-de-camp Gaston de Bonneval, decided to take the route through the suburb of Clamart. A dozen would-be assassins were waiting there, under the command of the mysterious organiser of the first assassination attempt at Pont-de-Seine the previous September.

Jean-Baptiste Bastien-Thiry was another disillusioned colonel. His soldier father had been posted to Metz when the General served there before the Second World War, and the son had gone to the same Jesuit school as Philippe de Gaulle. An intense personality and an ardent Catholic, Bastien-Thiry had gathered together a group of killers, including several Foreign Legion deserters. Three were Hungarians who had fled after the crushing of the 1956 rising in Budapest. By one account, they had planned seventeen attempts to kill de Gaulle. In one, they chased a presidential convoy through Paris and were about to open fire on de Gaulle's car when the driver of a Renault 4CV, which was alongside, saw an opening between the two cars and, with typical Parisian bravura, surged forward and unknowingly blocked the line of fire. Neither de Gaulle, nor his wife, nor any member of the security guard realised what had almost happened.

The assassination squad at Petit-Clamart, in three cars with a van as back-up, was armed with sub-machine guns and explosives. It remains a mystery as to how they knew the route the General was following; most probably they had a man watching the exit from the Élysée who tracked the direction taken. At 8.08 p.m., as light rain fell, the presidential Citroën and its escort vehicle, accompanied by two police motorcyclists, appeared driving towards the crossroads known as Petit-Clamart. Bastien-Thiry signalled to his men with a copy of the right-wing newspaper *L'Aurore* and they opened fire. De Boissieu told the driver, Francis Marroux, who had been at the wheel at Pont-de-Seine, to accelerate and turned to suggest that his parents-in-law put their heads down. On their left, he saw another Citroën parked at the side of the road; its windows were rolled down and two gunmen were pointing machine-gun pistols at the presidential car. 'Father, get down!' he shouted. De Gaulle later commended his son-in-law for having the right voice to give orders at important moments.

As the presidential car came under a hail of bullets, a Panhard saloon appeared, containing a family unconnected with the attack. With two tyres burst and the gearbox smashed, its interior sprayed with broken glass, de Gaulle's vehicle managed to get over the crossroads. Stinking of burnt rubber and swaying 'like a motor canoe at sea' as de Boissieu put it, it managed to get to Villacoublay, the General and his wife sitting upright in the back, covered with shards of glass. The President suffered minor cuts to his hand and left traces of blood when he ran his fingers over his collar. At the base, he reviewed the guard of honour as if nothing had happened. As he did so, his son-in-law checked his back for wounds. There was no blood. The General's only comment before boarding the plane was 'This time, it was close.' Madame de Gaulle exhibited just as much sangfroid as her husband. 'Don't forget the chicken,' she said; 'I hope it is all right' – reminding her son-in-law about packets of chicken she had placed in the boot of the car for lunch the following day. This somewhat surprised the security men present: the word '*poulets*' ('chickens') is slang for policemen.

Subsequent examination showed that the presidential DS had been hit by fourteen bullets, several of which must have passed within a few centimetres of the heads of the de Gaulles. In all, 187 shell cases were found in the street. The only person hurt, apart from scratches to the

General, was the driver of the Panhard who was slightly wounded on one hand – and, indirectly, the head of the police detachment for Colombey who died of a heart attack after going into a frenzy of activity to ensure the General's safe transport from the nearby air base to La Boisserie. Telephoning Pompidou after he reached his country home, de Gaulle said, 'My dear friend, those people shoot like pigs.' As he ate his soup at dinner that night, he kept grunting 'Damned gunmen!' Writing for posterity in his memoirs, he concluded a paragraph on the attack with the words 'So let de Gaulle continue his course and his vocation.'

As he watched the television news report on the assassination attempt, Bastien-Thiry remarked to his wife, 'Petit-Clamart, that's me'. He made no attempt to escape; to have done so would have been to diverge from the path he had decided to follow. De Gaulle was, to his mind, a devil incarnate and he was doing his Christian, patriotic duty. He compared himself to Claus von Stauffenberg, who had tried to kill Hitler. Calmly, he undertook an air force mission to Britain before being tracked down and arrested, appearing before a military tribunal at the beginning of 1963. His legal team included Jacques Isorni, from the Pétain trial, and Jean-Louis Tixier-Vignancour. Bastien-Thiry, who had a record of depression but was declared to be of sound mind by psychiatrists before the trial, argued that the President deserved death for the 'genocide' of the *pieds-noirs*, but claimed, improbably, that he had wanted to capture him alive to hand him over for trial.

Bastien-Thiry was sentenced to death, as were five of his companions, three in their absence as they fled France. The other got life imprisonment. De Gaulle commuted the executions of the two who had been in court, but refused clemency to the ringleader. According to de Boissieu, he had four reasons: the would-be assassins had fired at an innocent woman, his wife; Bastien-Thiry had put at risk the lives of the family in the Panhard; he had involved foreigners in the attack; and he had kept back from the front line himself, leaving it to others to do the shooting and to expose themselves to police counter-fire. On 11 March, Bastien-Thiry was driven to execution by a firing squad in the fort at Ivry-sur-Seine; security mounted to prevent an escape bid involved two thousand police. He refused to be blindfolded and died holding his rosary. De Gaulle said that he could be made into a martyr and 'he deserves it'. The following day, a letter reached the Élysée from Bastien-Thiry's father asking for his son's life to be spared.[1]

II
'No time to lose'

In *Le Monde,* Hubert Beuve-Méry expressed the hope that de Gaulle would build on the national emotion provoked by the Petit-Clamart attack to bring together supporters and critics to ensure the survival of the Republic. The President saw things differently. The regime had been, both literally and metaphorically, at the crossroads and for him it was now time for a major alteration to the constitution. The election of the head of state by a college of 60,000 people, including legislators and local representatives as laid down in the 1958 constitution, was too close to the way the Senate was chosen for his liking. The use of referendums had given him a taste for the direct link with the French people he had always sought.

'Frenchmen, Frenchwomen, it is to me that you are going to reply. This matter is between each of you and myself,' he said in his broadcast address before the 1961 ballot on Algeria. In June the following year, speaking to the nation from a studio set up for the occasion in the Élysée in which he sat at a reproduction Louis XV desk in front of a partition painted to look like a bookcase, he said that, when the right time came, a system of popular voting would be introduced to ensure that the Fifth Republic remained 'strong, well-ordered and continuous'. After the withdrawal of the MRP ministers from the government, he remarked to Peyrefitte that the system needed to be changed to minimise the importance of political parties further and to give the head of state legitimacy stemming directly from the sovereign people.[2]

There was also the question of what would have happened if Bastien-Thiry had succeeded. Since de Gaulle rejected the idea of creating a vice-presidency, the regime was an inverted pyramid depending on one man. What if he suddenly disappeared? His successor would not enjoy his historical stature, and would need explicit backing from the nation if he was to prevent a return to parliamentarianism. Mortality was crowding in. 'There's no time to lose,' he told the Cabinet. 'Perhaps I have only two months to live.' After the meeting, he remarked to Peyrefitte that Petit-Clamart had taken place at just the right moment.

The election of the President by the entire adult population was the way to ensure that the Republic would remain strong 'beyond the men who come and go', de Gaulle decided. The change should be brought about by a direct vote in a referendum, bypassing parliament, he determined. This was almost certainly unconstitutional, but he was not going to allow the legislature to become involved in his latest grand scheme.[3]

While he allowed his plans to mature, he paid a triumphant visit to West Germany during which he went to Ingolstadt, where he had been held as a prisoner of war in 1916. He made speeches in German, and vaunted his hosts as 'a great people', though, in typically caustic manner, he told aides 'It's not true. If the Germans were a great people, they would not acclaim me in such a manner.' Unaware of this, the weekly magazine *Der Spiegel* commented that he had 'arrived in Bonn as President of the French; he leaves as Emperor of Europe'.[4]

On 19 September, the General initiated a round-table discussion with ministers about constitutional reform. It was a fitting time to consider the question of how France could assure itself of strong leadership. The recent memory of the violence the regime faced had been reinforced by the sentencing to death, the previous day, of a leading OAS figure, André Canal, who was close to Salan and had headed the terrorist operations in metropolitan France. Another trial condemned Secret Army agents in western France. Internationally, there were crises, too: in the Congo and Yemen, East–West incidents in Berlin, tension between the United States and Cuba, clashes on the Chinese–Indian border and rows at the United Nations.

Only one member of the Cabinet, Pierre Sudreau, who was now Education Minister, came out in full opposition to the proposal for election of the head of state by universal suffrage. He considered the way the change was being introduced to be dangerous because it might instigate a period of constitutional instability. He also feared that the referendum campaign would turn de Gaulle into a divisive force. 'I thank you, *Monsieur le Ministre de l'Éducation nationale*,' de Gaulle replied, and then, in the face of this one-man revolt, sighed: 'How difficult it is to achieve unanimity.' Sudreau resigned, though he held back the announcement for several months.

The next day, the General went on television to announce a referendum on the change, to be introduced at the end of his term in 1965. The protests stretched from the Communists to the far right. Coty was indignant. Mollet warned of dictatorship and civil war. Reynaud accused de Gaulle of violating the constitution and insisted that 'France is here in parliament and nowhere else'. Trade unions were hostile. Eminent jurists were critical. Most of the press was with the critics, *Le Monde* foreseeing a crisis of the regime if the General did not bend. The President of the Senate, Gaston Monnerville, the second-ranking figure in the state, invited the National Assembly to vote a censure motion of 'what I call treachery [*forfaiture*]'. A majority of deputies adopted a censure motion in the National Assembly on 5 October, forcing Pompidou to submit the resignation of the government.[5]

In his memoirs, de Gaulle depicted all this as 'the clash of two republics, that of yesterday whose hopes of being born again lurked behind the rancours of its partisans, and that of today which I incarnate and which I would strive to prolong tomorrow'. Showing his disdain, he spent the day of the censure motion at a military exercise and did not receive Pompidou until late the following morning when he asked the Prime Minister to stay on. He then dissolved parliament pending elections in November. Before doing so, he called in the presidents of the two houses of the legislature, spending what he recalled as a 'cordial' thirty minutes with Chaban-Delmas. The session with Monnerville was very different.

Though aimed at Pompidou, the Senate President's 'betrayal' jibe had caused de Gaulle the gravest offence. The black French Guiana-born politician, who, like Pinay, annoyed de Gaulle by referring to him as '*Monsieur le Président*' rather than '*mon Général*', believed in the supremacy of the legislature. He also thought the President was a racist who was prejudiced against him. In unpublished notes cited by the biographer Éric Roussel he reported de Gaulle as remarking to Madame Monnerville about the Norman wife of President Senghor of Senegal, 'I don't understand a white woman marrying a coloured man.' Roussel comments that, given de Gaulle's habitual courtesy and gallantry, this seems unlikely. Receiving Monnerville at the Élysée, de Gaulle said the constitution obliged him to have the meeting. His guest replied that he thought the dissolution was correct after the censure motion, but believed a new prime minister should be named. '*Monsieur le Président du Sénat,* I thank you,' the General responded. That was all. The encounter lasted a mere two minutes and ended without a handshake. It was the last time Monnerville entered the presidential palace while de Gaulle was in office.

When the referendum campaign opened on 15 October, the President raised the stakes by going on television to say that he would step down if there was a weak 'yes' vote. In private, he spoke of the possibility of defeat as France 'went back to its little kitchen', but then declared to aides, 'I'll get them. I'll stick it up their arses.' Rejecting a final attempt by Sudreau to get him to change his mind, he told the resigning minister: 'Nobody after me will have the nerve to do what I am doing.'[6]

In the midst of the campaign, the General's attention was diverted abroad when the Cuban missile crisis erupted with its dramatic reminder of the very real dangers of the Cold War turning hot. Kennedy sent Dean Acheson, the grand old man of diplomacy, to brief the General; to keep the visit secret, he entered the Élysée through a side door. There was an awkward moment when de Gaulle asked if his visitor had come to inform or to consult him. 'To inform you,' Acheson replied. Still, the General said that, while he did not think there would be a military conflict, France would fight beside the United States if the Soviets attacked Berlin in an East–West war.

Seeing Acheson to the door of his office after the hour-long meeting, de Gaulle spoke in English to say that he would be happy if further exchanges on the subject could be channelled between the two of them. In fact, a subsequent message sent from Washington to inform the French leader of correspondence between Kennedy and Khrushchev went to the ambassador in Paris, Charles Bohlen, the man who had described de Gaulle to Franklin Roosevelt after Yalta as 'one of the biggest sons of bitches who ever straddled a pot'. The message arrived on a Sunday and Bohlen proposed to deliver it to de Gaulle at Colombey, only to be told that the General's weekends were not to be disturbed, which he saw as 'a clear example of de Gaulle's calmness in moments of crisis'.

However, the outcome of the Cuban crisis troubled de Gaulle. He wondered if Washington would react in the same way to a confrontation as far away from the United States as Cuba was from the USSR – that is to say, over Berlin. He was also concerned that the strength America had shown would reinforce its claims to global hegemony, and concluded that the time might have come when a weakened Soviet Union would be more welcoming to French friendship. The result of the détente likely to flow from the resolution of the crisis was also a double-edged sword for the General since he saw it raising the prospect of an understanding between the two superpowers that would cut out France and reduce to nothing his drive to raise France's standing in the world.[7]

*

The referendum on 18 October 1962 brought a 62 per cent 'yes' vote. There was a retrospective attempt by Monnerville to get the Constitution Council to declare the vote null and void – Auriol, a member of the watchdog body who had never sat on it, suddenly appeared to add his voice to the critics, as did de Gaulle's wartime companion René Cassin. But a majority of the Council decided that it had no authority to strike down a law approved by the electorate. Once again, de Gaulle had beaten the massed ranks of the political parties. Approval was strongest in the most economically advanced regions of northern France and the traditional Gaullist strongholds of Alsace and Brittany, while the 'no' did well in the old Radical stamping grounds of the centre and south-west. A third of voters considered that the outcome was down to de Gaulle's personal appeal rather than to the subject of the referendum.

But it was not the triumph for which he had hoped. The abstention rate of 23 per cent meant that the 62 per cent of those who voted positively represented only 46 per cent of the total registered electorate. The 'no' vote, which had amounted to 20 per cent of voters in 1958, rose to 38 per cent of those who went to the polls four years later. As de Gaulle confided: 'When I dreamed, I hoped for 70 per cent. When I was

Bettman/Corbis

allying France: the General tries to swing the nation behind him, here on the cliffs at Bruneval in Normandy in March 1947

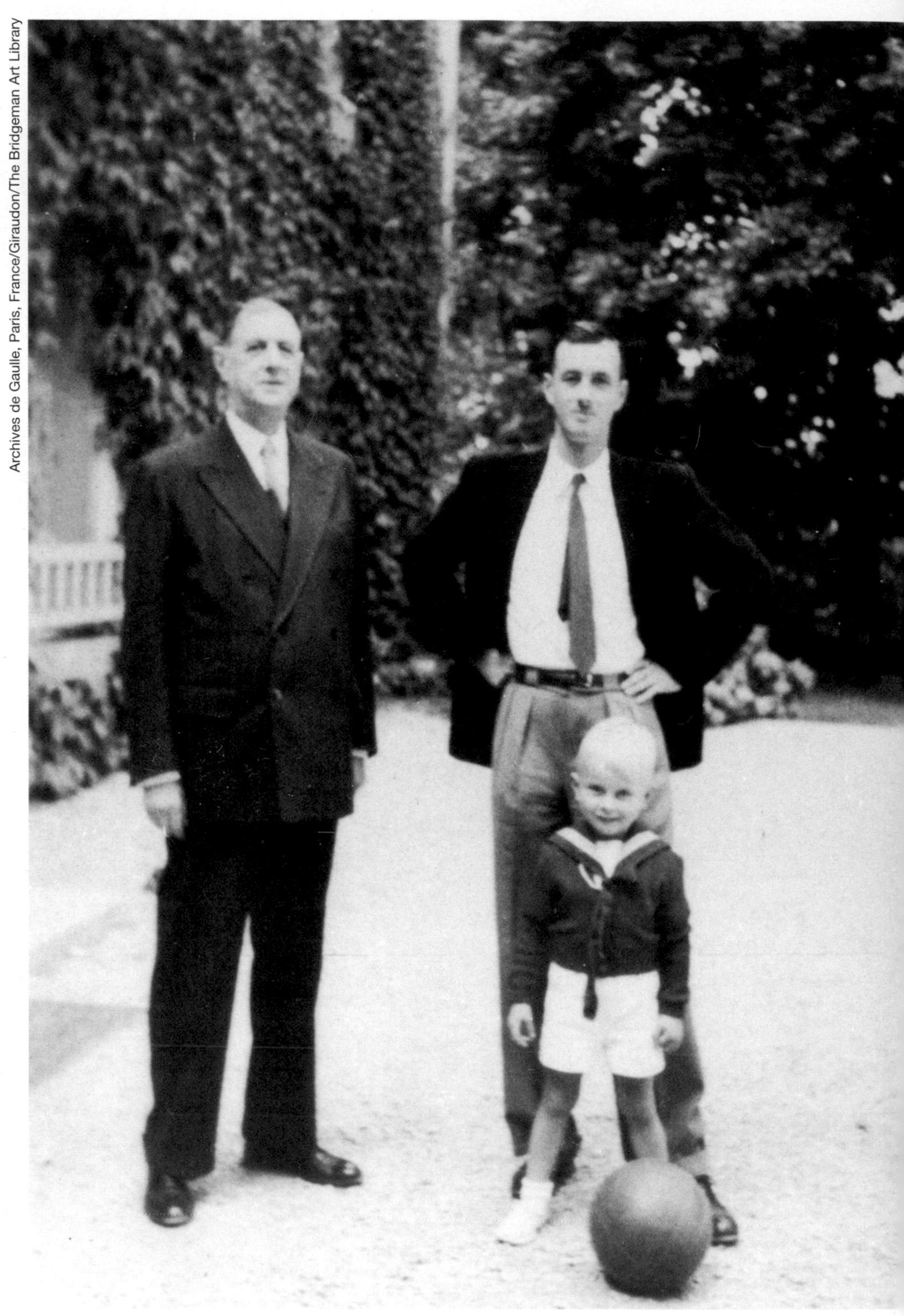

Father and grandfather: de Gaulle with his son Philippe and grandson Charles

Maurice Zalewski/Rapho/Eyedea/Camera Press London

Time and Life Pictures/Getty Images

Henri Bureau/Sygma/Corbis

ne return: de Gaulle putting himself at the disposal of
e Republic at a press conference as he manoeuvred his
ay back to power, and then assuring French Algerians
e had understood them after the revolt headed by his
ithful follower, General Massu (inset)

Europress/Sygma/Corbis

Foreign affairs: sealing the crucial friendship with Konrad Adenauer of West Germany and escorting Jacqueline Kennedy during a glittering state visit to Paris in 1961

AFP/Getty Images

Alain Dejean/Sygma/Corbis

ı chienlit: student riots and strikes shook the regime in May 1968, leaving de Gaulle nporarily floundering. But he regained the initiative with a sudden 'disappearance' and returned by helicopter to assert himself once more

Henri Bureau/Sygma/Corbis

Sygma/Corbis

Left-wing opponents headed by François Mitterrand and Pierre Mendès France (above) challenged for power, but were rebuffed after Gaullists staged a huge demonstration led by former Prime Minister Michel Debré (below, far left), the wartime Free French spokesman Maurice Schumann (second from left) and Culture Minister and writer André Malraux (centre)

Jacques Haillot/Sygma/Corbis

Alain Nogues/Sygma/Corbis

Waiting in the wings: by 1968, de Gaulle had a natural successor in the person of Prime Minister Georges Pompidou whom he promptly sacked

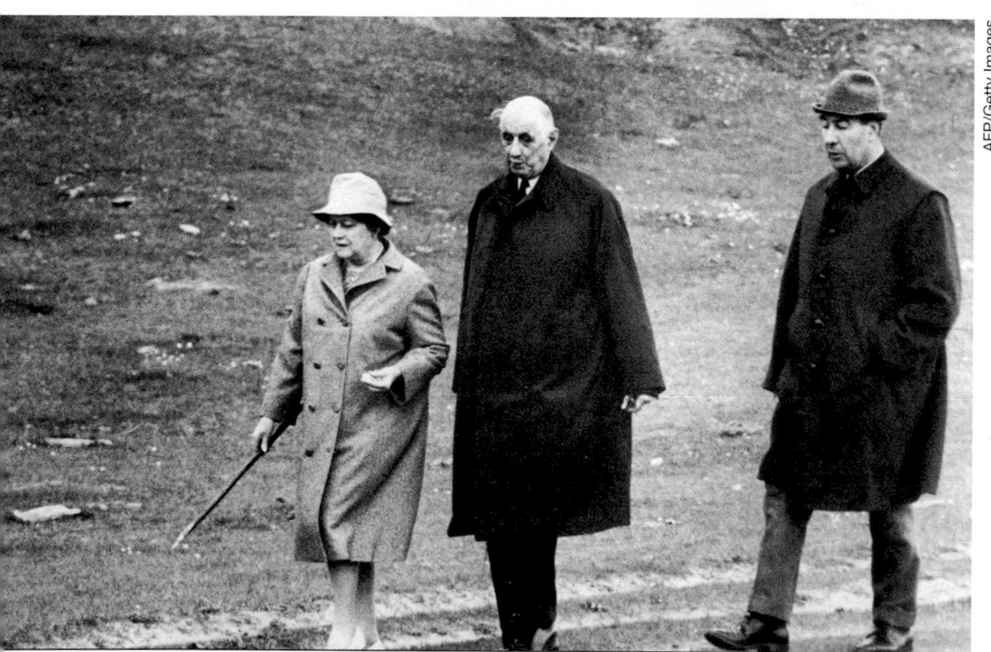

AFP/Getty Images

'aking his distance: Pompidou's emergence as a safe alternative led to de Gaulle's efeat and resignation. At the subsequent presidential election, he preferred to be out of France – in Ireland with his wife and long-time aide François Flohic

Henri Bureau/Sygma/Corbis

No fanfare: the General laid down that his funeral was to be a simple ceremony in his village of Colombey

Henri Bureau/Sygma/Corbis

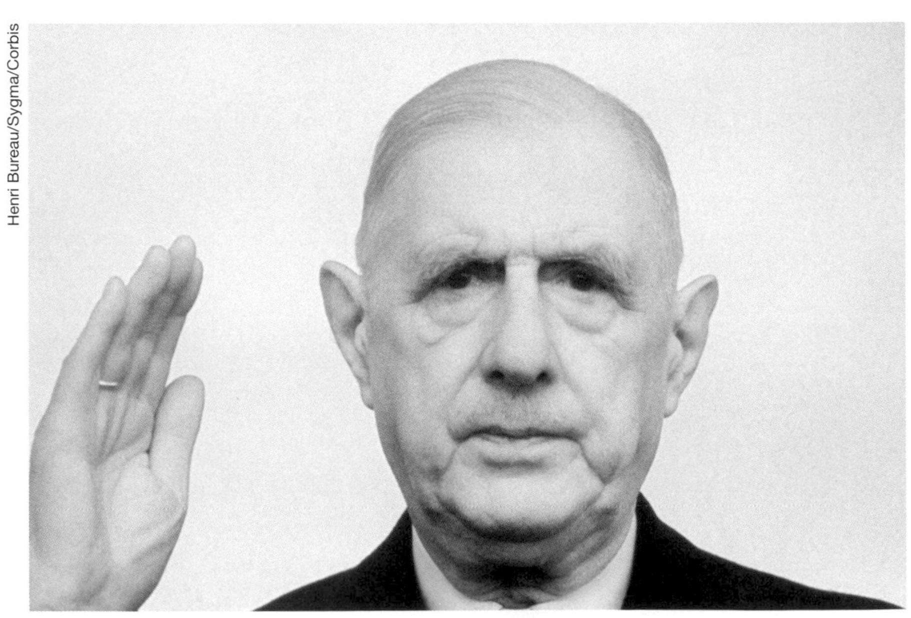

Au revoir: in death as in life, the General remained a potent presence and symbol of France

reasonable, I thought of 65 per cent. My disappointment was 62 per cent.' He had won a referendum but not got the plebiscite he wanted.

After the voting, he spent one day more than scheduled at Colombey considering his options. Then he launched into an offensive for the general election. He was no longer the arbiter above the political fray but a leader directly involved in the battle. His supporters emerged with 233 seats, only nine short of the absolute majority which the government could command with the support of 36 Independent Republicans. While the Left staged something of a revival by uniting their forces, the MRP did badly and Poujadist and pro-French Algeria candidates were wiped out. Among those beaten was Mendès France, defeated in the first round in Normandy.

At a Cabinet meeting, de Gaulle praised himself for having 'broken the parties', saying that only he could have achieved such a result and that he had 'been right against all the others'. As he boasted, while the party chiefs wanted to play a convivial couple of rounds of *belote*, he had taken them on at poker – and won. His disdain went as far as to lead him to refuse to shake the hands of either Auriol or Monnerville at the funeral of René Coty two days after the second round of voting. The government was dominated by Gaullist loyalists and civil servants, and the victors monopolised parliamentary commissions. Looking back in the last volume of his memoirs eight years later, the General called 1962 'the year of grace'.[8]

III
'Ne pleurez pas, milord'

With the electoral victories under his belt, it was time to turn back to Europe and Britain's bid to enter the Common Market. On 15–16 December 1962, Harold Macmillan travelled to the presidential château of Rambouillet to try to obtain some movement on the Common Market application. There had been progress between France and Britain in another field – the agreement to build a supersonic airliner together – but Macmillan was not optimistic, considering that de Gaulle's electoral victories would make him more difficult to deal with, 'grander and more patronising than ever', 'more mystical and remote, pontificating in general terms'. 'At the same time to protect the material interests (and short-terms interests) of French agriculture and commerce, he will bargain as hard and selfishly as any old French housewife in the market,' Macmillan noted in his diary. As for the other five member states, the Prime Minister judged that they were terrified by France's 'intellectual superiority and spiritual arrogance'.

The talks began after a big pheasant shoot in the cold rain, at which Macmillan recorded having bagged seventy-seven birds. De Gaulle did not participate but drove up in a black Citroën during the later stages and commented on the accuracy of the shooting. He and Macmillan then went inside for a three-hour conversation during which he said he wanted Britain to relinquish its special ties with the United States, and proposed nuclear cooperation to enhance Europe's independent military capacity. But Macmillan confided that he was about to conclude an agreement with Kennedy under which the US would sell Britain its Polaris underwater missile technology. The Prime Minister went further in saying that he saw Polaris as forming the basis for a multilateral NATO nuclear force, creating just the kind of European dependency de Gaulle rejected.

At one point, the two men went for a stroll in the park. Macmillan spoke French without an interpreter, which was almost certainly a mistake (as it had been for Churchill in June 1940). Things were made worse by the characteristically indirect fashion in which he approached the subjects. His private secretary, Philip de Zulueta, thought the President 'entirely misunderstood everything that was said'.

The next day, de Gaulle was very downbeat about British entry, leading Macmillan to speak, as he put it, 'somewhat emotionally'. When the two men were joined by their ministers for a plenary session, the General insisted that the Common Market should remain as it was. He recalled Churchill's remark to him before D Day that he would always choose America over Europe. British adhesion would lead other countries to try to join, changing the nature of the organisation. Macmillan recorded that Pompidou looked 'displeased' at what his leader was saying. 'I thought the discussions about as bad as they could be from the European point of view,' he added in his notes, attributing his host's attitude to his temperament and his 'personal and almost despotic control of France'. Subsequently, the General told the Cabinet that Macmillan, 'the poor man', had appeared sad and cast down. But what could he do about that, he asked, except to put his hand on his shoulder and intone the words of the Édith Piaf song of the time, '*Ne pleurez pas, milord*' ('Don't cry, My Lord')?

On 21 December, Macmillan met Kennedy in Nassau to conclude the agreement for Washington to sell Britain a dozen Polaris missiles. The British inserted language into the communiqué designed to show that their nuclear force was politically independent of the US, but de Gaulle deplored the deal. He rejected out of hand Kennedy's offer to extend the same deal to France; he told Peyrefitte the British had become vassals of Washington and had sold their birthright for 'a plate of Polarises'. France, he added, must not be influenced by what London did, blaming the Second World War on the readiness of pre-war governments in Paris to follow Britain's lead.[9]

At a press conference on 14 January, in front of a five-hundred-strong audience, the General rejected the British application which, he said, would lead to a 'colossal Atlantic Community dependent on and led by America which would soon absorb the European Community'. In private, he said Britain would not enter the Common Market in his lifetime. When news of the veto was relayed to the negotiators in Brussels, the British delegate, Christopher Soames, reacted furiously, growing red in the face and using vulgar French slang to upbraid French Agriculture Minister Edgard Pisani for the position his President had taken; the two men then retired to Soames' office and cooled down over whiskies and soda. Though British public opinion was far from enthusiastic about joining Europe, and the Labour Party leader Harold Wilson later told de Gaulle he had taken the right course, Macmillan was profoundly dejected. His government was running out of steam, and the sex scandal involving John Profumo, the Secretary of State for War, was looming. 'All our policies at home and abroad are in ruins,' the one-time Supermac noted. 'French domination of Europe is the new and alarming feature.' The outcome, he told the nation in a broadcast, was 'bad, bad for us, bad for Europe and bad for the whole Free World . . . France and her government are looking backwards, they seem to think that one nation can dominate Europe and, equally wrong, that Europe can or ought to stand alone.'[10]

A few weeks later, Macmillan reflected that 'the French always betray you in the end'. De Gaulle was 'absolutely crazy', he told Kennedy, retailing a remark by a French minister that, if Britain joined the Common Market, there would be 'two cocks on the dunghill', which would not be agreeable for the single Gaullist bird. The Foreign Office depicted the General as 'an almost impossible ally'. But all Britain could do was to cancel a visit to Paris by Princess Margaret for a film première.[11]

Luns and Spaak were confirmed in their view of the General. Yet de Gaulle was riding high enough to impose himself on them; the Common Market could not exist without France but could continue without Britain. The Brussels negotiations were abandoned at the end of January. Reynaud, Pleven, the Socialists and the MRP were strongly critical. The General was unmoved. When his patron of 1940 wrote him a letter to protest, he replied with an empty envelope addressed in his own hand, writing on the back: 'In case of absence, please forward to Agincourt (Somme) or to Waterloo (Belgium).'[12]

As usual, de Gaulle threw another ball in the air. A Franco-German friendship treaty was signed at the Élysée on 22 January 1963. The official photograph of the occasion contained high symbolism: the two heads of government, Adenauer and Pompidou, stood on either side of the President, who, as the monarchical figure, naturally occupied the central role. The treaty provided for regular meetings between the leaders of the two countries, and created a Franco-German youth organisation which would arrange visits between the two countries by hundreds of thousands of young people in the coming decades. But it did not provide any definition of what friendship across the Rhine entailed, or any formal mechanisms for exercising it. That said, its symbolism was clear, and enormous. In a speech later in the year, de Gaulle said the treaty was 'not a rose; it is not even a rose bush; it is a rose garden' capable of producing flowers for a long time. The historic rapprochement it embodies stands as one of de Gaulle's signal achievements, all the more striking in coming from a man who had survived Verdun and made his mark in refusing to accept Hitler's victory of 1940.

However, it did not meet with complete acceptance across the Rhine. The Gaullosceptic German Foreign Minister, Gerhard Schröder, whom

Adenauer had been forced to take into his government after suffering poor election results, criticised the treaty on the flight back to Bonn. To limit the possibility that France would use it as a lever to prize Bonn away from Washington, German proponents of a more Atlanticist policy held a meeting in the federal capital, secretly attended by Monnet, whose backing for European integration and close links with Washington had made him de Gaulle's *bête noire*. The result was a preamble to the treaty approved by the Bundestag, stipulating that the Franco-German agreement would not affect relations with the United States, thus ensuring that their country would not sign up to the General's vision of Europe.

De Gaulle reacted violently, seeing Washington's hand at work and describing the German politicians involved as behaving 'like pigs'. They deserved to see France denounce the agreement, quit the Western alliance and reach an understanding with Moscow, he said privately. Visiting West Germany in July, he made a pointed remark in a speech about treaties being like young girls: they lasted for as long as they lasted. If the Franco-German accord was not applied, it would not be the first time this had happened, he went on, quoting Victor Hugo: 'Alas, the young girls I have seen die.'

The preamble was, in fact, a reminder that, for all his commanding language and his success in vetoing British entry, the General was not as strong in Europe as might appear. His rhetoric and readiness to go to the brink created an exaggerated impression of power, which he nurtured to the full. But Spaak and Luns were still committed opponents. Italy wavered and West Germany did not want a conflict with its main protector across the ocean. When Adenauer was forced to step down in 1963, his successor, Ludwig Erhard, the 'father' of West Germany's recovery, was a strong Atlanticist who was less impressed by de Gaulle and more concerned with down-to-earth economic issues.[13]

In France, there were less lofty, if familiar, matters to be dealt with, such as a recurrence of the old dispute on state funding for religious schools, complaints from farmers about their incomes and unrest among coal miners as their industry was cut back. But, as he approached the fifth anniversary of his return to power, de Gaulle could congratulate himself on a string of achievements. There were, of course, nuances to them all – in Algeria, he had been obliged to bow to events; his foreign policy contained contradictions and was too often based on personal projection and the unrelenting pursuit of set ideas; some of the progress for which his regime claimed complete credit had its roots in the despised Fourth Republic; the positive referendum vote hid lower levels of support in the electorate as a whole.

Still, the General had gone a long way towards realising his fundamental aim of making France count again amid the multifaceted challenges of the early 1960s. As Mao Zedong had said when the Communists won China's civil war in 1949, the country could stand up again. The question now was what he would do next and, in particular, whether he considered his work largely done, leading him to step down in 1965 and hand the flame he had lit to a successor under the amended constitution.

32

FACING FRANCE

I
Changing times

Writing to his sister and Jacques Vendroux at New Year 1963, de Gaulle said that the outlook did not seem too bad for France. 'May it profit from the trumps at its disposal!' he added. The country, he judged, had been delivered from anxieties which had haunted it from the beginning of the twentieth century, free from the threat of invasion, civil war, economic ruin and the need for external assistance. He hoped for calmer seas ahead, but was to be disappointed for, as he also noted, France and the world around it had changed greatly.[1]

In the four and a half years since René Coty had called on 'the most illustrious of Frenchmen', his country had become a nuclear power, seen by its President as an essential element in rekindling its glory. The Algerian trauma was over, with occasional reminders such as the kidnapping by French secret agents of Colonel Argoud in Germany for delivery to the police in Paris tied up in the back of a car – de Gaulle commented that he did not like to see an officer trussed up like a sausage. The huge sub-Saharan African Empire had gone peacefully, even if the General harboured a lasting grudge against Guinea for having broken ranks from the start. Though little came of his vision of a community in which France would exert leadership over its former possessions, the franc currency zone acted as a bond; France retained troops in some of its former colonies and its aid, both financial and cultural, remained important.

The General's policy of keeping American influence at bay in French-speaking West Africa was largely successful. The link he had forged with the region during the war was strong. The Senegalese President, Léopold Senghor, spoke of a 'mysterious current', and ritual dances were performed in some former colonies to celebrate the General, complete with masks in his image. Foccart continued to exert significant influence from the Élysée, exploiting a network of contacts with heads of state and working with France's secret services to become the regime's leading cloak-and-dagger figure. African leaders were regular visitors to the palace. De Gaulle played the role of the sage; the dictator of the Central African Republic, Jean-Bédel Bokassa, insisted on referring to him as 'papa' – when de Gaulle said he should call him '*mon Général*' like everybody else, the former French army sergeant replied: 'Yes, papa.'[2]

Economically, the Rueff Plan had borne fruits, helped by the structural changes introduced in the planning system inaugurated by Jean Monnet under the Fourth Republic, even if the Gaullists gave them little credit. The currency was strong. France's growth rivalled Germany's and exceeded that in both Britain and the United States. State finances were far healthier than under the Fourth Republic. In its report on France's economy for 1962, the Organisation for Economic Cooperation and Development (OECD) paid tribute to its 'extraordinary vitality' that seemed to ride over the ups and downs of the international situation. The 170 leading publicly owned firms played a big role in the expansion of industry plotted by the minister responsible, Jean-Marcel Jeanneney. In keeping with his belief that the economy was best managed like a military campaign, de Gaulle strongly backed successive plans whose targets, he said, should have the character of 'an ardent obligation' for the nation.

The Caravelle airliner was a great success, as were the Mirage and Mystère fighter bombers produced by the Gaullist Marcel Dassault. The enthusiasm de Gaulle had shown for helicopters in the Algerian war helped to promote the Alouette produced by Sud-Aviation. A French train broke the world speed record. In February 1961, the President inaugurated the new Orly airport outside Paris, declaring that France knew no limits. Motorway construction expanded. A space programme was developed which led to the first French communications satellite being launched in 1965. In a broadcast in the summer of 1961, the General felt able to proclaim that the country had 'married its century'.

The DS Citroën limousine, in which de Gaulle had escaped from the bullets at Petit-Clamart, was the acme of style and engineering prowess, memorably described as being like a great oyster waiting to snap the legs off passing pedestrians. The big natural gas field at Lacq provided an important source of domestic energy supply. The soaring bridge over the Seine at Tancarville in Normandy kept alive the tradition of Gustave Eiffel. The origin of many of these projects dated back to the Fourth Republic, but the new regime presented them as evidence of the modernisation of the nation, a process that received a further boost as Giscard d'Estaing and Pompidou encouraged private industry and internationally competitive groups alongside the more traditional Gaullist backing for state planning.

Cities like Grenoble pioneered new forms of urban development. In keeping with de Gaulle's interest in modernising the capital, the former Delegate General in Algeria, Paul Delouvrier, was put in charge of renewing infrastructure and housing in the Paris region, laying plans for new towns to accommodate the rising population. Malraux launched a programme to clean up historic buildings, and established *maisons de la culture* (culture houses) in provincial cities. Guichard was put in charge of a regional programme designed to reduce inequalities between different parts of France.

At the Agriculture Ministry, Edgard Pisani tried to remedy low productivity. Spare land was bought up to amalgamate into larger and more efficient farms. A progressive young farmers' leader, Michel Debatisse, was appointed to the government's Social and Economic Council. Old farmers were given financial incentives to retire. Hard negotiating by the French produced favourable Common Market agreements. Farm output increased steadily and, by the 1970s, would be ahead of Germany and Italy, with the big holdings in northern France recording high levels of production though poorer areas of *la France profonde* continued to suffer as they always had, despite the romantic notions fostered about them by writers who had never endured an Auvergnat winter without heating or a dirt-poor existence in the flatlands of central France.[3]

The birth rate rose to an average of almost three children per mother thanks to generous family allowances. As well as repatriated *pieds-noirs*, two million foreign immigrants moved to France, mainly from Italy, Spain and Portugal, but then from North Africa, the men working in factories, the women often becoming home helps or concierges. The population grew younger and more urbanised, with 62 per cent living in towns and cities by 1962 compared to 53 per cent in 1946. In 1960, the number of pupils in secondary education was almost double the level of 1950, while university numbers had increased by 50 per cent. Farmers and farm employees who represented 27 per cent of the population in 1954, were down to 20 per cent by the start of the 1960s, and the proportion of industrial workers and staff rose from 44 to 49 per cent. People were spending less on food and clothing and more on accommodation, health, transport, telecommunications and culture.

Television changed the way people lived; instead of the café or the family gathering in the evening, the small screen ruled. Music-hall acts and popular singers of the new generation blanketed the nation. Television stars like Guy Lux and Léon Zitrone became household names while the newspaper veteran Pierre Lazareff and a highly talented team produced a ground-breaking reportage programme, *Cinq colonnes à la une* (Five columns on page one).

Following the work of Alain Robbe-Grillet, writers such as Michel Butor, Marguerite Duras, Claude Simon and Nathalie Sarraute rejected traditional narrative forms and experimented with the *nouveau roman.* Roland Barthes presented another challenge to orthodox thinking as he developed theories on semiology and structuralism. Communist renovators treading in the wake of Khrushchev's attack on Stalin set out to update their creed, while Sartre's *Critique de la raison dialectique* sought to present Marxism in a humanist form and disputed the objective nature of class. Claude Lévi-Strauss became an international celebrity with brilliant works stemming from his anthropological studies, and Michel Foucault published his ground-breaking research of social institutions, psychiatry, medicine and prisons.

The Nouvelle Vague revolutionised the cinema.* Classic singers, such as Édith Piaf, Charles Trenet and Maurice Chevalier, kept alive the

*A brief newsreel clip of de Gaulle and Eisenhower driving down the Champs-Élysées appeared in Jean-Luc Godard's *À bout de souffle.*

popular tradition of their art, backed by a solid post-war troupe of Yves Montand, Gilbert Bécaud and Charles Aznavour, and the troubadour Georges Brassens. Named after a pop music programme on the independent radio station Europe 1, *Salut les Copains!* (Hi, pals!) became the watchword for a new *yé-yé* generation that adopted rock 'n' roll with French characteristics under cover of assumed American-style names in a fresh example of France's fascination with transatlantic entertainment, among them Johnny Hallyday (Jean-Philippe Smet from Belgium), Eddy Mitchell (Claude Moine from Paris), Dick Rivers (Hervé Forneri from Nice) and Richard Anthony (Richard Btesh from Cairo). Hallyday appeared on *The Ed Sullivan Show* in the USA, and married a fellow singing star, Sylvie Vartan, from Bulgaria. France Gall, from Luxembourg and singing in French, won the Eurovision Song Contest, and became the 'French Lolita' in the words of her songwriter Serge Gainsbourg. Mireille Mathieu, from a family of fourteen children in Avignon, blasted her way to fame with her huge voice, provincial simplicity, echoes of Piaf and astute handling by Hallyday's manager, Johnny Stark.

With a few exceptions, such as the prim Mathieu, the new generation brought with it a more relaxed attitude to life and sex, epitomised by Gainsbourg and the Hallyday–Vartan relationship written up in the weekly celebrity press. With Brigitte Bardot as its cheerleader, Saint-Tropez became the epitome of a more hedonistic world to which French youth might aspire but which was still not accepted by their elders; as his political star rose, Pompidou found it expedient to stop spending his summer holidays at the Mediterranean resort and transfer to the more orthodox climes of Brittany. It was not a world with which de Gaulle was in touch, even if he told the wife of the writer Joseph Kessel that, though he did not know them personally, he had 'a lot of admiration' for the Beatles.[4]

While de Gaulle could celebrate strong growth numbers, there were political, social and economic problems. The Algerian war left a legacy of extra-judicial tribunals. In a speech, Mitterrand enumerated the powers of the regime: 'It has its own constitution, its government, its majority, its referendum, its television, its nuclear force . . . It has its Europe. Perhaps now it wants to have its own justice.' Long-forgotten legal provisions against insulting the head of state were invoked against demonstrators barracking the President. Life was made difficult for at least some critical writers.

Though publications such as *L'Express* and *Le Nouvel Observateur* maintained a lively climate of political debate alongside the gravity of *Le Monde* and the witty irreverence of *Le Canard enchaîné*, Agence France-Presse was run by loyalists under the Free French veteran Jean Marin, and its Élysée correspondent, Jean Mauriac, proved his reliability by not reporting scoops de Gaulle had confided to him. For the world media, the Paris bureau of Reuters was headed by an equally fervent Gaullist, Harold King.* The state broadcasting network was closely controlled. In a note to his press chief, Gilbert Pérol, the General said he would not allow any politicians, authors or critics to speak about him without his prior approval on the state broadcasting network, the *Office de Radiodiffusion Télévision Française* (ORTF). He inveighed against its news programmes as superficial, pessimistic and inclined to run reports that reflected badly on the authorities instead of 'what is approved, official and national'. The place needed to be cleaned out from top to bottom, he told the Information Minister, Alain Peyrefitte. Until that was done, he added, 'this magnificent instrument of support for the public spirit will remain a means of poisoning it'.[5]

While the school-leaving age was raised from fourteen to sixteen, increasing the number of pupils in state establishments from seven to nine million (plus two million in state-aided private schools), only a third of those in higher education left with a diploma of some kind, which the General classed as the lowest rate in the developed world. Louis Joxe's mission to simplify and harmonise the bureaucracy as Minister for Administrative Reform produced only limited results, particularly in bastions of civil service power such as education.

As de Gaulle noted in his memoirs, life for many of the French had become less individualistic. Factories grew in size; agriculture became more mechanised; chain stores and supermarkets rivalled traditional shops. The General lamented the effect of industrialisation and

*During the 1965 presidential election, King ordered that the present author should not be left alone in the agency's Paris office since he had shown his Communist sympathies by writing a 250-word story reporting a speech by Mitterrand critical of the General.

planning on farming as a component of French life. The economic battle, he noted, was one which never produced conclusive victories, and needed constant vigilance. The rural–urban imbalance widened and the birth rate fell in the countryside. The crush of people moving into big cities produced crowded urban estates and dormitory towns with little endemic life.

For all its technological progress, France remained quite backward in a number of ways. Contraception was still illegal, and, though nobody was prosecuted, birth control techniques were often primitive; surveys of hospitals showed that a third of pregnancies were not wanted. Abortions were estimated at 500,000 a year. The low divorce rate – half that in West Germany – could hardly be taken as evidence that French couples were that much happier than their counterparts across the Rhine.[6]

Economic policies veered to the right, penalising workers. Wages were no longer linked to the cost-of-living index and were low by the standards of a developed economy; hourly industrial earnings lagged 30 per cent behind those in Britain and West Germany. Public sector salaries fell below those in private companies that ignored instructions to practise wage restraint. The sales tax, which hit the poorest disproportionately, was higher than in many European countries, and income tax was lower. Employers paid far more into the social security funds than the state, depressing corporate profitability. Despite the efforts of Guichard's regional development agency, industrial progress in some areas accentuated the lag in others – the regions above a line drawn from Le Havre to Grenoble contained two-thirds of the population and most of the advanced industry. Though productivity rose significantly as factories were modernised, France spent little on research and development compared to other European nations. Unions were weak, and constantly at war with one another.

By the mid-1960s, the economic recovery launched in 1958 began to run into obstacles. In the first instance, de Gaulle blamed these on the 'abusive, monumental privilege' of the dollar, the size of the US gold reserve and Washington's domination of the International Monetary Fund (IMF). But he had to admit that there was trouble at home. Budgetary rigour was fraying, in part because of the cost of helping the *pieds-noirs* set up in France but also because of pressure for wage rises in the public sector to match those granted by private companies – Pompidou agreed to above-inflation increases in the public sector while Renault, the pace-setting state company, accorded workers a fourth week of holiday. As prices rose, the General saw inflation as the result of a national weakness for facile solutions – in economics, as in everything else, he preferred hard times.[7]

II
'Charlot, des sous!'

With the British negotiations ended and the Franco-German treaty signed in January 1963, de Gaulle's attention ranged far and wide – from the infrastructure of Paris to farm productivity, from the possible involvement of *pied-noir* guards in a prison escape by OAS convicts to the idea of building a tunnel under the Channel or a bridge across it. In foreign affairs, he ordered that France should not give Israel any undertakings of military support in the event of war in the Middle East, though he told the Prime Minister, David Ben-Gurion, that his administration would 'not remain indifferent' if there was a threat to his country's existence.[8]

In March, amid harsh late-winter weather, a big strike by coal miners presented the administration with a major challenge as it implemented a plan drawn up by the Industry Ministry to cut coal output from fifty-nine million tons to fifty-two million. In his memoirs, de Gaulle wrote that, with his family roots in northern France, he felt 'a particular esteem' for the miners. Still tens of thousands of protesters marched on Paris and the government faced a trial of strength with the Communist-led CGT, the union federation that led the stoppage. Declaring the action illegal, it demanded that the strikers go back to work while filling the gap in coal supplies with imports, showing that national production was not essential. But the committee which found a solution that ended the stoppage after thirty-five days reached a conclusion close to the miners' original demands.[9]

Economic problems increased as the year went on. The relative success of the miners encouraged action by employees of the railways, of power stations, rubbish collectors and other state sector workers. Inflation was rising and, with it, demands for wage increases that would set off a further spiral. There was a crisis over excess dairy production – Pisani was grabbed by protesters in Normandy and forced to drink litres of milk. On his provincial tours, de Gaulle was met with cries of '*Charlot, des sous!*' ('Charlie, cash!') – to which he replied, 'Cash and credits can only be allocated if we have them [and] if our country does not fall victim to inflation.'

The money supply was growing excessively, twice as fast as in West Germany. The budget balance, to which the General attached great importance, was under threat. The stability of the franc, which he so prized as a symbol of national greatness, was at risk – he saw the weakening of the currency as opening the door to waste, compromising the national effort and threatening France's independence.

He pressed Pompidou and Giscard d'Estaing to act – the economy was not exempt from his belief that he could impose his will wherever and whenever he wished. A Stabilisation Plan blocked prices, tightened credit and cut state spending. At the same time, de Gaulle ordered that France should build up its gold stocks and the Bank of France was told to insist that the United States settle 80 per cent of its trade payments for French goods in gold.

The result was positive. The growth in the money supply dropped sharply. Inflation declined. The trade position improved. Employment was high. 'For a second time,' the General wrote in his memoirs, 'the new Republic put the economy in order without stopping the march towards prosperity – very much the contrary.' However, the plan, which had been due to last for six months, had to be kept in place for twenty-eight, putting a brake on expansion and provoking recurrent strikes, protests and grumbling among small shopkeepers and artisans. In his memoirs, Pompidou says that he thought its duration 'excessive', but he could do nothing to lift it – he was, after all, only Prime Minister and de Gaulle was intent on imposing rigour on the French rather than allowing them to opt for an easy life, with Giscard acting as his ardent lieutenant as his own political career blossomed.

The procedure adopted by the government of imposing the economic measures directly without going through parliament marked a further move towards authoritarian rule. Opposition candidates gained ground locally and in by-elections. 'Few voices, it is true, were heard to recognise the general benefit of the exercise,' de Gaulle noted in his memoirs. 'But had I not learned that what is salutary for the nation does not go through without criticism and electoral losses?'[10]

III
Global star

When a journalist asked after his health, de Gaulle replied: 'Not bad. But, don't worry, I won't fail to die one day.' For a man in his mid-seventies, he remained extraordinarily active; in 18 months, from July 1963 to the end of 1965, he travelled to 28 French departments, presided over 110 Cabinet meetings and 180 other councils at the Élysée as well as receiving an average of 30 visitors a week. He made 24 trips abroad, and saw 57 foreign leaders who came to France. Familiar themes ran through his activity. In Europe, there were tricky Common Market farm negotiations, in which France broadly got what it wanted. The running dispute with Washington over its proposal for a multilateral force brought relations to a new low – Couve de Murville considered that the crisis it was the most serious the Gaullist regime had known because it went to the bottom of the transatlantic divergences. Kennedy's highly successful visit to Berlin in July 1963 also acted as an unwelcome counterweight to the Paris–Bonn relationship and encouraged the West German Atlanticists.

Still, the General's global fame rose steadily. In November 1963, at the funeral of Kennedy, who had been assassinated on the General's birthday, he towered over the heads of state and government, and insisted on walking to the cathedral beside Jacqueline Kennedy and the diminutive figure of Haile Selassie of Ethiopia despite the concerns of the US security service for his safety. He was seated in the eighth row, which he considered below the dignity of France. So, putting on his spectacles, he made his way forward, greeting fellow statesmen and royalty until he reached the front. 'Right, we can start,' he said to a protocol official and sat down where he was.

He was the first foreign dignitary Mrs Kennedy received after the service, reaching out to pluck a marguerite from a vase of flowers and handing it to him; he kept it carefully and took it from his pocket when he got back to the Élysée. After hearing of the assassination of JFK in Dallas, the General had saluted Kennedy at a Cabinet meeting as 'a true head of state'. He remarked that what had happened to the President, who had 'died like a soldier', could have happened to him; he pinned responsibility on the police, saw racism as the underlying cause and told Malraux that a new civil war could break out across the Atlantic. Jacqueline Kennedy, he added, was a star who would end up on the yacht of an oil tycoon.[11]*

The General dismissed Kennedy's successor, Lyndon Johnson, who received him for the briefest of meetings after the funeral, as a Texan Radical Socialist – 'a Queuille with loaded pistols'. His effort to chip away at America's global position ranged far wider than the initial confrontations over the Atlantic Alliance, though he pursued his drive against military integration by taking the French fleet out of the NATO command in the North Atlantic. He propounded neutrality for Indochina as US involvement there was rising steeply, offered military aid to Cambodia, and made lengthy trips to Latin America to urge its countries to stand up for themselves. His message was simple. While he differentiated between America, which represented freedom, and the Soviet Union, which might collapse if it did not allow its citizens their proper place, he refused the division of the globe into two blocs – the world, he said, was too rich and varied for that, and Paris would play its full part in developing new relationships.

He declined to sign the ban on nuclear tests in the atmosphere agreed by Washington and Moscow, depicting it as a carve-up between the two superpowers that placed unfair limits on countries like France, which tested above ground in the Sahara. He ended one discussion with Dean Rusk in 1964 with a two-edged remark that, when the *force de frappe* had been fully developed, the two countries should discuss cooperation, 'if we are still allies, as I hope'. In June that year, he declined to attend celebrations of the twentieth anniversary of the D Day landings in Normandy on the grounds that France had been excluded from

*When reminded of this by the present author six years later, de Gaulle expressed surprise and said he would have thought, rather, that she would have married Sartre – or Malraux (*Chênes*, p. 119).

Operation Overlord – participation would have been a painful acceptance that the Liberation had been the work of non-French forces. He did, however, join in similar ceremonies to mark the 1944 landings on the south coast, in which French troops had been involved; some time later, French newspapers reported the discovery of a bomb in a flower pot near the reviewing stand, apparently another attempt to kill the General though the US ambassador wondered if it had been planted in an effort to heighten de Gaulle's prestige.[12]

He inveighed against the United Nations as an instrument for American power and a threat to the world of nation states in which he believed. In the Middle East, he followed up on his unhelpful attitude to Ben-Gurion by cutting off France's military cooperation with America's ally, Israel, notably in cancelling an agreement to provide assistance in developing atomic weapons. He recognised Communist China after sending Edgar Faure on a preliminary mission. He also sought closer relations with Eastern Europe, receiving the President of the Supreme Soviet, Nikolai Podgorny, on a visit to Paris, exploring closer links with Poland and Romania, and telling Giscard d'Estaing to hold economic talks that led to a trade agreement with the USSR in October 1964; this was followed by an exchange of messages with Moscow in which, returning to an old theme, de Gaulle wrote of the lasting friendship, common heritage and reciprocal interests of the two nations.

In March 1964, he flew to Mexico to forge a 'special understanding' with France. Welcomed by a crowd of 300,000 in the centre of Mexico City, he spoke in Spanish as he called for the policies of the two nations to be 'attuned'. A committee was established to explore ways for them to work more closely together and to expand trade. But the President could make only limited progress; 3.5 per cent of Mexico's trade was with France compared to 60–70 per cent with the US, and the Common Market farm policy championed by Paris restricted its agricultural exports. His head pink from the sun, de Gaulle left Mexico City in a Caravelle, but discreetly changed planes on the Yucatan Peninsula to take a Boeing that would fly him more quickly to a tour of French possessions in the Caribbean. That was not the only secret of the trip: the General had travelled with a catheter inserted in his body.[13]

Back in Paris, he gave a television address devoted to the economy on 1 April, reeling off statistics as he had never done before and declaring that France had chosen 'effort, cohesion and success'. The following day, he was taken with great secrecy to the Val-de-Grâce military hospital in the capital for a prostate operation.

Before the operation, de Gaulle gave the Secretary-General at the Élysée, Étienne Burin des Roziers, who had succeeded Geoffroy de Courcel, a letter marked 'To be opened only after my death; but you will return this to me the day after tomorrow if, as I believe, everything goes well'. He also sent his son a letter with a statement to be unsealed and made public if things did go wrong. After the operation, Philippe and the presidential aide returned both letters unopened. The General probably destroyed them. The covering letter to his son contained a unique expression of family ambition. It said the General hoped that, if he died, a successor would be swiftly elected, but added: 'I hope that afterwards it will be you who will wish to and will be able to take on the task of running France in your turn.'[14]

While the General was temporarily out of action, Pompidou chaired a Cabinet session, further boosting his own stature. His heightened confidence may have been behind a remark he made in a speech to the National Assembly later that April in which he said that it was the elementary duty of a prime minister never to reveal in public differences that might occur between him and the President. He did not say that such differences had occurred, but merely raising the possibility showed that he regarded his job as more than that of a mere errand boy.

De Gaulle recovered swiftly, and was working at a desk in his hospital room in his pyjamas within a couple of days. He resumed his programme of tours of the French provinces and went to Bonn before picking up on his attempt to wean South America away from Washington with an exhausting trip to ten Latin American countries in the autumn, during which he spoke in Spanish. In January 1965, he attended the funeral of Winston Churchill in London. Then he switched to a new front in his campaign to reduce US supremacy by turning his attention to the dollar.

Encouraged by Jacques Rueff, a long-time advocate of using gold as the global monetary standard, the General decided it was high time to end the tacit agreement by which countries that had trade surpluses with America did not exercise their right to be paid in gold, but accepted dollars instead. Following his 'get gold' injunction to the government, France had converted dollar holdings worth $150 million into gold in January, and was intending to do the same again the following month.

On 3 February, de Gaulle told his economic adviser, Jean-Maxime Lévêque, that he intended to talk about monetary matters at a press conference the following day.

'I began to tremble,' recalled Lévêque, who was all too aware of the sensitive nature of such matters.

De Gaulle read out a draft of what he proposed to say. After criticising the US trade deficit, he concluded that a new system based on gold was required. What did his aide think? Lévêque objected that, though de Gaulle's criticisms of the existing system were justified, he had to realise that there was not enough gold available to sustain the arrangement he advocated.

'So what can I say?' the General asked.

Lévêque suggested that he put forward the idea of a profound reform of the global monetary system that would make gold more important but also include complementary credits operated by the international community.

The next day, de Gaulle raised the monetary issue at his press conference of his own accord. Apparently losing his way as he plunged into the subject, he said that the existing situation could not be allowed to continue. A decision had to be taken to return to the gold standard which had been abandoned in the 1930s during the Great Slump. The world needed 'an indisputable monetary base, and one that does not bear the mark of any particular country', he declared. 'In truth, one does not see how one could really have any standard criterion other than gold.' As a kicker, he added that American overseas investments in dollars were 'a form of expropriation'.

'Perhaps never before had a chief of state launched such an open assault on the monetary power of a friendly nation,' wrote *Time* magazine. 'Nor had anyone of such stature made so sweeping a criticism of the international monetary system since its founding in 1944.' Spain had just followed France's example in demanding payment from the US in gold while, in Washington, the Federal Reserve announced that the country's gold supply had fallen to a twenty-six-year low. With the six Common Market nations holding the same amount of gold as the United States, the transatlantic economic balance would change radically if they followed France's lead.[15]

But opposition from Washington, London and Bonn meant de Gaulle's proposal was a non-starter – France alone could not force a change. The US Treasury warned that it would set off economic warfare for the insufficient stocks of gold. There were other very real fears: governments would ban the sales of gold from their national reserves; tariffs would rise; protectionism along 1930s lines would destroy world trade; a rise in the gold price would mean the devaluation of currencies; big holders of dollars like Japan and West Germany would be affected significantly. But the gold issue was the kind of simple, apparently logical idea that naturally appealed to de Gaulle, and, above all, it provided a fresh arrow to fire at the United States in his endless quest for respect and recognition.

Accentuating France's multi-pronged advance, Couve de Murville announced that France would sponsor the People's Republic of China to replace the US ally, the Republic of China on Taiwan, in the Security Council. De Gaulle wrote to Ho Chi Minh about his disapproval of US involvement in Indochina – and the letter was immediately leaked. For Washington, Ho was a Communist dictator allied with Moscow and, to a lesser extent, with Beijing, who was set on pushing over the dominoes in Southeast Asia. For the French he was a man who had been brought up in their system, spoke French and, if they were honest, had been let down by Paris after the Second World War. There were personal links: Messmer had been in Indochina in 1945 while Jean Sainteny, who had concluded an agreement with Ho in 1946, was now Minister for Veterans. Supporters of US policy were few and far between in France. This was a cause on which de Gaulle could speak both for French history and for the nation.

In a conversation with Hervé Alphand, the ambassador to Washington, he forecast that 'the Atlantic Pact will go, too. It will be replaced, if our partners so wish, by lateral agreements; we will be able to conclude one with the United States, one with Britain, one with Germany.' When the ambassador objected that the United States would refuse to sign such an accord, the General replied: 'Bah! That is not very important. If things go badly – which I do not think will happen – we will still be together . . . NATO is of no use any more. Either there is war in Europe and we are destroyed or there is an exchange of massive reprisals, and it is a matter between America and the Soviet Union. So why the alliance?'[16]

The drive for national independence free from American influence extended into the economic and technological fields. The Concorde supersonic airliner was being developed with Britain to give them a lead over the United States, even if spiralling costs led de Gaulle to describe the project to ministers as a 'millions guzzler', and he repeated his habitual warnings about the perils of working with the British. France pressed ahead with its own colour television system, with its nuclear submarine fleet and with a national computer plan launched after Washington refused to allow the sale of electronic equipment needed for the *force de frappe*. Faced with redundancies at US subsidiaries in France and Chrysler's takeover of the Simca car company, the government adopted a more restrictive policy towards foreign investments, particularly from across the Atlantic.[17]

All his activity bolstered the French leader's status as a global star, and fitted in with his idea that France should be present on every global front. It was what he had always dreamed of, and he was now in a position to strut the world stage. The General was constantly in the headlines and on magazine covers. The French people seemed happy with his course – an opinion poll showed that only 29 per cent of those questioned thought their country's interests were close to those of America.[18]

What was actually achieved is questionable. The constant motion sometimes seemed to be an end in itself. Leaders of what was then known as the Third World might be flattered by de Gaulle's attentions, even if they sometimes came over as somewhat patronising. Yet he did not shake NATO or sway Washington's policy in Vietnam. He did not wean Latin American nations away from their dependence on the United States or establish a new gold standard, and he faced continuing divergences in the Common Market. For all his lofty admonitions, and the domestic appeal of the vision of a France reborn, the General could all too easily seem like a bad-tempered dog yapping at the heels of Washington and seeking to impose his views on the country's neighbours; Charles Bohlen described him to Lyndon Johnson as a man who was 'essentially egocentric with some touches of megalomania' and from whom it was pointless to expect any change of attitude, while the Under Secretary of State, George Ball, detected his absolutism increasing week by week. Most galling of all, Walt Rostow, Johnson's national security adviser, recalled that the President decided that, in public, the administration would 'ignore him and never be aggressive'.

Nor was de Gaulle quite as self-confident as he appeared. Meeting him after his operation, the former British ambassador to France, Gladwyn Jebb, found him looking 'old, tired, and ill. The sparkle had gone, and in a curious way, he seemed to me to be less confident. Gone too was the old roguishness, the *méchanceté*, which often enlivened our serious talks.' In public, he remained as impervious as ever; asked if he was tired after his long South American trip, he replied 'Why should I be?' But, with General Pierre Billotte, who had been with him in London and Algiers, he went through one of his reassurance-seeking exercises. He told the visitor he was going to resign, laying out his disappointments, inveighing against domestic politicians and saying that the Americans were insupportable. When Billotte played his role and urged him to stay on, de Gaulle replied: 'Better to leave in full form.' Following the expected script, Billotte argued that nobody could replace him. At that, the President's mood swung. 'For once, you are right. I will complete my septennate,' he said. 'Thank you for your visit. Come back to see me again.'[19]

IV
Challengers

The General's term did not expire until the end of 1965, but the centre-left opposition was invigorated by the protests against the Stabilisation Plan and the prospect of fielding a candidate who would make the President look old and out of touch, unresponsive to concerns at home and engaged in a foreign policy which was wilfully alienating France's partners. Gaullist control of parliament meant that discontent increasingly took the form of street action and strikes. The inclusion in the UNR of left-wing Gaullists anxious to find a 'third way' between capitalism and socialism did little to temper the administration's tilt to the right, whatever de Gaulle's long-standing dislike for bourgeois business. Wealth disparities grew. The tax system favoured the affluent. Progress in improving housing was slow. While a clear majority of those questioned expressed satisfaction with the way France was being ruled in general, an IFOP poll showed that 64 per cent of people thought they had become less well off, compared to 9 per cent who felt richer, while up to 70 per cent were unconvinced by the government's social policies.

In a draft for a speech in July 1964, the President noted 'the anxiety of the employers, the unhappiness of white collar employees, the revolt of industrial workers, the anger of farmers, the irritation of shopkeepers, the fury in the public services, the distress of the civilian population and the poverty of the military'. De Gaulle took all this in his stride. He later recalled seeing the protests as 'the best possible sign of balance in our expansion' because it meant that no section of the population was at an advantage and each one, after having gained something from the general growth of the economy, now wanted more. At home and abroad, he advised ministers to adopt an attitude of 'silence and serenity'.

There was speculation that he would consider that his work was done and open the way to the succession, most probably by Pompidou, who had raised his public profile with combative speeches in parliament and more frequent provincial appearances. But asides to ministers and aides left little doubt that he would stand; in 1963, he had written a note in which he described himself as the dyke that prevented the return of the 'ballets', 'games' and 'crises' which had cost France so much in the past. In keeping with his romantic attachment to royalty, he raised the possibility of the Comte de Paris seeking the presidency, telling him, 'Nobody would run against you.' But it was play-acting. He thought the pretender would have no chance at all of being elected. Why should France hark back to its old royalty when it had a new monarch?

All the more so given the definition of his powers set out by the

President at a press conference in December 1964, in which he laid claims to an authority which recognised no apparent limit, showing what he believed the introduction of direct election of the head of state entailed. From the relatively restrained version of the constitution approved at the referendum of 1958, France had moved towards a system which, at least in the eyes of its ruler, equated to the assertion by Louis XV in 1766 that the sovereign authority rested in his person or, as Louis XIV had put it, '*L'état, c'est moi*' ('I am the state'). The constitution as it now stood, de Gaulle said, meant that the supreme power emanated from the people, not from parliamentary 'partisans'. The head of state held this power thanks to his election by the nation; he alone delegated the 'indivisible authority of the state' in the ministerial civilian, military and judicial spheres.[20]

Against such a claim, de Gaulle's opponents faced a choice. Did they refuse to accept the system and leave him an empty victory in the election of the President by universal suffrage in 1965, or did they accept the new arrangements and run against him within the framework he had constructed? For politicians whose very existence involved playing whatever game was on offer, there could be no doubt, however much they continued to protest against the context set by de Gaulle. The weekly news magazine *L'Express* set the ball rolling by calling for a 'Monsieur X' who would unify the centre and non-Communist Left against the General. The candidate in question was Gaston Defferre, the Socialist former minister and Mayor of Marseille. A veteran of the Resistance, he had been in several Fourth Republic governments, but had not been associated with the repression in Algeria under Mollet.

A keen yachtsman who ran the influential Marseille newspaper *Le Provençal*, he was a poor speaker but had few enemies in the centre-left. After the Socialists named him as their candidate, he quickly gathered backing for a 'grand federation' of the MRP, the Radicals, Mitterrand's Convention group, and Mendès France. He offered a less combative attitude than the General towards Europe and travelled to Washington to see Johnson, promising that he considered discussion with Washington essential to try to solve outstanding problems and expressing understanding of US policy in Vietnam. De Gaulle did not go in for 'discussions', he noted. 'He prefers a monologue.' But Defferre was also careful to add that France should not be submissive to America.

The Defferre project ran into doctrinal difficulties with the MRP, notably over religious schools, and with the centrists over nationalisations preached by the SFIO. Conservative non-Gaullists found it hard to accept the continuing Marxism of the Socialists, and yearned for Pinay to stand, but their idol rejected the idea; anxious to preserve his halo as the embodiment of solid French value, he did not wish to end his career in defeat by de Gaulle. Then there was the Mollet factor: the former Premier remained in charge of the Socialist party and had no desire to see the Mayor of Marseille outdo him in influence. While Defferre tried to find fudges with the Christian Democrats, Mollet made noises about working with the Communists to unite the voters of the Left and enlist the big battalions of the PCF.

The initiative dragged on into the summer of 1965, but came to an end at a late-night meeting on 17 June in the home of an MRP leader, Pierre Abelin, where the scale of the internal divisions could not be ignored. A prominent Christian Democrat, Jean Lecanuet, a senator from Normandy, was preparing to step into the breach in the centre. Mitterrand raised the temperature by remarking that it would be a mistake for the federation to rule out accepting PCF votes. At that, Mollet broke in to ask whether those present would prefer to help a UNR candidate get elected rather than a Communist. 'Yes,' replied the Radical Maurice Faure. 'Well, that means there is no longer a federation,' the SFIO chief replied, delighted. Speaking to the left-wing Gaullist Louis Vallon, de Gaulle said he was optimistic about the election because he had 'an excellent secretary-general'. Vallon thought he meant the holder of that post at the Élysée, Burin des Roziers. 'No, Vallon, no!' de Gaulle replied. 'Guy Mollet, of course. An excellent secretary-general who intervenes at the slightest danger.'[21]

*

In public, at least, de Gaulle paid no attention to the approaching election. He cast his mind to higher things, telling reporters who accompanied him on a trip to Chartres in June: 'Very often I seem to hear a murmur – even if the voices are not raised loudly – I sense that it is a murmur which corresponds to a sentiment, a general call of "Go, France! Go, France! Go!"' He had plenty of matters abroad to occupy him.[22]

Relations with Germany were strained as France sought to buttress the benefits for its farmers in agricultural negotiations, the split aggravated by the incompatibility between the General and the fundamentally Atlanticist, free-trading Ludwig Erhard. De Gaulle had begun 1965 by telling Chancellor Erhard that closer cooperation was needed, but that the Brussels framework was not the right context in which to proceed. States should work among themselves rather than involving the Commission under Walter Hallstein, he proposed. There was good reason for him to press his views: the Common Market was due to adopt majority voting at the start of the following year, which raised the prospect of France being put into a minority. At the same time, Hallstein was seeking to extend the powers of the Commission and to allow surplus community funds to be spent outside the control of the member states.

In the summer, the Commission chief and his deputy, Sicco Mansholt of the Netherlands, overplayed their hand in seeking greater authority, and in making plain that this was aimed against de Gaulle. As difficult negotiations on the next stage of farm policy became bogged down, the General and Couve de Murville gave them plenty of rope before pouncing on 1 July with the announcement that France had had enough. Its representatives boycotted meetings in what was known as the 'empty chair' campaign, presenting the community with the most serious crisis of its eight years of existence but enabling the General to present himself as the ultimate defender of French farmers.

In the Third World, de Gaulle continued to put himself forward as the champion of decolonisation, though this was somewhat undermined by the dispatch of troops to shore up friendly dictators in French-speaking Africa. Despite his rhetoric about encouraging Africa towards peaceful development, he refused to join the United Nations effort in the Congo. France also took a less than firm line on sanctions preventing arms sales to South Africa, abstaining at the first United Nations vote and then drawing a distinction between weapons that could be employed for internal suppression and those used for external purposes – Pretoria was a big customer for Dassault's Mirage jet fighters. Nor did relations with Algeria live up to the hopes expressed at the time of independence as the Ben Bella administration chased out most of the remaining *pieds-noirs*: when the Algerian president visited France in 1964 for a meeting outside Paris, de Gaulle instructed that the ceremonial was to be kept to a minimum and that the talks were to be limited to two hours, without a banquet.

On the American front, de Gaulle condemned the US invasion of Santo Domingo to put down a putsch by colonels backing the left-leaning former president Juan Bosch. He continued his familiar line by withdrawing France's fleet entirely from the integrated NATO naval force. He then wrote himself a note laying down conditions for a Franco-American military treaty which would guarantee that there would be no subordination of French units to a foreign command but put US elements on French territory under French control; the idea got nowhere. A fresh row broke out with Washington after a US plane flew over the French nuclear centre at Pierrelatte, either to spy or by mistake. As always, de Gaulle was constantly on the watch for threats to France's independence, from the presence of British air force units at French bases to an attempted American purchase of the computer firm Bull. 'By which means, in which fields and to what extent is our national character threatened (particularly by the United States)?' he asked his advisers. 'However large may be the glass offered to us,' he said, 'we prefer to drink from our own, while clinking glasses all round . . . a different order, a different equilibrium, is necessary for peace. Who can maintain this better than us – provided that we remain ourselves?'

As part of this process, the crisis over NATO, inherent in French policy since 1958, was clearly coming to a head. In August 1965, de Gaulle told a visiting senior US official that all NATO's units based in France would be under French command within a year. At a press conference the following month, he pledged that France would remain 'the ally of our allies' but gave notice that, when the NATO treaty expired in 1969, 'the subordination known as integration will end, so far as we are concerned'. He had been particularly annoyed by the way in which US aircraft had taken off from bases in France to fly to the Congo during the United Nations' intervention there despite French opposition to the operation. If his statement was hardly a shock given his previous actions, there remained in the background the greater logic expounded in his remarks to Alphand earlier in the year, bringing into question France's membership of the alliance as a whole. But, for the moment, de Gaulle was content to have laid the groundwork for disengagement from integrated military structure. Action could wait till the following year. In the meantime, there was a presidential election to be won.[23]

*

Emerging as the main non-Communist contender to de Gaulle after the collapse of the Defferre project, Mitterrand knew that he would need the electoral backing of the PCF to be able to mount a significant challenge, but he was anxious not to become the puppet of the Party. So he put together a coalition encompassing the Socialist and Radical parties as well as four smaller groups, called the *Fédération de la Gauche Démocrate et Socialiste* (Federation of the Democratic and Socialist Left) (FGDS). Mendès France gave his support, saying that, while they had had disagreements, Mitterrand had always been 'on the right side of the barricade when it comes to serious issues' but that de Gaulle, even if he did not use his power in a bloody or cruel manner, ruled in a dictatorial fashion which did not belong to contemporary society.

The new formation felt strong enough to negotiate on equal terms with the Communists, now under the leadership of Waldeck Rochet after the long illness and death of Thorez. Waldeck wanted to move away from slavish adherence to Moscow and explore reform and modernisation along the lines being pursued by the PCF's sister party in Italy. That made things easier for Mitterrand but he was still careful to keep his distance, leaving the negotiations to others and having no direct contact with Waldeck.

The President and his main challenger had not got on from the time of their first meeting, during the war, in which Mitterrand had joined the Resistance but had also served Vichy, receiving its medal, *la Francisque*, being photographed with Pétain and developing a friendship with the collaborationist police chief René Bousquet, who had organised the mass round-up of Jews in Paris in 1942. Though never leading a major party, he had held a series of ministerial posts under the Fourth Republic. As Interior Minister and Justice Minister, he had gone along with repression and torture in Algeria, which he declared an integral part of France. The politician most critical of de Gaulle in 1958, he had established himself as a cutting, unrelenting opponent of the Fifth Republic in a series of speeches, books and pamphlets depicting the authoritarianism of the regime as contrary to the values of the Republic.

A sharp debater and inveterate womaniser, Mitterrand was seen by critics as a slippery politician for whom self-interest outweighed principles – de Gaulle described him as an opportunist and a 'crafty ruffian' and saw him as the epitome of the system he had displaced in 1958, likening him to the ambitious, unscrupulous but seductive figure of Rastignac in Balzac's novel *Le Père Goriot.* If the President was the Olympian lion, his main challenger was the sharp-toothed fox, though the polls put him far behind when he announced his candidacy on 9 September.[24]

They were even less encouraging for the pro-European, pro-Atlanticist Lecanuet when he formally became a candidate on 19 October, giving him only a few per cent of the vote. The senator's campaign chances seemed all the smaller since he had said only a week earlier that de Gaulle was unbeatable. Another senator, Pierre Marcilhacy, who was even taller than de Gaulle, entered the battle as the representative of conservative provincial opinion. The one-time Vichyite and *Algérie française* lawyer, Jean-Louis Tixier-Vignancour, ran for the far right in the hope of rallying support from the remnants of the Poujadist vote as well as from *pieds-noirs* who had crossed the Mediterranean and those who remained faithful to the memory of the Marshal.

De Gaulle had still not declared if he would run for re-election. His wife's view was clear. 'He has done his time,' she told Pierre Lefranc. 'He gets tired more easily. Everything has gone well so far. One does not know what may happen. I beg you, don't press him.' 'Charles, you have done enough,' she said as they went in to lunch with the aide, Flohic, at Colombey one weekend in October. 'It is time to leave things to somebody younger than you.' Walking in the forest that afternoon, de Gaulle turned to Flohic, and asked: 'Tell me, do I have the strength to continue?' The aide recalled a Venetian Doge he had heard about on a holiday in the Adriatic who ruled into his eighties.

On his return to Paris, the President searched history books for examples of people who had continued an active life into old age. He had the courage to run but not to leave. He still had plenty of unfinished business to deal with, and linked himself with the survival of the Fifth Republic. If he did not get the overwhelming backing of the people, he told Flohic, 'nobody can doubt that everything will collapse'. On 4 November, he announced his candidacy.[25]

Though Mitterrand's support in the polls had doubled, de Gaulle was still far ahead with 66 per cent support, pointing to a comfortable first-round victory with an overall majority. It seemed that the election would be largely a formality. If he was not in power, the President declared, France would fall back into decline and chaos as the Fourth Republic was born anew. Buoyed by the poll figures and led by his natural disinclination to lower himself to electioneering, he made a fundamentally flawed decision to stay above the fray which would contribute to his biggest reverse since returning to power.

*

As the election campaign gathered pace, a nasty reminder of the seamier side of the regime came to light with the kidnapping of Mehdi Ben Barka, a Moroccan opposition leader who had been about to play a prominent role in a Third World conference in Cuba. Ben Barka was picked up in Paris by police at a rendezvous arranged in Saint-Germain-des-Prés by a frontman who pretended that he wanted to talk to him about making a film on the non-aligned movement. He was handed over to gangsters at a villa outside the city. There, he was tortured under the direction of the Moroccan Interior Minister, General Oufkir, who was visiting France, in an attempt to get him to reveal details of a strongbox containing political documents. Though no body was found, Ben Barka was believed to have been flown back to Morocco and killed by Oufkir's police.

The affair came to light when one of Ben Barka's associates tipped off *Le Monde*, and gained in notoriety as a key figure was found dead after police raided his flat. Day after day, a drip feed of leaks about the connivance of the French police and secret services reached the press. Mitterrand was the only candidate to refer to the case during the presidential campaign.

At a press conference early the following year, de Gaulle dismissed it as a minor matter, but he could not shake it off, particularly given his all-embracing claim to preside over judicial as well as political affairs. Asked why he had not kept the country informed, he tried to get away with a joke: 'Put it down to my inexperience.' In fact, he was furious at the way the affair showed links between the police and the underworld, at the way in which the Moroccans had acted on French soil, and at the suspicion that Oufkir, who was close to the CIA, was in league with the Americans. He ordered a reorganisation of the French police and secret service.

Two police officers were convicted of taking part in the kidnapping of Ben Barka. Oufkir was sentenced to life imprisonment by a French court, but *in absentia*; his principal lieutenant was acquitted. King Hassan of Morocco ignored a warning from de Gaulle about the effect on Franco-Moroccan relations, and kept Oufkir in his post. Reflecting on the affair after de Gaulle's press conference, Defferre noted that, since the General held the reins of all the state's powers, he must have worried that the details would become known and so was content for the matter to be hushed up. The fear of what a thorough investigation might reveal about the regime's less savoury links was enough to contain the General's ire; forty-four years later, legal proceedings started by the Ben Barka family were still being blocked by French authorities.[26]

V

Down to earth

For the first round of the election, de Gaulle declined to make any television appearances or to hold any meetings. This left the field open for his opponents. They now numbered five, including a small businessman, Marcel Barbu, standing to express 'his anger and indignation'. To run, candidates had to put up 100,000 francs to cover election expenses and get the signatures of a hundred elected officials, who included mayors of rural villages. They each got two hours of television time, which would have cost three million francs if it had been bought as advertising.

The appearance of opposition candidates on the small screen was a revolution, exploding the pro-regime orthodoxy observed over the years by the ORTF under government control. Suddenly, critical voices had their say in live, unedited performances, overwhelming the comforting images rolled out on news programmes at the direction of the Information Ministry. Just as de Gaulle had used the new medium to enter French homes, so the opposition now did the same, gaining audiences far beyond those they could reach at election rallies.

Mitterrand appeared nervous to start with and argued with media experts who told him how to sharpen his performance, though he did improve bit by bit. On the other hand, Lecanuet was made for the small screen, coming over as a young, Kennedy-style figure with gleaming white teeth who reached out to those put off by the General's age and his intransigent foreign policy; though he could not hope to get as many votes as the left-wing candidate, he was a greater danger to de Gaulle because of his appeal to centrists who would otherwise have backed the President. To hammer home their message, Lecanuet and Mitterrand crossed the country with rallies as the Gaullist camp depended on huge posters that merely showed the President in profile, and manipulation of the state television news to try to get over the progress made in France since 1958.

The General wrote to his sister that he 'had done what was necessary'. That was hardly true. Had he chosen to do so, he could have pointed to an honourable economic record – though there was a shortage of modern housing and the telephone system was backward, France was the world's fourth-biggest exporter and state finances were healthy. Instead, he did nothing to counter the complaints aroused by the effect of the Stabilisation Plan on purchasing power and continued to back Giscard d'Estaing's tight policy against Pompidou's growing doubts, to the discomfort of the Prime Minister – Pisani recalled that the Finance Minister's competence and knowledge enabled him to exercise 'a real seduction' over the General who regarded him as a pupil consistently getting full marks.

Despite the reservations of those who wanted a more constructive approach to Europe and the United States, polls showed that Gaullist foreign policy was broadly popular. He could have vaunted his global stature, and pointed to his decolonising record. But Lecanuet appealed to pro-Europeans and pro-Americans, and the General left it to his opponents to make the running on issues that spoke to the changing country. He was a man of his generation on matters such as women's liberation; after Mitterrand had put down a parliamentary bill to remove the ban on advocating birth control, de Gaulle exploded to Peyrefitte: 'The pill? Never! One cannot reduce women to a machine to make love! You would be going against what is most precious to a woman, fertility. She is made to have children! If one tolerates the pill, nothing will hold any more, sex will invade everything!'[27]

*

The polls told an increasingly depressing story. By 27 November, a week before the first round, de Gaulle's standing had fallen below 50 per cent, condemning him to a run-off ballot. 'If I have to bite, I will bite,' he said at a Cabinet meeting, but he vetoed a proposal by the Interior Minister to publicise Mitterrand's service under Vichy and his continuing friendship with René Bousquet. He dismissed the two men as representing 'the ghost of anti-Gaullism springing from the deepest reaches of Collaboration', but said that publicity would risk tarnishing the office of President if his opponent came to occupy it.

He did allow Debré to engage in a series of radio debates with Mendès France which were, in many ways, the highlight of the campaign and ended in a draw. Finally, at the end of November, the General consented to speak on television. It was one of his least convincing performances, not helped by bad lighting and awkward camera angles. As he broadcast, Lecanuet held a meeting of eight thousand supporters in a sports stadium – the centrist candidate was shown speaking on a giant screen while a small television set beside it carried de Gaulle's address. The audience roared with laughter.

Election day, 5 December, being a Sunday, de Gaulle was at Colombey. Cold rain was falling, so he did not take his customary walk but sat in his study in the hexagonal tower at the side of the house, writing. At 5 p.m. he emerged to take tea with his wife. At 8 p.m. he sat down in front of the television to watch the reports after the polls closed. He was credited with 43–44 per cent of the vote, Mitterrand with 32 per cent or more and Lecanuet with around 16 per cent. At 8.30, he and his wife went into the dining room for supper. The telephone rang. From the Élysée des Roziers confirmed the bad news: there would be a run-off ballot.

The General said he would stay at La Boisserie the following day as he pondered what to do in the face of this rebuff. Two hours later, another telephone call came through, from Pompidou, Joxe and Peyrefitte at Matignon. The great fear of the Gaullists was that their leader would react as he had in January 1946, and walk out. Three years later, he spoke to a television interviewer of 'a wave of sadness that almost carried me far away'. The anonymous author of the introduction to his papers for this period says that he had thought of writing a resignation letter.

Pompidou spoke first, but did not seem to make much of an impression. When Joxe took the telephone, he was greeted with a string of lamentations on the lines of 'I am retiring. They don't want me.' When it was his turn to come on the line, Peyrefitte thought he heard 'an adolescent who has been punished, who has stumbled, and who is burning to inflict a further chastisement on himself'. As the results were confirmed, they gave de Gaulle 43.71 per cent of the vote cast (or 10.5 million), Mitterrand 32.23 per cent (7.5 million) and Lecanuet 15.85 per cent (3.75 million). Tixier-Vignancour took 5.27 per cent and Marcilhacy and Barbu 1–2 per cent each. The abstention rate of 16 per cent was low.

Having drawn 44 per cent, the General was sure of victory in the second round. The man who had caused him most harm, Lecanuet, was eliminated by having finished third. So there was everything to fight for, Peyrefitte told him in the telephone call. De Gaulle growled and hung up. But, when Pompidou called back an hour later, his mood had changed. As the Prime Minister read out a statement he planned to issue speaking of a 'division which had stood in the way of the national élan', the General broke in to correct the verb 'to put off'. De Gaulle the fighter was back. The next morning, as at other crucial moments, he had a visit from his brother-in-law, Jacques Vendroux, and then went for a long walk in the forest.

The outcome in the first round could be attributed to a variety of factors – the General's age and election tactics, discontent with the effect of the Stabilisation Plan among workers and small shopkeepers and artisans, unpopularity of France's European and Atlantic policy among Christian Democrats, residual resentment at the loss of Algeria on the far right, the emergence of Lecanuet as the representative of a new France backed by heavy promotional spending, and Mitterrand's success in holding together a left-wing coalition that brought the PCF into play.

On his return to Paris, de Gaulle rejected Pompidou's suggestion that he attack Lecanuet and denounce Mitterrand for heading a Popular Front. The Christian Democrat was out of the race and should be ignored, he reasoned; launching an anti-leftist campaign would solidify his opponent's support while he could count on 10 per cent or more of votes from the working class. Ignoring his miscalculation about the first round, the General was set on waging his offensive in his own way, keeping the Prime Minister at arm's length.

On 9 December, de Gaulle noted down the main points he would make in television appearances before the run-off against Mitterrand. The context had changed, he wrote; 'fear has disappeared. Necessary national measures have annoyed interest groups. The feudal political groups are hostile.' The choice was between continuing consolidation of the Fifth Republic or chaos, division, a social crisis and the loss of independence. 'Conclude by saying that nothing will be done without a stable and coherent regime, that is, without the Fifth,' he ended. In answer to accusations of authoritarian rule, he had a simple reply: 'Have you ever seen a dictator in a run-off ballot?'

For the second round, he continued to refrain from public meetings while Mitterrand held big rallies in Nantes, Nice and Toulouse, and paraded the support of Auriol, Monnet and Sartre, though the value of backing from the last was diminished by an article a month earlier in which he called the opposition candidate 'worse than de Gaulle'.

The principal duel was on the television, and de Gaulle did as well this time as he had done badly previously. He allowed himself to be interviewed by the Gaullist journalist Michel Droit and assumed a more human face than most of his audience had encountered before. While retaining his superior tone, he was direct and cutting, in contrast to Mitterrand, who tried to present himself in a statesmanlike mode but was increasingly caught out by the difficulty of appealing to the varied coalition behind him. In the programmes with Droit, the General spoke of everyday concerns in a manner he had never done before: on the front page of *Le Figaro*, the cartoonist Jacques Faizant showed the figure of Marianne telling him: 'Ah, if only you had always spoken to me like that.'

In one of his three appearances, he bounced up and down in his chair to imitate the 'kid goats who jump up and down, crying "Europe!", "Europe!", "Europe!"'. In another, he spoke of 'choir boys who have drunk the local wine and who shout in favour of a supranational Europe'. (That last passage was excised from the broadcast on the advice of his political counsellors.) Still, his disdain annoyed Lecanuet, but the centrist knew that most of his voters would opt for the General in the second round out of antipathy towards the Communists and so issued a mealy-mouthed recommendation that left them free to cast their ballots as they wished.

As set down in his note, de Gaulle's core message remained the one he had been developing since 1958: France faced a choice between him and a chaotic return to the past. On 19 December, he was re-elected with 54.5 per cent of the vote. The turnout was again high, with an abstention rate of only 15 per cent – the pop star couple Johnny Hallyday and Sylvie Vartan were photographed hurrying home from a provincial gig to cast their ballots. De Gaulle scored well among women and those aged over forty. Geographically, his majority was largest in the economically developed areas of northern and eastern France as well as in Brittany and Alsace-Lorraine. He won votes not only among Lecanuet supporters but, less palatably, from the Tixier-Vignancour camp. Though the PCF rallied industrial workers, the opposition was rooted in the more traditional regions south of the Loire.

*

The election had been a watershed in a number of ways. For the first time, the General had run in a national poll. He had been forced into a man-to-man battle in the second round with an opponent he despised. The opinion polls had come into their own. Television had taken the campaign into people's homes – 26 per cent of those questioned by the IFOP organisation said they had been affected by what the candidates had said on the small screen. Two million young people had voted for the first time. More money was spent than ever before by candidates – Lecanuet's high-profile campaign was estimated to have cost four to five million francs while the posters and leaflets for the General may have involved double that amount.

The new Republic was widely accepted; even among Communist voters, 58 per cent thought it preferable to its predecessor while IFOP polls showed that three-quarters of those questioned approved of the direct election of the head of state, though many regretted the imbalance between the executive and the legislature. De Gaulle's personality remained a major factor in his relationship with his countrymen, but something changed in December 1965. The Olympian figure of the early years of the Fifth Republic had been brought down to earth.

The Constable might still aspire to stride the world stage as the last survivor of the generation of Roosevelt, Stalin and Churchill, delivering messages from on high and seeking to mould Europe to his preferred shape. But, at home, he had become an electoral politician. He had been deconsecrated; the section devoted to his period in the history of the Fifth Republic by the eminent journalist Pierre Viansson-Ponté is entitled 'The Blasphemy'.[28]

In the short run, the election dashed his hopes of eliminating political parties as a major element in the national system. His principal opponents had run as representatives of major groupings. Under Mitterrand, the FGDS had brought together the non-Communist parties of the Left. The UNR might call itself a 'union' rather than a party, and contain different strands, but its role was similar to that of a classic movement intent on getting its candidate elected to office; its disparate elements were bound together by their fealty to the General for, as Albin Chalandon said, 'we are his thing; he is not ours – but that did not make it any less of a party'.

Forty-four per cent of those questioned in an IFOP survey in November 1965 thought that the General behaved like the chief of a party – that would rise to 67 per cent two years later. The vision of a head of state swept to office by a national wave of support ranging from Left to Right remained a chimera. Two major and long-established parties had managed to cooperate and gain the support of more than 40 per cent of voters. If they could stick together, that presaged another major challenge in legislative elections due in 1967 which Jacques Fauvet of *Le Monde* described as 'the third round' of the battle between the General and his opponents.

But, longer term, the logic of the Fifth Republic was coming into play. If Lecanuet was a classic representative of the centre who could have come from the Third or Fourth Republic, Mitterrand was different. Like de Gaulle, he was an ambitious outsider. So, for all his family's assumed aristocratic name, was Giscard, clearly a new man who saw the opportunities offered by the post-1958 institutional framework to a brilliant and determined politician intent on reaching the summit.

Surveys taken at election time showed that the French regarded the building of a strong state, France's international status and the resolution of the Algerian crisis as the main achievements of the General's seven years in power. But those were now givens of his rule, which were increasingly taken for granted. The number of those polled who mentioned the Algerian settlement among the General's major successes dropped from between 64 and 79 per cent in 1962 to 14 per cent three years later. The Fourth Republic and the war across the sea had been left behind.

While de Gaulle warned of a return to bad old times if he was defeated at the polls, the regime had to be judged on its own six-year record. A changing society had new demands; for most French people, everyday realities counted for more than the President's sweeping rhetoric about what had been achieved under his rule. As always, at least part of his head was above the clouds seeking out new summits to reach while voters were more concerned with their earnings, the state of their housing and the education of their children. Surveys showed dissatisfaction with the regime's record in social policy, in making France a more egalitarian nation, in improving living standards for workers and in looking after farmers, small shopkeepers and artisans.

To Debré the General described the result as '*peu brillant*' ('hardly brilliant'). To François Mauriac he observed that 'when no drama threatens, what can the "results" be?' To his sister he lamented that the French were opting for an easy life. In letters to others he put inverted commas around the word 'election' as if it had not been a valid event. But to his Cabinet he was honest: he had mistaken an election for a referendum. The man who, from 1958 to 1962, had embodied the General Will, as defined by Rousseau, could no longer ride above the divisions he would have liked to deny. As he said to Adenauer the following March, the electorate consisted of 'peasants, workers, white collar workers, shopkeepers, the poor, the middle class who all have their own complaints to make heard. In general, the French people are in favour of my policy, but this is less the case when it comes to their special interests.' The electoral path from 1958 had been mainly downhill. While the Algerian settlement had gained overwhelming backing, the 1962 constitutional vote had not been the plebiscite he had hoped for, only a simple referendum victory on fewer than half the registered electorate. Now, he had been brought further down to earth as the result of the only popular election he ever faced marked the start of a long divorce between the Constable and his people.[29]

33

TILTING AT WINDMILLS

I
Emperor's clothes

Despite the less than triumphant election result, de Gaulle told the nation in his New Year broadcast that 1966 would be 'the year of serenity, confidence and ardour' and pledged 'an end to doubts, to feeling our way, to giving up'. But the experience of being forced into a run-off ballot appears to have sharpened the General's behaviour. Far from moving towards moderation, he became more extreme, even more convinced that he was correct, even more committed to setting out his views on the world stage. His focus on developing France's military strength grew stronger as he insisted that it must move from atomic to thermonuclear weapons which would be tested at the Pacific site of Mururoa and would show the world that he and his country belonged in the first rank of world powers.

He was also goaded on by the remorseless oppression of age. 'Given the point I am at, how can I expect to be here for seven years?' he asked Alain Peyrefitte as he instructed the Information Minister what to tell reporters after the first Cabinet meeting of his second term. The Secretary-General at the Élysée, Burin des Roziers, recalled that he spoke of resigning after two or three years, but then changed his mind because he did not have sufficient confidence in any of the available successors to continue the Gaullist mission. In that context, he stepped up his efforts to fulfil the historic role he had set himself as if to deny his mortality. Even more than before, he recognised no limits, accepted no compromises, closing his eyes to the true global balance of power and to France's limited resources as he moved into overdrive, his global fame greater than ever – four biographies of him were published in English during 1966.

For all his renown and the shocks he caused, however, the outcome was too often that the emperor's clothes were shown to be full of holes as the old magician exercised his enormous skills to little avail. His pursuit of Shakespeare's 'great argument', or, rather, of several at the same time, rang increasingly hollow, while his lack of concern for ideological issues meant that he did not appreciate the depth of the divide between East and West. There were some successes and a major decision on NATO, but, viewed objectively, the overall results were far from happy. As Eisenhower noted to one of the General's biographers: 'It was all or nothing with him. He wanted it at the top, all the way, like Caesar. [But] he didn't have any means of exercising real world power.' Not that this would restrain the General from tilting at his chosen windmills or reading lessons to others. The comparison to Don Quixote is inevitable, particularly with the comforting, rotund figure of Georges Pompidou playing the role of Sancho Panza.[1]

*

The Prime Minister, who was reappointed after the presidential election, reshuffled his government. Giscard d'Estaing, who had been adamant about maintaining the Stabilisation Plan while Pompidou wanted to relax it, was replaced as Finance Minister, and concentrated on building up his independent position as a supporter of the administration who would still be free to criticise it as he wished. Debré moved into the ornate Finance Ministry on the rue de Rivoli; his title, Minister of the Economy and Finance, reflected his desire to run a wide-ranging portfolio which would include social affairs, entrusted to his friend Jean-Marcel Jeanneney.

Edgar Faure came in as Agriculture Minister. De Gaulle's long-time aide, Christian Fouchet, was put in charge of education, with the particular job of sorting out France's universities where a huge expansion of student numbers was putting great pressure on the old structures and teaching methods. Though Giscard went, another Independent

Republican, Raymond Marcellin, became Minister of Industry. A dour figure who had been a civil servant under Vichy, he had become an ardent supporter of the General and was on bad terms with his party leader.

Pompidou's nose had been put out of joint by the way de Gaulle had kept him at arm's length during the presidential election. Now he found himself at odds with the President's support for employee 'participation' to give workers a say in the running of their firms. As a banker who believed in private enterprise, the Prime Minister made sure that such ideas advanced by left-wing Gaullists were marginalised, though the General's hostility towards capitalism and search for national unity meant they would never go away.

Nor did Debré's attempts to establish a counter-power at the top of the government get anywhere; the former Premier ranked only fifth in the ministerial list and Pompidou kept a close eye on the economic programme, which provided for some liberalisation of prices, incentives for investment and reductions in the state deficit. Industrial mergers were encouraged to give France more companies which would be competitive on a European and global scale. Measures were introduced to boost the income of farmers who also benefited from the resolution of the crisis which had led to France's 'empty chair' boycott of Common Market proceedings; the outcome satisfied de Gaulle's insistence on sovereignty by granting member states the right of veto when their vital national interests were at stake. Other sections of the population were less content with the continuing depression of wages. Between January and April, there were strikes in the postal and telephone services, the big shipyard outside Marseille, in Paris public transport and the national railways as well as in the electricity and gas network.

*

At the end of February 1966, de Gaulle wrote a note to Pompidou, Couve de Murville and Messmer, at the Ministry for Armies, laying down the procedures to be followed to take France out of NATO's integrated structure on 1 March 1967. Two weeks later, the Foreign Minister handed the US ambassador a four-page handwritten letter from de Gaulle to President Johnson announcing the decision. The Americans were not surprised; the General had been signalling his intention for years, and the CIA had an agent in the Quai d'Orsay who kept them informed of the way French thinking was going. De Gaulle wrote in similar terms to the German Chancellor, Ludwig Erhard, the British Prime Minister, Harold Wilson, and President Saragat of Italy.

He said France planned to remain within the alliance and assured Washington it would be determined 'to fight on the side of its allies in the event that one of them should be the object of unprovoked aggression'. He did not want US troops to quit Western Europe altogether, given the need to guard against Soviet expansion, but all non-French military personnel would have to leave France and their installations would be shut down as the alliance's headquarters went from Paris to Brussels. NATO planes would not be allowed to use French air space without prior agreement. While hardly a surprise, de Gaulle's move aroused considerable emotion on the other side of the Atlantic; Johnson told Dean Rusk to ask de Gaulle if he wanted the American dead of two world wars to be removed as well. According to the Secretary of State, the question left the General embarrassed.

Withdrawal from the NATO structure was inevitably connected in the public mind with the General's efforts to develop closer relations with the Soviet Union; Hervé Alphand, the former ambassador in Washington who was now the top civil servant at the Quai d'Orsay, told Charles Bohlen that it was designed to foster détente with Moscow, a line also put forward by Couve de Murville. The move contained dangers; it was likely to give a greater role to West Germany, and de Gaulle's absolutist approach made it appear that the only alternatives for NATO were integration and withdrawal of countries which wanted change. But it was made inevitable by his deep and long-standing attachment to national sovereignty and to his abhorrence of the idea that French troops might go to war under US command.[2]

In his letter to Erhard, de Gaulle expressed the hope that Franco-German cooperation would become more evident in the defence field; he subsequently confirmed that French occupation troops would remain across the Rhine. But, without bringing the friendship treaty into question, Paris and Bonn were drifting apart. There were specific points of difference. West Germany declined to accept the French SECAM system for colour television – the General accused it of having reached a prior agreement with the Americans and British. Monetary proposals by the German central banker Otmar Emminger ran counter to France's championing of gold, and the General dismissed them as an effort to save the Americans from putting their house in order. In a paper on foreign affairs written before a visit to Paris by Erhard, de Gaulle attributed the 'growing difficulty' between the two countries to the fact that 'the Germans are no longer the polite and decent defeated power seeking to gain the favour of the victor. Today, the Germans feel their basic force being reborn and are motivated by new ambitions.'

While he said he supported the eventual reunification of Germany, the key word was 'eventual'. He continued to oppose redrawing the 1945 frontiers in the east as Bonn wanted. He looked with disfavour on any moves by the Erhard government to get access to nuclear weapons. Germany was a European nation whereas France had a global vocation, he continued in his note. So, while the two countries could cooperate on certain matters, there could be no true Franco-German policy.[3]

*

Increasingly insistent on promoting his vision of a continent stretching 'from the Atlantic to the Urals', de Gaulle set out on a ten-day visit to the Soviet Union in June 1966. He memorised Russian phrases while advance parties of French experts laid the groundwork for discussions on subjects ranging from oceanography to France's colour television technology. De Gaulle, whose interpreter was a White Russian prince from Paris, was accorded all the honours. He was greeted at the airport by Khrushchev's successors, the Communist Party chief, Leonid Brezhnev, the Prime Minister, Alexei Kosygin, and the President of the Supreme Soviet, Nikolai Podgorny. He was taken from Moscow to Leningrad, Kiev, Volvograd and Siberia, and became the first Western leader to be allowed into a Soviet space centre, where a satellite launch was laid on for him. Large crowds turned out, though the correspondent of *Le Monde* had doubts about the spontaneity of their welcome.

In speeches on the trip de Gaulle lauded the 'peaceful ardour' of his hosts and of a 'new alliance of Russia and France'. He looked forward to the end of the Cold War, and to a wider, more encompassing Europe. It was all very vague, and the Soviets made a point of flying de Gaulle to Siberia to demonstrate how far the USSR extended beyond Europe. There was an agreement to install a hotline between the Kremlin and the Élysée, but, since de Gaulle was disinclined to use such means of communication, it meant nothing in practice. The Soviets agreed to adopt the French colour television system and Renault set up a plant in the USSR. A further agreement provided for a Soviet rocket to launch a French satellite. But, in terms of achieving a new East–West equilibrium with France in the central position, there was no progress. As Couve de Murville remarked, the most important thing about the trip was that it had taken place at all.

The General pursued his courtship of the Russians; when Kosygin visited France at the end of the year, the de Gaulles attended a reception at the Soviet embassy, an honour previously bestowed only on Adenauer. But his basic loyalty to the West, his refusal to recognise East Germany and the tough line he took over Berlin put a limit on what he could get out of the relationship with Moscow. For the Kremlin, evocations of a historic Franco-Russian entente cut little ice. Moscow did not share the General's ambition to see Vietnam become a neutral state – it wanted its ally in the North to conquer the South and poured in aid to Hanoi. Brezhnev summed up the Russian view of the General to the Polish leaders – while he was 'an enemy', his policy had the advantage of weakening US positions in Europe. So he would be humoured. But when it came to Great Power politics, the reality was that he was not much further forward with the Soviets than he had been with Stalin.[4]

Nor did he make any more of an impression on Washington despite delivering his strongest attack on US policy in a speech to a crowd of 300,000 in Phnom Penh in September 1966 in which he spoke of the 'national resistance struggle' in Vietnam and urged the Americans to follow the example of the French in withdrawing from Algeria. There was an intriguing subtext to the speech. On the eve of the General's departure from Paris for the Far East, Dean Rusk sent a letter to Couve de Murville laying out two possible scenarios for an American withdrawal, and asking the General to use his influence to get the

Cambodian ruler, Norodom Sihanouk, to act as an intermediary between Washington, Saigon and Hanoi. De Gaulle took no heed of this. The French said later that the letter had arrived when the Foreign Minister was away from Paris, which seems an extremely feeble explanation. Rather, one can only wonder whether Vietnam had become such a hobby horse in the General's anti-American crusade that he preferred to ignore the letter from the Secretary of State so that he could go ahead with his speech in Phnom Penh. His course was certainly set; back in Paris, he spoke to a press conference of 'the bombing of a small people by a very large one' and then, in his New Year broadcast, castigated 'a detestable war since it leads a large nation to ravage a small one'.[5]

II
Electoral test

While the General had been globe-trotting, the Pompidou government was preparing for legislative elections to be held in March 1967. Growth was running at a more than respectable 5 per cent a year; household consumption was rising by 4.4 per cent; inflation was kept down to 2.8 per cent. But unemployment was at its highest level for a decade. Industrial output was faltering. Profit margins were low. There were recurrent strikes. Exports were hit by a downturn in demand elsewhere in the Common Market. The budget deficit grew. Major state companies announced big losses. At the Finance Ministry, Debré admitted that it seemed as if the objectives of the five-year economic plan would not be met. Reflationary measures were announced, but the public was morose.

For the fifty-six-year-old Prime Minister, who had established himself as leader of the parliamentary majority and chief manager of the Gaullist party, the poll would be his big national test. Though its member groups had differences, particularly over their relations with the Communists, the FGDS that had backed Mitterrand in the presidential election continued to link Socialists, Radicals and smaller parties. In December, it reached a pact for the coming elections with the PCF, which was then joined by the small left-wing ginger group, the

Parti Socialiste Unifié (Unified Socialist Party) (PSU), whose most illustrious member was Mendès France and which, while it brought few votes, contributed significant intellectual weight.

What Jacques Fauvet of *Le Monde* dubbed 'an open marriage' on the Left was facilitated by the rise of reformism in the PCF ranks as some prominent Communists explored a more open dialogue with outsiders. Critics might dismiss this as show, but Party thinkers such as the philosopher Roger Garaudy held out the hope of joining the 'EuroCommunist' trend. Membership figures showed an influx of young people as the PCF drew on discontent with the regime.[6]

Pompidou had other problems closer to home. Giscard d'Estaing, who was still only forty and had won points with the President for his pursuit of the Stabilisation Plan, waged a lengthy, though ultimately unsuccessful, campaign for Independent Republican candidates to be allowed to run against Gaullists while remaining members of the majority; Pompidou insisted on a united front. In the middle ground, Lecanuet had formed a new party, the *Centre démocrate* (Democratic Centre) and threatened to draw off voters alienated by the General's heightened intransigence on the international scene. Inside the government, Debré was always a potential challenger to the Premier and there was speculation that the General regarded the ever-loyal, unquestioning Couve de Murville as a successor at Matignon.

At the end of 1966, de Gaulle drew up a draft for an electoral statement for the legislative poll. He laid out what had been achieved in creating strong institutions, decolonisation and economic revival. Industrial modernisation should continue and agriculture should be renovated, with the state playing the guiding role. Educational reform was needed to improve the nation's skills. National independence must be safeguarded and the nuclear programme pursued – he had watched a bomb test in the South Pacific after his visit to Cambodia. Before the campaign opened, he went on television and radio to warn that an opposition victory would bring 'utter ruin'. He delivered a similar warning after the campaign closed. Even if the opposition gained a majority, he held that this would not affect the mandate he had received from the people in 1965. All that was taking place, he remarked, was '487 local elections'. In any case, the Gaullists expected to win easily, in line with favourable opinion polls. But the President got Pompidou to sign an undated resignation letter in case he decided to replace him.[7]

The Gaullist campaign was launched at a mass rally in Paris at which the Prime Minister sat between Malraux and Chaban-Delmas. Images projected on a giant screen showed 'France's victories', ranging from nuclear power stations to the skier Jean-Claude Killy – it included two Nobel prize-winners who backed the opposition. Couve and Messmer were pressed into standing for election for the first time to give them a popular legitimacy. Pompidou ran in the first election of his life in the Auvergne department of the Cantal, where his parents came from. He criss-crossed the country to speak at election rallies and did well in public debates with Mendès France and Mitterrand in their constituencies of Grenoble and Nevers.

The first round of voting on 5 March, which attracted an 80 per cent turnout, gave government candidates running under the banner of the 'Action Committee for the Fifth Republic' 37.7 per cent of votes. That was the highest score any French party had ever achieved, and induced a certain degree of complacency among government supporters. But there was a shock in store as highly effective agreements between Communists and Socialists to pool votes for the second round produced a knife-edge finish. The outcome was so close that the Gaullist high command had to wait for the result from the South Pacific territory of Wallis et Futuna to be sure that it had a parliamentary majority which could be calculated at anything from one to nine seats depending on how non-party deputies were classified.

Once again, de Gaulle's ambitions of seeing a large majority of the French unite behind him were dashed. His followers mustered only 42.6 per cent of votes cast while the Left took 46.4 per cent. The Gaullists lost 33 Assembly seats to end up with 200, while their main opponents raised their representation from 146 to 194. This made the government dependent on the 44 Independent Republicans for its slim majority – Giscard's group had gained 9 seats. Many of the constituency results were close; small last-minute swings in favour of the government would have produced a different outcome. But that had not happened, and the disavowal of the administration was unarguable. De Gaulle put a distance between himself and what had taken place. Alain Peyrefitte told Jean Lacouture that he snorted: 'So, you've won *your* elections. That's a pity.' If the Left had won, he added, 'We would have seen how we could govern using the constitution.'[8]

The President might have thought before the election of replacing Pompidou, but his preferred candidate, Couve de Murville, had been beaten by 250 votes by a conservative incumbent in the 7th *arrondissement* of Paris so was ruled out. In addition, to change Prime Minister could have been seen as an admission of weakness. So Pompidou stayed. His new government kept familiar faces at the top – despite an assurance the previous July that a minister defeated at the polls would have to quit, Couve kept the Quai d'Orsay and Messmer, who had also been defeated, remained as Minister for Armies. Two old Gaullists, Edmond Michelet and Maurice Schumann, returned, in charge of the civil service and research respectively, while Olivier Guichard took on the industry portfolio.

Several protégés of the Prime Minister got junior posts. They included Jacques Chirac, a hungry thirty-five-year-old politician who became number two at the Social Affairs Ministry. He had won a notable entry to parliament from the opposition bastion of the Corrèze after beating Mitterrand's brother with a campaign that included gaining the support of the provincial doyen, Henri Queuille, who remarked that the young man's suppleness qualified him to be a Radical Socialist. De Gaulle received him for thirty minutes at the Élysée, questioning him about local politics in the Corrèze, and then suggesting that he should be appointed as a deputy minister, an idea with which the Prime Minister was only too happy to agree.[9]

When the new National Assembly met, the opposition launched a series of violent attacks on the government during stormy debates which led to a Gaullist fighting a duel with swords with Defferre who had treated him as an idiot. (The Gaullist was slightly wounded in one arm.) Given its precarious majority, the administration used decrees to push through measures, particularly on the economy. The memorandum from Pompidou announcing this course was suddenly sprung on the Cabinet during a discussion about wine prices. Edgard Pisani resigned in protest from his post as Infrastructure Minister; he had other reasons to feel unhappy since Pompidou had tried to slim down his portfolio and de Gaulle had taken no notice of his advice to adopt a more open style of government.

There were strikes against the use of decrees, and three parliamentary censure motions which were only narrowly defeated. Though he did not speak out in public, Giscard was increasingly hostile, telling the American diplomat Charles Bohlen that de Gaulle was 'an era out of date'. However, there was some balm for the government when the federation headed by Mitterrand broke up over the disinclination of the Socialists to surrender their identity in a wider grouping while, among the centrists, Pleven and a rising figure, Jacques Duhamel, engaged in contacts with Pompidou.

Writing to his sister, de Gaulle regretted the 'mediocre' situation, and told Pompidou to focus on schemes for worker participation in companies and an alliance of labour and capital; but there was nobody in the Cabinet to press such ideas and the hostility between left-wing Gaullists and Pompidou ensured that nothing much was done. His latest plunge into domestic politics having proved a fresh disappointment, the President turned his attention back to international affairs, with ever more controversial effects.[10]

III
Israel

In the early summer, after a visit to London by Pompidou and Couve de Murville, Harold Wilson renewed Britain's bid to enter the Common Market, but got nowhere with the General who had already used a press conference to accuse the United Kingdom of lining up with Washington to subvert the continent. The Labour Party leader, who had approved of the veto on the Macmillan application in 1963, had changed his mind, in part because of a shift in domestic opinion, but the General had not. Speaking to Erhard's successor, the Christian Democrat Kurt Georg Kiesinger, he said that British membership would mean the end of the Franco-German relationship.[11]

The General's coolness towards the United States was on somewhat comic public display when he and Lyndon Johnson attended Adenauer's funeral in Cologne. The West German President, Heinrich

Luebke, had to take the hands of the two visitors, who stood on either side of him, and join them as they posed with other eminent mourners for a ceremonial photograph. The gesture ended awkwardly with de Gaulle grasping Johnson's outstretched thumb; the General looked no more enthusiastic than he had when Roosevelt got him to shake hands with Giraud in Casablanca. At the reception afterwards, he made it known that he would like to speak to the American. But he did not move towards him. Instead, emissaries fetched LBJ.[12]

As border clashes had escalated between Israel and its Arab neighbours, de Gaulle focused on the Middle East in the early summer of 1967. President Nasser of Egypt had expelled the United Nations Emergency Force stationed in the Sinai Peninsula since the Anglo-French Suez expedition of 1956. For the General, the situation represented an ideal theatre in which, as by far the most senior international statesman, he could act as a mediator. Since the Fourth Republic, France had been a big supplier of advanced weapons to Israel but had also built up relations with Arab nations and planned to go further with the big oil states.

When the Israeli Prime Minister, Levi Eshkol, wrote to him on 21 May asking for a declaration of support for his country's security and territorial integrity, and for Paris to try to get Moscow to restrain Nasser, de Gaulle did not reply for a week. Instead, on 24 May, he proposed that the United States, the Soviet Union, France and Britain review the mounting tension. On the same day, he received the Israeli Foreign Minister, Abba Eban, who was on his way to Washington, and told him: 'If Israel is attacked we shall not let it be destroyed, but if you attack we shall condemn your action.'

Though Washington and London accepted the French proposal to concert action, Moscow, which backed Nasser, turned it down. This showed plainly the limited results of the General's attempts to build a special relationship with Moscow. Far from playing the central role to which he aspired, he was left on the sidelines while the key diplomacy to try to avert war took place between Johnson and Kosygin.

As the crisis escalated, de Gaulle took an increasingly hostile attitude towards Israel. When Egypt closed a key southern maritime access route to Israel to ships flying Israeli flags or carrying strategic supplies, the General did not respond to suggestions that he should criticise the blockade of an international waterway. Nor did he reply to pressing appeals from Israeli leaders to speak out publicly. Eshkol wrote of his 'perplexity that, at such a grave moment, the voice of France, guardian of liberty and pioneer of civilisation, has still not been heard'. On 1 June, de Gaulle received at the Élysée the King of Saudi Arabia and the Syrian Foreign Minister, both avowed enemies of Israel's existence. At his meeting with the Saudi monarch, he noted that the existence of the Jewish state was a fact, but went no further, adding that France had had nothing to do with its creation.

On 5 June, Israel launched its victorious Six Day War. Despite Moscow's rejection of his mediation offer, de Gaulle backed a Soviet call for an emergency session of the UN General Assembly. His position was now quite plain, and was accentuated by the link between America and Israel. His private opinion of Arabs was not high, but he saw their countries as useful economic partners, and may have hoped that they would regard him as a guide independent of the two superpowers. On the other hand, he remarked to Jacques Foccart that the Israelis were 'unbearable'; he said they had caused problems at the creation of the state in 1948 and again at the time of Suez in 1956. 'It's not by force that they will resolve their difficulties,' he added.[13]

The General was left looking isolated and impotent. Some Gaullists were unhappy and, among non-Gaullist groups, only the Communist Party backed him. Giscard d'Estaing signed a statement of solidarity with Israel along with Mitterrand and Lecanuet. Gaullists in the National Assembly applauded Mollet when he defended Israel's right to exist. Three leading members of the government were reported to be in sympathy – Frey, Schumann and Debré. A poll showed 60 per cent support for the Jewish state.

'I think that . . . he has been forced to face reality and France's true lack of influence in international affairs,' Harold Wilson wrote to Johnson after a visit to Paris. At heart, the General understood that he had reached an impasse, the Prime Minister added, but he was too old and too tired psychologically to envisage a new approach. Forced back into a corner, the old soldier insisted that most French people did not want a quarrel with the Arab states, and then lashed out at his favourite target. At a garden party at the Élysée, he told parliamentarians World War Three had been set in train in Vietnam. The conflict there was the only thing that prevented Washington and Moscow reaching an understanding, he added. Then a blistering statement after a Cabinet meeting drew a link between America's 'fundamentally sterile' intervention in Vietnam and the Six Day War. The first, it said, had launched a 'psychological and political process' that led to the second. So peace would only be possible in the Middle East if US intervention in Vietnam ended. The link was stated as a fact, with no evidence.[14]

France voted with the Soviet bloc countries for an unsuccessful UN resolution demanding Israel's unconditional withdrawal from territories occupied during the conflict, rather than for a softer resolution, which was passed with backing from other Western countries. Receiving the Saudi Interior Minister and the Emir of Kuwait, de Gaulle expressed France's support for the Arab states and 'sympathy with the difficulties you have with Israel'. The refusal of the Eshkol government to follow his admonition not to go to war continued to rankle. 'What do you think they did with my advice? They completely ignored it!' he complained to Bohlen. Such *lèse-majesté* was clearly unacceptable.[15]

The payback came at a press conference in November, but, as so often with de Gaulle, there were two sides to what he said. He set off a storm by referring to Jews as 'an elite people, sure of themselves and domineering' who, once gathered into a state, were destined to show 'burning and conquering ambition'. He followed this with an account of the evolution of French policy, saying that, while supplying arms, the Fifth Republic had disengaged from France's previous very close ties because it believed that the 'warrior state of Israel' would take any opportunity to seize additional territory to house its growing population. Egypt's blockade of the Gulf of Aqaba had created 'a pretext to those who wanted war', he added. The occupation of land conquered in the Six Day War could not continue 'without oppression, repression, expulsions, while at the same time a resistance grows', he went on.[16]

Accusations of anti-Semitism flew about following his characterisation of the Jews. De Gaulle felt a need to reply. In a letter to Ben-Gurion, he insisted that he had meant nothing disparaging; on the contrary, the characteristics he had attributed to the Jews were the key to their survival through the centuries. Israel, he concluded, had become a state among others, its future depending on the policy it followed which, he added, had to be adapted to reality. Despite the provocative language the General used, the charge of anti-Semitism in the classic sense is hard to maintain against him. When they met in 1968, France's Grand Rabbi thought him genuinely surprised by the fuss he had caused, saying that his words had been intended as praise; indeed, in his mind, an elite was to be prized. But he showed a colossal blindness when he asked the Gaullist Léo Hamon how a non-practising Jew like him could have been offended, as if defining Jewishness by synagogue attendance.

The whole episode can best be seen as an example of his pique at being bypassed and reminded of the limits of his international sway. There were also two other elements in play. Their prospects under an Arab government had made many *pied-noir* Jews oppose his Algerian policy – an assassination attempt had been organised by one and Soustelle had close links with Israel. Some French Algeria figures such as Colonel 'Leather Nose' Thomazo had joined a demonstration in Paris in favour of Israel. These were not the kind of associations to be overlooked by de Gaulle, a man who was always on the outlook for enemies real or supposed; he said that a petition on behalf of Israel drawn up by members of the Élysée military staff reminded him of pro-*Algérie française* sympathies in his staff in the early years of his presidency.

More fundamentally, he allowed the people of France to have only one loyalty. He had castigated Jean Monnet and his fellow enthusiasts for European integration and the transatlantic alliance as having sold out to the United States. He classed the Communists as a foreign party. In that context, the evident identification with Israel of French Jews (and many gentiles) made them suspect in his eyes, particularly when tens of thousands demonstrated for a foreign country against his policy. He sent back to Marshal Koenig, who was a strong supporter of Israel, three Nazi trophies which the victor of Bir Hakeim had presented to him and which had been displayed at Colombey. In his conversation with Hamon, he said he had been shocked by pro-Israel statements on the war by the Rothschilds, and 'thought also of the Dassaults and those like them who do not even have the pride to keep their names', a remark his visitor could not have appreciated since his own name had originally been Goldberg.

Taken together, such factors created a network of resentments towards a country which, in many ways, echoed the General's vision of what a nation should be. In this, as in his tortured relationship with the United States, he was the prisoner of his own mindset to a degree that became more and more accentuated. Few episodes did more to reduce his status in the eyes of many of his countrymen and the world. According to Peyrefitte, Pompidou took it as a fresh sign of how age had changed the General. The most crushing verdict came from the most loyal of followers: the General displayed 'an infantile-psychological-senile' attitude, judged Debré, the grandson of a Chief Rabbi of France.[17]

IV
Quebec

The General's wilfulness was on display once again in July 1967, when he visited the French-speaking Canadian province of Quebec, where a movement calling for independence had been established in 1957. The trip had trouble written all over it from the start, trouble the General would relish. There were advance tremors. De Gaulle had refused to agree to extend the honours given to a head of state to the Governor-General of Canada on a planned visit to France because he was appointed by the British monarch; the visit to France was cancelled. At the start of 1967, he reacted angrily when the Canadians organised a ceremony at their First World War cemetery at Vimy Ridge in the Pas-de-Calais without asking for French permission, and invited the Duke of Edinburgh to preside over the occasion. Before leaving Paris for Quebec, he told his son-in-law, Alain de Boissieu: 'I will hit hard. Hell will happen, but it has to be done.' He added that he would be making up for France's abandonment of its colonists across the Atlantic in the eighteenth century.[18]

De Gaulle chose not to travel via the federal capital of Ottawa, but to board a French cruiser, the *Colbert*, in Saint-Pierre et Miquelon and sail up the St Lawrence River. Before boarding the ship, he told an aide: 'They will hear me over there, it will make waves!' Arriving in Quebec's biggest metropolis of Montreal, he went to the City Hall where he insisted on going on to the balcony earlier than planned to address the enthusiastic crowd gathered outside. He compared the welcome to the scenes in Paris at the Liberation, and ended with '*Vive Montréal! Vive le Québec!*' – then added '*Vive le Québec libre! Vive le Canada français! Et vive la France!*'

The speech, broadcast live on radio, prompted an immediate storm. Quebec separatists seized on his use of their 'Free Quebec' slogan. The Canadian government declared de Gaulle's words unacceptable, and a planned visit to Ottawa was called off. The Prime Minister, Lester Pearson, commented that 'Canadians do not need to be liberated. Indeed, many thousands of Canadians gave their lives in two world wars in the liberation of France and other European countries.' Justice Minister Pierre Trudeau, a native of Montreal, wondered how the French would react if a Canadian leader shouted 'Brittany for the Bretons'. (As it happened, Paris was soon to clamp down on autonomists in Brittany.)

Beuve-Méry in *Le Monde* detected 'an exaggerated self-importance and over-estimation of France's role'. A number of ministers were also worried. Without naming names, Peyrefitte quotes some of them as saying that the General had lost his bearings and been carried away by the crowd. Couve de Murville described the remark as 'bloody stupid' (*une connerie*). To show his disagreement, Edgar Faure did not join the welcoming party at the airport. But others approved, and Pompidou insisted that they must all show solidarity, though Peyrefitte recalled that the Prime Minister observed to him that the episode showed once more how the General had changed.[19]

De Gaulle exhibited absolutely no remorse. Flying home, he told his travelling companions that what he had said was 'a historical phenomenon' shaped by events. Others might have limited themselves to diplomatic courtesies, 'but when one is Général de Gaulle, one does not get away with those kinds of expedients. What I did, I had to do.' A statement issued at the end of the month stressed the 'immense French fervour' and the 'indescribable wave of emotion' the President had encountered, noting the desire of French Canadians to 'become masters of their own progress' with which France would associate itself.

At a press conference in November, de Gaulle made much of the fate of the French language in Canada. He hailed Quebec's 'rank of a sovereign state, master of its national independence'. However, when French-speaking Belgians asked him to declare himself for 'Free Wallonia!', he desisted, saying that he could not afford himself the luxury of breaking their country apart.[20]

*

After his forays into the Middle East and North America, he pursued another individualist, if largely covert, course by backing the secession of Biafra from Nigeria. France became a major arms supplier to the breakaway administration. Biafran oil was one motivation, but de Gaulle also welcomed the prospect of Nigeria becoming less powerful via-à-vis French-speaking states of West Africa. In Europe, meanwhile, he sought to augment his efforts to get closer to Moscow by building up France's links in east Europe – Couve had made eight visits to the region in two years, and his boss capped this by visiting Poland in September 1967.

He took care not to antagonise his hosts by avoiding the Polish Roman Catholic primate, Cardinal Wyszynski, an opponent of the regime – this led the Bishop of Krakow, the future Pope John Paul II, to refuse to receive him. From Krakow, he visited Auschwitz, where he sat at a small table in the open air meditating on what to set down in the visitors' book open in front of him. 'What sadness!' he wrote at last, then 'What disgust!' After a long pause, he added 'What pity!' and then 'What human hope!' Feeling the need to qualify those last words, he wrote in front of them 'And despite everything'. Slowly, he got up and walked away, telling a Polish woman that hope had not died at the camp because the nightmare had finally ended and those responsible for so many crimes had been defeated.[21]

In his speeches on the trip, de Gaulle repeated his call for cooperation on behalf of a Europe stretching from the Atlantic to the Urals. But the only response from Polish leaders was that their security depended on Moscow. The General also managed to annoy West Germany by referring to the city of Zabrze in Silesia, still known as Hindenberg by the Germans, as 'the most Polish of all Polish cities'. It was a pointless remark and, as a Polish newspaper wrote acidly, 'A guarantee of the Oder–Neisse border by France is not necessarily an event of major importance.' It was difficult not to conclude that the Frenchman was being carried away by his own rhetoric and his star status.[22]

After returning from Poland, he pursued his crusade against the dollar, while leaks to *Le Monde* put pressure on the British currency. But the ground was shifting at home. The government's essential ally, Giscard d'Estaing, spoke for many when he criticised 'the solitary exercise of power' and went on to define the support of the Independent Republicans for the General as 'yes but'. Cantonal elections, which strongly reflected local factors, brought further progress for the Communists and gave the combined forces of the Left an overall majority while the Gaullists and Independent Republicans could only attract 18.5 per cent of the votes between them.

The essentially conservative nature of the regime was evident and it was increasingly out of tune with society. In one telling case, the faithful Gaullist Lucien Neuwirth got the General's agreement to a bill to end the ban on contraception and the Cabinet approved a draft law. Then the proposal was referred to the Committee on Population and the Family which agreed to the measure only because it could prevent abortions. When the bill went to parliament, conservatives warned that contraception might lead to a decline in the morality of women and encourage them to become prostitutes. One speaker asked if men realised that legalising the pill would mean that women would control whether couples had children – 'Men will pose the proud consciousness of their virility,' he added, 'and women will be no more than the objects of sterile voluptuousness.' The law that eventually emerged was hedged round with provisos. At a Cabinet meeting, the President ruled out reimbursement of contraception under the social security system. He accepted that the French wanted freer moral standards, but 'the pill is for distraction,' he explained.[23]

Pompidou organised the Gaullists into a new party, *L'Union des Démocrates pour la Vème République* (UDVe), promoting young figures to replace wartime veterans, promoting a simplistic Manichaean picture of a France that had to choose between freedom and Marxist totalitarianism. De Gaulle insisted that the new party did not in any way affect his link with the French people. He, and he alone, had the mandate to rule. A decade after his return to power, he was not ready to cede any of his authority as he went into a year that would bring the most dramatic test of his relationship with the nation.

PART SEVEN
SHADOWS AND NIGHT

34

'GREAT THINGS ALWAYS END BADLY'

I
'France is bored'

De Gaulle's New Year broadcast to the nation for 1968 proclaimed that, though there would be trials ahead, the institutions of the Fifth Republic freed France from the kind of crisis that had afflicted it in the past; the nation, he added, would set an example to the world in the efficiency with which it ran itself. Despite the disappointment of the legislative election, 1967 had brought progress in a number of areas – the development of Concorde, the building of motorways and decentralisation of authority to big cities like Toulouse, Grenoble and Marseille, an important oil and gas accord with Algeria and the agreement on a single grains market for the Six. The Winter Olympics to be held in Grenoble in February 1968 would be a further cause for national pride. Preparations were going ahead for France's first test of a thermonuclear device in the South Pacific. All in all, the General might consider that everything was in order as the regime approached its tenth anniversary.

Personally, he took pleasure in the success of his son, who now commanded a missile-firing frigate, *Suffren*, which featured in a television documentary on the modernisation of France's forces. He sent Philippe money to help with his expenses during voyages his ship made to Africa, the Mediterranean and Latin America in November 1967. The following month, he assured him that he justified 'my proud fatherhood'. He gave his daughter-in-law five thousand francs to help pay for a winter sports holiday with her children, and promised Philippe the same sum when he got back to France.

He showered the Prime Minister with notes calling for action on everything ranging from help for repatriated *pieds-noirs* to judicial reform, from the number of aircraft used by ministers to the plan to move the food market of Les Halles out of central Paris. He insisted on the need to raise the birth rate, boost farm productivity and reduce the deficits of state companies, particularly the railway network. He pressed for the implementation of selection in universities to reduce overcrowding and produce more science graduates.

Following the precepts of his educational adviser, Jacques Narbonne, he saw the state controlling the educational destinies of the young, and overruled Pompidou's attachment to the traditional system that allowed them to find their own way. When Peyrefitte took over the education portfolio in April 1967, the General had spoken to him of his new job in military terms, remarking that soldiers obeyed orders whereas he was not sure that this was the case for the university establishment. A plan was drawn up to transfer the Education Ministry out of its sprawling premises on the Left Bank and into the former NATO headquarters at the Porte Dauphine, a move which Pompidou hoped would facilitate the reduction of the 'trade union squatters' who dominated the staff and impeded change.[1]

*

In a celebrated article in *Le Monde*'s issue of 15 March 1968, Viansson-Ponté echoed a remark by the nineteenth-century writer and statesman Alphonse de Lamartine that 'France is bored'. It was at peace and was not involved in any great global events, he wrote. While students elsewhere in Europe were demonstrating about the state of society and the war in Vietnam, its university population was merely bored. The eminent journalist was far from alone in his opinions. De Gaulle himself had written to his brother-in-law at the start of the year that things looked 'flat'. Visiting Washington, Giscard d'Estaing told the State Department that, while there was a wish for change in France, he did not see a political crisis erupting in the near future.

Nobody saw the potential for an uprising by the two groups which combined a growing set of grievances with a lack of political representation: the students and young industrial workers. De Gaulle's notes to the Education Ministry showed no awareness of what was bubbling up. All he wanted was selection, across the board and quickly. As for the economy, the President did not show much concern about the economy though growth was slowing down, the franc was too strong and the value of the minimum wage had declined steadily. As youth unemployment increased sharply, workplace militancy rose. There was a partial stoppage in the public services and fighting between strikers and police at several factories, including a pitched battle at a lorry plant in Caen in Normandy that went on till 5 a.m. – two hundred were injured. The CGT and the smaller labour group, the CFDT, held a joint day of action to protest against unemployment and social security policy. This led to street fighting between workers and the riot police of the *Compagnies Républicaines de Sécurité* (CRS) in Le Mans in which forty people were hurt.[2]

If Viansson-Ponté had travelled from *Le Monde*'s office on the Grands Boulevards to the provincial factories which had seen strikes turn violent, he might have written differently. Or if he had gone the shorter distance to the Paris suburb of Nanterre, he might have had an inkling of why boredom might not be the leitmotif of the summer of 1968. The thirty-five-hectare university campus there had been opened in 1964 beside an immigrant shanty-town. Its student numbers had soared from the original 2,000 to 15,000, nearly all of them taking courses in letters or law. It was more modern than most French colleges, but it became the symbol of the problems affecting the universities.

Overcrowding meant that students lived on top of one another. Transport links to the city were poor. Students did not have the local distractions enjoyed by their equivalents at faculties in Paris itself. The sociology department was a particularly active source of criticism of the established order and staged a sit-in strike at the end of 1967. The growing tension between students and the faculty administration resulted in the dean, Jean Grapin, agreeing to student representatives sitting on university councils for the first time in French history. This was the start of a revolt which spread beyond the Nanterre campus at the start of 1968, and in which sex played an important role.

French law ruled that any minors lodged in a group away from family residence were under the protection of the public authorities, giving them the right to dictate his or her way of life. Students in sexually segregated hostels were not allowed to receive visitors in their rooms or to make any alterations, such as hanging pictures. Since it was illegal to seduce a minor, a twenty-one-year-old who slept with a twenty-year-old was, in theory, subject to prosecution. The restrictions put on the legalisation of contraception in order to pass Lucien Neuwirth's bill were ridiculous to young people as the idea of free love gained ground. During 1967, male students staged symbolic occupations of female hostels at ten universities across the country. The police were called in. There was no negotiation to settle the dispute.

Though membership of the main student organisation, *L'Union Nationale des Étudiants de France* (UNEF), had fallen from 100,000 to 50,000 since 1961, small activist groups made the most of the growing discontent. Some were Trotskyites. Others drew inspiration from Che Guevara, Mao Zedong or a German philosopher in California, Herbert Marcuse, who saw the dynamic of revolution as coming from students rather than from a working class which had been subsumed into consumerism. Within the once powerful but now fragmented Communist youth movement, the 'Italians' who wanted to follow the example of the democratised party to the south formed a large dissident current.

The French students were following a movement that had spread through much of the Western world to try to overturn the status quo and obtain greater freedom. Flower Power had blossomed in California and showered its petals widely. In Britain, the Beatles had made *Sergeant Pepper's Lonely Hearts Club Band.* Experimentation and youth culture knew no bounds. Now it was France's turn, as the young people who had benefited materially from the years of economic growth and explosion in university numbers demanded a new social, human and political order which would have a greater place for the individual and reduce the top-down system epitomised by de Gaulle's penchant for military-style command.

II
The 'pranks' begin

At Strasbourg University, surrealist members of the Situationist International took control of the student organisation and set about destroying the existing structures as best they could. In November 1967, five thousand students marched in Paris. On 8 January 1968, the Minister for Youth and Sport, François Missoffe, went to Nanterre to inaugurate a swimming pool. When he had finished his speech, he was confronted by a red-haired, baby-faced German student, who asked him politely if he could give him a light for his cigarette. Then the young man launched into an attack on the government for not having made any mention of the sexual problems of young people in a six-hundred-page report on education. The swimming pool, he added, was only an attempt to divert the sexual energies of students into sport.

When Missoffe replied that sexual matters, like religion, were an individual issue, the student said all sociologists agreed that they were a social question; building a sports centre was a Hitlerian device to distract young people from real problems whereas the most important thing was to assure their sexual equilibrium. Having had enough of the conversation, the Minister remarked: 'With a head like yours you must have problems in that department. You can always jump into the pool to let off steam.' 'That's a Fascist response,' the twenty-three-year-old Daniel Cohn-Bendit shot back.

Ten days later, five thousand students at Bordeaux boycotted the university canteen. On 23–24 January, one hundred young female students occupied a university hostel for men at Nantes. Four hundred pupils at a Paris *lycée* clashed with police in the street. When Peyrefitte visited the university at Caen, a student threw an egg at the platform – it hit the minister's neighbour. Protesters against US policy in Vietnam staged a running series of demonstrations. On 26 January, police called in to Nanterre were forced to retreat; students denounced the dean, who had fought in the Resistance, as a Nazi. Fouchet, now Interior Minister, described the disturbances in his former domain of education as 'childish pranks'.

The hero of the swimming-pool incident wrote to Missoffe to apologise for his 'Fascist' accusation, explaining that the Hitler Youth had substituted sport for sexuality and that he had not meant to treat the Minister as a Nazi. In his reply, Missoffe wrote that he had completely forgotten the incident and invited the student to call on him for a personal conversation. That was enough to lead a university commission to reject a government attempt to get 'Danny the Red', as he would become known, expelled from France.

In keeping with Cohn-Bendit's focus on sexual freedom, student pickets took charge of hostels at Nanterre to ensure free circulation of men and women. Pompidou adopted a benevolent view of relations between male and female students – 'Let them sleep together,' he said over a lunch at Matignon. 'While they're doing that, they won't cause us any worries. And why should they go home at midnight? That's just the moment when it becomes most pleasant.' The rising disorder was another thing. The Prime Minister insisted that it must cease, but the militants became more and more active. Lectures were frequently interrupted and students set up strongpoints in university buildings.

At a Cabinet meeting, Peyrefitte noted that student agitation was flaming up all over the world. He said one cause of the trouble lay in the isolation of a campus like Nanterre; he preferred the British system under which teachers lived among students and residential quarters were part of an urban environment. De Gaulle, who continued to insist on the 'destocking' of student numbers, was not impressed. 'Your hostels are anarchic,' he said. 'This agitation is the result of the weakness of those in charge. Everybody lies down. Nobody has the courage to resist.' But, according to the Education Minister, when he described the protest leaders as 'subversives' and suggested using police raids, telephone taps and other methods employed against the OAS, the General replied: 'You think so? Against these kids, these clowns?'[3]

III
'Nothing heroic'

From his lofty perch, de Gaulle could not take the students seriously and could not understand why the troublemakers were not dealt with swiftly and effectively. For a statesman pursuing a great global role, the likes of Cohn-Bendit were below consideration. He was more interested in the evolution of one of his major concerns – Vietnam. A growing number of Americans were turning against the war. In March, the anti-war Democrat Eugene McCarthy did well in the presidential primary in New Hampshire, and Johnson halted bombing of the northern part of North Vietnam in an attempt to get Hanoi to the negotiating table. That was of far greater interest to the General than the agitation at Nanterre.

What he could not escape was that the state whose influence he had restored since 1958 was being rejected by the demonstrators, and that many French people, even if they did not go into the streets to protest, were also fed up with the hierarchies and bureaucracy that surrounded them. The order and conformity Gaullism demanded was at odds with an increasingly plural society. In a conversation with Jean-Marcel Jeanneney, the Social Affairs Minister, he agreed that there was a fundamental problem in the bureaucracy and the power of the Finance Ministry. But it was too late to change the nature of the system he had built over the previous ten years, and there was, too, a personal reason why the General could not act decisively.[4]

He could outwit conventional politicians, but the challenge he faced in 1968 was of a different order with very different actors. His strongly held standards had been formed at the start of the century and he remained true to the certainties he had reached early in life. He was isolated from the intellectual currents set off by Marcuse, the Structuralists and the other gurus of the protesters. Told at a Cabinet meeting that Che Guevara had become a model for some trade unionists, he had expressed surprise that beards should have become a revolutionary symbol.

He had been removed from ordinary life for too long, living in a cocoon of power. He spent his days on policy matters, on provincial and foreign visits, at banquets and formal occasions. Spontaneity had no place in his existence, let alone the free lives and loves sought by the new generation. He was interested in the fate of France's young people as a group, but did not view them as individuals.

His moral code was strict, buttressed by his wife's extreme conservatism. Peyrefitte recounts that, when he got into the plane taking the presidential couple to Poland in 1967, Madame de Gaulle asked him in what he called 'a sort of jubilation': 'So, it's true, you are going to ban miniskirts?' This was the result of a radio phone-in at which the minister had been asked whether girls wearing short skirts were conducive to boys concentrating on their studies, and had given a noncommittal answer. When he told France's First Lady that such a measure would not be feasible, he saw deep disappointment on her face. De Gaulle listened without a word. Peyrefitte thought he sympathised with '*Tante Yvonne*'.[5]

For all his confident words to the French people at the turn of the year, the old soldier was deeply tired and feeling his age, haunted by the memory of Pétain declining into senility. The lines on his face were etched ever deeper. He moved more slowly, his body ponderous, his eyesight feeble. In 1958, he had been intoxicated by the libido of power. During the ensuing years he had constructed a work of political art, but now the exercise of power, the thing he lived most for, was becoming routine and frustrating. The child of France was edging away from its pater-familias, who was thrown back on his familiar complaints that political parties were too powerful, and ministers eunuchs, the country too small for his ambitions, its people sheep. Peace was boring, war impossible, he lamented. 'Great things always finish badly,' he murmured to Maurice Schumann. To his goddaughter, Martine Lami, he wrote of having before him 'only shadows while waiting for the night'. 'There's nothing difficult left to do, nothing heroic,' he told Flohic.[6]

*

On 21 March, radicals stormed the American Express office in central Paris; one of the attackers arrested was from Nanterre and, in protest at his detention, students at the university occupied the room where the governing council met – their committee became known by the date of 22 March. There were other points of tension, including anti-imperialist rallies, a demonstration of support for the German leftist Rudi Dutschke, who had been wounded in an attempt on his life, and protests at the sacking of the director of the Cinémathèque, Henri Langlois.

On 1 April, several hundred students at Nanterre occupied the main lecture hall. While the dean said the university had to operate under rules, the 22 March Committee insisted that freedom should be unrestricted. On 19 April, two thousand young people marched through the Latin Quarter on the Left Bank of the Seine waving red flags and throwing a few stones at police cars. Two days later, a Sunday, the UNEF student union held a congress in Paris which saw a bitter argument over the line it should adopt. At the end of the day, after police had intervened to stop the factions fighting one another, the organisation's president resigned and was replaced by his deputy, Jacques Sauvageot, a twenty-six-year-old history student and a methodical organiser who came under constant pressure from revolutionary radicals.

In the following week, the extreme right-wing youth organisation, *Occident*, sacked the headquarters of UNEF and the main anti-Vietnam War body. This brought reprisal raids by leftists – a young man injured in the face lodged a complaint with police against Cohn-Bendit who, he said, had led the attack. There was also fighting at the university in Toulouse where police intervened to stop clashes between left- and right-wing students. At Nanterre, a student committee requisitioned a large lecture hall for a meeting, and chased away a Communist deputy, Pierre Juquin, after he started a talk in which he denounced 'agitators with rich daddies'. Some teachers sympathised with what they called 'a revolutionary class struggle'. A twenty-page bulletin put out by Cohn-Bendit's committee included instructions on how to make a Molotov cocktail.

On 27 April, Danny the Red was arrested following complaints by the injured youth and by the Nanterre authorities about the Molotov cocktail advice. He denied the aggression and was released for lack of proof. When Peyrefitte protested to Joxe, the Justice Minister, he was told Pompidou had agreed to free Cohn-Bendit. 'We cannot make fools of ourselves by locking up a student because of a prank,' the Prime Minister explained. His coolness was reinforced when he learned that, finding the students too radical, the Communist Party had decided to come out against the militants. He saw no reason to put off a planned trip to Iran and Afghanistan at the beginning of May.[7]

35

THE IDES OF MAY

I
'No weakness!'

May had a special significance for Charles de Gaulle three times in his life. In 1940, it had seen him go into battle at the head of his tanks and become a general before joining the Reynaud government, and then crossing to Britain. In 1958, it had seen his carefully controlled return to office. A decade later, he faced a country which seemed on the brink of revolution as hundreds of thousands of protesters shouted, '*Dix ans, c'est assez*' ('Ten years, that's enough').

The student rebellion and the strikes which accompanied it turned out not to be quite what they appeared from the headlines and television coverage. The late spring and early summer would show both the fragility of the General's position and his enduring appeal to the bourgeois France he deeply disliked – and the emergence of a dauphin to succeed him.

1–2 May. The traditional trade union march from the Place de la République to the Bastille on Labour Day was approved for the first time for fourteen years though there was a split between the Communist-led CGT and the independent CFDT that provoked a slanging match between their leaders. The following day, the faculty of letters at Nanterre was shut because of the continuing disorder, and eight members of the student 22 March group, including Cohn-Bendit, were summoned to appear before a disciplinary committee. The closure led protesting students to move to central Paris where they congregated in the Latin Quarter on the Left Bank around the college of the Sorbonne, France's most prestigious university establishment.

3 May. *L'Humanité* published a blast by Georges Marchais, a senior Communist Party official, against 'false revolutionaries' who had to be 'fought energetically'. The PCF had no time for what it regarded as an anarchist fringe of bourgeois youth. As the CGT union leader Georges Séguy, recalled, the leadership was completely overtaken by events.

Students demonstrated on an 'anti-imperialist day' and several hundred occupied the courtyard of the Sorbonne. The rector of the Paris universities, Jean Roche, called in CRS riot police to remove them; previously the police had not entered university premises. Young people stopped their vehicles in the street, and it took three hours to load the arrested students into the police wagons as fighting broke out, joined by pupils of neighbouring *lycées*. 'To be fifteen and to throw stones at the cops, while being protected by the crowd, what an absolute joy,' one schoolboy recalled. 'The cops were flabbergasted. The student leaders too.' The CRS staged violent charges and fired tear gas; made sinister by their visored helmets, batons and shields, they would become one of the hallmarks of the May–June events, denounced by the protesters in the slogan 'CRS = SS'.

Pitched battles surged in the streets and across the Place Saint-Michel. The driver of a police wagon, not wearing a helmet, had his head fractured by a stone hurled through the windscreen. The battle surged up to the Luxembourg Gardens, the police charges growing in intensity as did the hail of projectiles thrown by demonstrators. A huge barricade was stormed by the CRS who beat down anybody in their path. The Sorbonne was closed. Cohn-Bendit and Sauvageot were detained as responsible for the violence.

Amid all this came news of the agreement of the four parties in the Vietnam War – the United States, South and North Vietnam and the National Liberation Front (NLF – Viet Cong) – to meet for peace talks in Paris. Other venues had been considered, but the senior French diplomat dealing with Asia, Étienne Manach'h, negotiated in favour of the French capital. The stately conference centre on the Avenue Kléber was hurriedly prepared to receive the four delegations on 10 May. As host, France would have to remain above the debate and would play no part in the discussions.[1]

4–5 May (weekend). De Gaulle remained in Paris instead of going to Colombey. Joxe, who was acting as Prime Minister in Pompidou's absence, told the General that twelve of the 3 May demonstrators had been condemned to prison, though eight of the sentences were suspended. 'Well, that's better than nothing,' the President replied. Cohn-Bendit and Sauvageot had been released from detention, but the movement now had another group of martyrs to campaign for while criticism of Cohn-Bendit, which seemed to have an anti-foreign element, led to the cry, 'We are all German Jews!'

'No weakness!' de Gaulle told Joxe and Fouchet. 'Those who want to attack the state and the nation must be resisted.' He regretted that, due to insufficient selection, universities contained 'all kinds of odd customers who have nothing to do there'. 'We are dealing with an armed organisation whose object is subversion,' he added, ordering that the Sorbonne should remain closed for several days. 'When the child gets angry, the best way of calming him down is sometimes to give him a clout,' he added.

On the Sunday evening, the union of university teachers (SNESup) voted to go on strike. Its secretary-general, Alain Geismar, a twenty-nine-year-old science lecturer who led the left wing of the organisation, declared that the crisis in the universities could spread to the streets. It already had.[2]

6 May. After a university commission had voted for the exclusion from their colleges of militant student leaders, a protest demonstration marched through Paris. Fresh clashes broke out with police around the Sorbonne in the evening. Radio stations relayed blow-by-blow accounts from the scene, giving listeners across the country a vivid picture of the fighting as demonstrators smashed shop windows, trashed cars and hurled paving stones, metal from torn-down fences and anything else to hand. Police reaction was even more violent as the CRS attacked with tear gas, truncheons and high-velocity water cannon. Such a display of force, accompanied by five hundred arrests, had not been seen since the pogrom of Algerians in 1961.

The sharp-faced Peyrefitte went on television to condemn the violence while promising university reform. The police had clearly been provoked, but the force of their reaction sent a shiver through parents whose children were students as stories circulated of detained demonstrators being beaten up in police wagons or in temporary jails. What had started as a student rebellion over campus regulations turned into something resembling an insurrection, with the scale of violence in Paris and linked demonstrations in nine provincial cities. The administration also faced a new danger: Communist deputies from the Paris region made clear in private that, while they disapproved of the leftists, they did not want to be seen to be allying themselves with repression.

7 May. De Gaulle told the Education Minister that the only way to address street unrest was 'in a tone of command'. Taking Peyrefitte to task for having been too soft in his television appearance, he added: 'This is not the moment for explanation; this is the moment to fulminate.' *L'Humanité* switched tack to condemn 'the escalation of police violence'.

That evening, a large demonstration led by Cohn-Bendit paraded up the Champs-Élysées singing the Communist anthem, 'The Internationale', until they reached the Arc de Triomphe. Peyrefitte said that some urinated on the Tomb of the Unknown Soldier; Viansson-Ponté's history of the times makes no mention of this but speaks of one demonstrator trying to quench with his jacket the eternal flame which burned there. Fighting broke out around midnight when the demonstrators had got back to the Latin Quarter. The CRS staged violent charges, smashing up two big cafés and beating up those inside.[3]

8 May. 'Tonight, we take the Sorbonne,' Geismar declared on the radio. A telegram from five French Nobel prize-winners, including François Mauriac, called on de Gaulle to amnesty the jailed students and open the faculties. 'Contemptible demagogy,' the General told Joxe, Fouchet and Peyrefitte. 'This is a minor matter which must be settled with firmness . . . Neither truncheons nor tear gas should be spared.'

During a debate in the National Assembly, Edgard Pisani, who had resigned from the government ten days earlier, warned that the unrest reflected a much wider questioning of society by France's young people.

On the government benches, Fouchet whispered to Peyrefitte that protests by farmers and workers in Brittany had forced him to send riot police there, so he did not have enough men to contain the situation in Paris. The Education Minister added a couple of reassuring paragraphs to his speech to the legislature, saying that, if the students showed signs of calm, classes could resume at the Sorbonne and in Nanterre. That led the main evening newspaper, *France-Soir*, to rush out a special edition with the banner headline, 'The Sorbonne reopens tomorrow'. The evening demonstration was peaceful. Hearing the news in Afghanistan, Pompidou concluded that things were quietening down. But the CGT and CFDT trade union federations declared their solidarity with the 'struggle of the students and teachers'.[4]

9 May. The Latin Quarter was calmer as both sides drew breath. When the Communist poet Louis Aragon went to address the students, they booed him. Their leaders, including the *Jeunesse Communiste Révolutionnaire* (JCR), led by the twenty-six-year-old Trotskyite Alain Krivine, decided to continue the struggle even if the Sorbonne was reopened. The college, they vowed, would be occupied day and night. Sauvageot spoke of unleashing 'a cultural revolution'.

De Gaulle angrily told Peyrefitte that he had been wrong to speak of opening the Sorbonne. When the minister pointed out that he had actually said as much, the General relaxed. 'The conditions you laid down have not been met,' he said. 'That's obvious. So you will not reopen the Sorbonne. It is not us who have changed our minds. It's the *anars* [anarchists] who have rejected our proposals.'[5]

10 May. At 10.30, American and North Vietnamese delegates shook hands at the conference centre on the Avenue Kléber. They agreed to hold their first session of talks on 13 May. The occasion attracted a thousand correspondents from all over the world. In the three-day interval between two sessions, they had plenty of time to add to the media attention being paid to what was going on in the streets of Paris.

On the lunchtime news, the Gaullist René Capitant, deputy for the Latin Quarter, sounded the alarm about the degeneration of the situation and criticised the government. At 8 p.m., more than 10,000 demonstrators marched from the Place Denfert-Rochereau down the Boulevard Saint-Michel towards the Sorbonne, watched by strong police detachments on either side. The marchers threw up barricades made up of cars, railings, chunks of metal, paving stones and branches pulled from trees. One was three metres high and topped by barbed wire. In places, the barricades were so close to one another that they offered no means of escape – one was at the entry to a cul-de-sac.

If the authorities had used maximum force, they could have rolled over the demonstrators. But the Paris Prefect of Police, Maurice Grimaud, some of whose children joined the protests, was intent on avoiding any loss of life. 'Beating a demonstrator to the ground is like beating oneself, and brings the entire police force into disrepute,' he wrote to Paris police later in the month. 'It is even worse to strike demonstrators after arrest and after they have been taken to a police station for questioning.'

Demonstrations were also staged in major provincial centres. In Strasbourg, the red flag was raised over a university building. Ministers kept abreast of what was happening by listening to the reports on radio stations, particularly the private Europe 1 and RTL which, with their broadcasting transmitters situated outside France, were less inhibited than the ORTF. That evening, RTL was host to indirect and fruitless negotiations when it hooked up Geismar and a university representative who was not aware the conversation was being broadcast – nor did he recognise Cohn-Bendit when he put in an appearance.

In the Second World War and during the *pied-noir* risings in Algeria, the radio had been a powerful weapon in de Gaulle's hands; now it worked against him. The television was much less influential, both because of filming difficulties and because it was under state control – the government banned a report on the students for a weekly news magazine, leading to a protest by the producers of the main television programmes against the 'scandalous shortcomings' of ORTF coverage.

On the other side of the world, Pompidou arrived at the French embassy in Kabul by road late at night after a trip to the north of Afghanistan during which bad weather had prevented him flying back to the capital. He received a telephone call from Michel Jobert, his chief of staff at Matignon, urging him to return to Paris. The Prime

Minister took his advice. He concluded that de Gaulle did not have a grasp of the situation and that the ministers concerned could not reach an agreed position. He advised his colleagues in Paris that the time for concessions had not yet come. Joxe wondered if he was reserving these for his return; indeed, the Premier told Jobert that he would announce the reopening of the Sorbonne and play the pacification card.[6]

11 May. At 2 a.m., Joxe nodded when Fouchet ordered the police to go into action against the barricades on the Boulevard Saint-Michel. They advanced in solid lines, firing tear gas – in all, more than five thousand grenades were used, some containing chemicals which could cause blindness. One by one the barriers were taken, though some required ten assaults. Smoke billowed from burning cars as the demonstrators threw back paving stones and projectiles of all kinds, watched by local inhabitants from their windows. Having taken the barricades, the police indiscriminately beat people in the streets and stormed late-night cafés – Grimaud had not yet written his letter advising moderation, and, even if he had, as a paramilitary force, the CRS did not come under his orders.

A group of eminent professors telephoned the Élysée calling for an end to the attack before it degenerated into a massacre. But ministers had taken a crucial decision – that the security forces would not use guns. Nobody died. Still, the official casualty toll which spoke of 251 policemen among a total of 367 injured hugely minimised the reality. In all, 468 people were detained. The number of cars damaged in the Latin Quarter was put at 188. The CGT and CFDT trade union federations decided to call a strike in protest at the police action the following week.

Awakened to be told of the fighting, de Gaulle called a meeting for 6 a.m. which he began by asking if the army should be used. Messmer, who apologised for not having shaved, replied with an emphatic no. The police should be rewarded, the President said. The AFP news agency ran a story that government sources saw the demonstrations as the work of 'forces hostile to peace as the negotiations on Vietnam are taking place in Paris'. Other media were not misled.

II
The Dauphin steps out

After landing at Orly in the late evening, Pompidou went straight to Matignon. He called in Joxe, Fouchet and Peyrefitte. He asked them for their opinions but broke in almost immediately to tell them he had decided on radical action to defuse the tension. 'This is not a moment to skimp,' he added. 'I am lucky enough to be a virgin in this. I am the only one who can turn back the clock and reconcile us with the students.' So he was going to reopen the Sorbonne. When Joxe pointed out that this was contrary to de Gaulle's wishes, the Prime Minister replied, according to what Joxe told the biographer Éric Roussel in 1983: 'The General doesn't exist any more; de Gaulle is dead.'

Going to the Élysée, Pompidou swiftly got the President's approval for what he proposed. De Gaulle told Peyrefitte later that this was the moment the authority of the state crumbled. But he added that the Prime Minister forced his hand by threatening to resign if his plan was not accepted. That, the General said, would have thrown the regime into crisis. So he told Pompidou: 'If you win, so much the better, France will win with you. If you lose, too bad for you.' What was clear was that his own authority was seriously undermined while the Premier dictated policy, seeing it as a 'personal matter', as he told aides.

Pompidou recorded a television and radio address before going off for a good dinner. At 11:10 p.m., the ORTF broadcast his speech in which he finally stepped out of de Gaulle's shadow. He announced the reopening of the Sorbonne, and said appeals by detained demonstrators would be considered. Expressing 'deep sympathy for the students and trust in their common sense', he pledged to pursue university reform. 'I call on everybody to reject the provocations of a few professional agitators and to cooperate in the rapid and complete [restoration of] calm,' he concluded. 'I, for my part, am ready for this calm.'

Surrounded by a tight knot of aides plus his protégé Jacques Chirac, the Prime Minister took over decision-making in justice, the interior and education, causing tension with the ministers concerned. 'Say nothing, do nothing, I will handle everything,' he told Peyrefitte, whose offer of resignation he turned down. Jobert told ministers that his master would be the sole source of statements to the public.[7]

13 May. At 8.30 a.m. this Monday morning, the Sorbonne opened its gates. It was immediately occupied by students, and became the nodal point of the student action, a heaving festival of youth in search of freedom. It was the 'citadel of the revolution' and its 'ideological drugstore', as Viansson-Ponté put it.

Each evening an 'occupation committee' was elected which ran things for the next twenty-four hours. There was endless talk as students debated how to construct an ideal world in marathon debates in the lecture halls. Admirers of Mao, Lenin, Trotsky and Castro rubbed shoulders. Situationists preached their doctrine and regional autonomists set up their stalls. Sexual liberation was taken for granted. Revolutionary newspapers and a poster culture flourished proclaiming 'Power to the imagination', 'Take your desires for reality', 'Beneath the paving stones, the beach', 'It is forbidden to forbid', 'Be realistic, ask for the impossible', and 'I am a Marxist, Groucho faction.'

A jazz band sent by the Europe 1 radio station played in the main courtyard of the Sorbonne; an American ballet troupe gave performances. The statue of Louis Pasteur was topped by a red flag, and that of Victor Hugo by a Breton hat, followed by a pail. There were some less joyous elements: a young man from the Paris suburbs who claimed, falsely, to have fought with guerrillas in Africa and the Middle East organised a security service which specialised in extortion and robbery. But, for most of those involved, May 1968 brought a burst of unparalleled freedom. There were few clear aims, but an explosion of hope. It was, as the writer Claude Roy put it, 'a revolution that is something of a party, a party that is something of a revolution'.

Intellectual support for the students mounted: the journal *Tel Quel*, edited by the writer Philippe Sollers, who was surrounded by other adherents of the Paris cultural revolution, saw the events as leading to a crossing of barriers under the banner of Marxism and Leninism. Sartre expressed solidarity as did film-makers, including Jean-Luc Godard, who would lead sympathisers to close down the Cannes film festival.

At lunchtime on 13 May, a demonstration addressed by Cohn-Bendit and Sauvageot outside the Gare de l'Est called for the resignations of Fouchet and Grimaud and the creation of a 'people's tribunal to try the state police'. Transport and electricity went on strike in Paris in answer to a call from the CGT and CFDT. As reports in the press and on the independent radio stations told of the degree of CRS violence in the Latin Quarter, unhappiness spread among the police, many of whom saw Pompidou's broadcast as a slap in the face. This feeling was heightened when security forces were pulled out of the Latin Quarter.

In the afternoon, a vast procession marched to the Place de la République while demonstrations involving tens of thousands of people took place in big cities elsewhere. Students occupied several provincial universities. As well as proclaiming that power lay in the street, the protesters' slogans focused on the man in the Élysée – 'Ten years, that's enough', the old union call of 'Charlie, cash' and, to a staccato rhythm, 'Goodbye de Gaulle. Goodbye de Gaulle. Goodbye'.

The Paris demonstration was headed by student stars including Cohn-Bendit who laughingly resisted Communist attempts to sideline him. Trade union leaders were in the second rank. The politicians of the Left, including Mitterrand, Mollet, Waldeck Rochet and Marchais, were well behind, while Mendès France was lost in a group of young members of the PSU. The police kept away but, when the marchers reached the dispersal point at the Place Denfert-Rochereau, a potentially dangerous situation erupted as a group shouting 'To the Élysée!' sat in the street to block the throng behind them. A police wagon tried to get through to fetch an injured child. The crowd closed around it. Losing his head, the driver reversed and ran down several people. He was dragged from his seat. One of his companions fired three shots into the air. Then the CGT and several deputies wearing their scarf of office, including the Popular Front veteran Pierre Cot, intervened to diffuse the tension.

The marching order of the demonstration reflected the nature of the protests. Mainstream opposition politicians had been marginalised. Debates in the National Assembly on the situation took place in a vacuum; attacks on the government by Socialist and Communist deputies carried no weight with the students. Speaking that night to a rally at the Mutualité meeting hall, Cohn-Bendit was cheered when he criticised the leaders of the Left, including Mitterrand. 'What made me happy this afternoon was to be at the head of a procession in which the Stalinist scum were in the van at the back,' he exulted.

Across the Seine, the Vietnam peace conference began its search for a settlement. In the Élysée, de Gaulle debated whether to go ahead with a state visit to Romania due to begin the following day. Fouchet argued that he must stay in Paris – apart from anything else, the Interior Minister feared that his absence would allow Pompidou to pursue a soft line towards the protest. Couve de Murville said the prestige of France and of the General would be hurt if he put off the trip. Pompidou backed him up; his view was that the worst of the trouble was over and abandoning the visit would make the unrest appear more significant than it really was. The Prime Minister did not have much trouble persuading the General. De Gaulle saw Romania, which was showing some independence from the Soviet Union, as an important element in his attempt to break down Cold War divisions. He could hardly allow a gaggle of students to interfere with his global statescraft.

'The General is no longer the same man,' Peyrefitte recalled Pompidou as telling him in a low voice. 'He no longer has the same sensitivity about the consequences of the initiatives he takes, or the impact of the remarks he makes.'[8]

III
The workers join in

14 May. At 7.30 a.m., the presidential Citroën DS drove out of the Élysée for the airport at the start of de Gaulle's journey to Bucharest. The nation would have to wait to hear from him until 24 May, the Information Ministry announced.

At 8.30 a.m., workers occupied the Sud Aviation plant near Nantes where activity was threatened by a decline in production of the Caravelle airliner like the one in which the President was heading eastwards. They took the manager hostage though he was allowed a telephone to conduct a conversation with the leader of the CGT, Georges Séguy, which was broadcast live on Europe 1. A new stage in the upheaval had started. The workers had different claims from the students – they were primarily concerned with wages and conditions. Still, the flame of discontent and a readiness to take direct action were proving infectious. France was escaping from the absent President on several levels at the same time.

15 May. Employees at a Renault plant at Cléon in Normandy, who feared job cuts, followed the example of the Sud Aviation workers. Buses filled with representatives of the strikers drove to other Renault factories, including the company's headquarters at Boulogne-Billancourt outside Paris. At a Lockheed aircraft factory in Beauvais, 1,800 staff stopped work. On the Left Bank, the national theatre, the Odéon, was occupied by demonstrators, and its director, Jean-Louis Barrault, who had read the 'Ode to de Gaulle' in 1944, expressed his sympathy after trying to head them off.

Ministers, including Pompidou, became convinced that the protesters were being funded from abroad via Swiss bank accounts. According to Peyrefitte's recollections, the sources of finance were said to include the United States, Israel, China, Cuba and Bulgaria. There was talk of student leaders having been trained in insurrectionary techniques behind the Iron Curtain. But the revolt needed no external spur to action.[9]

16 May. At 5 p.m., 25,000 workers at the Renault plant in Billancourt voted to go on strike and take over the premises. The nationalised vehicle company's biggest factory was an icon of French industry. 'When Billancourt sneezes, France catches cold,' as the saying went. Whereas the action at Nantes and Cléon had been spontaneous, the Billancourt stoppage and occupation were the result of a call by the CGT shop steward. France's largest labour group led by the Communists could no longer stand aside, and the PCF was anxious not to be outflanked by factory-floor militants.

Occupations and the sequestration of management added a revolutionary tinge to the movement, evoking echoes of the Popular Front thirty-two years earlier. There was no particular pattern to the strikes. While north-east France was relatively little affected, the most militant areas were around Toulouse, Lyon, Grenoble and Nancy, and in the mines of the north. The strikers staged big demonstrations; in Le Mans, Clermont-Ferrand and Nantes, protesters attacked the prefecture.

There was a clear distinction between the approaches of the two main labour federations involved. The CGT stressed the classic demands for improved pay and conditions and made a point of exercising all the control it could over the strikers; the politically independent CFDT showed an interest in broader social and workplace reform. While Georges Séguy warned against 'irresponsible provocation', the CFDT engaged in talks with the Left Bank protesters.

Since the CGT was the dominant labour force, this meant that there was a gap between the strikers and the students. Workers at Billancourt closed the gates against a delegation from the Left Bank, and there were scornful jibes about the Sorbonne demonstrators driving sports cars and wearing cashmere sweaters. The May unrest would often be referred to as combining the student rising and strikes, and some younger strikers were motivated by the same kind of frustrations with the rigidities of French society that drove the university protests. But the gap between the two movements was the General's salvation. Had the CGT followed the CFDT's flirtation with the students, the regime would have been shaken much more radically, and government could well have become impossible.[10]

17 May. Work stopped at other Renault factories, at a big shipyard on the Seine and plants in Normandy, the south-west and central France. Stoppages began to affect railway and postal services. ORTF broadcasts were hit.

In Romania, de Gaulle made speeches calling for an end to the division of Europe. He visited the industrial centre of Craiova and gave a television address in which he looked forward to the day when the continent would 'finally breathe freely thanks to the independence of each nation, the end of opposing blocs and cooperation from one end to the other for peace and progress'. Naturally, he said nothing in public about what was happening in France, but the regular messages from the Élysée were sufficiently alarming for him to decide to cut his trip short by twelve hours and fly home.[11]

18–19 May (weekend). The President was in a thoroughly bad temper when he landed at Orly on Saturday evening. 'Playtime is over,' he told the ministers who welcomed him at the airport. For safety's sake, the presidential cortège had to follow a roundabout route into Paris. 'It's a shambles,' de Gaulle exclaimed to Pompidou when he called at the Élysée at midnight. The Prime Minister offered to resign. Shrugging his shoulders, de Gaulle replied: 'No question of that!'

'So, de Gaulle leaves and, when he returns, everything has collapsed,' he growled at a meeting with Pompidou, Fouchet, Messmer, Gorse and Grimaud the next day. The authority and dignity of the state had been ridiculed and his efforts over the previous ten years had been undone in five days, he went on, according to the account by the well-informed Viansson-Ponté. He ordered that the Sorbonne and the Odéon should be cleared immediately.

The others looked at Pompidou, who said nothing. So Fouchet jumped in to say that the only way of carrying out the General's order would be to use firearms. There would be deaths. Instead of running out of steam, the unrest would gain a fresh impetus. The Latin Quarter would have to be besieged. Any prospect of negotiations with the unions would be ruled out.

Raising his arms in exasperation, de Gaulle conceded that action should be taken only at the Odéon – but straight away. The Sorbonne could wait. Before the ministers left, de Gaulle gave Gorse a sentence to relay to journalists: '*la réforme, oui; la chienlit, non*'. It was another of the General's linguistic pirouettes but this time it fell flat. De Gaulle meant '*chienlit*' in its long-forgotten eighteenth-century sense of a carnival or masquerade. This fitted well with the rebellious student festivities. But the term was unknown to most people, some of whom may have assumed on first hearing that it meant 'shit in bed' – *chie en lit*. The President had been too erudite by half, but had given the events of May a new term.*[12]

20 May. The number of strikers was estimated to have reached six million. Households stocked food, and there were reports of rich people

*It was frequently translated into English as 'dog's breakfast'. The Collins–Robert dictionary translates it as 'havoc' while Larousse gives it as 'a disordered or chaotic situation'.

heading for the Swiss border with their cash and valuables. Petrol became scarce. The UNEF and the CFDT held a press conference to stress the link they saw between university and industrial reforms. But the CGT cancelled a meeting with the students' association.

Using the codename 'Monsieur Walter', Chirac, the Deputy Social Affairs Minister who was very close to Pompidou, established contact with the number three in the CGT, Henri Krasucki. The union leader told him to go to a square near the Place Pigalle. Chirac drove there in his own car rather than using an official vehicle. A man smoking a pipe approached and gave an agreed password. Chirac told him the government was ready to open talks on wages and welfare payments.[13]

21–22 May. Pompidou and Fouchet crossed swords with Mitterrand, Mollet and Waldeck Rochet in a parliamentary debate on a censure motion. Pisani accused the government of being more concerned with holding on to power than with governing effectively; he voted for censure and subsequently gave up his parliamentary mandate. Capitant announced that he was quitting the Gaullist party in the hope that de Gaulle would name a new government. The administration defeated the motion by 244 votes to 233.

It was announced that Cohn-Bendit, who had gone on a trip to West Germany, would not be allowed back. Receiving the faithful Gaullist Alexandre Sanguinetti, de Gaulle spoke of forming a 'combat government'. But some Gaullists were showing a worrying desire to put a distance between themselves and the General. Jacques Vendroux noted 'odious reflections' by some of his fellow deputies. He wrote that Albin Chalandon, the former Secretary-General of the Gaullist party, had gone as far as to tell a closed meeting that the President should step down; to make matters even worse, there was no outcry at this, only a few discreet murmurs, while some of those present expressed agreement.[14]

23 May. At a Cabinet meeting, de Gaulle criticised Pompidou for his strategy of letting events take their course. This had to end. The solution, he went on, was to launch a grand project to involve citizens more in the way the country was run, including the reform of the universities.

What he termed 'participation' was to be the subject of a referendum that would unite the people behind the administration. It was all very vague, but the President clearly thought that the best way out of the quagmire was to call a vote enabling him to deploy his familiar device of facing France with a choice between himself and chaos. Summing up, he said the essential thing was to head off the minority that was causing trouble, and to win a referendum followed by big reforms. 'And, on the third day, he was resurrected,' Joxe commented as he left the presidential palace.

There was a subtext to de Gaulle's decision. He was irate that his instructions had not been followed, and chafed at the authority Pompidou had acquired since his return from Afghanistan and during his absence in Romania. If a general election was held to regain the initiative, the Prime Minister would lead the Gaullist campaign and thus reinforce his standing. So, from de Gaulle's viewpoint, a referendum was much more preferable. If it was successful, he could impose Couve, his chosen candidate for Matignon, on the existing parliamentary majority.

Continuing his secret negotiations, Chirac drove from his office to a hotel in a poor part of northern Paris – some accounts said that it was used by prostitutes. He carried a revolver in his pocket because Pompidou worried that the Communists might try to kidnap him. Police agents watched from a distance. The junior minister was led to a room on the third floor where Krasucki was waiting. The two men began to hammer out the details of a meeting to settle the strikes.[15]

24 May. The number of strikers was estimated to have risen to ten million. Pompidou told Peyrefitte the PCF and the CGT were 'the last guarantors of a peaceful solution'. An agreement would be reached with them on pay and working conditions to end the agitation by workers. Still, the Prime Minister's strategy depended on the union leadership being able to impose itself on the worker base, and the past days had shown a high degree of independence on the shop floor. An additional wrinkle was the division within the PCF between reformers and Stalinists; while Georges Marchais incarnated a hard, traditional line, figures like the philosopher Roger Garaudy and, more discreetly, the apparatchik Roland Leroy advocated talking to the students – Garaudy was thrown out of the party as a result.

At noon, an ORTF team arrived at the presidential palace to record a seven-minute speech by the General promising 'participation'. It fell short of what was required, but he saw no need for a second take. When it was broadcast that evening, the reaction was lukewarm. His argument and language did not connect with his audience. The President himself acknowledged that he had not hit the nail on the head.

'It could have been worse,' Pompidou remarked to an aide. Guichard lamented that de Gaulle seemed to have nothing to say or, worse, had expressed himself badly and was out of step with the concerns of the nation. Peyrefitte's neighbour, a businessman, told him: 'What Pompidou is doing with the unions is what has to be done. He's a man! What de Gaulle has just said is worth nothing. In my circle, we all think the same thing, he has to go.'

The CGT held a march which passed peacefully, but the students organised a major demonstration to coincide with de Gaulle's broadcast address that ended in street battles on both banks of the Seine through the night. Clashes also broke out in Strasbourg and Bordeaux. Farmers protested in Brittany and central France, setting up roadblocks and fighting a five-hour battle with police in Nantes.

The first fatalities of the unrest occurred in Paris, where a young man died, probably as the result of being hit by a tear gas grenade, and in Lyon, where a police officer was fatally crushed by a lorry set rolling by demonstrators. Senior officials at the Interior Ministry considered a plan to bring in paratroopers to deal with the unrest, but Fouchet and Messmer maintained their opposition to using troops. The military chief of staff, General Fourquet, later recalled that the army commanders were worried at the prospect of their men being called in to deal with a political matter – memories of Algeria were still alive and Fourquet saw all too clearly the danger of young soldiers losing control in the face of the demonstrators and 'provoking a catastrophe'.

In Washington, the State Department and CIA took a dim view of the outlook for the General. If de Gaulle and Pompidou survived they would have to agree to wage rises which would weaken the franc, make monetary cooperation between the US and France easier and, perhaps, lessen French opposition towards British entry into the Common Market, presidential adviser Walt Rostow wrote to Johnson. The CIA judged that de Gaulle's broadcast had made things worse. The term 'arrogance' appeared repeatedly in US descriptions of his attitude.

In the Élysée, de Gaulle sat up all night listening to radio reports of the violence. He seemed a prisoner alone in his palace except for a few trusty officials while the capital and major provincial cities moved to their own rhythm, independently of him. He remarked on how he had become the target of the protesters – 'It's my departure they are calling for,' he acknowledged.[16]

25 May. At 2 a.m., Mendès France appeared at the Sorbonne to 'be a witness' to what was happening. That afternoon, a Saturday, Pompidou presided over the opening of talks with the unions and employers at the Ministry of Social Affairs and Labour on the rue de Grenelle. On the government side, he was accompanied by Jeanneney, his adviser Édouard Balladur and Chirac. At the Premier's insistence, Debré was not invited; he feared that his intransigence might be a problem, and de Gaulle backed him up despite the Finance Minister's extreme irritation.

Before the talks, Pompidou had telephoned the CGT leader, Georges Séguy, to raise a subject that would not be on the table but which the Prime Minister thought crucial. France's foreign policy risked being undermined by Washington if de Gaulle was weakened, he said. He hoped that the Communists were aware of the danger. The plea to the union federation to bear Moscow's interests in mind could not have been plainer. According to the union chief, Pompidou said he would rather be an ordinary official in a Communist regime in France than Premier in a government run by the Americans.

The employers began by accepting a 35 per cent rise in the minimum wage, far more than they had previously suggested. After that, negotiations bogged down as they stretched through the night. De Gaulle stayed in Paris for the weekend, showing the mood swings that would characterise him in the coming days. Calling at the Élysée, Missoffe was taken aback by his low spirits; the President said everything was done for and spoke of the Communist threat. The Minister for Youth and Sport telephoned Messmer to urge him to go to see the President. When he did so, the Armed Forces Minister found a man without a clear grip on what lay ahead as he explored permutations of what might happen.[17]

26 May. During a break in the negotiations, Chirac told Séguy he had just spoken to de Gaulle who stressed the dangers for French foreign policy and particularly for relations with Moscow if the talks broke down. Pompidou and Séguy agreed to hold tête-à-tête talks. The full session resumed in the afternoon but progress was laborious. Unknown to the Prime Minister, the President called Couve de Murville to the palace. The Foreign Minister entered the Élysée by a side door.

27 May. At 4 a.m. that Monday, a deal was reached in the corridor between Chirac and the CGT leaders, approved by Pompidou; they agreed on an average salary increase of 10 per cent in addition to the 35 per cent rise in the minimum wage. At 7 a.m., a full accord was reached. A small reduction in working hours would come into force in 1970. Strikers would be given half pay for the time they had been off the job. At 7.40 a.m., the delegations parted. Pompidou went home to get some sleep.

Twenty minutes later, the Renault workers at Billancourt assembled for their daily meeting. They had not yet got word from the rue de Grenelle. The CGT shop steward, Aimé Halbeher, presented a list of demands and a vote was taken to continue the strike. Then Séguy arrived and enumerated the points of agreement. This was received in silence. When the CGT leader said the employers had asked if the unions would instruct their members to return to work, a hostile cry went up. The strike continued, as it did at other major industrial plants.

At 11 a.m., the Matignon official Édouard Balladur woke Pompidou with the news. 'It's done for,' the Prime Minister said. As over the Sorbonne two weeks earlier, his strategy of seeking to work his opponents had come to naught. When the Cabinet met in the afternoon, he tried to make light of the outcome. De Gaulle concentrated on reading the text for the referendum set for 16 June. Messmer wondered what the administration would do if the vote could not be held because of strikes at printing works and in the transport system. Pompidou smiled.

Gaullists started to organise a big march in Paris. Despite the reaction of the Renault workers, the Prime Minister had not given up on the PCF. '"He" must not go,' Waldeck Rochet was heard to say of the General.

The students gathered once more for a night-time meeting, backed by the small but highly active PSU party, at the Charléty Stadium in Paris. Thirty thousand people cheered appeals for a revolution. Mendès France watched silently from the stands.[18]

28 May. Squinting through the smoke from the cigarette lodged in the left corner of his mouth, Pompidou told Peyrefitte it was time for him to step down as Education Minister; he would take charge of the portfolio for the time being, and form a commission of experts to inquire into ways to end the 'anarchy' and proceed to a true reform.

Demonstrators stormed the prefecture in Toulouse and only withdrew when the prefect apologised to them. Though banned from France, Cohn-Bendit made his way back to Paris and popped up at the Sorbonne with dyed hair and a broad grin. After Waldeck Rochet and Marchais visited him at his Paris home, Mitterrand said he would stand for the presidency if de Gaulle resigned, and called for a provisional government headed by Mendès France. Since the General had shown no sign of stepping down and Pompidou's government enjoyed a parliamentary majority, this could all too easily be portrayed as an unconstitutional move which would depend on Communist backing to succeed.

The PCF felt so confident that a member of its central committee sent a message to the Élysée offering support for the government if Communist ministers were appointed. The message was not passed to the General. To keep up the pressure and claim leadership of the Left, the CGT announced a massive demonstration for the following day. Rumours flew that the unionists had got weapons from an arms factory they occupied. Would they storm the Hôtel de Ville or even the presidential palace? Pompidou instructed that an 'armoured gendarmerie' force consisting of a thousand men with tanks stationed at Versailles should move to the Paris suburbs.

Shopping in the Madeleine quarter near the presidential palace, Yvonne de Gaulle was shouted at by a group of shop workers, according to General de Boissieu. Another report had a motorist bellowing insults at her. 'Things can't go on like this,' she said on her return to the Élysée. 'I was right when I told the General not to stand for re-election. It is becoming infernal.'

Visitors found the President extremely gloomy. Opinion polls showed support for him slumping while backing for Pompidou rose by 25 per cent. The old man said he had not slept for three days; at times he changed this to six. Some of the ministers and officials concluded that he might be on the brink of resignation as the country appeared to be disintegrating around him. At a session with the farmers' leader, Michel Debatisse, he insisted everything was lost as France's internal and external enemies ganged up with one another. The journalist Michel Droit, who was due to do a television interview during the referendum campaign, received a torrent of apocalyptic rhetoric. To Foccart the General said he had done all he could. Then he telephoned his son-in-law, de Boissieu, who was stationed in Mulhouse in eastern France, to ask him to come to Paris.

In the evening, he handed his son an envelope containing his last wishes. Over dinner in their private quarters, Madame de Gaulle spoke at length about her nasty experience that afternoon and of her worries about the safety of her daughter-in-law and the grandchildren whose home was surrounded by strike pickets. A military attaché was told to arrange for them to be flown with Philippe to French army headquarters in West Germany commanded by Massu. Yvonne went on so much about her experience that afternoon and her concerns for the family that Charles left the dining room and had his meal served in an adjoining salon.

After dinner, Pompidou came to the palace. He thought the General looked tired. 'Are you sleeping?' the President asked him.

'Yes, when I have time,' the Prime Minister replied.

'You're lucky.'

According to his own account, Pompidou said he doubted if the PCF and CGT were planning a revolutionary bid for power with their demonstration the following day. He thought public opinion had had enough of the agitation, and that the administration would emerge as the winner. De Gaulle accused the Prime Minister of having been too optimistic throughout the crisis. When the visitor proposed the dissolution of the National Assembly, the President asked 'What's the point? Everything is done for.'

In his memoirs, Pompidou wrote that he left without having realised how weary the President was. Rumours spread that the Prime Minister had either spoken of the General resigning or had offered to do so himself after undergoing another savage dressing-down. Though Pompidou denied this, the relationship between the two had entered a region of high tension. The younger man still held the President in great respect but he had already noted the effects of age and the General's faltering touch. His own policies might not have worked as yet, but the Prime Minister had taken charge as nobody else had done under de Gaulle. The son had become a man ready to challenge the father. For the good of France, and their own destinies, the monarch and the dauphin had to remain united, but divorce was inevitable.

The solid Fouchet, a companion since 1940, was the last caller of the day. The General compared the reopening of the Sorbonne to the cracking of the dam at Fréjus in southern France in 1959 which killed four hundred people. 'Sometimes I think I am going to collapse,' he added. But Fouchet recalled that his mood was not all downbeat – he even smiled at one point. Pompidou only learned of the visit when the Interior Minister telephoned him to say he had found de Gaulle's mood bizarre, as if he had some secret project in mind. Foccart remarked that the President was at a moment when he hesitated and waited, 'then he will take his decision'.[19]

IV

'We've lost the General'

29 May. The decision was not long coming. De Gaulle left his private quarters for his office on the first floor of the Élysée unusually early, at 7 a.m. He called in the senior palace officials, Bernard Tricot and Xavier de La Chevalerie, to tell them he was going to Colombey. Tricot telephoned Pompidou to inform him that a Cabinet meeting due to start at 10 a.m. was being postponed until the following day. When news of the President's departure became known, there was immediate speculation that, as in 1946, he was quitting.

That morning, *L'Humanité* ran an eight-column front-page headline calling for 'A government of the people and a democratic union with Communist participation'. Mendès France had said he was ready to head a new Cabinet as proposed by Mitterrand. Centrists and *Algérie française* veterans rallied to the opposition; Left–Right divisions dissolved in a common front against the General. Over the last ten years, de Gaulle had put so many noses out of joint that the list of those who wanted to see him go was long. According to Alain Peyrefitte, some members of the staff at Matignon joined Albin Chalandon in thinking it was time for a change at the top.

A little before 9 a.m., the President summoned one of his aides-de-camp, Pierre Tallon, to tell him that a helicopter should be waiting at the military base at Issy-les-Moulineaux outside Paris at 11.45 to take him to Colombey. The other aide-de-camp, François Flohic, would accompany him, and should be in naval uniform. Returning discreetly to de Gaulle's office at 9.45 a.m., Tallon glimpsed him sitting at his desk, leaning forward, his head close to his hands. He straightened up, turned to Tallon and asked him to help him open a locked box; he explained that he could not get the key to work, adding, 'You know I have always been very clumsy with my hands.' He gave the aide a letter and told him to take it to his son, Philippe, as soon as he left Paris. He seemed tired, his hands trembling slightly.

Pompidou had slept well and recalled that he awoke 'ready for action'. But the news of de Gaulle's departure shook him deeply. He thought the atmosphere in Colombey could encourage him to step down. Madame de Gaulle would be able to increase her pressure for him to resign. If he did, the Prime Minister would be in a tricky position since the hostile Gaston Monnerville would become acting president.

The Prime Minister now felt that the best course to rally the country would be to call a general election rather than pursuing the vague referendum proposal. He had the text of an appropriate decree typed and sent to the Élysée. At 11 a.m., having heard nothing from the palace, he telephoned Tricot to seek a meeting with the General. Tricot said the President had been closeted for an hour with his son-in-law, de Boissieu, who had arrived by helicopter from Mulhouse. He did not want to see anybody else.

No sooner had the Prime Minister hung up than de Gaulle telephoned him, something he did extremely rarely. He said he needed to go to Colombey to clear his mind; he would be back the following afternoon. When Pompidou raised the dissolution issue, he replied that, if the referendum looked risky, an election would be even more so. 'I am old, you are young, and it is you who represent the future,' he added. Then he suddenly stopped and said: '*Je vous embrasse*,'* before hanging up. Pompidou found the expression astonishing; did it signify an *adieu* rather than an *au revoir*?

When the line went dead, the Prime Minister called back and got Tricot who told him: 'He is leaving. It is too late.' The de Gaulles were driven out of the gate at the far end of the palace garden rather than through the usual exit into the rue du Faubourg Saint-Honoré. The General was only known to have used it once before, on his return to power ten years earlier. Was he going out the way he had come in?

At 2 p.m., Tricot arrived at Matignon, white as a sheet. 'We've lost any trace of the General,' he told Pompidou. 'He's not at Colombey.'[20]

*Once more, the expression has no exact English translation. Obviously 'I kiss you' or 'I embrace you' are out of place. Probably, the best equivalent is 'All the best'.

36

COUNTER-PUNCH

I
The last coup

'Surprise has to be organised . . . under a thick veil of deception,' de Gaulle had written in *Vers l'armée de métier* in 1934. 'Cunning should be used to make people believe that one is where one is not, that one wants what one does not want.' Throughout his career since 1940, he had used feints to outwit opponents. Now he was staging his last great coup against his followers as well, leaving Pompidou and his ministers completely in the dark.* The Prime Minister recalled the 'disarray' of those around him; the assumption was that the General had decided to quit though some guessed he had gone to the command post of France's nuclear force or to join de Boissieu in Mulhouse to prepare a military operation to regain control.

Receiving a group of pro-government deputies at 2.30 p.m., Pompidou spoke of the possibility of the PCF trying to stage a takeover. The 'jackals' of the Fourth Republic were on the prowl, he added. The President of the Gaullist group, Henri Rey, said the Premier would be the party's presidential candidate if the General stepped down. Albin Chalandon, who had shocked Jacques Vendroux by saying that de Gaulle should go, declared that the only solution was for Pompidou to take over. The Independent Republican Michel de Poniatowski agreed. The Prime Minister closed the meeting by saying that they had to wait

*The theory that the Prime Minister knew what was going on has been aired, notably by Viansson-Ponté. Without any solid evidence, it smacks of conspiracy theory pushed a stage too far.

for de Gaulle's decision. He could not rule out the General's resignation, in which case he would assume his responsibilities.[1]

As the politicians met in Paris, de Gaulle reached his secret destination, General Massu's headquarters in West Germany. He had decided to make the journey during his conversation that morning with his son-in-law. De Boissieu, who found the President weary, had tried to encourage him by saying that he was ready to put together a special unit to do whatever the General wanted to restore order. When the old man asked what the attitude of the troops would be if they had to use force, de Boissieu replied that the army had never been so disciplined. The soldiers were fed up with the students, he added.

'Right, I will go to see if Massu is in the same frame of mind,' the President replied with a smile. He had reasons for his curiosity. Most of France's leading generals had sent him a message of support a few days earlier, but the name of the 'bloody thick' man was missing. On 19 May, Massu had secretly dispatched an aide to Paris to assess the situation. Did the way he had been recalled from Algeria in 1959 still rankle? His attitude would be a litmus test, de Gaulle told de Boissieu; if it was positive, he could take the decisive step.[2]

He would fly by helicopter to the Vosges mountains in eastern France or to Alsace to meet Massu, who would cross the border from his command post in Baden-Baden. If conditions made landing impossible, he would continue to Germany. Flohic and Madame de Gaulle were to accompany him. His son and his family would travel separately.

The French state would be where he was. If the Communist demonstrators stormed the Élysée, they would find it empty. He gave de Boissieu two letters to be opened if an accident befell him. One was an address to the nation. The other contained instructions for Pompidou. His son-in-law was to go to Colombey and wait for him there. Should he have dinner prepared at La Boisserie? de Boissieu asked. 'No, we will look after ourselves,' de Gaulle replied.

Should he tell Massu the General was coming, de Boissieu inquired. Yes, but from Colombey, de Gaulle said. Having contacted Massu, he was to telephone the military base north of Colombey where de Gaulle would land after leaving Paris by helicopter. 'You must not say anything to anybody here,' the General added, setting out his strategy: 'I want to plunge the French, including the government, into a state of doubt and worry in order to be able to take control of the situation once again. I will win them back through fear.' When it became known, his journey to see France's best-known general could only fan speculation that he might be about to launch a military coup. The echoes of May 1958 were not far away in his manoeuvres to bring the nation into line.

Flohic, who was on a day off and was out shopping for food when he was called to the Élysée, was told to procure maps of France east of Colombey. He asked if they would have enough money; yes, the General said, he had made sure of a stock of cash. With Madame de Gaulle, they drove to the military base at Issy-les-Moulineaux, taking a route that avoided the Citroën plant in the suburb where workers were on strike. Two Alouette helicopters were waiting. The President, his wife and Flohic got into one; a bodyguard, a doctor and a police inspector climbed into the second. The General complained that they had too much baggage with them; loading it was slowing down their departure. 'Hurry up,' he said. 'We're being watched.'

They took off at 11.45 a.m., joined by an escort helicopter as they flew over factories sporting the red flag. The aircraft landed at a base north of Colombey to refuel. De Gaulle and his wife stayed in their seats during the stop. There was no word from de Boissieu who had run into a spot of difficulty. When he reached La Boisserie, he had called the switchboard in the nearby town of Chaumont asking to be put through to Massu. The operator refused to do so. Shortly afterwards, she called back to say that a trade union delegate had been sitting beside her and had told her not to meet his request. Connected to Foccart, de Boissieu told him not to worry about the General's whereabouts and to inform Pompidou that the President had been delayed. Then he went back to his base in Mulhouse.

The helicopters took off again, heading for Massu's two-storey home in the Black Forest. 'Can he [the pilot] find the residence?' de Gaulle wrote on the back on an envelope that he handed to Flohic. 'We are taking steps to find out,' the aide replied in writing. The pilot navigated with Michelin maps that the aide had obtained before leaving Paris, flying low so as to avoid the radar. Flohic told the escort craft to turn back as they reached the Rhine.

At 2.40 p.m., de Gaulle's party landed at the Baden-Oos base and Flohic went to telephone Massu's house.

'This is Flohic,' he told the general. 'We are here.'

'Who's we?'

'The General and Madame de Gaulle.'

Flohic recalled that the commander replied: 'Old boy, I am naked in bed having a siesta.' Massu wrote later that he had been snoozing, wearing a pullover and with a copy of *Le Figaro Littéraire* over his face. The previous night he had been up late drinking vodka with a visiting Soviet delegation.[3]

At 3.01 p.m., de Gaulle, who had not spoken during the three hours since leaving Paris, stepped from his aircraft on to the lawn of Massu's villa. His son and family touched down in another helicopter.

'Everything is done for,' the President told the general, who had telephoned Messmer to inform him of the sudden visit.

'Don't think that way, *mon Général*,' the long-time loyalist replied. 'A man of your standing still has means of action.'

The two of them talked on the lawn for fifteen minutes while Madame Massu took the First Lady inside the house for lunch. The men went into the study to continue their conversation for another twenty minutes, during which de Gaulle, who had missed lunch, was brought an omelette, a glass of water and two cups of coffee. As he ate, according to Massu, two other senior French generals made a brief appearance.

Afterwards, Yvonne was taken to an upstairs room to rest. With Massu, de Gaulle went into his familiar pattern of lamentation: the Communists had paralysed France and he was not wanted any more. He was, according to his host, in an apocalyptic mood and 'stubborn as a mule' in insisting that everything was done for. Massu reacted as the General must have known he would, saying it was not the habit of his visitor to look at such a shambles without doing anything. He appealed to the spirit of 1940 and added that the General had to fight to the end on a terrain of his choosing. According to the commander's account, de Gaulle looked up at him and his spirit seemed to revive as he murmured, 'Go on, go on.'

There would be a time to resign but this was not it, Massu continued. He should not flee when the battlefront was in France. The old fighter must carry on the struggle. The straight-talking Madame Massu was less supportive, however, telling Yvonne de Gaulle over lunch, 'It is not at the age of seventy-eight that one starts 18 June over again.'

'*Mon Général*, too bad, what do you want, you are in the shit and you have to remain in it a bit longer,' her husband said. 'Go back. There is nothing else to do. You are still in the game; you've got to stay in it.'

De Gaulle got up and walked towards his host.

'I'm going,' he said. 'Tell my wife. Philippe will do as he wishes.'

In a television interview a week later, de Gaulle admitted that 'Yes! On 29 May I was tempted to retire . . . I questioned myself.' The day before his disappearance went down with other moments when he had considered stepping down – after the failure of the Dakar expedition in 1940, during the revolt by Admiral Muselier in 1942, in 1946 when he had actually gone, in 1954 when the RPF was falling apart, and on the night of the first round of the 1965 presidential election. But, as then, he staged a vintage recovery, reaching out for comfort from military companions. The great puppet master was once again pulling his own strings to reassure himself and stun his country into awareness of what he meant to it.

Timing was all. The big CGT demonstration on 29 May would remind the French of the power of a party many still regarded as dangerous. Critics within the Gaullist ranks had to be taught a lesson and the Independent Republicans had to be reminded of the need for solidarity. The reinvigoration of the politicians of the *ancien régime* epitomised by the Mitterrand–Mendès France duo had to be choked off. The Communists on whom Pompidou counted had to be shaken by the prospect that 'he' might step down. The PCF was bound to continue its denunciations of 'personal power' and 'Gaullist dictatorship' and call for a 'people's government'. But, after Séguy's reversal at Billancourt, any good Marxist-Leninist could see that the situation demanded an objective tactical alliance with the enemy. In all, for a man of de Gaulle's temperament, action was irresistible, and he handled it perfectly.[4]

At 4.30, the General, his wife and Flohic took off again, Yvonne having entrusted her jewels to her daughter-in-law for safekeeping. Massu telephoned Messmer, and called de Boissieu to say that 'things are going to move'. Messmer told Pompidou the air defence system was tracking de Gaulle's helicopter which landed a kilometre away from La Boisserie.

Reaching his house, the President telephoned the Prime Minister and Tricot to confirm that the Cabinet would meet the following afternoon. To the civil servant he added: 'I have come to terms with my reservations.' To Pompidou he said he had been on a 'tour', without giving details. Everything had gone well, he added. He wanted to rest and reflect, and hoped to get a good night's sleep. '*Mon Général*, you have won,' the Prime Minister replied. 'After the scare the French had in seeing you disappear, we are going to see a prodigious psychological reversal.'[5]

The CGT demonstration in Paris brought out several hundred thousand protesters but passed peacefully. The PCF was not yet ready to try to launch a revolution. That was in keeping with the policy line laid down from Moscow which did not want regime change in France.

The other superpower was not so sure it wanted to see de Gaulle remain in power. The US embassy in Paris took a benign view of Mitterrand. At a meeting called by the ambassador, Sargent Shriver, on the afternoon of 29 May, a senior diplomat, Woody Wallner, was adamant that de Gaulle was finished whatever happened – he based this on a conversation with a senior journalist at *Le Monde*, André Fontaine, who had told him that his information from Pompidou was that the disappearance was the prelude to retirement. 'Write that,' Shriver instructed. Wallner dispatched a telegram to Washington where Dean Rusk sent a note to Johnson that de Gaulle would announce his resignation the following morning. The CIA predicted a presidential election which would take Mitterrand to the Élysée. Shriver noted the prospect of a new administration which would be 'more positive, less grandiose and more in harmony with American policy'.[6]

Back at La Boisserie, the General, Yvonne and Flohic took an evening walk in the grounds, discussing flowers, trees and poetry. Then they killed time in the library, waiting for the 8 p.m. television news. Normally de Gaulle would have used the interval to write or play cards, but he could not concentrate in his impatience to see the impact of his coup. At 7.30, he turned on the set. The screen was a snowstorm with background noise. The General thought there was something wrong with the television set, but Flohic explained it was the result of a strike at the ORTF.

When they went into the dining room for the evening meal, de Gaulle was in a good mood, reciting a poem about the Rhine. Flohic confessed that he did not know the author. 'It's me,' the General replied. Going to the drawing room after dinner, he said that if he had decided not to return to France, he would have gone to Ireland and then 'much further away. In any case, I would not have stayed in France.' Then he set about drafting the text for a broadcast to the nation he intended to make the following day. He began by stating that he had considered all the possibilities open to him and had determined that there would be no dissolution of the National Assembly since it had not voted a censure motion against the government. Nor would the government be altered; he paid fulsome tribute to the 'worth, ability and capacities' of the Prime Minister. If it was impossible to hold the referendum he had announced on 24 May, he would take other measures to maintain the Republic, that is by invoking the special powers under Article 16 of the constitution. France, he added, was threatened with the dictatorship of totalitarianism, but the Republic would not give way.[7]

In the morning, the President flew by helicopter to Issy-les-Moulineaux where a photographer took a shot of him walking to his DS. Arriving at the Élysée, he gave his aide, Pierre Tallon, a firm handshake. His look was lively. 'At last, I have slept,' he told Pompidou when they met before the Cabinet session.

The Prime Minister could not accept the way in which the head of state had kept him in the dark about his movements, particularly about leaving the country. 'I had been treated with what seemed to me at that moment a particular off-handedness,' he wrote in his memoirs. So he offered a three-sentence letter of resignation which de Gaulle waved aside; he might have longer-term plans to change the occupant of Matignon but this was not the right time. Pompidou resumed his argument in favour of a dissolution of the National Assembly and a general election rather than the referendum. De Gaulle repeated the view that, if the second was not going to succeed, neither was the first. The Premier said an election would enable them to focus on the nation's concerns after a month of turmoil. '*Mon Général*, you ask me to stay,' he added. 'I ask for a dissolution.' The threat of resignation was plain.

De Gaulle looked down at the draft of his speech that he had written at Colombey. With his fountain pen, he crossed out his pledge not to dissolve the Assembly and wrote in the line above that he was doing just that. At Pompidou's insistence, he also deleted the passage in which he had said he would not shuffle the government, merely retaining his tribute to the Prime Minister. The two men smiled at one another.[8]

But, having got back on top, the General was pitiless towards the Premier at the subsequent Cabinet meeting, tracing the troubles to his readiness to give way to the protesters, starting with the reopening of the Sorbonne. Watching them walk together through the Élysée corridors, Tallon thought he detected a certain stiffness in de Gaulle and a barely concealed vexation on the part of the Prime Minister.

The General went from the government meeting to record an address to the nation. Because the ORTF television service was still on strike, it was broadcast only on the radio. This was no bad thing for him. It meant that the French were not given a visual reminder of how old and tired he was. Also, it could go out in the afternoon, mobilising supporters for the Gaullist demonstration planned for Paris soon afterwards, and people could listen on transistor radios at work. His combative performance was in striking contrast to his unconvincing appearance six days earlier as he banged his fist on the desk in front of him, shaking the microphone. 'We saw the man of 18 June,' Tallon recalled. 'Why had he taken so long?'[9]

De Gaulle began by saying that he intended to continue his presidential mandate from the nation, and that Pompidou would remain at Matignon. Then his voice failed him. Tallon brought a glass of Évian water and a spoonful of linctus. Clearing his throat, the General announced that a general election would be held, and the referendum delayed. He denounced those who had prevented students studying through the 'intimidation, intoxication and the tyranny of groups organised from afar, and by a party which is a totalitarian enterprise'. He warned that if the situation did not improve he would be forced to invoke emergency powers.

In terms that harked back to the RPF, he called for civic action to be organised to combat the PCF which was playing on the 'ambition and hatreds of politicians on the scrap heap'. 'No, the Republic will not abdicate,' he concluded. 'The people will pull themselves together. Progress, independence and peace will carry the day together with freedom.'[10]

The 'civic action' the General had in mind was on display that afternoon when a huge crowd of supporters marched down the Champs-Élysées from the Arc de Triomphe. At its head were the fervent old partisans Malraux and Debré. Pompidou stayed away, but François Mauriac, now eighty-two, showed his loyalty by appearing at the front. The sea of demonstrators carrying huge tricolour flags surged into the Place de la Concorde. Outside the presidential palace, 50,000 cried: 'De Gaulle, you are not alone!' Gaullists claimed a million people took part; the police estimated 300–400,000.

Coming after the shock of the General's disappearance the previous day, the demonstration of 30 May was a masterly stroke. Doubters were sidelined. For the Independent Republicans, Giscard stated that de Gaulle should remain in power, though he also called for a new government which many understood he wished to head. In a message to de Gaulle sent via Tricot, the former Finance Minister added that he wanted to 'short-circuit Pompidou's manoeuvre'. A Soviet diplomat expressed satisfaction that things were coming under control and said the dissolution of the National Assembly met the essential demand of the opposition, including the PCF. Washington remained unconvinced, however; the CIA Director, Richard Helms, sent Johnson a report that France was on the brink of disaster and that there could be civil war.[11]

The previous evening at Colombey, alone with his wife and the faithful Flohic, de Gaulle had been genuinely happy, a feeling that he did not often experience. But, faced with the massive demonstration of support on 30 May, he reverted to his habitual scepticism. Highly excited, Fouchet telephoned the Élysée to instruct that de Gaulle should be informed of what was happening. When Tallon went to the General's office to deliver the news, he found the President standing by the window, trying to open it. 'Glad you came,' he said. 'I don't know why, but, with me, these things never work.' Opening the window, Tallon passed on the information from Fouchet, saying that the demonstration seemed to have succeeded.

'I am happy for you,' the aide added.

'Oh, you know, if it was only for me it would be of hardly any importance,' the President replied. 'What are they saying?

'They are shouting "*Vive de Gaulle*".'

'Of course.'

Then, his back curving, the General sat down to deal with the dossiers on his desk.

The next day, speaking to the newly appointed Junior Minister for Housing, Philippe Dechartre, he talked not of the residential construction programme but of the temptations of suicide, and confided that he had thought of doing away with himself after the fiasco in Dakar in 1940. Receiving Peyrefitte on 2 June, de Gaulle fell into one of his frequent lamentations about the tendency of the French to give up the fight: 'I cannot always hold them up,' he went on. 'I can't substitute myself for them. And the French will have to do without me one day.'

The Constable was not a man born to be happy. He knew his time was running out. He could not open the window. His hands had begun to shake. When he told Suzanne Massu during a dinner at the Élysée that providence had put her husband in his path on 29 May with what might be 'incalculable consequences for the future', a presidential official was struck by the way in which he grasped the tablecloth as if seeking a sheet anchor. Though he had delivered his counter-punch, the world was escaping him. He belonged to history but he still wanted to make it.

II
Electoral triumph

Smarting from unhappiness at the way the General had deceived him on 29 May, Pompidou rejected appeals to join the demonstration of 30

May. De Gaulle's prestige had been affected, he wrote. Throughout the month of May, 'it was I who spoke to the country, the Assembly, the unions and the politicians. For the mass [of the French] it was I who held on. The General was "absent".' The Prime Minister also worried about the economy; foreign exchange reserves were 'melting like snow in the sunshine' and the limits of Gaullist ambitions were clearly perceived abroad – as he would write in a frank passage of his memoirs published after his death, other countries saw 'the end of the war against the dollar, the end of lessons given to the great powers, the end of our leadership in Western Europe'. All of which caused him, he added, 'an immense sadness'.

The government was reshuffled. Old Gaullists like Fouchet and Joxe who bore responsibility for the handling of the events of May were dropped. Peyrefitte had already gone. The Independent Republican Raymond Marcellin, a tough advocate of law and order, took over the Interior Ministry. A civil servant, François-Xavier Ortoli, who had served with the Free French and was close to Pompidou, became Education Minister. Messmer remained in his job. So did Malraux. Three left-wing Gaullists entered the government in a sign of the General's reawakened interest in progressive policies. René Capitant, the ultra-Gaullist partisan of worker participation in running companies who was deeply critical of the Prime Minister, became Justice Minister; on the steps of the Élysée, he told reporters he was ready to 'swallow the Pompidou grass snake. I do not say it will be agreeable but it is my duty.'

The most important change was a switch between Debré and Couve de Murville, who left the Quai d'Orsay after ten years for the Finance Ministry. Couve had begun his career as a financial official and served Vichy in that capacity, but this was more than a return to his roots. He needed some experience in domestic and economic affairs if he was to become Prime Minister. In his memoirs, Pompidou says that the switch between Couve and Debré was at his instigation since he wanted to step down and knew who his successor would be.[12]

Strikes, factory occupation and student unrest continued. There were four deaths in the protests. On 11 June, the UNEF student organisation staged demonstrations in Paris, Toulouse, Lyon and Saint-Nazaire. The rally in the capital ended with violence on the Left

Bank, and police charges to take enormous barricades. Four hundred demonstrators and seventy policemen were injured. There were more than 1,500 arrests. Five police stations were attacked and seventy-five cars damaged.

Demonstrations were banned; leftist movements were outlawed and several foreigners expelled. On 14 June, the Odéon theatre was taken by the police. On the 16th, a Sunday, the CRS went into the Sorbonne which was then closed. Similar action was taken at other faculties though it was not until 27 June that the last student stronghold at the École des Beaux-Arts in Paris fell.

The industrial stoppages lasted until 17 June when the occupation at the Renault plants ended. The Grenelle agreements were accepted. The new government had marked its installation by ensuring that petrol supplies resumed for the Whitsuntide holiday. Whatever their sympathies for the students and strikers in May, the French rapidly opted for calm in June.

Yet the six weeks of turmoil in May and June 1968 left an indelible mark on France echoed by events elsewhere – the Prague Spring, which would be put down by Soviet tanks, the campus revolts and anti-Vietnam demonstrations in the United States and cries for freedom on their own terms by young people in many other countries, primarily in the developed world. (China was on a different course under the Cultural Revolution launched by Mao in 1966, and radicals in poorer countries tended to concentrate on attempting real revolution by force.)

Many reasons were advanced subsequently for the scale and nature of the revolt, known as '*les événements*'. For some it was either an exercise in subversion or a revolt by young people waging a new form of class struggle against their parents and the established order personified by de Gaulle. Those who delved deeply perceived a spiritual crisis in modern civilisation. For others, it simply reflected a crisis in the universities caused by the antiquated nature of the institutions and the lack of contact between teachers and students. Alternatively, the whole thing was simply an accidental chain of events without any overall form that evolved from demonstration to demonstration. In fact, the movement combined all these elements. As the commentator Alain Willener put it, the students wanted to 'affirm themselves as the creators of their own universe'. This meant killing God, the father figure. For the Fifth Republic, that role was played by de Gaulle. Later, the General referred to the events as the 'the call of nothingness' but he had felt the need to respond by resorting to extreme theatre to rally France behind him. It was no recipe for future stability.[13]

The election campaign waged by the *Union des Démocrates pour la République* (UDR), as the Gaullists now called themselves, was a one-note affair based on the fear conjured up at the end of May. The choice France faced was between order and anarchy, UDR candidates trumpeted. Despite its cautious record the previous month, the PCF was brandished as a scarecrow with dire warnings of 'Communist subversion'.

An amnesty granted to the OAS plotters placated the extreme right; Salan and Argoud were released from jail and Bidault and Soustelle returned from exile. De Gaulle weighed in with a televised interview with his chosen journalist, Michel Droit, in which he said he had stayed on at the end of May because, if he had gone, 'subversion threatened to sweep away the Republic'. The election, he went on, was of unique importance; if the outcome was good for him, freedom, progress, independence and peace would have won but if they went badly 'all would be lost'. The referendum on participation, he added, would be held in due course.

The opposition was in a spot. The Left could not argue against the restoration of order but had nothing else to offer. The PCF was under sustained attack. The way in which Mitterrand had put forward his presidential ambitions and advanced Mendès France as the next Prime Minister was painted as an example of overweening ambition, since there was a legally entitled holder of both posts and the constitution did not provide for a shadow administration. Centrists were caught between their desire to separate themselves from the Communists and Socialists and the need to put a distance between them and the Gaullists.

Driving to the celebrations of the anniversary of his 18 June broadcast, de Gaulle told Foccart it was certain that the UDR would win seats. Mitterrand's left-wing federation would be eaten up by other parties, he added, while the Communists would suffer. 'As for the centrists, my God, I don't know what they will do. They are not short of resources which come first of all from the employers and from our traditional enemies, which is normal, but also from the Jews and, I am certain, from the Americans.'[14]

His forecast proved quite accurate, if understated. The strength of the Gaullist tide was evident at the first round of voting on 23 June. Of the 154 seats won outright, 142 went to candidates of the UDR or the Independent Republicans. Between them, they scooped 46 per cent of the vote. The Left and the centrists each lost some 12 per cent of their votes at the previous year's general election. Having learned the lesson of its lassitude between the two rounds in 1965, the government kept up the pressure, with a fighting final broadcast by de Gaulle. Although the Left generally agreed on a single candidate for the run-off ballot, this did nothing to halt the Gaullist wave. The UDR and Independent Republicans ended up with 354 of the 487 National Assembly seats, a gain of 112 over 1967. Mitterrand's federation lost 64 seats to hold 57 and the PCF dropped by 34 to 39.

It was the first time in the history of France's republics that a single party had gained an overall parliament majority. The Left had suffered one of the worst reverses it had ever known, with the iconic Mendès France going down to defeat in Grenoble at the hands of Jeanneney. Despite his age and his fumbling performance in May, despite his self-doubts and his despair at the failure of the French to live up to his grand designs, de Gaulle had emerged as the great winner. The election had been, in effect, a referendum and his support appeared to be back to the level of the early years of the Fifth Republic.

III
Dropping the heir

With that under his belt, de Gaulle was free to put into practice his plan to change the occupant of Matignon. The election campaign had raised Pompidou's profile too high. In retrospect, his handling of the events of May did not look bad, and his position had been strengthened by repeated praise from the President. A meeting he had held with Gaullist deputies the day after the election led some to think that he envisaged turning the parliamentary majority into a force which could talk to the presidency on equal terms. What Jacques Vendroux described as a 'Pompidou clan' was clearly emerging.

A stream of visitors went to urge the Prime Minister to remain in office. Pompidou was in two minds. He had had enough of running the government under the wilful General, and did not relish the economic problems that lay ahead. He thought he would be called on to succeed de Gaulle one day and needed a period out of power before that. In a handwritten list of reasons why de Gaulle should step down, he noted that, first, he himself had to get away from government and 'to make myself wanted'.

Still, he was taken aback when a group of journalists told him over lunch that he was about to be replaced. After a family dinner at his flat on the Quai Béthune looking out at Notre-Dame, he did not sleep as he considered his situation and the political permutations. The next day, a Saturday and his fifty-seventh birthday, he telephoned Tricot to say that he would continue in his job if he could take a couple of weeks' rest, and have a proper discussion with the President about the meaning of worker participation whose vague character he considered dangerous. When the civil servant took this message to the President, de Gaulle cried: 'That's too stupid. He's too late.' The previous night, he had offered the job to Couve, who had finally managed to win a parliamentary seat in the smart 8th *arrondissement* of Paris. That night, the ORTF was ordered not to transmit an Alfred Hitchcock television film entitled *Au Revoir, Georges*; it was replaced with one called *Le Grand Silence*.

'Something in me was shaken,' Pompidou recalled. He felt 'as if I had ashes in my mouth'. De Gaulle wrote to him to pay tribute to his 'exceptional efficacious' work. 'Wherever you find yourself, know, my dear friend, that I will make a point of maintaining particularly close relations with you,' he added, signing off with 'feelings of faithful and devoted friendship'. On 11 July, Couve became Prime Minister. When he referred to Pompidou in his inaugural speech to parliament, his predecessor was cheered loudly; the former Premier remained impassive.[15]

The dropping of Pompidou had become inevitable, but it raised a major question. De Gaulle, who would be seventy-eight in November, was not immortal. He had discarded Pompidou, rather than smoothing his path to the succession. Couve was not a man to lead the Fifth

Republic, nor were other long-serving ministers. There was no fresh blood. The new Premier and the Interior Minister had both served under Vichy. The vote at the general election had been prompted by retrospective fear, not by support for a Gaullist vision of the future. More than ever, the regime was a one-man band, and the future loomed more uncertain than ever.

37

FINAL ACT

I
A lost cause

De Gaulle had two priorities for Couve de Murville's government when it took office on 10 July 1968 – to introduce reforms in the universities and to prepare for his referendum on worker participation. To carry out the first, Edgar Faure, the dome-headed Fourth Republic veteran celebrated for his ability to conjure up agreements, became Education Minister. Jean-Marcel Jeanneney took responsibility for the participation programme. Otherwise most principal ministries remained in the same hands except for Finance, taken by Pompidou's former chief of staff, François-Xavier Ortoli.

Working with a team of experts, many of them liberals, Faure came up with an education bill adopted by the Cabinet in mid-September. It granted autonomy to universities, and modernised the teaching and examination systems. This was not to the taste of conservative Gaullists whose numbers had been increased at the legislative election. But they did not dare to vote against the reforms when they came before parliament and the changes were approved by a margin of 440–0 with thirty-nine abstentions in November. De Gaulle, who judged that the minister had 'thrust a sword into the loins' of the conservative university establishment, was highly supportive, seeing the reform as the start of his crusade to enable the population at large to participate more in the way France was run.

Though unenthusiastic about Faure's programme, Pompidou avoided public criticism. Now simply the deputy from the Cantal department, he was the undoubted leader of the UDR in parliament while the party's new Secretary-General, Robert Poujade, was one of his protégés. De Gaulle had placed him 'at the disposal of the Republic', but the former Premier was increasingly detached from his former leader's policies, not only on education but also on participation, on which he had never been keen. However, his legacy was evident as the effects of the wage settlement he had reached in May were felt at a trying moment because of a new dismantling of Common Market tariff barriers. Inflation rose. The budget deficit was well above the target. Massive speculation built up against the franc as money flowed out of the country. On 10 November, the Paris Bourse had to be closed. De Gaulle blamed his former Prime Minister. 'The economy has been thrown to the ground for years to come,' he told Peyrefitte.

France secured an international loan, but the West Germans insisted that this was conditional on a devaluation; *Le Monde* was briefed on the precise amount of the change, which was relayed to Reuters and flashed around the world. But Jeanneney, backed by Faure, lobbied against changing the value of the currency. He called on the economic expertise of his former chief of staff, Raymond Barre, now Vice-President of the European Commission, who told the Élysée that, whatever the Germans said, the European banks would not insist on devaluation. On the afternoon of Saturday 23 November, the Cabinet decided to dig in their heels; only Chirac and Chalandon, now Minister for Infrastructure and Housing, argued in favour of a cut in the value of the franc.

Despite this assertion of France's ability to plough its own furrow, de Gaulle was not in the best of shape. The Soviet invasion of Czechoslovakia, to end the liberalisation of the Prague Spring, had been a major setback to his dream that a rapprochement with Moscow would open the way to a 'Europe from the Atlantic to the Urals'. At a summit in Bonn with Chancellor Kiesinger he blamed the whole episode on the Germans, since Moscow feared that, if it became embroiled in war with China, the Federal Republic would attack the Soviet Union 'in the back' and so felt it had to strengthen its hold on the satellite countries. That problem, he went on, stemmed from Bonn's failure to join wholeheartedly in cooperation with France, preferring to follow its own path in seeking reunification. 'I think that, if Germany had followed another policy, we would perhaps not be in this situation vis-à-vis the Soviet Union,' he added.

There was also the wider problem of France's influence after ten years of the Fifth Republic. In a conversation with the American politician William Scranton, de Gaulle lamented that none of the other countries of West Europe wanted to pursue his vision of independence from the United States. Further afield, his lobbying in favour of the recognition of Biafra's right to self-determination made no impact on the government of Nigeria, and Israel took no notice of his advice to avoid the use of force, provoking him to slap a total arms embargo on the Jewish state after its aircraft attacked Beirut airport on 31 December in reprisal for a terrorist attack on El Al planes.

Though it was headed off, the prospect of a devaluation threw the General into a depression, and his son told Foccart he found his father tired and lacking the kind of reactions needed for the challenges facing him. Madame de Gaulle continued to lobby for her husband's retirement, saying he shouldn't spend one more year in office. A growing number of the General's followers were of the same opinion. 'For years, the Gaullists watched a great man doing a trapeze act with a safety net,' Chaban-Delmas told an off-the-record lunch with foreign journalists. 'Then he did the act without a net. Today we see him carrying out a curious kind of gymnastics, without a net and without a trapeze. So it's logical that we are worried.' As for the ministers, Chaban commented: 'We have never had a government team made up of such serious and competent men but also so far from realities, so un-political.'[1]

The administration's position was all the more fragile because of the presence of Pompidou in the aisles. Left bitter by the way de Gaulle had treated him in May and June, the former Premier knew better than to put himself forward as an overt challenger, but it was enough for people to see him as the obvious Gaullist candidate for the succession to pull the rug from under the President's warnings that, if he went, France would descend into chaos. Then, in the winter of 1968, the discovery of the body of a Yugoslav hood set in train a series of events that estranged the former Premier from the General in a highly personal, emotive manner.

II
The Markovic Affair

The corpse of Stephan Markovic was found on a rubbish dump in the Yvelines department outside Paris; the dead man had been a bodyguard for the actor Alain Delon. A letter he wrote in his last days blamed the film star and a former criminal, François Marcantoni, for anything that might happen to him. Stories spread that he had been a lover of Delon's actress wife and had attended orgies with prominent figures whom he then blackmailed. While the police investigation got nowhere, the rumour mill began to talk of the wife of a former minister having been present at some of these parties. Prison authorities intercepted a letter from another Yugoslav called Akov, who was in jail, speaking of being taken to an orgy at a villa in the Yvelines after which he was told: 'You saw that big blonde woman. Silence! She is the wife of the Prime Minister.' René Capitant, the Justice Minister and an assiduous enemy of Pompidou, telephoned the Interior Minister, Raymond Marcellin, about the letter, guffawing as he did so.

Marcellin informed Couve de Murville and Bernard Tricot. The Élysée official took a helicopter to Colombey to tell the President, who was at his country house for the All Saints weekend. Returning to Paris the following Monday, de Gaulle called in the Prime Minister, Marcellin and Capitant. They decided that nothing must be done to interfere with the inquiry into Markovic's death by an examining magistrate. Couve was to fill in Pompidou. He did not do so.

The former Premier had heard rumours about a politician's wife being involved in orgies, but paid little attention. He was busy installing an office in the 7th *arrondissement* and preparing for the parliamentary session. He had met Delon but felt no reason to take any particular interest in the case. But, when he returned to Paris after passing the All Saints holiday with his family in the Auvergne, one of his former staffers who mixed in smart Parisian society came to see him and told him that the woman cited in the rumours was his wife, Claude. Pompidou summoned his closest aides, Jobert and Balladur, who confirmed this, as did an ex-staffer who now held a senior position at the Interior Ministry. The former Prime Minister reacted violently. He recalled that he had rarely felt so desperate; the magazine *Le Nouvel Observateur* described him as being like 'a wounded tiger'. He went to see Marcellin who said he did not believe the rumours. Matters became worse when a friend mentioned the allegations to his wife.

Pompidou demanded a meeting with de Gaulle. The rendezvous was kept secret, Pompidou entering the Élysée by the garden.

'I have three things to say to you,' he told the General. 'I know my wife well enough to know that it is unthinkable that she would find herself mixed up to however small a degree in this affair. Perhaps some people are trying to involve me. You won't find any trace of me. I can't say as much for all your ministers. Neither with Capitant, nor at Matignon, nor at the Élysée, has there been the slightest reaction of a man of honour.'

'But I, I have never believed all that,' de Gaulle replied weakly. 'I asked that you be warned.'

Pompidou said he was not putting de Gaulle's personal attitude in question and asked to see him again when he had pursued an investigation. As he left, he felt that the President 'did not seem very satisfied with himself'.

The examining magistrate, described by Chaban-Delmas as 'a nasty fool', had the bit between his teeth, attracting maximum publicity by interviewing glamorous film stars. Delon and his wife were held for questioning. The police appeared to be playing a tricky game: Akov turned out to be a police informer and had been visited by his detective handlers before he wrote his letter, which was in surprisingly good French. At the time of the alleged party, the man he said had taken him there was, in fact, in jail while the Pompidous were on holiday in Brittany.

In a New Year letter to 'my dear friend', de Gaulle urged Pompidou to ignore 'tittle-tattle even if it is grotesque and vile'. But the affair would not die down. A prominent lawyer, Roland Dumas, who was close to Mitterrand, flew to Belgrade to offer to represent the Markovic family. Lawyers on the far right, including Jacques Isorni, stirred things up. Pompidou found the possible involvement of secret service agents troubling.[2]

Then, in January 1969, matters became more complicated on the political front when the Deputy of the Cantal was asked about his plans by a group of journalists during a visit to Rome. He answered, as he always did, that when de Gaulle retired he would probably be a candidate for the succession. Having said this often in the past, he regarded his reply as routine and most of the journalists followed suit. However, one of them, Robert Mengin, who had formed a bad impression of de Gaulle in London in June 1940, and was now a correspondent in Italy for the Agence France-Presse (AFP), put together a report which made it appear that the former Premier was positioning himself as a rival to the General.[3]

A Paris evening paper played up the story, leading Couve to call for a strong reply. De Gaulle issued a statement asserting that he intended to stay until the end of his mandate in 1972. But Pompidou had reminded everybody that the dauphin was waiting in the wings. 'The fatal blow [to de Gaulle] was dealt by Pompidou in Rome,' Mitterrand told diplomats. 'He knows the journalists well and he is too crafty to let himself be surprised,' de Gaulle told an aide. 'He knew perfectly well what he was provoking.'[4]

The intermingling of low scandal and high politics, fanned by the former Premier's enemies among Gaullist ultras and some of the Left, continued when Markovic's brother claimed he had dined with Pompidou in the Delons' kitchen. The target of this accusation denied it and pointed out that, if he had dined with the actor, it would not have been in the kitchen. Still, the ORTF broadcasting network and the AFP, which got most of its revenue from the state, repeated the story. Posing as a defender of the politician, Isorni asked the examining magistrate to question the Pompidous about the kitchen dinner story ostensibly so that they could clear their name, but, in fact, to ratchet up the rumours.

Meanwhile, Pompidou heightened his implicit challenge to de Gaulle. In an interview on Swiss television he said that he might 'perhaps, and if God is willing, have a national destiny'. Realising that things were getting out of hand, the President asked the Pompidous to dinner at the Élysée on 12 March 1969, taking the precaution of also inviting the Debrés so that it could be presented as an occasion for former Prime Ministers. The atmosphere was cold. The President accused Pompidou of having renewed his offence with his Swiss statement, to which his guest replied that the position taken by the General and his government had forced him to stand up for himself. In his memoirs, he recalled that there had been 'no word from the heart' on the President's part about the Markovic allegation. He and his wife left early.*[5]

III
Losing Battle

The General's desire to make his worker-participation plans the subject of a national vote was stymied by the constitutional limitation of subjects on which a referendum could be held to matters dealing with the organisation of government or ratifying a treaty. So he fell back on a partial proposal to increase regional authorities and added a second proposition – to turn the Senate from an indirectly elected political body into an organisation made up of representatives of local organisations and of delegates from economic, social and cultural groups. This could be presented as conforming to the constitution and contained ideas that de Gaulle had advanced as long ago as 1946; but the second proposition appeared as an act of vengeance against a legislature which, while lacking effective powers, had been a hotbed of criticism and a home for opponents defeated in National Assembly elections.

On 2 February, the General announced the vote would be held on 27 April. This came at the end of a disappointing tour of Brittany during which he was met with cries of 'We are all Québecois!', 'Free Brittany!' and the May 1968 slogan 'CRS = SS'. The vague regionalisation proposition aroused little enthusiasm. A broad front of opposition rallied to the defence of the Senate, whose president, the comfortable centrist Alain Poher, elected in the autumn of 1968, stood in the Monnerville tradition, and would take over as interim head of state pending an election if de Gaulle stepped down. The issues at stake were less important than the key question of whether France wanted its republican monarch to continue his reign.

*The killer of Markovic was never identified as the investigation petered out.

De Gaulle had never lacked for critics but, by the beginning of 1969, they were even more numerous and vociferous as economic and social problems mounted. To maintain the parity of the franc, the Bank of France raised interest rates but this did not prevent the reserves falling sharply while the trade balance deteriorated. Austerity loomed as the General instructed Couve to cut state spending and slash subsidies in order to achieve a balanced budget. Public sector workers staged a one-day strike. Farm incomes fell and small shopkeepers staged a protest movement against the VAT sales tax and the expansion of supermarkets.

Conservatives lined up in defence of the Senate while *Algérie française* veterans had not forgotten what they saw as the General's betrayal. The 'Yes but' Independent Republicans were increasingly restive and their leader, Giscard d'Estaing, was building bridges for the future with Pompidou. The Jewish community had been shocked by the General's position on Israel, though the President had no second thoughts, as he showed with the arms embargo and in a suggestion to Foccart that ways might be found to damage the business of Edmond de Rothschild, who backed the centrist opposition, since he 'calls himself Jewish and French, but he is first of all Jewish which means . . . you cannot consider him as a Frenchman'.

All in all, it was far from the best context in which to ask people to vote. As Couve, who thought the referendum a mistake, remarked: 'How could the people not be, let us say, melancholic or neurasthenic or morose after all that has happened in the last six months?' Pompidou, who was not called upon to join the campaign for a Yes vote until the last minute, believed that the referendum would end in defeat and advised putting it off. The General considered doing this for a while but worried about the loss of face such a decision would entail; better to risk defeat than for the Constable to be seen to waver.

But he had no illusions. Taking Chirac aside at an official dinner, he said it was evident that the vote would be lost. A television address he delivered on 11 March to explain his proposals was lacklustre. Eleven days later, he told his military aide, General Lalande, that he would have to go one day or another. 'Things cannot hold eternally and it would be a very suitable departure.' Still, suddenly modest, he said that he would do his best.[6]

Amid this domestic uncertainty, the General kept busy with foreign affairs, receiving Richard Nixon in early 1969 for a visit during which the US President lavished praise on him as a historic giant; de Gaulle said France would give up its war on the dollar, a course on which he had little choice given the state of the economy. Remembering the Quebec clash, he told Debré that Paris had 'every reason to keep a large distance' from the federal government in Canada. In February 1969, France boycotted the Western European Union (WEU) defence grouping on the grounds that Britain had called a meeting without its agreement.

Then the President summoned the British ambassador, Christopher Soames, to put forward a proposal for secret talks on British entry into the Common Market on condition that NATO was dismantled, a larger free trade area established, and a directorate of the United Kingdom, Germany, France and Italy set up to run the western half of the continent. The notion died a quick death after the British leaked the story to the press; the French accused the ambassador of having relayed a distorted version of de Gaulle's words to London, and the incident caused fresh unhappiness among other members of the Six. At the end of March, de Gaulle flew to Washington for Eisenhower's funeral. The trip was notable for two things – the way in which, at the age of seventy-eight, he travelled back to Paris without sleeping and went straight to work, and the fact that, for the first time and despite Nixon's praise for him in Paris, he had to request a meeting with an American President, rather than being automatically invited.[7]

On 10 April, the General performed a television interview with Michel Droit that was far from his inspirational performances of the past as he presented a lengthy historical analysis of France's constitutions and the reasons why the Senate should be reformed. But he made one thing quite clear: if the No vote won, he would step down. That appeared more likely as, following the Left and the centre, Giscard joined the rejectionist camp. Yvonne foresaw a dramatic turn of events, advising her children to be ready to leave their homes with a suitcase containing their most precious possessions and making Foccart pledge to look after them if things went wrong with her and the General. After mass on 20 April, de Gaulle told his children that the referendum would go against him because of voters who would follow Giscard. He took a philosophical view: if he won, well and good, but if he lost he would also have won because of the mess that would follow; he still could not bring himself to recognise Pompidou as a worthy heir for he could have no successor.[8]

IV
'It's lost'

23 April. The atmosphere around the table at the weekly Wednesday Cabinet meeting is heavy. Debré delivers a report on foreign affairs in which he says that France's standing in the world will be compromised if the No vote wins. The General ends thc session by saying he hopes they will all meet again the following week – 'If it is not so, a chapter in the History of France will have ended,' he adds.*

Over coffee after a lunch with half a dozen advisers and their wives, de Gaulle remarks that he could have done without the referendum the following Sunday, but, if it is won, the future of the Fifth Republic will be assured. That afternoon, he listens patiently to reports by senior officials responsible for civil aviation and higher education. Receiving his four principal presidential aides as usual in the late evening, he tells them that, since the referendum will be lost, arrangements should be made to move his archives to 5 rue de Solférino in the early hours of Monday. His staff should leave the Élysée by noon that day. Nothing is to be said about these arrangements, but he is intent on making a complete break if he is forced out.

24 April. Shortly before noon, Debré arrives for a thirty-minute meeting. 'The dice have been rolled,' de Gaulle tells him. 'I can do nothing more. The French people don't want me any more. So I have nothing else to do but to leave.' After the former Premier argues that his final television broadcast the next day may change matters, the President insists: 'The French want to see me leave. I will go to the end. I will speak to them a last time. But I have no more illusions.'

*This account of de Gaulle's defeat and the following events up to his death draws substantially on Jean Mauriac's masterly reconstruction in his book, *Mort du Général de Gaulle*, to which I am greatly indebted.

After watching the start of the 1 p.m. television news, the de Gaulles lunch with Vendroux and his wife. Seeing the President in the afternoon, Foccart finds him 'already gone'. To the head of his private secretariat he speaks of the future after a negative vote, planning to find an office in Paris and visit the capital from time to time as in the years after his resignation in 1946. Some Gaullists discuss approaching Pompidou to try to induce him to announce that, if the No vote carries the day, he will not be a presidential candidate. The idea never takes shape.

At 7 p.m., the President receives Couve to tell him that, in the event of defeat on Sunday, Tricot will give him a personal letter and a resignation statement to be issued at 11 a.m. on Monday. Before the Prime Minister leaves, de Gaulle thanks him warmly for his services over the years.

25 April. Lightly made up, de Gaulle records his appeal for a Yes vote, saying that, if a majority vote against the proposals, his task as head of state will be impossible and he will immediately step down. 'Frenchwomen, Frenchmen, the decision of each of you will never have weighed so heavily in what is going to happen to France,' he concludes, '*Vive la République! Vive la France!*' As he watches a play-back, he mutters to the Information Minister, Joël Le Theule, 'We're fucked.' The de Gaulles eat a quick lunch and then, after the arrival of the first edition of *Le Monde*, go to their DS parked by the rose garden at the back of the Élysée. It has been loaded with more luggage than usual for a Colombey weekend. On the way out of the palace, Foccart intercepts them with news of a slightly more comforting last-minute opinion poll. 'No,' the General says. 'It's lost, I tell you, it's lost.' His attitude can only fuel subsequent speculation that the referendum has become a political suicide bid of a man who knows his time has passed.

At the gate on the Avenue Marigny, the General asks the driver to stop, winds down the window and, without saying anything, shakes the hand of the colonel in charge of the military detachment at the palace. Because of high winds, he has decided not to take a helicopter to the Haute-Marne but to go by road. On the way to the Porte d'Orléans, police block crossroads to let the DS through, saluting as the presidential couple pass. In the back of the car on the journey via Fontainebleau towards Troyes, de Gaulle reads *Le Monde* and then gazes silently at the countryside, sucking sweets and throwing the wrappers out of the window. At 4 p.m., he and his wife arrive at Colombey. 'We are coming back permanently,' he tells the maid at the door. 'This time, Charlotte, it's for good.'

At 8 p.m., the General watches his recorded speech on television. In Lyon to address a rally, Pompidou sees 'an old, disenchanted man'. At the former Premier's office on the Boulevard La Tour-Maubourg, lists of a future government are drawn up, with Chaban-Delmas as Prime Minister, and discreet consultations are conducted with Giscard and Edgar Faure. The chief of staff at the Quai d'Orsay tells American diplomats that they should be ready for the Left to take power. Because of this, Debré, who is in Alsace, will stay there, he adds.

26 April. De Gaulle spends the Saturday at La Boisserie. He does not receive a single telephone call. The faithful Flohic is lodged at a hotel in the nearby town of Bar-sur-Aube.

27 April. The weather is cold with occasional rain this Sunday morning. The de Gaulles hear mass in the house, in order to avoid onlookers and journalists outside. At 11.35 a.m., they go by car to vote in the municipal council office, walking up the wooden staircase to a booth behind a flowered curtain. The President shakes the Mayor's hand without saying anything. Outside people watch silently, and photographers take their pictures as the couple gets into the DS to be driven back to their house. De Gaulle does not invite Flohic, who has arrived from Bar-sur-Aube, to come back to the house – the aide thinks he wants to be alone when the referendum results come in.

The General works through the afternoon in his study. In the late evening, Tricot telephones. Taking the call himself, bent over in the cubbyhole under the stairs, the President hears that the indications are that the referendum has been lost. He asks the official to call him back at 10 p.m. By then, it is clear that the No vote has attracted 54 per cent of those who went to the polls. At the Élysée, staff gather round a buffet to follow the results, some in tears. The archives are already on their way across the Seine to the rue de Solférino.

When Tricot makes his 10 p.m. call, de Gaulle instructs that his resignation statement should be issued as soon as possible after midnight instead of waiting for Monday morning. At ten minutes past midnight, the French News Agency sends out a flash reporting the President's words: 'I cease to exercise my functions as President of the Republic. This decision takes effect today at midnight.'

At 00.30 a.m., the ringing telephone breaks the silence of the house. It is Debré. At first, de Gaulle sounds serene, but his former Premier recalls later that he was 'touched to the bottom of his being'. The following morning, when Flohic gets to the house, the General tells him that perhaps what has happened is just as well because the only alternative would have been the diminution of his historic stature. At the end of the year, Malraux asked why he had resigned on such a secondary issue – was it because of the absurdity of doing so? Looking fixedly at the writer, the General repeated 'because of the absurdity'.[9]

V
Afterlife

De Gaulle did not leave La Boisserie for eighteen days after his defeat. Lunching with him on 28 April, his brother-in-law found him 'calm and serene', hiding his sadness. In the following four days, he received three officials from the presidential palace to clear up administrative matters, and Foccart, who lost his job looking after Africa as Poher moved into the Élysée pending the presidential election set for June. De Boissieu, who was on a military visit to a nearby camp, took time off to see his father-in-law, recounting that his nine-year-old daughter, Anne, had gone to her room to cry when she heard the news of his departure. Philippe came on 4 May.

The General drew up an outline for a new volume of memoirs tracing events since 1958, and began to reply to the sackloads of letters that arrived at Colombey, writing by hand to Nixon, the Shah of Iran, the King of the Belgians, Presidents Senghor, Houphouët-Boigny and Boumédiène of Algeria as well as to the Comte de Paris. He sent Pompidou approval of his 'archi-natural' candidacy for the presidency, but could not refrain from noting that the former Premier's statements about being ready to run had cost the Yes camp some votes. While wishing him success, he concluded by saying that he would not show himself in any way during what he referred to in inverted commas as the 'campaign'.[10]

On 10 May, the former President, his wife and Flohic drove to a nearby military airfield and flew off in a Mystère jet from the government fleet. There was no announcement of the departure or of where they were going. The old man was once more showing his taste for secrecy, and it was only after he had arrived at Cork, in Ireland, that his whereabouts became known. His trip to a country where he could enjoy peace and quiet and from which some of his ancestors hailed meant that he missed the commemoration of his 18 June appeal and was out of France during the presidential election. 'You understand,' he remarked, 'that it is better for Pompidou that he doesn't say to himself when campaigning "he is there, in his drawing room, in front of his television. He is watching me." That would risk putting him out.' But his motivation was certainly more profound. Having been rejected, he had no desire to be in France when his successor was chosen.[11]

In County Cork he stayed in a modest hotel, the Heron Cove, where the tablecloths were paper and the guests drank from old mustard jars. He took long walks with Flohic and his wife, who sometimes found it hard to keep up. A posse of French journalists arrived but was kept at arm's length. The party then moved to a hotel set in the moors of Cashel where de Gaulle could walk in the park without being watched, before going on to Kenmare.

In his absence, Pompidou faced three main opponents – Poher for moderate, pro-Europe, pro-Atlanticist centrists, Duclos for the Communists and Defferre for the Socialists, running in tandem with Mendès France whom he pledged to appoint to Matignon if he won. Michel Rocard represented the PSU and Alain Krivine stood for Trotskyites. Pompidou emerged with 45 per cent of the first-round vote on 1 June. Duclos polled four times as many votes as the Defferre–Mendès ticket, but the split on the Left opened the door to Poher for the second round. The President of the Senate, an amiable second-rank politician, was no match for his opponent and the Gaullist machine. On 15 June, Pompidou strolled home with 58 per cent of the vote. De Gaulle sent him the tersest of messages: 'For every national and personal reason, I send you my very cordial congratulations'. In a longer reply, the new President pledged to keep to the General's foreign and defence policies – he made no mention of doing the same in domestic and economic affairs.

In the place of the General playing out the historic role he had assumed for himself, France was now led by a man who would operate on an ordinary human scale, who would balance alternatives to come up with a reasonable solution, who would give up dreams and stop telling the rest of the world how to behave. It was not a prospect the General could welcome, as he was reduced to remarking that Pompidou's score at the first round of the election was lower than his own losing count at the referendum, as if the two were comparable. 'I was wounded in May 1968,' he remarked. 'And then they got me. Now I am dead.' Speaking to the French ambassador to Ireland, Emmanuel d'Harcourt, he said that, if he had remained in office, he would have extended his support for the French Canadians to the Walloons of Belgium, the inhabitants of the Channel Islands and other groups which he thought should affirm themselves.

On 18 June, he was guest of honour at a banquet given by the Irish President, Eamon de Valera, at which he said that, in Ireland, he had found what he sought – 'to face myself'. The following day, he met thirty members of the MacCartan family, his distant Irish relations, one of whom had sought refuge in France from the victorious British army after the battle of the Boyne in 1690. At a lunch with the Prime Minister, Jack Lynch, and his government, de Gaulle raised his glass to 'united Ireland' – it could have been a minor repetition of *Vive le Québec libre*, but the microphone developed a fault during the General's toast and only those immediately around him heard it.[12]

*

Returning to France after Pompidou became president, de Gaulle seemed to his rare visitors to have been reinvigorated by his stay in Ireland. Still, he remained cloistered at Colombey, and did not visit the private office set up for him in Paris. He followed a strict routine, with lunch at 12.30 and dinner at 7.15, two walks a day, marking his way with his walking stick and particularly relishing his promenades when the wind was blowing. He concentrated on writing his memoirs, which he called 'my big work', writing and editing for three hours up to noon and for two more hours in the afternoon at his desk looking out at the valley below the house and across to the thick forest of Dhuits.

A small table beside him was covered with folders and documents. On the desk was a framed photograph of his grandchildren. The shelves opposite him were crammed with books and gifts, a small gold elephant from Houphouët-Boigny, an ancient Bible from Adenauer. When a visitor asked if he knew how to do nothing, he replied that he had trouble imposing 'a lazy routine' on himself but took time off to play patience, with the cat, called Grigri, beside him. Still, progress on the book was slow; as always he rewrote a great deal. 'What I am doing here in writing my memoirs is much more important for France than what I could have done at the Élysée if I had still been there,' he told the journalist Michel Droit.

Though he said nothing in public, his wife bore witness to the sadness he felt. His letters spoke of the 'crisis of mediocrity' in France. In Ireland, he had remarked to the French ambassador that since his departure from power, everything had come to a halt on the international scene. After Couve de Murville's defeat in a by-election outside Paris, he told his former minister nothing better could be expected in the prevailing context. France had reverted to the Fourth Republic, he remarked. While saying he found it natural that the new administration pursued policies of its own, he deplored the way it invoked his name. He attributed the referendum defeat to two of his recurrent foes – 'the doubt and tiredness of the French and immobilism'. 'I raised the corpse of France with my arms, making the world think it was alive,' Malraux recalled him saying when he called at Colombey at the end of 1969 for an hour-long conversation on which he based a book entitled *Les Chênes qu'on abat* (*The Oaks One Fells*).

The General wrote regularly to his son, sometimes enclosing money, and pledging 400,000 francs to help Philippe build a villa in the South of France. He also gave 3,000 francs to the Colombey gendarmerie in recognition of the way it had assured his security. Building work and repainting was done at La Boisserie. In June 1970, the de Gaulles visited Spain, where the General met Franco, telling him 'You *are* General Franco; that's something. Me, I *was* General de Gaulle.' He said he found his host very old, though, in fact, the Spanish leader was two years his junior. The trip ensured that he was out of France on 18 June which he spent in a hunting lodge of the sierra above Marbella working on his memoirs.

In August, the couple made a brief journey through the Vosges mountains, retracing the route of the advance Philippe's unit had made towards Germany at the end of the Second World War. Messmer came to visit, the two men taking a long walk in the forest; when they returned, Madame de Gaulle was looking out for them and the General commented to his former minister on the way she kept watch over him. In September, he was greatly saddened by the death of François Mauriac; in a letter to his widow he wrote that, with the writer's passing, 'a great cold grips us'. His former press secretary, Pierre-Louis Blanc, who went to La Boisserie to help with work on the memoirs, found the General reinvigorated by the country air, anxious to finish his work as he battled against the passage of time. But, visiting Colombey at the end of September, Philippe thought his father 'sadder and more melancholic than usual'. When they bade farewell after a walk during which they gathered mushrooms, his son reflected: 'Each time he left us, it was as if he would not see us again.'

In October 1970, the latest volume of de Gaulle's memoirs was published. Newspapers regretted the way in which it skated over difficulties he had faced and appeared less written from the heart than his account of the wartime years, but it was a huge popular success with750,000 copies distributed to bookshops. As well as starting the next volume, de Gaulle went on working his way through a collection of eight hundred of his speeches and messages being published in companion volumes. He made plans for more journeys, including one to China to meet Mao.[13]

VI
'Oh, it hurts'

2 November. The de Boissieus are at Colombey for the All Saints holiday. The General leads them to the village cemetery where they stand in front of Anne's tomb. He says that this is where he wants to be buried, 'but the gate to the cemetery is too narrow. Since there will perhaps be some visitors when I am here, it will be necessary to break down the wall and construct a second gate.' Looking at the gravestones he notes how many of the dead lived past eighty and adds, 'Eighty years, it's a heavy burden to bear.' After a hundred-minute-long walk in the forest with his son-in-law, his granddaughters present him with flowers in a ceremony set up by Yvonne for the Saint Charles holiday.

After Madame de Gaulle has gone to bed, the de Boissieus and de Gaulle watch the late television news. Then the old man says it is time for the younger ones to turn in, leaving him time to relish the solitude of the ground-floor rooms, the fire burning in the hearth, the doors left half open so that his ever-watchful wife can hear his movements through the bedroom door which she keeps open till he comes up.

3 November. A former Free French fighter, General Renourard, calls at La Boisserie to talk of the war. After he leaves, the General and the de Boissieus walk round the garden. Then the guests leave. De Gaulle calls out that he has not kissed their daughter, Anne, goodbye. She gets out of the car and her grandfather embraces her.

4–8 November. Quiet days at Colombey for a man who describes himself as having become a country dweller devoted to literary endeavours. The cook, Honorine, finds him 'very pale, his features drawn, his neck white'. She puts this down to the bad weather.

9 November. In the morning, de Gaulle, wearing a dark grey suit, works on his memoirs in his study. He eats well at lunch and walks round the grounds, once with Yvonne, once alone. The sky is dark, and a strong wind blows away the last autumn leaves. At 2.30, the General receives a young farmer to talk about some land he has exchanged with him; he plans to grow trees there. At 3.30 p.m., he telephones the aide in charge of his Paris office to fix an appointment at Colombey the following day. Yvonne is upstairs, her hair under the dryer after being set by Honorine. Charlotte, the maid, serves tea and cakes; de Gaulle takes them up to his wife. Then he returns to his study where he signs a tax form and writes half a dozen letters, including one to Philippe about the villa his son plans in the South of France. He wants confirmation of the cost so that he can supply the necessary funds and suggests that they deal with the details when the family comes to Colombey for Christmas.

Shortly after 6.45, he goes into the library after closing the shutters in the study. Yvonne comes down and sits at her desk to write letters. Her husband settles into the armchair at his green baize card table to play patience. Five to ten minutes later, he puts his right hand on his back and cries, 'Oh! It hurts here.' He slumps on his side against the arm of the chair, head forward. His glasses fall to the floor. He loses consciousness. His wife and the two servants prevent him from slipping off the chair. His face becomes very pale and his hands whiten. Subsequently, there would be speculation that he said something else, but this was never confirmed.

Madame de Gaulle tells Charlotte to call the doctor in Bar-sur-Aube. Honorine summons the driver, Francis Marroux, who is lodged in a house opposite the entrance to La Boisserie. The women lay the mattress from the divan in the library on the floor. With Marroux, they place the General on it. Then the driver goes to fetch the village priest, *l'abbé* Jaugey. Hurrying from his consulting room, the doctor, Lacheny, drives at full speed to Colombey, almost skidding off the road at one corner. He and the priest arrive at the same time. The doctor goes into the library, where a fire burns in the hearth. The General's heart is still beating, but his pulse is extremely weak. Staying in the next room, Jaugey hears moans which turn to groans and then to a death rattle. A few moments after starting the examination, the doctor looks at Madame de Gaulle and tries to signify with his eyes that nothing can be done. Still, he gives de Gaulle a morphine injection in case he is feeling pain.

Honorine goes to ask Jaugey to come into the room. The priest kneels by the body and gives the last rites. At 7.25, the General's heart stops beating. Raising her eyes from the corpse, Madame de Gaulle says: 'He suffered so much these last two years.'

The six people in the room all kneel in silence, the two servants crying. The doctor diagnoses the cause of death as a rupture of the abdominal aorta provoked by an aneurism. When Jaugey asks Madame de Gaulle if her husband was in pain, she replies firmly: 'No, no.' Reading a subsequent description of her as 'impassive', she notes that she was so terribly shocked that she felt as if she was no longer alive. Later, Vendroux tells Peyrefitte that a professor had described it as 'a psychosomatic death'; de Gaulle had had a heart weakness for years, his brother-in-law added, but it was the pain of rejection by the French people that provoked the attack. 'He was eaten away by grief,' his widow told the former minister. 'You can't image how much he suffered.'

She asks the priest to telephone de Boissieu in Paris to tell him the news and to get him to inform Philippe, who is reached at dinner in Brest where he was in command of a missile-launching frigate. At her request, the doctor, Marroux and the priest dress her husband's body in uniform and carry it into the drawing room. One of the servants combs the dead man's hair. Lacheny leaves to visit other patients in the area. Jaugey offers to stay by the body but Yvonne refuses. Jaugey goes to the church to pray. After he gets home, a policeman, who has been told of the comings and goings at La Boisserie, calls to ask him what is happening. 'Nothing alarming,' the priest replies. 'I assure you, nothing alarming.'[14]

10 November. De Boissieu and his wife arrive at Colombey at 1 a.m. The body lies on a divan, dressed in khaki uniform with two enamel Free French insignia on the tunic. The tricolour flag flown outside the house every 11 November covers it up to the chest. On a small table, lit by two candles, stand a crucifix and a twig of box wood in a saucer filled with holy water. In the dead man's hands is a rosary which Pope Paul VI had given to his wife, and which he kept in a drawer of his night table. At his feet lies a book recording the names of the Companions of the Liberation. The General's face is serene. 'It is as if he was twenty years younger,' one of those present said later, according to Jean Mauriac's account. Another visitor this day described the body as looking like that of a fallen king.

Yvonne insists that the death be kept secret so that family members can be told personally rather than learning the news from the media. Telephoning de Gaulle's office in Paris, de Boissieu says simply: 'I am in the country. Something very serious, irreparable has happened. You understand me . . . It is final, it is finished . . . My father-in-law.' He also calls the Élysée to inform Pompidou. Philippe is on his way to Paris by the night train, having decided not to commandeer a naval aircraft for reasons of discretion and because, by the de Gaulle family creed, it would be wrong to use state property for personal ends.

In the morning, the news spreads in the village after one of the servants tells the postwoman when she delivers the morning mail. Yvonne telephones Philippe at his Paris flat. He then calls the Élysée asking to be put through to Pompidou's close aide, Pierre Juillet. Juillet is not available, and the duty officer suggests connecting Philippe to the press secretary, Denis Baudouin. But Baudouin had worked for Lecanuet in 1965 and helped to organise the No campaign in the referendum. 'I do not wish to speak to M. Baudouin,' Philippe says. 'I cannot speak to him.' Instead, he asks the Gaullist loyalist Pierre Lefranc to go to the palace with the will which his father wrote in 1952 stipulating a simple funeral at Colombey. When Lefranc sees Pompidou, the President has already summoned Chaban-Delmas. Told the news, the Prime Minister says, 'Now we are alone.' As they meet, Reuters and the French News Agency send out a flash on the General's death. In Washington, Nixon pays tribute to de Gaulle as an ally in war and a real friend in peace. His loss is a loss for all humanity, the US President adds.

At 12.30, the French Cabinet declares 12 November a day of national mourning, with a requiem mass in Notre-Dame. Pompidou's office asks that the will should not be released until after the announcement of the Cabinet decision; the family goes ahead regardless. Lefranc is taken aback that the mass is decided on before arrangements have been made for the funeral at Colombey. After speaking to Colombey, he tells the palace no family member will attend the service at Notre-Dame. At 1 p.m., Pompidou appears on television, beginning his address by saying, 'French women, French men, General de Gaulle is dead. France is a widow.' Yvonne agrees that the President and Prime Minister may visit La Boisserie, but only the next day, to give Philippe time to arrive first.

He is still in his Paris flat. Nobody telephones him from the administration. Asked about this in 1972, he says that he would have thought that an appropriate official would have got in touch with him. 'I think that there was a misunderstanding and that in the disarray caused by the General's death, the fact that he had a family and a son was simply forgotten,' he added.

At Colombey, there is an emotional moment at the start of lunch when Madame de Gaulle, her daughter and de Boissieu face de Gaulle's empty chair in front of the dining-room fireplace; Yvonne asks Élisabeth to sit there. In the early afternoon, Philippe sets out to drive to Colombey with his wife and three of his children – the eldest son, named after his grandfather, is in the USA. A dozen other visitors arrive. Madame de Gaulle makes it known that she does not want any of her husband's former ministers to come to the house, but Debré, now Defence Minister, arrives.

At 8 p.m., the body is put in a coffin of light oak with aluminium handles. The village carpenter says later that it is a standard piece of work, but for its length of 2.05 metres. The lid is closed. Yvonne turns down suggestions that a death mask should be taken or that she should keep a lock of her husband's hair. She has his bed and linen, shoes and various personal effects burnt, explaining 'no relics, no relics!' However, she preserves his kepi and military cap and decorations for the museum dedicated to the Liberation.[15]

11 November. The Comte de Paris arrives at Colombey, driving himself from the capital. The General's sister is also there. She is handed a letter written to her by her brother which had not been posted; opening it as she stands by the coffin, she reads 'everything is very calm here'.

At 4 p.m., Pompidou and Chaban-Delmas get to the house, and go into the drawing room where they stand wordlessly with the family. Philippe takes them into the General's study where they spend a short time in silence. As they leave, Madame de Gaulle takes the Prime Minister's hand and tells him: 'You should know, he liked you.' There is no record of her saying anything to the President. Later, a stream of Gaullists come to pay their respects, including Couve de Murville, Lefranc, Palewski, Foccart and de Courcel.[16]

12 November. Thousands of people head for Colombey to be in the village for the funeral that afternoon. Two enormous wreaths are delivered bearing the names of Mao Zedong and Zhu Enlai. In Paris, thirty heads of state and representatives of foreign states attend the simple mass in Notre-Dame conducted by Cardinal Marty of Paris. They include Nixon, who brought de Gaulle's grandson, Charles, to Paris in Air Force One, the Shah of Iran, Haile Selassie of Ethiopia, the Emperor of Japan, Ben Gurion, Queen Juliana of the Netherlands, Harold Macmillan and Anthony Eden. As he leaves the cathedral while the organ plays 'La Marseillaise', Nixon turns back to look at the altar, raising his hand towards his heart. Another of the mourners grasps it.

Shortly after 2 p.m., the Colombey church bell begins to toll as it does at many churches across the country. At 2.50, an armoured reconnaissance vehicle drives out of La Boisserie, bearing the coffin, covered with a French flag. The crowd in the village is estimated at 40,000. Three hundred members of the Companions of the Liberation take their places in the church after travelling to Colombey in a special train and a fleet of buses. Among them are Resistance and Free French veterans Messmer, Schumann, Pineau, Cassin, Passy, Parodi and the Communist organiser of the rising in Paris in 1944, Rol-Tanguy. Just before the service begins, the sound of a car pulling up abruptly is heard from outside. Malraux, accompanied by the writer Romain Gary in his blue wartime uniform, surges into the church, his arms dangling, his face haggard as he walks unsteadily up the nave like 'a blind prophet', as Jean Lacouture put it. He hits the trestle table set for the coffin in front of the altar. Appearing overcome with surprise, he is led to a pew where he sits, hunched over and gnawing on his hands.

The coffin is carried in by a dozen young men from the village flanked by four cadets from Saint-Cyr, one of whom collapses at the catafalque. The ceremony is conducted by François de Gaulle, the General's priest nephew, *l'abbé* Jaugey and the bishop of the nearby town of Langres. The blue order of service is decorated with a Cross of Lorraine and a drawing of the church. As the service ends, security men stop an elderly peasant woman from entering. By his own account Malraux intervenes, telling the guard that the General would have been happy to let her through. The old woman limps up to the coffin to pay her last respects.

Just before 4 p.m., the twelve young men of Colombey bear the coffin into the graveyard, followed by fifteen members of the family. It is placed in the tomb where Anne had been buried twenty-two years earlier. On the pale stone is written simply her name and that of 'Charles de Gaulle, 1890–1970.' He had gone as he had wished, without a fanfare. 'How good to die without decay,' he had told Foccart.[17]

*

Charles de Gaulle poses an enormous problem for those who deny that history is shaped by great human beings. If only in reaction to extravagant Gaullist claims that everything changed in 1958, some writers have stressed the continuities between the Fourth and Fifth Republics, noting that economic growth, the construction of Europe and the development of France's nuclear weapons started before 1958 and linking the withdrawal from Algeria with the earlier dissolution of the French Empire in Africa and the loss of Indochina. Other accounts, including this one, have pointed to the way in which the General's achievements in foreign policy fell short of what he proclaimed, as did his attempts to rally the French people behind him on a lasting basis. The General himself provided plenty of fuel for such verdicts on him. His repeated lamentations were more than a simple search for reassurance, and, as a confirmed pessimist, he might have viewed his life as having failed to achieve the goals he set himself in the German prisoner-of-war camp in 1916, though he usually found somebody else to blame.[18]

However, the final judgement has to be that he was a man who made a huge difference, and put a lasting mark on his country. Though there were social and economic weaknesses, his decade as President of the Fifth Republic saw enormous changes as France adapted and modernised itself. His legacy is attested to by the hollowness of his claim that his departure would be followed by chaos. The institutions he created in 1958 still function. The spirit of his foreign policy endures, even if the edges have been softened. Twice, in 1940 and 1958, he offered France an alternative to disaster, overcoming huge odds by the force of his personality, his belief in his mission and his acute tactical sense. Twice, in 1946 and 1969, he showed that a natural autocrat can espouse democracy.

Though it opened him to mockery from those who saw him as ridiculously self-important, the key to his greatness lay in a very simple factor: his genuine belief that he incarnated France and could raise it to the status he believed it deserved. The different aspects to his personality, his policy shifts and the varied brands of Gaullism pursued by his followers reflected the currents in national life. That enabled him to save his nation twice, and depart when it was necessary despite all the pain this caused him.

Pompidou defined Gaullism as a refusal to accept reverses by people with a historical concept of events, who adopt demanding standards and show loyalty. The leader who was dubbed 'the man who said no' thus emerges as the opposite – a figure who constructed his own positive response to challenges that generally induced easy, and usually negative, escape routes from the mainstream around him. Gaullism therefore becomes a behaviour system rather than a collection of set beliefs – beyond the basic reverence for the nation state and a hope that all French people can be brought together.[19]

Viewed from outside, Charles de Gaulle appeared as a monument carved out of some ancient rock, above and beyond ordinary beings. For his own reasons, he made the most of this persona. But, behind the mask, the central role of his character and behaviour made him a highly human, and humanist, figure drawing on rigorous old values while recognising the need for change. His complex individuality meant that he stood alone, but also represented a common sense of destiny shared, in testing times, by his fellow countrymen and women. This made him unique in his time. The world would not see his like again.

SOURCE NOTES

For reasons of space, the following shorthand has been used in the notes. The author's surname is usually preceded by an aide-mémoire in the form of a word from the passage concerned or other pointer to the text, in inverted commas. Where there is more than one work by that author, an abbreviated form of the title of the work follows, in italic. Alternatively, when one of the works by any one author comprises two or more volumes, the numerals I, II etc., standing alone, indicate that it's the multi-volume work that's being referred to. Where a name is both an aide-mémoire and the author of the relevant work, it may serve both functions in the Notes. Full publication details can be found in the Bibliography.

Mémoires usually refers to de Gaulle's memoirs in the one-volume Gallimard edition; *Lettres* refers to de Gaulle's collected letters and notes in the Plon edition; *Discours* refers to the Plon collection of his speeches. Lacouture and Roussel refer to their biographies of de Gaulle except where otherwise stated. PRO, PREM, CAB and FO refer to files in the Public Record Office, London. FRUS refers to Foreign Relations of the United States, a series published annually by the US government.

INTRODUCTION

1 'historic', Rouanet, *Chagrins*, p. 2; 'assassination', Démaret and Plume; 'shells', Tournoux, *Jamais*, p. 284; 'decide', Oulmont, p. 52

2 'study', Cotteret and Moreau; *Lettres, 1962–3*, pp. 400, 405, Nixon, p. 79, Viansson-Ponté, *Gaullistes*, p. 41; 'shoulders', Tournoux, *Tragédie*, p. 432

3 'treaties', Peyrefitte, II, p. 228; Malraux, p. 166

4 'republic', 'statesman', Peyrefitte, I, p. 280, II, p. 93

5 'poker', Tournoux, *Tragédie*, p. 440, *Jamais*, p. 288; 'Clinton', John Heilemann and Mark Halperin, *Race of a Lifetime* (Viking Penguin, 2010); 'risks', Lacouture, III, p. 775

6 'Hamlet', Tournoux, *Tragédie*, p. 327, Rusk, p. 240

7 Nixon, p. 73

8 'doubts', Nixon, p. 79; 'Luns', Viansson-Ponté, *Histoire*, II, p. 53; 'chairs', Joxe, p. 144

9 I am indebted to Dr Gerald Woolfson for this analysis of de Gaulle's psychology.

10 'Foccart', Tauriac, *Vivre*, p. 216

11 'journalist', *Espoir,* no. 154
12 'ugly', 'pill', 'History', Peyrefitte, II, pp. 98, 99, 602, 'Bardot', Tauriac, *Vivre,* p. 366
13 'Chevalier', 'Trenet', 'soccer', Tauriac, *Vivre,* pp. 335, 338, 339
14 'polls', Berstein, *Gaullisme,* p. 269

CHAPTER ONE

1 'tanks', 'aircraft', Tooze, pp. 371–2, 376. I am indebted to André Villeneuve for information on military strengths
2 Churchill, II, pp. 40, 44
3 'old man', Jenkins, p. 597; 'Reynaud', Larebière, p. 20
4 'Pétain', Amouroux, I, p. 471
5 'velvet', Tauriac, *Vivre,* p. 32
6 *Lettres,* II, pp. 500–502, 'Reynaud', Lacouture, I, p. 188
7 Roussel, I, pp. 133–5, *Mémoires,* p. 59, Leca, p. 166; 'Darlan', Moch, *Darlan,* p. 92; 'Pétain', Spears, Assignment, II, 83–90; *Espoir,* December 1990, p. 11
8 'lunch', Tauriac, *Jours,* pp. 43, 84–5, *Espoir,* December 1990, p. 8, Lacouture, I, pp. 184–6, Roussel, I, pp. 121–2
9 'officers', Rémy, *Dix ans,* p. 422; 'reaction', *Espoir,* December 1990, p. 11; Leca, p. 102
10 *Mémoires,* p. 48, Tauriac, *Jours,* p. 92
11 'Brittany', Amouroux, I, pp. 443–4; 'London', *Mémoires,* p. 54, Spears, *Assignment,* II, p. 120; 'Paris', Tauriac, *Jours,* p. 97, Roussel, I, p. 142; 'cards', P. de Gaulle, *Père,* I, pp. 147, 156–7
12 'anguish', *Mémoires,* pp. 53–4; 'Hutzinger', *Mémoires,* p. 51, Amouroux, I, pp. 313–14; 'Pétain', Amouroux, I, p. 374
13 'summit', Pétain, *Mémoires,* p. 56; Bardoux, p. 358; Harvey, p. 387, Spears, *Assignment,* II, p. 139, Churchill, II, pp. 136–141; 'great deal', Colville, p. 124
14 'Auburtin', *Espoir,* June 1979, December 1990; 'Mandel', Moch, *Darlan,* p. 140, Spears, *Assignment,* II, pp. 222, 269
15 'meeting', *Mémoires,* p. 60, Fenby, *Lancastria,* Chapters 3–4, Churchill, II, pp. 158–9, 162; 'pale', Jeanneney, pp. 52–3; 'fish', Colville, p. 160; 'resignation', Favreau, pp. 385–6; 'Reynaud', 'situation', *Espoir,* December 1990, Spears, *Assignment,* II, pp. 195–6, 235–9
16 'Bordeaux', 'Reynaud', *Mémoires,* p. 64, Amouroux, I, pp. 464–5, Tauriac, *Jours,* p. 116, Raïssac, p. 186; 'mistress', Amouroux, I, p. 110
17 'Laval', Spears, *Assignment,* II, pp. 243, 258–9, 303; Bardoux, p. 363; 'meeting', Blum, p. 109; 'Bordeaux situation', Spears, *Assignment,* II, pp. 258–9, Amouroux, I, p. 477; 'de Gaulle', C. Mauriac, *Un autre,* pp. 48–9, 'Yvonne', *Paris Match,* 15 November 1970, P. de Gaulle, *Père,* I, pp. 158, 256; 'permits', P. de Gaulle, *Père,* I, p. 256; 'journey', 'sailor', Tauriac, *Jours,* pp. 119, 121; 'captain', Benoist-Méchin, II, p. 234; '*Richelieu*', Oulmont, p. 59
18 'Monnet', Roussel, *Monnet,* pp. 236–9, 241; 'diversion', *The Times,* 18 June 1940; 'union', Roussel, *Monnet,* pp. 241–2, Colville, pp. 159–60, *Mémoires,* p. 67;

'Reynaud', Spears, *Assignment*, II, p. 284; 'Portes', 'Cabinet', Amouroux, I, p. 484; 'Mandel', Tellier, p. 667, Spears, *Assignment*, II, pp. 315–17; 'message', Colville, p. 163; 'de Gaulle–Reynaud', *Mémoires*, p. 73; 'wrong', Roussel, I, p. 169; 'departure arrangements', *Mémoires*, p. 73, Spears, *Assignment*, II, pp. 311–12; 'staff', 'tribe', Lacouture, I, p. 210

19 'Harvey', Harvey, p. 392; 'departure flight', Spears, *Assignment*, II, pp. 304, 311, 318–23, *Mémoires*, p. 7, Roussel, I, p. 173, P. de Gaulle, *Père*, I, 169; 'suitcase', Amouroux, IV, p. 67

CHAPTER TWO

1 'cable', *Lettres*, II, p. 509; 'first day in London', *Mémoires*, p. 71, Roussel, I, pp. 179–81, Roussel, *Monnet*, p. 243; 'walked', Raïssac, p. 197, *The Times*, 7 June 1940; Cadogan, p. 302, Colville, pp. 159–60

2 Harvey, pp. 384–6, Roussel, *Monnet*, pp. 245–6

3 'Cabinet', Churchill, CAB 65/7, WM 171 (40) 11, Colville, pp. 163, 166, Kersaudy, *Churchill*, pp. 77–8

4 'preparations', 'broadcast', P. de Gaulle, *Père*, I, p. 177, Tauriac, *Vivre*, p. 20, Lacouture, I, p. 224. A. Briggs, *The History of Broadcasting in the UK* (Oxford: OUP), p. 242. Texts of speeches, *Discours, 1940–1946*, pp. 4–10

5 'radio', Cadogan, pp. 304–5, Oulmont, p. 97, Spears, *Two Men*, pp. 134–5, Gladwyn, pp. 98–9, Lacouture, I, p. 252, Roussel, I, p. 55

6 '*The Times*, 19 June 1940', Cadogan, p. 327, 'Vansittart', PRO, FO 954/8, Alanbrooke, pp. 101, 278, 295, 422

7 'water', P. de Gaulle, *Père*, I, p. 120

CHAPTER THREE

1 'conscious', Pouget, p. 20; 'representative', Tournoux, *Pétain*, opposite p. 22; 'thought', *Mémoires*, p. 5; 'satanic', 'distance', 'cars', 'pens', Tournoux, *Jamais*, pp. 17, 21; 'suffrage', 'army', 'revenge', Tournoux, *Pétain*, p. 5; Roussel, I, pp. 22–3

2 'intransigent', *Mémoires*, p. 5; 'songs', Tournoux, *Pétain*, p. 7; 'Blum', Roussel, I, p. 23; 'mother', *Espoir*, no. 39, p. 66.

3 'visits', 'play', Lacouture, I, p. 8; 'moved', *Mémoires*, pp. 5–6; 'Assembly', *Espoir*, September 1963, p. 16; 'tale', Larebière, p. 11; 'Germany', 'Jesuits', P. de Gaulle, *Images*, p. 20, Palmaert, p. 35, De Gaulle Museum, Lille

4 'story', Roussel, *Inédit*, p. 15; 'Black Forest', 'Germans', *Lettres*, I, pp. 29–30, P. de Gaulle, *Père*, I, pp. 128–9, De Gaulle Museum, Lille

5 'dogs', P. de Gaulle, *Père*, I; 'north', *Mémoires*, p. 5, 'speeches', 28.6.47, 1.10.47, De Gaulle Museum, Lille; Gorce, *Mondes*, p. 38; 'holidays', Palmaert, p. 31, P. de Gaulle, *Père*, I, pp. 43–4

6 'Ferry', Weber, p. 111; 'French situation', Blom, pp. 13, 181, 232, Tombs, p. 445, Caron, pp. 7, 9, 30, 129, 173, Johnson, p. 135

7 'army', *Mémoires*, pp. 6, 1235 note b, P. de Gaulle, *Père*, I, p. 56, 'Nationalist', Kedward, p. 44; Péguy, p. 14
8 *Lettres*, I, p. 109
9 *Mémoires*, p. 6, *Lettres*, I, pp. 50, 60
10 Saint-Cyr, *Mémoires*, p. 6, *Espoir*, March 1977, P. de Gaulle, *Père*, I, p. 32, Lacouture, I, pp. 20–21; Saint-Cyr, *Lettres*, I, pp. 45–8, *Mémoires*, p. 6
11 'irksome', *Lettres*, I, pp. 50, 60, *Mémoires*, p. 6; 'Joffre', Dallas, p. 431
12 'convinced', *Lettres*, I, p. 78; Noël, p. 115

CHAPTER FOUR

1 'advance', *Lettres*, I, p. 79, Pouget, p. 60
2 'Dinant', *Lettres*, I, pp. 29–30, P. de Gaulle, *Père*, I, p. 73; 'story', *Lettres*, I, pp. 106–7
3 'spell', de Gaulle, *Armée*, p. 94, 'extermination', *Lettres*, I, p. 126
4 'pigs', *Lettres*, I, pp. 113, 126; 'trenches', 'socks', 'gloves', *Lettres*, I, pp. 111, 127, de Gaulle, *Armée*, p. 97; 'politicians', *Mémoires*, pp. 6, 1235 note b, *Lettres*, I, pp. 416–17; 'Pétain', C. Williams, *Frenchman*, p. 133; 'grocers', Tournoux, *Jamais*, p. 27; 'Champagne', Roussel, I, p. 43, *Lettres*, I, p. 421; 'defences', *Lettres*, I, pp. 205–8, 213, 218, 227–8, 242, 276, 284; 'years', Tauriac, *Vivre*, p. 224
5 'Falkenhayn', Horne, *Verdun*, pp. 34–6; 'mistress', Serrigny, p. 45, C. Williams, *Pétain*, pp. 125–6; 'Pétain at Verdun', Horne, *Verdun*, p. 148; 'battlefield', Ousby, p. 16, 'Valéry', reply to speech of thanks to Marshal Pétain, French Academy, 1931; Brown, pp. 162–4, Horne, *Verdun*, p. 174
6 'engagement', *Lettres*, I, p. 313, P. de Gaulle, *Père*, I, p. 82, Lacouture, I, pp. 37–8.
7 *Lettres 1905–18*, pp. 311–12, 'prison camp', P. de Gaulle, *Images*, p. 41
8 Lacouture, I, pp. 45–6
9 'escape bids', *Espoir*, March 1978, June 2000, Pouget, pp. 102–03, 114, *Lettres*, II, pp. 295–320; P. de Gaulle, *Père*, I, Chapter 4, Lacouture, I, p. 44
10 *Espoir*, March 1978, p. 48; 'reunion', Pouget, pp. 125–7
11 'Plessy', Pouget, pp. 103–4, *Revue de la France Libre* in Lacouture, I, pp. 52–3; P. de Gaulle, *Père*, I, p. 582, 'chief', *Lettres*, I, pp. 336–7, Guy, p. 71
12 'post-war', 'Germany', 'Saint-Maixent-L'École', *Lettres*, I, pp. 526, 536, II, pp. 3–14, 16–18, 21–2, 31
13 Zamoyski, Chapter 1, Ascherson, pp. 45–59, Davies, Chapter 19
14 *Lettres*, II, pp. 24–8, 32–3, 37–40, 76–8; 'uniform', *Lettres*, II, pp. 42, 44; 'Jews', *Lettres*, II, p. 28; 'Countess', Roussel, I, p. 54, Lacouture, I, p. 59; 'shrugged', Peyrefitte, II, p. 99
15 'Bug', Roussel, I, p. 53, 'war and victory', Zamoyski, pp. 75, 228–9, Davies, pp. 291–7, Ascherson, pp. 58–60, *Lettres*, II, pp. 53, 79, 80–82, 87–8, 315, 321; *Complément*, pp. 226–7; 'tanks', *Lettres*, II, pp. 101–02; 'marry', Lacouture, I, p. 60

CHAPTER FIVE

1 'Giraudoux', Weber, p. 12; 'Clemenceau', Tournoux, *Pétain*, p. 43; *Mémoires*, p. 7; 'casualties', Johnson, p. 142; 'population', Larkin, p. 7, Pedroncini, p. 323, Weber, pp. 13–16 and note 26, p. 293; 'syphilis', 'wine', Brendon, p. 128; 'Socialists', P. Williams, *Politics*, pp. 6–10, 68; 'farms', Larkin, pp. 4–5, 386; 'economy', Caron, pp. 178–9, 248–9, Chastenet, III, pp. 213, 220, 224, Larkin, p. 9, Ahamed, p. 501; 'Maginot', Weber, p. 8, de Gaulle, *Armée*, p. 81; 'Pétain', Tellier, pp. 270–71; 'catastrophes', Lacouture, II, p. 58

2 'Kolb', *Lettres*, II, p. 35; 'lame', Roussel, I, p. 55; 'injection', Guy, p. 213; 'courtship', Vendroux, *Soeur*, pp. 74–7, Roussel, I, p. 55, Lacouture, I, pp. 61–3; 'reasons', *Lettres*, II, p. 90; 'bridge', Lassus, p. 39; 'wine', Vendroux, *Soeur*, p. 78; 'Investigation', Fondation de Gaulle, *1920–40*, p. 259; 'Wedding', Vendroux, *Soeur*, pp. 79, 82

3 Vendroux, *Soeur*, p. 83, *Lettres*, II, pp. 204–5

4 'Saint-Cyr', Tournoux, *Pétain*, pp. 74, 76; 'Xavier', Jackson, *De Gaulle*, p. 5; 'caricature', P. de Gaulle, *Images*, p. 53; 'École', Roussel, I, p. 59; 'Laffargue', 'destiny', Pognon, *Armée*, pp. 42–4, Vendroux, *Soeur*, p. 90; 'colonel', Roussel, I, pp. 59–61, Pognon, Armée, pp. 44–6; '*discorde*', Pognon, Armée, pp. 48, 52; 'ranking', Roussel, I, pp. 62–3, Tournoux, *Pétain*, p. 100, Pognon, Armée, p. 46

5 'Briand–Poincaré', Weber, p. 125; 'crisis', 'diplomacy', Chastenet, III, pp. 90, 106, 108–30, 326 note 3; de Gaulle's views, *Lettres*, II, p. 354

6 *Lettres*, II, pp. 285–6, Amouroux, I, p. 29, Lacouture, I, p. 76

7 'Anne', 'witness', 'friend', Lacouture, I, pp. 90, 106, 108, 'Daniel-Rops', 'officer', Tournoux, *Jamais*, pp. 5, 53–4, 'photograph', P. de Gaulle, *Images*, p. 64, Galante, p. 83, Lassus, pp. 76–7, botanical', Fondation de Gaulle, *1920–40*, p. 284, Peyrefitte, II, p. 94, 'car', P. de Gaulle, *Père*, I, p. 134; 'chaplain', Tauriac, *Jours*, p. 77

CHAPTER SIX

1 'Riffraff', Tournoux, *Pétain*, p. 134, 'letter', *Lettres*, II, pp. 331–3; 'response', 'praise', Pognon, Armée, pp. 62, 68

2 'Levant', Longrigg, pp. 140, 156–9, Fondation de Gaulle, *1920–40*, pp. 50–51, *Lettres*, II, pp. 355–6, 359; P. de Gaulle, *Images*, pp. 62–3

3 'study', Lacouture, I, pp. 123–5; 'radiators', P. de Gaulle, *Père*, I, p. 63

4 'Tardieu', 'economy', *Lettres*, II, pp. 355, 359, Chastenet, III, pp. 189–90, 192, *Espoir*, September 2004, Tardieu, p. 240; 'French governments', Vansittart, pp. 381, 473

5 De Gaulle, *Le Fil*, pp. 64–6

6 'Girardet', 'military life', 'Weygand', 'Auriol', 'routine', Fondation de Gaulle, *1920–40*, pp. 22–4, 29, 253–5, 271–9; 'piano', 'dinners', 'women', 'suit', 'sales', 'holidays', 'food', 'shirts', P. de Gaulle, *Mémoires accessoires*, pp. 78, 83, *Père*, I, pp. 105, 448, II, pp. 69, 253–4; 'pocket money', P. de Gaulle, *Père*, II,

pp. 59–60; 'life', Galante, pp. 74–5, Vendroux, *Soeur,* p. 83; 'children', De Gaulle Museum, Colombey; 'photograph', P. de Gaulle, *Père,* I, p. 448,'Calais', Lassus, pp. 67, 78

7 *Mémoires,* pp. 7–8, 10, *Revue historique des armées,* no. 1, 1980, no. 2, 1990

8 De Gaulle Museum, Colombey

9 'article', Lacouture, I, pp. 130–31; de Gaulle, *Armée,* pp. 155–6; 'reaction', *Espoir,* no. 154; 'fodder', Larkin, p. 68; 'Pétain', 'Reynaud', *Mémoires,* p. 439; 'pain', 'battering ram', *Mémoires,* pp. 10, 12, 'master', de Gaulle, *Armée,* pp. 248–9; 'crisis', *Lettres,* II, p. 393; 'Mayer', *Lettres, Complément,* pp. 256, 259–61, 263–4, 266–7, Lacouture, I, p. 130; 'Tukhachevsky', Pouget, pp. 127, 254: 'Guderian', *Lettres,* II, p. 465, 'Hitler', Fondation de Gaulle, *1920–40,* pp. 172–3

10 'revolution', *Lettres, Complément,* p. 16; 'army', Roussel, I, pp. 89, 87, Lacouture, I, p. 133, Pognon, *Armée,* p. 92

11 'Reynaud', 'Auburtin', *Espoir,* June 1979, *Mémoires,* p. 17, Reynaud, I, pp. 421–5, Tellier, p. 276, Palewski, *Hier,* p. 22, Fondation de Gaulle, *1920–40,* p. 379, *Lettres,* II, p. 414

12 'reaction', 'Reynaud–de Gaulle', Reynaud, II, p. 57, I, pp. 426–40; Lacouture, *Blum,* p. 336; *Mémoires,* pp. 18–19, *Lettres,* II, pp. 386, 391–2; 'idiotic', Tournoux, *Jamais,* p. 59

13 'embassy', 'Jouvet', Weber, pp. 244, 146

14 'Popular Front', 'reforms', 'consequences', in Jean Lacouture, *Front Populaire* (Paris: Actes Sud, 2006), which gives an excellent short account. Michel Marhairaz, Danielle Tartakowsky and Daniel Lefeuvre, *Le Front Populaire* (Paris: Larousse, 2009) is another accessible overview of this much covered period. Also see Larkin, pp. 59–60, 67, C. Williams, *Frenchman,* p. 68; 'prisoners', Fall, p. 38; 'Blum–de Gaulle', Blum, p. 114, *Mémoires,* pp. 23–5; 'impression', *Espoir,* June 1979; 'right', Serre, pp. 145–6; 'industrialists', Jeanneney, pp. 39–40; 'Pétain', Conquet, p. 283, C. Williams, *Pétain,* pp. 274–5

15 *Mémoires,* pp. 439–40, *Lettres,* II, pp. 440–41, 442–3; 'Pétain', P. de Gaulle, *Père,* I, pp. 552–4, Roussel, I, pp. 107–9, Lacouture, I, pp. 147, 160–65, Pouget, pp. 276–80, 282–3, Tournoux, *Pétain,* p. 90, *Lettres,* III, p. 429

16 'Bonnet', Brendon, p. 508; 'businesses', Jeanneney, pp. 49–50, Weber, p. 243

17 'horns', Weber, p. 134; 'Daladier', *Le Monde* obituary, 13 October 1970, Tournoux, *Jamais,* p. 59; *Lettres,* II, pp. 474, 476, 484; 'blame', Peyrefitte, I, p. 347

18 'Mayer', Fondation de Gaulle, *1920–40,* p. 250, Guichard, *Général,* p. 59; 'abyss', Werth, *Twilight,* p. 311

19 *Lettres,* II, p. 477, Galante, p. 75, Tournoux, *Jamais,* pp. 33–4, 55, Pétain, pp. 88–9, Pouget, pp. 58–61, Reynaud, II, p. 195

20 'Weygand', 'Danzig', Spears, *Assignment,* I, p. 190, Weber, pp. 260–61; 'situation', *Lettres,* II, pp. 486–7, 'Blum', Lacouture, *Blum,* pp. 337, 445, Roussel, I, p. 113

21 'Christmas', Moll, p. 87

CHAPTER SEVEN

1 'pamphlet', *Lettres, Complément*, p. 27, *Mémoires*, pp. 27–8, 31; Fondation de Gaulle, *1920–40*, p. 135, Lacouture, *Blum*, p. 445; 'majority', Favreau, p. 364; Fondation de Gaulle, *1920–40*, p. 369; 'de Gaulle', Amouroux, I, p. 110; 'Mandel', Bardoux, p. 160; 'Daladier', Amouroux, I, p. 342; Reynaud, I, pp. 294–5, 314
2 *Lettres*, II, pp. 491–2; 'Mandel', Favreau, p. 367; Spears, *Assignment*, I, pp. 190, 195, Amouroux, I, p. 41; Bloch-Morhange gives a devastating picture, especially in Chapter 2
3 'letters', *Lettres*, II, pp. 494–5, 497–9, 500, 502
4 'battles', 'bed', 'major', 'tanks', 'wood', 'chaplain', Tauriac, *Jours*, pp. 9–12, 17, 19, 20–21, 52, 56, 60–61, *Espoir*, December 1990, p. 7; 'Montcornet', 'casualties', 'Guderian', 'Abbeville', *Lettres, Complément*, pp. 275–6, Fondation de Gaulle, *1920–40*, pp. 180–99; 'Kleist', Raïssac, p. 171; 'radio', Rouanet, *L'inquiétude*, pp. 101–2, Oulmont, p. 79; 'write', *Lettres*, II, p. 497; 'fearlessness', C. Mauriac, *Un autre*, p. 18, *Espoir*, December 1990, pp. 7–8, Roussel, I, pp. 121–3; *Mémoires*, pp. 40–44; Lacouture, I, pp. 840–86

CHAPTER EIGHT

1 *Mémoires*, pp. 70, 72
2 Spears, *Two Men*, pp. 145, 148; *Mémoires*, pp. 142–4; 'Churchill', PREM 3 120/7, Churchill, II, pp. 451–2, 457; de Gaulle's relationship with Churchill and Roosevelt is expertly depicted in Kersaudy's books (see the Bibliography); Roussel, *Inédit*, p. 101; Alphand, pp. 88–9, Nicolson, p. 249, Borden, pp. 113–15, Pineau, p. 189
3 'reactions', Roussel, I, p. 681, 'Chalandon', 'Jacob', Tauriac, *Vivre*, pp. 21, 3, Bourdan, pp. 9, 32, Marin, pp. 219–20, Mengin, p. 62
4 'Committee', *Mémoires*, p. 82; 'fate', *Mémoires*, pp. 70–73; 'rooms', Marin, p. 219, 'de Courcel', Mengin, pp. 67, 90; 'expenses', *Lettres, 1940–41*, pp. 25, 20; 'Cassin', Pilleul, pp. 39, 43; 'Palewski', *Lettres, 1940–41*, p. 20; 'cohesion', Pilleul, p. 49, Barrès in Roussel, I, p. 483
5 'Cross', C. Mauriac, *Un autre*, p. 35, De Gaulle Museum, Colombey
6 'support', 'jewels', 'page', *Mémoires*, pp. 79, 86, 89; 'support', PRO FO882/7, 'Julitte', Roussel, I, p. 211, Aron, p. 101, Roussel, *Monnet*, pp. 249–54; 'absurd', *Lettres, Complément*, p. 277, 'diplomats', Tauriac, *Vivre*, p. 134, 'road', Spears, *Two Men*, p. 141
7 *The Times*, 24 June 1940, Cassin, p. 77, *Mémoires*, pp. 73–4, Larebière, p. 22, *Lettres, 1940–41*, p. 27, De Gaulle Museum, Colombey
8 'strings', Perrier, p. 209; 'Mers-el-Kébir', Tute, pp. 69–71, 92, Brown, pp. 186, 189, Spears, *Two Men*, pp. 162–5; 'outburst', 'speech', Hettier de Boislambert, p. 187; *Discours, 1940–46*, pp. 5–7, *Mémoires*, pp. 79–80; 'decades', Peyrefitte, I, p. 145
9 'constitutional', 'dog', Tournoux, *Pétain*, p. 202, Serrigny, pp. 180–81;

'Indochina', Fall, p. 42, O'Ballance, pp. 36–42, *Mémoires*, p. 139; 'Laval', 'printing', 'business', 'Claudel', 'acclaim', '1940', Azéma, *Munich*, pp. 193–4, Chapter 25, p. 241; Amouroux, II, pp. 370–71

10 'battle', *Discours, 1940–46*, p. 19; 'letters', *Mémoires*, p. 83; 'Passy', *Sunday Times* magazine, London, 15 March 2009, Roussel, I, p. 221, *New York Times* obituary, 22 December 1998, '1940', Azéma, *Munich*, p. 306; Moch, *De Gaulle*, p. 29

11 'Africa', Bourgi, pp. 53–4, *Lettres, 1940–41*, p. 102, *Discours, 1940–46*, pp. 31, 65

12 'capital', Passy, I, p. 68; 'luggage', P. de Gaulle, *Père*, I, pp. 277–8; 'voyage', Spears, *Two Men*, pp. 182–6, *Lettres, 1940–41*, p. 128; photographs, De Gaulle Museum, Colombey; 'Dakar engagement', *Espoir*, December 1990, *Lettres, 1940–41*, pp. 121–3, Bourgi, p. 72, Tournoux, *Jamais*, p. 87, Roussel, I, p. 247; 'explanation', 'match', *Lettres, 1940–41*, pp. 124–7, 130–32; Weygand, p. 110; 'conversations, aftermath', Tauriac, *Vivre*, pp. 236, 577–8, *Mémoires*, pp. 111, 127–8, *Lettres, 1940–41*, pp. 127–8; 'Pleven', Tournoux, *Jamais*, pp. 87–8, 'Dechartre', oral record, Fondation de Gaulle, Roussel, I, p. 261, Tauriac, *Vivre*, pp. 137–9; 'Schumann', Lacouture, I, p. 278; 'followers', *Lettres, 1940–41*, pp. 127–8, 142

13 'Cameroon', Tauriac, *Vivre*, pp. 84–5, Boisdeffre, pp. 69–70; 'Catroux', Lerner, pp. 156–7; 'storm', *Lettres, 1940–41*, p. 128; 'legend', Oulmont, p. 60; 'hopes', *Mémoires*, p. 114

14 'Montoire', '1940', Azéma, *Munich*, Chapter 31; 'Hitler', 'documents on German foreign policy', HMSO, London, Series D, vol. IX, no. 227; 'messages', Colville, *Fringes*, pp. 256, 276, Lacouture, I, p. 287; 'stoat', Kersaudy, *Churchill*, p. 127; 'Brazzaville', *Discours, 1940–46*, pp. 36–7, 38–9; 'motto', 'entity', 'order', *Lettres, 1940–41*, pp. 159, 167–8, 247; 'letter', Colville, *Fringes*, p. 174; 'radio', *Discours, 1940–46*, pp. 41–3; 'demonstration', '1940', Azéma, *Munich*, pp. 335–40; 'US', *Lettres 1940–41*, pp. 150–52; 'dreams', *Mémoires*, p. 123

CHAPTER NINE

1 Spears, *Two Men*, p. 146

2 'journey', P. de Gaulle, *Père*, I, pp. 257–8, *Espoir*, no. 157, Galante pp. 58–9, Roussel, I, pp. 193–4

3 'win', P. de Gaulle, *Père*, I, pp. 202–4; 'journalist', Barrès, p. 94; 'francs', Colville, *Fringes*, p. 175; 'photograph', P. de Gaulle, *Images*, p. 80

4 Geneviève de Gaulle-Anthonioz, *Espoir*, December 1990, pp. 49–51

5 'English residences', 'Connaught', *Mémoires*, p. 239; 'Yvonne', 'Muselier', Roussel, I, p. 266; 'English', *Lettres, 1961–3*, p. 108; 'island specialities', Lacouture, I, pp. 264–5; Barrès, p. 94; 'smoking', P. de Gaulle, *Père*, II, p. 373; Borden, p. 115

6 Spears, *Two Men*, p. 132; 'photographs', P. de Gaulle, *Images*, pp. 84–5; Lacouture, I, p. 216, *Lettres, 1940–41*, p. 127, *Lettres, 1941–3*, pp. 309–10, 321–3, 375, 538; 'Yvonne', P. de Gaulle, *Père*, II, p. 65; 'Hampstead', author's visit, December 2008 and conversation with subsequent owner

CHAPTER TEN

1 'turbulence', Passy, I, pp. 86, 121–2, 147; 'lunch', Colville, *Fringes*, p. 313; 'Churchill', Cadogan, p. 356

2 'officer', *Mémoires*, pp. 127–9, Passy, I, pp. 127–33; 'Muselier arrest', Accoce, Chapter 11, Cadogan, pp. 346–7; 'drugs', FO 954/8, Colville, *Fringes*, p. 383; 'Cassin', Accoce, p. 260; 'relations', Passy, I, pp. 135–6, 144–5; 'British', *Lettres, 1940–41*, p. 219

3 'Chequers', Colville, *Fringes*, pp. 312–13, *Mémoires*, p. 144; 'Messmer', Tauriac, *Vivre*, p. 269; 'Coulet', Pilleul, p. 44; 'Wavell', Kersaudy, *Churchill*, pp. 133–4, Spears–Churchill, 5 June 1941, Churchill Archives, Cambridge, Char 20/39/91–2

4 'command', Tauriac, *Vivre*, p. 87; 'campaign', 'rows', Spears, *Mission*, I, p. 121, *Mission*, II, pp. 132, 138, 151, *Mémoires*, pp. 160, 165, *Lettres 1940–41*, pp. 389–90; 'flag', 'fortress', Lacouture, I, pp. 303–4, Buis, p. 78, 'Lyttelton', telegram of 22 July 1941, Churchill College, Cambridge, Char 20/41, 35–6; 'agreement', *Lettres, 1941–3*, pp. 20, 30–31, 35–6, 41–2

5 'mad', Colville, *Fringes*, p. 422; '*Chicago Daily News*', 27 August 1941; 'Pleven', 'expulsion', *Lettres, 1941–3*, pp. 51–2, 57; 'caring little', 'Churchill', Colville, *Fringes*, pp. 350, 366–7, 'Eden', FO, 371/28545; 'British views', 'Morton', PREM 3 120/5, Roussel, I, pp. 323–4, Kersaudy, *Churchill*, p. 152; 'no one', FO, 371/28545; 'meeting', Colville, *Fringes*, p. 382, *Lettres, 1941–3*, pp. 59–63

6 'abdicated', Roussel, I, pp. 340–45; 'Moulin', Tournoux, *Jamais*, p. 98; 'Right', 'motto', 'Boris', Berstein, *Gaullisme*, Chapter 2, p. 43; 'Boris', Tauriac, *Vivre*, p. 254; 'Muselier', *Lettres, 1941–3*, pp. 70–71; 'sick', Colville, *Fringes*, p. 383; 'plot and outcome', CAB 65/25, WM 34 (42) 4, Kersaudy, *Churchill*, pp. 162–7, Cadogan, p. 406

7 'Pearl Harbor', Fenby, *Alliance*, pp, 79–80, 98; 'de Gaulle on US–UK', Pilleul, p. 52, Passy, *Souvenirs*, I, p. 236, Lacouture, I, p. 349, *Lettres, 1941–3*, pp. 268–9; 'anything', Roosevelt, *Saw It*, p. 115; 'worse off', Harriman, p. 265

8 'Saint-Pierre', *Lettres, 1941–3*, pp. 151, 156–70, Fenby, *Alliance*, p. 98, Kersaudy, *Roosevelt*, p. 97

9 'settlement', *Mémoires*, p. 217, *Lettres, 1941–3*, pp. 189–92, Kersaudy, *Churchill*, pp. 178–9

10 'Muselier', *Lettres, 1941–3*, pp. 218–19, 221–2, 225–8, 230, 236–7; PREM 3 120/2, FO 954/8; 'democracy', *Discours, 1940–46*, p. 194; 'testament', *Mémoires*, pp. 1214–15

11 'Magnificat', *Mémoires*, p. 261, P. de Gaulle, *Père*, I, p. 355; 'prostitutes', Peyrefitte, II, p. 99; 'Boegner', Roussel, I, pp. 421, 425; 'Soviet', *Lettres, 1941–3*, p. 270, Lacouture, I, p. 354, Harriman, pp. 231–2

CHAPTER ELEVEN

1 'Roosevelt', 'Churchill', Fenby, *Alliance*, pp. 161–2; 'hope', Billotte, p. 239; 'reaction', *Mémoires*, pp. 304–5, 309

2 'Giraud', 'Darlan', Eisenhower, pp. 110–12, 116, 143, Roussel, I, p. 451
3 'Roosevelt', FRUS, 1942, II, p. 547, State Department papers, 851.01/798; 'crockery', *Mémoires*, pp. 315–16; 'Jewish', Eisenhower, p. 142
4 Serrigny, pp. 227–8
5 'Eden', Harvey, pp. 192–3; 'broadcasts', *Mémoires*, pp. 330, 316; Kersaudy, *Churchill*, pp. 227–8; 'Soviet', Roussel, I, p. 459, drawing on Soviet archive
6 'pretender', Lacouture, I, p. 410; 'Roosevelt', Fenby, *Alliance*, p. 162; 'Eisenhower', Churchill College archive, Char 20/83; 'assassination and reactions', Cadogan, p. 500, Verrier, pp. 242–7, Peyrefitte, I, p. 438; 'Joxe', Pilleul, p. 54, 'Giraud', Verrier, p. 244; 'clumsiness', *Lettres, 1941–3*, pp. 490, 492, *Discours, 1940–46*, pp. 255–6, *Mémoires*, pp. 333, 336
7 'end', Cadogan; 'British reaction', FO 954/8; 'Roosevelt', Ward, p. 199
8 'De Gaulle', 'Anfa', FRUS, *Casablanca*, pp. 694–6, *Mémoires*, pp. 339–48, Roosevelt, *Destiny*, pp. 112–14, Kersaudy, *Roosevelt*, pp. 231–46, Sherwood, pp. 677, 685–8, 693, Moran, pp. 80–81, Macmillan, *Diaries*, p. 250, Fenby, *Alliance*, Chapter 10, Roussel, I, pp. 485–91, Lacouture, I, pp. 419–20
9 'imprecision', *Mémoires*, p. 342; Roosevelt, *Destiny*, pp. 112–14
10 Lacouture, I, p. 425
11 'roughest', *Mémoires*, p. 347, Moran, p. 81
12 Joxe, p. 141; 'Marrakech', Fenby, *Alliance*, p. 179; 'letter', Churchill Archives, Churchill College, 18 Feb. 1943; 'Tower', 'Peake', Nicolson, p. 284; 'British', 'Spellman', *Lettres, Complément*, pp. 360–67, Kersaudy, *Roosevelt*, p. 263, Lacouture, I, p. 430, *Mémoires*, pp. 348–50, 357–8

CHAPTER TWELVE

1 Amid the voluminous literature on the Resistance, Jean-Louis Crémieux-Brilhac's monumental account stands out, while Henri Amouroux's multi-volume work depicts everyday life during this period. Among English-language accounts, the works by Julian Jackson and Robert Gildea are outstanding and Patrick Marnham has investigated the mystery of Jean Moulin. 'meeting', Rémy, *Dix ans*, pp. 419–22; 'Méric', Amouroux, IV, pp. 432–4
2 'Thorez', Grosser, p. 25; Pineau, pp. 71–3
3 'choose', Lacouture, I, p. 384; 'Resistance', 'London meetings', *Mémoires*, pp. 235–7, 436; Astier de la Vigerie, pp. 269–72, Pineau, Chapters V, VI; photographs, De Gaulle Museum, Colombey, 'Geneviève', *Espoir*, December 1990, p. 51
4 'audience', Lacouture, I, p. 375: 'posters', De Gaulle Museum, Colombey
5 'Resistance', Pilleul, p. 69; 'Brossolette', Berstein, *Gaullisme*, pp. 55, 62; 'Moulin–Brossolette', Crémieux-Brilhac, Chapter 22; 'Jouhaux', *Lettres, 1941–3*, p. 415; Villon, p. 68; Pineau, p. 150, 'Jouve', Tournoux, *Jamais*, p. 139, Lacouture, I, pp. 322–3l; 'Communists', Crémieux-Brilhac, p. 625, Roussel, I, pp. 622–3
6 'conditions', Azéma, *Munich*, pp. 154–5, 214–18; 'economy', Tooze, pp. 410,

640; 'prices', 'Colette', 'Simenon', 'occupiers', Vinen, pp. 216–17, 233, 36; 'Jünger', *Mémoires,* p. 46. The cinema is covered in Joseph Daniel, *Guerre et cinéma* (Paris: Colin, 1972); '*Matin*', Werth, *France 1940–1955,* p. 88

7 Persecution of Jews is covered well in André Kaspi, *Les Juifs pendant l'Occupation* (Paris: Seuil, 1997). The Paris round-up is covered in Maurice Rajsfus, *La Rafle du Vél d'Hiver* (Paris: PUF, 2002). Paxton, *Vichy,* was among early works fixing responsibility. For Bousquet, Pascale Froment, *Bousquet* (Paris: Fayard, 2001). For Darquier de Pellepoix, Carmen Callil, *Bad Faith* (London: Cape, 2006)

8 'Moulin', 'advice', *Mémoires,* p. 354, Lacouture, I, pp. 437–8

CHAPTER THIRTEEN

1 '*tu*', *Lettres, 1943–5,* p. 251; 'Guichard', *Espoir,* no. 138

2 'Giraud', Lacouture, I, pp. 441–2; Harriman, p. 231; de Gaulle's speech, *Discours, 1940–46,* pp. 284–90, Roussel, *Monnet,* pp. 335–6; 'summit', Kersaudy, *Churchill,* pp. 276, 279–80, Fenby, *Alliance,* p. 193, Lacouture, I, pp. 431–3; 'Eden', PRO FO 954/8, *Mémoires,* pp. 364–5

3 'arrival', *Mémoires,* p. 366; 'meeting Giraud', Roussel, *Monnet,* p. 359, *Mémoires,* p. 68; 'exchanges', Catroux, p. 369, *Lettres, 1943–5,* p. 17, Lacouture, I, p. 447; 'Scot', Gladwyn, p. 230, Macmillan, *Blast,* pp. 345–6, *Lettres, 1943–5,* p. 28

4 *Lettres, 1943–5,* pp. 28, 31; 'Oliviers', P. de Gaulle, *Images,* pp. 102–3; 'Anne', *Mémoires,* p. 436; 'milk', 'dress', De Gaulle Museum, Colombey

5 'Jew', 'Paris', Lacouture, I, p. 494; 'Algiers', *Mémoires,* pp. 426–8, 437–8; 'Mendès', *Lettres, 1943–5,* p. 104

6 Kersaudy, *Churchill,* p. 245, Roussel, I, pp. 519–20

7 'de Gaulle–Giraud', *Discours, 1940–46,* pp. 309–13, Barrès, p. 398, *Mémoires,* pp. 431–2, 'Macmillan', PRO, PREM 3/182/6

8 'Algiers politics', *Mémoires,* pp. 412–19, *Lettres, 1943–5,* pp. 104, 158–9, Roussel, *Inédit,* p. 165, Berstein, *Gaullisme,* p. 64, Crémieux-Brilhac, p. 625

9 'Tehran', Fenby, *Alliance,* p. 238; 'trouble', Harriman, p. 265; 'embrace', *Lettres, 1943–5,* p. 124

10 *Mémoires,* pp. 1222–4, Lacouture, I, pp. 514–15

11 Lacouture, I, p. 500, *Mémoires,* p. 478, Fenby, *Alliance,* p. 271, Cooper, pp. 289–90

12 Destremau, *De Lattre,* pp. 276–8, 294

13 'Brazzaville', Bourgi, p. 114, *Mémoires,* p. 447; 'Algeria', Lacouture, I, p. 507, *Mémoires,* p. 446

14 'Lyon', Tournoux, *Jamais,* pp. 122–3; 'statistics', Azéma, *Munich,* pp. 301, 304–8; 'Pétain', 'Macmillan', C. Williams, *Pétain,* pp. 446–7, 449, 453–6, Serrigny, pp, 234–40

15 'eggs', De Gaulle Museum, Colombey; 'radicalisation', 'Pucheu', Pilleul, pp. 53–4, *Lettres, 1943–5,* pp. 156–7, 175–6, *Mémoires,* pp. 441–3, Tournoux, *Jamais,* pp. 103–15, Roussel, I, pp. 57–9, 591, Crémieux-Brilhac, pp. 603–5,

'Passy', in *Semaine économique, politique, financière,* 3 June 1949, quoted by Roussel, I, p. 743; 'blame', Peyrefitte, I, p. 148

CHAPTER FOURTEEN

1 'Parodi', Sébastien Studer, http://theses.enc.sorbonne.fr/document122.htmla, Amouroux, VIII, pp. 471–2
2 'ambassador', Roussel, I, p. 657, *Lettres, 1943–5,* pp. 212–13
3 'breakfast', 'limousines', Palewski, *Mémoires,* p. 215; 'Dufour', Cadogan, p. 633, *Lettres, 1943–5,* pp. 92–3, 100, 118, 123, 143, 267
4 *Mémoires,* p. 507
5 'lunch', Dixon, p. 91, Lacouture, I, p. 521, Kersaudy, *Churchill,* pp. 339–43, *Mémoires,* pp. 487–8; 'Bevin', *Mémoires,* p. 488; 'Eisenhower', Kersaudy, *Churchill,* pp. 344–5, *Mémoires,* pp. 448–9
6 'row', Cadogan, p. 634, Kersaudy, *Churchill,* pp. 346–52, *Mémoires,* p. 490, Lacouture, I, pp. 523–5; 'battle', *Discours, 1940–46,* pp. 407–9
7 Churchill Archives, Cambridge 20/166/25, PRO, FO 954/9 p. 233; 'Stimson', Stimson Diary, 11 June 1944, Library of Congress
8 'Normandy', *Mémoires,* pp. 494–5, *Lettres, 1943–5,* p. 250, Palewski, *Mémoires,* pp. 216–17, *Espoir,* October 2001

CHAPTER FIFTEEN

1 'visit', *Mémoires,* pp. 500–07, Aglion, pp. 205, 207–8, 210, Lacouture, I, Chapter 38, Roussel, I, pp. 614–16, Kersaudy, *Roosevelt,* pp. 415–25; 'convinced', *Mémoires,* pp. 501–3; 'Stimson', Cadogan, p. 640; 'Pershing', Aiglon, p. 211; 'New York', 'Canada', *Lettres, 1943–5,* p. 257, *Mémoires,* p. 507
2 Azéma, *Munich,* p. 324. Mémorial des Victimes Civils, Amouroux, VIII, pp. 335–8. I am indebted to André Villeneuve for research into the Normandy casualties
3 'Patton', Beevor, *D Day,* p. 384
4 'republics', Azéma, *Munich,* pp. 333, 336; Baumel, pp. 15–16; 'deaths', 'Comité d'histoire de la Deuxième Guerre mondiale', Aron, pp. 281, 348
5 'Tipperary', 'doctor', 'ultimatum', C. Williams, *Pétain,* pp. 467, 470; 'communications', Tournoux, *Jamais,* p. 124; 'Laval', Cole, pp. 290–97; 'passer-by', Noël, p. 16; *Mémoires,* pp. 846, 870
6 C. Williams, *Pétain,* pp. 471, 473, *Mémoires,* pp. 556–9, P. de Gaulle, *Images,* p. 120
7 'Syria', 'Corsica', *Mémoires,* p. 559, *Lettres, 1943–5,* pp. 274, 293–5
8 *Mémoires,* p. 555; 'conspiracy', *Mémoires,* pp. 551–2, 558–9, 'Herriot', de Tarr, p. 42
9 'Paris', Rol-Tanguy, pp. 198, 237–49, Astier de La Vigerie, pp. 344–6, *L'Humanité,* 24 August 1944; 'woman', C. Mauriac, *Un autre,* p. 13; 'son', P. de Gaulle, *Images,* pp. 106–7; 'nothing changed', *Mémoires,* p. 5681, 'Martyred',

Discours, 1940–44, pp. 439–40; 'bouquet', photograph, *Espoir,* 9; 'why', *Mémoires,* p. 580

10 'shooting', Hawkins, *BBC,* pp. 199, 202–4, *Lettres, 1943–5,* p. 297

11 C. Mauriac, *Un autre,* p. 36, *Lettres, 1943–5,* pp. 297, 300, 306; 'Yvonne, letter', P. de Gaulle, *Images,* pp. 110–11

12 'Senate', *The Times,* 28 August 1944; C. Mauriac, *Un autre,* p. 12; 'losses', Azéma, *Munich,* p. 348; Eisenhower, p. 326

CHAPTER SIXTEEN

1 'Lilliputians', F. Mauriac, p. 55

2 '1940', Malraux quoted by C. Mauriac, *Un autre,* p. 18

3 'Claudel', Noël, pp. 283–4; 'majority', Lacouture, II, p. 202

4 'destruction', 'difficulties', *Mémoires,* pp. 819–22, Baumel, p. 18, Rioux, *France,* I, pp. 35–9; 'telephone', 'shortages', Pilleul, pp. 64, 66; 'woman', C. Mauriac, *Un autre,* p. 16; Alanbrooke, p. 622; 'babies', Fauvet, p. 36; 'polls', Rioux, *France,* I, pp. 44–7

5 'house', C. Mauriac, *Un autre,* pp. 41, 45, 49, 155, *Mémoires,* pp. 714, 1336; 'son', *Lettres, 1943–5,* pp. 360–61; P. de Gaulle, *Images,* p. 117; 'Bidault', 'F. Mauriac', C. Mauriac, *Un autre,* pp. 165–8, 146, 160

6 'Palewski', C. Mauriac, *Un autre,* p. 122; 'paperwork', Pompidou, p. 38

7 F. Mauriac, pp. 16, 54–5; 'Chaillot', 'press conference', *Discours, 1940–6,* pp. 443–51, 467–8, C. Mauriac, *Un autre,* pp. 31–4; 'ingratitude', Villon, p. 117; 'Vianney', Lacouture, II, pp. 28–9; 'poll', Rioux, *France,* I, p. 84, Berstein, *Gaullisme,* p. 87; 'PCF', 'reeds', C. Mauriac, *Un autre,* pp. 45–6, 60

8 'In Bido', Beevor and Cooper, p. 129

9 'prefect', 'tour', C. Mauriac, *Un autre,* pp. 38–9, Lacouture, II, pp. 47–50; 'Starr', Beevor and Cooper, pp. 108–10; 'order', *Lettres 1943–5,* pp. 316, 319–20, 323; 'reasoning', 'Vichy', *Mémoires,* pp. 680–81

10 *Mémoires,* pp. 682–4, 704–8. The doctor-surgeon image is from Fauvet, p. 40. Mendès' resignation text is to be found in Fauvet, pp. 365–8

11 'cases', Amouroux, VIII, Chapter 9; 'petition', C. Mauriac, *Un autre,* pp. 79–82, 107–8; 'profits', Pilleul, p. 65

CHAPTER SEVENTEEN

1 'Leclerc', Roussel, I, pp. 653–4

2 'Eisenhower', Cook, p. 251

3 'US', C. Mauriac, *Un autre,* pp. 17, 22–3, 46–7, 55; 'Duff Cooper', Beevor and Cooper, p. 123

4 'Yvonne', 'photograph', P. de Gaulle, *Images,* p. 113; 'visit', Alanbrooke, p. 624, Cooper, p. 335, *Mémoires,* pp. 634–40, *Lettres, 1943–5,* p. 349

5 'visit, de Gaulle', *Mémoires,* pp. 641–5, *Discours, 1940–46,* pp. 486–91, *Lettres, 1943–5,* pp. 360–61, Tournoux, *Jamais,* pp. 136, 145, Fenby, *Alliance,*

pp. 344–5, Grosser, p. 27, Kersaudy, *Churchill*, p. 414; 'thigh', 'Thorez', Malraux, pp. 209–10

6 'Strasbourg', *Mémoires*, pp. 729–35, Alanbrooke, p. 642, Tournoux, *Tragédie*, p. 38, *Jamais*, p. 284

7 'US', 'Saigon', *Lettres, 1945–51*, pp. 57–9, 69–71; 'Yalta', *Mémoires*, pp. 667–74; 'Churchill', Robert Sherwood, *White House Papers of Harry L. Hopkins* (London: Eyre & Spottiswoode, 1948–9), pp. 775, 781–2; 'post-Yalta', *Mémoires*, pp. 674–5, Bohlen, p. 205; 'Congress', 'message', Kersaudy, *Roosevelt*, pp. 475, 479–80

8 Truman, p. 15; 'Stuttgart', *Lettres, Complément*, pp. 388–9, *Mémoires*, pp. 754–6

9 'Himmler', Peyrefitte, II, p. 93, *Mémoires*, pp. 761–2

10 'Tassigny', *Espoir*, June 2005, *Discours, 1940–46*, pp. 545–6

11 'poll', Rioux, *France*, I, p. 20; 'labourers', 'Clay', Giles MacDonogh, *After the Reich* (London: John Murray, 2008), pp. 12, 277

12 'clash', *Mémoires*, pp. 754–7, 766–6, Truman, pp. 158–60

13 *Discours, 1940–46*, pp. 532–4, *Mémoires*, pp. 749–52; 'veto', *Mémoires*, p. 814; 'analysis', 'Bao Dai', Cameron, I, pp. 41, 48–91; 'big slice', 'Leclerc', *Lettres, 1945–51*, pp. 73, 82–4, *Discours, 1940–46*, p. 605, *Mémoires*, pp. 814–18; 'events', Fall, pp. 55–9, O'Ballance, pp. 47–9; 'declaration', Cameron, I, pp. 52–4

14 'unpleasant', 'danger', Kersaudy, *Churchill*, p. 414, Truman, p. 160

15 Borden, p. 295

16 'infamy', C. Mauriac, *Un autre*, p. 170; 'press conference', *Discours, 1940–46*, pp. 558–80, *Lettres, 1945–51*, pp. 75–7; Grosser, p. 34, Lacouture, II, pp. 227–8

17 Lacouture, II, pp. 175–83

CHAPTER EIGHTEEN

1 Werth, *France, 1940–1955*, has pen portrait of de Brinon, pp. 126–30; 'lunch', C. Mauriac, *Un autre*, p. 26; 'camp', 'Vistula', *L'Express*, 17 April 2008

2 'trial', C. Mauriac, *Un autre*, pp. 139–43, *Mémoires*, pp. 834–9; *Lettres, 1964–6*, p. 256; 'de Gaulle and the trial', *Espoir*, June 2005; 'defence', C. Williams, *Pétain*, Chapter 28; Teitgen interview in documentary, *De Gaulle vu d'ailleurs*; C. Mauriac, *Un autre*, p. 139; 'imprisonment', 'nails', C. Williams, *Pétain*, Chapter 29

3 Decoux, pp. 476–81; 'Laval trial', 'execution', 'Pisani', Tauriac, *Vivre*, pp. 50–51, *Mémoires*, pp. 836–7, Lacouture, II, pp. 151–3

CHAPTER NINETEEN

1 'elections', *Lettres, 1943–5*, p. 410; 'Cabinet', Moch, *Vie*, p. 198

2 C. Mauriac, *Un autre*, pp. 72, 78, 115

3 'Assembly', *Discours, 1940–46*, p. 596; 'Jeanneney', Lacouture, II, p. 192

4 'visit', *Mémoires*, pp. 795–8; 'cartoon', 'drink', C. Williams, *Frenchman*, p. 310

5 'gifts', Tauriac, *Vivre*, p. 94, *Mémoires*, pp. 830–31
6 'politics', *Discours, 1940–46*, p. 596, *Mémoires*, pp. 844–6, Lacouture, *Blum*, pp. 507–8, 525
7 'Yvonne', P. de Gaulle, *Images*, p. 118
8 'transitory', *Mémoires*, p. 857; 'government', *Mémoires*, pp. 858–9; 'suit', P. de Gaulle, *Images*, pp. 118–19; 'poll', Berstein, *Gaullisme*, p. 97; 'crisis', *Lettres, 1945–51*, pp. 114–15, *Mémoires*, pp. 860–62, C. Mauriac, *Un autre*, pp. 149–59; 'speech', *Discours, 1940–46*, pp. 649–71; 'Canada', Tournoux, *Tragédie*, p. 16
9 '*Le Monde*', Sainderichin, pp. 15–16, 'situation', *Mémoires*, p. 866, *Lettres, 1945–51*, pp. 151–3, C. Mauriac, *Un autre*, p. 142; 'call', Elgey, I, p. 80; 'de Boissieu', Lacouture, II, p. 230; 'speech', *Discours, 1940–46*, p. 661, *Mémoires*, pp. 863–5, *Journal officiel*, 1 January 1945, p. 732
10 *Mémoires*, p. 869; 'Moch', Moch, *De Gaulle*, pp. 121–2, Moch, *Vie*, pp. 311–12, Lacouture, II, p. 235
11 'Herriot', *Mémoires*, p. 870
12 'meeting', *Mémoires*, pp. 870–72, Fauvet, pp. 369–70; 'Tanguy-Prigent', Lacouture, II, pp. 240–42; Tournoux, *Tragédie*, p. 152; de Gaulle, *Le Fil*, p. 82

CHAPTER TWENTY

1 *Mémoires*, pp. 871–3, *Lettres, 1945–51*, p. 188; 'sadness', *Mémoires*, p. 872, Tournoux, *Tragédie*, pp. 16, 544; 'poll', Werth, *France 1940–1955*, p. 283; 'Gouin', Moch, *Vie*, p. 312; 'Duclos', Fauvet, p. 72
2 'Marly', Guy, p. 36, C. Mauriac, *Un autre*, pp. 162–9; 'Cadillac', 'vegetables', 'goat', 'Debré', C. Mauriac, *Un autre*, pp. 171–2, 187; 'poem', de Boissieu, *Combattre*, p. 341; 'good thing', C. Mauriac, *Un autre*, p. 181; 'brasserie', 'decorate', Guy, pp. 40, 55; 'strange', Tauriac, *Vivre*, p. 457; 'cinema', Roussel, *Inédit*, p. 158, 'barriers', Tournoux, *Tragédie*, p. 26
3 'newspaper', C. Mauriac, *Un autre*, pp. 170–73, *Lettres, 1945–51*, pp. 195–6
4 'life', Tournoux, *Tragédie*, p. 17; 'mission', Lacouture, II, pp. 527–31; 'daisy', 'surrender', C. Mauriac, *Un autre*, pp. 195–6, 198
5 'optimistic', 'MRP', Guichard, *Général*, pp. 200–02, C. Mauriac, *Un autre*, p. 205
6 'circumstances', *Lettres, Complément*, p. 391; *Discours, 1946–8*, pp. 5–11; C. Mauriac, *Un autre*, p. 208, 'polls', Rioux, *France*, I, p. 156
7 'PCF', Berstein, *Gaullisme*, p. 105; 'Blum', *Populaire-Dimanche*, 26 June–3 July 1946; 'MRP', P. Williams, *Post-war*, p. 18
8 'Ramadier', Sainderichin, p. 36
9 'Vietnam', *Lettres, 1945–51*, pp. 184, 217–18; 'struggle', O'Ballance, pp. 71–81, Cameron, I, pp. 73–5, 89–99

CHAPTER TWENTY-ONE

1 Roussel, II, p. 61
2 'Colombey', 'sad', *Mémoires*, p. 873; 'Joxe', 'telephone', 'newspapers', Guy,

pp. 86, 207, 241; 'visitor', Lacouture, II, p. 402; 'silver', C. Mauriac, *Un autre,* p. 233; 'logs', 'radio', Tournoux, *Tragédie,* pp. 26, 31; 'food', 'archives', 'Yvonne', Tauriac, *Vivre,* pp. 127, 198, 558; author interview with local hotel owner, April 2009; 'laughter', P. de Gaulle, *Images,* p. 132; 'drinker', Viansson-Ponté, *Gaullistes,* p. 22

3 'speech', *Discours, 1946–8,* pp. 48–55, P. de Gaulle, *Images,* p. 134; 'Ramadier', Peyrefitte, I, p. 99, Tournoux, *Tragédie,* pp. 37–8; 'Strasbourg', *Lettres, 1945–51,* pp. 223–4; 'posters', De Gaulle Museum, Colombey

4 'RPF', Tournoux, *Tragédie,* p. 92, P. de Gaulle, *Images,* p. 135, C. Mauriac, *Un autre,* pp. 274–5, 277, Lacouture, II, pp. 308–10, 335, Berstein, *Gaullisme,* pp. 121–2

5 'economy', Rioux, *France,* I, pp. 243–4, 247, Larkin, p. 186

6 'advice', Lacouture, II, p. 307; 'hard times', Guichard, *Espoir,* p. 138; 'Friang', Tauriac, *Vivre,* p. 552; 'organisation', Charlot, *Opposition,* p. 140, Lefranc, *Avec,* pp. 67–8, 81; 'Solférino', *Espoir,* June 2002; 'secretaries', Tauriac, *Vivre,* p. 513; 'meetings', Tournoux, *Tragédie,* pp. 136–7, Lefranc, *Avec,* pp. 68–9; 'herrings', Tournoux, *Tragédie,* p. 19; 'paratroopers', C. Mauriac, *Un autre,* p. 296; 'rally', 'meeting', Serre, pp. 149–50

CHAPTER TWENTY-TWO

1 'results', Charlot, *Opposition,* p. 89; 'RPF', *Espoir,* 67; 'frogs', *Lettres, 1945–51,* p. 231; Moch, *Vie,* pp. 318–19

2 'de Gaulle', 'Boche', Oulmont, p. 27, Fauvet, p. 131, C. Mauriac, *Un autre,* p. 299

3 'Leclerc', *Lettres, 1945–51,* p. 241, *Lettres, 1951–8,* pp. 58–91, 'aide', Tauriac, *Vivre,* p. 347; Terrenoire, *Vivant,* pp. 49–50; 'smoking', Lacouture, II, p. 325, C. Mauriac, *Un autre,* pp. 300, 305, P. de Gaulle, *Père,* II, p. 356; 'pleasure', Tauriac, Vivre, p. 536; 'visitor', Viansson-Ponté, *Gaullistes,* p. 21

4 Rix, p. 163, Tauriac, *Vivre,* p. 97, *Lettres, 1945–51,* pp. 247–8, 363, De Gaulle Museum, Colombey; 'Élisabeth', *Lettres, 1945–51,* pp. 272, 374–5; 'Prefect', Tauriac, *Vivre,* pp. 100–01

5 'son', *Lettres, 1945–51,* pp. 399, 447, P. de Gaulle, *Images,* pp. 136–7; 'letters', *Lettres, 1951–8,* pp. 22–3, 32, 61, 64, 110, 122, 175

6 'plan', 'machine gun', 'interview', Tournoux, *Tragédie,* pp. 52–3, 543–5

7 'letters', C. Mauriac, *Un autre,* p. 330, *Lettres, 1945–51,* p. 279

8 'sports', 'age', C. Mauriac, *Un autre,* pp. 310–12, 328, 332; 'trips', Lefranc, *Avec,* pp. 74–5, Guichard, *Général,* Chapter 4

9 De Gaulle Museum, Colombey, Lefranc, *Avec,* pp. 71–2; 'Sartre', Seymour-Jones, p. 355; '*Le Monde*', Sainderichin, p. 34

10 'politics', Pompidou, pp. 57–8, Tournoux, *Tragédie,* p. 86; 'Cabinet', Fauvet, p. 152, C. Mauriac, *Un autre,* p. 331, *Lettres, 1945–51,* p. 315; 'Treason', Tournoux, *Tragédie,* p. 87; Auriol, *Journal,* 26 January 1949

11 'RPF', Pompidou, pp. 69, 73, 81, *Lettres, 1945–51,* p. 417; 'Soustelle', Guichard, *Général,* pp. 234–5; 'Plan', Tournoux, *Tragédie,* p. 545

12 'Bidault', Chaban-Delmas, *Mémoires*, p. 200; 'Pleven', Tournoux, *Tragédie*, p. 138; 'de Gaulle', Pompidou, pp. 129–30, *Lettres, 1945–51*, pp. 474–5
13 Chaban-Delmas, *Mémoires*, pp. 196–7; 'election', Lefranc, *Avec*, pp. 81–2, Rioux, *France*, I, pp. 227–31, Fauvet, pp. 172–7, P. Williams, *Post-war*, pp. 440–41; 'de Gaulle to Soustelle', *Lettres, 1951–8*, pp. 17–18; 'cheese', Tournoux, *Tragédie*, pp. 110–11; 'election outcome', 'press conference', Rioux, *France*, I, p. 230, Fauvet, p. 176, P. Williams, *Post-war*, pp. 446–7, C. Mauriac, *Un autre*, p. 347; 'bourgeoisie', Debû-Bridel, *Contestataire*, p. 95; 'fear', Tournoux, *Tragédie*, p. 110
14 'offer', 'crisis', Soustelle, *Ans*, pp. 83–8, Lacouture, II, pp. 382–4, Tournoux, *Tragédie*, pp. 127–9; 'worries', 'odious', *Lettres, 1951–8*, pp. 53, 61; 'Reynaud', 'hung up', Ullmann, pp. 168–70; 'deputy', Tournoux, *Tragédie*, p. 547, 'Colombey', Terrenoire, *Vivant*, pp. 50–51, Ullmann, pp. 168–70; 'jealousy', Soustelle, *Ans*, p. 91, 'letter', Pompidou, pp. 156–7
15 Pinay, pp. 28–31, 51–3, Tournoux, *Tragédie*, pp. 123–4
16 Larebière, p. 46, C. Mauriac, *Un autre*, p. 380; 'lunch', C. Mauriac, *Un autre*, pp. 379–82
17 'RPF', C. Mauriac, *Un autre*, p. 385, *Lettres, 1951–8*, p. 143, *Mémoires*, pp. 892–3
18 Guichard, *Général*, p. 303

CHAPTER TWENTY-THREE

1 'Koenig', Oulmont, p. 27; Chaban-Delmas, *Mémoires*, p. 236; 'meeting', Terrenoire, *RPF*, pp. 301–2, Lacouture, II, p. 409
2 'debate', 'speech', Fauvet, pp. 284–6
3 'archivist', 'translation', Tauriac, *Vivre*, p. 128; 'duty', 'Coty', 'niece', *Lettres, 1951–8*, pp. 162, 169, 176, 238; 'visitors', 'press conference', 'poll', Lacouture, II, pp. 420–21, 424; 'niece', Tournoux, *Tragédie*, p. 218; 'Yvonne', P. de Gaulle, *Images*, p. 153, Guichard, *Général*, Part Four, Chapter 1; 'Chad', Tauriac, *Vivre*, pp. 52, 86; 'soup', 'coup', Roussel, II, pp. 98–100, 104
4 'worst-paid', 'density', Horne, *War*, pp. 57, 184; Chirac, p. 34; 'Sahara', Jean Daniel in Rioux, *Portraits*, p. 460; 'visitor', Kettle, p. 94
5 'revolt', *Lettres, 1951–8*, p. 240
6 'deaths', Moch, *De Gaulle*, pp. 158–9
7 'inability', *Lettres, 1951–8*, p. 297; 'broadcast', 'British', Tournoux, *Tragédie*, pp. 209, 326, Roussel, II, p. 108
8 'Battle of Algiers', Horne, *War*, Chapter 9, Courrière, II, Massu, *Torrent*, Godard, *Paras*
9 Tournoux, *Tragédie*, pp. 210–11

CHAPTER TWENTY-FOUR

1 'Gallois', Tauriac, *Vivre*, pp. 242–4; 'photograph', P. de Gaulle, *Images*, p. 153; 'Mauriac', Tauriac, *Vivre*, pp. 494–5

2 *Lettres, 1951–8,* pp. 270–71, 298; Sulzberger, p. 31; Lacouture, II, pp. 428–9
3 'Soustelle', Horne, *War,* p. 269; 'Debré', Nouzille, p. 20
4 'arm', Tauriac, *Vivre,* p. 172; Vendroux, *Chance,* p. 433; *Discours, 1946–58,* p. 654
5 Guichard, *Général,* pp. 344–5, Tournoux, *Jamais,* p. 170, Sainderichin, pp. 65–6
6 'Emmanuel', *Atlantic Monthly,* June 1958; 'hand', Horne, *War,* p. 277; 'posters', 'Neuwirth', Elgey, I, pp. 739, 761–2; 'Hemingway', Malraux, p. 79; 'age', Tournoux, *Jamais,* pp. 186–7, Guichard, *Général,* pp. 343, 348; 'nephew', Lacouture, II, p. 446; 'Nora', Guichard, *Général,* p. 344
7 'libido', Lacouture, II, p. 455; 'Mitterrand', 'Beuve-Méry', see the titles of their books; Julliard, p. 219; 'Tim', *L'Express,* 29 May 1958; Buron, p. 90
8 'Delbecque', Lacouture, II, p. 505

TWENTY-FIVE

1 'Lacoste', Viansson-Ponté, *Histoire,* I, p. 20; Pflimlin, pp. 100–01, *Espoir,* October 1998, p. 15
2 'newspaper', Viansson-Ponté, *Politiques,* p. 20; 'Salan', Viansson-Ponté, *Politiques,* pp. 18–19
3 'Massu', Pellissier, pp. 262, 265
4 'Assembly', 'Lacoste', Pflimlin, pp. 114–17, Roussel, II, pp. 130–31
5 'reverse', Rémond, *Retour,* p. 21; 'Massu', Pellissier, p. 268; Guichard, *Espoir,* October 1998, p. 13, *Mémoires,* pp. 896–7; 'Pleven', Rémond, *Retour,* p. 15; Moch, *De Gaulle,* pp. 160–61, 170; 'banners', photograph in Kettle, after p. 622; 'Salan', Viansson-Ponté, *Histoire,* I, p. 47; 'statement', *Discours, 1958–62,* p. 3; 'Madame Massu', Pellissier, pp. 273–4
6 Buron, p. 84; 'Houghton', Nouzille, pp. 22–3; 'Vitasse', Tournoux, *Jamais,* pp. 174–5; 'Pflimlin', Poniatowski, p. 307
7 'Salan', Winock, *République se meurt,* pp. 55–6; 'Soustelle', Poniatowski, p. 311; 'Dassault', *Espoir,* October 1998, p. 9
8 'press conference', *Mémoires,* p. 898, *Discours, 1958–62,* pp. 4–10; Kettle, p. 201, Pflimlin, p. 120
9 'De Gaulle, activities', Guichard, *Général,* p. 356, *Espoir,* October 1998, p. 13; 'Salan', Horne, *War,* p. 293; Pflimlin, p. 121; 'US', Nouzille, pp. 24–6
10 *Mémoires,* p. 899, Pflimlin, pp. 128–9; 'plan', Massu, *Torrent,* pp. 120–25, Jouhaud, *Vie,* p. 53, *Le Monde,* 27 May 1958; 'Tunis', Pflimlin, p. 122; 'journey', Pflimlin, pp. 130–31
11 'meeting', *Mémoires,* p. 900, Pflimlin, pp. 130–35, *Espoir,* October 1998, p. 16; 'statement', *Mémoires,* p. 900, *Discours, 1958–62,* p. 11; Tournoux, *Jamais,* p. 457 et seq.; 'magnificent', Poniatowski, pp. 346–7; 'parliament', 'Cabinet', Pflimlin, pp. 136–7; 'Pleven', Ferniot, *13 Mai,* p. 448; 'Socialists', *Mémoires,* p. 901, Moch, *Vie,* p. 538
12 'Dulac–de Gaulle', Dulac, pp. 77–8; 'Auriol', *Lettres, 1951–8,* pp. 362–3; 'Messages', 'PCF', Tournoux, *Jamais,* pp. 174–5, 181, Horne, *War,* p. 296, Lacouture, II, p. 479
13 Moch, *Vie,* p. 287; 'action', Lacouture, II, pp. 483–4; 'son', *Lettres, 1951–8,* p. 364

14 'message', Tournoux, *Jamais*, p. 182; 'statement', *Mémoires*, p. 899
15 'Mollet', Moch, *Vie*, pp. 297, 303; 'Algiers', Kettle, p. 221
16 'say no', Pflimlin, p. 141; 'Mitterrand', Giesbert, p. 176, *Espoir*, October 1998, Lacouture, II, p. 492
17 'Assembly', *Mémoires*, p. 904, *Discours, 1958–62*, pp. 13–15; 'Messmer', Tauriac, *Vivre*, p. 429; 'decline', Lacouture, II, p. 540
18 Lefranc, *Avec*, p. 125
19 Dulac, p. 98

CHAPTER TWENTY-SIX

1 'Fauvet', Berstein, *Gaullisme*, p. 225
2 'constitution', Berstein, *Gaullisme*, p. 221; 'Vedel', Roussel, II, p. 158; 'bills', Viansson-Ponté, *Politiques*, p. 33. Discussion of constitution in colloquies reported October 1984 in *Espoir* and *Revue française de science politique*
3 'Africa', *Discours, 1958–62*, pp. 30–41, Lacouture, II, p. 578, quoting letter from J. Mauriac, 18 November 1984
4 *Discours, 1958–62*, pp. 41–5; 'demonstrations', *Le Monde*, 5/6 September 1958
5 'tax', Williams and Harrison, pp. 90–91; Viansson-Ponté, *Histoire*, I, pp. 69–73; Berstein, *Expansion*, p. 23; Olivier Duhamel, *Revue française de science politique*, 1985, p. 623; 'de Beauvoir', Seymour-Jones, pp. 400–01
6 'Napoleon', *Mémoires*, p. 1045; 'free trade area', Frances Lynch, *De Gaulle's First Veto*, European University, Florence, 1998, EUI Working Paper, HEC no. 98/8
7 'Dulles', Nouzille, pp. 34–7; Alain de Boissieu to Lacouture, Lacouture, III, p. 466; 'memorandum', Grosser, pp. 197–8, '1952', Walters, p. 253, 'foreign policy', 'Eisenhower', Grosser, p. 198, Gladwyn, p. 314, Galambos and Van Ee, XIX, pp. 917, 954–5
8 'Pierrelatte', Newhouse, pp. 16, 66; 'Adenauer visit', *Mémoires*, pp. 1031–7; 'good German', Pierre Maillard, *Espoir*, October 1998, p. 61; P. de Gaulle, *Images*, p. 173; 'de Gaulle–Adenauer letters', *Espoir*, no. 157
9 'plan', 'committee', 'Pinay', Fondation de Gaulle, Goetze oral history, Rueff, pp. 220–24, Lacouture, II, pp. 669–78, Roussel, II, pp. 179–82, Pinay, pp. 126–7, *Espoir*, no. 154, p. 55, Pflimlin, p. 176; Goetze, *Espoir*, no. 154; 'franc', Lynch, *Veto*, p. 29, Lacouture, II, p. 972, from *Colloque sur de Gaulle et le redressement financier*, 26 January 1985; 'success', Goetze, *Espoir*, no. 154, pp. 56, 42–8, Lacouture, II, pp. 672–4; 'speech', *Discours, 1958–62*, pp. 64–7
10 *Mémoires*, p. 909

CHAPTER TWENTY-SEVEN

1 'Mollet', Tournoux, *Tragédie*, p. 411; de Gaulle, *Le Fil*, pp. 82–3; 'telephone', Rusk, p. 196; Grosser, Chapters 6 and 7, gives excellent overview of de Gaulle's foreign policy

2 Viansson-Ponté, *Gaullistes,* p. 41
3 Viansson-Ponté, *Gaullistes,* p. 48; 'Martinet', Roussel, II, p. 288
4 'ghosts', 'money', Larebière, p. 63, *Mémoires,* p. 1139
5 Rusk, p. 243; Tauriac, *Vivre,* Chapter 16
6 'Madame de Gaulle', Tauriac, *Vivre,* Chapter 32
7 'Madame de Gaulle', 'frugal', 'suits', 'cars', 'children', 'barber', 'morning routine', Tauriac, *Vivre,* Chapter 32, pp. 174–5, 199–200, 201–3, 394–5, 515, 558; Dulong gives details of palace life, 'beds', p. 10; '*Le Monde*', Lacouture, III, p. 20; *Mémoires,* p. 1139; 'palace life', *L'Express,* 9 November 2006; 'bouillabaisse', 'sardines', *L'Express,* 7 August 2008
8 'Madame', Tournoux, *Tragédie,* p. 367; 'food', Tauriac, *Vivre,* pp. 539–40; 'Eisenhower', Walters, p. 260; 'age', Tournoux, *Tragédie,* p. 297
9 'Colombey', *Mémoires,* p. 1141, *Lettres, 1961–3,* pp. 26, 51, P. de Gaulle, *Images,* pp. 184–5; 'confession', P. de Gaulle, *Images,* p. 189; Nixon, p. 70
10 'Cabinet', *Lettres, 1962–3,* pp. 150, 392; 'authority', *Discours, 1962–5,* pp. 164–8
11 'Cabinet', Pinay, p. 132, Viansson-Ponté, *Gaullistes,* pp. 44–5; 'Pinay clash', Pinay, pp. 139–42, Viansson-Ponté, *Gaullistes,* p. 31
12 Pinay, pp. 139–42
13 'de Gaulle', Walters, pp. 254–9

CHAPTER TWENTY-EIGHT

1 Tournoux, *Tragédie,* p. 402, Faure, II, p. 688
2 'Chaban', Lacouture, III, p. 51
3 'reporter', Kettle, p. 237; 'speech', *Discours, 1958–62,* pp. 15–17; 'antique dealer', Démaret and Plume, pp. 3–7; 'shut up', Tournoux, *Tragédie,* p. 289, Berstein, *Expansion,* p. 53; 'French Canada', 'names', Lacouture, III, pp. 525, 531; 'return', Lefranc, *Avec,* p. 129
4 'Herzog', Tauriac, *Vivre,* pp. 476–7; 'press conference', *Discours, 1958–62,* pp. 51–60
5 'officers', Tauriac, *Vivre,* pp. 301–2
6 Soustelle, *Espérance,* p. 94
7 *L'Écho d'Oran,* 30 April 1959
8 'Jeanneney', Lacouture, III, p. 67l, *Mémoires,* p. 952
9 Argoud, p. 193; 'scorpions', Tauriac, *Vivre,* p. 54; 'visit', Lacouture, III, p. 70
10 'oil', Roussel, II, p. 199
11 *Discours, 1958–62,* pp. 117–23
12 'Pierre', Tauriac, *Vivre,* pp. 97–100, 'Jacquinot', *Lettres, 1961–3,* p. 143
13 'Massu visit', Flohic, p. 39; 'Argoud', Tournoux, *Tragédie,* pp. 355–6; 'Susini', Rioux, *Portraits,* pp. 356–8
14 'Narbonne', Tauriac, *Vivre,* pp. 133–4; 'astonishment', 'Cabinet', Tournoux, *Tragédie,* pp. 349–50, 352–4; 'Argoud', 'Challe', Lacouture, III, pp. 94–104
15 'Juin', Lacouture, III, p. 97; 'Bretons', Roussel, II, p. 221
16 'speech', *Discours, 1958–62,* pp. 162–6; Soustelle, *Espérance,* pp. 144–5

17 'poll', Roussel, II, p. 226
18 Faivre, *Archives*, pp. 80–81
19 'Si Salah', Roussel, II, pp. 237–8, Lacouture, III, pp. 116–22, Flohic, pp. 44–5; 'not very attached', Archives Nationales, Terrenoire Papers, July 1960

CHAPTER TWENTY-NINE

1 'link', Peyrefitte, I, p. 280
2 'Khrushchev visit', Viansson-Ponté, *Histoire*, I, pp. 282–6, Tournoux, *Tragédie*, pp. 364–6, 473, Taubman, pp. 448–9; 'old, fat', Hervé Alphand to Lacouture, Lacouture, III, p. 387; 'boat', Tauriac, *Vivre*, pp. 480–81; 'intelligent', 'cunning', Taubman, p. 449
3 'visits', 'speeches', *Discours, 1958–62*, pp. 175–8, 184–6, 187–208, 208–14; Nixon, p. 61
4 'summit', Walters, pp. 200–04, Bohlen, pp. 466–70, Taubman, pp. 460–68, Newhouse, pp. 109–10, Lacouture, III, pp. 390–91, Gladwyn, p. 247, 'Eisenhower', Galambos and Van Ee, p. 1532
5 'verse', Tournoux, *Tragédie*, pp. 397–8
6 Flohic, p. 46; 'birthday', 'poems', Tournoux, *Tragédie*, pp. 367–9
7 'address', *Discours, 1958–62*, p. 256; 'insertion', Viansson-Ponté, *Histoire*, I, p. 192; 'plots', Démaret and Plume, pp.14–16, Chapters 4–5; Laffont, *Expiation*, pp. 167–76; 'Cabinet', Terrenoire Papers, December 1960, Archives Nationales

CHAPTER THIRTY

1 'French Israel', Peyrefitte, I, p. 85
2 Argoud, pp. 237–8, 244, 253
3 'putsch', *Mémoires*, pp. 970–76, Viansson-Ponté, *Histoire*, I, pp. 351–64; 'Kennedy', Rusk, p. 244; 'grave', 'coup', Roussel, II, pp. 262–4; 'will', Larebière, p. 65; 'Colts', Lacouture, III, p. 167; 'speech', *Discours, 1958–62*, pp. 306–8l; 'Castro', Tournoux, *Tragédie*, pp. 375–6; 'Orly', Lacouture, III, p. 168; 'Ministry', 'masquerade', 'trucks', Viansson-Ponté, *Histoire*, I, p. 361
4 'Delegations', *Time* magazine, 2 June 1961
5 'Salan', 'Degueldre', Horne, *War*, pp. 483, 485
6 'visit', Dalleck, pp. 394–7; 'Eisenhower', Ambrose, pp. 490–91; C. L. Sulzberger, *New York Times*, 1 June 1961; 'UN', Newhouse, p. 130; Rusk, pp. 242–3
7 'Hallstein', *Mémoires*, pp. 1041–2; Rusk, p. 242; Tournoux, *Tragédie*, p. 462
8 'Couve–Luns', Heath, p. 230
9 http://www.hfienberg.com/ec/britapplywhy.html, Pickles, *Politics*, pp. 33–4
10 'plan', Fouchet, pp. 195–203
11 'negotiations', 'Bizerta', *Lettres, 1961–3*, pp. 98–110, 109, 111–15; 'Debré', *Lettres, 1961–3*, pp. 124–6; Flohic, pp. 59–60; *Discours, 1958–62*, pp. 333–49, *Lettres, 1961–3*, pp. 132–6, 143

12 'Pont-de-Seine', Démaret and Plume, Chapter 12; Terrenoire Papers, September 1961, Archives Nationales; *Lettres, 1961–3,* p. 149
13 'numbers', Jean-Paul Brunet, *Police contre FLN* (Paris: Flammarion, 1999), p. 330; 'Cabinet', Terrenoire Papers, Archives Nationales, in Roussel, II, p. 284; Peyrefitte, I, p. 89
14 'Cabinet', 'agriculture', Peyrefitte, I, pp. 298–9, 303–4; Heath, pp. 225–6, Newhouse, pp. 142–3
15 'De Gaulle', Terrenoire Papers, December 1961, in Archives Nationales, quoted in Roussel, II, pp. 286–7; 'Pinay', Roussel, II, p. 288
16 *Lettres, 1961–3,* pp. 167–9, 199–200; '*barbouzes*', Démaret and Plume, p. 73
17 SAC information from Bernard Edinger. For de Gaulle on OAS, *Mémoires,* pp. 985–6
18 Viansson-Ponté, *Histoire,* I, p. 270, Terrenoire Papers, Feb. 1962, Archives Nationales, in Roussel, II, p. 293
19 *Lettres, 1961–3,* p. 214; 'possible', Larebière, p. 68
20 *Lettres, 1961–3,* p. 220; Tournoux, *Tragédie,* pp. 399–400; Lacouture, III, pp. 229–31, Viansson-Ponté, *Histoire,* I, p. 278
21 'handkerchief': private information from the late André Passeron
22 'inevitable', *Lettres, 1961–3,* p. 224; 'speech', Terrenoire, *L'Algérie,* p. 281
23 'imbeciles', 'OAS', Terrenoire Papers, Roussel, II, pp. 281, 283, 289; 'not think like us', Tournoux, *Tragédie,* p. 403; 'Reynaud', Horne, *War,* p. 548
24 *Lettres, 1961–3,* p. 228
25 'head of government', 'Joffre', 'dossiers', 'transitional', 'told', Peyrefitte, I, pp. 101–2, 117; *Mémoires,* p. 1177; 'Mitterrand', Roussel, II, p. 311
26 'Couve', Peyrefitte, I, pp. 1–6; 'Pompidou', 'violet', 'abandon', Peyrefitte, I, pp. 129–30, Pflimlin, pp. 213–17
27 'unable', *Mémoires,* pp. 1045–6; '70 per cent', Viansson-Ponté, *Histoire,* I, p. 495
28 'Jouhaud', 'Salan', Peyrefitte, I, p. 169, II, Chapter 13, Roussel, II, p. 318, from Donnedieu de Vabres Papers, Archives Nationales, 539 AP5; *Mémoires,* pp. 991–2, Tournoux, *Tragédie,* pp. 413–18, Lacouture, III, pp. 269–70, Fouchet, pp. 175–7
29 'no question', Pflimlin, pp. 204–5; 'numbers', '*harkis*', Faivre, *Archives,* pp. 137–9; Lacouture, III, p. 260, Roussel, II, pp. 320–22; 'Cabinet discussions', Peyrefitte, I, Chapters 26, 27

CHAPTER THIRTY-ONE

1 Démaret and Plume give a detailed account of Petit-Clamart and Bastien-Thiry, Chapters 24–29, as does Alain de la Tocnaye, *Comment je n'ai pas tué de Gaulle* (Paris: Éditions Nalis, 1969). Also de Boissieu, *Servir,* pp. 165, 159, *Mémoires,* p. 993, Viansson-Ponté, *Histoire,* II, Lacouture, III, pp. 274–9, 213, Peyrefitte, I, p. 213; P. de Gaulle, *Images,* p. 178, *Minute,* 1 October 1970, map, photograph, Larebière, p. 71; 'father', Tournoux, *Jamais,* p. 293, *Tragédie,* pp. 443, 452
2 Peyrefitte, I, p. 183

3 'beyond', Viansson-Ponté, *Gaullistes*, p. 46, *Histoire*, II, p. 36, 'vote', Peyrefitte, I, p. 214
4 'visit', Viansson-Ponté, *Histoire*, II, p. 56, Grosser, p. 183
5 'Cabinet', Larebière, p. 80, Peyrefitte, I, pp. 226–9, Guichard, *Général*, pp. 386–8, *Lettres, 1962–3*, p. 264; 'Mollet', Tournoux, *Tragédie*, pp. 409–13
6 Roussel, II, p. 327, *Mémoires*, pp. 1164–9, Lacouture, III, p. 585; 'mood', 'Sudreau', Viansson-Ponté, *Histoire*, II, pp. 42, 47, Tournoux, *Jamais*, p. 464
7 Bohlen, p. 494; 'outcome', V. Jaubert, *L'Amérique contre de Gaulle* (Paris: Seuil, 2000), pp. 78–80
8 'election', Viansson-Ponté, *Histoire*, II, p. 47, Tournoux, *Tragédie*, pp. 407–8, Berstein, *Gaullisme*, p. 278; 'grace', *Mémoires*, p. 1147
9 'talks', Macmillan, *Day*, pp. 337–8, 345–55, Lacouture, III, p. 333; 'Zulueta', Horne, *Macmillan*, p. 431; 'Cabinet', '*milord*', Viansson-Ponté, *Histoire*, II, pp. 60–61, Peyrefitte, I, p. 333; 'birthright', 'war', 'vassals', Peyrefitte, I, pp. 347, 348, 361
10 http://www.ena.lu/press-conference-held-general-gaulle-14-january-1963–020000863.html, Lacouture, III, pp. 336–8; 'Wilson', Newhouse, p. 297
11 Pisani, pp. 106–7; Heath, p. 236; Macmillan, *Day*, pp. 365, 368–9, Horne, *Macmillan*, p. 446; 'Kennedy', Dalleck, p. 611, Peyrefitte, I, pp. 338, 346, 361
12 Letter, *Espoir*, no. 12
13 'garden', *Lettres, 1961–3*, p. 297; 'treaty', http://www.ena.lu/preamble_elysee_treaty_ratification_bonn_15_june_1963–020002910.html; Peyrefitte, II, p. 228

CHAPTER THIRTY-TWO

1 *Lettres, 1962–3*, pp. 289, 297, *Mémoires*, pp. 1175–6
2 'Senghor', 'papa', Lacouture, III, pp. 411, 419–20
3 'plan', *Mémoires*, pp. 1011–16; 'Orly', 'married', *Discours, 1958–62*, pp. 283, 327; 'oyster', 'farms', Larkin, pp. 184, 199–200
4 'statistics', Berstein, *Expansion*, Chapter 6; 'Sagan', P. de Gaulle, *Père*, I, p. 702; 'Beatles', *L'Express*, 9 November 2006
5 'Mitterrand', Viansson-Ponté, *Histoire*, II, p. 90; 'television', *Lettres, 1962–3*, pp. 311, 318, 326, *Lettres, 1964–6*, p. 67
6 *Mémoires*, p. 1022
7 'wages', 'tax', Larkin, pp. 179–80, 204; 'situation', *Mémoires*, pp. 1189–90
8 *Lettres, 1962–3*, pp. 289, 297, 299, 312, 335, 340, 344, 346
9 'strike', Peyrefitte, I, Part V, *Mémoires*, p. 1184, Roussel, II, p. 362
10 'economy', 'plan', 'gold', Larkin, p. 305, Peyrefitte, II, p. 334, *Lettres, 1962–3*, p. 345, Pompidou, p. 179, *Mémoires*, pp. 1204–8
11 'funeral', Tauriac, *Vivre*, p. 507, Viansson-Ponté, *Histoire*, II, pp. 73–4, Pisani, p. 131; 'yacht', Malraux, p. 119
12 'Queuille', Lacouture, III, p. 348; Rusk, p. 144, Bohlen, p. 517
13 'Caravelle', *Time* magazine, 27 March 1964
14 *Lettres, 1964–6*, p. 52
15 'Lévêque', Tauriac, *Vivre*, pp. 196–7, *Time* magazine, 12 February 1965

16 'Alphand', Lacouture, III, pp. 375–6
17 'Concorde', Peyrefitte, III, pp. 59, 61
18 'poll', Berstein, *Expansion*, p. 237
19 Noël, p. 471; Gladwyn, p. 325; 'Bohlen', 'Ball', Nouzille, pp. 103, 105; 'Rostow', Roussel, II, p. 385; 'Billotte', Tournoux, *Jamais*, pp. 342–3
20 'polls', Berstein, *Gaullisme*, pp. 320–21; *Lettres, 1964–6*, pp. 83, 103; Guichard, *Général*, pp. 404, 409; 'Comte', Tournoux, *Tragédie*, pp. 478–9, Peyrefitte, II, p. 532; Viansson-Ponté, *Histoire*, II, p. 115
21 'opposition', Roussel, II, p. 375, Nouzille, p. 113, Viansson-Ponté, *Histoire*, II, p. 141. Election covered in Derogy and Kahn
22 'murmur', Schoenbrun, p. 328
23 'Ben Bella', 'Bull', 'RAF', 'character', 'treaty', *Lettres, 1964–6*, pp. 19, 21, 39, 134, 141; 'speech', Newhouse, p. 281; 'press conference', 'Congo', Agence France-Presse, 9 September 1965, *Washington Post*, 10 September 1965
24 'Mendès', *Nouvel Observateur*, 27 October 1965; 'ruffian', Peyrefitte, II, p. 606. The lion and fox analogy is from P. de Boisdeffre, *Le Lion et le Renard* (Paris: le Richer, 1997)
25 'Flohic', 'Lefranc', Tauriac, *Vivre*, pp. 542–3
26 Peyrefitte, III, pp. 42–7, Roussel, II, pp. 410–15, Lacouture, III, pp. 628–32, 'proceedings', *Guardian*, 30 October 2009, p. 20
27 'campaign', Viansson-Ponté, *Histoire*, II, p. 183; Pisani, p. 130; *Lettres, 1964–6*, p. 210; 'polls', Berstein, *Gaullisme*, pp. 295, 303; Peyrefitte, II, p. 602
28 'polls', Berstein, *Gaullisme*, p. 279; 'dictatorship', Malraux, p. 167, Viansson-Ponté, *Histoire*, II, p. 177
29 'polls', Berstein, *Gaullisme*, pp. 269–70; 'result', 'reaction', 'Adenauer', *Lettres, 1964–6*, pp. 217–18, 220–21, 229–31, 237, 241, 271

CHAPTER THIRTY-THREE

1 Peyrefitte, III, pp. 11–12, 391; Viansson-Ponté, *Histoire*, II, pp. 212, 229; 'Eisenhower', Schoenbrun, p. 320
2 'agent', Nouzille, p. 135; 'NATO', *Lettres, 1964–6*, pp. 256–8, 263–7; Rusk, p. 243
3 'television', 'note', 'Germany', *Lettres, 1964–6*, pp. 241–2, 246–9, 267–73
4 'speeches in USSR', *Discours, 1966–9*, pp. 40–58, 'Couve', Viansson-Ponté, *Histoire*, II, p. 217; 'alliance', Newhouse, p. 291; 'enemy', Lacouture, III, p. 403
5 'letter', *New York Times*, 3 September 1966; 'broadcast', *Le Monde*, 2 January 1967, Viansson-Ponté, *Histoire*, II, p. 228
6 'Fauvet', Viansson-Ponté, *Histoire*, II, p. 263
7 *Discours, 1966–9*, pp. 147–9, *Lettres, 1966–9*, pp. 74–5; 'Mitterrand', 'letter', Peyrefitte, III, pp. 90–91
8 Lacouture, III, p. 230
9 Chirac, pp. 92–8, Tauriac, *Vivre*, p. 218
10 'Pisani', Lacouture, III, pp. 645–6, *Lettres, 1966–9*, pp. 106–7; 'Giscard', Roussel, II, p. 46
11 Ministère des Affaires Étrangères (MAÉ), 'De Gaulle–Kiesinger', 14 January 1967

12 'funeral', http://www.britishpathe.com/record.php?id=84842
13 'Eshkol', 'Saudi', Roussel, I, pp. 463, 468
14 Peyrefitte, III, pp. 275–83, *Lettres, 1966–9,* pp. 119–20; 'Wilson', Roussel, I, p. 469, MAÉ, de Gaulle–Wilson, 19 June 1967; Viansson-Ponté, *Histoire,* II, p. 330
15 MAÉ, de Gaulle–Emir, 5 September 1967
16 'press conference', *Discours, 1966–9,* pp. 227–47
17 Bohlen, p. 510, *Lettres, 1966–9,* pp. 129, 140, 170–72; 'press conference', *Discours, 1966–9,* pp. 227–47, http://www.dangoor.com/74049.html; 'Koenig', 'Hamon', Roussel, II, p. 494. I am indebted to Bernard Edinger for the information on Hamon's name; Peyrefitte, III, p. 514; 'Debré', Roussel, II, p. 491
18 'Vimy', *Lettres, 1966–9,* p. 62. Thomson gives fullest account of the visit, including the quotation from de Gaulle above. Also Roussel, II, pp. 480–86, Lacouture, II, Chapter 19
19 *Discours, 1966–9,* pp. 191–2; 'Canadian tour', Peyrefitte, III, pp. 330–59; 'Couve', Roussel, II, p. 486; 'Pompidou', Peyrefitte, III, pp. 338, 514
20 'Wallonia', Tournoux, *Jamais,* pp. 290–91
21 Tauriac, *Vivre,* pp. 91–2
22 *Discours, 1966–9,* pp. 204–16; 'newspaper', Newhouse, pp. 303–4
23 'Neuwirth', Tauriac, *Vivre,* pp. 78–9, Duchen, pp. 184–5, Peyrefitte, III, pp. 243–8

CHAPTER THIRTY-FOUR

1 'Philippe', 'notes', *Lettres, 1966–8,* pp. 127, 132, 184, 187, 195–201, 215, 143, 157, 172–3; 'education', Peyrefitte, III, pp. 383–5, 390–92; 'squatters', Pompidou, p. 181
2 *Le Monde,* 15 March 1968; *Lettres, 1966–9,* p. 184; 'Giscard', Nouzille, p. 201; 'historians', Capdevielle and Mouriaux, p. 24
3 'Nanterre', 'pranks', 'hostels', 'apology', 'Pompidou', Peyrefitte, III, pp. 422–5, 428–9, 437–8; Viansson-Ponté, *Histoire,* II, p. 403; Cohn-Bendit, p. 31
4 'Jeanneney', Lacouture, II, p. 666
5 Peyrefitte, III, pp. 74, 75–6, 248
6 'parties etc.', Tournoux, *Tragédie,* pp. 485, 490–91; 'shadows', *Lettres, 1966–9,* p. 264; Flohic, p. 172
7 'Cohn-Bendit', 'Pompidou', Peyrefitte, III, pp. 455–7, 460–62

CHAPTER THIRTY-FIVE

1 *L'Humanité,* 3 May 1968; 'Séguy', *L'Express,* 1 May 2008; 'schoolboy', Romain Goupil in the film *Mourir à trente ans, Le Monde,* 16 May 1998, Reader, p. 10; 'fighting', *France-Soir,* 4 May 1968; *Le Monde,* 5 May 1968; Viansson-Ponté, *Histoire,* II, pp. 439–40
2 'de Gaulle', Peyrefitte, III, pp. 467–8, 470

3 Peyrefitte, III, pp. 474–5, Viansson-Ponté, *Histoire,* II, pp. 449–50
4 'de Gaulle', Peyrefitte, II, pp. 479–80
5 Peyrefitte, III, pp. 484–6, Viansson-Ponté, *Histoire,* II, pp. 452–3
6 'Grimaud', 'obituary', *Guardian,* 29 August 2009; 'ministers', Peyrefitte, III, pp. 498–9
7 'injury figures etc.', Viansson-Ponté, *Histoire,* II, p. 700; AFP, 11 May 1968; 'Pompidou', Pompidou, pp. 183–4, 217–18, Peyrefitte, III, pp. 506, 521, 529–30, 573, Roussel, II, p. 516, 'Grimaud', *Espoir,* no. 158
8 'Roy', Marek Halter, *Mai* (Geneva: Éditions de l'Avenue, 1970); 'demonstration', 'Cohn-Bendit', Viansson-Ponté, *Histoire* II, pp. 471–2; 'same man', Peyrefitte, III, p. 514
9 'funding', Peyrefitte, III, p. 520
10 'strikes', *Le Monde,* AFP reports, May 1968; Jacques Frémontier, *La Forteresse Ouvrière: Renault* (Paris: Fayard, 1971), pp. 350–51
11 *Discours, 1966–9,* pp. 287–8
12 'second round', *Lettres, 1964–6,* pp. 216–17, ORTF, 7 June 1968, Derogy and Kahn, pp. 233–4, Lacouture, II, p. 638; 'cost', Viansson-Ponté, *Histoire,* II, pp. 199–201
13 Chirac, p. 112
14 Pisani, p. 246; 'Sanguinetti', Tournoux, *Jamais,* p. 318; 'Gaullists', Lacouture, III, p. 683; 'Chalandon', Berstein, *Gaullisme,* p. 281
15 'Cabinet', 'Couve', Peyrefitte III, pp. 533–40, 548, 578; 'negotiations', Chirac, p. 113
16 'de Gaulle', 'Pompidou', 'paratroopers', 'Fourquet', Lacouture, III, pp. 686–7, 692, Guichard, *Général,* p. 428; Tournoux, *Jamais,* p. 318; Peyrefitte, III, p. 543; 'US', Nouzille, pp. 209–10; 'radio', Lacouture, III, p. 687
17 'Grenelle', Pompidou, p. 160, Balladur, p. 153, Alexandre, *Péril,* p. 316; 'Séguy', *L'Express,* 1 May 2008
18 'Cabinet', Peyrefitte, III, p. 548
19 Peyrefitte, III, pp. 546, 552; 'responsible', 'experts', Pompidou, pp. 235–6, 191–2; Lacouture, III, p. 694; 'Madame de Gaulle', Foccart, *Mai,* pp. 142–3, Pompidou, pp. 191–2, Lacouture, III, p. 696; 'de Boissieu', Tournoux, *Jamais,* p. 317; 'Flohic', Tauriac, *Vivre,* p. 144; 'de Gaulle', Pompidou, pp. 190–92; 'Fouchet', 'Foccart', Roussel, II, p. 527
20 *L'Humanité,* 29 May 1986; Pompidou, pp. 192–3, Tournoux, *Jamais,* p. 323, Viansson-Ponté, *Histoire,* II, p. 535; Peyrefitte, III, p. 561; 'Tallon', Tauriac, *Vivre,* p. 143

CHAPTER THIRTY-SIX

1 Pompidou, pp. 193–5; 'officials', Tauriac, *Vivre,* pp. 143–4; Peyrefitte, III, p. 563; 'Gaullists', Tournoux, *Jamais,* pp. 327–38
2 'De Boissieu', Pompidou, pp. 249–51; 'conversation', Lacouture, III, pp. 702–3, Tournoux, *Jamais,* pp. 319–22; 'Massu', Nouzille, p. 206

3 'avoiding', 'Hurry', 'Flohic', Tauriac, *Vivre*, pp. 145–6
4 'Baden', Massu, *Baden*, pp. 87–92, 'Flohic', Tauriac, *Vivre*, pp. 147–9, Lacouture, III, pp. 705–11, *Le Figaro* magazine, 23 April 1983; Flohic, pp. 178–9; Flohic in *Espoir*, no. 158, Lacouture, III, pp. 704–5, Pompidou, p. 251; Tournoux, *Jamais*, p. 325, Tauriac, *Vivre*, p. 154
5 Tauriac, *Vivre*, p. 149, Tournoux, *Jamais*, p. 338
6 Nouzille, pp. 213–14
7 'Flohic', Tauriac, *Vivre*, pp. 149–50; 'draft', Peyrefitte, III, pp. 599–601
8 Pompidou, pp. 197–9; 'text', Peyrefitte, III, pp. 600–01, and Annexe 3
9 *Discours, 1966–9*, pp. 292–3; 'Tallon', Tauriac, *Vivre*, p. 152
10 *Discours, 1966–9*, pp. 292–3; Tauriac, *Vivre*, p. 152
11 'US', Nouzille, pp. 217–22; 'Giscard', Viansson-Ponté, *Histoire*, II, p. 540
12 'Dechartre', 'tablecloth', Tauriac, *Vivre*, pp. 137–8, 154; Pompidou, pp. 199–201, 203; *Le Monde*, 31 May 1968; 'switch', Pompidou, p. 200
13 Willener, *L'Image-Action de la société ou la politisation culturelle* (Paris: Seuil, 1970), Reader and Wadia, *Events*, p. 169, *Lettres, 1969–70*, p. 49
14 *Discours, 1966–9*, pp. 295, 310; Foccart, *Mai*, p. 243
15 Pompidou, pp. 203–7

CHAPTER THIRTY-SEVEN

1 'loins', 'economy', Peyrefitte, III, pp. 606, 610; 'Prague', 'Biafra', *Lettres, 1966–9*, pp. 236–7, 238–9; 'Kiesinger', 'Scranton', Roussel, II, pp. 556–8, MAÉ, *Entretien de Gaulle–Kiesinger*, 27 September 1968; Foccart, *Mai*, p. 410; 'Chaban', Viansson-Ponté, *Histoire*, II, pp. 598–9
2 'tittle-tattle', *Lettres, 1966–9*, p. 276
3 'Rome', Pompidou, pp. 266–7
4 'Mitterrand', Nouzille, p. 243; 'de Gaulle', Lacouture, III, p. 746
5 'Markovic affair', Pompidou, pp. 257, 269–71, 281–3, Haymann, pp. 87–103; 'statement', *Lettres, 1966–9*, p. 282; 'Geneva', 'dinner', Pompidou, pp. 270, 272
6 'referendum proposal', *Lettres, 1966–9*, pp. 232–3; 'social, economic conditions', 'austerity', 'Couve', *Lettres, 1966–9*, pp. 291–2, Viansson-Ponté, II, pp. 596–7; 'Rothschild', Foccart, *Mai*, pp. 615, 617, Roussel, II, pp. 573, 576–7; Jean Mauriac, 'Mort du Général de Gaulle', in Rioux, *Portraits*, pp. 661–2; Chirac, p. 126
7 'Canada', 'WEU', 'Soames', *Lettres, 1966–9*, pp. 297–8, 309; 'ask for', Roussel, II, p. 577
8 Foccart, *Mai*, pp. 723–4, 'Jean Mauriac', Rioux, *Portraits*, pp. 661–4
9 This account of de Gaulle's last days in office and subsequent events draws significantly on Jean Mauriac's detailed account in 'Mort du Général de Gaulle', Rioux, *Portraits*, pp. 661–76, plus personal information from André Passeron of *Le Monde*, and reports in that newspaper for 23–28 April 1969; 'television speeches', *Discours, 1966–9*, pp. 384–8, 389–403, 405–6; 'Le Theule', Viansson-Ponté, *Histoire*, II, p. 624; 'last day', Roussel, II, pp. 577–9, Lacouture, III, pp. 754–8; 'Flohic', Tauriac, *Vivre*, p. 572; 'absurdity',

Malraux, pp. 31–2
10 'calm', 'de Boissieu', Jean Mauriac, p. 680; 'Pompidou and de Gaulle', Pompidou, pp. 286–7
11 *Lettres, 1966–9,* p. 318
12 *Lettres, 1969–70,* p. 38; 'messages', Pompidou, pp. 290–91
13 'Colombey life', 'Messmer', Tauriac, *Vivre,* pp. 579–81, 583, Lacouture, III, p. 769; 'mediocrity', 'Couve', *Lettres, 1969–70,* pp. 31, 33, 63; 'scene', Roussel, *Inédit,* p. 295; 'foes', 'wounded', 'Fourth Republic', 'son', Jean Mauriac, pp. 684, 686, 688, 738; Malraux, p. 236; 'La Boisserie', 'gendarmerie', 'Spain', 'Vosges', *Lettres, 1969–70,* pp. 65, 109, 116, 137–8, 149; 'Franco', Roussel, *Inédit,* p. 297, Lacouture, III, pp. 777–8
14 Jean Mauriac, pp. 734–7, 743–6; Flohic, p. 216; Lacouture, III, pp. 786–7; Peyrefitte, III, pp. 617–19
15 Jean Mauriac, p. 755, Colombey Museum; 'king', Tauriac, *Vivre,* p. 582; 'Philippe', Lacouture, III, p. 790
16 Jean Mauriac, p. 757
17 'Nixon', Lacouture, III, p. 795; 'Foccart', Tournoux, *Jamais,* p. 375
17 See, for example, Berstein, *Expansion,* p. 347
19 'Pompidou', Chirac, pp. 119–20

BIBLIOGRAPHY

Unless otherwise stated, all French titles are published in Paris and all English titles in London.

Accoce, Pierre, *Les Français à Londres* (Balland, 1998)
Ageron, Charles-Robert, *Histoire de l'Algérie contemporaine* (Presses Universitaires de France, 1969)
Aglion, Raoul, *De Gaulle et Roosevelt* (Plon, 1984)
Ahamed, Liaquat, *Lords of Finance* (Heinemann, 2009)
Alanbrooke, *War Diaries* (ed. Danchev and Todman) (Weidenfeld & Nicolson, 2001)
Alexandre, Philippe, *Le duel de Gaulle–Pompidou* (Grasset et Tallandier, 1970
— *L'Élysée en péril, 2–30 mai 1968* (Fayard, 1969)
Alphand, Hervé, *L'Étonnement d'être. Journal 1939–1973* (Fayard, 1977)
Ambrose, Stephen, *Eisenhower: Soldier and President* (New York: Simon & Schuster, 1990)
Amouroux, Henri, *La Grande Histoire des Français sous l'Occupation*, 9 vols (Laffont, 1976–86 and 1999)
Anderson, Malcolm, *Conservative Politics in France* (George Allen & Unwin, 1974)
Andrieu, Claire, Braud, Philippe, and Piketty, Guillaume, *Dictionnaire de Gaulle* (Laffont, 2006)
Argenlieu, Thierry de, *Chronique d'Indochine* (Albin Michel, 1985)
Argoud, Antoine, *La Décadence, l'imposture et la tragédie* (Fayard, 1974)
Aron, Robert, *Histoire de la libération de la France juin 1944–mai 1945* (Fayard, 1959)
Ascherson, Neal, *The Struggles for Poland* (Michael Joseph, 1987)
Asselain, Jean-Claude, *Histoire économique de la France* (Seuil 1984)
Astier de La Vigerie, Emmanuel d', *De la chute à la libération de Paris 25 août 1944* (Gallimard, 1965)
Astoux, André, *L'Oubli. 1946–1958* (Lattès, 1974)
Auburtin, Jean, *Charles de Gaulle, soldat et politique* (Éditions universelles, 1945)
— *Le Colonel de Gaulle* (Plon, 1965)
— *Charles de Gaulle* (Seghers, 1966)
— 'Souvenirs sur le lieutenant-colonel de Gaulle' (*Espoir*, no. 27, June 1979)
Auriol, Vincent, *Journal du Septennat*, 7 vols (Armand Colin, 1971)
Azéma, Jean-Pierre, *De Munich à la Libération* (Seuil, 1979)
— and Bedarida, François, *La France des années noires* (Seuil, 1993)
Balladur, Édouard, *L'Arbre de mal* (Marcel Jullian, 1979)
Bardoux, Jacques, *Journal d'un témoin de la troisième* (Albin Michel, 1957)

Barrès, Philippe, *Charles de Gaulle* (Plon-Cartier, 1945)
Barthelet, Philippe, et German-Thomas, Olivier, *Charles de Gaulle jour après jour* (de Guibert, 1990)
Baumel, Jacques, *La liberté guidait nos pas* (Plon, 2004)
Bedarida, François, *La Stratégie Secrète de la Drôle de Guerre* (Presses de la Fondation Nationale des Sciences Politiques, 1979)
Beevor, Antony, *D Day* (Viking, 2009)
— and Cooper, Artemis, *Paris after the Liberation 1944–1949* (Penguin, 1995)
Benoist-Méchin, *De la défaite au désastre*, 2 vols (Albin Michel, 1966)
Berstein, Serge, *Le 6 février 1934* (Julliard, 1975)
— *La France de l'Expansion* (Seuil, 1989)
— *Histoire du gaullisme* (Perrin, 2001–2)
— *Léon Blum* (Fayard, 2006)
Beuve-Méry, Hubert, *Suicide de la IVe République* (Éditions du Cerf, 1958)
— *Onze Ans de règne 1958–1969* (Flammarion, 1974)
Billotte, Pierre, *Le temps des armes* (Plon, 1972)
Blanc, Pierre-Louis, *De Gaulle au soir de sa vie* (Fayard, 1990)
Bloch-Morhange, Jacques, *Le Gaullisme* (Plon, 1963)
Blom, Philipp, *The Vertigo Years* (Phoenix, 2009)
Blond, Georges, *Verdun* (Presses de la Cité, 1961)
Blum, Léon, *Œuvre 1940–44, 1945–47*, 2 vols (Albin Michel, 1963)
Bohlen, Charles E., *Witness to History 1929–1969* (Weidenfeld & Nicolson, 1973)
Boisdeffre, Pierre de, *De Gaulle malgré lui* (Albin Michel, 1978)
Boissieu, Alain de, *Pour Combattre avec de Gaulle* (Plon, 1981)
— *Pour servir le Général, 1946–1970* (Plon, 1982)
Bonheur, Gaston, et al., *De Gaulle Portraits* (Omnibus, 2008)
Borden, Mary, *Journey Down a Blind Alley* (Hutchinson, 1946)
Bourdan, Pierre, *Commentaires* (Calmann-Lévy, 1947)
Bourget, Pierre, *Paris 1944* (Plon, 1984)
Bourgi, Pierre, *Le général de Gaulle et l'Afrique noir* (Montchrestien, 1998)
Bréant, *De l'Alsace à la Somme* (Librairie Hachette et Cie, 1917)
Brendon, Piers, *The Dark Valley* (Cape, 2000)
Broche, François, *Les Hommes de De Gaulle* (Pygmalion, 2006)
Bromberger, Merry and Serge, *Les 13 complots du 13 mai* (Fayard, 1959)
Brown, Malcolm, *Verdun, 1916* (Stroud: Tempus Publishing, 2000)
Buis, Georges, *Les Fanfares perdues* (Seuil, 1975)
Burin des Roziers, Étienne, *Retour aux sources* (Plon, 1985)
Buron, Robert, *Carnets politiques* (Plon, 1965)
Cadogan, Alexander, and David Dilkes (eds), *The Diaries of Sir Alexander Cadogan* (Cassell, 1971)
Cameron, Allan W., *Viet-Nam Crisis*, vol. I (Ithaca: Cornell University Press, 1971)
Campbell, John, *Edward Heath* (Cape, 1993)
Capdevielle, J., and Mouriaux, R., *Mai 68* (FNSP, 1988)
Capitant, René, *De Gaulle dans la république* (Plon, 1958)
Caron, François, *An Economic History of Modern France* (Methuen 1979)
Cassin, René, *Les Hommes partis de rien* (Plon, 1974)

Castex, Henri, *Verdun: Années Infernales* (Éditions Albatros, 1980)
Catroux, Georges, *Dans la bataille de Méditerranée* (Julliard, 1949)
Chaban-Delmas, Jacques, *Charles de Gaulle* (Éditions Paris-Match, 1980)
— *Mémoires pour Demain* (Flammarion, 1998)
Challe, Maurice, *Notre révolte* (Presses de la Cité, 1968)
Chambrun, René de, *Laval devant l'Histoire* (France-empire, 1983)
Charbonnel, Jean, *L'Aventure de la fidélité* (Seuil, 1976)
Charlot, Jean, *Le Phénomène gaulliste* (Seuil, 1970)
— *Les Français et de Gaulle* (Plon, 1971)
— *Le Gaullisme d'opposition* (Fayard, 1983)
Chastenet, Jacques, *Histoire de la Troisième République*, vols 3–5 (Hachette, 1955–60)
Chirac, Jacques, *Mémoires, Chaque pas doit être un but* (Nil, 2009)
Churchill, Winston, *Second World War*, 5 vols (Penguin, 2005)
Clerc, Christine, *De Gaulle–Malraux* (Nil, 2008)
Cohen, Samy, *De Gaulle, les gaullistes et Israël* (Alain Moreau, 1974)
Cohn-Bendit, Daniel, *Le Grand Bazar* (Belfond, 1975)
Cointet, Jean-Paul, *Histoire de Vichy* (Tempus, 2003)
Cole, Hubert, *Laval* (Heinemann, 1963)
Colville, John, *The Fringes of Power: Downing Street Diaries, 1939–55* (Weidenfeld & Nicolson, 2004)
Conquet, Alfred, *Auprès du maréchal* (France-Empire, 1970)
Cook, Don, *Charles de Gaulle* (Secker & Warburg, 1984)
Cooper, Alfred ('Duff'), *Diaries* (Weidenfeld & Nicolson, 2005)
Cordier, Daniel, *Jean Moulin* (J.C. Lattès, 1989)
Cotteret, Jean-Marie, and Moreau, René, *Le vocabulaire du général de Gaulle* (Fondation Nationale des Sciences Politiques, Armand Colin, 1969)
Coulet, François, *Vertu des temps difficiles* (Plon, 1966)
Courrière, Yves, *La Guerre d'Algérie*, 4 vols (Fayard, 1968–71)
Courtois, Stéphane, *Le PCF dans la guerre* (Ramsay, 1980)
Couve de Murville, Maurice, *Une politique étrangère 1958–1969* (Plon, 1971)
Crémieux-Brilhac, Jean-Louis, *La France libre* (Gallimard, 2001)
Dallas, Gregor, *At the Heart of a Tiger. Clemenceau and His World 1841–1929* (Macmillan, 1993)
Dalleck, Robert, *John F. Kennedy: An Unfinished Life* (Allen Lane, 2003)
Daniel, Jean, *De Gaulle et l'Algérie* (Seuil, 1986)
Dansette, Adrien, *Histoire de la libération de Paris* (Fayard, 1966)
Daumard, Adeline (ed.), *Les Fortunes françaises au XIXème siècle* (Mouton, 1973)
Davies, Norman, *God's Playground: A History of Poland*, vol. II (Oxford: Oxford University Press, 2005)
Debré, Michel, *Mémoires* (Albin Michel, 1985)
Debû-Bridel, Jacques, *Les Partis contre de Gaulle* (Aimery Somogy, 1948)
— *De Gaulle contestataire* (Plon, 1970)
Decoux (Admiral), *À la Barre de l'Indochine* (Plon, 1949)
Delarue, Jacques, *L'OAS contre de Gaulle* (Fayard, 1981)
Démaret, Pierre, and Plume, Christian, *Objectif de Gaulle* (Laffont, 1973)
Derogy, Jacques, and Kahn, Jean-François, *Les Secrets du ballottage* (Fayard, 1966)

D'Escrienne, Jean, *Le général m'a dit* (Plon, 1973)
— *De Gaulle de loin et de près* (Plon, 1978)
D'Este, Carlo, *Eisenhower: A Soldier's Life* (Weidenfeld & Nicolson, 2003)
Destremau, Bernard, *Weygand* (Perrin, 1989)
— *De Lattre* (Flammarion, 1999)
Dixon, Piers, *Double Diploma* (Hutchinson, 1968)
Dreyfus, François-Georges, *Histoire de Vichy* (Perrin, 1990)
Droit, Michel, *Les Feux du crépuscule* (Plon, 1977)— *De Gaulle* (Hachette, 1987)
Duchen, Claire, *Women's Rights and Women's Lives in France, 1944–1968* (Routledge, 1984)
Duclert, Vincent, *L'Affaire Dreyfus* (La Découverte, 1994)
Duclos, Jacques, *Mémoires* (Fayard, 1968)
Dulac, André, *Nos guerres perdues* (Fayard, 1969)
Dulong, Claude, *La vie quotidienne à l'Élysée du temps de Charles de Gaulle* (Hachette, 1974)
Duroselle, Jean-Baptiste, *La France et les États-Unis* (Seuil, 1976)
— *La Décadence, L'Abîme* (Imprimerie nationale, 1985)
Duverger, Maurice, *La Cinquième République* (PUF, 1974)
Eisenhower, Dwight, *Crusade in Europe* (Heinemann, 1958)
Elgey, Georgette, *Histoire de la IVème République*, 3 vols (Fayard, 1992–2008)
Espoir (tri-monthly review, Paris: Institut Charles de Gaulle (Plon))
Fabre-Luce, Alfred, *Gaulle deux* (Julliard, 1958)
Faivre, Maurice, *Le Général Ély et la politique de défense* (Economica, 1998)
— *Les archives inédites de la politique algérienne* (l'Harmattan, 2000)
Fall, Bernard, *Street without Joy, Indochina at War 1946–54* (Harrisburg: Stackpole, 1961)
Faure, Edgar, *Avoir toujours raison . . . c'est un grand tort* (Plon, 1982)
— *Mémoires*, 2 vols (Omnibus, 1984)
Fauvet, Jacques, *La IVe République* (Arthème Fayard, 1959)
Favreau, Bertrand, *Georges Mandel* (Fayard, 1996)
Fenby, Jonathan, *The Sinking of the Lancastria* (Simon & Schuster, 2005)
— *Alliance* (Simon & Schuster, 2006)
Ferniot, Jean, *De Gaulle et le 13 Mai* (Plon, 1965)
— *De Gaulle à Pompidou* (Plon, 1972)
Flohic, François, *Souvenirs d'outre Gaulle* (Plon, 1979)
Foccart, Jacques, *Journal de l'Élysée*, 3 vols – *Tous les soirs avec de Gaulle, Le Général en Mai, Dans les bottes du Général* (Fayard, 1997–9)
Fondation Charles de Gaulle, *De Gaulle et le RPF* (Armand Colin, 1968)
— *Le Rétablissement de la Légalité Républicaine* (Éditions Complexe, 1996)
— *Charles de Gaulle, la jeunesse et la guerre, 1890–1920* (Plon, 2001)
— *Charles de Gaulle, 1920–40* (Plon, 2004)
Fouchet, Christian, *Mémoires d'hier et de demain* (Plon, 1971)
Friang, Brigitte, *Un autre Malraux* (Plon, 1977)
Frossart, André, *La France en général* (Plon, 1975)
Gaffney, John, and Holmes, Diana, *Stardom in Postwar France* (New York: Berghahn Books, 2007)

Galambos, Louis, and Van Ee, Daun, *The Papers of Dwight David Eisenhower* (Baltimore: Johns Hopkins Press, 2001)
Galante, Pierre, *Le Général* (Le Cercle du Nouveau Livre d'Histoire, 1968)
Gallo, Max, *De Gaulle*, 4 vols (Laffont, 1998)
Gaulle, Charles de, *La discorde chez l'ennemi* (Champigneulles: Berger-Levrault, 1944)
— *Vers l'armée de métier* (Champigneulles: Berger-Levrault, 1944)
— *Le fil de l'épée* (Bourg-la-Reine: M. Lubineau, 1963)
— *Discours et Messages*, 5 vols (Plon, 1970–71)
— *Lettres, notes et carnets*, 12 vols (Plon 1980–88)
— *Mémoires* (Gallimard, 2000)
Gaulle, Philippe de, *Mémoires accessoires* (Plon, 1997)
— *De Gaulle, Mon Père, entretiens avec Michel Tauriac*, 2 vols (Plon, 2003)
— *Mon Père en images* (Michel Lafon, 2006)
Giesbert, Franz-Olivier, *François Mitterrand* (Seuil, 1977)
Gildea, Robert, *The Past in French History* (New Haven: Yale University Press, 1994)
— *Marianne in Chains* (Macmillan, 2002)
Gillois, André, *Histoire Secrète des français à Londres* (Hachette, 1979)
Gladwyn, H.M.G.J., *Memoirs of Lord Gladwyn* (Weidenfeld & Nicolson, 1972)
Godard, Yves, *Les Trois batailles d'Alger: les paras dans la ville* (Fayard: 1972)
Gorce, Paul-Marie de la, *Deux Mondes* (Fayard, 1964)
— *De Gaulle*, 2 vols (Nouveau Monde, 2008)
Graham, Peter, and Vincendeau, Ginette, *The French New Wave* (Palgrave Macmillan, 2009)
Grimaud, Maurice, *En mai fais ce qu'il te plaît* (Stock, 1977)
Grosser, Albert, *Affaires extérieures* (Flammarion, 1992)
Guichard, Olivier, *Un chemin tranquille* (Flammarion, 1975)
— *Mon Général* (Grasset, 1980)
Guillemin, Henri, *Le Général clair-obscur* (Seuil, 1984)
Guy, Claude, *En écoutant de Gaulle* (Grasset, 1996)
Harvey, Oliver, *Diaries* (Collins, 1970)
Hamon, Léo, *De Gaulle dans la République* (Plon, 1958)
Harriman, Averell, *Special Envoy* (New York, Random House, 1975)
Hawkins, Desmond, *BBC War Report* (Oxford University Press, 1946)
Haymann, Emmanuelle, *Alain Delon: Splendeurs et mystères d'une superstar* (Favre, 1998)
Heath, Edward, *The Course of My Life* (Hodder & Stoughton, 1998)
Hettier de Boislambert, Claude, *Les Fers de l'espoir* (Plon, 1978)
Horne, Alistair, *The Price of Glory: Verdun 1916* (Macmillan, 1961)
— *A Savage War of Peace. Algeria 1954–1962* (NYRB Classics, 2006)
— *Macmillan* (Macmillan, 2008)
Irvine, William, *The Boulanger Affair Reconsidered* (Oxford University Press, 1989)
Jackson, Julian, *The Politics of Depression in France 1932–1936* (Cambridge University Press, 1985)
— *De Gaulle* (Haus, 2003)
— *France, The Dark Years* (Oxford: Oxford University Press, 2003)
Jeanneney, Jean-Marcel, *Une mémoire républicaine, entretiens avec Jean Lacouture* (Seuil, 1997)

Jobert, Michel, *Mémoires d'avenir* (Grasset, 1974)
Johnson, Douglas, *A Concise History of France* (Thames & Hudson, 1971)
Jouhaud, Edmond, *La vie est un combat* (Fayard, 1975)
— *Serons-nous enfin compris?* (Albin Michel, 1984)
Joxe, Louis, *Victoire sur la nuit* (Flammarion, 1981)
Julliard, Jacques, *La IVe République* (Calmann-Lévy, 1968)
Kahn, Jean-François, and Derogy, Jacques, *Les Secrets du ballottage* (Fayard 1966)
Kedward, Rod, *La Vie en Bleu* (Allen Lane, 2005)
Keiger, J. F. V., *Raymond Poincaré* (Cambridge University Press, 1997)
Kersaudy, François, *De Gaulle et Churchill* (Plon, 1981)
— *De Gaulle et Roosevelt* (Perrin, 2007)
Kettle, Michael, *De Gaulle and Algeria 1940–60* (Quartet Books, 1993)
Kupferman, Fred, *Laval* (Balland, 1987)
Lacouture, Jean, *Léon Blum* (Seuil, 1977)
— *Pierre Mendès France* (Seuil, 1981)
— *De Gaulle*, 3 vols (Seuil, 1984–6)
Lacroix-Riz, Annie, *Le Choix de la défaite* (Armand Colin, 2006)
Laffont, Pierre, *L'Expiation* (Plon, 1968)
Larcan, Alain, *Charles de Gaulle, itinéraires intellectuels et spirituels* (Nancy: Presses Universitaires, 1993)
— *De Gaulle inventaire* (Bartillat, 2002)
Larebière, Bruno, *Charles de Gaulle* (Trélissac: Éditions Chronique, 1997)
Larkin, Maurice, *France since the Popular Front* (Oxford: Clarendon Press, 1988)
Larminat, Edgard de, *Chroniques irrévérencieuses* (Plon, 1962)
Lassus, Robert, *Le Mari de Madame de Gaulle* (Lattès, 1990)
Lattre de Tassigny, Jean de, *Histoire de la Première Armée française* (Plon, 1952)
Leca, Dominique, *La rupture de 1940* (Fayard, 1978)
Ledwidge, Bernard, *De Gaulle* (Flammarion, 1984)
Lefranc, Pierre, *Voici tes fils* (Plon, 1974)
— *Avec qui vous savez* (Plon, 1979)
— *De Gaulle, un Portrait* (Flammarion, 1989)
Lerner, Henri, *Catroux* (Albin Michel, 1990)
Longrigg, Stephen, *Syria and Lebanon under French Mandate* (Oxford University Press, 1958)
Lottman, Herbert, *Pétain* (Seuil, 1984)
Loustaunau-Lacau, Georges, *Mémoires d'un Français rebelle* (Laffont, 1948)
Lynch, Frances, *De Gaulle's First Veto* (European University, Florence, 1998)
— *A History of the French Economy* (Routledge, 2007)
Macmillan, Harold, *Blast of War* (Macmillan, 1967)
— *At the End of the Day* (Macmillan, 1973)
— *War Diaries* (Macmillan, 1985)
— and Peter Catterall, *Diaries, 1959–66* (Macmillan, 2009)
Malraux, André, *Les Chênes qu'on abat . . .* (Gallimard, 1971)
Mangold, Peter, *The Almost Impossible Ally* (IB Tauris, 2006)
Marin, Jean, *Petit bois pour un grand feu* (Fayard, 1994)
Massigli, René, *Une comédie des erreurs* (Plon, 1978)

Massu, Jacques, *Le Torrent et la digue* (Plon 1972)
— *Baden 1968* (Plon, 1983)
Mauriac, Claude, *Un autre de Gaulle, Journal 1944–1954* (Hachette, 1971)
— *Aimer de Gaulle* (Grasset, 1978)
Mauriac, François, *De Gaulle* (Grasset, 1964)
Mauriac, Jean, *Mort du Général de Gaulle* (Grasset, 1998)
Mengin, Robert, *De Gaulle à Londres vu par un Français libre* (Table Ronde, 1965)
Méribel, Élisabeth de, *La Liberté souffre violence* (Plon, 1981)
Messmer, Pierre, *Après tant de batailles* (Albin Michel, 1992)
Michelet, Edmond, *Le Gaullisme, passionnante aventure* (Fayard, 1962)
Mitterrand, François, *Le Coup d'État permanent* (Plon, 1964)
— *Ma part de vérité* (Fayard, 1969)
Moch, Jules, *Rencontres avec Darlan* (Plon, 1968)
— *Rencontres avec Léon Blum* (Plon, 1970)
— *Rencontres avec de Gaulle* (Plon, 1971)
— *Une si longue vie* (Laffont, 1976)
Moll, Geneviève, *Yvonne de Gaulle* (Ramsay, 1999)
Monnet, Jean, *Mémoires* (Fayard, 1976)
Moran, Lord, *Winston Churchill* (Constable, 1966)
Moulin, Laure, *Jean Moulin* (Presses de la Cité, 1969)
Muselier, Émile, *De Gaulle contre le gaullisme* (Éditions du Chêne, 1946)
Nachin, Lucien, *Charles de Gaulle, général de France* (Plon, 1945)
Newhouse, John, *De Gaulle and the Anglo-Saxons* (André Deutsch, 1970)
Nick, Christophe, *Résurrection* (Fayard, 1998)
Nicolson, Harold, *The War Years* (New York: Atheneum, 1967)
Nixon, Richard, *Leaders* (Sidgwick & Jackson, 1982)
Noël, Léon, *Comprendre de Gaulle* (Plon, 1972)
Noguères, Henri, *Histoire de la Résistance* (Laffont, 1981)
Nouzille, Vincent, *Des Secrets Si Bien Gardés* (Fayard, 2009)
O'Ballance, Edgar, *The Indo-China War 1945–1954* (Faber & Faber, 1964)
Oulmont, Philippe, *De Gaulle* (Cavalier bleu, 2008)
Ousby, Ian, *The Road to Verdun* (Jonathan Cape, 2002)
Palewski, Gaston, *Hier et Aujourd'hui* (Plon, 1974)
— *Mémoires d'action* (Plon, 1988)
Palmaert, Albéric de, *Sur les Pas de Charles de Gaulle* (Rennes: Éditions Ouest France, 2007)
Parodi, Jean-Luc, *Les Rapports entre le législatif et l'exécutif sous le Ve République* (Armand Colin, 1972)
Passeron, André, *De Gaulle parle. 1958–1962* (Plon, 1962)
— *De Gaulle parle. 1962–1966* (Plon, 1966)
Passy (Colonel), *Souvenirs I et II* (Monaco: Éditions Raoul Solar, 1947)
— *Vichy France* (New York: Columbia University Press, 2001)
— *L'Armée de Vichy* (Seuil, 2006)
Paxton, Robert, *Vichy France* (New York: Norton, 1975)
— *French Peasant Fascism* (Oxford: Oxford University Press, 1997)
Péan, Pierre, *Vies et Morts de Jean Moulin* (Fayard, 1998)

Pedroncini, Guy (ed.), *Histoire Militaire de la France de 1871 à 1940* (Presses Universitaires de France, 1992)
Péguy, Charles, *Oeuvres complètes* (Gallimard, 1917–55)
Pellissier, Pierre, *Massu* (Perrin, 2003)
Perrier, Guy, *Rémy* (Perrin, 2001)
Perrol, Gilbert, *La Grandeur de la France* (Albin Michel, 1992)
Pétain, Philippe, *Mémoires* (Payot, 1929)
Peyrefitte, Alain, *C'était de Gaulle*, 3 vols (Gallimard, 2002)
Pflimlin, Pierre, *Mémoires d'un Européen* (Fayard, 1991)
Pickles, Dorothy, *French Politics* (London: Royal Institute of International Affairs, 1953)
— *The Uneasy Entente* (Oxford University Press, 1966)
Pilleul, Gilbert (ed.), *L'entourage et de Gaulle* (Plon, 1979)
Pinay, Antoine, *Un Français comme les autres* (Belfond, 1984)
Pineau, Christian, *La simple vérité* (Julliard, 1960)
Pisani, Edgard, *Le Général, indivis* (Fayard, 1974)
Pognon, Edmond, *De Gaulle et l'histoire de France* (Albin Michel, 1970)
— *De Gaulle et l'Armée* (Plon, Collection Espoir, 1976)
Pompidou, Georges, *Pour rétablir une vérité* (Flammarion, 1982)
Poniatowski, Michel de, *Mémoires* (Plon, 1997)
Pouget, Jean, *Un certain capitaine de Gaulle* (Aubéron, 2000)
Prate, Alain, *Les Batailles économiques du général de Gaulle* (Plon, 1978)
Raïssac, Guy, *Un combat sans merci* (Albin Michel, 1966)
Reader, Keith, *Intellectuals and the Left in France since 1968* (Palgrave Macmillan, 1987)
— and Wadia, Khursheed, *The May 1968 Events in France* (Palgrave Macmillan, 1993)
Rémond, René, *1958, Le Retour de De Gaulle* (Éditions Complexe, 1998)
— *La Politique est-elle intelligible?* (Éditions Complexe, 1999)
Rémy (Colonel), *De Gaulle, cet inconnu* (Monaco: Éditions Raoul Solar, 1947)
— *Dix ans avec de Gaulle, 1940–1950* (France-Empire, 1971)
— *Rognes et grognes du Général* (Versoix, 1978)
Revel, Jean-François, *Le Style du général. Mai 1958–juin 1959* (Julliard, 1959)
Reynaud, Paul, *Mémoires*, 2 vols (Flammarion, 1960 and 1963)
Rioux, Jean-Pierre, *La France de la Quatrième République*, 2 vols (Seuil, 1981, 1982)
— ed., *De Gaulle, Portraits* (Omnibus, 2008)
Rix, Pierre-Henry, *Par le portillon de la Boisserie* (Nouvelles Éditions Latines, 2008)
Rol-Tanguy, Henri, and Bourderon, Roger, *Libération de Paris. Les cent documents* (Hachette, 1994)
Roosevelt, Elliott, *As He Saw It* (New York: Duell, Sloan and Pearce, 1946)
— *Rendezvous with Destiny* (W.H. Allen, 1977)
Rouanet, Anne et Pierre, *Les Trois Derniers Chagrins du général de Gaulle* (Grasset, 1980)
— *L'inquiétude outre mort du général de Gaulle* (Grasset, 1985)
Roussel, Éric, *Jean Monnet* (Fayard, 1996)
— *Charles de Gaulle*. I. *1890–1945* (Gallimard, 2002)
— *Charles de Gaulle*. II. *1946–1970* (Perrin, 2007)
— *Inédit* (Gallimard, 2008)

Rousso, Henri, *Le syndrome de Vichy* (Seuil, 1987)
Rueff, Jacques, *Oeuvres complètes* (Plon, 1979)
Rusk, Dean, *As I Saw It* (New York, W.W. Norton, 1990)
Sainderichin, Pierre, *De Gaulle et le Monde* (Le Monde, 1990)
Salan, Raoul, *Mémoires* (Presses de la Cité, 1970)
Schoenbrun, David, *Les Trois Vies de Charles de Gaulle* (Julliard, 1965)
Schumann, Maurice, *L'homme des tempêtes* (Mail, 1946)
— *Un certain 18 juin* (Plon, 1980)
Serigny, Alain de, *La Révolution du 13 mai* (Plon, 1958)
— *Échos d'Alger* (Presses de la Cité, 1972)
Serre, René, *Croisade à coups de poigne* (Martel, 1954)
Serrigny, Bernard, *Trente ans avec Pétain* (Plon, 1944)
Seymour-Jones, Carole, *A Dangerous Liaison* (Arrow, 2009)
Sherwood, Robert, *Roosevelt and Hopkins* (New York: Harpers, 1948)
Soustelle, Jacques, *Envers et contre tout, de Londres à Alger 1940–1942* (Laffont, 1947)
— *Envers et contre tout, d'Alger à Paris 1942–1944* (Laffont, 1950)
— *L'Espérance Trahie* (Alma Mayenne, 1962)
— *28 ans de Gaullisme* (Table Ronde, 1968)
Spears, Edward, *Assignment to Catastrophe,* 2 vols (Heinemann, 1954)
— *Fulfilment of a Mission,* 2 vols (Leo Cooper, 1977)
— *Two Men Who Saved France* (Eyre & Spottiswood, 1966)
Sulzberger, C. L., *The Last of the Giants* (Weidenfeld & Nicolson, 1972)
Tardieu, André, *France in Danger* (Denis Archer, 1935)
Tarr, Francis de, *Henri Queuille* (Table Ronde, 1995)
Taubman, William, *Khrushchev* (New York: W.W. Norton, 2004)
Tauriac, Michel, *Les 30 jours qui ont fait de Gaulle* (Paris: Economica, 2001)
— *Vivre avec de Gaulle* (Plon, 2008)
Tellier, Thibault, *Paul Reynaud* (Fayard, 2005)
Terrenoire, Louis, *De Gaulle et l'Algérie* (Fayard, 1964)
— *De Gaulle vivant* (Plon, 1971)
— *Du RPF à la traversée du désert* (Plon, 1980)
— *De Gaulle, 1947–54* (Plon, 1981)
Thomson, Dale, *Vive le Québec Libre* (Toronto: Deneau, 1988)
Tombs, Robert, *France 1814–1914* (Longman, 1996)
Tooze, Adam, *The Wages of Destruction* (Allen Lane, 2006)
Touchard, Jean, *Le Gaullisme, 1940–69* (Seuil, 1978)
Tournoux, Jean-Raymond, *Secrets d'État* (Plon, 1960)
— *L'Histoire secrète* (Union générale d'éditions, 1965)
— *Pétain and de Gaulle* (Heinemann, 1966)
— *La Tragédie du général* (Plon, 1967)
— *Le Mois de mai du général* (Plon, 1969)
— *Jamais dit* (Plon, 1971)
— *Le Tourment et la Fatalité* (Plon, 1974)
Triboulet, Raymond, *Un ministre de Général* (Plon, 1986)
Tricot, Bernard, *Les Sentiers de la Paix* (Plon, 1972)
Truman, Harry, *Years of Decision* (New York: Doubleday, 1955)

Tute, Warren, *The Deadly Stroke* (Pen & Sword, 2007)
Ullmann, Bernard, *Jacques Soustelle* (Plon, 1995)
Unger, Gérard, *Aristide Briand* (Fayard, 2005)
Valette, Jacques, *Indochine 1940–1945: Français contre Japonais* (Sedes, 1993)
Vallon, Louis, *L'Anti de Gaulle* (Seuil, 1969)
Vansittart, Robert, *The Mist Procession* (Hutchinson, 1958)
Vendroux, Jacques, *Cette chance que j'ai eue* (Plon, 1974)
— *Ces grandes années que j'ai vécues* (Plon, 1974)
— *Yvonne de Gaulle, ma soeur* (Omnibus, 1991)
Verrier, Anthony, *Assassination in Algiers* (Macmillan, 1991)
Viansson-Ponté, Pierre, *Les gaullistes. Rituel et Annuaire* (Seuil, 1963)
— *Les Politiques* (Calmann-Lévy, 1967)
— *Histoire de la République Gaullienne*, 2 vols (Fayard, 1970–71)
Vigreux, Jean, *Waldeck Rochet* (La Dispute, 2000)
Villon, Pierre, *Résistant de la prèmiere heure* (Éditions sociales, 1983)
Vinen, Richard, *The Unfree French. Life under the Occupation* (Penguin, 2006)
Walters, Vernon A., *Services discrets* (Plon, 1979)
Ward, Geoffrey, *Closest Companion* (Boston: Houghton Mifflin, 1995)
Weber, Eugen, *The Hollow Years. France in the 1930s* (New York: W.W. Norton, 1966)
Werth, Alexander, *France 1940–1955* (Robert Hale, 1956)
— *The Twilight of France* (Hamish Hamilton, 1942)
Weygand, Maxime, *En lisant les Mémoires de guerre du général de Gaulle* (Flammarion, 1955)
Williams, Charles, *A Life of General de Gaulle, the Last Great Frenchman* (New York: Wiley, 1993)
— *Pétain* (Little, Brown, 2005)
Williams, Philip, *Politics in Post-war France* (Longmans, Green & Co., 1954)
— *Politics and Society in de Gaulle's Republic* (Longman, 1971)
— and Harrison, Martin, *De Gaulle's Republic* (Longmans, 1960)
Winock, Michel, *La République se meurt: chronique 1956–1958* (Seuil, 1978)
— *La Fièvre hexagonale: Les grandes crises politiques de 1871 à 1968* (Seuil, 1986)
— *L'Agonie de la IVe République, le 13 Mai 1958* (Gallimard, 2006)
— *1958* (Gallimard, 2008)
Winter, J. M., *The Experience of World War I* (Papermac, 1989)
Zamoyski, Adam, *Warsaw, 1920* (Harper Press, 2008)

GLOSSARY OF SIGNIFICANT PEOPLE

Abetz, Otto (1903–58) Proconsular German ambassador in France during the Second World War.

Argoud, Antoine (1917–2004) Army officer. Organiser of the unsuccessful military putsch in Algeria in 1961 after which he joined OAS. Kidnapped by French agents in Germany, he was given a life sentence but was amnestied in 1968.

Auriol, Vincent (1884–1966) Socialist politician. President of Republic 1947–54.

Barrès, Maurice (1862–1923) Right-wing theorist. His exaltation of France fuelled de Gaulle's own extreme attachment to his nation.

Bastien-Thiry, Jean-Marie (1927–63) Military officer. Set up several assassination attempts against de Gaulle, notably at Petit-Clamart in 1962, after which he was caught and executed.

Bidault, Georges (1899–1983) Resistance leader and Christian Democrat politician. Foreign Minister in de Gaulle's post-war government and Prime Minister 1949–50. Supporter of French Algeria, he joined the OAS and went to live in Brazil before being amnestied in 1968.

Blum, Léon (1872–1950) Socialist politician. First Jew to be Prime Minister at head of 1936 Popular Front which introduced major labour and social legislation. Deported to Germany in the Second World War, he refused to serve under de Gaulle after Liberation. Prime Minister again 1946–7.

Briand, Aristide (1862–1932) Eleven times Prime Minister under the Third Republic and a fixture at the Foreign Ministry. Best known for pursuit of détente in Europe and promotion of peace which won him the Nobel Peace Prize.

Catroux, Georges (1877–1969) General. Joined the Free French in London in 1940. High commissioner in the Levant in 1945 and Minister for Africa in first de Gaulle government.

Chaban-Delmas, Jacques (1915–2000) Gaullist politician. Resistance general who established a political bastion in Bordeaux. Defence Minister 1957–8. President of National Assembly 1959–69. Primé Minister 1969–72.

Challe, Maurice (1905–79) General. One of the four leaders of the 1961 Algiers putsch. Sentenced to fifteen years in jail. Amnestied in 1968.

Chirac, Jacques (1932–) Gaullist politician. Protégé of Pompidou, he was later twice Prime Minister and President of Republic 1995–2007.

Clemenceau, Georges (1841–1929) Politician known as 'the Tiger'. Led France at end of First World War and negotiated the Treaty of Versailles in 1919 but was then voted out of power.

Couve de Murville, Maurice (1907–99) Civil servant-turned-politician. Minister of Foreign Affairs 1958–68. Prime Minister 1968–9.

Coty, René (1882–1962) Conservative politician. President of Republic 1954–9 when he appealed to de Gaulle to return to power.

Daladier, Édouard (1884–1970) Radical Socialist politician. Prime Minister 1938–40, signing the Munich Agreement with Hitler.

Darlan, François (1881–1942) Head of the French navy. Became the second-ranking figure in Vichy regime before being ousted at Germany's instigation. Moved to Algiers where he worked for the Americans. Assassinated at the end of 1942.

Darnand, Joseph (1897–1945) Commander of the Vichy paramilitary *Milice*. Executed in October 1945.

Debré, Michel (1912–96) Gaullist politician. Firebrand 'Father' of the constitution of the Fifth Republic of which he was Prime Minister 1959–62. Later Finance, Foreign and Defence Minister.

Defferre, Gaston (1910–86) Socialist politician. Deputy and Mayor of Marseille. Badly defeated at the presidential election of 1969.

Delouvrier, Paul (1914–95) Civil servant and economist. Appointed by de Gaulle to administer Algeria in the late 1950s. Then supervised the modernisation of Paris.

Dreyfus, Alfred (1859–1935) Soldier. Falsely convicted in 1894 of treason, the Jewish captain was sentenced to life imprisonment in French Guiana. '*L'Affaire Dreyfus*' divided France. In 1906 he was cleared of all the charges.

Duclos, Jacques (1896–1975) Communist politician. Sharp-tongued parliamentarian who ran for presidency in 1965.

Faure, Edgar (1908–88) Centrist politician. Adroit Prime Minister under the Fourth Republic. Put through education reforms after 1968 riots.

Foccart, Jacques (1913–97) Gaullist backroom operator and well-connected chief adviser on Africa, constantly accused of being at the centre of a web of dirty tricks on the General's behalf.

Fouchet, Christian (1911–74) Veteran Gaullist who drew up the unsuccessful Fouchet Plan for Europe in 1961. Minister of Education 1962–6, and of Interior in 1967–8 during 1968 riots.

Gamelin, Maurice (1872–1958) Generalissimo. Cerebral, ineffective commander of French military at outbreak of Second World War.

Giraud, Henri (1879–1949) General. Unsuccessful US-backed rival of de Gaulle in North Africa in 1943.

Giscard d'Estaing, Valéry (1926–) Centre-right Finance Minister 1962–6, President of Republic 1974–81.

Herriot, Édouard (1872–1957) Radical Socialist politician. Thrice Prime Minister and long-time President of the National Assembly.

Isorni, Jacques (1911–95) Lawyer. Tribune of the far right who defended Pétain.

Jouhaud, Edmond (1905–95) General. One of the four leaders of the 1961 Algiers putsch. Joined OAS leader before being captured. De Gaulle commuted his death sentence. Freed in 1967.

Joxe, Louis (1901–91) Gaullist politician. Joined de Gaulle in Algiers. Negotiated the Évian peace agreement in 1962. Justice Minister during 1968 riots.

Juin, Alphonse (1888–1967) Marshal (awarded posthumously). Joined de Gaulle in 1943 after serving Vichy. One of the very few people the General called '*tu*', but disapproved of his Algerian policy.

Koenig, Pierre (1898–1970) Marshal (awarded posthumously). Free French commander who became a Gaullist politician. Defence Minister under Mendès France and Faure, earning de Gaulle's disapproval.

Lagaillarde, Pierre (1931–) Leader of barricades revolt in Algeria.

Lattre de Tassigny, Jean de (1889–1952) Marshal. Served under Vichy before joining the Free French. Led French forces into Germany in 1944, and then in Indochina.

Laval, Pierre (1883–1945) Politician. Prime Minister under the Third Republic and second-ranking figure in Vichy regime. Executed 1945.

Lecanuet, Jean (1920–93) Centrist politician who held eleven ministerial posts in ten years, the 'French Kennedy' was a presidential candidate in the 1965 election.

Leclerc de Hauteclocque, Philippe (1902–47) Marshal (awarded posthumously). Free French commander who led the 2nd Armoured Division into Paris in 1944. Subsequently sent to Indochina. Died in plane crash in North Africa. Had been regarded by de Gaulle as his natural successor.

Mandel, Georges (1885–1944) Politician. Appointed Interior Minister in 1940, he strongly opposed surrender. Despite being Jewish, he refused British attempts to get him to go to London after Fall of France. Assassinated by Vichy *Milice* in 1944.

Massu, Jacques (1908–2002) General. Free French/Fighting France soldier and Indochina veteran who won the Battle of Algiers against the FLN in 1957 and became leader of the revolt the following year. Sidelined after criticising de Gaulle, but the President made secret trip to seek reassurance from him in the 1968 crisis.

Mauriac, Claude (1914–96) Writer son of François Mauriac. De Gaulle's private secretary after Second World War.

Mauriac, François (1885–1970) Writer and Nobel literature prize-winner. Much admired by de Gaulle.

Mauriac, Jean (1924–) Son of François Mauriac. Political correspondent at Agence France-Presse (AFP) news agency. Rare journalist de Gaulle trusted.

Maurras, Charles (1868–1952) Right-wing thinker. Proponent of xenophobic nationalism.

Mayer, Émile (1851–1938) Free thinker. Military theorist who influenced de Gaulle in 1930s.

Mendès France, Pierre (1907–82) The de Gaulle of the Left. Economics Minister after the Liberation. As Prime Minister in 1954–5, withdrew France from Indochina. Rigorous approach earned many enemies, with particular venom from far right and anti-Semites. Opposed de Gaulle's return to power and remained in opposition.

Mitterrand, François (1916–96) Long-time anti-Gaullist. Fourth Republic stalwart with two-sided war record. President of France 1981–95.

Moch, Jules (1893–1985) Socialist politician. Joined Free French in London. Minister under de Gaulle after Liberation. Interior Minister 1947–9 and 1958.

Mollet, Guy (1905–1975) Socialist leader. Prime Minister 1956–7. Backed de Gaulle's return to power but then went into opposition.

Monnerville, Gaston (1897–1991) Centrist politician. Grandson of slaves. President of upper house of parliament 1947–68. Became strong anti-Gaullist, privately accusing de Gaulle of racism.

Monnet, Jean (1888–1979) Architect of European unity. Launched French economic planning after Liberation. Generally on bad terms with de Gaulle.

Muselier, Émile (1882–1965) Admiral. Head of Free French naval forces and unsuccessful rival to de Gaulle.

Palewski, Gaston (1901–84) Gaullist loyalist. De Gaulle's chief of staff during the Second World War and after the Liberation. Supervised development of French nuclear industry. President of Constitutional Council 1955–74.

Papon, Maurice (1910–2007) Civil servant. Paris police chief 1958–67, ordering repression of Algerians and demonstrators. Went on to become Budget Minister before his Vichy past caught up with him and he was convicted of crimes against humanity for authorising deportation of Jews from Bordeaux.

Pétain, Philippe (1856–1951) Marshal and head of state in Vichy regime. Viewed as a hero for his military leadership in First World War, including the battle of Verdun. Condemned to death in 1945. Sentence was commuted by de Gaulle to life imprisonment.

Peyrefitte, Alain (1925–99) Close to de Gaulle, he was Minister of Information 1962–6 and of Education in 1967–8.

Pflimlin, Pierre (1907–2000) Centrist politician. Prime Minister 1958. Minister of State under de Gaulle. Quit over the General's European policy.

Pinay, Antoine (1891–1994) Conservative politician. Middle-class provincial idol for his careful economic and financial policies. Prime Minister 1952–3. Finance Minister 1958–60 but fell out with de Gaulle.

Pisani, Edgard (1918–) Gaullist politician who went into opposition. Agriculture Minister 1961–6. Public Works Minister 1966–7. Turned against administration in 1968.

Pleven, René (1901–93) Centrist politician. Prominent in Free French. Prime Minister 1950–51 and 1951–2.

Poincaré, Raymond (1860–1934) Five times Prime Minister and President of France 1913–20.

Pompidou, Georges (1911–74) Gaullist politician. Aide to de Gaulle after Second World War. Prime Minister 1962–8, President of Republic 1969–74.

Queuille, Henri (1884–1970) Extreme centrist. Worked with de Gaulle in Algiers. Three times Prime Minister under Fourth Republic.

Ramadier, Paul (1888–1961) Skilful Socialist politician. As Prime Minister in 1947 he dropped PCF from government.

Reynaud, Paul (1878–1966) Conservative politician with troublesome mistress. De Gaulle's first major political backer. Prime Minister and Foreign and Defence Minister as France fell in 1940, appointing de Gaulle as his deputy at Defence. Replaced by Pétain on 17 June 1940. Resurfaced under Fourth Republic but estranged from de Gaulle.

Rochet, Waldeck (1905–83) Communist politician. Would-be reformist PCF General Secretary 1964–72 hemmed in by Moscow-aligned hardliners.

Rueff, Jacques (1896–1978) Free market advocate and gold bug. Economic adviser to de Gaulle drawing up plan that balanced the budget and strengthened the franc, underpinning prosperity of Fifth Republic.

Salan, Raoul (1899–1984) General. Nicknamed 'the Mandarin'. Leader of the 1961 Algiers putsch. Then joined OAS. Caught, he was sentenced to life imprisonment but was amnestied in 1968.

Schuman, Robert (1886–1963) Pro-European politician. Dry, lifelong bachelor. Twice Prime Minister. A founder of the Common Market and Council of Europe.

Schumann, Maurice (1911–98) Gaullist and Christian Democrat politician. De Gaulle's spokesman and frequent broadcaster from London during Second World War. President of MRP party. Minister of Scientific Research 1967–8, Social Affairs 1968–9 and Foreign Affairs 1969–73.

Séguy, Georges (1927–) Trade unionist. General Secretary of CGT, Communist-led labour federation, and member of PCF political bureau. Key negotiator in 1968 strikes.

Soustelle, Jacques (1912–90) Gaullist politician and French Algeria supporter. Joined Free French in Latin America. Secretary-General of Gaullist RPF movement but fell out with de Gaulle over Algeria after 1958, joining OAS.

Susini, Jean-Jacques (1933–) OAS ideologue. Twice sentenced to death in absentia. Amnestied in 1968.

Terrenoire, Louis (1908–92) Gaullist. Christian Democrat politician who switched to Gaullism, became Secretary-General of the RPF and Information Minister in 1960.

Thierry d'Argenlieu, Georges (1889–1964) Admiral and monk. One of leading Free French military figures but an inept politician who sowed trouble in his wake.

Thorez, Maurice (1900–64) Communist leader. As PCF General Secretary, he backed the pre-war Popular Front in 1934, deserted to the USSR in 1940 and joined de Gaulle's post-war government.

Weygand, Maxime (1867–1965) Proud Generalissimo. In charge of French forces in later stages of German invasion in 1940. Defeatist. Leading figure in early Vichy regime. Demanded death sentence for de Gaulle.

Zeller, André (1898–1979) One of four generals in the 1961 Algiers putsch. Sentenced to fifteen years in prison. Amnestied in 1968.

GLOSSARY OF ABBREVIATIONS

ALN ***Armée de Libération Nationale*** – Army of National Liberation
CFDT ***Confédération Française Démocratique du Travail*** – French Democratic Confederation of Labour (left-wing)
CGT ***Confédération Générale du Travail*** – General Labour Confederation (Communist)
CNIP ***Centre National des Indépendants et Paysans*** – National Centre of Independents and Peasants (Conservative)
CNR ***Conseil National de la Résistance*** – National Council of the Resistance
FGDS ***Fédération de la Gauche Démocrate et Socialiste*** – Federation of the Democratic and Socialist Left
FLN ***Front de Libération Nationale*** – National Liberation Front
GPRA ***Gouvernement Provisoire de la République Algérienne*** – Provisional Government of the Algerian Republic
JCR ***Jeunesse Communiste Révolutionnaire*** – Communist Revolutionary Youth
MRP ***Mouvement Républicain Populaire*** – Popular Republican Movement (Christian Democrat)
OAS ***Organisation de l'Armée Secrète*** – Secret Army Organisation (terrorist)
PCF ***Parti Communiste Français*** – French Communist Party
PSU ***Parti Socialiste Unifié*** – Unified Socialist Party
RPF ***Rassemblement du Peuple Français*** – Rally of the French People (Gaullist)
SAC ***Service d'Action Civique*** – Civic Action Service (Gaullist strong arm force)
SFIO ***Section Française de l'Internationale Ouvrière*** – French Section of the Workers' International (French Socialist Party)
UDF ***Union pour la Démocratie Française*** – Union for French Democracy (Gaullist)
UDR ***Union des Démocrates pour la République*** – Union of Democrats for the Republic (Gaullist)
UDSR ***Union Démocratique et Socialiste de la Résistance*** – Democratic and Socialist Union of the Resistance
UNEF ***Union Nationale des Étudiants de France*** – National Union of French Students
UNR ***Union pour la Nouvelle République*** – Union for the New Republic

INDEX

NOTE ON THE AUTHOR

Jonathan Fenby has edited the *Observer* and the *South China Morning Post* and is a former bureau chief in France for the *Economist* and Reuters. He is the author of ten books including the acclaimed *Generalissimo* and *The Sinking of the Lancastria.* He lives in London but is frequently to be found across the Channel where he is a Knight of the French Order of Merit